GRAY ZONES

Studies on War and Genocide
General Editor: Omer Bartov, Brown University

Volume 1
The Massacre in History
  Edited by Mark Levene and Penny Roberts

Volume 2
National Socialist Extermination Policies: Contemporary German
  Perspectives and Controversies
  Edited by Ulrich Herbert

Volume 3
War of Extermination: The German Military in World War II, 1941/44
  Edited by Hannes Heer and Klaus Naumann

Volume 4
In God's Name: Genocide and Religion in the Twentieth Century
  Edited by Omer Bartov and Phyllis Mack

Volume 5
Hitler's War in the East, 1941–1945
  Edited by R.D. Müller and G.R. Ueberschär

Volume 6
Genocide and Settler Society: Frontier Violence and Stolen Indigenous
  Children in Australian History
  Edited by A. Dirk Moses

Volume 7
Networks of Nazi Persecution: Business, Bureaucracy, and the
  Organization of the Holocaust
  Edited by G. Feldman and W. Seibel

Volume 8
Gray Zones: Ambiguity and Compromise in the Holocaust and Its
  Aftermath
  Edited by Jonathan Petropoulos and John K. Roth

Volume 9
Robbery and Restitution: The Conflict over Jewish Property in Europe
  Edited by M. Dean, C. Goschler, and P. Ther

GRAY ZONES
Ambiguity and Compromise in the Holocaust and Its Aftermath

Edited and Introduced by

Jonathan Petropoulos and John K. Roth

Berghahn Books
New York • Oxford

First published in 2005 by
Berghahn Books
www.berghahnbooks.com

©2005 Jonathan Petropoulos and John K. Roth

All rights reserved. Except for the quotation of short passages for the purposes of criticism and review, no part of this book may be reproduced in any form or by any means, electronic or mechanical, including photocopying, recording, or any information storage and retrieval system now known or to be invented, without written permission of the publisher.

Library of Congress Cataloging-in-Publication Data

Gray zones : ambiguity and compromise in the Holocaust and its aftermath / edited and introduced by Jonathan Petropoulos and John K Roth.
    p. cm. — (Studies on war and genocide ; v. 8)
  Includes bibliographical references and index.
  ISBN 978-1-84545-302-2 (alk. paper)
    1. Holocaust, Jewish (1939–1945)—Congresses. 2. Holocaust, Jewish (1939–1945)—Historiography—Congresses. 3. Holocaust, Jewish (1939–1945)—Influence—Congresses. 4. Holocaust, Jewish (1939–1945)—Moral and ethical aspects—Congresses. I. Petropoulos, Jonathan. II. Roth, John K. III. War and genocide ; v. 8.

D804.18.G73 2005
940.53'18'01—dc22

2005041086

British Library Cataloguing in Publication Data

A catalogue record for this book is available from the British Library

Printed in the United States on acid-free paper

ISBN 1-84545-071-X hardback

To
Leigh Crawford and AnneMerie Donoghue

... we are in this world to do good ...

—Primo Levi, "Lorenzo's Return," in *Moments of Reprieve*

The greater part of historical and natural phenomena are not simple, or not simple in the way that we would like.

—Primo Levi, "The Gray Zone," in *The Drowned and the Saved*

Contents

List of Figures	xi
List of Abbreviations	xiii
Prologue: *The Gray Zones of the Holocaust* Jonathan Petropoulos and John K. Roth	xv

Part One: Ambiguity and Compromise in Writing and Depicting Holocaust History

Introduction — 1

Chapter 1
The Ambiguities of Evil and Justice: Degussa, Robert Pross, and the Jewish Slave Laborers at Gleiwitz — 7
Peter Hayes

Chapter 2
"Alleviation" and "Compliance": The Survival Strategies of the Jewish Leadership in the Wierzbnik Ghetto and the Starachowice Factory Slave Labor Camps — 26
Christopher R. Browning

Chapter 3
Between Sanity and Insanity: Spheres of Everyday Life in the Auschwitz-Birkenau *Sonderkommando* — 37
Gideon Greif

Chapter 4
Sonderkommando: Testimony from *Evidence* — 61
Michael Berenbaum

Chapter 5
A Commentary on "Gray Zones" in Raul Hilberg's Work — 70
Gerhard L. Weinberg

Chapter 6
Incompleteness in Holocaust Historiography — 81
Raul Hilberg

Part Two: Identity, Gender, and Sexuality During and After the Third Reich

Introduction   93

Chapter 7
Choiceless Choices: Surviving on False Papers on the "Aryan" Side   97
Robert Melson

Chapter 8
"Who Am I?" The Struggle for Religious Identity of Jewish Children Hidden by Christians During the Shoah   107
Eva Fleischner

Chapter 9
Hitler's Jewish Soldiers   118
Bryan Mark Rigg

Chapter 10
A Gray Zone Among the Field Gray Men: Confusion in the Discrimination Against Homosexuals in the *Wehrmacht*   127
Geoffrey J. Giles

Chapter 11
Pleasure and Evil: Christianity and the Sexualization of Holocaust Memory   147
Dagmar Herzog

Chapter 12
The Gender of Good and Evil: Women and Holocaust Memory   165
Sara R. Horowitz

Part Three: Gray Spaces: Geographical and Imaginative Landscapes

Introduction   179

Chapter 13
Hitler's "Garden of Eden" in Ukraine: Nazi Colonialism, *Volksdeutsche,* and the Holocaust, 1941–1944   185
Wendy Lower

Chapter 14
Life and Death in the "Gray Zone" of Jewish Ghettos in Nazi-Occupied Europe: The Unknown, the Ambiguous, and the Disappeared   205
Martin Dean

Chapter 15
"Almost-Camps" in Paris: The Difficult Description of Three Annexes of Drancy—Austerlitz, Lévitan, and Bassano, July 1943 to August 1944   222
Jean-Marc Dreyfus

Chapter 16
Alternate Holocausts and the Mistrust of Memory 240
Gavriel D. Rosenfeld

Chapter 17
Laughter and Heartache: The Functions of Humor in Holocaust Tragedy 252
Lynn Rapaport

Chapter 18
The Holocaust in Popular Culture: Master-Narrative and Counter-Narratives in the Gray Zone 270
Ronald Smelser

Chapter 19
The Grey Zone: The Cinema of Choiceless Choices 286
Lawrence Baron

Part Four: Justice, Religion, and Ethics During and After the Holocaust

Introduction 293

Chapter 20
Gray into Black: The Case of Mordecai Chaim Rumkowski 299
Richard L. Rubenstein

Chapter 21
Catalyzing Fascism: Academic Science in National Socialist Germany and Afterward 311
Jeffrey Lewis

Chapter 22
Postwar Justice and the Treatment of Nazi Assets 325
Jonathan Petropoulos

Chapter 23
The Gray Zones of Holocaust Restitution: American Justice and Holocaust Morality 339
Michael J. Bazyler

Chapter 24
The Creation of Ethical "Gray Zones" in the German Protestant Church: Reflections on the Historical Quest for Ethical Clarity 360
Victoria J. Barnett

Chapter 25
Gray-Zoned Ethics: Morality's Double Binds During and After the Holocaust 372
John K. Roth

Epilogue: *An Intense Wish to Understand* 390
Jonathan Petropoulos and John K. Roth

Select Bibliography	395
About the Editors and Contributors	399
Index	407

List of Figures

Images accompanying Hans Haustein, "Contra Nostalgie,"
    Konkret (January 1975)   148

Wartime Film footage of the Voksdeutsche Colony Halbstadt,
    Nazi occupied Ukraine (date unknown)   186

Reich Führer of the SS and Police Map of the Reich Commissariat
    Ukraine (May 1942)   193

German officer inspects a crate packed for transport to Germany   234

Jewish women inmates at Lévitan mend clothes, seized from Jews
    in France, before the goods are shipped to the Reich   235

List of Abbreviations

BA	Bundesarchiv Berlin-Lichterfelde
BAMA	Bundesarchiv-Militärarchiv Freiburg
BDL	Bund Deutscher Mädel
BdO	Befehlshaber der Ordnungspolizei
BHSA	Bayerisches Hauptstaatsarchiv
BRSA	Brest Regional State Archive
CAHS	Center of Advanced Holocaust Studies
CCP	Central Collecting Point
DAF	Deutsche Arbeitsfront
DGW	Deutsche Gasrusswerke
DM	Deutschmarks
DUA	Degussa Unternehmens-Archiv
ERR	Einsatzstab Reichsleiter Rosenberg
FSU	former Soviet Union
GARF	State Archives of the Russian Federation
HHSAW	Hessisches Hauptstaatsarchiv Wiesbaden
HSF-USA	Holocaust Survivors' Foundation—USA
JCS	Joint Chiefs of Staff
JDC	Joint Distribution Committee
JTA	Jewish Telegraphic Agency
KdO	Kommandeur der Ordnungspolizei
MG	Military Government
MPG	Max-Planck-Gesellschaft
NARA	U.S. National Archives and Records Administration
NSV	Nazi Party Welfare Society
OSS	Office of Strategic Services
RKU	Reichskommissariat Ukraine
RMEL	Reichsministerium für Ernährung und Landwirtschaft
RM	Reichmarks
SHAEF	Supreme Headquarters Allied Expeditionary Force
SPD	Social Democratic Party
UGIF	Union générale des Israélites de France
VoMi	Volksdeutsche Mittelstelle

VSS	Vorstandssitzung
WJC	World Jewish Congress
ZSA	Zhytomyr State Archives
ZSL	Zentrale Stelle der Landesjustizverwaltungen

Prologue
The Gray Zones of the Holocaust

Jonathan Petropoulos and John K. Roth

I know what it means not to return.
—Primo Levi, "Sunset at Fossoli," in *Collected Poems*

Born in Turin on 31 July 1919, Primo Levi, an Italian-Jewish chemist, joined a partisan resistance group after the Germans occupied northern Italy in the autumn of 1943. He was arrested as a suspect person by Fascists on 13 December 1943. Fearing that confirmation of his partisan identity would lead to torture and death, he admitted his status as an "Italian citizen of Jewish race," unaware of what that identification held in store for him. Levi was sent to a concentration camp at Fossoli, near the city of Modena, which had been intended for British and American prisoners of war. By mid-February 1944, more than six hundred Jews were imprisoned there. The arrival of German SS men meant that Levi and the other Jews at Fossoli would be deported.

On the evening of 22 February 1944 Levi's transport left the train station at Carpi. By then, Levi knew that its destination was Auschwitz. That name, he said, was "without significance for us at that time," but soon enough he realized that going there was "a journey towards nothingness."[1] After reaching Auschwitz on the night of Saturday, 26 February, Levi was spared for labor, received the tattooed number 174517 on his left arm, and endured Auschwitz for eleven months. For most of that time, he worked at Monowitz, a subcamp in the vast Auschwitz complex. Monowitz—also called Auschwitz III or Buna—provided slave labor for the construction of

Notes for this section begin on page xxi.

an I. G. Farben plant, the Buna factory, whose name was taken from the synthetic rubber that the Germans wanted to produce there. Liberated by Russian troops on 27 January 1945, Levi eventually got back to Italy, where he resumed his life as a chemist and also became one of the most perceptive and respected writers about the Holocaust.[2]

Plagued by bouts of depression and by what he called "survivors' disease," Levi died on 11 April 1987—probably by suicide—leaving behind a remarkable authorship that proved to be as diverse as it was penetrating. Although largely ignored at first, his Auschwitz memoir, *Se questo è un uomo* (1947 and 1958), which was translated into English as *If This Is a Man* (United Kingdom, 1959) and as *Survival in Auschwitz* (United States, 1961), has become a widely read classic. In *Il sistema periodico* (1975), which appeared in English as *The Periodic Table* (1984), Levi used chemistry's basic elements as points of departure for further reflection on his Holocaust experience. His essays in books such as *I sommersi e i salvati* (1986), translated into English as *The Drowned and the Saved* (1988), are also required reading for anyone who studies the Holocaust in depth. Furthermore, Levi wrote significant fiction—some of it science fiction—and gave interviews that are among the best of the oral history that comprises what is often called survivor testimony.

Levi described himself as "split in two."[3] Neither his life nor his thought were without fracture and contradiction, but the splitting to which he referred—it was one result of Auschwitz, his survival, and a return-that-was-no-return—was also a blending that contributed to the masterful poetry that added to the variety and brilliance of his writing.[4] His verse epitomizes qualities that characterize his other works: a restless questioning, an economy and clarity of mind, a persistent sense of irony and paradox, a keen eye for detail and a love for sensitively crafted language, a patient consideration of historical and psychological complexity, a carefully nuanced moral judgment, an unrelenting honesty, and an unvanquished humanism infused with lucid realism, to mention a few. Poignant yearning also marks Levi's thought, a theme and feeling that appear in one of the poems he wrote not long after World War II ended. In the eight brief lines that comprise "Sunset at Fossoli," which is dated 7 February 1946, Levi recalls seeing the sun go down through the barbed wire that imprisoned him in that Auschwitz antechamber. He notes how the sun's return is expected, but Levi says that he saw the sun die and that he knows "what it means not to return."[5] For Levi, the sun both died and lived; he returned and yet did not. Both during and after the Holocaust, Levi realized, his existence was marked by versions of such tension and the inescapable ambiguity and compromise they contained.

This book is not primarily a study of Levi's life and thought, but its chapters have been inspired and focused by threads in them both. Showing how the Holocaust shattered the world in ways that made it problematic, if not impossible, for human existence to return to what it had been before Auschwitz, let alone to return to "normal," Levi's Holocaust experiences led him, for example, to reflect on language. "If the Lagers had lasted longer," he observed, "a new, harsh language would have been born: and only this language could express what it means to toil the whole day in the wind, with the temperature below freezing, wearing only a shirt, underpants, cloth jacket and trousers, and in one's body nothing but weakness, hunger and knowledge of the end drawing nearer."[6]

Arguably, the Holocaust did not last long enough to produce fully the new language of which Levi spoke, but as survivors and scholars continue their struggle to describe, analyze, and explain what happened during those dark times, new and, in their own way, harsh concepts have emerged. One thinks, for instance, of Lawrence Langer's *choiceless choices,* a term now used to identify the dilemmas created by Nazi Germany and its collaborators, who often put Jews and other victims in circumstances where they had to make decisions among hideous options that could not even be described as involving so-called "lesser of evils."[7] Or, to cite a second example, there is Terrence Des Pres's *excremental assault,* the concept he created to refer to the ways in which lack of sanitation in the Holocaust's ghettos and camps—whether intended by the Germans or not—humiliated and besieged every prisoner and killed many of them.[8] Even *genocide,* the word coined by Raphael Lemkin, was added to humanity's vocabulary only while the Holocaust raged.[9]

No list of terms belonging to the new, harsh vocabulary required by Holocaust studies could begin to be complete if it failed to include Primo Levi's *gray zone.* He used that phrase specifically to refer to the "incredibly complicated internal structure" of Auschwitz, which created moral ambiguity and compromise in ways large and small. He was struck particularly, but not only, by the ways in which the German organization of the camp led Jews, however reluctantly, to become complicit in the destruction of their own people. Focusing attention especially on the *Sonderkommando,* the Jews who were conscripted to work in the gas chambers and crematoria at Auschwitz-Birkenau, the camp's killing center, Levi said that "Conceiving and organizing [those] squads was National Socialism's most demonic crime."[10]

Levi's gray zone, however, was not restricted to such radical examples. Emphasizing "the extreme pressure of the Lager," he noted that the number of "gray, ambiguous persons, ready to compromise" was—and remains—more the rule than the exception in any time or place. In Auschwitz those ranks swelled, for survival depended on finding or taking some advantage that made nearly all survivors—Levi included himself—"the rightful owners of a quota of guilt."[11] Levi amplified those feelings in a chapter on "Shame," which is an important sequel to the reflection on "The Gray Zone" that precedes it. "The 'saved' of the Lager were not the best," said Levi. "What I had seen and lived through proved the exact contrary. Preferably the worst survived, the selfish, the violent, the insensitive, the collaborators of the 'gray zone,' the spies. It was not a certain rule (there were none, nor are there certain rules in human matters), but it was nevertheless a rule. I felt innocent, yes, but enrolled among the saved and therefore in permanent search of a justification in my own eyes and those of others. The worst survived, that is, the fittest; the best all died."[12]

Levi's understated philosophical view held that "Each of us is a mixture of good and not so good,"[13] but his interpretation of the gray zone rejected invidious moral equivalencies. "I do not know," he wrote, "and it does not much interest me to know, whether in my depths there lurks a murderer, but I do know that I was a guiltless victim and I was not a murderer."[14] As Levi made clear by his analysis of a man whom he identifies as Muhsfeld, a German perpetrator who momentarily, but only momentarily, showed pity when a Jewish girl somehow remained alive in Auschwitz after gassing, the gray zone could include a very wide range of men and women, but immense differences remained among them. Compared to Muhsfeld, Levi could rightly call himself a guiltless victim. Considering himself from other angles, Levi could not exempt himself from guilt, relatively minor though it might be.

In the main, however, Levi did not intend his analysis of the gray zone to result in condemning judgments but instead to show how Auschwitz could "confuse our need to judge"[15]—and rightly so—and then to warn his readers about the ambiguities and compromises that could be lurking for them, a point driven home at the end of his famous chapter on "The Gray Zone" in *The Drowned and the Saved*. That chapter extends the gray zone beyond the confines of Auschwitz as it concludes with reflection on Chaim Rumkowski, whose fate it was to lead the Jewish Council that the Germans forced the Jews to establish in the Lodz ghetto. Suggesting that Rumkowski's story contains "in an exemplary form the almost physical necessity with which political coercion gives birth to that ill-defined sphere of ambiguity and compromise" that constitutes the gray zone, Levi's chapter concludes that "like Rumkowski, we too are so dazzled by power and prestige as to forget our essential fragility. Willingly or not we come to terms with power, forgetting that we are all in the ghetto, that the ghetto is walled in, that outside the ghetto reign the lords of death, and that close by the train is waiting."[16]

Levi spoke of the gray zone in the singular, but his analysis made clear that this region was multi-faceted and multi-layered. It was not confined to one time or place. With that insight in mind, during the spring of 2003 Michael Berenbaum, Jonathan Petropoulos, and John Roth began to plan the inaugural conference for the Claremont McKenna College Center for the Study of the Holocaust, Genocide, and Human Rights, which had been established that March. Following Levi's lead, we thought about the Holocaust's gray *zones,* the multitude of ways in which aspects of his gray-zone analysis might shed light both on the Holocaust itself and also on scholarship about that catastrophe. With key support from Claremont McKenna College President Pamela Gann and Dean of the Faculty William Ascher, who provided funding from the Podlich Distinguished Visitor endowment that had supported Berenbaum as a scholar-in-residence during the 2002–3 academic year, invitations were extended to the scholars who have contributed to this book. Their papers were critically discussed at the conference on "Gray Zones: Ambiguity and Compromise in the Holocaust and Its Aftermath," which took place in Claremont, California, on 5–7 February 2004, and then the papers were revised for publication.

Both the conference and this book have tried to reach a significant goal, which is to deal with Levi's claim that the Holocaust in particular shows that "The greater part of historical and natural phenomena are not simple, or not simple in the way that we would like."[17] The Holocaust and its aftermath are too vast and complicated for any book, however many contributors it might contain, to yield completeness and closure on that theme, which serves as this volume's governing epigraph. It is possible, however, to illustrate how the Holocaust and scholarship about it grapple with ambiguity and compromise at their deepest and often most excruciating levels.

Levi argued that nothing revealed the gray zone more grimly than the *Sonderkommando*'s plight. In the years since he made that claim, new testimony and scholarship about those tragic units have appeared. Early on, then, we identified the *Sonderkommando* as one of the topics of Holocaust history and scholarship that the conference and this book must encounter. Berenbaum, Petropoulos, and Roth soon added other cutting-edge subjects that not only deserved attention in their own right but also could be linked together to show both the complexity that Levi had in mind and the ways in which scholars have responded to it with thoughtful responsibility. As indicated by the book's table of contents, those topics include ambiguity and compromise in writing and depicting Holocaust history; issues about identity, gender, and sexuality during and after the Third Reich; inquiries about what we call "gray spaces," those regions of geography, imagination, and psychology that reflect the Holocaust's impact then and now; and dilemmas that have haunted the pursuit of justice, ethics, and religion during and after the Holocaust.

Levi began his chapter on "The Gray Zone" by asking the following question: "Have we—we who have returned—been able to understand and make others understand our experience?"[18] He went on to suggest that there could be no "return," at least not in the sense that understanding could be obtained if "what we commonly mean by 'understand' coincides with 'simplify.'"[19] The human mind tends to equate understanding with simplification, and Levi thought the desire for simplification was justifiable because there can scarcely be any understanding unless there is some simplification of experience. Both understanding and the communication that make it possible depend on paying attention to *this* instead of to *that*. Every declarative sentence that one speaks or writes leaves out more than it grasps. Nevertheless, the Holocaust negates the equation between understanding and simplification; it resists the belief that any *this* can be fully understood without attending to virtually every *that*. The challenge the Holocaust poses, neither alone nor exclusively but in distinctive ways because of the extent and degree of the atrocity it contained, is how to keep awareness and analysis of complexity from overwhelming one's ability to understand and yet to make awareness and analysis of complexity yield understanding instead.

Accomplishing such work is easier said than done, and not least because, as shown by Levi's work and the essays that supplement it in this volume, our efforts to understand the Holocaust require reconsideration of *understanding* itself. In the gray zone, Levi maintained, "The two camps of masters and servants both diverge and converge."[20] If there is to be sound and growing understanding of the Holocaust, grappling with a multitude of factors of that kind will be its hallmark. The readers of this book will have to judge for themselves whether that goal has been at least partly achieved in these pages, but the hope of those who have created them is that these essays will contribute to such understanding and also model scholarship that can produce more understanding of that kind.

Credit for any success enjoyed by this book goes to many more people than the scholars who have written its chapters. Already we have mentioned Pamela Gann and William Ascher, who were instrumental in the creation of the Claremont McKenna College Center for the Study of the Holocaust, Genocide, and Human Rights. We owe much to them. As also indicated above, Michael Berenbaum provided expert guidance in developing the conceptual framework for this project. Omer Bartov encouraged Petropoulos and Roth to approach Marion Berghahn so that the book could be considered for publication in the series on War and Genocide that Bartov edits for Berghahn Books. Both have encouraged and supported our work enormously, and we are especially grateful to Marion Berghahn for publishing the book. Kimberly Petropoulos served brilliantly as the manager of the Gray Zones conference. While she ensured that the finished essays arrived in a timely manner, our superb editorial assistant, Amy Walter, worked long, hard, and with stellar attention to detail as she put the manuscript into publishable form. Her accomplishments were augmented by those of Garrett Hodge, who assisted with the book's bibliography and line edits. At Berghahn Books, the project's production editor, Michael Dempsey, handled every detail with care and efficiency. Lori Rider's copyediting and Lynda Stannard's indexing were superb as well. To all of these helpful people, we give profound thanks.

In *Moments of Reprieve* (1986) Primo Levi recalled his friend Lorenzo, a gray-zoned figure in his own right and the person whom Levi had identified in *Survival in Auschwitz* as the one to whom he owed his life. Lorenzo Perrone, an Italian civilian and a skilled mason, was technically a voluntary civilian worker who had been recruited to help build the industrial plants that the Germans were constructing at Auschwitz III. In fact, he was more like a labor conscript, and he despised the German cruelty that he saw there. After meeting Levi in late June 1944, he decided to help his fellow Italian, even though it was a crime with grave consequences for Lorenzo even to speak to an Auschwitz prisoner. For months Lorenzo saw that Levi received extra food, which was the physical difference between life and death. "I believe that it was really due to Lorenzo that I am alive today," Levi would write, underscoring that his help meant more than food alone.[21] What also sustained Levi was what he called Lorenzo's "presence . . . his natural and plain manner of being good, that there still existed a just world outside our own, something and someone still pure and whole, not corrupt, not savage, extraneous to hatred and terror; something difficult to define, a remote possibility of good, but for which it was worth surviving."[22]

When liberation came, Levi lost track of Lorenzo, but later he became determined to learn what had happened to his life-saving friend. They reconnected for a short time in Italy after the war, but soon Lorenzo died. At one of their postwar meetings, Levi learned that he was not the only Auschwitz prisoner whom Lorenzo had helped, but Levi's friend had told that story to scarcely anyone. In Lorenzo's view, wrote Levi, "We are in this world to do good, not to boast about it."[23] Those words fit Lorenzo in unique ways, but we also find them fitting for a final expression of appreciation and gratitude, which goes to Leigh Crawford and AnneMerie Donoghue, the special friends to whom this book is dedicated. In their generous ways, they are like Lorenzo. Without them neither the Claremont McKenna Center for the Study of the Holocaust, Genocide, and Human Rights nor this book on *Gray Zones: Ambiguity and Compromise in the Holocaust and Its Aftermath* would exist.

Notes

1. Primo Levi, *Survival in Auschwitz: The Nazi Assault on Humanity,* trans. Stuart Woolf (New York: Simon and Schuster, 1996), 17.
2. For further detail on Primo Levi's life, consult the major biographies that have been published in recent years: Carole Angier, *The Double Bond: Primo Levi, a Biography* (New York: Farrar, Straus and Giroux, 2002), Myriam Anissimov, *Primo Levi: Tragedy of an Optimist,* trans. Steve Cox (Woodstock, NY: Overlook Press, 1998), and Ian Thomson, *Primo Levi: A Life* (New York: Henry Holt, 2002). A concise and worthwhile overview of Levi's thought is provided by Massimo Giuliani, *A Centaur in Auschwitz: Reflections on Primo Levi's Thinking* (Lanham, MD: Lexington Books, 2003).
3. See, for example, Levi's interview with Edoardo Fadini in Primo Levi, *The Voice of Memory: Interviews, 1961–1987,* ed. Marco Belpoliti and Robert Gordon; trans. Robert Gordon (New York: The New Press, 2001), 85.
4. See Primo Levi, *Collected Poems,* trans. Ruth Feldman and Brian Swan (London: Faber and Faber, 1988). This collection appeared originally as *Ad ora incerta* (*At an Uncertain Hour*) in 1984.
5. Ibid., 15.
6. Levi, *Survival in Auschwitz,* 123. From his hiding place in Dresden, the German Jewish scholar Victor Klemperer documented how the Nazis themselves had contributed to a new, harsh language of violence and atrocity. See Victor Klemperer, *The Language of the Third Reich (LTI—Lingua Tertii Imperii): A Philologist's Notebook,* trans. Martin Brady (New York: Continuum, 2002).
7. See, for instance, Lawrence L. Langer, *Versions of Survival: The Holocaust and the Human Spirit* (Albany: State University of New York Press, 1982), 67–129. Choiceless choices, writes Langer, do not "reflect options between life and death, but between one form of abnormal response and another, both imposed by a situation that was in no way of the victim's own choosing" (72).
8. See Terrence Des Pres, *The Survivor: An Anatomy of Life in the Death Camps* (New York: Oxford University Press, 1976).
9. See Raphael Lemkin, *Axis Rule in Occupied Europe: Laws of Occupation, Analysis of Government, Proposals for Redress* (Washington, DC: Carnegie Endowment for International Peace, 1944).

10. Primo Levi, *The Drowned and the Saved,* trans. Raymond Rosenthal (New York: Summit Books, 1988), 53.
11. Ibid., 49.
12. Ibid., 82.
13. Primo Levi, "The Duty of Memory," in *The Voice of Memory,* 232. This article is based on Levi's interview with Anna Bravo and Federico Cereja, which was first published in Italy in 1983.
14. Levi, *The Drowned and the Saved,* 48.
15. Ibid., 42.
16. Ibid., 67, 69.
17. Ibid., 37.
18. Ibid., 36.
19. Ibid.
20. Ibid., 42.
21. Levi, *Survival in Auschwitz,* 121.
22. Ibid.
23. Primo Levi, *Moments of Reprieve: A Memoir of Auschwitz,* trans. Ruth Feldman (New York: Penguin Books, 1987), 160.

– *Part One* –

AMBIGUITY AND COMPROMISE IN WRITING AND DEPICTING HOLOCAUST HISTORY

"I did not choose to be a writer," said Primo Levi, "I was turned into one."[1] His deportation, his awareness of the gray zone in Auschwitz, his observation of the suffering of others—these were among the experiences that compelled him to write. *Survival in Auschwitz* contains a brief but poignant episode that reflects these impulses. Levi recalls Dr. Pannwitz's chemical laboratory, a warm and privileged place for an Auschwitz prisoner as winter bears down upon the camp. "To work," he writes, "is to push wagons, carry sleepers, break stones, dig earth, press one's bare hands against the iciness of the freezing iron."[2] Levi's verbs "push, carry, break, dig, press" denote exhaustion and the death that follows. "But," says Levi, "I sit all day."[3] He has a notebook, a pencil, and a comrade, too. The comrade is not exactly another person, and yet he is, for the comrade is part of Levi himself: an aspect of himself that has been revived by the privileges that are his. In its own way, this self-revival involves gray-zoned ambiguity, compromise, and more because it contains "the pain of remembering, the old ferocious suffering of feeling myself a man again, which attacks me like a dog the moment my conscience comes out of the gloom."[4] With that companion close by, Levi says that he takes his pencil and notebook and writes "what I would never dare tell anyone."[5]

Levi could not keep the words he wrote in Auschwitz. To do so invited death. But even after he was liberated and able to write freely, were there things that he would never dare tell anyone? Levi was an eyewitness to the Holocaust. He wrote about it with the precision and curiosity of the empir-

Notes for this section begin on page 5.

ical scientist. In that process, Levi revealed much about himself as well. His need to tell the story of his Auschwitz experience was very strong. Devoting himself to that work, he tried hard to maintain "a careful balance between the essential and the superfluous," which he regarded as "the decisive element for narrative procedure."[6] Levi found writing to be "a way of creating order," the best one he knew, and he added that he felt "an immense need to put things in order, to put order back into a world of chaos, to explain to myself and to others."[7] But aspects of the chaos, things that he remembered, could elude telling and thus leave the order incomplete, however much the writing might create or restore it.

Levi often thought of himself as a storyteller. His craft was not that of the historian, although few persons have done more than Levi to advance historical understanding of the Holocaust. Indeed, Levi and Holocaust historians have much in common, for they have long struggled with challenges about memory, documentation, and representation. How does one capture events that transpired in the past, especially if there are evidentiary lacunae? In the case of the Holocaust, there are other, special challenges that grow out of the enormity and horror of the events, perhaps including things that a person would never dare tell anyone. Echoing Levi from time to time, the authors in this section identify many of the challenges and also explore some of the reasons for them. They offer strategies that hold the most promise as Holocaust scholars formulate a collective methodological and philosophical response. Their historical findings also complement and supplement what Levi revealed about the Holocaust and the gray zone in particular.

Forced to work at the I. G. Farben construction site at Monowitz, where the Germans hoped to manufacture synthetic rubber, Primo Levi knew firsthand that German industry was deeply involved and implicated at Auschwitz. At the time, however, his perspective was necessarily limited. He could have had no idea of the full extent of industry's relationships to the Holocaust and the many gray zones that obtained within them, including his own. Only later, with the scholarly expertise of historians such as Peter Hayes, could that story be told. Hayes's chapter explores this gray-zoned terrain by analyzing a German chemical corporation called Degussa, whose products included carbon black, "a sootlike granular substance," Hayes explains, "that, when added to rubber, increases its durability." Absent German industry's role, the Holocaust and its reverberations would have been very different, if they had existed at all. Hayes's opening essay sets a tone for all that follows in *Gray Zones*, for he shows how accurate Levi was in saying that "the greater part of historical and natural phenomena are not simple, or not simple in the ways that we would like."[8]

Decisions that were made at a distance from Auschwitz and other Holocaust sites had devastating consequences far and wide. Careful study of them provides new insight, just as Levi supplied when he wrote about the gray zone. Christopher Browning's essay combines the study of both a network of slave labor camps (in the factories at Starachowice) and a nearby ghetto (at Wierzbnik). By grounding his investigation in a specific geographic context—sites in the Radom district of the General Government—Browning provides valuable empirical evidence concerning key issues, including survival and resistance strategies among Jews, the comportment of *Judenrat* members, solidarity among victims, and the usefulness of postwar survivor testimony. His findings do not always conform to expectations (or wishes), but Browning remains faithful to the evidence he has found—even if this results in surprising conclusions ("life outside the camps was less safe for Jews than inside") or the placement of certain individuals in uncomfortable gray zones.

Primo Levi thought that survivors of the *Sonderkommando* would not be likely to speak much about their experiences. Nor would their terrible plight be one that most people would want to dwell upon. The Israeli historian Gideon Greif has found neither of those positions to be entirely accurate. He has conducted path-breaking research by interviewing surviving members of the *Sonderkommando*, the squads of victims who labored in the gas chambers and crematoria and did so much to focus Levi's conception of the gray zone. In securing the testimony of these former commandos at Auschwitz-Birkenau, Greif has performed a great service to the historical profession. After all, these men were at "ground zero" of the Holocaust and saw things that no one else alive has seen. Levi knew and thought about them, but Greif has done firsthand research that Levi was unable to do. As he seeks to convey their experiences, which may well include things that they would never dare tell anyone, Greif conceives a gray zone between a common industrial plant and an "insane" system that produced death (or more precisely, human ashes). Besides exploring this centaur-like connection between rationality and madness, Greif identifies other gray zones that existed in the lives of *Sonderkommandos:* for example, in the tension between an unfeeling, numb, and even robotic mind-set on the one hand, and a compassion for other victims. He looks at the ambiguous relationship between the commandos and the SS guards, where fear and familiarity would coexist. Among the *Sonderkommandos*, the impulse towards suicide and the desire to survive and bear witness also existed simultaneously amidst a rush of conflicting emotions.

Michael Berenbaum also explores the experiences of the *Sonderkommandos*, as he utilizes testimony gathered for the documentary film *Evidence*. He pursues a conscious strategy of permitting surviving members to relate their experiences in their own words. As with the subjects of Greif's study, certain themes recur: the contemplation of suicide, the sense of abject powerlessness, the refuge in numbed feelings, robotic behavior, and the outrage they felt at the fate of children. Levi's analysis of the gray zone alludes to these realities; the voices of the men themselves, amplified by Berenbaum's scholarship, add much more detail, much more anguish, than Levi was in a position to provide. Due to defense mechanisms that have prevented them from engaging certain topics and ideas, and because of the relatively few survivors, the *Sonderkommandos* pose special challenges to scholars. While most observers would absolve them of any guilt for what they did in order to survive—this was also the viewpoint of Primo Levi, himself a tough judge—the *Sonderkommandos* occupy a gray zone in that they defy understanding. It is indeed difficult for historians to gain a clear picture of their experiences or put them in a larger philosophical and ethical context.

Gerhard Weinberg explores some of the methodological challenges he has encountered during his distinguished forty-plus–year career by surveying his engagement with Raul Hilberg's work. Weinberg, the author of the definitive study of Hitler's foreign policy and a magisterial volume on World War II, among other books, has persuasively advocated the need to examine the Holocaust in the context of war, a reality that Levi experienced but did not grasp as Weinberg's global study has been able to do. Besides an awareness of the mutability of the front lines and a sensitivity to the manner in which military fortunes changed the attitudes of both leaders and masses, Weinberg emphasizes the importance of ideology. In an analysis of the 20 January 1942 Wannsee Conference protocol, he concludes that the important document reveals an intention on the part of the top Nazi leaders to pursue a more geographically expansive genocidal program—one that would go beyond, to use Hilberg's words, "the destruction of European Jews" and extend to the Middle East. But lest he be categorized in the "intentionalist" camp of Holocaust scholars, Weinberg stresses the importance of contingency: not everything was planned by the Nazi leaders and their accomplices. As with Hilberg and Levi, too, Gerhard Weinberg stresses the importance of understanding specifics and details; and like Hilberg, he points to the importance of contemporaneous documentation. Among the most knowledgeable authorities when it comes to the archives, Weinberg shows that there is still much to be discovered and learned.

Another of the "deans" among Holocaust scholars, Raul Hilberg is acutely aware of the limitations of representation. When Levi says that there were things "I would never dare tell anyone," Hilberg understands that there are memories that "cannot be expressed.... How does one describe the utter deprivation of possessions and privacy in a camp, the filth, the smell, the exhausting labor and endless roll calls, the cold, the heat, the persistent hunger, the thirst, the confrontation with the sudden loss of a wife, a husband, a child, the momentary fear of being gassed, the constant anxiety interrupted only by deep sleep?"[9] Hilberg's point and Levi's confession are not identical, but they are close enough to complement each other as they identify key problems in representing and depicting the Holocaust. As for Hilberg in particular, despite an approach that is sober and in many ways pessimistic about the potential for human understanding, he struggles on with a lifelong project as Levi did with his. One manifestation of this battle is his repeated rewriting of his classic, *The Destruction of the European Jews,* for which there have been two major revisions since the book was first published in 1961. While Levi and many notable scholars have usually developed a career strategy that entails writing a series of books, Hilberg has attempted to refine his magnum opus: to make it as accurate, as "right" as it can possibly be. Hilberg has, of course, also written other books; most recently, he has reflected on the sources available to Holocaust scholars and explored the concomitant methodological issues. His essay here continues in the vein of this most recent, methodologically oriented work. Yet, by reflecting on recent historiographical trends, Hilberg also raises, or returns to, some of the psychological factors that have influenced scholarship on the Holocaust. He notes the "inhibition to study the invisible victims," and the challenges posed by probing the lives of ordinary people. Especially daunting are topics where researchers are confronted by a "gray zone" laden with sensitive issues carrying the implication that particular groups of people, specifically among the victims and the Jewish Councils in particular, could have been guilty of wrongdoing. For a scholar who employs such a rigorous and explicit empirical approach to the Holocaust—one grounded in contemporaneous documents—Hilberg is remarkably attuned to the influences of psychology, language, and narrative approach, among other factors, as they affect scholars in pursuit of "imagined perfection."

Recalling the notes he had written in the chemical laboratory at Auschwitz in 1944, Levi emphasized that they were real, even though they "never amounted to more than twenty lines," but at the same time they were not real because "there was no way I could keep them. It was materially impossible. Where could I hide them? In some container, but which? In my pockets? We had nothing, they changed our beds, the mattresses were continually being moved, even our clothes. There was no way of holding on to anything. Except in our memory."[10] Hayes, Browning, Greif, Berenbaum, Weinberg, Hilberg, and Primo Levi: each has contributed much to Holocaust understanding by highlighting the complexity of that event. They share a commitment to make up for the absence of words, the lack of writing, the silence that the perpetrators of the Holocaust sought to impose on their victims.

Notes

1. See Primo Levi's 1984 interview with Rita Caccamo De Luca and Manuela Olagnero in Primo Levi, *The Voice of Memory: Interviews, 1961–1987*, ed. Marco Belpoliti and Robert Gordon; trans. Robert Gordon (New York: The New Press, 2001), 161.
2. Primo Levi, *Survival in Auschwitz: The Nazi Assault on Humanity*, trans. Stuart Woolf (New York: Simon and Schuster, 1996), 141.
3. Ibid.
4. Ibid., 142.
5. Ibid.
6. See Levi's 1987 interview with Robert Di Caro in *The Voice of Memory*, 171.
7. Ibid., 174.
8. Primo Levi, *The Drowned and the Saved*, trans. Raymond Rosenthal (New York: Summit Books, 1988), 37.
9. Raul Hilberg, *Sources of Holocaust Research: An Analysis* (Chicago: Ivan R. Dee, 2001), 167.
10. See Levi's 1983 interview with Anna Bravo and Federico Cereja in *The Voice of Memory*, 225.

– Chapter 1 –

THE AMBIGUITIES OF EVIL AND JUSTICE
Degussa, Robert Pross, and the Jewish Slave Laborers at Gleiwitz

Peter Hayes

Thanks to more than three decades of intensified research, historians now generally think a great deal differently about the German corporate world in the Third Reich than they used to. Largely gone are the once prominent shibboleths depicting industrial and financial magnates as major players in Hitler's appointment as chancellor, as monolithically or even predominantly pro-Nazi and antisemitic in the early years of the regime, and as molders of domestic and foreign policy throughout the period 1933–45. The once common contention that German big business sought and pursued the dispossession of Jews and their exploitation as slave laborers as means of making windfall profits is increasingly questioned. But this does not mean that current scholarship absolves Germany's commercial elite of responsibility for the crimes of Nazism. Rather, the prevailing view now traces executives' liability not to their supposed congruence of purpose with Hitler's government but to their reflexive adaptability. Managers' nearly universal readiness to try to tame or tap into Nazi assaults on liberty and morality almost invariably made these worse. As a result, the leaders of German industry and finance became deeply complicit in promoting the horrors their country visited on Europe and especially its Jews from 1933 to 1945.[1]

Yet recent efforts to obtain compensation for the victims of this complicity have shown little awareness of this historiographical maturation. Plaintiffs' lawyers, who presumably would blanch at the thought of a layman discoursing on the tax code after reading a few old treatments of the subject for a popular audience, apparently think nothing of assembling ama-

Notes for this section begin on page 21.

teurish renditions of economic and corporate history in the Nazi era from a smattering of dated accounts by nonspecialists. Consider the fanciful picture painted by Burt Neuborne before the Committee on Banking and Financial Services of the United States House of Representatives on 14 September 1999:

> Imagine the economic benefit to a wartime economy of being relieved from the obligation of paying wages to more than 50 percent of your labor force. The fruits of the unpaid slave and forced labor were realized in enormous wartime profits, most of which was [sic] paid out to large shareholders as dividends, much of it was reinvested in capital equipment that paved the way for [German] post-war corporate profitability.[2]

"Imagine" indeed. Although there is some truth in Neuborne's remark about capital equipment, every other historical claim in this passage is vastly overstated. Employers of forced laborers—that is, of the non-Jewish Europeans who were lured or lassoed into composing 80 to 90 percent of Germany's nonnative workforce between 1939 and 1945—were not "relieved . . . of paying wages to" such people. They were, in fact, paid, albeit at variably discriminatory rates, and the potential "savings" to firms in comparison to domestic levels of compensation often were reduced considerably by the expense of housing and guarding such personnel. To be sure, slave laborers—that is, the Jews from ghettos and camps who made up the remaining roughly 10 to 20 percent of foreigners put to work for the Reich—usually got no recompense. But they were paid *for*, and the rates that the SS charged per head, along with the costs of barracks and guard forces, required substantial outlays.[3] Moreover, until mid-1944, the great majority of such slave laborers were exploited by German government agencies, not private industry. Of those allotted earlier to corporations, most toiled on construction projects that were never completed and/or never gave off returns. Finally, most of the "enormous wartime profits" accrued by German industry during World War II were not in fact paid out to shareholders, since dividends were capped by Nazi law at 6 to 8 percent of net profits. Rather, they either were reinvested in plants and machinery that the fighting often obliterated, or they accumulated in reserves that war damages and government-bond depreciation later exhausted.

In short, the most conspicuous recent discussion of industrial complicity in the Holocaust has proceeded in the reductionist, black-and-white terms that adversarial proceedings before courts of law (and in the court of public opinion) foster, but that erase the nuances or "gray zones" of the historical record. Neither the contribution of forced and slave labor to the wartime profitability of German industry, nor the extent of that profitability, for example, approached the levels posited by many plaintiffs' attorneys. But experience with American civil suits is an apparently irresistible inducement for these lawyers to hype the wages of criminality in order to magnify its just deserts. Not for nothing did Gerald Feldman once feel driven to the exasperated remark that "the briefs in some class actions sometimes make me feel that our worst history students have decided to take up law."[4] That comment is surely too sweeping—many of these people probably were excellent students before succumbing to the temptations of legal debate. But Feldman's comment highlights two unfortunate by-products of the way justice has been pursued for Holocaust victims in the United States. The repeated deployment of outmoded, simplistic models of German corporate behavior and experience in the Nazi context has cheapened this pursuit and distorted public perceptions of why and how the slave labor system developed. This essay attempts to repair some of the damage in the latter respect.

A powerful illustration of the gap between historical and legal approaches to gauging corporate complicity in slave labor is provided by the story of an Upper Silesian factory of the Degussa concern, the plant's up-and-coming young manager, and the male and female Jewish slave laborers who increasingly built and operated it in 1942–44. This is a tale replete with ironies, a story of how an installation the firm did *not* want entangled it with Auschwitz, of how an executive's self-interested but growing *solicitude* for his workers contributed to worsening their existences, and of how lawyerly preoccupation with the "disgorgement" of *phantom gains* fails to make the appropriate case for Degussa's obligations to those it victimized. In short, the history of the Deutsche Gasrusswerke site at Gleiwitz during the latter half of World War II exposes not one but three different "gray zones" of behavior (corporate, personal, and legal) in the context of the Holocaust and its aftermath.

The Corporate Gray Zone—Degussa and Gleiwitz

The Deutsche Gasrusswerke (DGW), an equal partnership between the Degussa chemical corporation of Frankfurt and a consortium of German tire manufacturers, made carbon black, a sootlike granular substance that, when added to rubber, increases its durability. During the prewar years, the Nazi regime encouraged domestic output of the product, driving the capacity at the nation's principal existing plants (Degussa's own at Kalscheuren and DGW's at Dortmund) up from a mere six hundred metric tons per year in 1934 to some twenty-two thousand in 1939, despite Degussa's repeated objections that such growth far exceeded any conceivable estimate of prospective civilian demand.[5] With the outbreak of the war, the government redoubled its efforts. Johannes Eckell of the National Office for Economic Expansion resurrected his plan for a third factory, a notion that Degussa's chief executives, Hermann Schlosser and Ernst Baerwind, had fought off the year before, only now with a twist. In "extraordinarily sharp" terms, Eckell urged the businessmen to select a location in Upper Silesia, which was beyond the reach of aerial assault from Western Europe but about to become, with the fall of Poland, comfortably within the Reich's expanded frontiers.[6] Because current carbon black production seemed likely, even by the government's own calculations, to overshoot the absorptive capacity of the German rubber industry until at least mid-1941, the undertaking struck Baerwind as "from a commercial point of view somewhat absurd." But Eckell nonetheless insisted that "for military reasons, the project . . . must be so worked out that it can be pulled ready from the drawer at any time" and directed Baerwind in November 1939 to present such a plan in the latter half of the coming January.[7] After Eckell reiterated this demand a month later, Baerwind resignedly noted that "We will not be able to get out of an inspection of locations in Upper Silesia" early in the new year, only to be rescued briefly by other developments that caused Eckell to relent for the time being.[8]

Once the failure of the Reich to bring Britain to terms over the summer of 1940 indicated that a long war was in the offing, Eckell returned to his pet project. In September he threatened Degussa and DGW that, in the event of further foot-dragging, "the National Office will have to call upon other carbon-black makers . . . to provide for the expansion of capacity." As usual in the Third Reich, the gambit of playing producers against each other worked. The managing board in Frankfurt promptly deduced that "in order to preserve its leading position in the carbon-black field, Degussa must take an active part" via DGW, even though, as Baerwind pointed out, the feedstocks on which an Upper Silesian plant would depend were both twice as expensive as those in western Germany and heavily contested by other claimants.[9] By the end of the year, Baerwind and Georg Kemnitz of DGW concluded that the best available eastern site was one offered by Borsig Coking Works (*Kokswerke*) adjoining its factory in Gleiwitz, the former border town where World War II had begun.[10] Their attention apparently had been drawn to the spot already in 1939 because of the usefulness of the gas given off by the existing plant to the operations of a new facility.[11]

Once again, as in the 1930s, the unwanted expansion required the owners of DGW to put up considerable capital. The initial cost estimates for a new plant at Gleiwitz that could fabricate six thousand tons of active carbon black annually came to RM 12 to 13 million, more than Degussa had expended on the two earlier installations combined. Just under half of the appropriation was to be raised in cash from the partners and the balance from mortgages and bank loans.[12] But Eckell remained sure that buna output soon would outstrip carbon black production, and in autumn of 1941 an explosion at Kalscheuren and an air raid near the Dortmund plant presented him with another rationale for even greater growth: the urgent need to have replacement capacity in the German east in case of "accidents in the west."[13] Though DGW's leaders still doubted the reliability of raw material supplies, they knuckled under in November and approved an increase in Gleiwitz's capacity to some fourteen thousand yearly tons at a cost of a further RM 10.7 million, RM 2 million from another stock issue and the rest from additional borrowing, which brought the firm's total indebtedness to RM 21.2 million.[14] To lighten the burden, the Reich then agreed to renounce taxes due on up to RM 3 million in annual postdepreciation profits at the Dortmund plant so long as they were invested in the new one at

Gleiwitz, to cover it under the protections against superfluity afforded by the regime's "war risk clause," and to throw in supplemental relief from local taxes.[15] But, as often occurred in the Third Reich, what the Nazi state gave with one hand, it took back with the other. In May 1942, with Gleiwitz now projected to equal Dortmund in size, Eckell sought still more output of carbon black in Upper Silesia. By once again indicating readiness to turn to a competitor, he won DGW's agreement to an eventual capacity of seventeen thousand tons per year.[16] As a result, by the turn of 1942/43, DGW and Degussa foresaw the final cost of Gleiwitz as between RM 27 and 30 million.[17] Just over eight million of these were to come from the owners of DGW, 11.5 million from the profits of the plant at Dortmund, and the rest from borrowing by the company.

This was the setting in which the Degussa/DGW carbon black factory at Gleiwitz embarked on what became a three-year-long, ever-expanding, and highly ambiguous linkage to the Holocaust. Notably, the initial allocation of Jewish prisoners to the site, which occurred in April 1942 and consisted of some two hundred men from Annaberg and other forced labor camps in Upper Silesia, does not appear to have occurred at Degussa's request.[18] In view of the massive German labor shortage, the firm planned throughout 1941 on constructing the plant with some three hundred workers, roughly two hundred of them foreigners. By September, three months after the ground-breaking, a workforce of 280 men had been arduously pulled together. The non-Germans came primarily from Bulgaria and Italy, received the prevailing local wages for Germans of the same skill classifications, and were housed temporarily nearby in a well-outfitted former camp of the German Labor Service (*Arbeitsdienst*) pending the completion of on-site barracks.[19] But the ever-impatient Johannes Eckell had remained unsatisfied. In July, he proclaimed that "no other building project . . . is going so wrong," and he insisted at the end of the year on a tripling of Gleiwitz's workforce during the following spring, not least because of his recent success in forcing an increase in the originally planned production capacity by 133 percent.[20] To this end, his aides told Degussa's architect that "It is unavoidable that Russian prisoners of war also be used on the project" and countered fears of possible sabotage with reassurances "concerning the quality of this human material." Degussa's man reluctantly gave in, concluding that "We therefore will have no choice but to cover a portion of the labor requirements with Russians."[21] By late January 1942, however, Soviet prisoners of war were no longer sufficiently available to reach Eckell's target of nine hundred workers. Accordingly, at a meeting in Gleiwitz among himself, along with nine additional government officials, Kemnitz of DGW, architect Ziegler and one other Degussa representative, and Robert Pross, the man already destined to take over the plant in July, "The use of Jews was suggested and accepted in principle by the building supervisors."[22] Though such phrasing is purposefully vague, both it and Eckell's zeal regarding the factory imply that the management was on the receiving end of the idea.

The Personal Gray Zone—Robert Pross and Slave Labor

Born in 1906 and trained as an engineer, Robert Pross enjoyed a meteoric rise at Degussa after joining its construction office in May 1936. The following year, he began supervising the erection and operations of the Dortmund carbon black factory, and he supplemented his résumé by joining the Nazi Party. Politics appear to have played no role in his subsequent ascent, and little in the surviving evidence suggests that he was either active in or fervent about the Nazi Party, aside from the romantically nationalist overtones of his retrospective description of the Gleiwitz factory in 1945 as a "once flourishing . . . German workplace."[23] Instead, at the age of only thirty-six he won the assignment to build and direct so expensive and politically important a facility on the basis of his track record in bringing Dortmund rapidly to profitability, despite constant increases in its scheduled capacity.

Whatever Pross's political attitudes, they probably had little to do with the lack of concern that he and Degussa's chief architect initially showed for the welfare of the slave laborers that began to arrive at the Gleiwitz site. Although these managers clearly viewed the work habits and skill levels of their foreign workers and especially their first round of Jewish personnel as handicaps to be overcome, the parent firm quickly imposed a policy of shirking responsibility for the conditions that helped make such people relatively unproductive.[24] Ewald von Retze, a member of Degussa's managing board, laid down the general line that the corporation should avoid getting entangled in disputes over such matters by delegating them.[25] Thus, Frankfurt made arrangements at one time or another between 1941 and 1943 with the Organisation Todt, the National Labor Service, and the Deutsche Arbeitsfront (German Labor Front; DAF) to supervise the Gleiwitz workers' room and board, oversee their labor, and guard the barracks in return for monthly and/or daily fees.[26] The executives then left the matter at that, even though they suspected or knew that the deals provided considerable room for chicanery, especially with regard to food purchasing.

As a result, one survivor of the first shipment of Jews recalls that "the food was catastrophic," the clothing insufficient during winter, the footwear made of wood, and the labor both hard—largely because it consisted of excavating deep foundations for a subcontractor (the Allgemeine Hochkonstruktions-Ingenieure firm of Düsseldorf) with only shovels—and, on occasion, murderous.[27] In addition, the housing appears to have been overcrowded during most of 1942 (as it would be again later) and sometimes flimsy, since barracks were partially recycled from other building sites.[28] By the time Coen Rood, a Dutch Jewish tailor who also managed to survive the factory, arrived in November, only the accommodations, which included showers and adequate toilet and washing facilities, had improved. They were still lice-infested, however, and the rations consisted of pumpkin and cabbage soup, along with bread adulterated with sawdust. Put to work without gloves moving ice-cold iron and steel containers, Rood soon had reason to discover that the infirmary possessed only the most basic of medicines and bandages and that bartering whatever he could for extra food would be indispensable to survival. By the end of January 1943 eight of the men who had accompanied him from Holland were dead, two from beatings; a month later, six others were among the twenty-two men in the infirmary who were taken away in a truck, supposedly for work elsewhere.[29] Altogether, at least 246 Jews arrived at the Gleiwitz factory camp in 1942, and the number may have gone as high as four hundred; only 166 remained as of 26 February 1943.[30] In the factory management's records, one finds but faint echoes of this grim reality, as when Pross remarked in his annual report for 1942 that "special concern was directed at . . . the implementation of effective means to call lazy foreigners or those who have fled to account. The educational effect of the methods applied has resulted in a notable decline in loafing."[31]

Moreover, at the end of October 1942 DGW's leaders acquired another reason not to expend any thought on improving the Jewish prisoners' situation. According to Ziegler's summary of his and Pross's conversations with officials of the Armaments Ministry branch in Breslau,

> At the moment a transfer of Western [European] Jews to the East is in process. Among them are quite usable skilled workers, who can achieve even better performance with further, intensive direction. Before the allocation of these Jews, however, the present Eastern Jew camp is to be dissolved. Since we already have been contemplating giving the Eastern Jews back soon, this exchange corresponds closely to our way of thinking and fits into our plan. It was therefore agreed that DGW, in combination with the local building office, will immediately make the labor requirements known to the Department for Armaments Expansion in Breslau. . . . Director Pross already has telegraphed this information to Gleiwitz, Dr. Shenk, and given instructions that the necessary steps are to be taken immediately.[32]

Having been coerced into including Jews among their workers only seven months before, DGW's leaders no longer needed coaxing. Despite having a workforce on the site during the last quarter of 1942 that averaged 1,343 people (310 more than the need projected during the preceding April), they now jumped at the chance to obtain additional such unfortunates, while dispensing with the ones who had been worn down in the interim.[33]

The anticipated exchange took place in March 1943 and brought a second, augmented round of Jewish deportations to the Gleiwitz factory camp, but not according to the plan formulated in October 1942. Most of the 130 Jews shipped out were Western Europeans, of whom only thirty-two Dutch seemed to have remained. Their replacements, whose number provided for "a considerable expansion of the Jewish labor force," consisted almost entirely of Yiddish-speakers from Eastern Upper Silesia, many from the last ghetto liquidated there in Sosnowitz.[34] Gleiwitz now received 379 workers, at least 330 but probably almost all of them Jews, in return for 335 laborers transferred away, primarily to armaments projects.[35] A month later, 209 foreign women, almost certainly all of them Jews also from Eastern Upper

Silesia, appeared on the plant's roster. There the total number of Jews at the end of the month came to 535, 46 percent of the 1,152 foreign personnel and 38 percent of the total workforce, including Germans, of 1,393.[36] In preparation for these changes, the inmate labor camp was extended to include several of the barracks formerly for foreign workers, and a twelve-foot-high barbed wire fence was erected both around the compound and between the sectors henceforth reserved for men and women.[37]

Robert Pross later maintained that the Gleiwitz Labor Office suggested the use of Jewish women, but affirmed nonetheless that "The responsibility for this decision lay on my shoulders alone."[38] There is no reason to doubt him on either count. His retrospective version of the rationale for his actions is surely incomplete, however. Given the consideration that he (and his secretary) later began to demonstrate for the workforce, it may be true that he "saw . . . the possibility . . . of perhaps saving these people from worse," but his overriding thought at the time was probably self-interested.[39] As he wrote shortly after the first section of the plant commenced producing at the end of April 1943, "Only because of the success in obtaining female Jewish forced laborers through the good offices of the Plenipotentiary for Building was the chief prerequisite for the start-up even present."[40]

When the use of Jewish women was broached, Pross was both under enormous pressure to reach the spiraling production targets at Gleiwitz and conscious of the potential rewards of doing so (in 1944, as the second part of the plant was being finished, he received the War Service Cross, First Class).[41] His reputation as a "vertical starter" within the Degussa concern was at stake, and he could only benefit from his colleagues' appreciation of "what it means to the plant leaders to start a factory with a workforce that consists, aside from a few German craftsmen and foremen, exclusively of Polish Jewesses."[42] In this context, and since he already had acquiesced without recorded comment in the decision more than a year earlier to use Jewish male laborers to build the plant, the idea of rescuing Jewish women through putting them into the production line presumably functioned, if it occurred to him at the time, more as a rationalization than a reason for his decision.

Whatever the mix of Pross's motives, the cost of Jewish labor is unlikely to have been one of them. He took Jewish men and women because they were the only workers he could get, not because they came cheap. On the contrary, DGW's leaders always listed their dependence on low-performing foreign or forced labor as an—admittedly convenient—part of the explanation for the "excess expense" of building at Gleiwitz. And experience during the first year, as recorded in the profit and loss statements for 1943, largely bore them out. This document, the only surviving one that throws appreciable light on the overall and relative charges incurred for forced labor at Gleiwitz, includes statistics covering the nonsalaried workforce during that calendar year, when the average number of non-Jews actually working on the site came to 611 and the average total of Jews to 480, as well as data for the month of December in particular.[43]

The comprehensive figures show that during 1943 the non-Jewish workforce received RM 716,205, including an annual supplement, and that RM 117,574 went to subcontractors, presumably non-Jewish laborers, for a total of RM 833,779. For the Jews DGW paid RM 584,159, plus a charge of RM 124,878 for management of their barracks, which yields a sum of RM 709,037.[44] It appears, then, that the non-Jews, who made up on average 56 percent of the wage force, received 54 percent of the firm's disbursements for labor, but the Jews who constituted on average 44 percent of the workers cost DGW 46 percent of the bill. If one takes into consideration the 66,480 RM expended during the year on "legally required and other voluntary social welfare contributions," which went exclusively to non-Jews, the percentages come almost into alignment. Thus, the per capita costs of workers from Degussa's point of view work out for 1943 to RM 113.67 per month for non-Jews without benefits and RM 122.73 with these and, rather astoundingly, RM 123.20 for Jews.[45]

From the company's perspective, this amounted to an even greater relative *disadvantage* of using Jewish forced labor than meets the eye for two reasons: (a) the productivity difference, since Jewish men, in particular, were generally thought to contribute less work product per hour than non-Jews, even foreigners (and were, of course, worked and fed in such a way that this was likely to be so); and (b) the gender gap, since the non-Jewish labor force was almost universally male, while the Jewish one was about 40 percent female, which means that the base wages for the latter group should have been proportionately lower, according to German regulations.

Upon closer examination, however, this startling pattern turns out to be characteristic only of the construction phase at Gleiwitz, when the prevailing wages of civilian unskilled building workers, German and foreign, were relatively close to those that the SS demanded of companies for Jews (generally RM 3 to 6 per day, depending on sex and skill level, minus allowances for food and housing). In February, construction workers constituted 82 percent of all workers on the site; by June, the figure was 47 percent, and in December it came to only 41 percent. As the share of skilled workers bulked larger among the Germans (and the non-Jewish foreigners), their average hourly wage diverged increasingly from the costs of each Jewish forced laborer. The trend was reinforced by the gradual and related increase of the share of women among the Jews during the year. Thus, by December, when non-Jews barely outnumbered Jews on the Gleiwitz site on average (468 to 463), the relative shares of the outlays for wages, benefits, and barracks were 65 percent and 35 percent, the relative monthly costs per capita RM 192 to RM 104, and the relative daily ones RM 6.86 to RM 3.71. On an hourly basis, the discrepancy stood out still more sharply: Whereas the cost to the company of non-Jews, including benefits, averaged out to between RM 0.80 and 0.86 per hour in December 1943 (it is not clear whether they were working 60- or 56-hour weeks at this point), that for Jewish men came to only RM 0.33 per hour, given their twelve-hour workdays, and that for Jewish women was only slightly higher at RM 0.38 per hour, despite the fact that their shifts on the production lines were limited to eight hours.[46] In other words, the purely financial benefit of Jewish labor to DGW emerged only as the plant matured.

Of course, arithmetic of this sort is uncertain and cold, and it ought not divert attention from the ghastly realities of inmate labor, including the fact that its victims saw none of the income, which went partially to those who confined and underfed them and primarily to the SS and thus ultimately the Reich Treasury. But such statistical analysis does highlight the inaccuracy, at least in this instance, of two aspects of popular opinion concerning "slave" labor, namely, that its attraction was its cheapness, and that its cheapness made German employers spendthrift regarding it. For the factory managers at Gleiwitz, the use of inmate labor was not at the outset a considered decision based on or buttressed by cost calculations; it was an act of selfish and desperate improvisation, a reflex response to the desire "to do what had to be done," as American usage would put the matter today, in a context that afforded few other means to that end. Moreover, and ironically, this sort of idealized egocentrism also had much to do with a perceptible shift in the Gleiwitz management's attitude toward the installation's Jews during 1944. Though they had not been sought after because they were cheap (indeed, the fact that they were not may have prompted resentment that strengthened DGW's indifference to their plight in 1942–43), the fact that they obviously were becoming so enhanced their value to the firm.

Robert Pross in particular appears to have grown increasingly attentive to the ways in which the administration of the inmate labor camp on the factory grounds undermined his own efforts to complete and operate it. In November 1943, "One hundred Jews had to be given up in the construction sector," allegedly owing to a lack of guards, and there were other signs of increasing mismanagement by the DAF.[47] Survivors report a decline in the already poor quality of the food around the turn of the year and, consequently, a mounting incidence of illness and the trucking away of inmates from the infirmary to Auschwitz. Pross later attested that his growing suspicion that "much was going into the wrong channels" prompted him to remonstrate with the relevant officials.[48] In mid-January 1944 Gauleiter Bracht of Upper Silesia, Colonel Hueter of the regional Armaments Inspection Office, and two officials of the Labor Front visited the factory and held a discussion with Pross "of all the difficulties concerning personnel, especially the longer stay of the Jewesses," which had been threatened by a short-lived general order for the removal of Jews from the region toward the end of the preceding year.[49] With his works only half complete, and Jews comprising 44 percent of his total personnel and just over 50 percent of his effective workforce at the time, Pross no doubt underlined the importance of their labor—and of ensuring that they, in fact, could perform it. Whether humanity played as large a role as pragmatism in his stance is impossible to say on the basis of the records that have come to light.

Either way, Pross's dependence on Jewish labor provides an explanation for the pleasure with which he greeted the sudden takeover of DGW's factory camp by the SS on 3 May 1944 and its incorporation into Auschwitz's network of branches.[50] The extant sources contain no indication that he sought this development; he claimed later that "One day we were surprised by the announcement"; and it occurred amidst a general extension of the Auschwitz subcamp system in early 1944 and a sharp increase in the number of forced laborers at the neighboring Borsig Kokswerke, part of the Schering concern, who were also housed in DGW's barracks.[51] Yet one cannot exclude the possibility that Pross's dissatisfaction with the previous operation of the labor camp in some way helped precipitate the changeover. It was surely welcome to him, providing a virtual guarantee of the supply of inmates to the site. And, hard as this is to credit in retrospect, the transfer of authority seemed to promise an amelioration of conditions for the workers. Along with the "considerably reinforced guard force (*Waffen*-SS)" and the electric fences that the SS ordered erected around the prisoners' compound and the factory grounds came at first, even survivors attest, much better food, clothing, and bedding and much greater attention to the cleanliness of the barracks. The improved diet reflected, in part, DGW's agreement with the SS to assume direct responsibility for provisioning the inmates, which led to an immediate increase in the firm's budget for that purpose by RM 10,000.[52] There were, however, ominous signs: the prompt tattooing of the prisoners and shaving of their heads, the requirements that they put on striped inmate uniforms and attach stars of David to the jackets and legs, and the suicide of two terrified women, whose memory of previous encounters with the SS drove them to despair.[53] But these events did not dent the near euphoria of DGW's managers. They were so delighted with the new situation that they reported at the beginning of June 1944, a day before Auschwitz Commandant Rudolf Höss paid them a visit, "We are striving little by little to replace the foreigners entirely with Jewish inmates."[54] Indeed, already by the end of that month, the number of Jews working on the site had risen from 506 to 724 when the SS took over, their proportion from 50 percent to 67 percent. And both figures kept climbing: the raw number peaked in November 1944 at 813, the percentage a month later at 76 percent.[55]

Pross thus secured his flow of labor at a troubling human cost. The latter fact does not appear to have been his chief preoccupation amidst the excitement of completing the plant, bringing it into full operation, and beginning to turn a regular, indeed widening, operating profit—all of which occurred in October 1944.[56] But neither could the worsening treatment of the prisoners by the SS altogether escape his attention, nor could what awaited them at Auschwitz, with which DGW's intensified relationship pulled Pross into direct contact. He went at least twice in the second half of 1944 to choose laborers from the concentration camp, and he learned either there and then or by other means at roughly the same time of the mass murder being perpetrated.[57] Closer to home, he admitted later to having known of the increasingly wanton and debilitating cruelty meted out toward the male laborers and the petty restrictions that harassed the female ones—even though, as survivors confirm, he and his managerial colleagues never entered the barracks and appeared in the compound rarely, even then under escort—and claimed to have interceded to change things.[58] Given the workers' importance to him, his contention is plausible that he took the opportunities of visits to Auschwitz to argue for the replacement of successive camp commanders whose brutality cut into the workers' productivity. The story is not, however, corroborated by his admittedly sketchy diary for 1944, and, if it happened, the first change of leadership in September backfired. SS-*Oberscharführer* Bernhard Becker's successor, a beast of the same rank named Konrad Friedrichsen, tormented the laborers with after-hours calisthenics and savage beatings for trivial infractions, which he forced inmates to witness during extended evening roll calls.[59] By the time he was relieved of command in January 1945, he had taken a terrible toll, even though most of his murders were delayed—that is, they occurred via the now-weekly pickups from the infirmary as a result of the pain he ordained in plain view on the DGW site.

The genuineness of Pross's concern for at least one segment of his Jewish workforce is suggested by its unusual fate. Although the surviving statistics provide no sure basis for calculating the mortality rate among workers at Gleiwitz, it clearly differed pronouncedly between women and men. Virtually none of the females, who worked indoors in eight-hour shifts manipulating important machinery and packing the carbon black, died between 1943 and the evacuation of the plant in January 1945. This is not to say that they were treated well; survivors recall being constantly terrified, cold, hungry, and plagued by skin sores resulting from vitamin deficiency. The threat of infection due to the omnipresent soot and the absence of medicines was constant.[60] Attrition among the men, most of whom performed interchangeable tasks outdoors on the building site, was another matter, however. A rough and conservative estimate is that at least three hundred of them died at Gleiwitz or shortly after being carted away from it between 1942 and 1945, not counting those who were "exchanged" in early 1943 and "given up" later in the year (about 230 individuals).[61]

Something more than relatively advantageous working assignments seems necessary to account for such divergent fates. It appears that the plant management at Gleiwitz recognized the difference between expendable workers, for whom it would take few risks in dealing with the Labor Front or SS, and nonexpendable ones. Willing usually to turn a blind eye to malnutrition, illness, and murder on the construction site, the plant's leaders tried to prevent the wasting away and culling out of the more valuable female workers. This attitude may have been fortified by what women survivors experienced as almost chivalrous behavior toward them by senior managers on certain occasions, as, for example, during one tour of the facility by visiting dignitaries, when an executive even held a door open for the Jewish forewoman of a work shift, who was accompanying the group to explain the operations being observed.[62]

The Legal Gray Zone—Assessing Degussa's Liability

Both the criminality of the Nazi forced labor system and the complicity of firms such as Degussa and DGW that made use of involuntary, unpaid laborers are reprehensible facts regardless of whether any party made money on the arrangements. However, an unfortunate side effect of the quest for restitution for slave laborers in recent years, as asserted at the outset of this essay, is the implication that the evil of the system lay in its profitability, as if the conduct described here would not be subject to condemnation and restitution but for the wealth it generated. In part, this is a distortion imposed by a form of "path dependency" in the American judicial system, where the language of civil suits emphasizes the "disgorgement" of unjust proceeds from unlawful conspiracies as the principal means of making them good. Whatever its origins, however, the emphasis on profits gleaned from slave labor is simply inappropriate to cases such as the DGW plant at Gleiwitz.

For the reasons given above, there was probably no cost advantage to the use of Jewish construction laborers at Gleiwitz during 1942. For 1943/44, although calculating what the company's retained labor costs might have been is extremely difficult, a very rough way of proceeding is to say that the sum of the average monthly numbers of Jews working on the site in 1943 comes to 5,755 and their cost, as noted above, was RM 709,037. The wage bill for the total of 7,880 Jewish workers obtained by summing the figures given in the individual monthly plant reports during 1944 would thus have been RM 970,845, for an overall, two-year cost of almost RM 1.7 million. Assuming that the wage bill for native German laborers would have averaged out to a figure about three times this high if they had worked the same number of hours, we may conclude that the Gleiwitz factory "gained" on the order of RM 3.4 million from the use of "slave" labor—about US$ 13.6 million in early twenty-first-century values.

While this is an unhistorical calculation, since Gleiwitz either would not have been built or would have been completed much more rapidly under normal conditions in the labor market, the arithmetic does convey some sense of the extent of what Degussa would have implicitly pocketed by virtue of the inmate labor system, if Germany had won World War II. To the sum should be added whatever percentage of the completed value of the installations at Gleiwitz could be attributed to the Jewish portion of the labor force that helped build them. That value, however, would not have been very great. In the course of 1943 Degussa researchers discovered that employing hydrogen rather than coke-oven gas in the making of carbon black increased yields by 75 percent and that alterations to improve air flow to the burners produced a further gain of 15 to 20 percent.[63] In short order, the capacity of all existing installations doubled to twice the level that Germany's rubber manufacturers conceivably could absorb, even according to Eckell's predictions. DGW's executive committee therefore concluded that "after the war, we will have trouble keeping Dortmund and Gleiwitz afloat" and decided early in 1944 to stop work upon completion of the first half of the latter plant, only to reverse itself in view of the mounting aerial threat to the former.[64] Had Germany won the war, the Gleiwitz plant would have been largely superfluous.

But the factory was finished only three months before the Red Army conquered it, and one cannot label the relative "savings" on labor "profits." Gleiwitz's construction costs aggregated to RM 10.5 million and its total expenditures to over RM 21 million as of the end of 1944, by which time its total sales to date had come to RM 2.3 million in 1943 and, at most, twice as much in 1944. The plant did not begin to produce at a profit over its unit costs until 1944 and "made" money in the simplest sense for some four months, showing an operating profit for the year of RM 1.2 million.

All things considered, including accelerated depreciation of the plant and equipment, Gleiwitz was still RM 3 million in the red when it was overrun by the Soviets, who may also have collected the RM 800,000 that the firm had on deposit in local banks.[65] Not only did the plant lose money; it also consumed RM 11.4 million of the profits of the DGW's Dortmund factory.[66] Neither did Degussa or DGW retain the physical results of the inmates' labors, since the plant was stripped by the Soviets, then nationalized and run by the Poles until the early 1990s, when a new joint venture agreement returned the only remnant of the initial project, the shells of the buildings, to Degussa's control.[67] By any measure, no "profits" on inmate labor remained to disgorge in 1945, though assuredly justified claims to compensation for unremunerated work and extraordinary physical and mental anguish remained to be paid.[68]

Making money was not the reason that the Reich's increasingly counterproductive, cruel, and chaotic program of labor exploitation came into being, and it is neither morally nor historically sound to measure its evil by its lucrativeness. Precisely because the "slave" labor system emerged out of a vortex of macropolitical forces, international law consistently has defined the German state—and thus its citizens collectively—as the primary party responsible for answering to the financial claims of people exploited under Nazism.[69] It is thus entirely fitting that the German state now carries most of the burden under the German Remembrance Initiative (*Stiftungsinitiative*) of paying restitution claims from former forced and slave laborers.[70] But German corporate leaders, including Degussa's, showed little hesitation about making use of the system Nazism ordained. By cooperating, they encouraged and perpetuated it; in many cases, they aggravated it as they attempted to twist the regime's actions into economically rational and politically beneficial forms.[71] That is why there is also no injustice in the bill that has fallen on German industry fifty years later, regardless of how little a firm such as Degussa may have "profited," in the end, by the sweat and blood its goals exacted.

That said, the popular perception that firms such as Degussa and individuals such as Robert Pross escaped punishment after 1945 for their complicity in Nazi criminality is also overstated and ignores another "gray zone" of reality. Total net war damages to Degussa, including the value of destroyed buildings and equipment and confiscated precious metals, stockholdings, patent rights, and other assets came to approximately RM 111 million by the firm's own postwar calculation, a sum that equates to almost one-half billion U.S. dollars in today's values.[72] Even if one allows for some exaggeration in arriving at this estimate, Degussa clearly did not walk away from the Third Reich unpunished for having participated in it. As for Robert Pross, his career continued after 1945, but not on the same high-flying basis as before. When he retired from Degussa in 1970, he noted his disappointment at never having achieved his ambition of being elected to the managing board and remarked that "The odium of having been professionally successful during the Thousand Years . . . seems never to have left me."[73] Whether such forms of retribution were adequate is open to debate; but whether these complicitous parties paid at least some price for their actions is not.

Notes

1. The principal articulators of the once standard views were Franz Neumann, *Behemoth: The Structure and Practice of National Socialism* (New York: Octagon Books, 1963), and Arthur Schweitzer, *Big Business in the Third Reich* (Bloomington: Indiana University Press, 1964), as well as a host of explicitly Marxist writers. Of course, the pivotal figure in altering this received picture was Henry Turner, especially through his monumental *German Big Business and the Rise of Hitler* (New York: Oxford University Press, 1985) and his meticulous *Hitler's Thirty Days to Power: January 1933* (Reading, MA: Addison-Wesley, 1996), but a number of other scholars were instrumental in the transition. For recent summaries of the state of research, see Harold James, "Banks and the Era of Totalitarianism: Banking in Nazi Germany," and Peter Hayes, "Industry Under the Swastika," in Harold James and Jakob Tanner, eds., *Enterprise in the Period of Fascism in Europe* (Aldershot: Ashgate, 2002), 14–37.
2. Quoted in Michael J. Bazyler, *Holocaust Justice: The Battle for Restitution in America's Courts* (New York: New York University Press, 2003), 59.
3. The basic, essential works on this subject remain Edward L. Homze, *Foreign Labor in Nazi Germany* (Princeton: Princeton University Press, 1967), and Ulrich Herbert, *Hitler's Foreign Workers* (Cambridge, U.K.: Cambridge University Press, 1997), the original German edition of which appeared in 1985. More recently, see also Mark Spoerer, *Zwangsarbeit unter dem Hakenkreuz* (Stuttgart: Deutsche Verlags-Anstalt, 2001).
4. Gerald Feldman, "The Business History of the 'Third Reich' and the Responsibilities of the Historian," Occasional Paper, Center for German and European Studies, University of California, Berkeley, January 1999, 15.
5. See Peter Hayes, "Market Assessment and Domestic Political Risk: The Case of Degussa and Carbon Black in Nazi Germany, 1933–1939," in Per Hansen and Christopher Kobrak, eds., *European Multinationals and Dictatorship* (New York: Berghahn Books, 2004), 62–77; and Peter Hayes, *From Cooperation to Complicity: Degussa in the Third Reich* (New York: Cambridge University Press, 2004), chapter 4.
6. Degussa Unternehmens-Archiv [hereafter: DUA], PCA 2/3, Baerwind's Gespräch mit Dr. Kemnitz . . . betreffend Aufforderung der Reichsstelle, 11 September 1939, and his Notizen betreffend . . . das Projekt einer dritten CK3-/CK4-Fabrik, 18 September 1939, where the quoted words appear on 3.
7. See DUA, DL3.Baerwind/23, Aussprache bei der Reichsstelle für Wirtschaftsausbau, 23 September 1939; and PCA 2/10, Baerwind's Russwerke Dortmund-Sitzungen in Berlin, 20 November 1939. The two quoted passages appear in the latter document, 3.

8. DUA, PCA 2/3, Baerwind's Aussprache ... über das Projekt einer dritten CK3-/CK4-Fabrik, 27 December 1939, and Baerwind's Aktenvermerk betreffend die Aussprache beim Reichsamt, 18 July 1940, and Auszug aus dem Bericht des Herrn Dr. Kemnitz vom 10. Juli 1940.
9. DUA, DL 2/1, Niederschrift über die Vorstandssitzung [hereafter: VSS] am 7. Oktober 1940, 125, and Anlage 1, Baerwind's Besprechung mit Dr. Eckell, 23 September 1940, 1 and 3.
10. Ibid., VSS am 4. November 1940, 140, and Anlage 8, concerning the expansion at Kalscheuren; am 2. Dezember 1940, p. 147, on the probable choice of Gleiwitz. As background, see PCA 2/3, Baerwind's Verhandlungen in Berlin ... über die zweite R.D. Fabrik, 11 November 1940, and his Berliner Besprechungen, 25 November 1940.
11. Ibid., Baerwind's Aussprache bei der Reichsstelle, 27 December 1939.
12. DUA, DL 11.5/40, a collection of the loan agreements between July and October of 1941, which also outlines the overall financing, 17–25 and 35–46.
13. DUA, BET 9/46, Baerwind's Verhandlung im Reichsamt, 20 October 1941, and his Sitzung der Erweiterten Arbeitsausschusses der Deutschen Gasrusswerke, 1 December 1941, which is the source of the quotation.
14. Ibid., Bernau's Deutsche Gasrusswerke GmbH, Dortmund, 14 November 1941.
15. DUA, BET 9/46, Kemnitz to the Reich Finance Ministry, 25 November 1941; Kemnitz to Bernau, 22 December 1941; Kemnitz to the Reich Finance Minister, 22 December 1941; and Kemnitz to Römer (RWM) and Mundt (RFM), 22 December 1941, with Anlagen. The tax exemption on reinvested profits applied originally to 1941–42 only, but was extended through 1944.
16. DUA, PCA 2/4, Baerwind to Eckell, 27 May 1942.
17. DUA, BET 9/48, Kemnitz to Gesellschafter der Deutschen Gasrusswerke, 1 December 1942, Anlage 1 (for the higher figure, as of September 1942); and DL3.Baerwind/26, Deutsche Gasrusswerke GmbH, 22 January 1943 (for the lower total).
18. On the arrival of the Jews at Gleiwitz, see DUA, PCA 2/4, Ziegler's memo of 21 April 1942.
19. On the projected workforce, see DUA, PCA 2/3, Nagel's Besuch bei den Borsig-Kokswerken in Oberschlesien, 12 December 1940, 3, which also sets the average wages at 50–60 pfennig per hour; Herrmann's Bericht über die Verhandlungen in Gleiwitz, Kattowitz und Breslau, 17 March 1941, 4; Ziegler's Notiz betreffend Russwerke Dortmund G.m.b.H., Werk Gleiwitz, Barackenlager, 25 March 1941, 2. On the accommodations, PCA 2/4, Ziegler's Deutsche Gasrusswerke ... Notiz über die Besprechung beim Stadtbauamt, 21 May 1941; and Mühlschwein's Notiz Betrifft: R.-OS., Werk Gleiwitz, 21 August 1941. That the minimum wage for Italian workers was 67 pfennig per hour is established in PCA 2/4, Mühlschwein's Notiz Betreffend: R.-OS. Werk Gleiwitz. Einsatz ital. Arbeitskräfte, 21 July 1941. On the workforce in September, PCA 2/4, DGW Bauleitung to Arbeitsamt Gleiwitz, 2 September 1941; Mühlschwein's Notiz. Betrifft: R.-OS., Werk Gleiwitz, Arbeitereinsatz, 10 September 1941; and Ziegler's Notiz ... über meinen Besuch in Gleiwitz, 20 September 1941.
20. DUA, PCA 2/4, Ziegler's Betrifft: Deutsche Gasrusswerke G.m.b.H., Werk Gleiwitz, 7 July 1941, for the quotation.
21. Ibid., 7 December 1941.
22. DUA, PCA 2/4, Pross's Besprechung über Material- und Arbeitseinsatzfragen in Gleiwitz am 27. Januar 1942, undated.
23. DUA, PCA 2/2, Pross's Betr. Entwurf zum Jahresbericht Gleiwitz 1944, techn. Teil. 24. Fassung, 14 December 1945, 2.
24. For a litany of complaints about the "underperformance of the foreign workers," see DUA, PCA 2/1, Monatsbericht Nr. 18 für September 1942, 21 October 1942, as well as BET 9/48, Monatsbericht Nr. 16, 26 August 1942.
25. DUA, TA 2/78, Retze's Notiz. Betr. Fürstenberg: Verpflegungsfrage, 28 October 1942; and TA 2/87, Retze to Deneke, 12 July 1943.
26. On the initial arrangements with the DAF for foreign workers, see DUA, PCA 2/3, Herrmann's Bericht über Verhandlungen in Gleiwitz, Kattowitz und Breslau, 17 March 1941,

7–8; but I have found no document recording subsequent agreements. Survivors recall being guarded in 1942–43 by men in a succession of uniforms, first brown, then blue, then green.
27. Interview with Martin Sojka, Frankfurt, 22 October 1998.
28. By the end of 1942, there were twenty-four structures in the barracks camp, twelve residential, each built for one hundred people, and twelve ancillary structures for supplies, washing, and toilets. On this and the repeated delays in obtaining them, see DUA, BET 9/48, Jahresbericht 1942 über den Aufbau Werk Gleiwitz, undated [after 27 April 1943], 2, as well as PCA 2/3, Ziegler's Notiz betreffend . . . Barackenlager, 25 March 1941 (which reports the cost of the first three residential and first five support barracks as RM 131,490); PCA 2/4, Ziegler's Notiz über die Besprechung mit der Abteilung Rüstungsausbau, 21 April 1942, 2–3; his Notiz über mein Besuch beim Reichsamt für Wirschaftsausbau, 18 May 1942; and his Besprechung mit Herrn Direktor Pross, 31 July 1942.
29. Coen Rood, *"Wenn ich es nicht erzählen kann, muss ich weinen": Als Zwangsarbeiter in der Rüstungsindustrie* (Frankfurt am Main: Fischer Taschenbuch Verlag, 2002), 46–70. Rood wrote down his recollections in 1945–49, but they have been considerably edited and shortened for publication. For corroboration of his memory concerning the clearing of the infirmary, see Robert Pross's handwritten contemporary record of the camp's population, DUA, BU Robert Pross, Russ-Tagebuch, final, unnumbered pages.
30. On the final count, see Pross (note 29 above). The figure of 246 is the sum of the two hundred initially reported and forty-six Dutch Jews accounted for by Rood (eight dead, six sent from the infirmary, and thirty-two still present in March 1943), but Rood's is not likely to have been the only group of Jews to reach Gleiwitz during these months, especially since the workforce totals given in DGW's Monatsberichte for the latter half of 1942 do not disaggregate the category of "foreigners," which increased by some three hundred. The supposition draws some strength from the comment of an official in the Breslau branch of the Department for Armaments Expansion to Degussa's architect that "skilled workers cannot be provided, just 300–400 Jews, who are to be used as unskilled workers"; PCA 2/4, Ziegler's Notiz über die Besprechungen am 25.3.42, 29 March 1942, 1–2.
31. DUA, BET 9/48, Jahresbericht 1942 über den Aufbau Werk Gleiwitz, undated [after 27 April 1943], 2.
32. DUA, PCA 2/4, Ziegler's Notiz über den Besuch bei der Abteilung Rüstungsausbau . . . Aussenstelle Breslau, 2 November 1942.
33. See PCA 2/4, Ziegler's Notiz über die Besprechung mit der Abteilung Rüstungsausbau, 21 April 1942; BET 9/48, Pross and Dreske's Verwaltungsbericht und Personalstandsmeldung, 1 October 1942, and Monatsbericht Nr. 19, 1 November 1942 (1329); and PCA 2/1, Personalstandsmeldung zum 31. Dezember 1942.
34. On the number transferred out, see DUA, PCA 2/1, Monatsbericht Nr. 24 für März 1943, 12 April 1943; on those remaining and their replacements, Rood, *"Wenn ich es nicht erzählen kann,"* 75. For the quotation, DUA, BET 9/43, Protokoll über die Arbeitsausschuß-Sitzung der Deutschen Gasrusswerke GmbH am 4. März 1943, 4.
35. DUA, PCA 2/1, Monatsbericht Nr. 24 für März 1943, 12 April 1943.
36. Ibid., Personenstandsmeldung zum 30. April 1943, 6 May 1943; and BU Robert Pross, Russ-Tagebuch, entry for 30.4.43.
37. Rood, *"Wenn ich es nicht erzählen kann,"* 74.
38. DUA, PRO 01/0012, Pross's Erinnerungen an die Zeit meiner Tätigkeit bei den DGW Gleiwitz 1941–1945, 25 July 1963, 1; and BU Robert Pross, Betr. DGW—Werk Gleiwitz—Einsatz von Häftlingen, 23 January 1996, where the quotation appears on 2.
39. Pross, 23 January 1996 (note 38 above). On his kindness and that of his secretary Fräulein Mittas, see Rood, *"Wenn ich es nicht erzählen kann,"* 84–85 (where his name is remembered erroneously as Prost and hers as Marx) and 115.
40. PCA 2/2, Betriebsbericht Nr. 1 für Mai 1943, 5 June 1943, 6.
41. See DUA, BU Robert Pross, which contains a copy of the award of the medal, dated 1 September 1944. See also his Russ-Tagebuch, 64, where the entry for 4 November 1944 reads, "Honored by the workforce on the occasion of the award of the KVKI."

42. This is the stunningly self-absorbed comment of Ernst Baerwind; DL3.Baerwind/26, Besuch im Werk Gleiwitz der DGW, 21 April 1943, 2.
43. For the labor force figures, see DUA, PCA 2/1, Monatsbericht für Januar 1943, 11 February 1943, and BU Unterlagen Robert Pross, Ruß-Tagebuch, workforce entries for 5 February 1943 to 1 January 1944. All such figures in this and subsequent paragraphs exclude workers ill or absent for any reason (and the figures for January 1943 have been estimated accordingly).
44. DUA, PCA 2/2, Gewinn- und Verlustrechnung, Deutsche Gasrusswerke GmbH, Gleiwitz, 31 December 1943.
45. DGW's profit and loss statement for 1943 also includes a reference to an additional amount of RM 119,904 paid out in "manufacturing wages," but there is no telling how these were divided. The line entry for "Jews' wages" includes the notation "without manufacturing wages," an addition that would be superfluous if Jews were excluded altogether from them. In view of the uncertainty about the allocation, I have left this category of compensation out of my calculations.
46. On the length of the women's workday, interview with Manya Friedman and Helen Luksenberrg, 14 August 1998; and DUA, DOK 1/05, Sándorné Orosz and Judit Varga to Direktion der Deutschen Gasrusswerke GmbH, 7 November 1990.
47. DUA, PCA 2/2, Betriebsbericht Nr. 7 für November 1943, 9 December 1943, 8.
48. Rood, "*Wenn ich es nicht erzählen kann,*" 84; DUA, PRO 01/0012, Pross's Erinnerungen an die Zeit meiner Tätigkeit bei den DGW Gleiwitz 1941–1945, 25 July 1963, 1.
49. DUA, PCA 2/2, Betriebsbericht Nr. 9 für January 1944, 5 February 1944; on the short-lived directive, BET 9/50, Kemnitz to Baerwind, 9 December 1943, and, as background, Sybille Steinbacher, "*Musterstadt*" *Auschwitz: Germanisierungspolitik und Judenmord in Ostoberschlesien* (Munich: K.G. Saur, 2000).
50. For the date of the takeover, DUA, Geschichte Werke, Bescheinigung (Zur Vorlage beim Wirtschaftsamt), signed by SS-Hauptsturmführer Schwarz, 15 May 1943.
51. For the quotation, DUA, PRO 01/0012, Pross's Erinnerungen . . . Gleiwitz 1941–1945, 25 July 1963, 2. On the sequence of subcamp foundings or takeovers by the Auschwitz administration in early 1944, see Aleksander Lasik, Franciszek Piper, Piotr Setkiewicz, and Irena Strzelecka, *Auschwitz 1940–1945*, vol. I (Oswiecim: Auschwitz-Birkenau State Museum, 2000), 122–26.
52. DUA, PCA 2/2, unsigned and undated Kommentar zur Zwischenbilanz des Werkes Gleiwitz per 31.5.1944; and, for the quotation, Betriebsbericht Nr. 13 für Mai 1944, 5 June 1944. On the building of the fence and the initial improvement of conditions, Rood, "*Wenn ich es nicht erzählen kann,*" 86–89 and 98–99, and interview with Manya Friedman and William (Wolf) and Helen Luksenberrg, 14 August 1998.
53. Rood, "*Wenn ich es nicht erzählen kann,*" 86–91. Rood recalls one suicide (88) and Pross two (his accounts of 1963 and 1996), but they agree on the means: jumping out of a high window in the packaging building of the factory. Lasik et al., *Auschwitz 1940–1945*, vol. I, p. 125, report two deaths.
54. DUA, PCA 2/2, Betriebsbericht Nr. 13 für Mai 1944, 5 June 1944, signed by Pross and Dreske.
55. Ibid., Betriebsberichte Nr. 13–14, 19–20, 5 June, 5 July, and 5 December 1944, and 5 January 1945.
56. DUA, PCA 2/2, Betriebsbericht Nr. 18 für Oktober 1944, 4 November 1944, and Pross's Betr. Entwurf zum Jahresbericht Gleiwitz 1944, techn. Teil, 14 December 1945, and the attached graph showing Produktion u. Gestehungskosten in Gleiwitz 1944.
57. See the statement of Pross's daughter Brigitte Axster reporting her father's admission of the visits in her afterword to Rood, "*Wenn ich es nicht erzählen kann,*" 213–14. On his knowledge in 1944, see DUA, BU Robert Pross, his Betr. DGW—Werk Gleiwitz—Einsatz von Häftlingen, 23 January 1996, 5.
58. Interview with Manya Friedman and William (Wolf) and Helen Luksenberrg, 14 August 1998; DUA, PRO 01/0012, Pross's Erinnerungen . . . , 4 July 1963, especially 4–5.

59. Pross's Erinnerungen . . . , 4 July 1963, especially 6; and his Notiz betr. . . . Besuch von Mr. Coen Rood, 3 May 1999; Rood, *"Wenn ich es nicht erzählen kann,"* 103–6, 113, and 115 (where he gives the camp commanders' names as Friedrichs and Backer and also notes that rations improved unaccountably in autumn of 1944); and Lasik et al., *Auschwitz 1940–1945*, vol. I, p. 125.
60. Interview with Manya Friedman and Helen Luksenberrg, 14 August 1998.
61. If at least as many construction workers died on average per month at the Gleiwitz site after April 1943 as before, the minimum toll was between 240 and 300, but considering the worsening conditions in the *Lager* as the war went on, and the more brutal discipline after the SS took the barracks over in May 1944, it was in all probability higher. Rood also notes that the SS shot the last remaining eight men in the camp as it was being evacuated; *"Wenn ich es nicht erzählen kann,"* 120.
62. Interview with Manya Friedman, 14 August 1998.
63. DUA, PCA 2/144, Baerwind and Bonath to Forschungsführung des Reichsministers der Luftfahrt, 8 October 1943.
64. DUA, PCA 2/143, Oelmann's Besprechung über Russfragen, 2 February 1944 (on the supply to demand ratio), and BET 9/50, Herrmann's Niederschrift über die Besprechung des Arbeitsausschusses, 29 March 1944 (on the decisions regarding Gleiwitz); Achterath's Betr.: Russ, 20 June 1944 (for the quotation), and Kemnitz to the Gesellschafter der Deutschen Gasrusswerke GmbH, 27 June 1944.
65. DUA, PCA 2/1, Endabrechnung der Bauarbeiten, Stichtag 31. Dezember 1944, 26 July 1945; PRO 1/12, Schlussabrechnung DGW Gleiwitz, 8 October 1945; PCA 2/2, Gegenüberstellung von Gestehungskosten und Erlösen [for 1943]; PCA 2/2, Bisherige Betriebsergebnisse des Werkes Gleiwitz, 14 August 1944; and, for the profit and deficit figures, BET 9/5, Bericht über die Prüfung der Bilanz nebst Gewinn- und Verlustrechnung per 31. Dezember 1944, 5 November 1945. On the outstanding RM 800,000, see PCA 2/2, Achterath's two memos headed Betr. DGW—Gleiwitz, 31 January and 1 March 1945.
66. See BET 9/51, Treuhand- und Wirtschaftsprüfungs-Gesellschaft mbH, Bericht über die Prüfung der Bilanz nebst Gewinn- und Verlustrechnung per 31. Dezember 1944 der Deutsche Gasrusswerke GmbH.
67. On the stripping of the plant (and the arrest of Fräulein Mittas, Pross's secretary), PCA 2/2, Schenk's Betrifft Schicksal der Gleiwitzer Russfabrik, 24 August 1945. On the joint venture between Degussa and the Polish government, Brigitte Axster's afterword in Rood, *"Wenn ich es nicht erzählen kann,"* 214.
68. For a similar conclusion, based on a distinct but related line of argument, see Cornelia Rauh-Kühne, "Hitlers Hehler? Unternehmerprofite und Zwangsarbeiterlöhne," *Historische Zeitschrift* 275 (2002), 1–55.
69. On the macrocausation of the forced labor system, see especially Herbert, *Hitler's Foreign Workers*, 154.
70. See Susanne-Sophia Spiliotis, *Verantwortung und Rechtsfrieden: Die Stiftungsinitiative der deutschen Wirtschaft* (Frankfurt am Main: Fischer Taschenbuch Verlag, 2003).
71. See especially Lutz Budraß and Manfred Grieger, "Die Moral der Effizienz. Die Beschäftigung von KZ-Häftlingen am Beispiel des Volkswagenwerks und der Henschel Flugzeug-Werke," *Jahrbuch für Wirtschaftsgeschichte* 2 (1993), 89–136; and Neil Gregor, *Daimler-Benz in the Third Reich* (New Haven, CT: Yale University Press, 1998).
72. See DUA, DL 11.5/61, Zusammenstellung der Kriegs- und Kriegsfolgeschäden und Vermögenswerte gemäss Gesetz Nr. 53 der Militärregierung bzw. Nr. 5 des Alliierten Kontrollrates per 20. Juni 1948 nach Vermögensarten, as well as Anlage V5.
73. DUA, BU Robert Pross, Anrede, 16 December 1970.

– Chapter 2 –

"ALLEVIATION" AND "COMPLIANCE"
The Survival Strategies of the Jewish Leadership in the Wierzbnik Ghetto and Starachowice Factory Slave Labor Camps

Christopher R. Browning

I have often been asked how I first became interested in the study of the Holocaust. The short answer to that question is very simple. I read a book and it changed my life. That book was Raul Hilberg's *The Destruction of the European Jews,* in this case the 1967 Quadrangle paperback printing of the original 1961 edition, which I first read in June 1969. Hilberg's interpretive framework of the destruction of the European Jews as an administrative/bureaucratic process, moving through the specific functional phases of identification, expropriation, concentration, and annihilation and spanning the continent, struck me with the force of revelation and produced what might best be called an "academic conversion experience." The destruction of the European Jews was not some aberrational outburst of sadism more of voyeuristic than historical interest. Rather, it was a pivotal event of the twentieth century that spoke to the human condition in the modern world and merited exacting historical scrutiny. I became what we now call a Holocaust historian, though of course there was no such term or recognized field of study at that time. Since then I have mostly worked in the subfield of "perpetrator history," where the standard of expectation, approach, and subsequent agenda all traced back to Hilberg's work in one way or another.

When I turned to my current project, a study of the factory slave labor camps of Starachowice utilizing survivor testimony as the primary evidentiary source, I did not initially realize that here, too, writing more about the victims than the perpetrators and using postwar testimonies more than contemporary documents, I would still encounter the long shadow cast by Hilberg's work. I should have known better, of course, for I had already found

Notes for this section begin on page 34.

his edition of the Czerniakow diaries an absolutely fundamental source for my work on Nazi ghettoization policies.

In autumn of 2002 Raul Hilberg called my attention to a short article in the *Yad Vashem Quarterly* by David Silberklang, which related the "precarious liberation" of the Janiszow forced labor camp in southern Poland. On 6 November 1942, weeks after the liquidation of the nearby ghettos on the Vistula River border between the Lublin and Radom districts of the General Government, partisans of the Gwardia Ludowa broke into the Janiszow forced labor camp. The partisans killed the German commandant, chose some ten to fifteen young men to join them, and before departing for the forest, urged the other Jews to flee. Some local Jews familiar with the region ventured into the forest, but many of them returned to the camp before nightfall. The bulk of the Janiszow prisoners, however, remained in the camp. They sent a delegation to the local German police station to report the incident and were told to wait in camp for further instructions. The following day the Jewish prisoners were transferred to the camp at Budzyn. Needless to say, virtually none of the Janiszow Jews, whether they chose to escape to the forest or remain in camp, survived the war.[1]

I had already heard a similar story from a former Jewish partisan. His band had broken into a Jewish slave labor camp and urged the prisoners to escape. To the partisans' astonishment, and to this man's clear disgust when telling the story to me later, the Jewish prisoners had refused to leave. Ironically, this same man in the same conversation expressed his anger at Raul Hilberg because Hilberg had characterized the typical Jewish responses in the Holocaust as "alleviation" and "compliance" and had downplayed both "flight" and especially "resistance."[2] The former partisan experienced no perceptible cognitive dissonance between his anger at what he perceived to be Hilberg's personal insult and his anger at Jews who had behaved in a manner that seemed to confirm Hilberg's analysis of typical Jewish response.[3]

Clearly any historian who wades into the terrain of Jewish response, particularly the dilemmas that confronted Jews (and above all Jewish leadership) in German-occupied Poland, is dealing with a phenomenon that is historically complex, emotionally conflicted, and morally freighted. As in the case of the "precarious liberation" of the Janiszow prisoners, this is for the most part a terrifying landscape dominated by Lawrence Langer's grim notion of "choiceless choices," where all paths led to death. In the case of my current research project, the factory slave labor camps of Starachowice, however, we encounter a somewhat different landscape, a "gray zone" of "ambiguity and compromise"—to borrow the language of the editors—where through the combination of a fortuitous conjuncture of outside factors on the one hand and Jewish choices on the other, an unusually large remnant or cluster of Starachowice prisoners ultimately survived. My own collection of postwar testimonies of Starachowice survivors has now reached 238, and of course many others who survived left no account. For hundreds of Jews from one relatively small complex of camps to have survived the ghetto liquidations of the Radom district in autumn of 1942, twenty-one months of slave labor in Starachowice, and after evacuation an additional six months in Auschwitz-Birkenau, and finally the horrific death marches of 1945, is to say the least an unusual Holocaust story. In what way did the choices of the Starachowice Jews to pursue a desperate survival strategy of "alleviation" and "compliance" lead to a partially different outcome than for those of Janiszow and elsewhere?

I must emphasize most emphatically that it was not within the power of the Starachowice Jews to make decisions that taken alone could have saved even a remnant of their group. The beginning point of my account must be the conjuncture of four fortuitous but key external events that provided a very narrow window of opportunity for partial survival. First, Starachowice was a town containing steel and munitions works confiscated by the Hermann Göring Werke. Its managers met Himmler's three specific requirements for retaining Jewish labor, namely, they were producing for the war economy even in the strictest sense, they built special camps for their Jewish workers, and they paid the SS the required 5 and 4 zloty per day for male and female Jewish workers, respectively.[4] The result was that while routinely 90 to 95 percent of the Jews in the Radom ghettos were taken to Treblinka in autumn of 1942, in Starachowice nearly 30 percent were kept as workers. Second, after Himmler had relentlessly liquidated the Jewish slave labor camps of East Galicia and Lublin to the east, culminating in the great *Erntefest* massacre on 2–3 November 1943, the labor camp liquidation campaign stopped just short of Starachowice, where the camps remained in existence until their evacuation in summer of 1944. Third, unlike the Jewish work camps of Silesia and Krakow to the southwest, the Radom district slave labor camps were not taken over by the SS but remained under factory management to the end. And fourth, upon evacuation to Auschwitz-Birkenau in late July 1944 the Starachowice transport was taken into camp in its entirety without a decimating selection on the ramp. It is against the background of these crucial external events that we must examine the survival strategies of the Starachowice Jews.

With the outbreak of war, the Jewish community concentrated in the old town of Wierzbnik adjacent to the new factory town of Starachowice fled en masse, for they all feared German bombing of the steel and munitions factories and the destruction of their town. The Germans in fact did not bomb the factories, as they wished to capture them intact. Once the German army quickly swept through the Radom district, and before there was any Soviet zone not too distant to the east to which they might have attempted to escape, virtually all of those Jews who had fled returned to Wierzbnik. As elsewhere in German-occupied Poland, the provincial, Orthodox, Yiddish-speaking Jewish community of Wierzbnik was then compelled to create a *Judenrat* in autumn of 1939. It was headed by Simcha Mincburg, an educated, cosmopolitan, Zionist banker.[5] Other members of the *Judenrat* were more representative of the average Wierzbniker, such as the draper Rachmiel Wolfowicz[6] and the shoe store owner Shlomo Enesmann.[7]

Faced with paralyzing random labor roundups on the one hand, and ceaseless plundering on the other, the *Judenrat* sought to bring some order and equalization of burden. As elsewhere in Poland, they organized a Jewish labor office under the Vienna-educated and German-speaking Izak Laks to provide labor as the Germans demanded, while permitting Jews with means to avoid their turn at hard labor by paying needy Jews to substitute for them.[8] The *Judenrat* levied assessments on propertied Jews to finance the endless "contributions" imposed by the Germans and authorized Jewish police to arrest those who failed to pay their assessed share.[9] Through the *Judenrat*'s liaison to the German police, Wolfowicz, it helped arrange for the ransom of numerous arrested Jews.[10] On a much larger scale, four weeks after a large contingent of male Jews had been taken to Globocnik's notorious work camps in the neighboring Lublin district in summer of 1940, the *Judenrat* paid for the return of those who were married. Unmarried male Jews had to continue working there until the camps were closed as winter approached.[11]

The *Judenrat* also pursued a strategy of bribery with the insatiable German chief of police, Walter Becker, attempting to create a vested interest in its community's continued survival, but this was a clear and inevitable failure.[12] While Becker may have held the power of life and death over individual Wierzbnik Jews, he was in the greater scheme of the German occupation a total nonentity—a minor police official of Social Democratic Party (SPD) background whose application to join the SS was never approved—and the fate of the Wierzbnik Jews as a community clearly lay in other hands.

But in pursuing a strategy of survival through work, the *Judenrat* was at least partially successful. The decisive turning point was the hiring of Jews to work in the steel and munitions factories, where they had been excluded from employment before the war. The *Judenrat* paid German management of the Hermann Göring Werke, particularly the man in charge of Polish and Jewish workers, Leopold Rudolf Schwertner, to increase the number of Jewish employees. Moreover, they facilitated Schwertner's own brisk private business of touring surrounding villages to sell individual work cards and smuggle Jews into the Wierzbnik ghetto.[13] The *Judenrat* reputedly also prevailed upon German authorities, presumably once again through bribery, to create an "open" rather than a "closed" ghetto in Wierzbnik in spring of 1941.[14] Other than for work, Jews could leave the ghetto—whose boundaries were marked with signs—only at some risk, but Poles could enter at no risk, a circumstance that greatly facilitated the maintenance of economic ties with the outside world as well as the entry of Jewish refugees from the surrounding region.[15]

In short, while the Jewish workers of Wierzbnik produced munitions for the army whose military defeat they prayed for, and the *Judenrat* lined the pockets of individual German authorities who ruthlessly oppressed and exploited them, nonetheless the Jewish community—following a strategy of compliance and alleviation—experienced such significant tangible benefits in comparison to elsewhere in the Radom district that Wierzbnik became one of the towns to which increasingly beleaguered Jews flocked in desperation as offering the last and best hope of survival. Those Jews of the Radom district adopting flight as a survival strategy fled to, not from, Wierzbnik.

As the German ghetto-liquidation squads swept through the Radom district in the late summer and early autumn of 1942, Wierzbnik Jews made their last preparations for the inevitable. Entire families bought work cards when possible, in effect purchasing their own future enslavement as the price of survival, and placed property with Polish friends. For families with children too young for work cards, many made arrangements to hide them with Poles. Deliberate German disinformation about the prospective date of deportation, however, meant that some of these children had not yet been placed in hiding when the ghetto was liquidated on 27 October 1942.[16] Some Jews with work permits were included in the deportation, such as the chief rabbi whose work card was demonstrably ripped up in the marketplace, as well as some preteens whose recorded ages were obviously false. And some young Jews without work cards were selected for labor anyhow. By the end of the day, nearly four thousand Jews had been dispatched to their deaths in Treblinka, but some 1,500 to 1,800 Jews had been marched off to prepared labor camps with a precarious chance to survive.[17]

Several hundred Jews were sent to Tartak, an "Aryanized" sawmill and lumberyard, which constructed munitions shipping crates and other wood products under military contract. Strictly speaking, this was not a camp, for there were no guards and no fences.[18] Under the management of the so-called decent German Fiedler and his assistant Piatek, Tartak was a relative sanctuary. Escape would have been a simple matter, but there was virtually no safer place for Jews in central Poland. Hence Jews sought, at the cost of bribes, to be transferred there, not to get out.[19]

Less fortunate were the vast majority of Starachowice Jewish workers, who were sent to one of two factory slave labor camps—Strelnica and Majowka—constructed by the Hermann Göring Werke, guarded by a *Werkschutz* detachment of Ukrainians, and administered by the factory security department, initially headed by the sadistic mass killer Willi Althoff. The sanitary conditions in these hastily constructed camps were horrific, and both camps were continually swept by epidemics, especially typhus. The factory management, reluctant to pay to the SS the modest 5 or 4 zloty per head per day for even temporarily incapacitated Jews, adopted the simple policy of periodically killing those too ill or too weak to work. These continual killings were carried out with gusto and enthusiasm by Willi Althoff, who often staged them theatrically for his own greater amusement and even for the entertainment of occasional guests.[20]

In addition to the external regime of terror, personified by Althoff, the Jewish slaves also experienced the internal governance of the prisoner community in the form of a *Lagerrat* (camp council) and *Lagerpolizei* (camp police), personified by the unsavory Jeremiah Wilczek. His prewar legal problems and resulting prison time had allegedly prepared him to adapt quickly to the German occupation.[21] He had served as a bag man for payoffs to the German police in Starachowice before the liquidation of the Wierzbnik ghetto,[22] and was the Germans' man in charge of the prisoner community thereafter. He co-opted three members of the old *Judenrat* (Wolfowicz, Enesmann, and Birenzweig) and built up a cohort of privileged prisoners—mostly from families related to his own—who held the key positions of camp police, block elders, and kitchen staff. He also formed a *Konsum* of skilled artisans who were exempted from factory labor and produced for both the Germans and the camp elite.

For survivors who had experienced many camps, Starachowice was notorious in two regards—the utter filth and infestation of the hastily constructed camps on the one hand and the notoriously inegalitarian camp culture on the other. The latter was in part systemic. The Wierzbnik natives were still in their own town, and many had access to property they had left with friends. The many Jews who came from elsewhere, both before the liquidation of the ghetto and after, entered the camps without any comparable wealth. But this structural inequality was greatly intensified by the tone set by the Wilczek regime, under which everything had a price and required a payoff and incoming prisoners were frequently deprived of the few possessions they may still have had. None felt more disadvantaged and discriminated against than these transfers from other camps, who despite their veteran status suddenly found themselves at the bottom of a steep pecking order.[23]

If native Wierzbnikers generally expressed less bitterness about the camp elite in their postwar testimonies than outsiders, virtually all portrayed Wilczek in particular in a negative light. In addition to the accumulation of power he wielded and privilege he flaunted, he was specifically accused of extorting sexual favors from female prisoners and participating in selections.[24] On the other hand, on occasion Wilczek used his position in ways that benefited the entire prisoner community. Like the *Judenrat* in the pre-camp period, Wilczek continued a strategy not only of survival through labor but also of bribery vis-à-vis the factory management. This paid off significantly in many ways, but several benefits deserve particular mention. Wilczek reached an agreement with the factory management that the Ukrainian guards were to remain outside the camp fence, and internal security would be in the hands of his *Lagerpolizei*. This alleviated the threat from Ukrainian guards who had entered the women's barracks at night and raped women prisoners, even if it did not end sexual extortion by Wilczek and some of his clique.[25]

Above all Wilczek established a relationship or alliance with one of the factory managers, Kurt Otto Baumgarten. In Baumgarten the enslaved Jews encountered a corrupt German who sought to both maximize company profits and line his own pockets, an end that was best achieved through exploitation and extortion rather than extermination of his Jewish workers. Though the evidence is slight, it was at least suggested that Baumgarten was paid to help get rid of the murderous commandant, Willi Althoff.[26] Not coincidentally, with the departure of Althoff, the factory management announced to the prisoners its reversal of the policy of killing sick workers.[27]

Later the Baumgarten-Wilczek alliance helped unseat Althoff's successor, Walter Kolditz, whereupon Baumgarten took charge of the camps himself.[28] His head of the Ukrainian *Werkschutz,* Willi Schrott, also received *Lagerrat* bribes.[29] As a result, on occasion the *Lagerrat* was able to buy the lives of prisoners who otherwise would surely have been executed. When Wilczek's elder son, Avraham, was caught having purchased a gun from a Ukrainian guard, his life was bought.[30] And when a young female prisoner, Guta Blass, courageously attacked *Werkschutz* chief Willi Schrott while urging other prisoners to escape, her life was also spared after a hefty payoff to Baumgarten.[31]

The survivors' memories of the *Lagerpolizei* are also ambivalent. With the exception of Szaja Langsleben,[32] a vicious collaborator and German loyalist to the end who was killed under unclear circumstances in Lodz after the war, most of the individual policemen were remembered more for whom they saved than for whom they mistreated.[33] Perhaps most complex was the gradual transformation of Wilczek's elder son, Avraham. In the early phase of the camp, he was despised for his arrogance and brutality toward prisoners, as privilege and apparent power went to the head of the eighteen-year-old policeman. Over time, however, Avraham mellowed and increasingly used his position to help others.[34] As the evacuation of the camp became imminent, he and several other policemen were among the organizers of a planned breakout. Avraham was among the very few who got away to the forest, found a friendly partisan unit, and survived until the Red Army arrived six months later. After the war, while working for the Soviet authorities, he helped many returning survivors in Lodz and undoubtedly saved the lives of some by warning them not to return to Starachowice, where one night right-wing Polish partisans murdered a number of Jews who had gone back to their hometown.[35]

For most of the period of the Starachowice camps, no one planned resistance and few attempted escape. Life outside the camps was less safe for Jews than inside, and people who had purchased their slavery as the price of survival were not eager to abandon their strategy or endanger their investment. The physical act of getting out of camp was not a major obstacle, but there was certainly no inclination for Wierzbnik prisoners who still had family members in camp to abandon them. On the contrary, after the departure of the murderous Althoff in the late spring of 1943, some parents who had successfully hidden children who were too young for the purchase of work permits managed to have them smuggled into camp, thus reuniting their families.[36] And for newcomers transferred into the camp, the prospect of trying to survive on the outside in unknown territory was too daunting. In short, those who knew the terrain were held in camp in part by family ties, and those without family ties were in part deterred by unfamiliarity with the terrain.

All these calculations for remaining in the Starachowice camps as an island of relative safety in a sea of danger lost relevance in the summer of 1944, as the approach of the Red Army and evacuation of the camps became imminent, and all prisoners were moved to a new camp directly on the munitions factory grounds.³⁷ Key members of the *Lagerpolizei* and other young prisoners began planning for a mass breakout, and contact was made with the partisans who were to shoot out the camp searchlights and facilitate escape to the forest. Many of the prisoners remained unaware of the breakout plans, and many others who were aware decided not to take the risk. All plans seemed moot in any case, when a train suddenly arrived and prisoners were herded into waiting boxcars on Wednesday, 26 July 1944. Just as suddenly and without explanation, the loading was broken off and the prisoners were returned to the barracks. That night the desperate breakout was attempted without help from the partisans. In most testimonies, based on hearsay, this was portrayed as a betrayal by Polish partisans who had been paid for their services but failed to perform them. However, one man who talked to the leadership before the breakout attempt was told that the partisans, upon learning that the camp contained many women and children with whom they did not know what to do if the breakout were totally successful, had already backed out earlier. In any case, the attempt to cut through the double ring of fences was detected, and the first wave of escapees—bunched in the narrow passageway between the first and second openings—was cut down in a hail of machine gun fire and grenades, and the next waves still awaiting their turn fled back to the barracks. A second attempt in broad daylight the next afternoon, with prisoners scattering in all directions and scaling the fences at different points, proved somewhat more successful. Still, only a small number of prisoners escaped, and even fewer survived the next six months before the arrival of the Red Army in January. Undoubtedly, a higher percentage of prisoners who did not attempt to escape ultimately survived than those who did.³⁸

The remaining Starachowice Jews were once again loaded onto the train on Friday, 28 July, and arrived in Birkenau on Sunday morning, 30 July. The train ride proved tragic on two counts. First, many prisoners—having survived twenty-one months of slave labor—perished from dehydration, heat prostration, and suffocation in the stifling, overloaded train cars. Second, with the end of the camp's control system, tensions within the prisoner community erupted into violence. In spring of 1944 a final transfer of prisoners had arrived in Starachowice from Majdanek. This was a group of men, some from Warsaw and some from small towns in the Lublin district, who had somehow survived ghetto liquidations, numerous selections, and the *Erntefest* massacre. They were held in Majdanek for several weeks before being sent to Starachowice.³⁹

The new arrivals, dubbed the "KZs" or "Lubliners" in camp parlance, could not believe that there was a place where Jewish men, women, and children were still alive, and where food was sold openly on the camp's black market. As one astonished Lubliner testified many years later,

> that, I would never believe. I saw a few thousand Jews . . . women and men, and they had everything there. They had food. They had stores, you could have bought food for money, for anything. And it was like a different kind of world.

> ... [W]e were surprised. Some of the eldest of the Jews, the machers, they were living very good. They were getting nice civil dress. . . . [T]hey had their own women and they had everything there.[40]

The Lubliners also could not accept the shabby treatment they received at the hands of the camp elite, whose control they unsuccessfully challenged and whose victory they never forgave. When the train was being loaded in Starachowice, a group of Lubliners forced its way into the front car that carried Wilczek and many of the camp elite. In the dark and crowded train car fighting broke out. Wilczek, his younger son, the head of the camp kitchen, and other members of the camp elite, as well as bystanders who tried to intervene and stop the fighting, were strangled. Upon arrival in Birkenau their bodies were piled on the ramp for all to see, before the Starachowice Jews entered camp without selection and were merged into the general prisoner population.

It is understandable that those who write about the terrible ordeal and the fate of Polish Jewry should be tempted to cast their narratives in terms of victim solidarity, heroic resistance against hopeless odds, and moral redemption through unequaled suffering. This is, however, a temptation that historians should resist, even though (as the reaction to Raul Hilberg's work has shown) to do so is to invite harsh reaction. The Jews of Starachowice pursued strategies of survival through compliance and alleviation, in the form of labor and bribery, over resistance and flight. In this particular case, these choices not only seemed the last and best hope at the time, but they actually saved lives and allowed a remnant to survive. The precarious benefits of these policies were not equally shared, and those who benefited most were seldom individuals who stir our admiration. A few striking exceptions notwithstanding, persecution, exploitation, hunger, enslavement, and mass murder do not turn ordinary people into saints. My history of the Starachowice Jews is one of horrific suffering, incredible endurance, and partial survival. But it cannot be a narrative of redemption and edification while remaining faithful to the evidence.

Notes

1. David Silberklang, "'Jews, Save Yourselves!' The Precarious Liberation of the Janiszow Forced-Labor Camp," *Yad Vashem Quarterly* 28 (Fall 2002), 9.
2. Raul Hilberg, *The Destruction of the European Jews* (Chicago: Quadrangle, 1961), 14–17.
3. Scholarly response to Hilberg's treatment of Jewish resistance has taken two divergent forms. The first is an attempt to show that Jews had indeed engaged in numerous acts of armed resistance. But however tireless, such research could not alter the overall picture that armed resistance—even if exemplary, inspiring, and more frequent than previously documented—was nonetheless still confined to a small minority of victims. The second approach, which Yehuda Bauer initiated, redefined the concept of resistance, broadening it from armed resistance to include any concerted actions aimed at thwarting German intentions. This makes the debate at least in part a semantic issue, for what Bauer catego-

rizes as resistance denotes many of the same activities and survival strategies that Hilberg includes under "alleviation." Of course the two terms still resonate with different connotative meanings.

Ironically, German historians have attempted a similar reconceptualization of our understanding of resistance by Germans to the Nazi regime. Martin Broszat in particular introduced the notion of *Resistenz* to denote the impermeability of the German population to certain policies and propaganda messages of the Nazi regime as opposed to *Widerstand*, the traditional notion of opposing the regime and working for its overthrow. Needless to say, those who favor a broadened notion of Jewish resistance are not necessarily sympathetic to a broadened notion of German resistance.

4. Christopher R. Browning, *Nazi Policy, Jewish Workers, German Killers* (New York: Cambridge University Press, 2000), 78–79.
5. Interview, Chris L., 2001.
6. *Zentrale Stelle der Landesjustizverwaltungen Ludwigsburg* (hereafter ZStL), AR-Z 39/62, Hamburg StA 147 Js 1312/63, investigation of Walter Becker (hereafter Becker case), 1006 (Mendel M.).
7. Goldie Szachter Kalib, *The Last Selection: A Child's Journey Through the Holocaust* (Amherst: University of Massachusetts Press, 1991), 123.
8. Becker case, 405 (Fred B.), 866 (Anna W.); United States Holocaust Memorial Museum (hereafter USHMM), RG 50.030*0396 (Chris L.); interview, Chris L., 2000.
9. Becker case, 405 (Fred B.), 460, 1290–92 (Anna G.); Survivors of the Shoah Visual History Foundation (hereafter VHF), Interview 2643 (Howard K.).
10. Becker case, 775 (Faye G.), 822 (Ben Z.), 1006 (Mendel M.), 1197 (Helen W.).
11. Becker case, 879, 1269 (Morris Z.), 1295 (Irene L.); Fortunoff Archives, Sterling Library, Yale University (hereafter FA), T-1683 (Meyer K.); VHF, Interview 13514 (Saul M.).
12. Becker case, 508 (Dina T.), 1006 (Mendel M.), 1021 (Riwka G.).
13. Becker case, 736–37 (Toby W.), 796 (Abraham R.), 938 (Zvi Hersh F.), 956 (Israel E.), 961 (Sarah P.), 970 (Rachmiel Z.), 1053 (Pinchas H.); VHF, Interviews 2651 (Toby S.), 3948 (Irene H.), 3916 (Rochelle E.), 15716 (Joseph F.), 16492 (Eva H.), 33025 (Joseph T.); Kalib, *The Last Selection*, 129; interview, Joseph and Gitta F., 2002.
14. Jerahmiel Singer, "Dark Days of Horror and Ruin," in M. Shutzman et al., eds., *Wierzbnik-Starachowitz Book* (Tel Aviv, 1973), 27.
15. They constituted a second wave of newcomers to Wierzbnik, following the arrival of entire transports of Jews from Lodz (in 1940) and Plock (in 1941). This first wave of refugees, for whom the *Judenrat* and native Wierzbnikers had provided both accommodations and soup kitchens, were victims of Nazi Germany's campaign of "ethnic cleansing" in the so-called incorporated territories of western Poland that had been annexed to the Third Reich. On the help provided to them by the Wierzbnik Jewish community: VHF, Interviews 1983 (Martin B.) and 943 (Harold R.)
16. Interview, Regina N., 2001.
17. Landgericht Hamburg, Urteil (50) 35/70 in der Strafsache gegen Walter Becker, 17. According to a letter kept by the German gendarme Max Strasser, the figure 3,748 was written in chalk on the side of the train. According to Alan N. (Becker case, 732), about twelve hundred men and four hundred women were taken to Starachowice. According to Simcha M. (Yad Vashem Archives [hereafter YVA], M-49E/155), about fifteen hundred Jews from Starachowice were interned in the labor camps. According to Mendel M. (Becker case, 82) and Zvi F. (Becker case, 67), fifteen hundred men and three hundred women were interned.
18. Becker case, 810 (Helen W.), 1271 (Morris Z.); YVA, O-3/2860 (Chava F.) and M1E.2469 (Josef K.); interview, Martin B., 2001.
19. YVA, M-49/1172 (Mendel K.); Becker case, 800 (Avraham R.), 880–81, 1271 (Morris Z.); interview, Martin B., 2001.
20. Some killings were arranged as target practice: Becker case, 866 (Eva Z.) and 896 (Anna B.). More often, he conducted runs or stair-climbing competitions and shot those who fell behind: Becker case, 417 (Celia N.), 436 (Toby W.), 503 (Helen S.), 732 (Alan N.), 778

(Fay G.), 792 (Leib R.), 840 (Zelda W.), 860 (Eva Z.), 868 (Anne W.), 875 (Adrian W.), and 896 (Anna B.). For entertainment of guests, see Becker case, 792 (Leib R.) and 831 (Ben L.). Althoff also made various "visits to the sick" (*Krankenbesuchen*) and shot all those in the hospital barracks: Becker case, 29 (Israel A.), 83 (Mendel M.), 407 (Fred B.), 435 (Toby W.), 631 (Mania B.), 749 (Leonia F.), and 896 (Anna B.); FA, T-91 (Israel A.). In March 1943, Althoff had a mass grave dug in the nearby Bugaj forest and had 140 Jews shot there: Becker case, 83–84 (Mendel M.), 425 (Jack S.), 491 (Ralph C.), 505 (Max S.), 509 (Dina T.), 515 (Ruth W.), 732 (Alan N.), 859 and 1239 (Eva Z.), 865 (Anna W.), 987 (Anna B.), 1388 (Pinchas H.); YVA, M-49E/155 (Simcha M.). Alan N. (interview, 2001) states that he was in Strelnica when such a selection and massacre occurred, but that he had been transferred to Majowka before March 1943, so there may have been more than one such event.

21. Interviews, Howard C., 2001, and Fay G., 2002.
22. Becker case, 370 (Moshe R.).
23. YVA, M-49/1172 (Mendel K.), an extremely early testimony from summer 1945, is the most outspoken critical account by a "newcomer" to the camp. Other "newcomer" bitterness is expressed in VHF, Interviews 4255 (Tola P.) and 5190 (Ceil S.). The *Lagerrat*'s confiscation of the possessions of newcomers is confirmed by VHF, Interview 36226 (Toby K.), and my interview with Alan N., 2001.
24. On Wilczek as "the rooster of the camp" extracting sexual favors, FA, T-1884 (Regina N.). For a similar accusation against Wolfowicz, interview, Joseph F., 2002. On Wilczek's participation in selections, see YVA, M-49/1172 (Mendel K.) and Becker, 654–65 (Mayer G.).
25. VHF, Interview 4272 (Tema L.); interview, Chris L., 2001.
26. Becker case, 65 (Rywka G.), 84 (Mendel M.), 406 (Fred B.), 592 (Mina B.).
27. Becker case, 818 (Faye G.) and 828 (Ben L.); VHF, Interview 43397 (Louis F.); interview, Joseph F., 2002.
28. ZStL, II 206 AR 125/68, Investigation of Kurt Otto Baumgarten, 23 (Kurt Baumgarten). Becker case, 692 (Paul F.).
29. Becker case, 873–74 (Adrian W.).
30. Interview, Anna W., 2001.
31. USHMM, David Boder Interviews (Kalman E.); Museum of Jewish History, RG-1383 (Pola F.) and RG-1165 (Guta Blass W.). USHMM, RG 50.030*250 (Guta Blass W.).
32. YVA, M-49/1172 (Mendel K.); VHF, Interviews 28993 (Chaim W.) and 40881 (Salek B.).
33. Becker case, 425 (Jack S.), 804 (Syma R.), 896 (Anna B.); VHF, Interviews 16492 (Eva H.), 12728 (Ann S.), 3196 (Rachelle E.).
34. For negative assessments of Avraham Wilczek, see FA, T-91 (Regina N.); interview, Henry G., 2000. For positive assessments: interviews, Alan N., 2001, and Fay G., 2002; Becker case, 717 (Ida G.); VHF, Interview 37728 (Tovi P.). For mixed assessments: interviews, Howard C., 2001, and Joseph F, 2002.
35. Interview, Anna W., 2001.
36. Kalib, *The Last Selection*, 174; VHF, Interviews 3916 (Rochelle E.), 37728 (Tovi P.).
37. For a detailed analysis of the events of the "Final Days" of the Starachowice factory slave labor camp in July 1944, including the attempted breakouts and the evacuation to Birkenau, see Christopher R. Browning, *Collected Memories: Holocaust History and Postwar Testimony* (Madison: University of Wisconsin Press, 2003), 60–85.
38. This is the emphatic judgment of Joseph F., interview, 2002.
39. There are only a few testimonies from surviving "Lubliners": VHF, Interviews 9567 (Morris B.), 9390 (Henry E.), 2589 (David G.), and 6071 (Harry W.). None of them mention the death of the camp elite during the train ride to Birkenau, much less the "Lubliners'" specific role in that event.
40. VHF, Interview 9390 (Henry E.).

– Chapter 3 –

BETWEEN SANITY AND INSANITY
Spheres of Everyday Life in the Auschwitz-Birkenau Sonderkommando

Gideon Greif

The killing installations in the concentration and extermination camp at Auschwitz-Birkenau functioned according to the patterns of common industrial plants: machines, production lines, workers, simple managers, senior managers, a general director, and so on. Only two major differences exist between regular factories and Nazi death camps: the raw materials in the Nazi camps were human beings, and the only end product was human ashes. The workers in the death factories were in most cases Jewish prisoners. In Auschwitz-Birkenau they were unofficially called the *Sonderkommando*.

There are various reasons for the creation of a Jewish battalion of death factory workers. The explanation given by Primo Levi in his brilliant book, *The Drowned and the Saved,* stresses one of the crucial motives: "Behind the pragmatic aspect (to economize on able men, to impose on others the most atrocious task) other moral subtle aspects can be perceived. This institution represented an attempt to shift onto others—specifically, the victims—the burden of guilt, so that they were deprived of even the solace of innocence."[1] The Germans decided to create the squads in order to share the burden of responsibility for their crimes with their victims. The Jews not only had to be murdered but also had to become perpetrators in their murder, according to this way of thinking. This explanation reflects the typical distorted Nazi way of thinking and acting toward the Jews: breaking all kinds of existing barriers between perpetrators and victims, between good and evil, between morality and immorality, between civilization and havoc.

They did the "black work of the Holocaust," as Yaakov Gabai, one of the *Sonderkommando* survivors, defined it.[2] The killing action itself, namely,

Notes for this section begin on page 58.

the pouring of the gas crystals inside the gas chamber, was exclusively and always done by the Germans. Such a "profession" has never been practiced by a human being, anywhere, anytime. The six extermination camps had no precedence in human history and can be considered as a purely Nazi invention. The Germans based their confidence that Jewish prisoners would be capable of doing everything needed in the killing installations on the assumption that they had the techniques of breaking the spirits of every human being and could achieve by terror every goal through their slaves. Once confronted with the horrible reality at the killing site, those prisoners would undergo a "shock treatment" and break mentally, and subsequently they would fulfill their tasks obediently. This aim of the Germans was realized. Rudolf Höss states in his memoirs, "[I]t was all done in such a matter-of-course manner that [the *Sonderkommando* prisoners] might themselves have been the exterminators."[3]

Survivors of the *Sonderkommando* remember that the first encounter with the heaps of twisted corpses traumatized them so severely that most of them began to act as "robots" (Gabai) or passive "machines" (Cohen). Some survivors, such as Chazan, for instance, also testify that they "stopped being human by then" (this aspect will be discussed in detail later on). In many sources, including the historical ones written at that time,[4] this kind of characterization of the *Sonderkommando* as emotionless, heartless, rude, beastly, brutal, and apathetic people is very common and widespread: "They are described as crude, repulsive, frightening sights. . . . [They] became even more nauseated at their own condition."[5]

This situation in which an installation for mass killing functions like a regular production facility but in which the workers are more like robots already creates an odd and bizarre atmosphere resembling a science fiction story. While reading the testimonies of the *Sonderkommando,* especially the chilling technical details of the "production line," the reader's impression is of experiencing a nightmare. The two channels—on the one hand the purely technical operation and on the other the extreme crime committed there—scarcely can be combined into one entity.

Naturally, in an environment of daily mass murder, where gas chambers, suffocated cries, corpses, and ashes are omnipresent, it is unrealistic to expect people who work in this place for a long period of time to act as they characteristically would have otherwise. Each had to adapt to the rules of this odd factory if he wanted to survive. Several *Sonderkommando* members worked in the crematoria for more than two years, like the brothers Abraham and Shlomo Dragon, and it is hard to believe that such a long period would pass by without leaving deep scars in the souls of the *Sonderkommando* prisoners. Every member of the unit must have gone through some metamorphosis of the soul because of the nature of the work. The personality of each member must have been reshaped and remodeled to enable the individual to fulfill the day-to-day missions that contradicted the values and laws used and respected by the civilized world.

The goal of this essay is to present the two spheres of the crematoria reality: the sane and the insane. The aim is to test the assumption that all *Sonderkommando* members indeed had turned into living machines who had lost contact with reality and to explain the ability of some to retain their sanity and continue to act as human beings in the midst of the inferno in the crematoria.

The *Sonderkommando* and Their Environment

Many sources speak about the trauma that was inflicted upon the *Sonderkommando* prisoners as a result of their duties inside the killing centers.[6] The pictures they had seen in the gas chambers and crematoria ovens were unendurable. Yet most of them managed to overcome the first immediate shock and gradually "got used to" the work with the corpses, retaining their job for days, weeks, and even years. The work became routine, the tears dried up over time, the mind grew numb, cries of the murdered were ignored, and the corpses became like pieces of wood. When a new transport arrived, the most significant factor was not its human cargo but the food and possible valuables for exchange that these doomed people would bring into crematorium compounds. Sometimes, when people were called back again to work, the *Kapo* encouraged them by shouting, "A French transport has arrived with nice things from the Champs-Elysées."[7]

Primo Levi correctly defines the invention of the *Sonderkommando* as "the most demonic crime of the NS regime."[8] The *Sonderkommando* represents the most evil and distorted aspect of the National Socialist mind. The Germans intentionally forced the Jewish prisoners to assist them in running the operation that aimed at exterminating all traces of their brethren. The Jewish *Vorarbeiter* (foremen), *Kapos*, and *Oberkapos* gave orders to the hundreds of their subordinates. The killing factory was directed by the victims of the crimes: this indeed was the goal of the real murderers—to put the burden of blame on the Jews. A foreigner who would have come to the crematoria building would have never guessed that all the many workers were merely puppets on a string. In reality they were just slaves, the slaves of the death factory at Auschwitz-Birkenau.

It is painful that the German mind could create a scene in which a Jew had to cremate the body of his wife or child, pull out the corpses of his beloved ones from the gas chamber, and ignore the questions that other Jews posed to him in the undressing room.

The members of the *Sonderkommando* were without choice. Refusing to continue working automatically meant death, while continuing to work was to live in hell. Sanity and insanity could be easily mixed in that atmosphere, intensified by the fact that the *Sonderkommando* was isolated from other prisoners. Its members were doomed to be murdered after they finished their obligations. They knew that they were living on borrowed time. Every day could be decisive for their lives.

The Idea and Its Implementation

The Germans, who tried to create a new world based on new rules and a new ideology, regarded the gas chambers and crematoria ovens as a necessity. The crematorium itself was the peak of the dehumanization process of the victims. In a system whose aim is to wipe out the *Untermenschen* (subhumans), mass-killing installations are irreplaceable ingredients. The gas Zyklon B fits perfectly into this ideology: in order to get rid of the *Ungeziefer* (vermin), one uses poison. One cleanses the world and liquidates the unwanted parasites. "Race theory" had paved the way to a crime against humanity, endorsed and encouraged by scientists, physicians, biologists, and geneticists.[9]

The Nazi regime introduced patterns of thought, behavior, morality, and culture, which distorted, ruined, and liquidated the already existing values of civilization. In this context we should see the invention of an extermination camp and the *Sonderkommando* as tools through which the revolutionary new ideas of the Nazis could be implemented. In other words, the invention of the death camps and the way in which they were conducted corresponded to the National Socialist *Weltanschauung* (world view).

Apart from the fact that they were considered "bearers of the secret" and were isolated from the other prisoners, other aspects mark the *Sonderkommando* as unique in the context of the death camps. Since the *Sonderkommando* prisoners were involved in the killing process, they were not meant to become *Muselmänner* (people on the verge of death from lack of food and exhaustion), at least not too quickly. Apart from their daily rations, which were similar to those of the other camp inmates, they were allowed to partake of significant amounts of food that the gassed victims had brought into the crematoria compound. This is a part of the insanity: the Jews sentenced to death, who have to kill other Jews sentenced to death, must be fed properly in order to be capable of fulfilling the murderous action. Valuables found in the clothes of the victims gave them opportunities to trade for comparatively high-quality food. In the context of the camp life the area in which more than a million people were murdered also served as a place of commerce and exchange. A kind of a "Persian market" existed in the heart of the killing houses between the gas chambers and crematoria halls.

Between Benefits and a Death Penalty

These aspects of the *Sonderkommando* reflect the duality of the prisoners' daily life: on one level there was the "Final Solution," the full-scale genocide—corpses, ashes, cries, despair; but on another level, life continued in a normal, routine manner. In this reality, the *Sonderkommando* were provided "benefits" that included sufficient nourishment and protection from brutality and bodily punishments. Indeed, one may assume that the *Sonderkommando* prisoners lived a "double life." This world included professional habits, physical work, hours of work, and hours of leisure. The other world was artificial, created by the Germans. In this world the Jews had nothing to say.

The *Sonderkommando*, of course, were victims, too. They can easily be defined as the most miserable of the miserable. The workers of the death factory had to witness day by day the extermination of their own people. There was nothing they could do about it. Their hearts and souls were broken by sorrow and despair. In the undressing room they were forced to be part of the system of deceit and misinformation about the real purpose of the "disinfections." There are testimonies about cases in which *Sonderkommando* prisoners had to push their own families into the furnaces or had to rip gold teeth out of their own mothers' mouths. Any lack of obedience or resistance on their part was immediately punished with death.

Rudolf Höss, the commander of Auschwitz, describes such a situation in his memoirs:

> It often happened that Jews from the *Sonderkommando* discovered close relatives among the bodies and even those who went into the gas chambers. Although they were visibly affected there never was any kind of incident. This incident I witnessed myself: As the bodies were being pulled out of one of the gas chambers, one member of the *Sonderkommando* suddenly stopped and stood for a moment as if thunderstruck. He then pulled the body along, helping his comrades. I asked the *Kapo* what was wrong with him. He found out that the startled Jew had discovered his wife among the bodies. I watched him for awhile after this without noticing anything different about him. He just kept dragging his share of bodies. After awhile I again happened upon this work party. He was sitting with the others and eating as if nothing had happened. Was he really able to hide his feelings so completely or had he become so hardened that something like this didn't bother him?[10]

A Mental Metamorphosis: From Shock to Adaptation

When looking more specifically at their mental conditions and responses, one can see that many *Sonderkommando* prisoners went through a kind of metamorphosis: from shock and paralysis to getting accustomed to the permanent horrors surrounding them, sometimes even enjoying the luxuries donated to them by the crematoria staff. When questioned about their feelings on their first day in the *Sonderkommando*, all survivors describe experiencing an indescribable jolt: "How did I react? I was confused. I thought I was going insane. I told myself 'This is the end,'"[11] recalls Joseph Sackar. Leon Cohen says, "What can I tell you? It was terrifying. I can't describe it in words. Just terrible."[12]

These two statements correspond to the memories of Shaul Chazan, also a former member of the *Sonderkommando*, who relates,

> We had a gut feeling that we couldn't identify. We didn't know a thing. On the one hand, I saw the bodies down there; on the other hand, the *Kapo* and the SS men

were beating me and cursing at me all that time, to the accompaniment of barking dogs. It was hell on earth. If there's a hell after death, I think it must look like that. It was hell, real hell. There it wasn't a question of whether to believe or not.[13]

A detailed report on the experiences and feelings of the first day in the *Sonderkommando*, on which the "normal" prisoner crossed the line between sanity and insanity by becoming a member of this doomed unit, can be found in the testimony of Eliezer Eisenschmidt:

> They led us into the yard and opened the door of the building that was used as a gas chamber, and we were overwhelmed with grief. We were in absolute shock. We'd never seen anything like this in our worst nightmares. To this day, I can see in my mind's eye what we saw behind the doors as they opened. A dead woman stood there, naked, her body doubled up. We froze. We couldn't grasp what was happening there. We saw the bodies in the gas chamber. When we began to remove the bodies, we saw how they'd become a single mass.[14]

Eisenschmidt belonged to that group that had to load the dead bodies onto the wheelbarrows. When he received this order for the first time, he was "stung to the quick. . . . For a few minutes, I was too revolted to touch a body. Such a thing never happened to me. Obviously I wasn't the only one in the group who felt revulsion. I couldn't work until someone hit me hard on the back with a rod."[15]

Shlomo Dragon, who was just seventeen years old when he was forced to join the *Sonderkommando,* reports similar feelings when he remembers Otto Moll, the crematorium chief, beginning to explain what they were supposed to do: "You have to remove the dead people from the house. There are corpses there, and you have to take them out in wheelbarrows, throw them into these big pits, and incinerate them."[16] Subsequently Moll opened the door. Shlomo Dragon recalls:

> We smelled gas. We saw corpses of both sexes. The whole place was full of naked people on top of each other, falling out . . . almost all of us went into shock. We stared at each other without uttering a sound and fell silent. We were too terrified to make a sound. We were like that for a couple of days and then we pulled ourselves together again. We'd never seen anything like it before.[17]

But despite their inconceivable activity, most of the members of the *Sonderkommando* eventually got used to their work within a short period of time. Yaakov Gabai remembers, "For the first few days, it was just terrible. But I told myself, 'You mustn't lose your sanity.' I knew from then on I'd have to see these sights day in, day out. This would be our job, so we'd better get used to it. A tough job, but get used to it."[18]

Finally, the service for the death industry became partly a technical task, as Lemke Pliszko describes: "Sometimes one could believe it was a common workplace and not a crematorium."[19] He continues:

> We took nothing too seriously. Nothing could move us anymore. When we wanted to eat our bread, then you were sitting on a body and eating the bread. You got

used to the place so much, you thought it was always your home. I could see a lot of corpses and nothing moved in my heart. Here in the Kibbutz, where I live [today], when I see a dead person, I'm shivering. Even crying with tears. In the camp when I saw corpses, I thought to myself: "Today the other man is dead. Tomorrow you'll be dead." You get used to everything. We had to sit somewhere when we were eating and the floor was full with bodies. The process of getting used to it was very quick and began immediately. Only one person whom I knew "went to the fence." Only one person. All the others wanted to live. Working in the crematoria I didn't feel as if I were working inside a nightmare. We accepted the reality as it was. Life was that this is a place where people are killed. That was life. For this reason I could go on working there.[20]

The numbing of the prisoners' feelings and the mental repression were in this context a self-protection mechanism against the horrible reality around them. The process of becoming an "automaton"[21] happened rather quickly—in the case of Leon Cohen it took only two days. To turn the prisoners into puppets, they were taken at the beginning to a pile of corpses that were to be cremated. For young people who have never seen a dead body in their life, this was a real shock. Two or three days later, when the sights of death increased, the prisoners mentally succumbed, becoming paralyzed and numb. The inner change was inevitable.

Becoming Accustomed or the Only Alternative

The mind of every person has its limits, however. The minute that the new *Sonderkommando* prisoners felt the real nature of the work they were forced to do, some of them saw only one outlet: suicide. Shaul Chazan remembers "a Greek Jew from the *Sonderkommando* who jumped into the fire. He saw what was going on and leaped into the pit."[22] Shlomo Dragon also testified on suicides: "There were several cases where people among us would 'run to the fence' in the morning. But not often."[23] This statement accords with Lemke, adding to his remarks above, "After a few days we got used to the situation. Those who got depressed went to the fence [and committed suicide]. Yet there were also those who, even later, never got used to the situation."[24]

For several psychological reasons very few chose to commit suicide. Those who did usually committed suicide in a very early stage of their "service" in the commando.[25] They understood it would be beyond their power to bear the distorted, insane reality to which they had been brought. The shock was too monstrous to be tolerated after just arriving from a relatively "normal" world. The psychological switch that all other members of the *Sonderkommando* must have made to survive and not go crazy must have been tremendous. The minority who decided to put an end to their lives had supposedly comprehended what their expected role in the Nazis' crime was to be.

For the majority that succeeded in getting used to the situation, there was one main principle: the gruesome tasks had to be executed meticulously. The orders, however, did not come directly from the Germans. The

Jewish leadership—the *Vorarbeiter* and the *Kapo*—received them from the SS staff and passed them on to their workers. The death plant functioned well even without the presence of the SS men. The Jewish workers were experienced professionals who knew exactly what they were expected to do and worked with efficiency. Each shift arrived on time, and the slight technical problems were not serious enough to sabotage such an important undertaking as the liquidation of the Jewish people.

The common "madhouse" is usually characterized with a bitter sarcasm. The same mood prevailed in the crematoria, a place that the German killers liked. The crime of genocide against the Jewish people was always accompanied by irony, cynicism, humor, and laughter—even when the gas Zyklon B was poured into the chambers. Eliezer Eisenschmidt recalls such a scene:

> After the room filled up with people, the doors were closed. Next, an SS man came over with the Zyklon gas in his hand. He put on a gas mask, opened the canister of gas, and threw the contents in. Shortly after the gas was thrown in, the people began to smell it and then we heard them shout "*Sh'ma Yisrael* . . ." from the interior of the gas chamber. The German called out to his comrades scornfully, "They're calling '*schmeiss rein, schmeiss rein*'—'throw it in, throw it in. . . .'"[26]

The perpetrators had lost their sense of humanity. But did the same happen to the *Sonderkommando* prisoners? Did all of their emotional and human sentiment vanish, too? A closer look at the testimonies reveals a different aspect of their daily life.

Keeping Human Mannerisms

The many hundreds of *Sonderkommando* prisoners were not a homogenous group, and many different prisoners displayed very different patterns of behavior. Indeed, many of them lost the capacity for human sensitivity and developed a cold, emotionless attitude. Others were different and tried to retain their former selves. Auschwitz did not create new characters: it strengthened existing character lines and sharpened others. Such were, for instance, religious Jews in the *Sonderkommando,* who became instructors and advisors for many members of the *Sonderkommando* who felt lost and desperate. Leading figures in the commando were ultra-Orthodox Jews such as Zalman Gradowski, Leib Langfuss, Zalman Lewental, and others. Yaakov Silberberg reports on a consultation he once had with one rabbi who did not desist in his spiritual practices even as a prisoner in the camp:

> I had a problem with myself. I was confused, didn't know what to do, how to behave. Personally I had a big problem: I belong to a "Cohen" family, the priests, and at that time, I was religious! I am a priest and, according to the Jewish religion, a "Cohen" has to be outside of the grave, far away from the dead, in order

not to get impure. . . . Shlomo Kirszenbaum told me, that in one of the big crematoria, there was the *Dayan* [religious judge] of Makow, and it was worthwhile talking to him.²⁷

Silberberg went to the *Dayan,* who responded: "Don't worry, we are here, in order to fulfill the mission of God. He wants it this way, and we have to act exactly as He orders us to do, this is God's will."²⁸ Silberberg goes on: "Then he also told me, that what we do here, would be—from his point of view—a *Mitzvah* [commandment], because by this way the Jews received some kind of burial."²⁹

Despite the routine and the numbness in the death factory, there are many accounts of how *Sonderkommando* prisoners exhibited respect for the victims, how they mourned the dead around them. One example of their enduring sense of sympathy is found in Zalman Gradowski's unpublished manuscript:

Here are lying now again two [bodies] . . . young women who once were extremely beautiful. They have filled two complete worlds on this earth. They have given so much happiness and pleasure. Each smile was a comfort, each look was happiness, each word was a heavenly and charming poetry. Everywhere, where they have only put their foot, they have brought with them happiness and contentment. Many hearts loved them. And now the two are lying on a plate made of iron and soon the crater will be opened and within minutes there will be nothing left of them.³⁰

The *Sonderkommando* men were tremendously saddened when they realized how many young lives were going to be eliminated:

No remnant and no memory will be left of all those who are standing here, all those who filled complete cities. They had a place in the world and soon they will be wiped out together with their roots. As if they have never been born. Our hearts are tearing out of pain. We are feeling, we are undergoing in reality their agony of transition from life to death.³¹

The *Sonderkommando* members documented their lives in the crematoria with the intention of leaving evidence for posterity. In fact, many testimonies reveal that a prime factor in their will to survive was the motivation to give evidence and in so doing to take revenge on the Germans. The members of the *Sonderkommando* also assisted other prisoners to escape from the camp in order to disseminate the truth about Birkenau in the free world. There were two pairs of Jewish escapees—Alfred Wetzler and Rudolf Vrba (Walter Rosenberg), as well as Czeslaw Mordowicz and Arnost Rosin— who managed to escape in mid-1944 after having obtained important information from members of the *Sonderkommando.*³²

Another unique group was the one that founded the underground movement in the *Sonderkommando.* This group initiated the uprising on 7 October 1944, the only armed uprising in the history of Auschwitz, during the course of which they destroyed the crematorium building No. IV, attempted a mass escape, and killed and wounded several SS men.[33] There was a sense of solidarity among the members of the *Sonderkommando*. Cases of betrayal and treason are unknown.

The *Sonderkommando* members acted in different ways in regards to the usage of belongings taken from the murdered: some became greedy and corrupt, while others did not take anything from the luggage of the dead Jews. Joseph Sackar, a Jew from Greece, told this with pride in his testimony.[34] The intention of the Germans to ruin the soul of the *Sonderkommando* prisoners failed—they did not quite succeed in pulling their victims with them into the abyss. In *Reading the Holocaust* Inga Clendinnen rightly points out that the *Sonderkommando* squads of around fifty members were small enough to develop some kind of esprit de corps: "some small sense of community and some recognition of the other as a comrade seems to have bloomed in that unlikely place, and that blooming lightened one corner of the darkness that was Auschwitz."[35]

Undermining the Borders— Working Together in the Crematoria

Auschwitz—the site where death, destruction, and extermination reigned supreme—also allowed some space where a pseudo-normal "working relationship" between the SS personnel and the *Sonderkommando* prisoners emerged. One of the most intriguing aspects in this research involves the encounters between the prisoners and their masters.

As mentioned, one aspect peculiar to the *Sonderkommando* was the relative proximity of the prisoners to their SS guards. Typical camp inmates did not necessarily see much of the SS. The SS man was somebody from whom the prisoner ran away, even when the SS man was still at a distance. Whenever an SS guard approached a prisoner it was almost always for torture or punishment.

Prisoner life was, as it is known, largely run and supervised through the system of prisoner functionaries: the *Kapos,* block seniors, and so on. This distance between the SS and most of the inmates was intentional: to prevent any softening effect that encounters with victims might have on SS guards. Distancing was one of the dehumanizing techniques that made the starving and dying people appear like a mass of anonymous *Untermenschen*. The pictorial instruction book of the SS described precisely how far the SS should be kept separate from single prisoners.[36]

In comparison to the whole camp, the situation in the crematoria was special. Only a handful of SS men were usually guarding and supervising the *Sonderkommando* during their work in relative proximity and over prolonged periods of time. More senior SS guards showed up whenever new transports arrived and when people were gassed. Those visits were made for the purposes of robbery and amusement. But for the most part during their shifts the *Sonderkommando* worked in the vicinity of very few SS guards. Hence, in the crematoria compound the distancing effect and the concomitant dehumanization of the prisoners were somewhat reduced. To the SS, the well-fed *Sonderkommando* members in proper clothing must have indeed appeared more like human beings than the emaciated and dying prisoners in the camp, who disgusted and frightened them.

In this context it seems worthwhile to shed some light on the range of interaction between the *Sonderkommando* and their SS oppressors.

Forms of Interaction

The same system of prisoner functionaries in the camp also structured life in the *Sonderkommando*. It was mainly the prisoner functionaries, that is, the *Kapos* or the *Vorarbeiter*, who had contact with the SS. They received the orders and passed them on to the *Sonderkommando*.[37] The common *Sonderkommando* worker did not actually interact with any of the SS. Survivors recall that they were mortally afraid of even getting near them. Georg van Ryk, a former member of the *Sonderkommando*, once said, "The SS were like gods. We did not even dare to look at the SS, otherwise they would have started to beat us immediately."[38]

The SS were unsurpassed in their cruelty and sadism. Otto Moll,[39] Friedrich Stiewitz, Walter Quackernack, Johann Gorges, Josef Schillinger, Josef Hustek, Kurschuss, and Scheinmetz (the first names of these two people are unknown) stand among the most despicable murderers who not only executed orders but also took great pleasure in their positions as "gods of the crematoria." They could maltreat, torture, and kill at will. No rules and boundaries restricted the barbarism of these people.

The era of Auschwitz was the "great opportunity" for the people on the lower rungs of German society: the baker, the gardener, the waiter, the little clerk—all of these "nobodies" in normal society suddenly became important, mighty figures who were responsible for life and death in Auschwitz. Their sadistic ideas were translated into practical realities, since the camps allowed the most extreme idea to be practiced, even those ideas that in any normal society before the Nazi time would be considered insane.

Accordingly, the camps were laboratories for the practice of cruelty that knew no bounds. The tendency toward acceptance and adaptation to the most barbarous crimes was widespread. This can be seen in many episodes, described, for instance, in *Seven Departments of Hell* written by Tadeusz Stabholz, a Jewish physician and survivor of three extermination camps: Treblinka, Majdanek, and Auschwitz. Such scenes are, for example, the killing of the prisoner Fink, the cruelty of chief physician Zentkeller, the slaughter of the Jews of Block 7 who tried to defend themselves before being gassed, and the running of the naked Jewish women to the gas chamber.[40] All of these scenes are characterized by beastly cruelty, which was aimed at humiliating the Jews and causing them the utmost suffering.

Moll—The Spawn of Insanity

The ultimate example of the cruel "Nazi spirit" is that of Otto Moll, the crematorium manager, who zealously sought to perfect the killing methods in Birkenau. The obsession with which he undertook the project of digging large pits near crematorium V to accelerate the corpses' burning is typical of the boundless insanity in the camps: the more extreme and cruel the innovation, the more the killers enjoyed it. Moll recruited members of the *Sonderkommando* and accompanied them to the excavation site. As long as his plans were not realized in a perfect manner, he would not be satisfied. The following observation is taken from Filip Müller's memoirs: "Even before work began, Moll paced nervously up and down the site. He inspected the area, going from place to place, consulting a large drawing which he had unfolded and comparing it with smaller drawings of the pits as well as of the rest of the extermination installations."[41]

Indeed, Moll was very excited and wanted the trench to be dug as fast and as well as possible. When the two large pits were finally finished—both forty to fifty meters long, about eight meters wide, and two meters deep—they were not yet ready for use, since "there followed the realization of the refinements thought up by the arch-exterminator's warped ingenuity."[42] Moll took great care with this project: together with his assistant, Eckardt, he climbed down into the pit and marked out a strip to be dug, "running lengthways down the middle from end to end."[43] This channel, which sloped to both sides from the middle, was thought to catch the human fat that would run from the burning corpses into two collecting pans. In his memoirs Müller comments, "The whole concept seemed quite inconceivable: a drain channel to catch human fat which in turn was to be used as fuel in order to obliterate as fast as possible all traces of these murderous deeds."[44]

But Moll was fascinated by this idea, which could mean a paramount improvement considering the effectiveness of one of his main tasks: the burning of the corpses. After all of the refinements were completed, Moll excitedly ordered two buckets of water to test whether the channel would work. But before reaching the collecting pan, the water slopped back and stopped. As Müller recalls, Moll was shocked:

> When he realized that something was wrong with the fall of the channel he grabbed the empty bucket and brought it down to the heads of any prisoners unfortunate enough to be standing within reach. . . . Moll too flung himself on the wretched prisoners in the pit who were cowering together with fright and kicked them viciously, shouting at the top of his voice: "You stupid shits, what's the matter with you, can't you even manage a simple job like that?"[45]

Finally Moll, the manager of the crematoria himself, climbed down into the pit, dressed in blue overalls, and supervised the alterations. Having finished, he ordered again the buckets of water and splashed them. This time the water drained completely. When Moll noticed the success, he relaxed, and as Müller remembers: "His face showed satisfaction and round his lips hovered something like a fleeting smile. He was obviously relieved and convinced that he had taken a big step forward on the road towards a solution of his task."[46] According to Müller, Moll didn't leave the scene immediately. Still standing at the pits he relished his success but, simultaneously, thought about possible problems that could prevent his system from working (e.g., the viscosity of the human fat).

Yaakov Gabai also witnessed Moll enjoying the sphere of insanity. He reports:

> A large transport from Lodz came in on 30 August 1944, and that month 250 Polish *"Muselmänner"* were sent from several camps on the outskirts of Auschwitz. By that time, they were unable to move. Right then the commander of the crematorium, Moll of the SS, came and said, "Don't send these ones to the gas." He wanted to butcher them personally. First he beat them with the metal rod that he used to shatter the remaining bones of people who had died. Afterwards, he came down and asked one of the soldiers to give him a rifle and some bullets. He began to shoot. After he shot four or five of them, one of the *"Muselmänner"* called out, "Commander!" and Moll, who was a brutal sadist, answered, "Yes?"
> "I've got a request."
> "What do you want?"
> "As you shoot my friends, I want to sing the Blue Danube Waltz."
> "Be my guest! How jolly! It's even better to shoot with musical accompaniment," Moll answered. So the man sang—la-la-la—and Moll shot them all until it was the singer's turn. The last bullet hit him and finished him off.[47]

Scene of Amusement and Surrealism

The border between sanity and insanity is also demonstrated by the shocking fact that the crematoria building and the gas chambers also served as a site of entertainment and amusement. Senior SS people and high-ranking Nazi officials were attracted by this place. Indeed, the testimonies tell us, from time to time delegations arrived, wishing to be present at the dreadful killing of the Jews. The peephole in the door of the gas chamber enabled the dignified VIP guests to watch "live" how the victims choked and died inside. Actually most guests were pleased and enjoyed the "show." As we see, the killing centers were not only places of painful death but also a scene of circus and theater, like a cabaret stage—an insane mixture of crime, murder, and barbarism with laughter and satisfaction. This contradiction between cruel death and enjoyment is very similar to the bloody fights of the gladiators in the Roman amphitheaters.

Another example of the mixture of sanity and insanity concerning the relationship between the SS men and the prisoners is the existence of some Lithuanian SS men who fluently spoke Yiddish[48]— a language that was not only comprehensible to the German perpetrators, but was also one used by millions of Jews all over Europe; indeed, it was the language in which they expressed their sentiments, sorrows, and dreams. Moreover, the expressions with which these SS men chose to describe their actions denied the humanity of the murdered. They were referred to as *Stuecke* (pieces) and *Dreck* (dirt) that had to be *bearbeitet* (processed). We should keep this in mind as we now attempt to describe the surreal proximity that existed between some *Sonderkommando* and the SS guards in the crematoria.

The Meeting of Perpetrators and Victims

Conversations between SS guards and *Sonderkommando* members were not uncommon. Lemke Pliszko relates that SS men would usually start conversations. There was little time to talk during the hard work, but sometimes during lunch breaks an SS guard would sit with the prisoners.[49] In his testimonies Pliszko describes an atmosphere that is more suggestive of an office environment. If we did not know the identity of this place, we would assume we were dealing with a friendly, polite place of hospitality. Pliszko says:

> We were sitting with the Germans round one table in the crematoria building. We were talking about several topics, including the work we were doing. An especially good mood prevailed when only one German was sitting with us. He himself did not murder Jews. He did not pour the gas inside the chambers. As long as he was alone—he was even friendly. The minute a second German came—he changed his attitude immediately. Being alone he spoke totally differently.[50]

But even though the prisoners used to sit together with the SS men, even at one table, there was always a certain feeling of insecurity: "When they came in the morning, they said 'Good morning!' to us. On the other hand, the same man who said 'Good morning' also could beat us when he was ordered to. Usually we did not get beatings, but sometimes we did get hit with a stick. One of the Germans even sent us to bring the stick to him."[51]

Pliszko recalls one particular SS guard who even emphasized that he would regret what he did, and that he was forced to do it. "Almost everybody said that, at least those that were good, not the evil bastards, of course."[52] This seems like the typical statement from an SS man, heard a thousand times over in the Nuremberg trials, but in the immediate context of the encounter between the prisoner and the SS, such talk—and already the fact that they talked to each other at all, in a relatively normal, human manner—seems surprising. In describing this "humane manner," Lemke Pliszko points out, "Mainly the SS men with lower ranks hinted to the *Sonderkommando* prisoners from time to time that they were dissatisfied."[53]

There are other examples: Morris Kesselman describes that, naturally, he distrusted most of the SS, except for one guard from Holland, with whom he even talked in a more personal manner, about their families, where they came from, and so on. After being bribed with alcohol, this SS man even assisted Morris in smuggling food from the *Sonderkommando* to other camp inmates.[54] Kesselman's statement concurs with Gabai's description illustrating that they interacted with their guards quite well: "They were with us all the time and they were really OK. We had no problems at all with them.

Everyday Life in the Sonderkommando

One of the guards was from Holland, a good guy, really fine. We always asked ourselves how this Dutchman could possibly be an SS man."[55]

Gabai goes on talking about this specific SS guard: "The SS man from the Netherlands . . . was still a boy—twenty-two, twenty-three at the most. . . . He never said a bad word to anyone. A friend, a buddy . . . he even gave me his weapon and said, 'Take it. You may play with it.'"[56] This Dutch SS man is often mentioned with overtones of appreciation by survivors of the *Sonderkommando*. Such statements also align with those of Miklos Nyiszli, the Jewish doctor who worked in the crematoria and who writes in his memoirs, "Taken individually, any SS guard in the crematorium could be bought."[57] The feeling about the vulnerability of almost every SS man to bribery was an opinion shared by other survivors, too.

Indeed, there was a kind of familiarity between the *Sonderkommando* and the SS, as Nyiszli stresses in a different context: "Three months in the same camp and in the same milieu had created, in spite of everything, a certain intimacy between us [Nyiszli and Muhsfeld, SS-*Oberscharführer*]. Besides, the Germans generally appreciate capable people, and, as long as they need them, respect them to a certain extent, even in the KZ."[58] This "intimacy" even encouraged Nyiszli to ask *Oberscharführer* Muhsfeld to save the life of a young girl who had amazingly survived the gassing in the gas chamber (account follows below).

The special kind of familiarity between the SS guards and the *Sonderkommando* prisoners is also well expressed by Lemke Pliszko, who testified: "The Germans who worked with us knew our first names. . . . The Germans called me Lemke and I called him with his rank. He knew the names of everybody. . . . The relations with the Germans were normal like in normal factories. When one of them wanted to call me, he said: '*Lemke, komm her!*' ['Lemke, come here!']."[59] In this context one should mention that the *Sonderkommando* prisoners actually invented nicknames for the guarding SS men—although Eliezer Eisenschmidt stresses that "giving nicknames didn't mean we felt closer or more confident with them."[60]

The prisoners and the SS men met almost daily, worked physically proximate to each other, and thus knew each other quite well. These nicknames—mostly relating to the physiognomy of the Germans ("The Small One," "The Big One," and "Roiter" because of his red face[61])—were intended to alert fellow prisoners before the appearance of a brutal SS man. As Morris Kesselman explains, it was thereby also possible to speak about the SS men, even behind their backs, without them realizing it. Besides, it was a kind of relaxation from the heavy, constant pressure that ruled over the work in the crematoria. In a way, the nicknames enabled the prisoners to undermine the power and authority of their tormentors. Taking into consideration the fact that a phenomenon typical of social relations between people in normal times was also adapted inside the killing centers leads to the conclusion that giving nicknames was part of a psychological self-defense in order to survive. Even in the darkest areas of the crematoria, the sense of humor did not disappear.

As mentioned above, as long as the low-ranking SS men were alone with the *Sonderkommando*, relationships would seem quite relaxed. The moment other guards or higher-ranking officers showed up the atmosphere changed swiftly. The plane on which this kind of more intimate interaction occurred was brittle and could collapse at any instant. Again Lemke Pliszko describes relatively personal encounters with one SS man from Lithuania: "We [the *Sonderkommando*] did not have any bad intentions, neither did he [the Lithuanian SS]. But we were also careful with those that were not too dangerous to us. Because one slip, one wrong word could still mean your death."[62]

Treading this thin red line—working "together" with the SS men for months or even years, talking to them but also fearing death—illustrates the paradoxical mixture of normality and abnormality that the prisoners experienced in the crematoria. Usually, the members of the *Sonderkommando* were afraid of approaching SS men. Thus they were even more surprised when the SS people then acted in an unexpectedly humane manner. Nyiszli remembers such a situation in the crematoria dormitory after a "social" evening with alcohol and talk, when SS men making rounds stopped and reminded the prisoners it was time to go to bed. Normally such reminding was delivered with punishment. Here it almost seems to be a polite request to switch off the lights.[63] Lemke Pliszko reports on a similar experience: "In 1944 once a German came to our block and he wished us all the best. So the *Blockalteste* [the prisoner supervisor of the block] answered: 'We wish you the same.'"[64]

This "friendly" treatment did not occur by accident. Apart from the constant reign of terror, the SS certainly also had an interest in playing "good guys" vis-à-vis the *Sonderkommando* prisoners so as to be able to enrich themselves on a personal level and more generally to keep the *Sonderkommando* operations running smoothly without any disturbance. This twisted intention also shines through in the following scenario, mentioned by Yehuda Bacon. He recalls that "prisoners, block seniors, and the SS used to play football and ping-pong together in the Gypsy Camp, when they were offduty on Sundays."[65] Primo Levi also refers to this unusual event:

> Nyiszli tells how during a work break he attended a soccer game between the SS and the *Sonderkommando,* that is to say, between a group representing the SS on guard at the crematorium and a group representing the Special Squad. Other men of the SS and the rest of the Squad are present at the game. They take sides, bet, applaud, urge the players on as if, rather than at the gates of hell, the game were taking place on the village green.[66]

The following scene also illustrates the grotesque coexistence of annihilation and a seemingly normal social interaction between the perpetrators and the victims. Gabai, who was forced to work as a *Heizer* (stoker) and who was accordingly ordered to burn the corpses in the ovens, recalls:

> Once they brought a girl from Hungary who had a two-day-old baby. She knew she was about to be murdered. We had nothing to do that night. We sat around

idly and offered her a chair to sit down, some food, and cigarettes. She told us that she was a singer and talked for about half an hour. We sat in front of the furnaces. Next to us sat a Dutch SS man (the one mentioned above), a rather nice, likeable guy. He also listened in. When the story was over, he stood up and said, "Very well, we can't sit here like this forever; now it's death's turn." She was asked what she preferred, that we kill the baby first or her. She said, "Me first. I don't want to see my child dead." Then the Dutchman stood up, brought over the rifle, shot her, and threw her into the furnace. Then he picked up the baby, bang-bang, and that was that.[67]

This horrible story contains the seeds of insanity that prevailed in the undressing rooms and gas chambers. We find in it the quick charge between politeness and bestiality, the ability of the SS man to be human and murderous almost at the same time, the mixture and duality of life and death in one location.

Considering the more exceptional and extreme statements, where *Sonderkommando* survivors talk about a "relaxed" attitude and even show some kind of "solidarity" and understanding vis-à-vis the SS, one should bear in mind that such victims often spoke well of their tormentors in later testimonies. Filip Müller, for example, writes in his memoirs, "We prisoners and [the SS man] Starck were worlds apart. . . . [But] I often wondered how it was possible for this young man, scarcely older than myself, to be so cruel. . . . He was no doubt a *victim* of the Nazi propaganda."[68]

The partial identification with the tormentor, the portrayal of both (oneself and one's tormentor) as victims, all of these are ways to ease the trauma and to make sense of the crime and the suffering. Psychologists have examined such phenomena, referring to them as the "Stockholm Syndrome," to mention but one name.[69] Nevertheless, Müller's statement is exceptional—no other *Sonderkommando* survivors share his attempt to find some kind of understanding toward the German perpetrators.

Yet, in depicting instances of human interaction between the SS and the *Sonderkommando*, we intend to point out an apparent paradox. In the very center of the inferno, in the crematorium compound, there also existed a certain margin that helped the prisoners deny and repress to some degree the unimaginably horrible acts in which they were forced to participate.

In fact, this seemingly paradoxical aspect also extends to the ways in which the *Sonderkommando* prisoners related to each other. As mentioned in the beginning of this essay, on the one hand the survivors recall themselves as having acted as human machines, shell-shocked, traumatized, unable to act or do anything about their situation. On the other hand, they also tell of scenes that appear in stark contrast to that of the human robot—moments of friendship and mutual solidarity, evenings with social gatherings and songs, and, of course, the underground activities leading up to the uprising in the *Sonderkommando* in autumn of 1944. We shall now map out these human spaces inside the inferno, which helped the *Sonderkommando* prisoners to retain their sanity, to keep their strength, and, ultimately, to survive.

Relationships Within the *Sonderkommando*

Survivors' testimonies about their daily routine in the *Sonderkommando* show the immense pressure exerted on the prisoners during their work shifts. It was sheer physical toil under the most traumatic and gruesome conditions that one can imagine. Yaakov Gabai remembers: "We worked like robots there. I had to stay strong in order to survive and relate everything that had happened in this hell. Reality proves that people are crueler than animals. Yeah, we were animals. We didn't have emotions. Sometimes we doubted whether we were still human."[70]

Chazan recalls the same experience: "I'd stopped being human by then. If I'd been human, I couldn't have endured it for even one minute. We kept going because we'd lost our humanity."[71] Leon Cohen makes a similar argument: "During that time we had no emotions. We were totally drained. We blocked up our hearts; we were dehumanized. We worked like machines. We were human beings devoid of human emotion. We were really animals, not people." Finally Cohen concludes, "We'd become robots."[72]

Yet, time and again their accounts also reveal aspects about everyday life in the crematoria, where the *Sonderkommando* did not quite feel like numb and passive human ghosts. Even when acting like machines and repressing their inner feelings, the death that ruled over the scene was covering all. The pain, sorrow, and grief were certainly penetrating the prisoners' hearts.

Those prisoners on day-shift duty were principally free and could do in their barracks whatever they wanted after the evening roll call. We would expect them to be depressed, broken, and on the edge of insanity. Yet there were also times when they had conversations, when they talked about their past lives, when they sought some consolation in the solidarity that existed among them. They were not totally alone in this horror.

A Sense of Solidarity and Familiarity

Describing the sense of solidarity among the *Sonderkommando* prisoners, Lemke Pliszko recalls: "I knew everyone in our block—we were together like a family."[73] This is illustrated by the fact that prisoners usually addressed each other personally by their names, as Kesselman remembers.[74] The survivors generally confirm that the camaraderie among the *Sonderkommando* prisoners was greater than in other units of the camp because they were so isolated and shared the same fate: the verdict of death.

Prisoners in the *Sonderkommando* gathered in small groups, often being from the same town or area with a similar background. They knew that they could trust each other. Yet the sense of solidarity very much emerged from the feeling that they were all together in this traumatic inferno and also, in a way, from the certainty that none of them would survive—although this awareness was mostly suppressed.

The *Sonderkommando* was, however, not a homogenous unit. Rather, it consisted of people from many different countries and backgrounds.

Everyday Life in the Sonderkommando

Whenever conflicts occurred, it was usually between such groups, and cases of concrete violence among prisoners are described mainly between Jewish prisoners and the small group of Christian Poles in the *Sonderkommando,* who held the position of *Vorarbeiter.*

Jewish prisoners, although from different countries of origin, could generally speak Yiddish with each other. The only exception was the large group of the Jews from Greece who spoke only Greek or Ladino, with whom the others could initially hardly communicate. The Greeks were a relatively closed group and mostly kept to themselves due to language and cultural differences. Despite such difficulties with communication, the relations between groups from different countries are described as relaxed and friendly. Even with their many different backgrounds, people somehow found their accepted places in the *Sonderkommando,* as Abraham Dragon confirms:

> We got along fine with all the people from different countries. We communicated [with the Greeks] largely by using gestures. They could do as much physically demanding work like us, because they had suffered at home and had become hardened. People from Germany or France could not work as hard, and the *Kapo* arranged for them to work as hair cutters or sorting clothes, things that did not involve hard physical labor.[75]

"Social Evenings"

As already mentioned, after work hours the prisoners were mostly so exhausted that they just had something to eat and went to sleep. One would converse mainly with the people in the neighboring bunks. Nevertheless, Joseph Sackar states: "One cannot say [that] we had lived like robots."[76] After having finished work, the *Sonderkommado* prisoners could sit together and talk and think about their situation, their work in the crematoria, their experiences, and what was done to them.[77] There was space to think about what happened to them—and the prisoners indeed reflected on their fate. Those were moments of self-awareness and self-reflection. In an interview Eisenschmidt reports on a feeling of sadness that crept back in when he saw groups walking toward the crematoria building since they reminded him of his family.[78]

The existence of religious life in the killing center also contradicts the picture of passive human machines. Gradowski reports in his secret writings that the religious Jews insisted on continuing the tradition of making a *Minyan* three times a day in one of the crematoria buildings.[79] It seems that the description of the "robot-like" routine would mainly refer to the actual working process, where emotions had to be suppressed to be able to stand the work among all the corpses. In the evening after work some prisoners tried to abandon their "robot behavior."

Sometimes there were also social occasions where prisoners would come together and sing, as Yehuda Bacon recalls, "mainly sentimental songs, about our previous lives and about freedom."[80] Many other survivors highlight the regular singing of the Greek groups in the evenings after work, where even some of the German SS guards were present. Lemke Pliszko, among others, confirms that "the Germans often stood at the door and listened when the Greeks were singing."[81] He goes on recalling: "After duty in our barrack, we were singing Yiddish songs. The Greek prisoners were singing and dancing until late at night. They knew how to sing. They sang for many hours."[82]

Nevertheless, from time to time the members of the *Sonderkommando* who had become accustomed to their work in the crematoria were reminded of their former life, the life outside of the crematoria, when prisoners from other units appeared. Indeed, the link between the "normal" world and that of the *Sonderkommando* is illustrated by the few prisoners who succeeded in entering the barracks of the *Sonderkommando*. Yehuda Bacon, Mordechai Ciechanower, Stanley Glogover, and the other curious, naïve youngsters were mainly interested in the food but also in the human warmth that the *Sonderkommando* prisoners could provide. As Bacon remembers, it was very dangerous for members of the *Sonderkommando* to be in contact with other prisoners, due to their knowledge of every detail of the killing process.[83]

Despite this, contact between the *Sonderkommando* and other prisoners continued. Children working at the nearby "Canada," such as fourteen-year-old Yehuda Bacon, sometimes received permission from the *Sonderkommando* prisoner on duty to enter the *Sonderkommando* block. Although some prisoners were unwilling to speak about their work in the crematoria, Bacon got information about what was going on there. A few people told him about their experiences and even about their feelings at this unique place, where sanity and insanity are so close to each other that it is nearly impossible to distinguish one from the other.

The gap between sanity and insanity is well demonstrated by the astonishing and rare case of a young girl who survived the gas chambers.[84] When the gas pellets were thrown inside the chamber, she fell on the floor and, by chance, was not poisoned. After the gassing, when the *Sonderkommando* prisoners started taking the dead bodies to the ovens, they suddenly discovered that the girl was still breathing. All of the members of the *Sonderkommando* were shocked—this definitely was the first time that something like this had happened. The chief of the gas chamber commando ran to Dr. Miklos Nyiszli, a physician who was both a member of the *Sonderkommando* and simultaneously Mengele's pathological expert. He gave the girl injections and after a few minutes she regained consciousness. Of course she was confused, since she could not grasp what had happened to her. Nyiszli asked her a few questions and learned that she was from Transylvania and was sixteen years old. Immediately the question arose about what to do with her. It was clear that a girl could not stay with the crematorium's *Sonderkommando*. Suddenly SS-*Oberscharführer* Muhsfeld appeared supervising the work and saw the gathering of prisoners. When he entered the room he also noticed the girl. Nyiszli knew there was almost no chance to save the life of the girl, but since he felt respected by Muhsfeld because of his work as a physician, he tried to explain the situation and asked Muhsfeld to do something for the child. When the SS man asked him what he proposed to do, Nyiszli pointed out the possibility of putting her in front of the crematoria gate, where a commando of women always worked. Nyiszli suggested that it would not be hard for her to disappear in the crowd. But Muhsfeld was convinced that a girl of sixteen years would not understand the circumstances of her survival and instead would immediately start telling where she just had come from and what she had experienced in the gas chambers. Finally Muhsfeld concluded: "There's no way of getting round it. The child will have to die."[85] Half an hour later the girl was shot dead.

Epilogue

"It must sound terrible and it's hard to understand how we lived together with our murderers. But anything was possible in Auschwitz."[86] These words of Yaakov Gabai are a concise description of the problem that forms the basis of this article. The extermination camps were sites in which the Nazi spirit flourished and bloomed in its most extreme way: the camps were the essence of the Nazi regime and Nazi ideology and the crimes committed there against Jews and other victims were a compulsory outcome of this ideological belief. The creation of the death factory commandos, the *Sonderkommando*, must be considered one of the worst crimes perpetrated by the Nazis, as Primo Levi justifiably wrote in his famous chapter on "The Gray Zone" in *The Drowned and the Saved*. In the daily activity of those *Sonderkommando* prisoners was a combination of normality and abnormality. The decision to eliminate all Jews in the world was insane in and of itself. The practical way of executing this intention was a direct continuation of this madness. The statements about the seemingly ongoing everyday life in the crematoria, and especially about the relations between some *Sonderkommando* prisoners and the SS, are surprising.

For a deeper understanding of the reality of the *Sonderkommando*, it is important to consider not only the aspects that describe how these innocent people were turned into paralyzed human machines. One should also link this image of the *Sonderkommando* to that of the heroic fighters who organized the uprising in the crematoria, or that of the *Sonderkommando* prisoners who assisted others to escape, or those who wrote down all of the horrors with persistence in order to deliver to the next generations a record of what took place. Survivors frequently claim that those who did not go through the same horror will never be able to understand what they experienced in the camps. The case with the *Sonderkommando* is even more difficult to comprehend. The technical aspect of the death factories is comprehensible, but what lies beyond our empirical abilities of understanding is how the *Sonderkommando* people could persevere. It seems impossible to grasp how a human being could have been able to work for months and even for years in the death factory. Nevertheless, we must make an effort and try to shed light onto each of these unprecedented phenomena that happened in the Shoah. The few survivors of the *Sonderkommando* are unique

Auschwitz survivors, and through their testimonies we gain a deeper insight into the Shoah, into ourselves, and into the world in which we live.

Notes

1. Primo Levi, *The Drowned and the Saved,* trans. Raymond Rosenthal (New York: Summit Books, 1988), 53.
2. Gideon Greif, *We Wept Without Tears,* trans. Naftali Greenwood (New Haven, CT: Yale University Press, 2005). See the German edition, *Wir weinten tränenlos . . . : Augenzeugenberichte des jüdischen "Sonderkommandos" in Auschwitz* (Frankfurt am. Main: Fischer, 1999), 221. Hereafter I cite mainly the page numbers of the German edition.
3. Auschwitz-Birkenau State Museum, *KL Auschwitz Seen by the SS* (Warsaw, 1991), 77.
4. Some members of the *Sonderkommando* wrote clandestine notes, which they buried at Birkenau. Those notes were partly discovered after the war. Among the main chroniclers were Zalman Gradowski, Leib Langfuss, and Zalman Lewental.
5. Ber Mark, *The Scrolls of Auschwitz,* trans. Sharon Neemani (Tel Aviv: Am Oved, 1985), 125.
6. See Wolfgang Sofsky, *Die Ordnung des Terrors—Das Konzentrationslager* (Frankfurt am Main, 1997), 307–10. The English edition is *The Order of Terror: The Concentration Camp,* trans. William Templer (Princeton, NJ: Princeton University Press, 1997). See also Ota Kraus and Erich Kulka, *The Death Factory: Documents on Auschwitz* (New York: Pergamon, 1966).
7. Yehuda Bacon, interview with Gideon Greif (G.G.), Jerusalem, 30 May 2003.
8. Levi, *The Drowned and the Saved,* 53.
9. See Eugen Kogon, Hermann Langbein, and Adelbert Rückerl, eds., *Nazi Mass Murder: A Documentary History of the Use of Poison Gas,* trans. Mary Scott and Caroline Lloyd-Morris (New Haven, CT: Yale University Press, 1994).
10. Rudolf Höss, *Death Dealer: The Memoirs of the SS Kommandant at Auschwitz,* ed. Steven Paskuly and trans. Andrew Pollinger (New York: Da Capo Press, 1996), 160–61.
11. Greif, *Wir weinten tränenlos . . . ,* 68.
12. Ibid., 341.
13. Ibid., 303–4.
14. Ibid., 244.
15. Ibid., 245.
16. Ibid., 123.
17. Ibid., 124.
18. Ibid., 196.
19. Interview with G.G., Kibbutz Givat HaShlosha, 21 November 2003.
20. Interview with G.G., 21 May 2004.
21. Greif, *Wir weinten tränenlos . . . ,* 353.
22. Ibid., 303.
23. Ibid., 171.
24. Interview with G.G., Kibbutz Givat HaShlosha, 25 July 2000.
25. Greif, *Wir weinten tränenlos . . . ,* 197–98.
26. Ibid., 247.
27. Greif, *We Wept Without Tears,* Hebrew edition (Jerusalem: Yad Vashem, 1999), 354.
28. Ibid.
29. Ibid.
30. Ibid., 83–84.
31. Ibid., 58.
32. See, for example, Henryk Swiebocki, *London Has Been Informed: Reports by Auschwitz Escapees* (Oswiecim: Auschwitz-Birkenau State Museum, 1997); Rudolf Vrba, *I Escaped*

from Auschwitz (Fort Lee, NJ: Barricade Books, 2002); Erich Kulka, *Escape from Auschwitz* (South Hadley, MA: Bergin and Garvey, 1986).
33. Andreas Kilian, *"Der Sonderkommando-Aufstand in Auschwitz-Birkenau . . ."* ("The Uprising of the *Sonderkommando* in Auschwitz-Birkenau . . . "), published in the bulletin *Lagergemeinschaft Auschwitz—Freundeskreis Auschwitz* (Camp Community Auschwitz—Circle of Friends Auschwitz), 2002–3.
34. Greif, *Wir weinten tränenlos . . .* , 84
35. Inga Clendinnen, *Reading the Holocaust* (Cambridge: Cambridge University Press, 1999), 74.
36. The original is at the Auschwitz-Birkenau Museum archive, MPMAB, section "Höss Trial."
37. On the functionaries in Auschwitz see Hermann Langbein, *People in Auschwitz*, trans. Harry Zohn (Chapel Hill: University of North Carolina Press, 2004).
38. Interview with G.G. and Andreas Kilian, Amsterdam, 8 May 1996.
39. For a biographical sketch see *KL Auschwitz Seen by the SS*, 245–46.
40. Greif, *We Wept Without Tears*, Hebrew edition, 136, 146, 149–50.
41. Filip Müller, *Eyewitness Auschwitz: Three Years in the Gas Chambers*, ed. and trans. Susanne Flatauer (Chicago: Ivan R. Dee, 1999), 129.
42. Ibid., 130.
43. Ibid.
44. Ibid.
45. Ibid., 131.
46. Ibid., 132.
47. Greif, *Wir weinten tränenlos . . .* , 203.
48. Lemke Pliszko, interview with G.G., Kibbutz Givat HaShlosha, 16 December 2003.
49. Ibid.
50. Interview with G.G., 21 May 2004.
51. Ibid.
52. Interview with G.G., Kibbutz Givat HaShlosha, 9 May 2002.
53. Interview with G.G., Kibbutz Givat HaShlosha, 25 July 2000.
54. Morris Kesselman, "Memorials Aren't All in Stone," as told to Arlene Lehto, unpublished manuscript, 124.
55. Greif, *Wir weinten tränenlos . . .* , 217.
56. Ibid., 219–20.
57. Dr. Miklos Nyiszli, *Auschwitz: A Doctor's Eyewitness Account*, trans. Tibère Kremer and Richard Seaver (New York: Arcade Publishing, 1993), 75.
58. Ibid., 117.
59. Interview with G.G., 21 May 2004.
60. Interview with G.G., Givatayim, 12 December 2003.
61. Interview with G.G., Kibbutz Givat HaShlosha, 21 November 2003.
62. Interview with G.G., Kibbutz Givat HaShlosha, 16 December 2003.
63. Nyiszli, *Auschwitz*, 46.
64. Interview with G.G, Kibbutz Givat HaShlosha, 25 July 2000.
65. Interview with G.G., Jerusalem, 19 July 1999.
66. Levi, *The Drowned and the Saved*, 54–55.
67. Greif, *Wir weinten tränenlos . . .* , 204.
68. Müller, *Eyewitness Auschwitz*, 30.
69. Encarta, *World English Dictionary* (1999), 1759.
70. Greif, *Wir weinten tränenlos . . .* , 221.
71. Ibid., 312.
72. Ibid., 356.
73. Interview with G.G., Kibbutz Givat HaShlosha, 16 December 2003.
74. Interview with G.G., Miami Beach, 6 December 1999.
75. Interview with G.G., Ramat Gan, 2 January 2004.

76. Interview with G.G., Holon, 26 December 2003.
77. Eliezer Eisenschmidt, interview with G.G., Givatayim, 12 December 2003.
78. Ibid.
79. Greif, *We Wept Without Tears,* Hebrew edition, 88–91.
80. Interview with G.G., Jerusalem, 30 May 2003.
81. Interview with G.G., Kibbutz Givat HaShlosha, 25 July 2000.
82. Interview with G.G., 21 May 2004.
83. Interview with G.G., Jerusalem, 30 May 2003.
84. Nyiszli, *Auschwitz,* 114–20.
85. Ibid., 120.
86. Greif, *Wir weinten tränenlos . . . ,* 220.

– Chapter 4 –

SONDERKOMMANDO:
TESTIMONY FROM EVIDENCE

Michael Berenbaum

You tell me to what point are you ready to compromise those things that are against your conscience and sense of ethics, that would jeopardize your standing in the community, your job, your salary. When do you keep quiet when you shouldn't? What price do you give to squealing when you shouldn't, when if there were a risk, your livelihood, not your life never mind. Let me ask you, when do you compromise—when your life is threatened. I don't know. Do you? I don't know. I only know that the price was too high.[1]

Sonderkommando, the special prisoner units that operated in the vicinity of the gas chambers, were intimate with the act of killing. They observed the murderers—and the act of killing—directly, closely, and over a long period of time. They were in the presence of the condemned in their last moments, when they entered the undressing room, when they lined up to go into the gas chambers; and they were with the corpses minutes after they were gassed, when their bodies were removed from the chambers and they were processed. At Birkenau as elsewhere, *Sonderkommando* pulled gold teeth from the dead victims' mouths, searched the inner cavities for hidden valuables, removed rings from fingers and clipped hair which was then bundled and shipped, burned the corpses either in open pits or in the crematoria's ovens, crushed the bones, and brought the accumulated ashes to the Vistula River, where they were deposited in the river to flow downstream.

One member of the *Sonderkommando*, Sam Itzkowitz, was born in Markov, Poland, in 1924 and arrived in Auschwitz on 10 December 1942 at the age of eighteen. Soon after his arrival he was selected to work in the vicinity of the *Sonderkommando* and could observe his surroundings. It

Notes for this section begin on page 68.

was not work he chose but a task imposed upon him. He was not alone in contemplating suicide shortly after he began his work. When asked, "Did you think of going to [the electrified barbed wires surrounding the camp]?" Itzkowitz responded, "Plenty of times. I didn't have the guts. . . . I kept on thinking to myself I wish I had the guts to do it. I just didn't, couldn't get myself together to do it."[2] Death was certainly easier and simpler than the life he was to live.

The temptation to commit suicide did not easily pass. Another *Sonderkommando,* David Nencel, described one moment when he opted to die: "I took the elderly woman in my hands and I was walking and crying, and I throw her into the bunker there and I didn't go out . . . I felt that I'm carrying my own mother in there. I just didn't want to go on with something like it. I wanted to go together with them and finish."[3] But he was permitted no such choice. "Before they locked the gas chamber door, they count the prisoners, and they count and they see one is missing, so they pulled me out."[4]

Ya'akov Zilberberg was a *cohain,* a member of the priestly tribe forbidden to desecrate its unique status by being in contact with the dead. He was a religious Jew and thus prohibited from taking his own life. He offered a rationale: "What benefit would there be if I committed suicide? Who would know what went on?"[5] Zilberberg talked with a rabbi who also served as a *Sonderkommando,* the *Dayan* (judge) of Makow. He told the *Dayan,* "'I am going to the wires.' [The *Dayan*] said to me [that] it would be a bigger sin if I should kill myself than if I should do this work. . . . One adjusts. Then I said, 'Tomorrow morning I go to the electric fence.' . . . In the morning I began to think differently. It was difficult to live, but then you adjust."[6] Repeating the *Dayan*'s words, Zilberberg said, "For [suicide] there is always time."[7] Shaul Hazan said, "To kill yourself you need a reason. We had no reason to kill ourselves."[8]

The Germans were in charge. In the undressing room they presided. They told the incoming Jews that they were going to the shower and then to work. They instructed them to remember the hook upon which they hung their clothing so that they could retrieve it afterward. An SS man would drop the gas. Sam Itzkowitz described the process of killing: "A German doctor would come by after the gassing and pronounce the words: 'Everything is finished.' He would then leave in a Red Cross vehicle."[9]

> First the women had to go in, into the gas chamber. They led them in and packed them as tight as they could. Then the men had to go after that, and . . . the chamber was filled to capacity. But they knew it was going to be filled, so they held back a lot of youngsters, boys and girls, and they held them back. As the chamber was filled to the capacity, the *Sonderkommando* had to grab kids by their legs and their arms and the legs and shove them in on the heads of the people, of the victims in the gas chamber, and kept poking them . . . so they would go further, and the scream of the victims that were walked on was horrendous, but the kids had to move further in until they got all of them in, and then they slammed the door, and gave the signal to the SS man upstairs to put the gas in.[10]

He was asked: "Did people know they were going to die?" Itzkowitz replied, "They knew. They knew but couldn't do anything. They were naked, they were one against the other, and nowhere to go and . . . you couldn't move an arm or a leg. What can you do?"[11]

Eliezer Eisenschmidt tried to allude to the fate that awaited his victims. Seeing an entire community about to be murdered—"liquidated" is the term the Nazis deceptively used—he turned to its rabbi. He warned: "Say *viddui* [the final confession in Jewish liturgy] with your congregation." "No!" the rabbi responded. "God will help us."[12]

Some *Sonderkommando* were reticent to tell the prisoners what awaited them: "I did not say the truth. What could I say, that you are going to die? I am thankful that I did not say the truth."[13] Others presumed that the prisoners knew their fate.

> Most of them knew they were doomed [and] there was nothing they could do about it. And most of them did not believe. Somehow their human instinct is so strong that they see death in front of them and they tried to wipe it off. No, that cannot be! This cannot happen. But in reality, finally they had to face it.[14]

Rudolph Reder has a unique stature as a former member of the *Sonderkommando*. He is one of only two known survivors of Belzec, the death camp that operated between February and December 1942 at which approximately five hundred thousand Jews were murdered. Since Chaim Hirzchmann, the other known survivor, was killed on the day he bore witness, Reder is literally the only survivor of Belzec to tell his story. He was born 4 April 1881 in Dębica, Poland, and was thus more than sixty years of age when he worked in the *Sonderkommando* at Belzec. Educated as a chemist, Reder moved to Lwow in 1910 where he owned a soap factory. During the German occupation Reder was incarcerated in the ghetto with his family. His daughter was a doctor in the Jewish hospital. The SS captured Reder during the *Grosse Aktion* 16 August 1942 and deported him to Belzec.

Upon arrival he was selected to work in the *Sonderkommando*. At the beginning, he operated an excavator digging mass graves; later he worked as a mason. Thanks to his job he could move about the entire territory of the camp and witness the entire killing operation. Reder escaped from the camp, when he went in a company of two SS men to Lwow in order to buy building material. Until the end of German occupation his former worker Anastazja Hawryluch hid him. He moved together with his wife to Krakow in 1945 and he lived there until 1950. He emigrated to Israel and then to Canada. His date and place of death is unknown.

His brief narrative was taken in 1946 and has vividness not found in many later testimonies. Reder described a unique tension between knowing and not knowing. The victims went back and forth between hope and despair, knowledge of what awaited them and a willingness to be deceived. It began on the train: "No one was talking to anyone; no one was consoling lamenting women, no one was stopping sobbing children. We all knew: we were going to certain and horrible death."[15]

Primo Levi reports a similar dread on the train. "Now in this hour of decision, we said to each other things that are never said among the living. We said farewell and it was short: everybody said farewell to life through his neighbor."[16] Upon arrival Reder described the tension between hope and despair:

> Immediately after the victims were unloaded they were gathered in the courtyard surrounded by armed *askars* for Irrman to give a speech. The silence was deadly. He stood close to the crowd. Everyone wanted to hear. Suddenly there was hope: If they talk to us, maybe they want us to live. Maybe there will be work . . . maybe?
>
> Irrman talked loud and clear: "You are going now to bathe. Later you will be sent to work. That's all." Everybody was glad, happy that, after all, they will be working. They even applauded. The men went straight ahead to a building with a sign, *Bade und Inhaletionsräume* [bath and inhalation rooms]. The women proceeded twenty meters more to a large barrack about thirty by fifteen meters to have their head shaved. They entered quietly not knowing what to expect. Silence was everywhere.
>
> After a few minutes they were made to line up and made to sit on wooden stools, eight at a time. When eight Jewish barbers entered and silently like automated figures started to shave off hair completely to the skin with shaving machines, that's when they realized the truth. They had no doubts then. Everybody—young and old, children and women—everybody went to certain death. Little girls with long hair were herded into the shaving barracks. Those with short hair went to the barracks with the men.
>
> Suddenly, without even a transition from hope to despair—came the realization that there was no hope. People began to scream—women became hysterical, crazed. . . .[17]

There were efforts to deceive the Jews: Irrman's speech, the SS telling the victims to remember where their clothing was hung, even an officer swearing in the name of Hitler that they would return from the shower.

Certain tasks were restricted to the Germans. They alone decided who should live and who should die. They alone placed the gas in the chambers. They alone declared the dead, dead. At Auschwitz work hours were long; twelve-hour shifts were the norm. The personal situation of *Sonderkommando* was paradoxical, surely compromised. As long as transports continued to arrive, the *Sonderkommando* were needed. When they were needed, they would be kept alive. When the arrival of transports slowed, however, they were the most vulnerable and the first to die because they were the most dangerous eyewitnesses to the killing process.

Gideon Greif's masterful collection of *Sonderkommando* interviews as well as the still unpublished ones that I read from the testimonies gathered for the film *Evidence*—some of which overlap with the Greif material—finds a recurring theme of self-justification: "I had no choice!" The statement is technically incorrect but psychologically potent, for indeed there were choices. What is remarkable is the sense of battle between conscience and life, as well as the ability of many within the *Sonderkommando* to shut down their feelings and to acclimate to their routine.

The *Sonderkommando* repeatedly speak of having no choice:

> You went along and did not have a choice. You went along under the pressure of beatings.[18]
>
> Like I said, a person adjusts.[19]
>
> You have no choice, and we continued like that, even did not think [for] a moment that we were going to leave from here, a moment we did not think we would live to see.[20]
>
> I did not have a choice and I lied. There was nothing wise about it.[21]
>
> We knew we had no choice. It's either commit suicide or go with them or do what you have to do.[22]

Again, Reder is authoritative but not alone in his recollection of the emotions that had to be denied. "How did it feel to work in this atmosphere?" Reder was asked.

> When the barracks were locked for the night and the lights were out one could hear a whisper of prayers for the dead, the *Kaddish* [the Jewish prayer for the dead], and then there was silence. We did not complain—we were completely resigned. We moved like automated figures just one large mass of them. We just mechanically worked through our horrible existence. Only when I heard children calling, "Mommy, haven't I been good? It's dark." My heart would break. Later we stopped having feelings.[23]

Words recur, almost in a pattern. Note the descriptors "robot," "automaton," and "mechanized living." Feelings were shut down or anesthetized. When *Sonderkommando* were asked, "How did you feel?" they responded:

> No more feelings. For one thing I said to someone I don't remember that I was no longer a human being. I couldn't cry. So this tells me that everything is dead inside. I am not a human being. Like some kind of robot.[24]
>
> I was very afraid, worried, stressed. You didn't have enough time to think about it and you just went in like robots.[25]
>
> No then I was not a human. I told you I was not a human. I could not cry. I could not think. Like a robot.[26]
>
> Human beings entered in a certain routine and you already work like a robot.[27]

In his enduring treatment in *The Nazi Doctors,* Robert Jay Lifton has spoken of the psychological mechanism of doubling, of creating an Auschwitz-self and a non-Auschwitz-self. This strategy was not limited to the killers; it may also have been practiced by the victims.

Because they dealt with death, it was inevitable that religious questions were asked. Death pushes toward the absolute—either toward God or away from God. The *Sonderkommando* gathered for prayers on Yom Kippur (the

Day of Atonement) 1944, which was the year 5704 in the Jewish calendar. They had scavenged everything that was needed, including prayer books and Torahs. They were left alone to pray on the evening of Kol Nidre. They also observed the Passover seder, celebrating the miraculous exodus of the ancient Israelites from Egypt. Matzo, the unleavened bread, were baked. In the entire history of exile, one cannot imagine a place of exile so complete.

Sam Itzkowitz was blunt as to the impact of his work on his faith. When asked, "Did you feel the presence of all those dead souls?" he replied immediately. "Do you believe that there were souls? I didn't see any.... Once you close your eyes you are dead. All that malarkey that you're going to come back when the Messiah comes, please don't hold your breath on that." He became insistent, almost defiant:

> I lost my faith right there because when I saw—you know, when I saw people die, it bothered me, but that wasn't too bad. When I saw innocent children, babies being thrown in the fire just like kindling wood, then I kept on hollering, "Why did you have those children born if you wanted to dispose of them in this kind of way? What have those innocent souls done to you? Why do they have to suffer an agonizing death?" This is what broke me away from it. I didn't see any explanation. I didn't see any miracles. I didn't see anything.[28]

He asks the difficult questions. "What's the use? Where is justice? Where is God? I just didn't have [faith]."

Others maintained their faith, as Itzkowitz observed:

> One day I was in the crematorium, and I see a middle-aged man, very lean, very skinny, going up to the—to the door where they were pulling out the bodies, and the mature bodies, the big bodies couldn't be picked up, they were so heavy. The *Sonderkommando* went up and put a buckle on the arm or the leg, whichever, and pulled them toward—to the ovens. But the small children were laying there and he walked through the dead bodies, through the corpses, and he picked out the small children, and every one he picked up was just like a limp—and he'd kiss every one of the children and recited the *Kaddish*. I could see his lips moving, and he walked it to the ovens and laid it on the top of another prisoner that was shoved in, in the fire.

"Did you look into the oven?" Itzkowitz was asked.

> Have you ever seen what a body looks like when the fire hits it? This is the most blood-curdling feeling. The arms and the legs and the head rise when the flame hits the dead body. The muscles relax and the arms and the legs and the head, you believe that minute the corpses are coming back to life, and all of a sudden the skin starts to peel just like the bark on a birch tree peeling off, and the stench is horrendous.[29]

His description of the dead is echoed by a very different source, one who witnessed the death at Belzec. Kurt Gerstein (1905–1945) was at once a perpetrator and an invaluable witness giving vital information to the West about the Nazi killing centers while there was still time to save the victims.

As head of the Technical Disinfections Department of the *Waffen*–SS, he worked directly with Zyklon B. He justified his continued participation in the killing by the secret information he passed on to the West. If anyone lived in the gray zone, it was Gerstein, whose career has been powerfully depicted in Saul Friedlander's *Kurt Gerstein: The Ambiguity of Good*.

In August 1942 he visited the *Aktion Reinhard* camps of Treblinka, Sobibor, and Belzec. Thereafter, he made contact with neutral diplomats from Sweden and the Vatican, members of the Dutch underground, and a bishop of the anti-Nazi German Confessing Church without much success. He died in prison in 1945 apparently by suicide; in actuality fellow SS officers may have murdered him. His testimony is now an invaluable insight into Belzec, but he was ineffective in halting the killing. Of his visit to Belzec, Gerstein reported:

> Some Jewish workers on the far side opened the wooden doors. . . . Inside, the people were still standing erect, like pillars of basalt, since there had not been an inch of space for them to fall in or even lean. Families could still be seen holding hands, even in death. It was a tough job to separate them as the chambers were emptied to make way for the next batch. The bodies were tossed out, blue, wet with sweat and urine, the legs soiled with feces and menstrual blood. A couple of dozen workers checked the mouths of the dead, which they tore open with iron hooks. "Gold to the left, other objects to the right!"[30]

Unlike ordinary prisoners in Auschwitz, the *Sonderkommando* did not suffer from hunger. Their food was ordinary concentration camp provisions but it was supplemented by the food that they could scavenge from newly arrived transports. Arriving prisoners brought with them food on the trains, food that reflected what was eaten in their native lands. Thus, Polish *Sonderkommando* ate olives and dates when the Greek Jews arrived in 1943. Some Jews arriving on the eve of Passover even brought matzo. Transports of Polish Jews arrived without provisions, we were told. The explanation may be simple. Ghettoized Polish Jews were already starving before deportation. *Sonderkommando* slept on mattresses in heated bunks built on top of the ovens. They wore civilian clothes. Some carried knives, as they were not searched. Although they had roll calls and had to follow a rigorous routine, the Germans seem to have left them mostly alone. Some participated in the resistance. A crematorium was set on fire in October 1944, just before gassing at Auschwitz-Birkenau was halted.

How did people behave in the moments before their death? Joseph Sackar, a Greek Jew who arrived in Auschwitz on the eve of Passover 1944, reports, "Children behaved like children looking for their parents' hand. Parents embraced their children. Children didn't know anything."[31]

What did people say inside the gas chambers? Shlomo Dragon, one of two brothers who worked as *Sonderkommando,* said, "People called one another by name. Mothers called their children, children, their mothers and fathers. Sometimes we could hear 'Sh'ma Yisrael: Hear, oh Israel, the Lord is our God, the Lord is One,' the traditional line recited by Jews at death."[32]

Rudolph Reder reported, "I heard the noise of sliding doors, moaning and screaming, desperate calls in Polish, Yiddish—blood curdling screams. All that lasted fifteen minutes. Screams of children, women, and finally one common, continuous, horrible scream. All that lasted fifteen minutes. The machine ran for twenty minutes and after twenty minutes there was silence."[33]

Death took on a routine character, the monotony of a daily assignment—but not always. When death was individualized it was recalled vividly. Sam Itzkowitz recalled such death: Tobias Segal was working the *Sonderkommando*. His job was to carry out the clothes from the victims once they got undressed. Bess Platka was there in the undressing room, getting undressed. Tobias walked up to her and started taking the clothes. She says to him, "Tobias, what's going on here? I'm going to come out and I'm going to want my clothes." He says, "You won't need it. In the next five minutes you will be dead."

> ... Well, she got hysterical. She went berserk. As she took her panties off, she threw it in the SS man's face and she called him, "You murderer." He tried to get to her to shut it up and pulled out his gun and tried to pistol-whip her. While he was pistol-whipping her, she said, "You are not going to kill my child. I gave it life and I'll take its life," and she choked the baby to death and threw the baby in his face....
>
> She reached, and she had a big—the European beer bottles were very thick, heavy glass, and she had one of those bottles. She didn't have any beer. It was a bottle with water.... She grabbed that bottle and hit him over the head with the bottle and knocked the bastard out. As he fell to the ground, she grabbed his gun and emptied the whole chamber into him ... blood flying all over the place. And the guards outside came in and shot everyone who didn't want to go in the gas chamber.[34]

When they saw her body and the SS officer Schillinger's together, one *Sonderkommando* commented, "We had genuine joy at *his* death."[35]

In the undressing room people asked where to go after the showers. What were the Germans' plans for them? "Ordinary questions, always the same questions," is the way one witness described it. Another got annoyed when asked by an interviewer, "What did you say?" He answered sharply, "What could we say?"[36] Some of the victims understood what was about to happen. Others went to death not knowing, still not comprehending the destructive process that was unfolding. One feels the abject powerlessness of the *Sonderkommando* in these situations. They knew more directly, more clearly than anyone how vast and murderous were the killers—and there was nothing they could do. Only later at Treblinka, Sobibor, Belzec (according to only one report), and Birkenau did armed resistance break out.

Notes

1. Testimony of Anna Heilman who worked in the Union workshop that helped supply gun powder for the resistance at Birkenau, gathered for the film *Evidence*, book 2, tape 56, 24.

2. Interview with Sam Itzkowiz, *Evidence*, book 2, tape 45.
3. Interview with David Nencel, *Evidence*, book 1, tape 26.
4. Ibid., tape 28.
5. Interview with Ya'akov Zilberberg, *Evidence*, book 1, tape 21, 3.
6. Ibid., 3–4.
7. Ibid., tape 21, 5.
8. Interview with Shaul Hazan, *Evidence*, book 1, tape 9, 14.
9. Itzkowitz, book 2, tape 22.
10. Ibid., tape 24.
11. Ibid., tape 25.
12. Interview with Eliezer Eisenschmidt, *Evidence*, book 1, tape 2, 10.
13. Joseph Sachar, *Evidence*, book 1, tape 10, 9.
14. Itzkowitz, tape 25.
15. *Belzec: The Testimony of the Only Documented Escapee, Rudolph Reder*, translated from the Polish and edited, with additional notes and glossary, by Anna M. Levin-Ware and Robert G. Ware. Unpublished manuscript, 1991. Cited hereafter as Reder.
16. Primo Levi, *Survival in Auschwitz*, trans. Stuart Woolf (New York: Summit Books, 1986), 19.
17. Reder, 20.
18. Eisenschmidt, book 1, tape 3, 3.
19. Zilberberg, book 1, tape 3, 9.
20. Ibid., tape 4, 3.
21. Sachar, book 1, tape 26, 1.
22. Interview with Morris Kesselman, *Evidence*, book 2, tape 35.
23. Reder, 37.
24. Gideon Greif, *We Wept Without Tears: Testimonies of the Jewish Sonderkommando from Auschwitz* (Hebrew) (Jerusalem: Yad Vashem, 1999), 123.
25. Ibid., 306.
26. Ibid., 339.
27. Ibid., 358.
28. Itzkowitz, tape 81.
29. Ibid., tape 82.
30. Saul Friedlander, *Kurt Gerstein: The Ambiguity of Good* (New York: Alfred A. Knopf, 1969), 110.
31. Greif, *We Wept Without Tears*, 121.
32. Ibid., 164.
33. Reder, 21.
34. Itzkowitz, tape 82.
35. Greif, *We Wept Without Tears*, 189.
36. Ibid.

– *Chapter 5* –

A COMMENTARY ON "GRAY ZONES" IN RAUL HILBERG'S WORK

Gerhard L. Weinberg

In the April 1962 issue of the *American Historical Review*, I began my review of the first edition of Raul Hilberg's book, *The Destruction of the European Jews*, with the comment: "This is an impressive and depressing work."[1] That view has in no way changed in the intervening forty-two years and two further editions. The aim of this commentary is to raise some issues that Hilberg either could not or did not engage fully.

First, it remains essential in my judgment to recall that Hitler's belief in the stab-in-the-back legend was sincere and was widely shared by Germany's military and political leaders in the 1930s and 1940s and that it influenced German policies in many ways. The reluctance to impose massive and early hardships on the German population during the first years of war; the willingness to fight the United States once more since that country's military role in enabling the Western Allies to win in the West in 1918 was considered a legend; the deferral of what became the first systematic killing program, the killing of handicapped Germans, until 1939; and the killing program's decentralization in 1941 are only a few examples. Policy toward Jews was no exception.

Since Hitler expected to wage a series of wars, one obvious way to ensure victory this time and to avoid any repetition of what he believed had caused defeat in 1918 was to drive as many Jews out of the country as possible *before* Germany started its first war. There was certainly persecution and there were individual killings; but for fear of domestic repercussions, there could be no systematic program of killing either the handicapped or the Jews during the prewar period. While the Nazis sterilized the handi-

Notes for this section begin on page 80.

capped in great numbers during the 1930s, they did not begin to kill them until 1939. It is within this broader context that one must evaluate Hitler's support of the arrangement by which Jews who emigrated to Palestine had less of their property taken from them than others, a scheme to which many in the Nazi Party objected at the time.[2] From Hitler's point of view it would be less likely to arouse the German public's opposition to future wars on the home front if these Jews were killed in Palestine rather than in Germany, a subject to which I will return in a moment.

Throughout World War II the prewar flight and expulsion of about half of Germany's Jewish population, followed in and after 1941 by the systematic murder of all Jews whom German arms could reach, was seen by the political and military leaders of Germany as a guarantee that defeat was impossible and victory certain this time. In his speech to a large assemblage of generals and other officers on 26 May 1944 Hitler reviewed precisely this point to the enthusiastic cheers of his audience.[3] The editor's notes to the text of the published speech list numerous other references by Hitler, Heinrich Himmler, and others to the killing of the Jews as an assurance that there could be no repetition of what the Nazi leadership and many other Germans imagined had happened in 1918. Hitler and his fellow German leaders acted on what they believed to be the "lesson" of 1918, whether or not their interpretation of Germany's loss of World War I had any basis in reality.

A second field in need of further exploration is a problem inherent in the title of Hilberg's book. Were Hitler and his associates interested only in the destruction of Europe's Jews? This is surely an unlikely view and one on which the title is potentially misleading. When in April 1920 Hitler explained to an audience in Munich that Jews had to be extirpated, the term he used was *"auszurotten"* ("exterminated") completely *"mit Stumpf und Stiel"* ("with root and branch").[4] Whatever Hitler may have known in detail about the realities of the history of Jews in Europe, he was certainly aware of the fact that in the preceding centuries various German and other European cities and states had expelled Jews; but that in subsequent centuries some Jews had been allowed to return to the very places from which they had been driven. Is it entirely fanciful to suggest that a man whom we know to have been concerned about the optical appearance of the ruins of the thousand-year Reich in subsequent centuries might have given some thought to a return of Jews to Europe at some time in the future in a manner somewhat similar to what had occurred in the past?

It is true that when Hitler explained Germany's policy toward the Jews to the visiting war minister of the puppet state of Croatia on the evening of 21/22 July 1941, he spoke of emptying Europe of Jews, one country at a time, and predicted that the Hungarians would be the last to surrender their Jews.[5] But whatever Hitler may really have anticipated at the time that the "Final Solution" was just getting under way, we do know that by November 1941 at the latest he was clear in his own mind on the subject and was prepared to explain his views for the record. In his conversation with the

Grand Mufti of Jerusalem Hitler described the then ongoing emptying of all of Europe of Jews. Hitler then explained his expectation that a similar process would affect all Jews living in what he called non-European countries, that is, the rest of the world. More specifically, Hitler promised that the Germans would arrange the destruction—"*Vernichtung*" is the word he used—of all Jews in Palestine and other parts of the Middle East.[6] Since he made it a habit to check the official accounts of his conversations for accuracy, there is no reason to question that this was his expectation at the time. The same Jews that he had earlier allowed and even encouraged to move to Palestine would be killed there, together with all other Jews in the British mandate, when the German armies reached the area by moving through the Caucasus mountains from the north or the Libyan desert from the south.

We know today that the Red Army in 1941 and again in 1942 stopped the German armies in the north and that the British Army in 1941 and once more in 1942 stopped them in the south. There was, however, no certainty beforehand that Hitler's expectation that the approximately one million Jews of the Middle East would be killed was not to be realized. The survival of the Jewish communities in the Middle East was very much in doubt, especially in the summer of 1942 as the Germans pushed into the passes through the Caucasus and advanced deep into Egypt. According to German plans, the region was to become a part of Italy's colonial domain, but its Jewish inhabitants were to be killed first. It did not work out that way, but the outcome of the fighting could not be predicted with any degree of certainty.

A somewhat similar development took place later in 1942 after the landing of American and British forces in French northwestern Africa in early November. The Germans and Italians immediately began to build up a substantial army in Tunisia with the instruction and expectation of driving out the Allies and taking over the whole area, thereby exposing the more than half a million Jews there to the German killing program.[7] The Soviet offensive at Stalingrad two weeks after the northwest Africa landings put a halt to the Axis buildup of forces in Tunisia. That buildup had been sufficient to halt the Western Allies before they could quickly seize their main objectives, Tunis and Bizerta, but then further Axis reinforcements could not be sent to North Africa. The Germans were obliged to rush forces to the southern portion of the Eastern Front to relieve the situation there, and these proved as inadequate for their mission as the ones in Tunisia were insufficient for theirs. Just as the landings of the Western Allies in northwestern Africa facilitated the Red Army's great victory at Stalingrad, so the Soviet offensive at Stalingrad facilitated the victory of the Americans and British forces in Tunisia. The large Jewish population of northwest Africa, like that of the Middle East, was saved by the armies of the Allies in desperate fighting.

Although hardly ever commented upon in this connection, a somewhat similar situation affected the survival of a substantial portion of the Jewish population of France. In August 1944 trains with Jews crammed into them were leaving Paris for the killing centers. It was the physical advance of the Allied armies after the breakout from the beachhead in Normandy that put a stop to this procedure before large numbers of additional Jews could be sent to their deaths by the Germans. What had made this halt in deportations possible? In late 1943 the British and American air offensive against Germany was increasingly curtailed by the heavy losses suffered by the fleets of Allied bombers. It looked as though the whole project might have to be called off as the Germans reclaimed control of the air over Central Europe. It was the addition of fighters equipped to escort the bombers that changed the dynamic of the air war once again. In February and March 1944 large numbers of bombers were sent to targets that the Germans absolutely had to send up their fighters to defend, and it was in the struggles between the escorting fighters and the German air force that the Allies in those months attained the control of the skies over Western and Central Europe, providing one of the two essential prerequisites for any attempt at an invasion across the English Channel.

The other prerequisite was the defeat of the German submarines so that troops and supplies could be gathered and employed for an invasion of northwestern Europe. That victory had been attained in May 1943 so that by the end the year, Allied construction of shipping exceeded losses, while the German efforts again to turn the tide in the Battle of the Atlantic were effectively blocked. Even so, the invasion had to be postponed one month to make sure that there would be enough shipping for the assault wave. Each month that the launching of the exceedingly risky invasion attempt could be moved up or had to be postponed meant, in effect, the rescue or the loss of thousands of Jewish lives in France. This relationship rarely, if ever, appears in any of the literature. Just as the discussion of the Holocaust is far too divorced from its wartime context, so the debates over the strategic bombing offensive and the Battle of the Atlantic rarely allude to the fact that the Germans did not fight to see the Eiffel Tower, to move the pyramids to Berlin, or to float a "Strength-through-Joy" cruise ship on the Caspian Sea, but rather to carry out a demographic revolution on the globe, a revolution of which the murder of all Jews was a central part.

The details of military operations lead to a point that has to be central to future discussion of the Holocaust. About 95 percent of the Jews actually murdered came within reach of the Germans because of the military course of the war. It is obvious but generally ignored that, had the Germans advanced further, the percentage would have been even greater, but had they been held sooner, the percentage would have been smaller. We know today what no one knew or could have known beforehand. The element of contingency is far greater than usually imagined. This is especially obvious if one looks at an aspect of the protocol of the Wannsee Conference on the implementation of the "Final Solution" that neither Hilberg nor, as far as I know, any other scholar has explored.

Included in the listing of those to be killed are the Jews of England, estimated at thirty-three thousand, along with those of Ireland, estimated at four thousand.[8] No one present thought this worthy of discussion: victory was assumed. A German occupation of the British Isles would make it possible to kill all Jews there, and no participant in the conference thought that any other possibility needed to be considered. We know today that it did not work out that way, but another group of Jews quite definitely *not* included in the list was reached by the German military during the war, and they were murdered. The listing for Italy includes the Jews there, and there is a separate entry for Jews in Albania, then under Italian control. It was tacitly assumed that these Jews would be included in the killing program that was discussed at the conference. The Jews then living on the island of Rhodes and the other Dodecanese Islands in the Aegean Sea, however, are *not* on the list, but after the Germans occupied those islands following the surrender of Italy, these Jews were deported to Auschwitz and killed there.

The omission of the Jews living in these portions of Italy's empire, as contrasted with those living in Albania, should, in my judgment, be seen in conjunction with the way in which the Jews of Turkey are treated in the same list. The text reads, *"Türkei (europ. Teil),"* or "Turkey, European portion, with an estimated number of 55,500." Are we to deduce from this that the Jews on the other side of the Straits would be permanently safe to live out their lives? Is it not much more likely that what we have in this document and its list is in fact a first, immediate installment of a worldwide killing program, to be followed, when possible, by further ones? In January 1942, at the time of the Wannsee Conference, substantial German armies were very much closer to England and Ireland than to Rhodes. Who could predict that the nearer ones would be saved and those further away murdered in 1944? In this connection, what is one to make of the preposterously high number of Jews specified in the list as being in France (850,000)? Is the assumption that Jews in Algeria, an area that was then considered in the French governmental structure an integral part of metropolitan France, were assumed to be in Europe by some quirk of National Socialist geography? And the Jews of Morocco as well?

If the Holocaust is to be understood, it is important that scholars try to look beyond what the Germans did and how they went about doing it, even though these are certainly subjects of immense importance. It is in the elucidation of these two critical topics that the enormous strength of Hilberg's work is to be found. But in order to understand what those in charge wanted to do and what they thought they were doing, one also needs to pay attention to their direction and their goal in addition to the mechanics of the actual operations that they were able to carry out before the victory of the Allies put a stop to their efforts. In order to comprehend a revolution halted in its tracks, attention must be paid to where the tracks were heading. This may make it a little easier to understand both the inclusion of Jews outside Europe in the killing program on the one hand, and the occasional deferral of murdering Jews in such parts of Europe like Finland and prewar Bulgaria on the other. It must be remembered that those in charge in Berlin operated on the assumption that after Germany's victory in the war, such temporary accommodations to the exigencies of wartime diplomacy could quite easily be revoked.

This emphasis on contingency and on the specifics of military operations in the war brings up an issue on which Hilberg's work has, in my judgment, been very drastically misinterpreted and misused by some authors and commentators. The Jewish Councils, the *Judenräte*, are discussed in considerable detail in Hilberg's book, but, I would suggest, without sufficient attention to the other side of the fate of the Jews of Rhodes. Whatever questions about the Holocaust may be open, unknown, or in dispute, one thing that is not now in dispute but that no one knew at the time is when the war ended. One should, for example, consider an entirely possible alternative scenario of the fighting. In the winter of 1941/42 the German armies on the Eastern Front were very badly defeated, first at the southern end of the front at Rostov, then in the middle before Moscow, and soon after at the northern end at Tikhvin. The German Army Group Center came extremely close to being destroyed by the Red Army in early 1942—as actually did happen to it in the summer of 1944. What if Joseph Stalin's hopes of a decisive victory in early 1942 had been realized and, as a result, the ghettoes of Vilna, Kovno, Lodz, and perhaps even Warsaw, as well as many others, had been liberated in the spring or summer of 1942? Would not those who had been trying to keep the Jews in the ghettoes alive as long as possible subsequently have been hailed for their efforts? This is not by any means designed to deflect all criticism from the *Judenräte*. There are numerous issues in this aspect of Holocaust history that would benefit from further research. Rather, this point is made in order to remind those who discuss the *Judenräte* that it makes little sense to attack their leaders and members for not knowing what no one else on earth knew at the time: precisely how the tide of battle on the Eastern Front would shift and when and how the war would end. Our knowledge of the fact that the war continued until practically all Jews who had been herded into the ghettoes were killed—along with the members of the *Judenräte* themselves—ought not to distort the account of events and our assessment of individuals acting under horrendous pressures.

Next, it is important to call attention to an aspect of research that in many important ways supplements the work of Hilberg and, when continued, is likely to add further nuances to the picture offered in *The Destruction of the European Jews*. There have been a number of careful, thoughtful, and well-documented studies of the Holocaust on a local level, with the works of Dieter Pohl, Thomas Sandkühler, Susan Zuccotti, Christian Gerlach, and Radu Ioanid providing excellent examples.[9] The recent book of Wolf Gruner on the role of local German municipal administrations in the persecution of Jews may well open up another field deserving of further research.[10]

A somewhat different but very important way in which further research can supplement and in some cases perhaps revise portions of Hilberg's work is related to the opening of hitherto classified American records under the Nazi War Crimes Disclosure Act. Two aspects of the newly opened materials are especially important in this regard. They will become obvious with the publication by Yad Vashem of papers from the June 2003 conference in New York on the Holocaust and Intelligence, and by the appearance of the volume of papers by professional historians on the materials newly declassified under the Nazi War Crimes Disclosure Act that the National Archives Trust Fund was scheduled to publish in 2004. Nevertheless, a brief overview belongs within the context of this volume.

There are, in the first place, substantial records pertaining to intelligence sources and methods that were not reviewed for declassification earlier, which now have been reviewed under the new law and, in many cases, opened for research. Included in these records are extensive materials pertaining to the interest of Allied intelligence agencies in the rescue efforts. By definition, such efforts required contacts of Jewish representatives and organizations on the one hand with Nazi officials and the officials of Axis satellites or neutrals on the other. Allied intelligence agencies were necessarily interested and at times involved directly or indirectly in these matters. The whole story of those efforts, especially with regard to the attempts to rescue Jews from Hungary in 1944, will have to be reexamined on the basis of these records. Shlomo Aronson has made a start on this, and some of his findings will appear in the aforementioned book on the Holocaust and Intelligence conference. In addition, important relevant and newly declassified materials are included in his 2004 book, *Hitler, the Allies, and the Jews,* but further work will be necessary on the German side of the issue. In addition, the possibility that negotiations with the Germans, especially in Hungary, may have led to delays in deportations that were then affected by the course of the war and other developments will need to be factored into future analyses of events.

Another example of intelligence records newly made available for research are voluminous materials pertaining to the utilization of, or refusal to utilize, German and other individuals who may have been war criminals by American intelligence agencies at the end of the war and in the following years. There will be extensive reviews of this issue in the volume on the European aspects of the Nazi War Crimes Disclosure Law. Much of this deals with events of the postwar years, but there is certainly important information on the fates of many individuals who had played roles in the Holocaust.

A second category of records not reviewed for possible declassification previously but now becoming accessible is what is officially called Foreign Government Information. These are materials provided to the United States by other governments and that were secret at the time but have now been opened with the consent of the government that originally provided them. For the period of World War II and the immediately following years, these documents are primarily from the United Kingdom. What has this to do with the subject of the Holocaust? Three examples of the types of documents released will serve to illustrate the connection. In the first place, there are the reports of the Chilean consul in Prague who was evidently very close to high-level SS officers. His reports home, surreptitiously copied by the

British and subsequently furnished to the United States, provide new insight into what the then central figure in the Holocaust, Reinhard Heydrich, was planning in the winter of 1941/42, the time between his arrival in Prague and his assassination.

As a second example one should note the summaries of the interrogations of Otto Ohlendorf. It has long been known that this commander of *Einsatzgruppe* D was turned over to the United States by the British late in 1945, that he testified at the main trial at Nuremberg, and that he was subsequently tried and hanged by the Americans. What was not previously known is that while in British custody in the summer of 1945, Ohlendorf was extensively interrogated, and the summaries of the interrogation reports were provided to the American authorities. In these there is information on the pre–June 1941 orientation provided to the *Einsatzgruppen* commanders, a subject that has been much discussed in the literature. Hilary Earl will cover this topic in the forthcoming conference book on the Holocaust and intelligence. It may, however, be safe to predict that information of this type will cause some rewriting of aspects of the Holocaust, just as the 1996 declassification of Order Police reports on mass killings of Jews in the early weeks of the invasion of the Soviet Union has already required.[11]

A third example would be that many of the documents recently opened are again, like the Order Police reports, copies in German or in English translation of British intercepts of German radio communications pertaining to the Holocaust that were provided to agencies of the United States, primarily the Office of Strategic Services (OSS). In important instances these intercepts are the only surviving records because the relevant records of neither the German sending nor receiving agency have survived. For example, if one wants to see details of the efforts of German agencies to collect and deport to their deaths Jews from Italy after that country surrendered to the Allies and most of it was occupied by the Germans, this is where much of the paper trail is to be found.[12]

The agreement of the British government to the opening of copies of intercepts, interrogation summaries, and many other documents that they provided to the Americans during or after World War II obviously raises an additional major question for scholars. What about those records of which the British did not give copies to the Americans? Clearly the government of the United States could ask only for agreement to the declassification of the ones of which it has copies in its own archives. That process leaves open the possibility, in my opinion the likelihood, that there will be further substantial releases from British archives of intelligence records that had not been shared with the United States. One can only express the hope that these will be opened before the end of *this* century. And again, in the case of decoded intercepts of German messages, these will likely turn out to be the only surviving texts. In spite of the massive amount of documentation currently available for research on the Holocaust, there is much more to come.

The release of documents from British archives naturally raises the question: what about the archives of the former Soviet Union? There has been some progress in this regard, but very little in the field of intelligence. This is of significance for research on the Holocaust because, for most of the years in which the Holocaust took place, Soviet listening stations were in a far better geographical position to intercept German radio communications than those of the British. This suggests that the collections of intercepts could be more complete, and that the individual intercepted texts would most likely have fewer gaps and garbles. No firm predictions can be made in this hazy field. It is, however, surely reasonable to suggest that we may learn a great deal if and when those in charge of the records conclude that no security interests whatsoever are being protected by keeping them closed until the paper disintegrates physically.

In this connection, one should also note the massive quantities of captured German records in the archives of the Russian Federation, some of which have been utilized by scholars, for example the recent book by Avraham Barkai on the main organization of German Jews.[13] As for relevant records formerly in the German Democratic Republic and now accessible to scholars, these will be described in the contribution by Alexandra Wenck in the conference volume on the Holocaust and intelligence mentioned earlier.

The prior references to the German killing of the Jews of Rhodes as well as their efforts to collect and deport to killing centers the Jews of Italy brings up a further aspect of the contingencies of war that needs to be included in studies of the Holocaust. Just as the Allied armies prevented the Germans from reaching and killing the Jews of the Middle East and northwestern Africa and interrupted the deportation of French Jews to their deaths, so, by one of the great ironies of the war, the success of those same armies in removing Italy from the war opened Rhodes and Italy to the Germans. Furthermore, the surrender of Italy in September 1943 made it possible for the Germans to enter other refuges from the Nazis' Jewish killing program. The Italian zones of occupation in France, Yugoslavia, and Greece had been generally safe for both Jews living there as well as Jews who had fled to them precisely because of their knowledge of Italian policy.[14] It was the defeat of Italy that made it possible for German forces to enter these areas and to extend, or at least try to extend, their single-minded devotion to murdering Jews to places where many had found refuge in the preceding years.

There is one further area in which the great work that Hilberg has done for the history of the Holocaust and our understanding of it could easily lead readers astray. One of the major strengths of the book is that it dissolves the anonymity of the actors on the German side. Whatever the complicated jurisdictions and quarrels about this subject, and whatever the peculiar organizations of the bureaucracy that he unravels and explains in great detail, the perpetrators are not faceless cogs in some automatically moving mechanism, which is a preposterous misreading of reality that occasionally appears in the literature. There were real actors at various levels with plenty of opportunity to exercise their imagination, to push for acceleration or delay, and to demonstrate their initiative. There is a striking example. The officials in the German Ministry of Finance, who proposed in April 1938 that the exemption from the dog tax allowed to blinded war veterans be taken away from Jews blinded while serving in the German army in World War I, have their names recorded for posterity in Hilberg's book.[15] On the other hand, the very nature of the focus on the perpetrators entails two risks.

First, there is the danger that the account would imply that individuals working in the program for the systematic killing of Jews had it all worked out beforehand. There was certainly intention and planning, but in this regard also the factors of contingency and of experimentation should not be omitted. Those in charge, as well as many of the participants, were feeling their way forward into what was essentially uncharted terrain. Like many other governments, the governments of Germany as well as of its states had carried out capital punishment, and there had been occasions when a substantial number of persons considered internal enemies had been killed. But here was a very different project involving the collection and killing of thousands, even hundreds of thousands. The Germans had experimented in many ways in the program for killing the handicapped, as Henry Friedlander has shown.[16] How would they define those to be killed? How would they collect those to be killed from wherever they were located? How would they kill on a vast scale? How would they dispose of colossal numbers of corpses? How would they recruit people who will kill others all day long, every day, for months, even years, on end? These and many other questions confronted the perpetrators. A retrospective account of the answers they found can too easily lead to the erroneous conclusion that they had it all worked out beforehand, when in fact they knew themselves to be pioneers in an especially horrendous but novel enterprise.

The other risk is that of anonymizing the victims of the killing program. While the victims are not the focus of Hilberg's work, the emphasis on individuals on the murderous side of the action, along with organizational and statistical information, could make the reader lose sight of the fact that each Jew who was murdered was an individual with hopes and talents, family and feelings. At the University of North Carolina at Chapel Hill, this problem is engaged at Holocaust remembrance time by the public reading aloud of names of persons murdered in a continuous sequence for hours on end. Whether or not this is the best way to deal with a very difficult problem, it is at least one way to reassert a degree of individuality for the victims. These persons were not just numbers, either as physically marked on their bodies or as analyzed in statistics, whether by Hilberg himself[17] or in the careful work edited by Wolfgang Benz.[18] It was always specific human beings who were killed. Whatever his or her age or gender, geographical location, or social status, each had a life to lead, a life that was cut short by the deliberate actions of others. And how much could these men, women, and children have contributed to the wider world? "Gray zones" indeed.

Notes

1. Gerhard L. Weinberg, "Review of Raul Hilberg's *The Destruction of the European Jews,*" *American Historical Review* 67 (April 1962), 694.
2. Gerhard L. Weinberg, *The Foreign Policy of Hitler's Germany: Starting World War II, 1937–1939* (Chicago: University of Chicago Press, 1980), 247. The account in Edwin Black, *The Transfer Agreement: The Untold Story of the Secret Agreement between the Third Reich and Jewish Palestine* (New York: Macmillan, 1984), has some supplementary details but is flawed by the influence of hindsight, the dominance of the author's messages, and a title that reveals the author's ignorance of the published literature.
3. Hans-Heinrich Wilhelm, ed., "Hitlers Ansprache vor Generalen und Offizieren am 26. Mai 1944," *Militärgeschichtliche Mitteilungen* 20, No. 2/76, 123–70, esp. 134–35, 1557.
4. Eberhard Jäckel, ed., *Hitler: Sämtliche Aufzeichnungen 1905–1924* (Stuttgart: Deutsche Verlags-Anstalt, 1980), 120.
5. *Akten zur deutschen auswärtigen Politik 1918–1945,* Series D, Vol. 13/2 (Göttingen: Vandenhoeck & Ruprecht, 1970), 838.
6. Ibid., No. 515.
7. Gerhard L. Weinberg, *A World at Arms: A Global History of World War II* (Cambridge: Cambridge University Press, 1994), 434–35.
8. *Akten zur deutschen auswärtigen Politik 1918–1945,* Series E, Vol. I (Göttingen: Vandenhoeck & Ruprecht, 1969), No. 150, 270.
9. Dieter Pohl, *Von der 'Judenpolitik' zum Judenmord: Der Distrikt Lublin des Generalgouvernements 1939–1944* (Frankfurt am Main: Peter Lang, 1993); Christian Gerlach, *Kalkulierte Morde: Die deutsche Wirtschafts- und Vernichtungspolitik in Weissrussland 1941 bis 1944* (Hamburg: Hamburger Edition, 1999); Thomas Sandkühler, *"Endlösung" in Galizien: Der Judenmord in Ostpolen und die Rettungsinitiative von Berthold Beitz, 1941–1944* (Bonn: Dietz, 1996); Radu Ioanid, *The Holocaust in Romania: The Destruction of Jews and Gypsies Under the Antonescu Regime, 1940–1944* (Chicago: Ivan R. Dee, 2000); Susan Zuccotti, *Under His Very Window: The Vatican and the Holocaust in Italy* (New Haven, CT: Yale University Press, 2000).
10. Wolf Gruner, *Öffentliche Wohlfahrt und Judenverfolgung: Wechselwirkung lokaler und zentraler Politik im NS-Staat (1933–1942)* (Munich: Oldenbourg, 2003).
11. An excellent example is Richard Breitman, *Official Secrets: What the Nazis Planned, What the British and Americans Knew* (New York: Hill and Wang, 1998), which utilizes the police intercepts that had been released.
12. A chapter by Richard Breitman in the volume to be published by the National Archives Trust Fund deals with this issue. A work that utilizes some of the newly declassified documents is Robert Katz, *The Battle for Rome: The Germans, the Allies, the Partisans, and the Pope, September 1943–June 1944* (New York: Simon & Schuster, 2003).
13. Avraham Barkai, *"Wehr Dich!": Der Centralverein deutscher Staatsbürger jüdischen Glaubens 1893–1938* (Munich: Beck, 2002).
14. On the general subject, see Jonathan Steinberg, *All or Nothing: The Axis and the Holocaust, 1941–1943* (London: Routledge, 1990).
15. The reference with the names will be found in the first edition on 100–101, n. 7; in the third edition on 148, n. 7.
16. Henry Friedlander, *The Origins of Nazi Genocide: From Euthanasia to the Final Solution* (Chapel Hill: University of North Carolina Press, 1995).
17. Third edition, Appendix B.
18. Wolfgang Benz, ed., *Dimension des Völkermords: Die Zahl der jüdischen Opfer des Nationalsozialismus* (Munich: Oldenbourg, 1991).

– Chapter 6 –

INCOMPLETENESS IN HOLOCAUST HISTORIOGRAPHY

Raul Hilberg

No empirical work of historiography is complete. The condition of incompleteness in such a literature is inherent in the sources themselves. An entire flow of events in all their complexity cannot be carried in the memory of witnesses. It cannot be stored with all of its attributes in remaining artifacts, and it is not replicated in all of its facets in contemporaneous records. All that has gone on in the world, which in theory is the whole of history, can be preserved only in fragments, and these leftovers constitute our material. The attempt to recapitulate anything at all is therefore an exercise that cannot be encompassing, no matter how large or small the subject of investigation may be. The effort will be a compromise between imagined perfection and something that can possibly be accomplished. Empirical historiography is by definition salvage. It cannot be more.

    Historians are people who, for whatever reason, decide to pursue a project about the past. They employ resources with which they have to work as best they can. They may be different in their knowledge and intellectual capabilities, but empirical research demands its due. The researcher will inevitably traverse three phases. The first is a certain bewilderment as original sources are examined. Who took this photograph? What does it show? Who wrote this letter? To whom? What do the abbreviations mean? What is the content about? After a while—sometimes a long time—connections are seen, meaning is drawn from something that had been incomprehensible, insights are added to insights, and a picture emerges. The work continues in a quest for fulfillment—the elimination of errors, the closing of gaps, the clarification of conclusions. Then the researcher encounters the principle of diminishing returns. More and more searching is required for fewer and fewer results. Resources are exhausted, time limits are reached, inspiration is used up. A compromise is made: the work stops.

These two realities, the one embedded in a preordained impossibility, the other in the limitations of human beings, are well known to practitioners in any field of historical research, and in other disciplines as well. They are reiterated here, because nowadays the words "Holocaust" and "compromise" are usually not found in the same sentence. One should remember, however, that in the early years after the war, the Holocaust had no place in academic life, that it was not even acknowledged as a topic, and that special claims later had to be made for its importance.

The claims are not baseless. It has dawned on the Jewish community that the sudden loss of nearly a third of its numbers in the space of a few years ranked with the expulsions from Spain of 1492 and with the destruction of the Temple in Jerusalem of 70 C.E., that it was a catastrophe that was bound to have consequences in the life of Jewry for many generations. To Germans it gradually became clear that in the midst of all the havoc that the Nazi regime had wrought, the annihilation of European Jewry was a special act that defied understanding and that raised questions about the nature of a society in which such events could occur. This concern surfaced also in countries where governments or volunteers had collaborated with the Germans. And finally, wherever there was a tendency inside or outside of postwar Europe to stand by and do little or nothing, the age-old query, "Am I my brother's keeper?" acquired new meaning as new threats arose to the stability of humanity in a shrinking world. Clearly, all these reflections had spawned or catalyzed a growing Holocaust literature, but they did not erase the compromises with which historians must wrestle. Holocaust research still entails the familiar problems of research, and writing about the Holocaust still requires the usual skills of writing.

The evolution of Holocaust historiography had its bare beginnings more than fifty years ago and it is far from finished. What has not been accomplished in the aggregate so far is attributable to two basic factors. One represents the researcher's inability to be more comprehensive, accurate, or descriptive. The other is a form of self-restraint in confrontation with sensitive subject matter. There is an element of insufficiency in the first case and of distancing in the second, but neither is always self-evident.

When an omission is involuntary, the reason may often be found in at least one of several circumstances. An entire segment of the facts may have been bypassed because the researcher could not recognize their relevance. A factual finding may be in disarray, because a piece of the puzzle was not at hand. A skeletal picture may have been drawn, because a close-up view was blocked. The following are a few illustrations of these difficulties.

Detecting particular aspects of the Holocaust, such as the background of the perpetrators or the connections of the Holocaust with other developments, has been remarkably slow. Even basics that may now be regarded as obvious had to be discovered, and each discovery was a change of a common impression. It is in the nature of things that these accomplishments do not tell us how many revelations are still in the offing. One can only assume that whatever none of us has observed so far, one of us may notice in the future. Here, then, are some advances of the past that serve as a reminder not to conclude at any time that nothing more has to be done.

At the very beginning references to the Holocaust were cloudy. The phenomenon had no name and could not be distinguished from hostility to Jews in prior centuries or from acts of contemporaneous aggression against other groups. The vocabulary generally used in discourse about the Jewish catastrophe was limited to such expressions as "anti-Semitism," "persecution," "atrocities," "Nazis," or "beasts." The words were limited and could not encompass what had happened. They were obsolete, because the German outburst could only be perceived in a fog. Its unprecedented character could not be grasped. Its actuality was unimaginable.

Consequently, many initial attempts at understanding were misguided shortcuts. The SS and the Gestapo were conspicuous, but in one of the Nuremberg trials it came as a surprise that the officers of the *Einsatzgruppen*, which were responsible for the deaths of hundreds of thousands by shooting, were not hooligans but lawyers or other professionals with academic degrees.[1] Again, the leadership of the ministerial bureaucracy in Vichy France, which drafted and signed many anti-Jewish decrees, and which at first was thought to be a throwback to the nineteenth century, turned out to contain a number of young technocrats who wanted to modernize the country.[2] The Romanian Iron Guard, viewed after the Bucharest revolt of 1941 only as a bunch of street battlers excelling in brutality, had, among others, poets and mystics in their midst.[3]

Nazi Germany as a whole was crudely described as a totalitarian regime, operating under the leadership principle and demanding blind obedience by automatons. Then Uwe Adam showed how the system was developing without many new laws and how it was spewing out "implementation decrees" that did not necessarily implement the old laws.[4] Christopher Browning, in turn, found an incident that literally tested the presumption that absolute, uncompromising orders were indispensable. In the Polish town of Jozefow the commander of a newly deployed German police battalion had actually given his men a choice between shooting Jews or stepping aside. A sufficient number were ready to carry out the action.[5]

In the web of decision-making by all sorts of agencies, the Holocaust was a distinct undertaking, but one that was not unseparated from other concurrent operations. The links had to be uncovered, one by one, and that is an ongoing effort. Götz Aly, who is an exceptionally astute practitioner of this art, revealed the strands between the Holocaust and resettlement policies and between the Holocaust and the search for funds to finance the war.[6] Susanne Willems, following on this path, showed how the concentration and deportations of the Jews in Berlin were planned in conjunction with the housing program for the German capital.[7] Walter Manoschek and Ulrich Herbert observed a confluence of goals in military reprisals and the shooting of Jewish men.[8]

In the realm of studies exploring the Jewish communities, Isaiah Trunk's dissection of their reactions was a major step forward. Trunk discovered something that no one had looked for: a Jewish political culture so deeply rooted that it emerged in the closed-off ghettos of Eastern Europe, notwithstanding their geographic isolation from one another and the lack of direct contacts between them. Trunk did not write his massive work as a history of individual ghettos. He cut across all of them to deal with the way in which they approached problems of housing, labor, health, and other challenges. In that manner he demonstrated that atomized Jewry had a common mode of reacting to restrictions and danger. Trunk did not proclaim his conclusions, but they leap from his chapters. More than thirty years after his book was published, nothing of this scope about the ghetto Jews has yet appeared in print.[9]

Discernment cannot be programmed. One must wait for a researcher who can detect the characteristics of a phenomenon, or explore its environment, or draw its Gestalt. But what if someone is already pursuing a project and something goes wrong? We almost never have all the sources that we might like at our disposal, and sometimes a single missing document may generate a problem. If the historian believes that the item cannot be found or that it no longer exists, what then? Months, years, or decades may be spent in conjectures about its content. Indications may be gathered from other, albeit inconclusive materials, and in a compulsive attempt to complete the picture, something may be said to take the place of the elusive fact. A date may be offered, or the identity of a person—anything that one might wish to know. In lieu of certainty, assumptions will be inserted and extrapolations may be built on them, thereby compounding the author's vulnerability.

The following two cases are examples of what may happen. Both pertain to numbers. This selection is deliberate, because the finding of an error in numerical manipulations is unambiguous. The first illustration deals with calculations of the Jewish death toll in Belzec, which was the destination of many transports of Jews from Polish cities and towns, and which did not receive non-Jewish deportees.

The Israeli historian Yitzhak Arad used a variety of estimates prepared in Poland and Israel to construct a table of deportations to the Belzec camp. The approximate figures pointed to an overall sum of somewhat more than 500,000, including some 280,000 from the Galician district alone. Arad also assumed that German Jews who had been deported first to the Lublin district and only then to Belzec were not counted in his sources. The Jews in small villages, he thought, had not been taken into account, either. Therefore, he believed that at least one hundred thousand people should be added to the list, bringing his total to six hundred thousand.[10] There was in fact no such dark area and his upward adjustments were in error. I myself did not make that particular mistake. I made a different one.

Shortly after I began my work in the late 1940s I examined two documents. One was the report about the results of the "Final Solution," which covered deportations in Poland to the end of 1942, by the SS statistician Richard Korherr.[11] The other was a "Final Solution" report by the SS and police leader in the Galician district of the so-called *Generalgouvernement* of conquered Poland, Fritz Katzmann, dated 30 June 1943, about operations in his territory.[12]

In the Korherr report I noted two figures:

"Dragged through" the camps of the *Generalgouvernement* by 31 December 1942:	1,274,166
Remaining in the Galician district on 31 December 1942:	161,514

In the Katzmann report I noted:

Deported or killed in Galicia by 27 June 1943:	434,329
Remaining in labor camps within Galicia on 27 June 1943:	21,156

My initial focus was on the number 1,274,166. I knew that three camps were definitely included in this total: Belzec, Sobibor, and Treblinka. I had also found out that gassing had ceased in Belzec on 8 December 1942, but I could not disaggregate the overall figure.[13]

Many years later, when I learned more about the flow of deportees to this camp complex, I surmised that the majority of the Belzec victims must have arrived from Galicia and that virtually all of the Galician deportees must have been sent to Belzec. By 1971 I computed a total of roughly 600,000 dead in the camp,[14] and by 1985 I scaled my estimate down to 550,000.[15] In pursuing the number, I had arranged the three other "Final Solution" figures reported by Korherr and Katzmann in the following manner:

Maximum number of Galician Jews killed in 1943:
161,514 (alive 31 December 1942) – 21,156 (alive 17 June 1943)
= 140,358

Maximum of Galician Jews killed in 1942 after the start of deportations:
434,329 (total killed) – 140,358 (number for 1943) = 293,971

Maximum number of Galician Jews killed in Belzec:
293,971 – the number shot in 1942 = ?

At this point, however, I did not follow the subtractions to their logical conclusion, even though I might have obtained a reasonable approximation. My problem was the 140,348 who vanished between 31 December 1942 and 27 June 1943. Some were undoubtedly in hiding and others had succumbed to typhus and other diseases, but at least 130,000 must have been killed. I could not confirm the sparse witness testimony of Galician deportations to other camps in any German document, and I could not substantiate shootings of such a volume from the fragmentary records at my disposal. Therefore, I set aside Korherr's year-end figure of 161,154. It was not the product of a census, after all, and the local reports from which it must have been constructed were not at hand. Perhaps these reports were rounded, or late, or both. Only after the appearance in 1997 of a highly detailed monograph by Dieter Pohl, who visited archives in Galicia after they had been opened in the 1990s and whose knowledge of their holdings was greater than mine, did I realize that many of the 1943 shootings had escaped my notice. More ghettos than I had suspected were still in existence early in 1943, and several of the larger ones were thinned out more than once.[16]

The actual Belzec toll was revealed in 2001 by Peter Witte and Stephen Tyas. It was 434,508, and the German report containing this number had been unearthed only shortly before among radio intercepts that the British government had kept secret for more than fifty years.[17] I had overshot the mark by more than one hundred thousand.[18] Needless to say, when the breakdown of a sum is incorrect, more than one other constituent number will be wrong. In my case, there were two more: those for Treblinka and Lublin (Majdanek). My suppositions regarding the number of people killed at these facilities were too low. As to Majdanek, I had hesitated to include it as a *Generalgouvernement* camp, because it was not under the same jurisdiction as Belzec, Sobibor, and Treblinka. The new document set matters straight also on this point. Majdanek's victims were to be included in part.

A more complicated anatomy of a faulty numerical compilation is exemplified by a table in a book by Yisrael Gutman about the ghetto of Warsaw.[19] Gutman states that the source of the table, which lists the number of Jews deported daily from the ghetto to Treblinka, is a 1951 issue of a bulletin published by the Jewish Historical Institute in Warsaw.[20] His heading for the table is "German Statistics of the Deportations." The data cover the dates from 22 July to 21 September 1942, and his total is 253,741. For 19 to 24 August a single entry is a round twenty thousand with the notation "estimate," for 26 August a round three thousand (again an "estimate"), and for 11 September a round five thousand, a third estimate. In addition, two intermissions are indicated as well.

What is unusual about this tabular enumeration is that it conflicts with another number that Gutman must have found in a report made by the SS and police leader of Warsaw, Jürgen Stroop, after the ghetto battle of 1943. There, Stroop states that 310,322 Jews had been deported in the summer of 1942.[21] Could the fact that the table used by Gutman was a detailed accounting, and the number by Stroop only a solitary sum, have been the reason for choosing the former and discarding the latter? His choice, whatever its basis, was fraught with multiple mishaps.

Gutman was evidently not aware that his figures were not German to begin with. They came from the Jewish Council in the ghetto. To the extent that his August numbers were precise, they coincided—except for incorrect copying of a few insignificant digits—with those of the council report for that month. Inasmuch, however, as he did not have that document, he was ignorant of a sentence in its text stating, "We have no statistic of those persons who volunteered to be resettled."[22] The "volunteers" were a large component of the total.

There is a second, partially countervailing complication. Whenever Gutman's table contains an approximation, it is a rounded multiple of the preceding exact figure. Thus, for 19 to 24 August the twenty thousand are roughly five times the 3,926 for 18 August, and for 26 August the three thousand are taken from the 3,002 for 25 August, but in the report of the council there are mere dashes beside the dates for which Gutman inserted his estimates. That forcible substitution is negated by entries in a ghetto diary by Abraham Lewin, which Gutman cited repeatedly in other contexts, and which includes explicit statements to the effect that no transports left on 19 and 20 August as well as on other specific dates.[23]

Errors, like breakthroughs, are the acts of individual authors. They may be spread when they are copied. It should be stressed, however, that missteps of this sort are not altogether unusual, either in Holocaust historiography or the writing of history generally. They do not invalidate an entire work, unless they are the foundation of everything their creator had to say. When they do arise because a specific item of information was missing, overlooked, or misconstrued, knowledge is not impaired for all time and progress is not foreclosed.

The situation is different when the historian wishes to step closer to the scene of the action, to be inside its space. Most of the sources are essentially dry, not reaching the senses. Generally, they do not have the quality of something that is visible, audible, or palpable. Official correspondence in particular tends to be telescopic, purposeful, and problem-oriented. In such writing, mention may be made in a clinical manner of the psychological burdens carried by shooters, or comments could be added without elaboration to the effect that Jews were literally collapsing in the course of forced labor, but there is seldom more. Witnesses, especially Jewish victims, struggle with language to express what they saw. Consequently, neither Germans nor Jews will convey much about the atmosphere of the time. In this respect, the inadequacy of the sources is a common limitation affecting all historians in all fields, but the problem is more acute in attempts to deal with an event like the Holocaust, which is far removed from ordinary experience.

Although survivors have greater motivations than their tormentors to provide details about the impact of the blows inflicted on the Jewish community, the results are nevertheless meager. A former inmate of the Croatian camp network at Jasenovac, where many Jews, alongside Serbs and others, were held and killed, wrote about his observations at length. His account, however, is filled only with repetitious statements that Jews were "flogged," "killed," "gunned down," "killed behind the kitchen," "clubbed to death," "shot," "bayoneted," "hit," "murdered right then and there," and so on.[24] In the extensive survivor testimony this kind of rendition is fairly typical.

Less ordinary is the commentary of Stanislaw Adler, a lawyer who served as a police officer in the Warsaw ghetto, that is, its Jewish police. In his memoir he relates that toward the end of spring of 1941, when thousands of Warsaw Jews labored in water regulation and other outdoor projects, the returning workers were escorted by Polish police to the "Dulag" (*Durchgangslager*, or transit camp), a spacious school building outside the ghetto boundaries at 109 Leszno Street. Many who were dying or ill with infections rested there, segregated from the others, on bare stone or cement floors. Adler heard their testimony uttered in "monotone." He does not attempt to repeat exactly what they said. We are shown only shadowy figures in tattered clothes. He wonders "when, during their tortures" these people had time to work. He is "unable to explain by what miracle" some of them survived after having been chained and dragged on the ground for several kilometers. In short we see the men in a mirror. The reflector is Adler, who tells us what he perceived and to what he reacted.[25]

In the testimony of a German policeman who participated in mass shootings, there are denials and hints that raise suspicions but leave little certainty. Yes, he stood *in* the ditch when the victims, lying down, were shot. No, he did *not* stand on bodies. Yes, he shot children but told the mothers to hold a child tightly during the shooting. Yes, he smoked during these actions, but there was no alcohol. And no, he did *not* eat at the site. Eating would have been impossible because of the odor. Then he described what kind of odor it was.[26]

Infrequently, a shimmering sentence in a report evokes presence. "Barley soup with chunks of beef was served," a captain of the Order Police, who had accompanied a transport of Jews from Düsseldorf to Riga with a small detachment, noted in his report. He did not forget to praise the German Red Cross, which fed his men when the train had halted, after three days, in Siaulai, Lithuania, during a wet and cold December night in 1941. The Jews, who had to manage with provisions they had brought with them, were allowed only water en route.[27]

Rare also is the description of food purchased in the Lodz ghetto in February 1944, after the Germans had decreed that during work hours no Jew would be allowed in the streets or an apartment. To obtain their weekly ration of two kilograms of bread, the workers, many of whom had not eaten during the previous day, hurled themselves after 5:00 P.M. at the distribution centers to avoid having to wait at the end of a line outside in the snow and in fear that a "shortfall" would leave them empty-handed. They banged at the windows, shouted, and pressed against each other tightly, eyeing the loaves. The passage about this scene, which was written in the official Jewish Lodz ghetto chronicle for posterity, has remained unpublished.[28]

Through lengthy searches it is possible to uncover other scattered images, but such descriptions cannot be manufactured by the historian. It is for this reason that novelists and film directors step in. To fill the gap they promise an imaginative reconstruction, but given the manifest difficulties it is often imaginary.

In sum, when we consider the inabilities of observers to recognize a pattern in a maze, or to steer around a missing link, or to penetrate the blackness surrounding the nucleus of an event, we surmise the existence of an elusiveness—a quality that is unreached and unachieved. Yet there are also questions that are consciously avoided. To this day, one topic that is noticeably underdeveloped touches on an issue of prime importance, and that is the story of how specific groups in the Jewish community, caught in the grip of destruction, reacted daily to restrictions and danger. What did coping look like? In their dilemma, what did lawyers do, or illiterates? How were family relations preserved or transformed? What was the significance of age? What role did money play? What might have been the personal budget of working Jews in the Berlin of 1941, or 1942 Saloniki, or the Theresienstadt ghetto of 1943? Information about such seemingly mundane matters in published essays and books is rather fragmentary or presented in outline form.[29]

One reason for this dearth is plainly the loss, in the course of ghetto clearing operations or the clearing of Jewish apartments, of the great bulk of Jewish records, including private diaries and letters, as well as correspondence and reports of Jewish councils. Another is the failure, especially during the initial postwar years, to question Jewish survivors in detail about conditions and occurrences that were antecedent to climactic moments. Ultimately, however, there is a persistent reluctance to approach the subject of interpersonal relations among the Jewish victims. The "No Trespassing" signs were placed at the boundaries of this topic by the researchers themselves. For some, the markers set up by the British army in Bergen-Belsen in April 1945, "Here Lie Buried 2,000 Bodies," "Here Lie Buried 2,500 Bodies," "Here Lie Buried 5,000 Bodies," were the final word. Nothing more could be said about these people, united and indistinguishable in death. Others, like Primo Levi, called upon everyone to heed the command not to make judgments. Who, after all, could step into the shoes of those victims? No one. For still others, the psychological limit had been reached. There were some things they did not *want* to know.

Still, when Primo Levi wrote about a "gray zone," he placed the problem on the agenda. Levi, the chemist and Auschwitz survivor, measured freedom of action and gradations of behavior. Moreover, he had to have symmetry between victims and perpetrators in his analytical commentary. Although he would not allow any merging of "prisoners" and "custodians," as he called them, he did not hesitate to attribute weaknesses to the former and to grant saving graces to the latter. He cites the case of two merchants, one who was the Jewish "Elder" of the Lodz ghetto, Chaim Rumkowski, the other the ghetto's German manager, Hans Biebow.[30] Both were ambitious and both had a vested interest in preserving the ghetto from deportations. Rumkowski sacrificed even children to maintain the ghetto as a manufacturing enterprise, and Biebow—with his staff of 198 employees—concerned himself with food rations, production, and ghetto exports until the last moment, that is, just before the transportation of the Lodz Jews to Auschwitz, when he told them in a duplicitous manner that they would be resettled for their safety from Allied bombs. Rumkowski perished in the camp and Biebow was executed after the war. Levi did not know the whole story of the strange symbiosis that paired the two men, but he understood that each played his role consistently. They may have been self-serving, but they pursued the same goal. In the end they failed, and that failure sealed also their personal fate.

Rumkowski has received considerable attention because he is commonly regarded as the most notorious ghetto leader. With few exceptions his counterparts in other places remain indistinct. They are described in the aggregate but seldom as individuals. Noteworthy is the fact that an extensive memoir by the last Slovak Jewish council chairman, Oscar Neumann, written in the spring of 1946 and published ten years later in the original German language, never appeared in English,[31] and that the diary of the French Jewish leader, Raymond-Raoul Lambert, published in France, is also unavailable in English translation.[32] We hardly have to remind ourselves that such firsthand accounts are not abundant.

The inhibition to study the invisible victims is even greater. Information about them is not completely unattainable, since it may be located, at least in the charts and tables of remaining Jewish council reports, as well as in other sources, but its implications have not been seriously addressed. Unanswered are principally those questions that hint at fissures and breakdowns in the Jewish community and that point to differential vulnerabilities of its component groups. These variations emerged during the earliest anti-Jewish constrictions and became more pronounced in the ensuing years. When, for example, only half of the Jewish school-age children in France or Czestochowa received an education, which ones were selected and which were in the other half? When Jewish men were impressed for labor in Poland or Romania, who had to work and who was exempt? When the number of calories consumed on average in a ghetto was such and such, which families were near or above that line and which fell to the bottom? Primo Levi raises this question briefly when he alludes to Auschwitz survivors as having eaten more than the usual camp ration.[33]

A handful of authors probed the lives of ordinary people at some depth. One was Stanislaw Adler, who wrote his sophisticated memoir at the end of the war in Polish. He committed suicide in 1946 and a friend brought his manuscript to Israel. An English translation was published by Yad Vashem thirty-six years later, but the book was not distributed in the United States.[34] Another was the American sociologist John K. Dickinson, who spent several years in Germany during the 1950s, where he interviewed 172 persons about the life and death of a single unknown Jewish victim. He wrote a biography of this man, giving him a fictional name. The publication of the account in 1967 did not attract much public or academic interest.[35] In 2001 it was still one of a kind. Reissued that year by a small publisher who had edited the book thirty-four years earlier, but this time with an appendix identifying the place of the story and revealing the real names of the victims and witnesses, the monograph was largely ignored again.[36] The relative silence that greeted the insightful work of Adler and Dickinson is symptomatic of an extraordinarily low receptivity to issues at the core of the Jewish catastrophe and of an unmistakable psychological unpreparedness to examine them.

We have always known that the progress of research depends, in the first instance, on accessibility of source materials. What we did not readily admit to ourselves for several decades is that even sizable stockpiles of records in wide-open archives do not guarantee any substantial growth of interest. We have had to learn the hard way that advances of knowledge are not automatic. They become possible when someone steps out of a habitual framework of thought to recognize complications or connections not seen before, or when fortuitously a missing fact is found, or when patient sifting through large collections of records allows glances at life as it was lived. All this is part of a process that may span several generations of researchers. The sheer passage of time governs also the slow disintegration of inhibitions that have blocked questions and answers with respect to the behavior of victims in extreme situations. But the reticence that persists will be overcome, and the ambiguities that it produced will disappear.

Notes

1. See the opening paragraphs, listing the academic and professional qualifications of the accused, in the sentencing portions of the judgment rendered in *United States v. Ohlendorf* (the *Einsatzgruppen* case), in Nuremberg Military Tribunals, *Trials of War Criminals* (Washington, DC: U.S. Government Printing Office, 1946–49), vol. 4, 510–96.
2. See Jean-Pierre Azéma, *From Munich to Liberation, 1938–1944* (New York: Cambridge University Press, 1984), 56.
3. Radu Ioanid, *The Sword of the Archangel: Fascist Ideology in Romania*, trans. Peter Heinegg (Boulder, CO: East European Monographs, 1990).
4. Uwe Adam, *Judenpolitik im Dritten Reich* (Düsseldorf: Droste Verlag, 1972).
5. Christopher Browning, *Ordinary Men: Reserve Police Battalion 101 and the Final Solution in Poland* (New York: HarperPerennial, 1994).
6. Götz Aly, *Endlösung: Völkerverschiebung und der Mord an den Europäischen Juden* (Frankfurt am Main: S. Fischer, 1995), and his unpublished essay "Die Bekämpfung der Inflation in Griechenland und die Deportation der Juden von Saloniki," part of a project on finance still in progress, 2003.
7. Susanne Willems, *Der entsiedelte Jude: Albert Speer's Wohnungsmarktpolitik für den Berliner Hauptstadtbau* (Berlin: Edition Hentrich, 2002).
8. Walter Manoschek, *"Serbien ist judenfrei": Militärische Besatzungspolitik und Judenvernichtung in Serbien 1941/42* (Munich: R. Oldenbourg, 1993); Ulrich Herbert, "Die deutsche Militärverwaltung in Paris und die Deportation der französische Juden," in Christian Jansen, Lutz Niethammer, and Bernd Weisbrod, eds., *Von der Aufgabe der Freiheit* (Berlin: Akademie Verlag, 1995), 439–40, 447.
9. Isaiah Trunk, *Judenrat: The Jewish Councils in Eastern Europe Under Nazi Occupation* (New York: Macmillan, 1972).
10. Yitzhak Arad, *Belzec, Sobibor, Treblinka: The Operation Reinhard Death Camps* (Bloomington: Indiana University Press, 1987), 126–27, 383–89. Arad also referred to a German court judgment setting forth six hundred thousand. The number appears in a Polish handbook as well. See Glowna Badania Zbrodni Hitlerowskich w Polsce, *Obozy hitlerowskie na ziemiach polskich 1939–1945* (Warsaw: Panst Wydaw Naukowe, 1979), 293–94.
11. Korherr to Himmler [March 27, 1943], Nuremberg trials document NO-5194.
12. Katzmann to Higher SS and Police Leader Friedrich Krüger, 30 June 1943, Nuremberg trials document L-18.
13. I listed only "hundreds of thousands" for each camp. Raul Hilberg, *The Destruction of the European Jews* (Chicago: Quadrangle Books, 1961), 572.
14. Raul Hilberg, ed., *Documents of Destruction: Germany and Jewry, 1933–1945* (Chicago: Quadrangle Books, 1971), 206.
15. Hilberg, *The Destruction of the European Jews*, 2nd ed. (New York: Holmes & Meier, 1985), 893, 1219.

16. See Dieter Pohl, *Nationalsozialistische Judenverfolgung in Ostgalizien 1941–1944* (Munich: R. Oldenbourg, 1997), 245–65.
17. Peter Witte and Stephen Tyas, "A New Document on the Deportation and Murder of Jews During 'Einsatz Reinhardt' 1942," in *Holocaust and Genocide Studies* 15 (2001), 468–86. The item was a radiogram by an SS officer, Hermann Höfle, who was stationed in Lublin, to another SS officer, Franz Heim, in Krakow, 11 January 1943, decoded by the British Code and Cypher School. "Reinhardt" was the German code name for the operation that eventuated in 1,274,166 Jews dead by the end of 1942. The figure in the radiogram was the same as Korherr's.
18. I corrected the error in the third edition of *The Destruction of the European Jews* (New Haven, CT: Yale University Press, 2003), 958, 1320.
19. Yisrael Gutman, *The Jews of Warsaw, 1939–1943* (Bloomington: Indiana University Press, 1982), 212–13.
20. *Biuletyn Zydowskiego Instytutu Historycznego* 1 (1951), 81, 86, 90, as cited by Gutman with his table.
21. Stroop to Higher SS and Police Leader Krüger, 16 May 1943, Nuremberg trials document PS-1061.
22. Chairman of the Jewish Council in Warsaw, Marek Lichtenbaum, to the German Kommissar of the ghetto, Heinz Auerswald, 5 September 1943, Zentrale Stelle der Landesjustizverwaltungen in Ludwigsburg, Akten Auerswald, Red Series 365e.
23. For an English-language translation of the diary, see Abraham Lewin, *A Cup of Tears— A Diary of the Warsaw Ghetto* (Oxford and New York: Oxford University Press, 1989), 160ff. Gutman's error also had reverberations. Thus, his underestimate of the deportations is coupled with his corresponding failure to gauge the actual size of the ghetto population just before their start. That figure must have been over 380,000 rather than his 350,000. See the census count (397,016) for 1 March 1942 in a report by *Regierungsdirektor* Curt Hoffmann (Labor Office, Warsaw District), 12 June 1942, Zentrale Stelle in Ludwigsburg, Red Series 365d. Gutman did not have that statistic, either.
24. Duro Schwarz, "The Jasenovac Death Camps," in *Yad Vashem Studies* 25 (1996), 383–430.
25. Stanislaw Adler, *In the Warsaw Ghetto, 1940–1943* (Jerusalem: Yad Vashem, 1982), 211–12. The author committed suicide in 1946.
26. Excerpts from the testimony by Adolf Petsch, a member of the Security Police in the area of Pinsk-Stolin who participated in massacres during 1942 at Janov, in the indictment of the prosecutor at the Landgericht Frankfurt am Main, 4 Js 901/62, dated 28 March 1968, 64–66.
27. Report by Captain Paul Salliter, covering 11–17 December 1941, in H. G. Adler, *Der verwaltete Mensch* (Tübingen: Mohr, 1975), 462.
28. Typescript of the entry of 26 February 1944, with the initials of Alice de Bunom. Courtesy of Lucjan Dobroszycki.
29. See, for example, the fragmentary description of conditions affecting Parisian Jewry by Renée Poznanski, *Jews in France during World War II* (Hanover, NH, and London: University Press of New England, 2001), 327–32.
30. Primo Levi, *The Drowned and the Saved*, trans. Raymond Rosenthal (New York: Vintage International, 1988), 60–69.
31. Oscar Neumann, *Im Schatten des Todes: Vom Schicksalskampf des slowakischen Judentums* (Tel Aviv: Edition Olamenu, 1956). The book has three hundred tightly printed pages.
32. Raymond-Raoul Lambert, *Carnet d'un témoin* (Paris: Fayard, 1985).
33. Levi, *The Drowned and the Saved*, 41.
34. Adler, *Warsaw Ghetto*.
35. John K. Dickinson, *German & Jew: The Life and Death of Sigmund Stein* (Chicago: Quadrangle Books, 1967). "Stein" is a pseudonym. The publisher, Quadrangle Books, is now extinct.
36. The publisher was Ivan R. Dee, the editor of Quadrangle Books in the 1960s.

– *Part Two* –

IDENTITY, GENDER, AND SEXUALITY DURING AND AFTER THE THIRD REICH

Primo Levi described himself as a centaur.¹ That mythological figure—half-man, half-horse—mirrored his gray-zoned sense of identity. Just as the centaur represents two realities that are improbably, even impossibly, fused into one, Levi's life was a fusion, at times a confusion and collision, of elements—the Italian and the Jew, the chemical plant manager and the writer—that were inseparable from the Holocaust that split him and left his identity enigmatic.

In ironic ways, Levi's knowledge of chemistry saved him from an Auschwitz death. Anticipating that production of synthetic rubber might soon begin at Buna/Monowitz, the German "logic" that governed Auschwitz in 1944 resulted in a late spring call for prisoner-chemists. Sensing that some advantage might await him, Levi was among the prisoners who applied and was accepted to work in *Kommando* 98, the so-called Chemical *Kommando*. Levi knew, however, not to let his hopes rise very high. Even after passing the examination administered by a German official whom he identifies as *Doktor Ingenieur* Pannwitz, Levi knew only that he had "spent a day without working, so that tonight I will have a little less hunger, and this is a concrete advantage, not to be taken away."²

No synthetic rubber was ever produced at Buna/Monowitz. Nor did the Chemical *Kommando*'s work have much to do with science. It consisted largely of endless moving of back-breaking sacks of caustic chemicals, which often burned the skin and made the prisoners prone to infection.³ The Holocaust entailed that one thing led to another in strange and unexpected ways. For a time the Chemical *Kommando* worked near the British POW camp,

Notes for this section begin on page 96.

where black-market bartering was favorable. In addition, Levi's assignment to the Chemical *Kommando* also resulted in work with a bricklaying unit, where he was befriended by Lorenzo Perrone, the Italian civilian who gave him life-saving rations.[4]

Levi's account of the gray zone emphasized its "incredibly complicated internal structure," which brought immense and often irresistible pressure to bear on the people within its Auschwitz grip. That structure, however, was complicated and incredible partly because it involved so much contingency and chance. Levi's fate was and was not his own. Within his personal gray zone, things happened to him arbitrarily as much as, or even more than, he controlled what took place. Sometimes he could seize chance opportunities that were unavailable to others; sometimes unexpected advantages just came his way. In the late autumn of 1944, as Auschwitz's deadly winter took hold, one of those strokes of luck arrived. Inexplicably, Levi was one of three Chemical *Kommando* prisoners chosen to work in *Bau* 939, which was a real chemical laboratory set up by Dr. Pannwitz. This new assignment improved Levi's chances considerably. The threats of hunger, exposure to the cold, disease, and selections that would condemn one to the gas chambers and crematoria at Birkenau might be kept at bay. "In these conditions," Levi observed, "those less expert than us about things in the *Lager* might even be tempted by the hope of survival and by the thought of liberty. But we are not, we know how these matters go; all this is the gift of fortune, to be enjoyed as intensely as possible and at once; for there is no certainty about tomorrow."[5] The Holocaust's contingencies favored and burdened Levi in ways that most of those who entered Auschwitz never returned to feel. Although *Häftling* 174517 knew that he was the Holocaust's innocent victim, Levi also felt shame, a key component in what he called the survivors' disease.

La chiave a stella (The Star-shaped Key, 1978), translated in the United States as *The Monkey's Wrench* (1986), is Levi's semifictional work about a construction worker named Tino Faussone and a chemist-writer who swap stories about their everyday pursuits. At one point, the chemist-writer says of himself: "In distant times I, too, had got involved with gods quarreling among themselves; I, too, had encountered snakes in my path, and that encounter had changed my condition, giving me a strange power of speech. But since then, being a chemist in the world's eyes, and feeling, on the contrary, a writer's blood in my veins, I felt as if I had two souls in my body, and that's too many."[6]

In Part 2 of *Gray Zones,* versions of such "double experience," combined centaur-like in Levi's life and thought, find expression in studies that explore identity, gender, and sexuality during and after the Third Reich.[7] The experiences these chapters report are "double" for various reasons, all of them shadowed by the Holocaust. Sometimes these studies involve split identities and multiple personalities, including the ambiguities and compromises that accompany them. In other cases, they emphasize male/female differences and the complications that arise when gender and sexuality unavoidably fit

Levi's claim that "the greater part of historical and natural phenomena are not simple, or not simple in the way that we would like."[8] In still other circumstances, the accent falls on the difference between what has been said and can be said and on what resists saying, even to the point of being taboo, a factor that still haunts attempts to retrieve experience and analyze testimony about sexual activity and abuse in the Holocaust, a gray-zoned area if ever there was one.

As they address under-researched issues in Holocaust studies, the six scholars who contributed chapters to this part of *Gray Zones* base their analyses on years of scholarly research, which is often informed by personal experience relevant for their chosen topics. In that sense, there is another dimension of "double experience" in these essays and in all Holocaust scholarship, for the identities of the scholars and the devastating terrain of their fields mix and mingle to make Holocaust studies a rich, thickly layered, often painful and sometimes contested blend of passionate engagement, dispassionate inquiry, sorrowful melancholy, and determination not to despair. Thus, Robert Melson writes autobiographically in a study that focuses on the traumatic complexity of Jewish survival on the "Aryan" side and its aftermath. He explores the gray zones of deception: what it meant to conceal one's identity and to behave in misleading ways in order to survive. Eva Fleischner, whose identity contains both Jewish and Catholic roots, explores the gray zones of identity by directing attention to the crises faced by Jewish children who were hidden by Christians, raised as Christians, and who, in some cases, even became Christian clergy and yet discovered in adulthood that they were Jews. Fleischner also explores ambiguities with regard to the motivations of those who baptized Jewish children: did they act to save lives or win converts, or both?

Drawing upon his recent book, *Hitler's Jewish Soldiers: The Untold Story of Nazi Racial Laws and Men of Jewish Descent in the German Military*, Brian Mark Rigg explores the dilemmas of identity and survival that faced the so-called *Mischlinge*, half- or quarter-Jews, who served in the Third Reich's military. Rigg explores the complexities of related issues: what did the *Mischling* soldiers know of the Holocaust, what role did Hitler play in personally certifying "Aryanizations," and what does "*Mischling* policy" say about the relationship between ideology and *Realpolitik?* Geoffrey Giles's chapter continues the focus on the *Wehrmacht*, but he draws attention to the gray-zoned position of homosexuals in the German armed forces under Hitler. Giles notes that most homosexuals led very private lives and that, in comparison to Jews and Socialists, they were difficult for authorities to identify. Moreover, the inconsistent policies of the various branches of the *Wehrmacht* and the SS, the variable punitive measures, and the failure to reach agreement about the nature of homosexuality created a series of gray zones marked by tension and confusion.

His essay teams with Dagmar Herzog's to advance awareness that understandings of the complexities of sexuality and gender are not peripheral but central themes if fuller insight about the Third Reich and the Holocaust is to be obtained. Her way of challenging the conventional wisdom that Nazi attitudes about sexuality were repressive is bound to stimulate debate and further research in largely unmapped territory. Herzog argues that the combination of "sex and death, pleasure with evil, was at the very heart of Nazism's own project." In the postwar Federal Republic, public debates surrounding sex and National Socialism—both issues coming to the fore with the relatively emancipatory spirit of the 1960s—also proved contentious and defied resolution. These issues also ultimately centered on collective identity.

Sara Horowitz asks us to think about ways in which gender differences affect something as basic, and at times as ambiguous and problematic, as our understanding of good and evil. Turning to Holocaust-related literature and film, including recently published memoirs by women, her essay echoes a theme from Primo Levi's analysis of the gray zone when she laments the fact that gendered images of good and evil have often affected interpretation of women's choices and behavior during the Holocaust in ways that "simplify complex and ambiguous moral questions, insisting on ultimate judgment, rather than on compassion."

The research and reflection of these authors go in paths different from the ones that Levi took. Nevertheless, as these six writers do their work, they show that there is and must be fusion between Primo Levi's gray zone and the gray zones of their accounts. Only such encounters with complexity can untangle needless confusion about the Holocaust.

Notes

1. See Primo Levi, *The Voice of Memory: Interviews, 1961–1987*, ed. Marco Belpoliti and Robert Gordon; trans. Robert Gordon (New York: The New Press, 2001), xvii–xxvi, 84–86; Carole Angier, *The Double Bond: Primo Levi, a Biography* (New York: Farrar, Straus and Giroux, 2002), 529–90; Massimo Giuliani, *A Centaur in Auschwitz: Reflections on Primo Levi's Thinking* (Lanham, MD: Lexington Books, 2003), 27–35.
2. Primo Levi, *Survival in Auschwitz: The Nazi Assault on Humanity*, trans. Stuart Woolf (New York: Simon and Schuster, 1996), 107.
3. See Angier, *The Double Bond*, 324–27.
4. See Ian Thomson, *Primo Levi: A Life* (New York: Henry Holt, 2002), 171–72.
5. Levi, *Survival in Auschwitz*, 140.
6. Primo Levi, *The Monkey's Wrench*, trans. William Weaver (New York: Summit Books, 1986), 52. The British edition is entitled *The Wrench*. In all cases, the reference is to the socket wrench that Faussone carries with him. Levi's biographers agree that this book is the happiest and most humorous that he wrote. Nevertheless, there are gray-zoned motifs within it. With specific reference to his remark about two souls, Levi commented in a 1986 interview with the author Philip Roth that "my statement that 'two souls . . . is too many' is half a joke, but half-hints at serious things." Levi's centaur-like qualities remained in play. See Primo Levi, *Survival in Auschwitz*, 183.
7. Levi uses the phrase "double experience" in *The Monkey's Wrench*, 52.
8. Primo Levi, *The Drowned and the Saved*, trans. Raymond Rosenthal (New York: Summit Books, 1988), 37.

– Chapter 7 –

CHOICELESS CHOICES
Surviving on False Papers on the "Aryan" Side

Robert Melson

In his essay "The Gray Zone," Primo Levi suggests that even in the camps, where lives were circumscribed to sheer survival or mass murder, prisoners and guards had choices to make that placed them in the "gray zone" of moral ambiguity.[1] In contrast, Jews in hiding on the "Aryan" side seemed less constrained in their lives and hence more likely to make morally ambiguous choices. I shall argue that during the Holocaust, whether in the camps or outside of them, Jews were most often presented by "choiceless choices" in that the decisions they made were inescapable and dictated by circumstances.[2] However, those who survived on the Aryan side sometimes experienced small moments of satisfaction when they succeeded in deceiving or humiliating their pursuers. Such moments were largely denied to prisoners in the *Lagers*. On both sides of the barbed wires survivors experienced pangs of shame, remorse, and guilt after their liberation, even though in most cases such feelings did not necessarily derive from prior moral transgressions.

My parents and I survived the war because my mother through sheer *chutzpah* and bravado was able to get her hands on false papers of identification that allowed us to pose as Polish aristocrats on the "Aryan" side, and because my father, who was an intrepid *macher* and operator, hooked up with a German war-profiteer of the Schindler type. I've told the story of our survival elsewhere.[3] Here I wish to pause and reexamine a few events from our experience from the perspective of Primo Levi's assertions in "The Gray Zone" concerning the moral ambiguities attending on survival and the shame and guilt that followed.

Notes for this section begin on page 106.

According to Levi, the *Lager* was a factory for producing corpses, while extracting hair and gold teeth from the dead and labor from the still living. The infernal genius of this industrial process was that the camps were largely run by the prisoners themselves, under the close and brutal supervision of the guards. The gray zone for the prisoners lay in those areas of activity that implicated them in the running of the camp: to survive, each prisoner soon learned that he or she was in competition with every other victim for space, food, and influence (*protektzja*) with the *Kapos* and other "prominents"—a competition whose outcome was life or death. When confronted with a new, confused prisoner, Levi tried to instill in him some hard-won truths about survival:

> I tried to convince him of a few recent discoveries of mine (in truth, not yet well digested): that down there, in order to get by, it was necessary to get busy, to organize illegal food, dodge work, find influential friends, hide one's thoughts, steal, and lie; that whoever did not do so was soon dead.[4]

Those who couldn't compete died or were killed, those who survived were usually just plain lucky, but all were left with feelings of shame and guilt, shame for having been assaulted and dehumanized without being able to respond and guilt for surviving, possibly at the cost of another's life. The prisoner who stole a chunk of bread from his dying bunkmate to live one more day may be forgiven by others who recognize him as a victim of circumstances monumentally beyond his control, but he, especially if he is a decent person like Levi, may not be able to forgive himself when he is a free man and memories come to haunt him.

Of course there were "gray zones" of what might be called moral triage on both sides of the barbed wire: to survive on the "Aryan" side one had to throw overboard precepts and behaviors such as truth-telling, honesty, and the maintenance of personal integrity. As they tried to evade the Nazi dragnet, my parents too had to steal, lie, and find influential friends. We were foxes fleeing the howling pack of dogs trying to rip us apart, but our passing for gentiles on the outside cannot be compared to Levi's horrifying experience inside the *Lager*.

Although we too were sentenced to death and had to rely on our wits to survive, the situation for Jews living on false papers on the "Aryan" side was radically different, because in our daily lives we were not confronted with the diabolic competition for survival with other Jews and other prisoners that the *Lager* enforced on its inmates. Our fate was to elude the hunters—and those who would help them, the bystanders—who wished to capture and kill us. We never had to elbow people out of the way in order to fall on a crust of bread that fell out of the hands of a dying prisoner. However, like the prisoners in the camps, we too were confronted with choiceless choices, and we too practiced a moral triage that led to feelings of shame and guilt that continued to haunt us after the war. Let me illustrate my points by turning to four episodes told to me by my parents when I interviewed them.

My parents, Wolf "Willy" Mendelsohn and Natalia "Nacia" Ponczek, were a stylish, attractive, highly assimilated couple who had met in Warsaw before the war. Although my mother's father, Leon "Leib" Ponczek, was a religious Jew, my grandmother Stefania ("Stefcia") and my mother were largely secular. Nacia was Slavic looking and Polish speaking. She was blond, blue eyed, had been a singer in a nightclub, and had won two beauty contests before she was married. My father was the classic tall, dark, and handsome type. His native tongue was German, not Polish. He had been educated in Switzerland and Berlin, and before the war had owned a business that had dealt with the Polish government from which he had been barred because he was a Jew. He was energetic, enterprising, a *macher,* whose dream had been to come to America "to make it big," as he put it. It was a dream deferred for a few years until the war was over.

In 1936 they married, and a year later I was born as Sylvio Mendelsohn. In August 1939, a month before the war, we left for Stanislawow in Polish Galicia where Willy was going to join his father and uncle in running the family-owned woolens factory. Hence when the war broke out we were first occupied by the Soviets. Then in 1941, after the Germans attacked their erstwhile allies, we came under German occupation.

On 12 October 1941 the Germans ordered the Jewish population of Stanislawow to assemble in the center of the city. It was said that the Jews were going to be deported to somewhere else in Poland. Those who failed to report would be shot. Some ten thousand people came. They were shoved onto trucks, driven out of town, and massacred by units of the *Einzatsgruppen* and the German Order Police. The shooting lasted well into the night under the lights of trucks. Later the bodies were buried by Ukrainian laborers. The Jews who remained were ordered to move into a ghetto. On 22 February 1943, the ghetto was liquidated, and the inhabitants were killed at Belzec.

We had survived thus far because, following my mother's intuition, we disobeyed the Germans and did not go to the place of assembly, and, following my father's refusal, we did not enter the ghetto. Instead we stayed in hiding with Hela, a red-headed Ukrainian young woman who had been my governess. But by late October 1941, our time at Hela's was running out. Her friends were asking her leading questions about her strange guests, and it was only a matter of time before we, including Hela, would be denounced, arrested, and killed. It was at this juncture that my mother went to see the Zamojskis with a desperate appeal.

My parents had met Jan and Janina Zamojski by chance at a café before the war. They were a young Polish couple with a son, Boguslaw (Bobi), about my age, and the two families became acquaintances, if not friends. What distinguished the Zamojskis from everyone else was their name. They were a provincial branch of one of the leading noble families in Poland. Their ancestors had been high dignitaries, including prime ministers, although at the time Jan Zamojski was a low-level functionary in the town administration.

My mother's plan was to ask the Zamojskis for their documents of identity. We would leave Stanislawow and survive by posing as them. At first they were taken aback, but upon further reflection they agreed to give up their documents, but there would be a price: twenty thousand zlotys (about five thousand dollars), an astronomical sum. When my mother came back to Hela's empty-handed, my father was furious. Here is how my mother remembered the scene:

> "So it's a simple business proposition!" exclaimed Willy with anger. "Our lives for twenty thousand zloty. And where are we supposed to find this treasure? Maybe we can sell the bicycle and the sewing machine, we'll throw my suits and your dresses into the bargain, and then we'll have about five hundred zloty! What the hell are we supposed to do, take Sylvio by his sweaty little hand while he drags his potty behind him and start marching down the road in winter?"
>
> I started to cry. The Zamojskis were our last chance. Now that was gone. We were sentenced to death. We didn't know why, and we didn't know where to turn next.
>
> That night I couldn't sleep. I had taken drops of valerian, hoping that they would settle my nerves, but all they did was to increase my restlessness. The next morning I got up with a desperate plan: I would go back to the Zamojskis. I didn't tell Willy, because I didn't want to disappoint him should my plan fail, and I was afraid that he would stop me from going. I left in the afternoon, after making a lame excuse that I needed to go shopping.
>
> When I knocked on their door, the Zamojskis were in a good mood. They may have assumed that I was bringing the money and that their economic problems were over. Once again the three of us sat in the living room. . . .
>
> "My dear friends," I started, "I spoke to Willy about your proposal. He thinks the price is a bit steep, but he can raise the money. There is no problem from our end. In the meanwhile, I've come to inspect the merchandise, you understand. I need to see what your birth certificates and other documents look like. I hope you don't mind." I smiled. I tried to exude calm and confidence.
>
> The Zamojskis looked disappointed. They exchanged knowing glances, but after a moment's hesitation he [Jan] said, "You'll have to excuse us for a few minutes." Then they both disappeared into the bedroom. A few minutes later they came out with the documents. There were birth certificates and wedding certificates. These were passes to life. How I envied their being Polish and "Aryan" and not Jewish! But I tried to look as nonchalant as possible as I inspected the merchandise. While the Zamojskis left me alone and busied themselves in the kitchen, I tried to memorize the pertinent information: names, dates, places. I scratched whatever facts I could on the flap of my worn brown leather shoulder bag, breaking a nail in the process.
>
> After a few minutes they returned with a bottle of schnapps and some glasses, which I refused because I needed to keep a clear head. As I left I told them that I'd be back with the money in a few days.
>
> "It's a large sum," I said, "but Willy will manage to raise it. Don't you worry."
>
> When I heard the door of their apartment close behind me, I descended to the ground floor. I sat on their pitch-dark staircase, and by the light of matches I wrote furiously into a child's small lined notebook that I had brought with me just for this purpose. I copied whatever facts I could remember and make out from the scratches on my pocketbook: Jan Ferdynand Zamojski, Boguslaw Marian Zamojski, Janina Victoria Zamojska, born in Lwow on such and such a date, baptized in Stanislawow at the church of so and so. Good.[5]

The next morning Nacia Mendelsohn went to the local church where the Zamojskis had been baptized; there she convinced the priest that she was Janina Zamojska, a Polish countess, and that she needed a new set of documents, birth certificates and marriage certificates, for herself, for her husband, Jan, and for her son, Boguslaw. She explained that the Soviets had confiscated our papers, and that the family needed them to survive under the Germans. The extraordinary thing is that the priest believed her and made out the documents that she asked for.

> On the way home, I stopped every few minutes to look into my purse to make sure that the documents were still there. I felt I'd burst like a balloon. I had pulled it off! Now we had a slim chance.
> When I got home, I took Willy aside. "Willusiu, darling," I whispered, "I've got the papers."
> "What?" He almost shouted. "What papers?"
> "Willy dear here's your new birth certificate. You're now Count Jan Ferdynand Zamojski. I'm Countess Janina Zamojska. You can call me Nina from now on. And Sylvio is little Count Boguslaw 'Bobi' Zamojski."
> Willy took the documents to the window and for a few moments studied them carefully. Then he hugged me gently to him, and like a small child I started to bawl.[6]

A few days later we escaped Stanislawow for Krakow. And then, a year and a half later, when Polish blackmailers discovered our identity, we managed to get to Prague, where we survived the war. My mother's false papers had saved our lives.

When years later I asked my mother, "What ever happened to the Zamojskis?" she looked annoyed and with a wave of her hand dismissed the question and dismissed them: "Who cares—they would only help us for a price, money we didn't have." At first I agreed with her, but in time I have come to see the situation as more nuanced. I think she was dismissive of the Zamojskis because she must have realized that her request had been outrageous, and their refusal not to give up their papers for free could not have been a total surprise. What angered her and my father was that the Zamojskis seemed to have put money before friendship. However, while the Zamojskis may not have been generous and noble, their reactions had been human and understandable. They themselves were in dire economic straits and in mortal danger, and they were not wrong to have imagined that my father—the son of the wealthy Julius Mendelsohn—might have had money enough to buy the documents.

As for my mother, her angry dismissal of the Zamojskis may have covered over a guilty conscience: in effect she had stolen their identities and had put them at risk as well, and her story might seem less admirable on closer examination. But she need not have worried: what was she supposed to do? Hers was a choiceless choice forced on her by the murderous Nazis, and she reacted with uncommon ingenuity and courage. That she felt some shame for her actions only shows that she had a conscience like so many other survivors in the camps and outside of them.

When we got to Krakow from Stanislawow we were helped by a generous landlady who, not knowing we were Jews, let us temporarily stay in her home and even fed us, while my father got the *Kennkarten,* the official identity cards demanded by the German occupation. Next, the problem was how to make money to survive, and here my father took over. He linked up with Herr Bonneberger, a German war-profiteer operating from Warsaw who needed a German and Polish representative to hustle and sell his products in Krakow. Bonneberger was selling plastic goods, including raincoats and industrial-length aprons. Showing him Bonneberger's samples, Willy persuaded Herr Siegel, the head of Spolem, a German-run consumer distribution network whose sphere of operations was all of Poland and the Ukraine, to buy thousands of Bonneberger's plastic raincoats and other products by splitting his commission with him. Bonneberger was very pleased. When they met in Krakow, he and Willy, calling himself Jan Zamojski, of course, hit it off famously. It was then that Willy persuaded Bonneberger to open a joint bank account and to help him find a new apartment in the German section of the city. (Both my parents realized that it was easier to deceive the Germans than the Poles, who might see through their Zamojski masquerade.) It was there that we met our neighbor, Colonel Kruk. My father tells the rest of the story. It illustrates not shame for actions done to others but shame as humiliation for abuses suffered by himself.

> *One morning, soon after we had moved in, Nina and I were finishing breakfast, Bobi was playing on the floor, and the maid was cleaning up in the kitchen. Suddenly there was a loud banging on the door. Nina, who was closest, opened it, and in barged a Gestapo officer. He wore a black uniform and the cap with the death-head insignia. Carried two pistols on him. "What the hell?" I said, but he ignored me completely.*
>
> *"I'm Colonel Kruk, your next-door neighbor," he said to Nina in German. "Starting tomorrow morning, you're going to clean my place. The first things that need to be done are the floors and the windows. My wife is coming in a week. I want the place to be spotless."*
>
> *I felt the blood drain from my face. I was trembling I was so mad. "Colonel Kruk," I said, "I am Count Zamojski. My wife is not a maid, and she's not going to be your servant. You will be civil the next time you speak to her. Is that understood?"*
>
> *Kruk turned to me dumbfounded. "What did you just say? What tone are you using with me?"*
>
> *"Just as you hear it," I said coldly.*
>
> *He turned on his heels and left, slamming the door behind him.*
>
> *"Jan, you're totally insane," Nina said trembling. "We've got to fix the situation."* [Nina called Willy "Jan" during the war, and Willy called Nacia "Nina," even in their most private moments.]
>
> *She was right, of course, but I couldn't act "Count Zamojski" one minute and then behave like a frightened little man the next. But I'm no fool. That evening when we heard Kruk come back, I grabbed a bottle of cognac and banged loudly on his door. When he appeared wearing jodhpurs and an undershirt over his scawny chest, I waved the bottle of cognac in front of him and invited myself in to have a drink. Kruk mumbled something like, "Come in."*

> That evening Nina and I sat with him, toasting each other and going through the bottle. After that we became great "friends."
>
> Kruk used to drop by our place every evening after work. His mission, plain and simple, was to murder Jews. He'd brag: "Today I got rid of twenty Jews. Tomorrow I have another batch to hang."
>
> Often he'd come in late at night or early in the morning. When Bobi was still awake, Kruk especially liked to play with the child. He said that Bobi reminded him of his own little boy whom he had left in Hamburg. He'd bounce Bobi on his knees and let him play with his Gestapo cap. The child would put on Kruk's huge cap over his little head so that his face and ears would disappear, and then he'd march around the room giving the "Heil Hitler!" salute like a little Gestapo midget. Kruk found it all very amusing.
>
> One day he asked Nina if it would be okay to bring some of his colleagues to dinner. What to do? The guy is our neighbor . . . a Gestapo official. So I said, "Ja. Of course. With pleasure."
>
> A few days later the maid Nina prepared a feast. That night as Kruk and his cronies were sitting around the dinner table, most of their conversation was about killing Jews. They were all bragging about it. This one had hung thirty people that day. The other had one hundred shot. A third drowned a whole crowd of Jews. That was the main theme of the evening. Meanwhile we're eating, drinking, laughing. Nina had made a Hungarian goulash. They loved her and her cooking. We couldn't get rid of them. They were happy and contented—just the kind of people you'd see in a Munich beer hall. When they saw me bring in the cognac after dinner, they cheered and clapped. Nina and I were a big hit and so was Bobi. They were normal, ordinary Germans having a great time. When they left, Nina and I avoided looking at each other. That night we went to bed without exchanging a word.[7]

Why did Nacia and Willy avoid looking at each other? Why did they go to bed without exchanging a word? This was the shame not of chagrin or embarrassment; it was the shame of humiliation and degradation. They had done nothing wrong. They had to go through with the dinner if they wanted us to survive, but they had to repress their feelings of horror and contempt and act as if they enjoyed the situation and implicitly approved of their guests' actions both at the dinner and at their work. Theirs was a choiceless choice. They were able to pull off the deception but at the cost of their own worth and integrity.

As for me, like a little pup, I picked up subtle signs from my parents, especially their anxiety and fear when Kruk was around. I tried to do what was expected of me, which was to be a little clown, a little charmer. As long as Kruk was laughing, he wasn't harming us. I couldn't have put it that clearly then, but in retrospect that's what I felt. Today I still feel the anxiety of the situation: my parents, afraid for their lives, afraid for me, and I sensing their fear, acting up, giving the "Heil Hitler" salute while wearing Kruk's Gestapo cap. I don't feel ashamed, but I feel degraded and humiliated by the situation. I also feel something else: Kruk was a brutal fool, and we tricked him to believe that we were the noble Zamojskis, instead of the Jews he hated and despised. I'm not sure that I can call it a feeling of pride or triumph—the whole situation was so pervaded by fear and death—

but we had eluded the hunters one more time, and I had helped in the deception.

That feeling of pride and gritty triumph in deception was even more apparent after my parents pulled off another dinner party. It so happened that while we were passing ourselves off as the "noble Zamojskis," we were joined by three women, Wanda and Irena Godlewska and their mother, Pani Maria Godlewska, whom I called Pani Marylka when she lived with us. The two young women were lively and beautiful, while their mother seemed to be a typical aristocratic lady from the Polish upper strata. It took a little time, but after a while we realized that we were all Jews living on false papers. In the meantime, my uncle Tadzo, my mother's younger brother who was living with us in Krakow, had fallen in love with Wanda, and the young couple decided to get married.

It was an obvious, if unwritten, rule of survival on false papers that one had to act as normally as possible: if a young couple was going to get married, they would have a wedding ceremony and a party. Thus it was that in the winter of 1942, in the midst of war and genocide, in order to keep to the plan and improve our chances, my parents gave a dinner party in honor of the bride and groom. Here is how my mother recalled the event:

> We planned a big wedding feast for the young couple. Among our guests were Hauptmann Gottfried, a big shot in Die Werke des Generalgouvernement. He was the chief inspector of all the factories in occupied Poland. Jan let him make a lot of money by selling him raincoats below the market price, which he resold and then became very rich. Gottfried was a correct but corrupt former Austrian army officer. He became an essential contact for us later when we desperately needed him. Although he was married, he came with his girlfriend, a tall, stunning blond. Bonneberger and Herr Siegel from Spolem came. [There were other German contacts that my mother mentions], and of course Colonel Kruk and his wife. She had finally come from Hamburg with their little boy.
>
> By the way, Frau Kruk had volunteered to cook the meal. She was an excellent chef who had worked for a German nobleman before the war, and the meal was scrumptious. They were all there, our German "friends," to celebrate the wedding of Wanda and Tadzo, two Jewish kids from Warsaw![8]

I doubt that at the time my parents or any of the family relished the irony of the situation, as they carried on with the merriment while being terrified of being discovered. But after the war when I interviewed her about it, my mother laughed at the recollection. The wedding feast had been a dangerous but successful deception, quite different from the dinner party that had been forced on her by Kruk and his murderous comrades. At the first, she and my father had felt degraded by having to entertain Nazi killers, but at the second, she had deceived her pursuers and savored a small but sweet moment of triumph, a rare enough occurrence for Jews during the war.

While we were living on false papers on the "Aryan" side my grandparents, Leon (Leib) and Stefania (Stefcia) Ponczek, my mother's parents, were trying to survive in the Warsaw ghetto. Three times my uncle Tadzo smuggled himself into the ghetto and tried to persuade them to leave with him, but they refused to follow him. My grandmother looked Polish and spoke the language without a Yiddish accent. Not so my grandfather. He both looked Jewish and spoke Polish with an accent, which would have given him away to the Polish blackmailers surrounding the ghetto. They would have seized him and handed him over to the Germans. I suspect he refused to leave because he didn't want to endanger the rest of the family, and my grandmother refused because she didn't want to leave him. Before the deportations of summer/autumn of 1942, neither my parents nor my uncle insisted forcefully enough that my grandparents come and join them in Krakow; when they finally acted, it was too late. Here is how my mother recalled the events:

> By the spring of 1942, we heard rumors—Jan had contacts in the Polish underworld—that the Jews were not only being shot as in Stanislawow, but that they were being deported to camps where they were gassed and their bodies burned. For the first time we head of places like Auschwitz, Majdanek, and especially Treblinka.
> Then in July 1942 we heard that there was major deportation of Jews out of the Warsaw ghetto to Treblinka and certain death. Tadzo wanted to go back to Warsaw to try to save our parents. Despite my protests—I was terrified that they would both be killed—Jan decided to go with him.
> They took the train to Warsaw and stayed in a pension on the Aryan side. There was this high wall, barbed wire, broken glass. They tried to get in, but it was too late. The Jews were being deported, parts of the ghetto were burning, and the entrance was closed. They wouldn't let you in, even if you had the right papers, but Tadzo tried anyway.
> Tadzo was going to go in with false papers, changes of clothes for my parents, and money to try to bribe the guards at the gate. Meanwhile, Jan was to wait for him on the Aryan side. He also had money on him and a gold cigarette case. The plan was that Jan would take a seat on the tram that ran by the ghetto and wait for the three of them to come out. The tram was crowded. Many of the passengers were hanging out of the windows to get a better view of the burning ghetto. The second time the tram went by, Tadzo hopped in. He was alone. He had not been able to get in, and they had failed in getting my parents out.
> When they got back to Krakow neither wanted to talk about it. Tadzo locked himself in his room. Jan said very little, but when we were alone, and I embraced him, he began to speak.
> "I did it for you," he said. "I hate to see you suffer. We were too cautious. We had the money. We could have gotten them out earlier. This trip was all for nothing."9

When briefly after the war we were in Brussels, waiting for the affidavits that would allow us to come to America, my mother ran into Kazik, a first cousin, who had been in the Jewish police in Warsaw during the deportations and had witnessed what had happened to her parents. Kazik told her that her father had been beaten to death in the street in plain sight of my grandmother, and that Stefcia, when her turn came to join the march to the *Umschlagplatz*, had gone insane.

My mother deeply regretted that she had heard Kazik's story, because, as she put it: "The knowledge of how they died lies heavy on my heart. I can see their murder. I can feel it. He told me all the details, Bobi. I won't repeat them to you . . . I can't . . . I won't."[10] But she did. My father and uncle, both of whom were willing to talk to me about other experiences during the war, refused to discuss what had happened the day they had failed to rescue my grandparents.

Gradually after the war my mother drifted into a deep clinical depression, which left her speechless. It was only after a series of electroshock treatments that she regained some of her verve and her long-term memory. I don't know to what extent her depression was a result of her wartime experiences, but I suspect that she, my father, and my uncle were ravaged by guilt for not having done enough to rescue my grandparents. By the time they attempted a rescue, it was too late, and this may have appeared in their eyes as self-serving. They might have gotten Stefcia and Leib out of the ghetto, but they would have endangered the rest of the family, including me, in the process. In effect they had abandoned my grandparents to their fate, but that choice, too, like so many choices during the war, was a choiceless and tragic choice.

Both inside the *Lagers* and outside of them, survivors were left with feelings of guilt and shame, but such feelings should not be confused with moral blame for their behavior. Survivors such as Primo Levi did engage in self-blame for the tragic choices they had to make or even when they had not transgressed any moral code of principles. Given an apparent choice between life and death, a person cannot be blamed for choosing life. Indeed, we are glad that Levi chose life when he did and became the witness that he was. Yet we also grieve for his suicide, which suggested that he felt unnecessary blame and guilt for having survived.

Notes

1. Primo Levi, *The Drowned and the Saved,* trans. Raymond Rosenthal (New York: Vintage Books, 1989), 36–69.
2. The term was coined by Lawrence Langer. See, for example, *Admitting the Holocaust* (Oxford: Oxford University Press, 1995), 46. Although he does not use the term "choiceless choice," Levi himself was well aware of the moral situation that faced the prisoners in the *Lagers:* "In reality, in the vast majority of cases, their behavior was rigidly preordained. In the space of a few weeks or months the deprivations to which they were subjected led them to a condition of pure survival . . . in which the room for choices (especially moral choices) was reduced to zero" (*The Drowned and the Saved,* 49–50).
3. Robert Melson, *False Papers: Deception and Survival in the Holocaust* (Urbana and Chicago: University of Illinois Press, 2000).
4. Primo Levi, *Survival in Auschwitz,* trans. Stuart Woolf (New York: Collier, 1993), 92.
5. Melson, *False Papers,* 54.
6. Ibid., 56.
7. Ibid., 70.
8. Ibid., 82.
9. Ibid., 78.
10. Ibid., 115.

– *Chapter 8* –

"Who am I?" The Struggle for Religious Identity of Jewish Children Hidden by Christians During the Shoah

Eva Fleischner

The great majority of Jewish children who survived the Holocaust were hidden by Christians, either in Christian institutions (schools or convents) or by individuals and families. Many were baptized either to save their lives or because of the rescuers' desire to convert them. Regardless of the motive, many of these children faced an identity crisis as they grew into adulthood after the war. Who were they, Jew or Christian? Who were their "real" parents—those who gave them birth and then "abandoned" them, or those who had saved their lives and whom they often had come to love?

Having been taught to act as Christians, they had to switch identities once more after the war as their biological parents, or the Jewish community, reclaimed them. Some returned to Judaism after years of struggle while others never returned. Their lives are among the most poignant legacies and the most striking "gray zones" left by the Shoah.

When we speak of survivors of the Shoah we usually think of men and women who today are in their seventies, eighties, or nineties who survived the ghettos, the concentration camps, or even the *Sonderkommando*. These are the survivors whom many of us invite to speak to our classes, congregations, or communities. These are the survivors of whom we often say nowadays, "This is the last generation of survivors, the last generation of eye witnesses."

But there is another group of survivors of whom we do not often speak or think: those who survived as children—some as infants only a few months old. Since the early 1990s we have begun to hear and learn more about these "hidden children of the Holocaust," largely through their own efforts, sparked by their desire that the world should know that they too had experienced

Notes for this section begin on page 117.

traumas and nightmares—traumas and nightmares that many of them still carry with them forty or fifty years later.

A brief historical note here: in prewar Nazi-occupied Europe there were about 1.6 million Jewish children. During the war 1.5 million of these children were murdered, so that only 6 to 7 percent were alive at war's end. This figure compares with a survival rate of 33 percent for adult Jews. The difference is easy to understand. Children were a special target of the Nazis because they represented the future of the Jewish people. They were also, of course, the most helpless and vulnerable of all the Nazis' victims; they depended entirely on others for their survival. This meant that they could live only by being hidden.

Jewish children were hidden in convents throughout Europe. They were also hidden, even adopted, by gentile families or individuals, which in Poland invariably meant Catholics. But in other countries, too, there were thousands of Christians who took in Jewish children, passing them off as their own. Whether hidden in convents or with families or individuals, the children had to conceal their Jewish identity and assume a Christian identity, which sometimes included baptism. If the children were very young or came from nonreligious Jewish families, they had as yet no Jewish identity. The only identity that they came to know was the Christian/Catholic identity of their rescuers, the nuns or their foster parents, who in some cases were the only parents they had known. If at the end of the war parents or relatives had survived and returned to claim them, the children once more had to leave behind their identity and learn to become Jews. What was for most of the world the "happy ending" of World War II was, for many of the hidden children, neither "happy" nor an "ending" but rather the beginning of a fragmented, confused existence.

The traumas that these children experienced were numerous: loss of family and home; a sense of abandonment and even of betrayal; in the case of very young children no memories at all of who they were and where they came from; constant exposure danger; forced silence and secrecy; loss of their former name and assumption of a new name; the need to hide Jewishness and to learn to pretend to be Christian; the list goes on and on.

This is how Abraham Foxman many years later described the painful transition from being hidden in a Catholic home to being reclaimed by his Jewish parents:

> When I was an infant growing up in German-occupied Poland I was called Henryk Stanislas Kurpi. To all the world Bronislawa Kurpi was my mother. Actually, she was my Polish Catholic nanny who had promised my parents she would take care of me. I was baptized and raised as a Catholic. My parents survived the camps and returned to claim me. A custody battle with my nanny ensued, but my parents won. Eventually my family and I moved to the United States.
>
> Imagine the confusion and pain this turn of events inflicted on all involved. There was I, a Jewish child, making the sign of the cross in the home of my parents, who were observant Jews. Slowly I had to reclaim my identity and learn about Judaism and what it meant to be a Jew.[1]

In Poland today—to consider only one occupied country—there are men and women, born during the Shoah and now in their fifties and sixties, who grew up as Catholics but who have lived for years with the suspicion that they are not who they, and the world around them, think they are. They always felt that something was missing and that they didn't quite fit in. Here is the story of one of these "modern Marranos,"[2] as told in the documentary film *The Secret*.[3]

Romek

Romek is a Catholic priest in Warsaw. When we first see him he is preparing to celebrate Mass, donning his vestments. In a long interview with the narrator, an American rabbi, Michael Shudrick, he gradually tells his story.

He had devoted and devout Polish Catholic parents, but he always worried that he didn't look like them. One day, as the family stood together in front of a mirror, Romek thought he detected some likeness between himself and his father. Turning to his mother the boy said, "Mom, don't you think I look a little like Dad?" (As he tells this he adds that his mother was a simple woman who never lied.) She made as if to speak, then said nothing. Her silence told him that the answer was no, he did not resemble his father. He blurted out, "If I am a Jew, I don't know what I would do to myself!" To this day he does not know where these words came from deep inside of him.

When he grew up he wanted to become a priest. His father was strongly opposed and tried to talk him out of it. But Romek went ahead anyway and entered the seminary. He was eventually ordained. His father died two years later. Fast forward: Romek is now thirty-five years old and has been a priest for twelve years. His mother is old; they are close, and he visits her whenever he can. One day he asks her about the town where he was born, Swieciany. This is how the conversation went:

"Mom, were there any Jews in the town?"

She looked at him. "Romek," she started to say and stopped.

"Mom, I am not a child anymore. I won't love you any less, I'll love you more. This is *my* truth, and I have to know."

And then, for the first time in his life, he heard these words: "You had wonderful parents [who] loved you very much. They were Jews. They were murdered. I saved you from death."

(Long pause)

"Why do you tell me this only now, so late?"

"Do you remember the scene in front of the mirror? You said, 'If I am a Jew I don't know what I would do!' I felt that you could not live if you knew. Now you are mature, and you can handle it."

Then she tells him how his birth mother came to her, begging her to save her baby. "But we live in a rented apartment, we have only two rooms, everyone would notice. We are afraid. . . . " The Jewish mother: "You are a person of faith, you are a Christian! You believe in Jesus, and Jesus was a Jew. Please! Save my Jewish baby! In the name of the Jew Jesus in whom you believe!"

In her desperation the Jewish mother had hit upon the one argument that the Polish woman, a devout Catholic, could not refuse. "Take him, in the name of the Jew Jesus!" What else could she do but take the baby and raise him as her son?

A little later in the film Romek takes the rabbi to his apartment. On a special shelf he has pictures of his Polish mother and of his Jewish mother, a picture of Christ, and a menorah. "Everything together!" he says. "The most important thing here is the Sh'ma." The rabbi: "If I were to ask you, 'Who are you?' what would you say?"

"I am the son of Jakob and Batia. Maybe because I miss them so much, I am still waiting to meet them. Of course, I am also the son of Pjotr and Leah. I am just a normal man, I hope, whose name is Wechsler-Waszkinel. Nothing more."

All the time he speaks he is on the verge of tears, and at times he cannot go on. He seems, finally, to have made peace with his strange, mixed heritage. He now studies Jewish tradition, but he has remained a priest.

There are thousands of men and women in Warsaw today (and probably in many other places, too) who are not sure who they are. Some are devout Catholics who have discovered that they were born to Jewish parents and have decided to remain Catholic. Some have been able to embrace their newfound Jewishness with enthusiasm. Others are afraid to acknowledge their Jewishness publicly because there is still antisemitism in Poland. They are afraid to "come out" as Jews.

There are as many stories as there were hidden children. Each experience was unique, and some experiences were more painful, or tragic, than others. Much depended on how old the children were at the time, how much of a sense of self and of their Judaism they had when they were hidden, how they were treated by the rescuers (whether nuns or a family), if they were able to maintain some contact with their parents, and so on.

Renée

Renée was born in Mulhouse, Alsace, in 1932.[4] As the persecution against Jews grew, the family fled to France, arriving in Paris in 1940. In the summer of 1942, after the roundup of sixteen thousand Jews by the French police, they went into hiding. The parents found a secret maid's room while the three girls were sent to a convent in Flers, a small town in Normandy. Theirs was not the usual kind of hiding—they did not live in an attic or basement but rather remained in plain sight. They were hiding their Jewishness. In order to pass as Catholics the three girls learned catechism and Catholic ritual. "Actually, I found it comforting," Renée wrote later. Her Jewishness had meant little to her, and she had resented suddenly being labeled a Jew when she didn't feel like one. "Still, I had some scruples. I tried not to cross myself often, and not to go in [the church] through the front door, because that meant having to genuflect."

What she loved was the hymn singing every evening. Singing gave her a feeling that she belonged. "It wasn't so much about God—I didn't believe in God. He had been lousy to the Jews!" The singing made her feel less alone and less scared. Still, she often felt depressed. At such times she used to go and sit at the feet of a Virgin Mary statue. "She was a mother, I told myself. She would understand. One time, when I hadn't heard from my own mother for several weeks, I sat at the base of the statue, picking the petals off a daisy—'She loves me, she loves me not.' A daisy is *marguerite* in French, and that was my mother's name. It was symbolic. When my petal-plucking game ended on 'Loves me not,' I felt terrible. . . ."

The nuns were good to the children who they knew were Jews. When the Germans invaded the town the nuns had the girls baptized. Renée knew it was for their greater safety, but still, she was afraid. "I thought: once you're baptized, that's it. I had guilty visions of flying up to heaven without my parents." After the Allies invaded Normandy, they bombarded the town for three days. Renée was sure she was going to die. On 6 June, D-Day, she made a vow: "God, if you get me out of this I promise to become a nun!"

Soon after the war the children were reunited with their parents. But even though she no longer needed to hide her Jewishness, Renée felt ashamed of being a Jew. For years she told people that she was Catholic; she was afraid that if they found out the truth they would ridicule her. "It was painful keeping that secret," she said. One of her sisters, who had remained in France, never acknowledged being Jewish; she was afraid of antisemitism.

For a long time she was haunted by her vow to become a nun, but eventually she was free of it. In New York, where she settled, she met Jews who were comfortable with their Jewishness, and gradually she began to accept her own. She became a social worker. "Maybe that was my way of being a nun after all!" she says, by being good to her clients, and helping people who were suffering. She now had Jewish colleagues who made her feel less like an outsider.

Let me elaborate on two aspects mentioned in Renée's story because they are of wider relevance to our subject.

1. "Actually, I found it comforting." We find similar sentiments expressed by other hidden children: they found comfort in their Christian/Catholic milieu. This is not surprising. Saul Friedländer tells in his autobiography[5] how he not only came to feel at home in the French convent where his parents had taken him, but that he began to feel a desire to become a priest. (It was a young Jesuit who brought him back to his Jewish roots.[6]) Children who had lost everything—family and home—who had lived in constant danger because they were Jews, often found a new home in the Christian milieu in which they now lived, a milieu that meant security and safety, especially if their rescuers were kind.

The long-term effects of this fragmented childhood in the children's lives varied. Some broke off all relations with their rescuers after the war (though in some cases they reconnected many years later). Others remained in touch and retained fond memories of the Christian environment they had once known. I encountered one example of this when I met Rita.[7]

During the war nine-year-old Rita was hidden in a convent of the Sisters of Notre Dame de Sion in Grenoble. Across the street was a pharmacy owned by a woman whom I interviewed many years later. As we talked she kept referring to "my little Rita," whom she had befriended during the war—the child used to spend time with her during the school holidays when other children went home. After my return to the United States I contacted Rita, who lives in Montreal. She was delighted to have the latest news of her old friend, Mlle Luzet, whom she had been visiting regularly over the years. Rita often came to New York and suggested we meet in St. Patrick's Cathedral. When I arrived there she was sitting quietly in one of the side aisles, obviously comfortable and at ease.

During our lunch together Rita told me how much she had loved the beautiful chapel at the convent, and that she would often go there to be quiet and alone. She spoke fondly of one of the nuns, who used to tuck her into bed every night—"it made me miss my mother much less!" The nuns never made any attempt to convert her. Rita remains a Jew and has raised her two sons as Jews.

2. The baptism of Jewish children by rescuers remains controversial. We know that thousands of hidden children were baptized. The controversy centers on the rescuers' motivation: was it to save the children's lives or to win new converts for the Church? The Roman Catholic Church in particular has a long history of forced conversion. It is not surprising, therefore, that many Jews suspected Catholics of proselytism even during the Shoah. Their fear of losing their children through conversion is illustrated by the following incident:

A Jewish group concerned with the rescue of Jewish children visited several Catholic and Protestant houses that sheltered them. On seeing only crucifixes on the wall and no symbol that recalled to the children their Jewish origin, the group concluded: "When all is said and done, these works [of rescue], however admirable, are only a means to an end: the end is religious propaganda and proselytism."[8] While this conclusion overlooks the fact that the display of any Jewish symbols would have put not only the children but also the rescuers at grave risk, we know nonetheless of many instances where conversion was indeed the goal.

This was not always so. I sometimes encountered a very different attitude—one of utmost respect for the children's Jewish faith—in my research on Catholic rescuers in France.[9] Two instances follow:

In the first I interviewed a nun who was director of a large boarding school in Paris during the war and who had hidden many Jewish children in the school, sending them across the demarcation line at the earliest opportunity. In response to my question of whether she had thought of having the children baptized, I received an emphatic "No" and the following story:

> A woman who was a friend of the school came to see me one day; this is what had happened to her: She had been walking in the street, when a policeman came out of the metro carrying a little Jewish boy in his arms. He looked around furtively and, seeing no one else in the street, came up to the woman. "Madame, won't you please take him? I am supposed to take him away; they have already arrested the parents. I can't get myself to do it, please take him!" She did, and she took him home with her.
>
> Then she came to see me.
>
> I asked her what she intended to do with the child—he was perhaps three years old, very beautiful. "I'll keep him and raise him as if he were my own son." And she did. A year later she came to see me again and said, "You know, Sister, I have been thinking that we really ought to have the boy baptized." "I don't agree," I said. "We don't have the right, since neither of us is his mother." She did not understand, and we began to argue. "You understand nothing," she angrily told me. And I told her, "Madame, you are the one who doesn't understand. You are not the child's mother. He won't be an adult for another fifteen years or so. Only then can he say, 'I am a Jew, and I want to remain a Jew.' Or, 'I don't.'" She went away in anger—she did not understand.[10]

In the second I interviewed Rolande Birgy, who was in her seventies at the time. She had spent much of the war in the French Alps bordering Switzerland. While waiting to send Jewish children across the border she had to find temporary homes for them. She always made sure, first, that the families hiding the children would respect their Jewish faith. She also arranged that on the weekday when French children went to catechism class, priests would instruct the Jewish children in their own scriptures.[11]

The question as to the motivation for baptism on the rescuers' part must remain open. The opinion of the Jewish group quoted above, however, cannot be universally supported.

Pete

I want to speak of one other group of children, some of whom also suffered a crisis of faith as adults. They are the lucky ones who managed to escape and emigrate, with their parents. The family remained intact, they were spared the horrors of the Shoah, and they did not have to go into hiding in order to survive. And yet many of them, too, had doubts about their religious identity. Their parents had been so traumatized that they determined to protect their children against antisemitism and persecution at all costs. They raised them as non-Jews without even letting them know that they were Jews. These are not the "hidden children of the Holocaust" in the sense of Romek or Renée. And yet another type of hiding took place: the children's Jewishness was hidden from them.

Here is part of the story of one of them: F. Peter ("Pete") Sabey, a personal friend, Protestant minister, and therapist for many years, successful and happy in his work. For much of his life he was not allowed to know that he was a Jew. What follows is part of our interview.[12]

Pete was four years old when he, his brother, and his mother emigrated to the United States to join their father, a doctor, who had gone ahead and after many difficulties succeeded in bringing over his family. They settled in Rochester, New York, where Pete's father established his medical practice. "We were enemy aliens," Pete remembers. "We were Germans. I was ashamed of being German—not of being Jewish. I had absolutely no idea that we were Jews." Yet there were small signs now and again that puzzled him.

> There was my Auntie Kate, my father's youngest sister, whom I loved. She lived in Buffalo with her husband, but family gatherings were infrequent. I found out years later that my father had made them solemnly promise never, never to tell me and my brother that we were Jews. Only on that condition were they allowed to visit us. They were secular Jews, but I learned about that only later.
>
> Then there was my Israeli cousin Yardena, who had moved to New York and married an American. Much later we became great friends. They too were secular Jews. I never knew what to make of that. Asking anything about our family history had been taboo—a bit like a child asking about sex and being brushed off. We simply didn't ask or even think about it. At that point I just couldn't incorporate their Jewishness into my life. My family's Jewishness was like the invisible elephant in the middle of the room.
>
> And I remember the time when I came across this strange name in the back of one of my father's books—Sabatzky. I said to Auntie Kate, "That sounds Polish!"
>
> "No, not Polish, absolutely not Polish!" she answered emphatically. I know now that my father was trying to protect us—those were the days of Fr. Coughlin, of quotas in the universities, when Jews couldn't join country clubs.
>
> My mother was pretty, with blond hair and blue eyes. In hindsight I realize she was not only in denial of her Jewishness, but also that she had internalized antisemitism so completely that she was antisemitic herself. When I was seven or eight I remember my mother asking me, "Do I look Aryan?" I had no idea what the word meant, but the question felt weird. And I recall being on a bus with my parents, my mother looking at all the passengers, and then whispering to my father: *"Jod! Jod!"* The implication was that being Jewish was something ugly, something shameful. At the same time I liked many of my Jewish classmates. . . . My parents divorced when I was twelve; my brother and I chose to stay with our father.

Although the family had joined the Methodist church when they first came to Rochester, Christianity was a marginal part of Pete's growing up. He went to Amherst College, "a happy pagan." Gradually, through friendship with the college chaplain, he began to think that maybe there was something to Christianity after all. He decided to go to Union Theological Seminary "for one year only!" he told himself. But as a result of fieldwork in the East Harlem Protestant parish, his world was turned upside down. He decided to return to Union, immersing himself in New Testament studies. Eventually he became chaplain at Lafayette College in Pennsylvania, a Presbyterian school. He became a Presbyterian himself.

As chaplain, Pete always worked ecumenically with students of all faiths. He remembers several times when students from Hillel came to his chaplain's office to ask if he could fill in so that they could have a minyan. "I did it gladly, it was interesting." Those were the late 1960s with Vietnam and the assassinations. Pete fought racism of any kind wherever he encountered it in his subsequent campus ministries at the University of Massachusetts at Amherst and at the University of California at Davis. His parents died within a year of each other in 1988 and 1989. All this time he still had only tortured intimations that his family might be partly Jewish.

> After my father's death we cleaned out his place with my Auntie Kate, and we came across a small book he had written, in which he traced our family history—all the way back to the Crusader Frederick Barbarossa! I was excited! Auntie Kate took the book from me, took one look, and threw it down in anger. "Lies, lies, nothing but lies!" she yelled, stamping her foot on the book again and again. I stood there in a state of shock, completely dumbfounded. Our father had invented our entire family history.

Only after his parents' death did Aunt Kate feel free to tell him all about their family:

> I eventually learned the truth about my grandmother's death—my father's mother. I remembered her from before we left Germany. We had been told that she had died in the bombing of Berlin. Now I found out—from an Israeli cousin who had done research at Yad Vashem—that she had been put on a train to Lithuania with other Jews. When they arrived in Riga after a frightful journey, they were all shot. My father had tried desperately to bring her over in time, but he had failed. How heavily his mother's death must have weighed on him. . . .
> I understand, today, that he wanted to protect us. He wanted to make sure that we would never be victims, would never be exposed to antisemitism; that we would never even know the fate that had befallen my grandmother.

Pete's extended family in Israel, the children and grandchildren of his father's younger sister, were a wonderful expansion of his family life. He visited them a few years ago with his wife Judy. "My cousin Ester is a real Jewish mother, she hugs you, takes you into her arms. They love us, but they could not understand that all this time we had not known we were Jews. While I was in Israel I was almost ashamed of being a Christian—a kind of reversal."

> When I first found out that I was Jewish I was in shock. At one level there was my Auntie Kate, my cousin Yardena, and my dear Jewish friends. At another, deeper level there were all the stereotypes. I used to wonder, Do I look Jewish? What would my therapy clients feel if they knew that I am Jewish? Would some of them no longer want to see me? And there was also a sense of danger: If people found out that I am Jewish, would they want to kill me? A therapist once told me, "If you scratch a Jew you find terror!" All this is much diminished over the years.
> It has taken me a long time to come to terms with my Jewishness. I was able to be public about it only a few years ago. After my parents' death Aunt Kate

encouraged visits with my cousin Yardena. I invited her to come and visit me in California. "I'll come only when you are able to introduce me as your Jewish cousin!" she retorted.

Today I don't want to have any secrets. And when I think of many of my fellow Jews—of Einstein, of Freud, the list is endless—I tell myself, How could I *not* be proud of being Jewish? After I read Cahill's *The Gifts of the Jews* I thought, We really are a wonderful people!

So, I think I have now made peace with my Jewishness. But it is quite clear to me that I'll never become Bar Mitzvahed or join a Jewish congregation—though I enjoy the Seder and have met some wonderful rabbis. If you ask me, "Who are you?" I'd probably say: first a Christian, then a husband and father, and third, maybe, a Jew.

When I think of the hidden children of the Holocaust I am so grateful to have been spared what they went through.

Still, Pete has had his own struggles.

Postscript

Confusion about religious belonging is one of the legacies of the Shoah. And it will not disappear with the death of the last survivor, because in many cases it has been passed on to the children and perhaps even to the children's children. Of Pete's three children, his daughter is happily married to a Jew. The couple has membership in a very progressive United Church of Christ congregation, but they are also active in the Jewish community. Their four-year-old twin daughters are at home in both communities, at least for now. Pete's older son is nonchalant, and his youngest son does not want to think or speak about it.

It was not only Jewish children who had escaped with their parents who were unaware of their Jewish identity. Children born to survivors in the United States (or in other countries where the parents had built new lives) also sometimes suffered from the same confusion of religious identity. The following lines were written by Helen Fremont after she had become a successful lawyer in Boston:

> Lara and I were raised Catholic in a small city in the Midwest. In 1960, at the age of three, I went to nursery school at the convent of the Saint James Sisters, and at six I wore Lara's hand-me-down itchy white petticoat dress to my First Communion. It was the first and last time I would ever swallow a wafer, however, since our family always tiptoed out of church every Sunday before Communion. "It's not an important part of Mass," my mother explained, and for a long time we believed that Communion was a curious American addition to Catholicism.[13]

This is the opening paragraph of *After Long Silence*. The rest of the book tells the amazing story of how the two sisters gradually, over many years, uncovered their parents' secret history and invented lives. After the Shoah, their experiences resonate with those of others who continue to cope with similar gray-zoned realities.

Notes

1. Abraham Foxman in Jane Marks, *The Hidden Children: The Secret Survivors of the Holocaust* (New York: Fawcett Columbine, 1993), ix.
2. The term *Marrano* seems apt to me in this context. It originally referred to the "secret Jews" of Spain who, in 1492 under the reign of Ferdinand and Isabella, were given the choice between expulsion or baptism. The majority chose expulsion, but many accepted baptism, yet continued, secretly, to live as Jews, practicing Jewish customs. As generations passed, many of their descendants were no longer aware of their Jewish origins, nor of the meaning of some of the family rituals still practiced (such as lighting candles on Friday night). Among descendants of Marranos were some famous Catholic saints, e.g., John of the Cross and Teresa of Avila, as well as many of the conquistadores of Mexico. There are descendants of Marranos today in several countries, e.g., Portugal and Mexico, and in New Mexico.
3. *The Secret,* produced by the Ronald E. Lauder Foundation, the Steven Spielberg Foundation, and the Righteous Persons Foundation. Belshir International, Israel.
4. Renée Roth-Hano tells her story in *The Hidden Children,* 34–42.
5. Saul Friedländer, *Quand vient le souvenir . . .* (Paris: Éditions du Seuil, 1978).
6. Ibid., 126–29.
7. In 1985 I received a research grant from the Vidal Sassoon Foundation and Hebrew University to study Catholic rescuers in France. My first interview with Mlle Luzet, which led to my encounter with Rita the following year, took place on 28 October 1985 in her house on a mountainside outside Grenoble.
8. Jacques Duquesne, *Les Catholiques Français sous l'Occupation* (Paris: Grasset, 1966), 262.
9. This research first appeared in my paper titled "Can the Few Become the Many? Some Catholics in France Who Saved Jews During the Holocaust," given at the first "Remembering for the Future" Conference, held in Oxford, July 1988. It is published in the proceedings of the Conference, Yehuda Bauer et al., eds., *Remembering for the Future* (Oxford: Pergamon, 1989, Vol. I), 232–47.
10. Ibid., 241.
11. Ibid.
12. Eva Fleischner, interview with Pete Sabey, Claremont, California, 19 and 25 January 2004.
13. Helen Fremont, *After Long Silence* (New York: Delta, 1999), 7.

– *Chapter 9* –

HITLER'S JEWISH SOLDIERS

Bryan Mark Rigg

Recently, the interest in World War II and the Holocaust has grown dramatically. Books on these topics frequently hit the best-seller list and newspapers run articles nearly every week on some aspect of this time period. Whether it is a controversial study calling the vast majority of Germans "Hitler's willing executioners" or an exposé of IBM's role in the Holocaust, it seems that the general public cannot get enough of the subject matter. With the release of films such as Steven Spielberg's *Schindler's List* and *Saving Private Ryan,* the thirst for knowledge about the Third Reich, World War II, and the Holocaust has only increased.

It is true, however, that there are numerous areas relating to the Holocaust and the Nazi era in general that remain largely unexamined or poorly understood. This research about Jews and *Mischlinge* (partial Jews) in the *Wehrmacht* represents a close study of one such area and, while it does not presume to offer the final word, it is hoped that it will provide its readers with a new way of looking at one of the central issues of the history of the Third Reich and the Holocaust, namely, Jewish identity.[1]

To understand this research, one must first be aware of Jewish law, *Halacha,* and how it defines a Jew. For most Jews today, especially those who are observant, a Jew is a person who is born of a Jewish mother or who converts to Judaism.[2] Knowing this will help one understand the confusion surrounding the individuals researched here and whether they are considered to be Jewish or not.

For the purposes of this essay one must also have a fundamental understanding of the Nazi racial laws. In 1935 the Nazis issued the Nuremberg

Notes for this section begin on page 126.

Laws, which created the categories of Jew, "half-Jew," and "quarter-Jew." The Nazis defined a Jew as a person who had three or more Jewish grandparents. "Half-Jews," according to the Nazis, had two Jewish grandparents. A "quarter-Jew" had one Jewish grandparent. The Nazis also called these people *Mischlinge,* which is a derogatory term loosely translated as "mute," "half-breed," or "bastard." Much confusion surrounded these racial laws. Although the Nazis called the Jews a race, they ultimately had to use religious criteria to define that race. Birth, death, and marriage certificates in Germany always noted the religion of the person involved. As a result, the Nazis relied on these documents to prove someone's "race" instead of looking at his "blood" or physical traits such as large noses or flat feet. Knowing this, one sees how bankrupt the Nazi racial laws were. Also, if a person had converted to Judaism, although his ancestry was purely gentile, the Nazis would view him as a full Jew. However, if a Jew converted to Christianity, then for the Nazis he remained a Jew.[3]

A telling story to illustrate this confusion surrounding these racial laws happened to Erwin Fuchs in 1937. In 1937 half-Jew Erwin Fuchs was five years old. He boarded a streetcar with his older brother. Both boys had been informed that Jews were no longer allowed to sit in public transportation, so they remained standing. A woman sitting near the boys made a little room for Erwin on her seat and said, "Here's half a seat for you, little one." Doubtful, little Erwin looked up at his brother and asked, "Which side of me is Jewish, the right or left?"[4]

When people hear about these Nazi racial laws, they often ask, "How could these people serve in the *Wehrmacht?* I thought everyone of Jewish ancestry was killed." This is where this research becomes very interesting. When full Jews served in the *Wehrmacht*—I estimate their numbers to be a few thousand—it was only with false documents. As far as their superiors were concerned, they were "Aryans" and were treated accordingly.

Half-Jews were required to serve. The conscription laws of 1935 included half-Jews in the draft. However, these men could not become NCOs or officers without Hitler's personal consent. In other words, these men could not become professional soldiers. On the one hand, perhaps Hitler drafted half-Jews because the *Wehrmacht* needed the additional manpower. Hitler knew how many men could be lost in one battle from his experience in World War I, and maybe he felt like he had to field every German he could in the coming war without bending his racial ideology too much. On the other hand, it is often difficult to find rational explanations for Hitler's behavior, and allowing tens of thousands of half-Jews to serve in the *Wehrmacht* did not make sense when looked at through the lens of Nazi racial ideology.

Such ideological problems would soon cause Hitler some difficulties. After the successful defeat of Poland, thousands of decorated half-Jewish soldiers felt disturbed by how the Nazis treated their Jewish family members. Traditionally parents of soldiers were honored by their communities, but Jewish parents of soldiers were excluded from such praise and glory in 1939 and 1940. *Mischling* soldiers found that their mothers and fathers had lost their jobs and could not shop in certain stores, and that Nazis spit on some of them in public. Such mistreatment added insult to injury for *Mischling* families and soldiers who had risked their lives fighting for Germany. Although families of *Mischling* soldiers did enjoy some protection from persecution in the late 1930s and early 1940s, they felt they deserved more. Many *Mischling* soldiers complained to their commanders about the mistreatment of their parents. To the credit of thousands of Aryan officers, they sent such complaints up the chain of command. Complaints also poured into military offices from families whose sons fought in the Polish campaign. Clara von Mettenheim, a Jew, wrote Army Commander-in-Chief General Walther von Brauchitsch on 8 December 1939 on behalf of all half-Jewish soldiers asking him to work with the Nazi Party to alleviate the problems families like theirs experienced. She said:

> I speak to you as the mother of three soldiers, and as an old army wife. . . . My boys are soldiers from head to toe. The god-father of one of my boys is Germany's Crown Prince, and my old friend [General von] Seeckt held the other one at his christening. My sons are *Mischlinge* because of me. During the war, when my sons were fighting in Poland, we were tortured here on the home front as if there were no more important tasks to be done during the war. . . . Please stop this mistreatment of half-Jewish soldiers and their parents.[5]

Frau von Mettenheim felt desperate and did not understand why a family of their social standing had to endure such persecution. She felt responsible for the misfortune that had visited her family and pleaded with Brauchitsch to remove the obstacles her sons faced. She described how angry her son Dieter had become when he returned from the war in Poland to find that his sister had been expelled from certain organizations and his mother was constantly being persecuted. Dieter also accompanied his mother to the Office for Jewish Affairs to pick up her Jewish identification papers. On this particular day he wore his uniform with his decorations. He did so not to provoke anyone but because he was about to return to his unit, never imagining how this would shock the people working in that office. He returned to the front deeply upset and worried about his mother.

Having heard this story and others, Hitler pronounced such events intolerable. Either all half-Jews must immediately leave the *Wehrmacht*, Hitler stated, or the government must protect their Jewish parents. Hitler did not want to protect full Jews, so he ordered the "half-Jews" discharged. The discharge order was not issued until 8 April 1940. Since the next day Hitler invaded Denmark and Norway, all half-Jews in these units remained. Most half-Jews in units preparing for the French campaign that Hitler launched in May 1940 also remained untouched due to bureaucratic mishaps or the secrecy surrounding the plans for the attack on France and the fact that many were not known to be half-Jews.

After Hitler successfully defeated France in six weeks, many half-Jews were located and discharged. According to one source, about seventy thousand were probably discharged at that time. According to this study, 50 percent of all the half-Jews documented were still serving in spring of 1941. In other words, many of them were not affected by the discharge order of April 1940. Hitler allowed those who had proven themselves in battle to apply for clemency, and those half-Jews remained with their units until he decided on their application. This was the policy affecting "half-Jews" in the *Wehrmacht* during the Third Reich.[6]

With the conscription laws of 1935, Hitler also made it mandatory for quarter-Jews to serve, but like half-Jews, they could not become NCOs or officers unless Hitler granted them special permission. This policy remained the same throughout the entire war. How many *Mischlinge* served in the *Wehrmacht*? According to assimilation and mixed-marriage records, birthrates in Germany and Austria, and military records and other government documents, and with the help of a few statisticians and mathematicians, this study conservatively estimates that at least sixty thousand half-Jews and ninety thousand quarter-Jews served in the *Wehrmacht*. Since many historians have not studied the *Mischlinge* in depth before, many have failed to uncover the large number present in Germany during the Third Reich. However, 150,000 *Mischling* soldiers represent only a small percentage of the *Wehrmacht*'s personnel. By 1945 more than seventeen million men had passed through the ranks of the German Armed Forces. Therefore, 150,000 represents less than 1 percent of Germany's total manpower.[7]

Nevertheless, the number of *Mischlinge* serving in the *Wehrmacht* is both startling and important for what it tells us about how Jewish identity was viewed, constructed, and contested by German citizens, Nazi leaders, military commanders, and the Jewish community within German borders, and also for what they tell us about how these perceptions saved some while condemning others to the death camps. Even more startling, this study demonstrates that Hitler played a direct role in permitting *Mischlinge* to serve in the *Wehrmacht*. This essay has already mentioned exemptions and special permissions that Hitler granted *Mischlinge*. Generals, admirals, navy ship captains, fighter pilots, and thousands of ordinary soldiers who were *Mischlinge* served in the *Wehrmacht*, and they did so with Hitler's personal approval.

There were three types of exemptions from the racial laws that allowed a half-Jew to stay in the *Wehrmacht*. One form allowed him simply to remain in the armed forces. The second allowed him to remain and be promoted. These forms were generally called *Genehmigungen* (special permissions). In both of these forms Hitler had included a clause that he would decide after the war whether the *Mischling* was worthy to be declared "Aryan." The third allowed a *Mischling* to describe himself on official documents as *deutschblütig* (of German blood). It gave the recipient all the rights of an "Aryan" except the right to join the Nazi Party or to own farmland. Some quarter-Jews tried for the second and third types just as aggressively as the half-Jews. How many received such exemptions? It is difficult to document the exact number since the different departments that handled these cases did not produce any central database. However, according to Hans Heinrich Lammers, head of the Reich Chancellery, Hitler granted thousands. This study concurs with that assessment, especially since Hitler had decreed that some half-Jews who died in battle were to be posthumously declared "Aryan." He claimed that he did not want to be ungrateful to those half-Jews who had "shed blood" for the Third Reich.[8]

Another question that is often asked about the findings of this research is "Did these men know about the Holocaust?" Jewish and *Mischling* soldiers not only served in armed forces controlled by a government hostile to them as "racially inferior" beings, but many also witnessed the disappearance and occasionally the death of their relatives. During this research, the question of whether or not these men knew about the Holocaust was carefully considered. It was expected at the beginning of this research to find that the majority of these men did know. It turns out, however, that the opposite was true. Many did indeed know about some atrocities, deportations, and executions, but that many of their relatives, once deported, met their fate immediately in a gas chamber and then were burned in a crematorium was beyond their powers of imaginations. The fact that these men might ultimately follow their relatives also remained unknown or unacknowledged by most of them.[9]

The most important evidence to support their ignorance was the half-Jews' experience with the Organisation Todt (OT) forced labor camps. By late summer of 1941, thousands of half-Jews were discharged. In 1944 Hitler decided that this pool of workers should be sent to forced labor camps. Unbeknownst to the half-Jews, this was the last step before their final destruction. If half-Jews knew about the Holocaust, why did they report to their OT deportation stations? The answers to this question are complex. Since most reported to their OT deportation stations when ordered, this is a possible indication that they did not know about the Holocaust. If everyone knew about the Holocaust, one might assume that they would have tried to hide, escape, or possibly commit suicide rather than report at the OT gathering point. It is true that few foolproof hideouts existed in Nazi Germany. Also, the Swiss border was heavily patrolled on both sides, and Sweden was difficult to reach, being separated from Germany by the Baltic Sea. Still, though the odds were stacked against those who attempted to hide or escape, one would think that had half-Jews known what eventually awaited them, they would have tried their luck no matter what the cost. Most received their deportation notices from either the Gestapo or local government employment offices, which gave them several days, if not weeks, to report. This would have given them time to plan an escape. Most reported as ordered because they did not fear for their lives. One half-Jew claimed he knew about Nazi atrocities but still reported to his OT deportation station. He did not know where he was going or why half-Jews were being drafted. He heard about Auschwitz only after the war and did not fear for his life at the time. He does not know why he was not scared, "But that's the truth of the matter—I simply did not think it was dangerous."[10]

When another half-Jew was deported to an OT camp, he recalled another train parked near his own in which he heard people crying and groaning, "a true sound from Hell."[11] However, he still did not think his own life was in danger. One would think that if they had known their deported relatives had probably been murdered, their survival instinct would have taken over and most of them would have tried to flee Germany or gone underground. Nonetheless, the majority were unaware of what lay beyond the OT camps. One half-Jew said that "very few knew or even suspected [that their Jewish relatives had been murdered] at that time."[12] Thus, the majority reported when called to OT. They did not know that this was the beginning of the end for them. Historian Ian Kershaw eloquently explains the difficulty of knowing about the Holocaust.

> During the war years interest in the "Jewish Question" declined still further. The deportation passed off apparently little heeded by the population. Most people seem to have asked little and cared less about the fate of the Jews. The war, its worries and deprivations, dominated opinion. The Jews were out of sight and out of mind. Knowledge of shootings and atrocities in occupied territories was widespread, and rumors about extermination circulated. Details in particular about the systematic gassing program in the camps, appear, however, to have been largely unknown.[13]

This research offers several historical insights besides showing that it was difficult to know about the Holocaust. It shows that the Third Reich cannot be understood in extremes of black and white. Not everyone who wore a uniform with a swastika was a Nazi as we use that word today. Not everyone who had Jewish ancestry was a victim of the death camps. This research shows that there were hundreds of thousands of people persecuted by the Nazis not because they called themselves Jewish, but because the Nazis called them Jewish and treated them accordingly. With this in mind, it is interesting to note that the half-Jews in the eastern territories were labeled as full Jews by the Nazis, although most of these people who were sent to the death camps would not have called themselves Jews; however, the Nazis killed them because they considered them to be Jews. Not every German officer was a pure "Aryan," and not every Aryan officer was a rabid antisemite. The *Mischling* experience clearly demonstrates the complexity of life in the Third Reich. Nazi policy toward these people was a maze of confusion and contradictions that reflected the regime's uncertainty about how to deal with Germans of partial Jewish descent.

Mischling policy was difficult to enforce for many reasons. One reason was that the Nazi ideology of "race" came into conflict with the goal of maintaining power. If Hitler had treated the *Mischlinge* too harshly in the 1930s and early 1940s, he might have lost support from thousands of Aryans in key positions in the economy, armed forces, and government who had *Mischling* relatives. Another reason for the difficulty of enforcing *Mischling* policy was that, since they did not exist as a category of people before 1935, bureaucrats had to rely on church and city or county registry records, denunciations, and honest confessions to identify *Mischlinge*. In the *Wehrmacht*, enforcement, particularly of discharge orders, was often hindered by officers who valued trained soldiers more than the racial laws. The fact that Hitler reserved the right to grant exemptions from these laws reinforces the perception that even he recognized how impractical these laws and how contradictory his goals were. However, as historian Henry Turner wrote, Hitler was driven by "the unshakeable conviction that reality would eventually conform to his will."[14] Hitler had complete faith in his abilities to change reality to conform to his irrational philosophy. Diplomatic and military triumphs from 1933 to 1940 reinforced his belief in his own infallibility as a leader, prophet, and racial hygienist. Hitler perverted Germany's legal system and forced it to implement his racial ideals as laws.

In light of how aggressively Hitler pursued the extermination of the Jews, it is surprising how much time he spent reviewing applications for exemptions from the racial laws submitted by *Mischlinge*. One can understand his careful analysis of the pros and cons of removing a *Mischling* general from his post, but many to whom Hitler granted these coveted exemptions were common soldiers with the ranks of private or NCO. Hitler's exemptions and the actions of thousands of Aryan officers, including men close to Hitler, in support of *Mischlinge* contradicted the Nazis' *Weltanschauung*. What is particularly difficult to believe is that the arch antisemite Hitler himself granted even one exemption from the racial laws. But he personally issued many. As Kershaw wrote, "Nothing was as it seemed in the Third Reich."[15]

Some of Hitler's actions suggest that he believed Jewish "blood," even in minute amounts, could ruin a person. Other actions suggest that Hitler believed Gregor Mendel's theory of genetics by which a *Mischling* could be 100 percent "Aryan" if he inherited all of his "blood" from the Aryan parent. But Hitler consistently wavered on his views about race. Many of his decisions regarding *Mischlinge* do not reflect the pure categories of race so central to Nazi rhetoric and philosophy.

Mischling policy also demonstrated the triumph of ideology over reason. Hitler should have focused his efforts on winning the war first and then he could have implemented whatever racial policy he wanted in the territories he dominated. The *Wehrmacht* discharged tens of thousands of "half-Jews" on Hitler's orders throughout his regime. If winning the war had been his top priority, Hitler could easily have recalled all of these soldiers to active duty on the Russian front. But even in the winter of 1942, when Germany needed every able-bodied man to fight, Hitler still ignored the thousands of *Mischlinge* previously discharged from the *Wehrmacht*. Instead, Hitler focused upon whether a few hundred *Mischlinge* deserved exemptions. Hitler was giving exemptions even in 1944 as his regime crumbled before his eyes. If the war was more important than the destruction of the Jews, then Hitler could have allowed thousands of *Mischlinge* to serve in the *Wehrmacht*. The vast majority would have fought bravely for their homeland, and even the worst soldier would have been useful as cannon fodder. Hitler apparently valued a pure Aryan society more than victory. Hitler took this exemption process seriously and believed he had the power to discern a person's true racial makeup. For Hitler, carrying out racial policy was simply more important than winning the war. Hitler once said, "The Jewish question takes priority over all other matters."[16]

After the attempt on his life in July 1944, Hitler revoked many of the exemptions he had granted earlier. He needed to blame someone for this attack, and *Mischlinge* presented an easy target. To order the discharge of so many high-ranking officers late in 1944, even generals who had received the *Ritterkreuz*, simply because they were partially Jewish, did not make strategic sense.

But as the war worsened, Hitler's persecution not only of full Jews but also of *Mischlinge* dramatically escalated. *Mischlinge* often found themselves the losers in a game where the rules changed at the whim of their opponent. Many of these men, who had served loyally and had been awarded some of Germany's highest honors, would eventually have been subjected to the same fate as the Jews. Had the war continued, or had Germany won, most half-Jews would have been exterminated. Quarter-Jews would have suffered further discrimination, and probably selective extermination.

This research also departs from pure historical research to enter the more existential realm of questions of identity. The following story illustrates some of the identity issues that this study often confronted. When I interviewed "half-Jew" Heinrich Hamberger in Munich, he explained that he and his army buddies met in a pub once a month. After discussing the matter, he agreed to take me there, but only on two conditions: first, under no circumstance would I tell anyone about his Jewish descent, and second, I would tell them I studied something else besides *Mischlinge* who fought in the *Wehrmacht*. I agreed.

When we entered the pub, loud voices greeted us, and the smell of smoke smarted our nostrils. I watched the years melt away as these former soldiers relived the "good old days." After a while, Hamberger left me alone and I started to talk with his former company commander. He wanted to impress upon me how honorable the *Wehrmacht* had been. I mentioned that during my studies I had come across an anomaly that Jews and men of Jewish descent had fought in the *Wehrmacht*. "Have you ever heard about this?" I asked. The commander looked around, spotted Hamberger on the other side of the room, and nodded his old, scarred head. He lowered his raspy voice to a conspiratorial tone: "Don't tell Hamberger, but we know he's a Jew." I acted surprised and promised not to tell. This event illustrates the universal fear present among many *Mischlinge* who feel insecure about their "Jewishness."

Moreover, Hamberger's comrades did not appear to have cared that he was Jewish. To them, he was simply a member of the unit; he was a comrade. This story highlights the irony inherent in the fact that most *Mischlinge*'s fellow soldiers viewed them as brothers-in-arms, which created strong bonds of friendship. Many non-Jewish *Wehrmacht* soldiers did not view "Aryan" and *Mischling* unit members differently. This fact, with time, greatly influenced the way *Mischlinge* came to view themselves and their time in the armed forces. Whether they felt their comrades knew about their true identity or not, they started to feel like they were among close friends who were loyal to one another regardless of circumstances.

Notes

1. For additional detail and citations, see Bryan Mark Rigg, *Hitler's Jewish Soldiers: The Untold Story of Nazi Racial Laws and Men of Jewish Descent in the German Military* (Lawrence: University Press of Kansas, 2002).
2. Ibid., 277 n. 17.
3. Ibid., 94–100.
4. Ibid., 19.
5. Ibid., 113.
6. Ibid., 116–19, 209.
7. Ibid., 51–65.
8. Ibid., 172–235.
9. Ibid., 247–66.
10. Ibid., 262.
11. Ibid.
12. Ibid.
13. Ian Kershaw, "Popular Opinion in the Third Reich," in Jeremy Noakes, ed., *Government, Party, and People in Nazi Germany* (Exeter: University of Exeter Press, 1980), 71.
14. Henry Ashby Turner, *Hitler's Thirty Days to Power: January 1933* (London: Bloomsbury, 1996), 36.
15. Ian Kershaw, *Hitler 1936-45: Nemesis* (New York: W. W. Norton, 2000), 406, 709.
16. See George Victor, *Hitler: The Pathology of Evil* (Washington, DC: Brassey's, 1998), 197.

– Chapter 10 –

A GRAY ZONE AMONG THE FIELD GRAY MEN
Confusion in the Discrimination Against Homosexuals in the Wehrmacht

Geoffrey J. Giles

Already in June 1927, more than five years before Hitler came to power, the Nazi parliamentary deputy (and later Interior Minister) Wilhelm Frick railed against homosexuals in the Reichstag, who would inevitably bring about the "downfall of the German people." He called for tough measures against homosexuality, which was especially fostered by "Jewish sex criminals and Jewish moral contamination."[1] Homosexual victims of the National Socialist regime were indeed treated appallingly later, but they lay in what was probably the ultimate gray zone of the Holocaust because they were so difficult to identify. From official government or seized institutional records it was fairly straightforward to track down a Jew or even a Socialist. But how to find the elusive homosexuals? It is true that there were extensive police records, and a broad range of gay and lesbian clubs and societies kept membership lists during the Weimar Republic. But they by no means covered the whole, or even the majority, of the homosexual population of Germany. Most homosexuals only emerged into the public eye if they were unfortunate enough to fall foul of the police; otherwise they led very private lives. Just how many homosexuals were there in Nazi Germany? Even if we take the lowest likely estimate of 5 percent of the population, that still means a group of more than three million individuals, a figure hugely in excess of the half-million Jews in Germany at the start of the Third Reich.

This essay was prepared during a fellowship in Munich from the Alexander von Humboldt Foundation, for whose backing I am deeply grateful. Thanks are also due to the United States Holocaust Memorial Museum, the German Marshall Fund, and the University of Florida, without whose support some of the earlier research would not have been possible.

Notes for this section begin on page 144.

The armed services or *Wehrmacht,* as a homosocial institution, offer an example both of long experience with and confusion over homosexuality.[2] With the coming of World War II, we can say that the majority of the most sexually active young German men served in its ranks. Its handling of the homosexual question, the target of almost paranoid police campaigns in the years following Hitler's murder of the homosexual SA leader Ernst Röhm, is therefore illuminating. The *Wehrmacht* tended to treat homosexual offenses differently from Heinrich Himmler's police. One important distinction was that relatively few offenses within the military involved young teenagers, so that homosexuals could not be characterized *tout court* as child molesters and thus automatic outcasts from society. The generals regarded the phenomenon as a regrettable but probably inevitable concomitant of the isolation of men, and did not prosecute it with much vigor, except where an abuse of rank had occurred in carrying out a sexual assault.

Certainly the Fritsch Affair, involving (entirely false) charges of homosexuality against the commander-in-chief of the army in 1938, was a great embarrassment. Yet the army was not receptive to the blacklists of arrested homosexuals and male prostitutes that the Gestapo pressed upon it that year. Noting the danger that many of these young men could be disadvantaged for the rest of their lives on the basis of a rather harmless youthful indiscretion, it declined to set up a permanent card index on homosexuals, noting rather archly that it had more important things to do.[3] Certainly the exaggerated masculinity and militarism of Nazi society as a whole carried with it a certain, simmering homoeroticism, which has been rather overemphasized by Klaus Theweleit.[4] In Joanna Bourke's excellent study of male bonding among British soldiers in World War I, she shows vividly (in part through photographs) the uninhibited physical closeness of the men. Yet even though she writes of men kissing each other, she refrains from suggesting any sexual activity between them.[5] Indeed, she claims that "the strain of war had 'de-sexed' men, rendering them impotent," and elsewhere that "many men were too tired even to masturbate."[6] My research on Nazi Germany casts doubt on these assertions. While the known cases are only small in number, that is probably because most such activity was consensual and private and did not attract the attention of third parties. Certainly it is not something that would be mentioned in letters or memoirs, which are the most important sources for Bourke.[7]

As Germany steered toward war in the spring of 1939, the chief psychiatrist of the army, Professor Otto Wuth, gave a lecture to air force and navy military judges on "The Psychopath Problem in the Armed Services" during a short training course on military law in wartime. He included homosexuals in this category and provided detailed comments on the topic.[8] A genetic disposition to homosexuality had not yet been proven, according to Wuth. Research on twins to this end had been inconclusive. Rather, every person was born bisexual, he claimed, with personality traits of both his or her father and mother. During adolescence youths were in a state of flux. Initially they focused more on their own bodies through masturbation, but gradually, through such worthy institutions as ballroom dance classes, their interest and infatuation with the opposite sex grew and settled along the normal path of heterosexual attraction of its own accord.

Wuth, however, confidently pronounced homosexuals as a group to have clear psychopathic traits on the basis of their "frequent" alcohol abuse and a 3 percent suicide rate, ignoring the intense societal pressures that might have driven them to the latter. Their "frequent insincerity, well-known to every expert" simply reinforced the conclusion for him, based on very sloppy reasoning though it was.[9] With homosexuals there was a developmental flaw. Their sex drive could be easily misdirected. "Masturbation can persist, the focus on one's own sex can become anchored by experiences with comrades or by seduction, and then we have homosexuality." Reminding his audience that this was no small problem, Wuth put the number of homosexuals in Germany at the time at two to three million, or 4 percent of the population. Young men who had been temporarily "derailed" through seduction held promise of being susceptible to corrective measures, though no one had yet figured out how to distinguish conclusively between "real" and merely "temporary" homosexuals. The bottom line for the judges, however, was that it didn't really matter whether a homosexual was suffering from a permanent or a temporary, curable condition. Homosexual *acts* were punishable by law one way or the other, and it was with these that they should concern themselves.

Already in the early months of the war, Field Marshal Keitel warned in a memorandum that excessive drinking could lead to homosexual offenses, citing the case of one lieutenant who had disgraced himself with Hitler Youths on twenty-five occasions.[10] A few weeks later soldiers were reminded that inebriation could not be used as a mitigating circumstance if the person had knowingly made himself drunk. One example given was of a sergeant who was aware that he felt homosexual urges under the influence of alcohol but had nevertheless drunk to excess and then had sex "with a willing young man."[11] Such memos had little effect. Army chief Brauchitsch was still complaining in June 1941 (on the eve of the invasion of the Soviet Union) that homosexual incidents were regrettably on the rise, owing to excessive alcohol abuse.[12]

The German air force did not simply follow Wuth's general directives on the treatment of homosexuals, despite the fact that the army's chief psychiatrist counted as the senior adviser to all three services. "Not every homosexual is a psychopath!" wrote the inspector of the Luftwaffe Medical Corps in October 1941, in apparent contradiction to Wuth. Yet if that statement sounded hesitant, a more sweeping condemnation followed shortly after: "Sexual perverts are liable to undermine the *Wehrmacht* and must be removed from it." It became clear that the Luftwaffe was using the word "homosexual" to describe everyone who engaged in homosexual activity, even on a single occasion. "The only exception among the homosexuals are very young soldiers with a still-unstable sex drive, if it is indisputably evident that they have been seduced and a genuine homosexual disposition can be regarded as out of the question." The inspector, however, gave no instructions on how to determine this.¹³

As always, a rather offhand remark by Hitler himself could set in motion a whole shift of policy. In August 1942 Hitler responded to a request for clemency that had been brought all the way up to him for adjudication. The appeal, lodged by a first lieutenant deemed to be a "true" homosexual, sought to substitute military service at the front for the remaining prison term. You simply cannot not change nature, responded Hitler, and it was "therefore *wrong to permit a man to prove himself before the enemy*" [emphasis in original]. In the case of such offenses carried out while a man was on active service, the guilty must undergo the entire punishment and then be expelled from the ranks. On a second occasion he repeated the same sentiment: "Anyone convicted on the grounds of unnatural indecency, even if [committed] in a state of total inebriation, *may never be offered [the option of] proving himself before the enemy* and rehabilitation" [emphasis in original].¹⁴ The latter statement sounded somewhat more comprehensive and caused a flurry of activity, because it did not accord to practice hitherto, which had sought to distinguish between "real" and "temporary" homosexuals, in order not to occasion too many discharges or provide too easy a way out from military service.

Until 1942 the practice of the air force had been to punish severely only those cases where an ingrained homosexuality *(Veranlagung)* could be established. These men were packed off to a prison camp and dishonorably discharged. The same thing happened for cases involving a serious abuse of rank in sexual assaults. On the other hand, if a man could show that he had been seduced, or had performed homosexual acts "as a result of sexual overexcitement," he was not normally expelled. Those men deemed to be "temporary" homosexuals *were* reintegrated into the service after serving out their sentence. They were "as a matter of principle offered the possibility of proving themselves at the front."¹⁵ Hitler's blanket statement on the treatment of offenders now threatened to quash this more pragmatic *modus agendi* and result in a significant further depletion of the ranks. The army admitted that it didn't really know whether Hitler's statement was meant to be applied across the board, or whether it was simply intended to target the "true" or genetic homosexuals. Field Marshall Keitel was evidently too timid to ask Hitler directly and expose himself to the suspicion either that he did not understand the policy or that he was criticizing it. He decided to find out what other ministries and agencies thought the policy was. The results of the rather embarrassed "confidential personal inquiries" showed considerable variation all along the line about the target group and their treatment. Army officials summarized the main practice of the different agencies involved.¹⁶

The Reich Ministry of Justice assumed that "every homosexual act of an *adult* person" [emphasis in original] was the real thing and not just a passing phase. It was the result of a genetic fault, and the guilty parties would always pose a danger to the community. The ministry felt that the commuting of sentences or granting of pardons was generally "out of the question." Leniency was only feasible in the case of errors committed during puberty, *if* "after a suitably long time" the development of healthy feelings could be documented.

Gestapo headquarters, on the other hand, believed that it was possible to distinguish, even among adults, between those of a fixed homosexual disposition and those who had been seduced or merely "derailed" on a single occasion. It agreed that the former were hopeless cases and it was useless to think that they might reform themselves. The second group, however, were viewed by the Gestapo as altogether capable of reintegration into the community, and here a milder punishment was entirely appropriate. The Gestapo expert (presumably Erich Jacob) revealed to the army that the estimate of "men with a homosexual disposition (including borderline cases)" now ran at four million. Not even Himmler believed that, so this figure must rest on a misunderstanding by the *Wehrmacht* in conflating the "nature and nurture" categories (the incurable with the curable). On the other hand, the Gestapo may have been trying to frighten the *Wehrmacht* into a realization that it could not afford to expel such huge numbers of men from service, which would have created a logistical nightmare for the police at the height of its Holocaust involvement.

Policy among Himmler's other activist institution, the criminal police, in the fight against homosexuality was of course similar, but more details emerged here. Even the apparent single derailments fell under continued surveillance. Multiple offenders, either those with several convictions or those who were known to have seduced several other men, were shipped off for "preventive detention" in a concentration camp; that is, they were incarcerated without trial outside the normal justice system. The criminal police announced that it had already released some homosexuals from preventive detention and sent them off for military service. It did not want them back again. The principal problem was that it had no room for them. There was "barely any space left" in the concentration camps, and if the military was going to start expelling all these suspected homosexuals, then it would have to build its own camps. We have to see these remarks in context. They were made only about six months after the Wannsee Conference had shifted the "Final Solution" into top gear. Himmler needed in 1942 to concentrate all his efforts on the death camps, rather than expanding the concentration camp system, for which financing would have been difficult to obtain at this stage of the war.

Homosexuals in fact formed a tiny proportion of the concentration camp population. With some four million of them on the loose, however, they could easily overwhelm the capacity of the camp or prison system if indiscriminate arrests were made at a time when the logistics of the "Final Solution" against the Jews were proving difficult enough to cope with. And Heydrich, the master coordinator of that program, had just been murdered a few weeks earlier. Wuth warned against discharging homosexuals after they had completed their punishment. That would lead to a rush of homosexual acts committed by soldiers purely in hopes of escaping frontline service. It should be noted, then, that the army was taking a tougher line than the actual protagonists on this issue, Himmler's police.

The Nazi Party's own policy was to expel both the "true" homosexuals from its ranks as well as all those who had committed any type of homosexual act. Here there was to be no compromise, and indeed Martin Bormann upheld this strict interpretation to the very end, as countless rejected requests for reinstatement show. Himmler's SS sounded the most radical of all agencies, because its disciplinary courts (which also covered the police) in theory punished the homosexuality of its members with a mandatory death sentence. That, however, was infrequently carried out, and Himmler did sometimes order *Frontbewährung* following appeals for clemency, in apparent contradiction with his own policy and Hitler's specific instructions.[17]

There were, then, important differences here, and Keitel's adviser, Dr. Lehmann, felt that a more formal statement than this should be required from the various agencies before the policy of the army could be set in place. Until then, he advised that convicted soldiers with a presumed homosexual disposition should on no account be permitted to prove themselves at the front, but rather they should be sent away to a military prison camp in order to safeguard military discipline. Beyond this he suggested that the army, too, should consider introducing the death penalty for severe offenses of the type that in civilian courts would earn a penitentiary sentence. That sounded rational, yet many more convictions were now leading to the penitentiary than in normal times due not to the increasing gravity of the crimes but rather to the growing harshness of judicial practice. Though nothing came of this radical and quite unjustified idea, it does indicate that influential military officers, generally taken to be less fanatical than their Nazi counterparts, did not fall far behind them when it came to homophobia and the desire to execute offenders.[18]

As the discussion about the nature of homosexuality continued in the following months, a surprisingly frank memorandum emerged from the pen of Wuth, summarizing the current state of knowledge, or more correctly, the lack of it. He admitted that there was no certain knowledge about the deeper causes of homosexuality and that no proof existed of the inheritability of sexual anomalies. Repeating the line he had taken three years earlier, which itself was based on the research of Emil Kraepelin and others, Wuth affirmed everyone's initial bisexuality and attributed a homosexual tendency to "unfavorable sexual experiences." In his view, however, such experiences would not have a lasting effect on most people. He saw a psychopathic disorder of "unstable drives" as a precondition for a lasting deviation. Wuth made two important points in his report. First, he stressed that the question of "nature or nurture" *(anlagebedingt oder umweltbedingt)* was wrong. It was more a case of "predominantly nature or predominantly nurture." Both played a role, and the individual had to "fight" both, as he put it in a phrase typical of his time. His second important point was that those men in whom a genetic disposition had come to the fore were not certain to commit illegal sexual acts. They faced not an "unalterable destiny" but merely a "threatening destiny." Wuth did grant them a measure of free will. Adult homosexuals could do nothing about being homosexuals, but they could, and of course should, do something about restraining themselves from carrying out homosexual acts.

Unfortunately, it was extremely difficult to identify the irremediable homosexuals by looking at their sexual activity alone. So, too, with their physical appearance: the arguments advanced by a number of doctors that homosexuals had an unusual and identifiable physique had not been proven. Sometimes they were even married and had children. The trick was, according to Dr. Wuth, to remember that they were psychopaths who would also reveal their lack of control in other criminal ways. A look at their police records demonstrated neatly that "true" homosexuals as a group were criminals. More than one-third of them either had convictions or were under suspicion of a crime. Ignoring the fact that the police often trumped up charges against people who had fallen foul of them, Wuth seemed to be using this as a means of justifying the punishment, rather than the treatment, of homosexuals. So while he avoided some of the dogmatism of other experts in the field about the nature of homosexuality, he was far from giving suspects the benefit of the doubt. Even a random homosexual act carried out in a state of drunkenness was enough to strip the culprit of any rank. It was a sign of such decay that the person was totally unsuited to stand in a position of authority over others.[19]

Wuth repeated the same sentiments in a similar memo to Field Marshal Keitel the same day, cautioning, however, that it would be unwise to expel everyone from the military who had committed any kind of homosexual offense, especially on a mere single occasion. That was how Hitler's will ought to be interpreted: no position of authority for homosexuals but no automatic escape from service, either. Sterner measures in Party organizations were perhaps appropriate because their membership was selective, where the military was meant to embrace the entire male population. The most drastic punishment, the death penalty, should only be used for "crass seducers of the young" and in cases of an abuse of rank. Even then, thought Wuth, its deterrent effect would be limited unless there were full reporting of these cases in the press, which was unlikely because it would provide unwelcome fuel for enemy propaganda such as had occurred in the past around Ernst Röhm. If the latest Gestapo estimate of four million homosexuals leaked as well, the effect would be disastrous, creating an impression of a creeping homosexualization of the country. Wuth thought that figure much too high, but if there had been a notable increase, then it must be a statistical fluke caused perhaps by the expansion of the scope of German law, especially §175 of the Reich penal code, regarding what constituted a homosexual act. Or perhaps it was due to the "systematic poisoning of youth" that had occurred in the *Wandervogel* and other pre-Nazi youth movements, now that those "infected youths" were reaching adulthood. Again we see here that even an educated expert outside the Nazi movement could utterly accept the mendacious vilification meted out by the Nazi propaganda machine about its rivals, when only a few moments earlier he had been downplaying the importance of adolescent episodes. What steps did the military need to take to address the homosexual problem? He suggested pep talks by medical officers, but on a more practical level, sexual frustration should be alleviated by the provision of more leave (was he so unaware of the military situation that he thought this a possibility?) and by the construction of brothels.

When it came to punitive measures, however, Wuth now outdid himself in radical proposals. Agreeing with Hitler that heroic behavior in battle could not rehabilitate a homosexual, he nevertheless argued that the guilty should be sent to the front to face the enemy in special punishment battalions rather than languishing in military prison camps. These would presumably be deployed in the most dangerous parts of the line, as Himmler ordered for his Dirlewanger Brigade, service in which left a poor chance of survival. Wuth also wanted a comprehensive evaluation, preferably psychiatric, of every single case—no easy task with the hundreds of offenders each year in the military. He repeated that there was no objection to the death penalty for those who seduced minors, but he urged that castration should be applied more often. Even though he admitted that it was not 100 percent effective, he thought it worked 70 to 80 percent of the time in reducing both criminal and sexual activity. Wuth also urged the field marshal to introduce some "visible physical marking" *(sichtbare körperliche Kennzeichnung)* of recidivists. That, in the discourse of the time, suggests some form of permanent tattoo for the repeat offenders. Given his own admission regarding the uncertainty of identifying the "true" homosexuals, this appalling idea went even further than the SS administration of the concentration camps, for whom a cloth pink triangle was quite sufficient. We have evidence that some homosexual camp inmates managed to exchange their pink triangle for one of a different color, thus lessening their chance of arbitrary maltreatment. With a tattoo, the prisoner would be marked for life. This radical notion suited Wuth very well.[20]

Now that the issue of castration had been raised again, the army had the opportunity to put it into practice a few weeks later. The soldier Viermund B. had been punished on two occasions for homosexual offenses and had now (it is unclear under what coercive circumstances) submitted a request to be castrated in order to avoid "further conflicts with the law." To remove himself from further temptation, he also requested his discharge from the army. The latter was a very bad idea, thought Wuth, because in civilian life he would be given an "opportunity for homosexual activity that might possibly even remain undetected." No, he needed to remain on active service. It was pointless to take an oath from him to refrain from further such acts, because the promise of a homosexual was worthless. Wuth upheld his prejudice that homosexuals were "in general notoriously unreliable" in this regard.[21] But castration was certainly a desirable option.

Ignoring his recent remarks about the only partial success of castrations, Wuth now went further and claimed that research had shown a 97.78 percent success rate in the castration of sex offenders. And he declared that in another study almost three-quarters of those castrated reported that their libido and potency had been extinguished after only one or two months with the doctors reporting "relatively small" physical or psychological side effects. I have discussed elsewhere how untrue such claims were, but they provided a strong argument for the advocates of this cruel procedure. Wuth's only reservation here was that military field hospitals should not get into the business of carrying out castrations and sterilizations. Viermund B. should be castrated in a civilian hospital (at his own expense!) and return for duty as quickly as possible.[22]

By now the policy of the army was being standardized in a way that went against Hitler's apparent call for expulsion from the ranks. The generals feared a widespread depletion of personnel at a time when the tide of war was beginning to turn. They therefore sought ways to control, to punish, and yet to retain homosexual offenders in uniform, if only as cannon fodder. Yet for all the discussions going on in the medical corps, it was clear that they still did not understand homosexuality.

Wuth warmed to his task as chief advisory psychiatrist by collecting a large amount of statistical data on homosexual offenders in the military, presumably to convince his superiors of the enormity of the problem. He was somewhat frustrated in his attempt at totality by the refusal of the Justice Ministry to pass on the names of *all* men involved in homosexual incidents. The ministry felt it unfair that someone who had been seduced into a temporary lapse might be branded for life as a homosexual. Wuth had to content himself with notification of male prostitutes and seducers of minors, otherwise falling back on the cases occurring within the ranks of the armed services. This, then, was a reversal of the situation in 1938, when the army itself had rejected such lists over concern about lifetime stigmatization.

Armed with these numbers Wuth drew up a substantial memorandum aimed at further regularizing procedures against such offenders. The statistics on homosexual offenses did not say precisely what Wuth wanted them to, but that did not stop him from forging ahead with his own interpretation. Police investigations of suspected homosexuals skyrocketed in the years immediately before the war. Wuth's figures showed the following details about military personnel arrested by the civilian authorities:

1937	32,360	arrests (of whom 308 were *Wehrmacht* members)
1938	28,882	(102)
1939 (first half)	16,748	(327)
1942 (second half)	4,697	(332)

He was cheered that the investigations of the police were now only one-quarter of what they had been in 1939 and suggested that this meant the situation was coming under control. The practice of sending multiple seducers to a concentration camp after the completion of their prison sentence was having a positive effect here, he argued. His figure of such pink triangle prisoners dated from 1940, when there were 2,284 of them, and he assumed the numbers would now be greater. He ignored altogether the fact that the numbers of *Wehrmacht* soldiers being charged was not dropping but increasing significantly. Even before the outbreak of the war there were more soldiers charged in the first half of 1939 alone than there had been for the whole of 1937.

The number of soldiers in wartime, against whom charges of homosexuality had been brought by the military authorities, was rising as well:

1939	
August to December	185
1940	
First quarter	229
Second quarter	241
Third quarter	291
Fourth quarter	373
1941	
First quarter	405
Second quarter	474
Third quarter	451
Fourth quarter	370
1942	
First quarter	401
Second quarter	403
Total	3,823

Again shutting his eyes to his own figures, Wuth claimed that the problem was evidently declining. His explanation was that the stresses and strains of frontline combat gave less opportunity for such acts. Yet the figures for the summer of 1941, when Operation Barbarossa began, are the highest of all, which seems to puncture his theory. Wuth had an answer for that: he claimed that records showed the majority of cases occurring in the rear areas, under the influence of alcohol, and not at the fighting front. That may have been the case, though it may also be true that units at the front did not have time to report such incidents or that they could not afford to pull men out of the line. For Wuth, then, the situation was not as bad as previously assumed. There was too much exculpatory talk of sexual deprivation leading to homosexual acts, in the way this had long been observed among sailors on board ships or prisoners in jails. Wuth repeated his view that the fighting troops at the front line were too busy to worry about sex at any cost. "If a [homosexual] perpetrator among the troops approaches a normal man, the latter will soon tell him what he thinks of him and will report him. If he approaches a like-minded man, then both of them are punishable."

If we assume that Wuth was not so entirely ignorant of the sex drive of the average virile young soldier as he appeared to be, then we must assume that he was following a particular agenda here. His aim was not like that of Dr. Matthias Göring, who claimed to be able to cure many homosexuals; rather, he sought to capture and punish as many homosexuals as possible, even merely suspected homosexuals. The willing victim was just as guilty as the "perpetrator." And when they were sent off to a punishment unit, he now recommended not a "bodily marking" as before but rather "a badge of a particular color attached to their uniform." He felt confident that this would really turn the other prisoners against them. Wuth cited the experience with the pink triangle in the camps, which the postwar testimony of victims has confirmed: "It has been apparent in the concentration camps that criminals such as burglars, thieves, and so on sharply reject those people who are interned because of §175. Such a badge, which enables observation by all the [other] prisoners, also makes the formation of any groups or cliques among these perpetrators impossible." The outlawing and thus complete emotional isolation of homosexuals from other types of prisoners, as well as from other homosexuals, should be deliberately encouraged, in Wuth's view.

That such desolation would contribute to the high death rate among pink triangle camp inmates must surely not have escaped the attention of a senior psychiatrist. Wuth, however, wanted to get rid of a problem that he did not really know how to solve. He was less interested in the fate of the men themselves than in the reputation of the army and indeed of Germany. Repeatedly he mentioned the fuel that could be given to enemy propaganda by revelations about this issue in Germany, even though he thought Britain, with its own contingent of three to four million homosexuals (according to his reading of Havelock Ellis), would be wise to keep quiet on this matter. Wuth therefore strongly urged that no discussion of homosexuality take place even in scientific journals. The safest procedure was for the military and the Nazi Party to exchange confidential notes on the phenomenon.[23] Even his own files on the topic were kept locked in a secure safe.[24]

In the spring of 1943 Field Marshal Keitel finally issued a set of guidelines for handling cases of homosexuality, having waited for an opportune moment to show them to Hitler beforehand. His instructions were brief and to the point. Suspects had to be dealt with in three categories. The first were those men deemed to have a genetic disposition, the "true" homosexuals. Every effort should be made to investigate this well before the trial itself, including the interrogation of his fellow soldiers, in order to avoid mistakes. For these men the punishment should be harsh, with a penitentiary sentence for serious cases and the death penalty itself a possibility. They were to be handed over to the civilian authorities to serve out their sentence (which Keitel must have known would lead to a concentration camp after the completion of the formal sentence).

The second group of offenders included those with only a single incident occurring, especially if they had been seduced. They also needed thorough investigation because they too might be "true" homosexuals who had simply been fortunate enough to escape detection thus far. Drunkenness at the time of the offense was no proof that a disposition was not firmly in place. Yet if it were certain that the deviation had been isolated and temporary, then this group might be sent off to the front to prove themselves and then reintegrated into their units. The third group consisted of those for whom a genetic disposition could not be proven. They would be kept for further surveillance in punishment units. If unsuitable for military service they could be simply handed over to the civilian law authorities for punishment there. Or they might be reclassified under the first or second category.[25] Hitler's presumed blanket rejection had now been circumscribed in light of urgent, practical demands for workers. A subsequent memo clarified that a preexisting genetic disposition was not a *sine qua non* for assignment to category 1. Men with an "acquired, evidently incorrigible tendency" could be placed in line for the death penalty in the first category as well. The determination of "evident incorrigibility" was of course an undefined, rather loose, and subjective affair. Worse still, it could now be applied retroactively to any of the 5,806 cases of homosexuality investigated in the military thus far during the war.[26]

Meanwhile Wuth kept pressing for the introduction of compulsory castration for homosexuals due to their "very high rate of recidivism (35.2 percent)." This was the "only suitable means of allowing such people to pursue some occupational activity without permanent incarceration and without danger to the community." And his definition of the target group was expanding to include the "incorrigibles" with merely an acquired (rather than inborn) disposition, who were going to be expelled from the *Wehrmacht* anyway. He now began to refer to this group as the "neurotic" homosexuals. If they could not control themselves and repeated the offense, then they too should become candidates for castration, for they were "just as dangerous as a 'true' homosexual." Just how widely Wuth wanted to cast the net is apparent from his next statement: "Homosexuality itself is not being punished, but rather someone is being called to account when his inclination to offend against §175 becomes manifest. For the rest it certainly seems questionable whether the deliberate further procreation of such "neurotic" homosexuals is really so desirable for the community."[27] Even though medical science was unable to determine how, whether, and by whom a genetic disposition toward homosexuality could in fact be passed on, some doctors like Wuth thought that much broader preemptive measures should be undertaken, even against men who *might* in the future commit homosexual offenses but had not in fact done so.

These evaluations by military psychiatrists continued to occupy a good deal of their time. For example, the official diary kept by one of the army's team of advisory psychiatrists, Professor Kurt Schneider, for August 1943 shows that four out of the fourteen evaluation reports he had to prepare that month dealt with cases of homosexuality, a larger number than for any other problem.[28] Homosexuality continued to puzzle the experts. Another of the army's psychiatrists noted that summer that offenses occurred with some regularity right after men had returned from leave, even from a honeymoon. The only conclusion he could draw from this was that the heightened heterosexual activity during leave had left certain men not sexually satisfied but rather oversexed. An "organic relationship" seemed to exist between the two.[29] Decades of scientific literature about prisons had noted that men under confinement sought sexual release with one another as a substitute for heterosexual acts that were not available to them. Yet in evaluating the pending castration of a lance corporal in July 1944, Wuth's office dismissed this idea as a possible excuse: "It is well known that during imprisonment there exists for various reasons no great inclination anyway for homosexual activity, or indeed none at all."[30]

An exception to this trend toward radicalization may simply reflect the circumstance that the accused was a doctor himself. Dr. Helmut B. was a sergeant in the army medical corps who had been convicted of homosexual offenses before the war. His colleagues evidently found him a good physician and colleague and did not want to lose him. The advisory psychiatrist, Dr. von Baeyer, testified that a "normalization of his behavior, not of course of his disposition, seems to have come about" and had no hesitation about recommending his promotion. Baeyer seemed more dubious, however, about another case a couple of weeks later that involved a plea of "sleep drunkenness." He wanted the fellow soldiers of the accused to be interrogated more closely about his habits.[31]

Wuth was not the only *Wehrmacht* expert on homosexuality, even though he ranked as the senior psychiatrist. In June 1944 the head of the Luftwaffe's medical corps issued a closely printed, fourteen-page memorandum on the "evaluation of homosexual acts" for military doctors. It was far more detailed and wide-ranging than anything the army had come up with. Unfortunately, it also deviated in part from the insights propounded by Wuth. This was a polished report, not merely typed but printed up for distribution, and it fell like a bombshell on the army psychiatrists' office.[32] As the result of closer cooperation with the psychotherapeutic institute of Matthias Göring, the favored nephew of Luftwaffe chief Hermann Göring, the air force medical corps was much more open to the beneficial effects of psychiatric treatment. Beyond this the memo provided a sober and surprisingly balanced view of the possibilities for success in this area, although it also supported drastic solutions in certain cases. That in turn revolved around definitions of homosexuality, and here the Luftwaffe differed from the army, in part through a more richly defined schematization (faulty though it was).

The long document started by explaining the law and stressing that mere touching or kissing now constituted a homosexual act. Schröder also pointed out that, although women were not formally covered by §175, there were ways of prosecuting lesbians, too, and they should be used without hesitation: "'Indecency' between women cannot be excused by the fact that the law makes no special provision for them." He meant that women could still be trapped by the broader reach of the penal code over issues of coercion, abuse of rank, or creating a public nuisance.

How could one spot a "temporary" or "sham" homosexual? Luftwaffe physicians were reminded that most adolescents fell into this category and often displayed all the passion of first love. Particularly noticeable was the "strongly idealistic attitude" of sham homosexuals, in which physical sexual aspects receded. But doctors should be careful about jumping to conclusions: "This criterion is however deceptive, for such sublimations also occur with [genuine] homosexuals of worthy character [*bei charakterlich wertvollen Homosexuellen*]." Another extraordinary and highly unusual statement, going against the grain of automatic vilification: an admission that real homosexuals *could* be men of estimable character. The Luftwaffe believed, again in contradiction to other agencies, that inebriation did not automatically reveal the hidden perversions within a man. Such lapses might be telling in this way, though that was where the expertise of the psychiatric personnel was required through a comprehensive assessment of the accused.

Born homosexuals were still frankly a mystery. The Luftwaffe admitted that most of the theories put forward had not panned out. Physical appearance offered no certain clues: after spending a whole page detailing the popular image of the usually effeminate gay man, Schröder warned that you simply could not tell by looking at someone whether he was a homosexual or not. In saying this, the Luftwaffe was opening the gates to a panic fear of homosexuals that could only increase homophobia. However, Schröder offered a few clues. Not always, but "so relatively often that it cannot be overlooked," homosexuals had the soft skin and facial expression of a woman, narrow shoulders and broad hips, a peculiar gait and a high-pitched voice. Their skin was the real giveaway: again and again it turned out to be fattier and softer than average and therefore *warmer*. Perhaps that was why they were prone to blush so easily. Furthermore, Schröder speculated, this was possibly the origin of the popular term for a homosexual, a "warm brother" *(warmer Bruder)*, not to mention the word *"schwul,"* which was doubtless a derivation of *"schwül"* or sultry.

Occupation could be a clue, because homosexuals were found with particular frequency as hairdressers, ladies' tailors, bath attendants, masseurs, nurses, actors, dancers, waiters, cooks, and servants, but also among the skilled professions such as educators (especially in boarding schools and youth groups), doctors, clerics, and soldiers. Here was a real laundry list of ill-informed, popular prejudices. A couple of the categories hit rather close to home and brought an immediate and vigorous rebuttal from the army psychiatrists: "The author's assertion that homosexuals are to be found in particularly large number among doctors and soldiers is new and does not accord with the facts."[33]

Schröder did not, however, allow himself to be swept away by the usual scare tactics about the disgusting *practices* of all homosexuals but discussed these in almost uniquely measured tones. "The nightmare vision of the wild pederast throwing himself with unrestrained lust on the backside of his victim occurs in reality just as seldom as the heterosexual lecher before whose physical impetuosity even the most vigorous female resistance must collapse." He explained that it should not be regarded as the norm. Indeed, in terms of sexual practices, "anal intercourse (pederasty) between homosexuals is by no means the rule. In fact it is relatively rare (albeit naturally much more frequent than among heterosexuals) and remains almost completely restricted to primitive and crudely insensitive, born homosexuals. Not every homosexual is a pederast. To equate the two betrays either thoughtlessness or ignorance." He went on to point out that, far from having an out-of-control sex drive, homosexuals were as capable of true love as anybody else. Of course they could behave like adolescents when they had a crush, but they were "capable of the greatest loyalty and sacrifice and of genuine lifelong comradeship." In mid-1944 when one would expect to hear nothing but the diabolization of Germany's putative enemies, these were extraordinary comments indeed.

The final guidelines suggested by the Luftwaffe begin with the following statement in bold type: "The interests of the conduct of war, of manly discipline in the military, of the protection of youth, in addition to concerns of population policy, demand unconditionally the suppression of all homosexual acts, the detection of the homosexuals, their punishment and their removal from the *Wehrmacht*." That sounds like a sweeping statement, aimed at banishing every participant in any type of homosexual activity from the armed services. We have already seen how impractical that was deemed to be, in the wake of Hitler's pronouncement to this effect, and in fact the paragraphs immediately following suggest that only a selective permanent removal was being proposed. As for "sham" homosexuals, removal from the *Wehrmacht* was recommended only for those "of inferior character," above all those who were deliberately using sex for the purposes of blackmail or preferment.

Beyond that, what the "sham" homosexuals needed was "special education, leadership and care." The army had a much cruder view than the Luftwaffe of what form that should take, and one of its psychiatrists scribbled "KZ" (concentration camp) in the margin of his copy. While born homosexuals were incurable, they might be brought round to act with self-control and responsibility; if not, they should be castrated. Those men with acquired homosexuality, on the other hand, were definitely curable, and their castration was "biologically pointless, and questionable from the point of view of population policy." Here was a flat rejection of Wuth's policy.

In the end, all the control mechanisms came down to a correct identification of the type of homosexual one was dealing with, and unit commanders and courts-martial needed that information in order to determine the most appropriate action to take. Schröder warned that "the correct diagnosis is often very difficult." It entailed use of two areas neglected in contemporary medical training (unjustly in his view): sexual psychology and sexual pathology. If the regular Luftwaffe physicians did not feel comfortable with these, then they should by all means call in a psychiatrist to assist with the diagnosis.[34]

By November 1944 Wuth had retired and was replaced by an old Austrian Nazi, Professor Max de Crinis. The homosexual question was a priority for him, too. De Crinis introduced a far-reaching change in military practice. A committee set up by him reported a significant difference of understanding regarding the term "homosexual tendency" *(Hang)*. For physicians, this meant either a constitutional condition with which the subject had been born or an acquired sexual peculiarity. Experience now showed that this was not how judges understood the term. In the legal world, the focus lay more on the character of the person and whether the nature and number of criminal offenses committed suggested that he or she was a "habitual criminal." In many cases, then, the expert witness and the judge had been talking past each other. The doctor spoke of "tendency" in a biological sense, whereas the judge was merely interested in criminological probability. De Crinis's committee decided to recommend that the courts should *not* consult medical experts about the *Hang* in future but should seek such appraisals from the Criminal Police Central Office for Combating Homosexuality, "which in light of its special experience is the most likely [agency] to assist the judge with an evaluation on the question of a tendency."

Since the certification of a "homosexual tendency" could already lead under existing guidelines to the severest of punishments, including the death penalty, this was a quite fateful concession to make to the police. It implies a greater readiness to accept the radicalization of the treatment of homosexuals, a complete dereliction of duty in protecting the men thought by doctors to be reformable homosexuals, and perhaps the desire of the physicians to remove themselves from any share of guilt in the passing of unjustified death sentences (at a time when many Germans realized that the war was lost).[35] Doctors should still always be called as expert witnesses, the committee insisted, if there was a suspicion of mental illness such as schizophrenia or manic depression, some kind of brain damage, or even some damage to the inner organs such as testicles or pituitary or thyroid glands. Yet they weakened to a mere recommendation their presence in cases involving alcohol, "sleep-drunkenness," or when the accused was under the age of twenty-one. This surrender of authority by medical experts in "routine" cases of homosexuality would have had devastating, and often fatal, consequences under the legislation planned by the regime for after the conclusion of the war. It left the definition of a gray zone of sexual orientation up to the whim of the very police organization charged with stamping out homosexuality in Germany completely.

The capitulation of the *Wehrmacht*'s medical corps to the police over the issue of identification of homosexuals is a curious one in that it goes against some six decades of attempts by physicians in the opposite direction. Starting in the 1880s, psychiatrists had striven to prove themselves the decisive expert witnesses in the courtroom in a variety of cases involving the mental competence of the accused. This is a not atypical story in the history of professionalization. Why this deviation from the norm, then, this denial of expertise?

The answer may lie in the frustration over the failure to reach agreement over the nature of homosexuality. After all, much work lay ahead, at least for those who did not accept that the war was lost. Most of the Jews of Europe were now dead, but here stood a potentially dangerous and subversive enemy group of enormous proportions. The authorities had only just scratched the surface of its control or suppression. Identification was much more problematic than with Jews. Here you could not simply pull the man's pants down (a common and humiliating practice with circumcised Jewish men) and tell that he was a homosexual. The pseudo-scholarship about distinctive physical attributes, such as the funnel-shaped anus of passive homosexuals that scientists had seriously debated, had been rejected by the 1940s. There was surely a huge need for medical experts here to sort out the four million homosexuals into categories of risk to the community. Yet perhaps it was the daunting size of the problem that gave the psychiatrists pause.

In truth, this had not given pause to those involved in the Jewish question. But the sorting out of Jewish victims was of a quite different nature. The few remaining German Jews were no longer regarded as fellow countrymen, having been stripped of their full citizenship. As aliens they could be rounded up indiscriminately and shipped off to the camps. The more than three million homosexuals were men who were desperately needed for military service now, and the army would continue to make huge personnel demands for the postwar maintenance of the gigantic empire that was planned, not to mention for "the next war" of which Himmler was already speaking.

Categorizing homosexuals as irremediable or reformable was no easy task, as experience had shown. It required at a minimum an *individual* psychiatric evaluation. The *Wehrmacht* medical corps simply did not have enough staff for such an undertaking on a large scale, and there were no signs that a massive expansion might be granted. Besides, the psychiatrists already had their hands full with other pressing issues: as the German defeat grew closer, there were more and more soldiers under suspicion of going berserk and shooting their superiors or comrades, or shooting themselves (often in the foot or leg) in order to remove themselves from the danger zone. The mental state of each one of them needed individual attention, not to mention cases of battle fatigue or shell shock. The easy way out, then, was to give in to the claims of the police that the sure way to identify a real homosexual was to see if he already had a criminal record, because most of them were actually criminal types of a much broader kind.

Was Professor Max de Crinis satisfied that he had carried out his job as the *Wehrmacht*'s chief psychiatrist in a responsible fashion? On 30 April 1945, as the Soviet forces were capturing Berlin, he committed suicide.[36] Even before de Crinis, the military psychiatrists had not been very helpful or sympathetic toward suspected gay men. But they had at least placed some of them in the consequential category of reformability. Alongside the recent debates about the brutality of the army in the East toward noncombatants, we should note that the military was becoming progressively less compassionate toward a significant segment of its own men.[37] Let us be clear that this surrender of authority to the criminal police meant that at least some homosexuals who had been spared the concentration camp or the gallows would in future not avoid the ultimate fate. Were Hitler to win the war, Germany's three million homosexuals faced a bleak future.

Notes

1. Frick explicitly named Magnus Hirschfeld as the worst offender. Burkhard Jellonnek, *Homosexuelle unter dem Hakenkreuz: Die Verfolgung von Homosexuellen im Dritten Reich* (Paderborn: Schöningh, 1990), 53.
2. I have briefly touched on the views of the military in Geoffrey J. Giles, "'The Most Unkindest Cut of All': Castration, Homosexuality and Nazi Justice," *Journal of Contemporary History* (January 1992), 41–61.
3. OKH Burdach to Heeres-Sanitätsinspektion, 5 September 1938, Bundesarchiv-Militärarchiv Freiburg (BAMA) H20/479. I have adhered to the original call numbers at the time of my use of documents. BAMA has subsequently redesignated all the call numbers of these files and even made two different files out of a single one, and I have not had the opportunity to recheck all the documents.
4. Klaus Theweleit, *Männerphantasien*, vol. 2: *Männerkörper: Zur Psychoanalyse des weissen Terrors* (Basel/Frankfurt am Main: Stroemfeld/Roter Stern, 1986).
5. After pointing out that "in sleep, their bodies easily 'spooned' together," in reference to one of the photographs, she then gives evidence of the nonsexual nature of this, quoting a letter of one soldier to a lady friend: "I must close now as my *wife* is in bed . . . & wants me to keep her warm but it is only a Palestine wife, another Sussex boy, & we are both Jacks so there is nothing doing . . ." Joanna Bourke, *Dismembering the Male: Men's Bodies, Britain and the Great War* (Chicago: University of Chicago Press, 1996), 135.
6. Ibid., 166, 161.
7. Most of the sources for the Third Reich are police and court records. For an examination of wartime homosexual activity at the front, see Geoffrey J. Giles, "The Denial of Homosexuality: Same-Sex Incidents in Himmler's SS and Police," *Journal of the History of Sexuality* (January/April 2002), 256–90.
8. He also discussed Jehovah's Witnesses. While conceding that they were "not in general mentally ill," he did hold a psychiatric evaluation of each one to be desirable. "Das Psychopathenproblem in der Wehrmacht nebst Besprechung einiger einschlägiger Fragen." Vortrag Professor Dr. O. Wuth, Oberfeldarzt an der Militärärztlichen Akademie Berlin, 9/10 March 1939, BAMA H20/128.
9. This was a reflection of a common view, espoused, for example, by Himmler, that homosexuals were "pathological liars." He based this principally on the fact that homosexual suspects, having fallen into the clutches of the police, would vigorously deny having committed any crime. In his long speech on homosexuality to SS-Gruppenführer on 18 February 1937, Himmler remarked, "I don't even think of asking a homosexual any more: 'Can you give me your word on this?' I don't do it any more because I know I'll get a false word. At the moment when the homosexual says something with tears in his eyes, he's convinced that it is true. In my experience homosexuality leads to an absolute, I would almost say mental, unsoundness and insanity." Bradley F. Smith and Agnes F. Peterson, eds., *Heinrich Himmler: Geheimreden 1933–1945 und andere Ansprachen* (Frankfurt am Main: Propyläen Verlag, 1974), 96–97.
10. Rundschreiben Keitel "Erziehung des Offizierkorps," 18 December 1939, BAMA RH 53-7/v.709.
11. Another soldier, a 23-year-old driver, was punished for buggering a young calf while drunk. Rundschreiben Wehrkreiskommando XVII, "Straffälle durch Trunkenheit," 17 February 1940, BAMA RH21-2/v.60.
12. Rundschreiben Brauchitsch "Alkoholmissbrauch," 6 June 1941, BAMA RH54/95.
13. "Anleitung zur Erstattung gerichtspsychiatrischer Gutachten," Inspekteur des Sanitätswesens der Luftwaffe, 1 October 1941, BAMA H20/827.

14. Vortragsvermerk Lehmann für Herrn Feldmarshall, 12 August 1942, BAMA H20/479.
15. Vermerk "Die Entwicklung des Homosexuellen-Problems in der Wehrmacht," n.d. [after July 1943]. Thanks are due to the late Hans-Georg Stümke for sharing this document with me, and to Geoffrey Cocks for correcting its attribution to BAMA H20/474.
16. The following viewpoints from Vortragsvermerk Lehmann für Herrn Feldmarshall, 12 August 1942, BAMA H20/479.
17. See Giles, "The Denial of Homosexuality," 256–90.
18. Vortragsvermerk Lehmann für Herrn Feldmarshall, 12 August 1942, BAMA H20/479.
19. Vortragsvermerk für Herrn Generaloberstabsarzt Prof. Dr. Handloser, 4 November 1942, BAMA H20/479.
20. Zum Vortragsvermerk für Herrn Feldmarshall, Chef WR, 4 November 1942, BAMA H20/479.
21. See above, n. 9.
22. See my discussion of the dubious medical opinions in Giles, "'The Most Unkindest Cut of All,'" 41–61; Wuth to Heeres-Sanitätsinspektion/Wi G I, 22 January 1943, BAMA H20/486.
23. Otto Wuth, Aide-Mémoire betr. Verbrechen und Vergehen §175 RStGB. Statistische und andere Bemerkungen, February 1943, BAMA H20/479.
24. Most of the documents in Wuth's file are stamped not merely confidential but secret *(Geheim)*, and some are marked specifically for storage in the *"Panzerschrank Homos,"* such as Wuth to Blankenburg, 16 April 1943, BAMA H20/479, with which letter he sent Bormann's office copies of literature emphasizing the effectiveness of castration.
25. Richtlinien für die Behandlung von Strafsachen wegen widernatürlicher Unzucht, Chef OKW Keitel, 19 May 1943, BAMA H20/479.
26. Erlass OKH, "Entlassung von Soldaten aus dem aktiven Wehrdienst wegen widernatürlicher Unzucht," 22 July 1943, ibid.
27. He was thinking of *Tarnehen*, marriages undertaken by male homosexuals with a woman (often a lesbian) in order to conceal their homosexuality. Beratender Psychiater to Heeres-Sanitätsinspektion, 26 July 1943; Beratender Psychiater to Lehrgruppe C (Forschungsgruppe) der militärärztlichen Akademie, 7 September 1943, ibid.
28. Only three cases of self-mutilation, one sexual assault on children, one murder, one manslaughter, three thefts. Tagebuch August 1943 Schneider, 31 August 1943. His notes for October 1943 show that three out of the five evaluations he was called upon to write that month concerned homosexuality. Tagebuch Oktober 1943 Schneider, 31 October 1943, BAMA H20/502.
29. Erfahrungsbericht Wilke, 14 July 1944, BAMA H20/122.
30. Beratender Psychiater to Lehrgruppe C, 26 July 1944, BAMA H20/479.
31. *Schlaftrunkenheit* had frequently been accepted as a mitigating circumstance in a variety of crimes since the 1880s. Kriegstagebuch Dr. von Baeyer, 16 September 1944 and [9?] October 1944, BAMA H20/500.
32. Chef des Sanitätswesens der Luftwaffe Schröder, Anweisung für Truppenärzte zur Beurteilung gleichgeschlechtlicher Handlungen, 7 June 1944. The memo bears the accession date stamp of 11 November 1944 (though there is another copy stamped 23 January 1945, so the army apparently requested further copies). It is possible that Wuth received a copy before this, and the November date stamp may simply reflect delays in keeping up with incoming materials, caused by Wuth's retirement and his replacement by de Crinis. Yet Wuth does not appear personally to have kept back any of his professional files and materials. In September 1944 he was engaged in a petulant exchange with his former office, trying to get hold of a film of the carrying out of an execution, which he claimed was a "personal gift of the Luftwaffe" and not the property of the institute. His successor refused to surrender the film for Wuth's private viewing. BAMA H20/479. Günter Grau unfortunately chooses to reproduce in his collection only a small section of this fascinating document, on the steps to be taken by the Luftwaffe physicians, rather than excerpting the whole. Even then he dismisses it as being of rather marginal, merely "historical interest," having little practical result for the lives of soldiers. In fact we do not know what

effects it had, because the records of the Luftwaffe advisory psychiatrists have not survived the war like those of the army. See Günter Grau, ed., *Homosexualität in der NS-Zeit* (Frankfurt am Main: Fischer Taschenbuch, 1993), 213, 230–31, 233–37.
33. Unsigned, undated copy of memo from a *Beratender Gerichtsmediziner*, BAMA H20/479.
34. He admitted that brothels at the front, sanctioned by the military, were a necessary evil. But they should only be used by "older, sexually experienced men with a fixed sex drive," not by young soldiers who might be turned off by the sordidness of the experience and find the solicitations of an older, male comrade more appealing. Chef des Sanitätswesens der Luftwaffe Schröder, Anweisung für Truppenärzte zur Beurteilung gleichgeschlechtlicher Handlungen, 7 June 1944, BAMA H20/479.
35. Schulte, Becker, Rodenberg, Frentzel-Beyme and Boehm to Beratender Psychiater beim Heeres-San. Inspekteur, 15 December 1944, BAMA H20/482. Günter Grau misses the significance of this document in his brief comments about it in *Homosexualität in der NS-Zeit*, 213. And Florian Mildenberger misreads the document, which does not state that doctors should talk about an *Anlage-Homosexueller* rather than a *Hangtäter* in future. What it does say is that judges see the latter not only in the former (that is, "true" homosexuals) but also among those men "originally of normal sexuality" who have been brought to "this perverse form of sexual activity" by external factors such as seduction in early youth. Florian Mildenberger, *In der Richtung der Homosexualität verdorben: Psychiater, Kriminalpsychologen und Gerichtsmediziner über männliche Homosexualität* (Hamburg: Männerschwarm Skript-Verlag, 2002), 270.
36. The information on de Crinis's suicide is from Mildenberger, 204, though he unfortunately neglects to give sources for any of his detailed biographical footnotes.
37. See, for example, Hamburg Institute for Social Research, *The German Army and Genocide: Crimes Against War Prisoners, Jews, and Other Civilians in the East, 1939–1944*, trans. Scott Abbott (New York: New Press, 1999).

– Chapter 11 –

PLEASURE AND EVIL
Christianity and the Sexualization of Holocaust Memory

Dagmar Herzog

I begin with a juxtaposition of two pictures. They were published in *Konkret*, the well-known West German New Left news magazine, in 1975.[1] This juxtaposition makes me intensely uncomfortable. But it also offers an important entry point into my topic, which concerns the complex connections between sex and mass murder in the Nazi and post-Nazi German imagination. One is a painting by a Nazi-approved artist (Otto Roloff); it is of the mythological Leda about to be raped by the swan (the god Zeus in disguise) but at this time just lying in the sunshine in sensual languor for the benefit of the viewer. The other is one of the iconic photographs from the Holocaust killing fields: Jewish women in the *Reichskommissariat* Ukraine waiting in line to be executed.

There is a somewhat long prehistory to this juxtaposition; the article in *Konkret* is actually a review of an art exhibit, launched in Frankfurt in 1974, the first exhibit ever of Nazi art in the postwar period.[2] The exhibit was strongly didactic, determined throughout to place the "pretty" surfaces of Nazism (the paintings and sculptures) alongside photographs of the Third Reich's horrible realities. Thus a Nazi sculpture of strong healthy men was juxtaposed with a photo of piles of skulls, a painting of a farmer in harmony with nature was set beside photographs of toiling slave laborers, a painting of war heroes was contrasted with a photo showing the actual misery of warfare, and a painting of attractive naked women was paired with a copy of the Nuremberg race laws and a photo of Jewish women in their underwear about to be murdered. But this particular juxtaposition appearing in *Konkret* was not in the original exhibit; this was,

Notes for this section begin on page 159.

Images accompanying Hans Haustein, "Contra Nostalgie," *Konkret* (January 1975)

rather, *Konkret*'s own invention. Yet the *Konkret* article had nothing at all to say about the accompanying images. It is obvious that the juxtaposition was designed to elicit a visceral shock effect, but it is also—as I will go on to explain—indicative that the article demonstrated absolutely no capacity to theorize what the juxtaposition might mean.[3]

What do these images, and *Konkret*'s apparent speechlessness in the face of them, have to do with my announced topic—Christianity and the "sexualization" of Holocaust memory? What I want to bring into focus in this essay are not only some important aspects of the still inadequately understood relationships between Nazism and the Christian churches. I am above all concerned with indicating the key roles played by postwar West German Christian theologians, clergy, and lay activists in formulating a particular version of Christianity after the defeat of Nazism. And within this particular formation of post-Fascist Christianity, I am interested in identifying how the memory of Nazism was subtly reshaped; that is, how moral debate in postwar Germany was directed away from discussions of complicity in mass murder and toward a narrowed conception of morality as solely concerned with sex.

This essay has three parts. First, in order to explain how this redirection of moral debate in postwar Germany was possible, I need to backtrack into the Third Reich itself. I challenge the standard notion of Nazism's sexual politics as repressive and conservative for everyone and instead offer a revised interpretation that highlights the links between the pro-sex elements of Nazism and its antisemitism and genocidal violence. Against this background, then, the essay turns to the influential efforts of postwar Christian commentators to rewrite the Nazi past and suppress Christianity's own entanglement with Nazism while presenting the restoration of sexual conservatism in the 1950s as an *anti*-Nazi project. And third, the essay traces the intergenerational misunderstandings about Nazism caused by the postwar conservative restorationist settlement, along with the ensuing efforts of liberal and New Left activists to reconceptualize entirely the perceived relationships between pleasure and evil. At the end, I will return briefly to the pictures in *Konkret*.

Most scholars continue to presume that Nazism was somehow at its core anti-sex. The standard periodization suggests that the Third Reich's sexual politics should be seen as a reactionary backlash against the liberality of the Weimar Republic. The Third Reich is routinely described in a sort of assertive shorthand as "sex-hostile," "unhappy, lifeless, pleasureless," marked by "rigid bodily-sexual norms of behavior" and "official German prudery."[4] The visceral intensity of Nazi antisemitism is said to have had its source in an external projection of "unconscious guilt produced by repressed sexual desires" in "innumerable" Germans.[5] Indeed, as Jeffrey Herf summarized the problem in 1999, "Historians of German society and culture under the Nazis" have proceeded as though "the connection between Nazism and sexual repression" was simply "intuitively obvious."[6] A German book from the 1990s, for instance, characteristically portrays the Third Reich as a time when "eroticism as a sensibility was suppressed," bedrooms were depressingly "gloomy" spaces, and "whatever Weimar had thought and partially practiced as progress was radically denied or terminated."[7] The persistence of this basic conceptualization is evident in studies published in 2002–4 as well.[8] My work seeks to reconceptualize this frame.

Let me be clear. There were indeed in the Third Reich countless sexually repressive tendencies: from the torture and murder of homosexual men to the prosecution of Jewish–gentile sex in the so-called race defilement trials to the grotesque reproductive experiments and sexual sadism practiced on Jewish and other prisoners in the concentration and death camps. But none of these horrific facts justifies the conclusion that the Third Reich was repressive for everyone. What has routinely been downplayed since the 1960s is evidence that Nazi policy and practice, for the majority of the population, was anything but sexually repressive. Also, Nazi homophobia was not part of a larger prudish agenda but rather was inseparable from injunctions to happy heterosexual activity among those ideologically and "racially" approved by the regime—and *not* just for the sake of reproduction, but also for the sheer sake of pleasure.[9]

Sexually conservative Nazi publicists did exist, and for them references to Jews functioned as a negative counterpoint to underscore the value of a sexually conservative agenda. Thus, "race specialists," medical doctors, and the like celebrated Germans' conversion to avid antisemitism but worried that Germans remained ensnared in (what they called) "Jewish" ways of thinking in at least one respect: sex. "There are no two sides to the Jewish question," one physician asserted, "and it is not admissible to damn the Jew in his political, economic, and human manifestation while secretly, for personal convenience, maintaining the customs he has suggested in the realm of love- and sex-life."[10] Similarly, other sexually conservative Nazis also blamed Weimar-era Jewish writers and filmmakers for their "glorification of adultery and sexual uninhibitedness," or they complained that otherwise properly Nazified Germans continued to "repeat the Jewish or Jewish-influenced vulgarities concerning the relations of the two sexes."[11] Yet as these arguments themselves already imply, sexual conservatives were not exactly winning the day.

Instead, for much of the populace, Nazism brought with it a further expansion of the liberalizing trends begun even before Weimar and which had intensified during Weimar. In part, the liberalization of mores would be the result of the monumental disruptions caused by total war, labor mobilization and population transfers, and the general climate of moral anarchy as mass murder escalated. But the liberalization was also, long before the war, actively advanced as part of official Nazi Party policy. Jews were strongly associated with an accepting, celebratory attitude toward pleasurable (and not inevitably reproductive) heterosexuality. While some Nazis did want a return to conservative values, the bigger drama involved the effort to detach emancipatory impulses from their association with "Marxism" and "Jewishness" and to redefine sexual liberation as a "Germanic," "Aryan" prerogative.

This pro-sex Nazi agenda was especially put forward in the context of attacks on the Christian churches (and this explains a great deal about what would happen *after* the war). Over and over, Nazis aligned themselves with young people's impatience with traditional bourgeois mores. Race theorist Hans Endres, for example, argued in 1941 that "we have been raised in criminal bigotry, because the Oriental Christian mentality has suppressed our healthy Germanic instincts in sexual matters. Our younger generations . . . must become proud of their bodies and enjoy the natural pleasures of sex without being ashamed."[12] The physician Carl Csallner argued that only "priestly cant" had turned the sexual drive, which was "wanted by nature and spontaneously presses toward activity," into something "base and mean"; the sexual drive, in Csallner's view, was "great" and "holy."[13] For these pro-sex Nazis, references to the supposed shamelessness and impropriety of "Jewish" versions of sexuality functioned more as a technique of disavowal and distraction. Consider the wildly popular SS journal *Das Schwarze Korps* (The Black Corps). Here "clerical 'moralists'" were accused of having "pathetic complexes," and Nazi journalists raged against "the denominational morality . . . that . . . wants to interpret what are natural processes as *sinful drives*."[14] In article after article, the paper denied that it was advocating "free love," which it associated with Marxism and Jewishness. But simultaneously, often in the very same articles, the paper enthusiastically celebrated nudity and nonmarital heterosexuality. The fiercely hyperbolic attacks on Weimar-era cultural arbiters for *their* purported advocacy of extramarital sex, pornography, and nakedness simply served to deflect attention from the Nazis' advocacy of those very same things. Incitement and disavowal were inseparable.

Already a few years into the Third Reich, it was well known both domestically and internationally that Nazis encouraged premarital sex among teenagers. Nazi commentators dealt with the ensuing controversy both by refuting the idea that they were doing any such thing and by avidly defending their own policy and practice. While in 1934 leaders in the Bund Deutscher Mädel (Federation of German Girls; BDM) still received a directive to encourage their young charges to have premarital love affairs under "top secret" conditions, by 1935 at the latest there was nothing particularly secret anymore about what went on in some (though surely not all) of the local BDM chapters.[15]

In Dresden, for instance, Victor Klemperer noted the following in his diary in 1935: "Annemarie Köhler tells us in despair that the hospitals are overcrowded with fifteen-year-old girls, some pregnant, some with gonorrhea. The BDM. Her brother has vehemently refused to allow his daughter to join."[16] As of 1937, the Social Democratic Party in exile reported the news that in the Hitler Youth, "promiscuity is the concretely accepted situation."[17] The international press also reported that parents were frequently devastated by news of what went on in the Reich Labor Service and the encouragement to pair off for sexual encounters that young people received while away from home.[18] But by the early 1940s the regime was so unconcerned with international opinion on these matters that it was openly publicizing its encouragement of marital infidelity as well, not just for the elite.[19]

What historians have missed (perhaps because historians of religion do not talk much with historians of sexuality) is the intense rivalry that raged in the Third Reich between Nazis and Christians, especially Catholics, precisely over sex, rather than over anti-Jewish attitudes or policies. Numerous church leaders and laypersons initially championed the Nazi ascension to power. Protestant pastors praised Hitler as a "marvelous gift from God" and "a through and through decent, clean character," and celebrated the Nazis' rise to power as a "miracle." "The immense power of international Jewry" was deemed a "frightening" threat, while Hitler was providential: "It is absolutely certain that God sent us this man and through him protected us from a great danger."[20] Catholics, who had often been skeptical about Nazism during Weimar, were now thrilled to find a government that shared their hostility to both communism and liberalism. Many Protestants and Catholics shared Nazi disdain for Jews and the view that Jews were responsible for the sexual immorality that purportedly pervaded Weimar culture. Indeed, distress over what they identified as Weimar's debauched sexual climate was a major reason for some Christians' early endorsement of the Nazi regime.

Clergymen and lay activists believed they had finally found the ally they needed to combat Germany's sexual dissolution. As a Catholic scholar put it in 1933, not only was National Socialism "by its nature an opponent of

Bolshevism, liberalism, relativism," but in addition, "National Socialism is an outspoken opponent of . . . public indecency" and of the "liberalistic permissiveness" which was "dominating" modern civilization:

> We Catholics have protested tirelessly in countless press campaigns, pamphlets, sermons, conference resolutions, and parliamentary proposals against trash and smut [*Schund und Schmutz*]. But this effort remained mainly in the theoretical realm, because we were not the state. But now, National Socialism has the power to be effective and in its attacks against the cesspool of the big city we already see the result.[21]

In that same year, Protestant activist Adolf Sellmann of the Western German Moral Purity Association was no less enthusiastic, and for the same reasons. "Overnight things became different in Germany. All smut and trash disappeared from public view. The streets of our cities became clean again," Sellmann said. He saw his organization's fifty-year battle for "the morality and strength of the *Volk*" as finally achieving its aims.[22] The churches especially welcomed early Nazi actions to shut down brothels, gay and lesbian bars, and nudist organizations and to clean city kiosks of pornography.[23] A Catholic journal effused about these "sharp measures against the different forms of public immorality" and declared "we stand behind the efforts of the government 100 percent."[24] Another Catholic journal raved about "the new government's level-headed yet firm approach toward filth wherever it is visible . . . therefore *Siegheil!*"[25]

Christian observers also interpreted Nazism as a force for improving the status of marriage and embraced Nazi racialism as fully compatible with Christianity. In this spirit, for instance, a Protestant pastor in 1934 touted "the great national shift" and "different perspective" in sexual values brought by the Nazi ascension to power and adumbrated in Hitler's *Mein Kampf*. While in Weimar advice writings had emphasized specific sexual techniques such as those promoted by the Dutch advice writer Theodor van de Velde, Hitler was now showing the way to "a completely different understanding of wedlock than in the era of individualism." This pastor did not feel that Nazi "racial hygiene" might conflict with Christian values; instead he wrote, "Naturally, in the *völkisch* state racial hygiene will be the highest principle for the formation of marriage and the ethos of marriage in the *völkisch* state will in essence receive its content from the *Volk* and from the race."[26] Along related lines, the Jesuit Hermann Muckermann authoritatively rejected Jewish–gentile marriages and argued that for the sake of the preservation of the "untouched, elemental nature of the German people" he wanted to "push back racially foreign, particularly Jewish influence in the shaping of our culture."[27]

However, within just two to three years, Christian spokespersons found reasons to feel disillusionment over the Third Reich's sexual politics. Increasingly they assailed Nazism's apparent intention to reintroduce the very "culture of nakedness" it had claimed it would abolish. In 1936, for instance, a Protestant pastor wrote to the *Völkischer Beobachter* (Racial Observer) to chastise it for printing "obscene pictures" and demanded to know whether images of nude women were really proper objects for "German art." For his part, he said, he had "been ashamed, as I held the paper in my hands, and immediately I cut out two pictures and shredded them. After all, you should consider that this paper gets into the hands of the simple folk and children."[28] Similarly, when the Nazi Party's Office for Racial Policy published a calendar with nudes, Catholic priests in Westphalia organized a campaign against its sale, arguing that the pictures were "piggish [*schweinig*]" and "indecent [*unanständig*]."[29]

Catholics in particular began to sound the alarm about Nazi promotion of sex outside of marriage. One Catholic journal editor in 1935 explicitly lamented that although "at first we believed that morality would improve in the Third Reich—today this *hope* reveals itself *more and more as false*." He further charged that "fleshly lust" and a "spirit of uncleanness" were at work in the Third Reich. (Yet notably he also went out of his way to validate the Third Reich's "message about race, blood, and soil" as "at least in part valuable and true."[30])

Christians also continued to share Nazi antisemites' assumptions of an intrinsic link between Jewishness and sexual liberality, even as they suggested that Nazism was turning out to be no better when it came to sex. The Catholic priest Matthias Laros in 1936 praised the Nazis for their dedication to race and *Volk,* but he also held Nazism responsible for the dissolution of sexual mores. "The era has succumbed to a horrifying barbarism and overstimulation of the sexual drive." The "false prophets" of a relaxed sexual morality were carrying their pernicious teachings "everywhere, into the smallest village." The "entirety of public and private life has today been gripped" by an "insane overvaluation of the sensual-sexual." Distancing himself from *both* Nazis and Jews (even as he reinforced the association of Jews with un-Christian sexual values), Laros declared that "the church, unconcerned by all semitic or antisemitic fashions of the day, holds fast to the ... Christian structure of marriage."[31] There were Protestants who joined in the Nazis' antisemitism as well but who publicly dissented from the regime's evolving sexual politics. Protestant publicist Wilhelm Stapel protested in 1935 the new Nazi "tendency toward nudism" (and was promptly attacked by a Nazi newspaper as a result).[32] Yet in 1933, in his contribution to an antisemitic anthology, Stapel had seen fit to complain about how Jews were constantly criticizing Germans and denigrating "*our* moral concepts: reputation, modesty, bravery, patriotism, fidelity to the Führer, loyalty to the *Volk,* and so forth. . . . Continually they are objecting to our natural morality [*Sittlichkeit*]. . . . Jewish domination is the most insufferable form of rule. There would be no antisemitism if only Jews could keep their mouths shut."[33]

There is far more that could be said about the increasing dissolution of traditional sexual mores under the impact of total war. And it is indeed significant that Germans would come to associate sex with war and genocide not least because quite literally the war was the context in which they experienced sexual infidelity.[34] But what I want to emphasize most here are the meaning-making processes engaged in by postwar Germans.

The immediate postwar moment was, as is well known and widely acknowledged by both scholars and popular commentators, a time of considerable hedonism and sexual liberality in Germany, preeminently but not exclusively because of the involvement of German women with U.S. and other occupation soldiers. And while many scholars have noted that the prevalence of fraternization with Americans was due not least to the millions of German male war deaths and the resulting disproportion of young women to men (rather offensively called at the time a "surplus of women [*Frauenüberschuss*]"), what must also be acknowledged is the powerful appeal of the Americans in particular precisely because they were the victors.[35] For demographics alone cannot explain behaviors or values. What is less well understood is that the much-noted "libertinism" of the postwar moment was also consistent with the loosening of mores that had been produced by both Nazi encouragement and by the dynamics of war. In this postwar situation, what requires our attention is the way in which Christian commentators, in their eagerness to reestablish traditional sexual and familial mores, talked about Nazism—and how they quite directly worked to refocus moral debate away from genocide and toward matters of sex.

The narrow emphasis on sexual morality to the exclusion of other moral concerns was not merely a matter of political expediency but also one of deeply held belief. Under Nazism sexual licentiousness and genocide had in truth become linked. Catholic Anton Hofmann urgently made this point when in 1951 he not only criticized the way "National Socialist schools and the like" had forced "premature sexual contact" on young people under the guise of "'natural-free experiencing' of the erotic event," but also directly connected Nazi encouragement of sexual activity to Nazism's other transgressions. Hofmann contended that the disrespect for the spiritual dimension of life evident among people overly obsessed with erotic pleasure was intimately associated with disrespect for the bodies of others and therefore facilitated brutality and mass murder; as Hofmann put it, in juxtaposing the "overvaluation of the body" with "godlessness and cruelty," what needed to be understood was "the paradoxical matter that the same person who raises the body to dizzying heights, in an instant can sacrifice the bodies of a hundred thousand others."[36]

Yet the postwar Christian emphasis on calls to restore conservative sexual mores also worked to obscure Christian accommodation to and support for Nazism. For every earnest effort to deal with the metaphysical crisis that the Third Reich had indisputably caused there were many other Christian spokespersons who took the occasion to advance self-exculpatory narratives about the churches' relationship to Nazism.[37] Christian spokespersons often presented sexual propriety as the cure for the nation's larger moral crisis, at times suggesting that sexual immorality under Nazism, as much as popular complicity in disenfranchisement and murder, was a main source of that crisis. One Protestant synod, in its postwar call to its flock to turn away from the godlessness of Nazism, expressed equal if not greater concern about the "forgetting of respect and modesty between man and woman . . . the crumbling of chastity"—and the way these supposedly made Germany a "laughingstock among foreign nations"—than about "the violence and murder" that "arose in our land."[38]

Some Christian commentators explicitly elaborated moral equivalencies between Nazi crimes and postwar hedonism. Thus one Protestant statement in 1946 stressed that it was the church's responsibility to speak out not only against "the sin of yesterday" (here it referred obliquely to the "horrors and crimes" of the Nazis) but just as much against "the sin of today": "the licentiousness and lack of dignity with which women and girls today surrender themselves and men profane female honor."[39] Similarly, the Catholic bishop of Passau declared,

> I have described how during the war years disgrace was heaped on the name of Germany. I must now add that no less disgrace has been brought to the name of Germany through all those careless women and girls who, in frivolous disregard for the Sixth Commandment, through their shameless attitude humiliate not themselves but the entirety of the *Volk*.[40]

Some commentators made the displacement of attention away from the immorality of killing to the need for postwar sexual morality quite explicit. The popular Catholic priest Johannes Leppich, for example, in his open-air sermons attracting tens of thousands of listeners, announced provocatively (as he chastised his listeners for both fraternization and intra-German promiscuity and blamed "hackneyed Goebbels phrases" for popular denigration of female virginity):

> It is true: we have a terrible war behind us, a war which has left behind demolished churches and houses and a multitude of war dead. But destroyed churches and houses can be rebuilt, and every day enough human beings are born. No—that is not what is ruining Germany. And if one asks me: is our *Volk* being ruined, or does it still have a future, then there is only one answer: We are dying once more at the hands of our women and girls, who every day throw what is most sacred in them into the dirt.[41]

In short, there was quite a lot of expediency as well. Indeed, shifting moral debate away from mass murder and onto sexual matters became one of the major tactics used by West Germans both in domestic politics and international relations.

Moreover, a main effect of the new emphasis on sexual propriety was precisely that gradually, over the course of the 1950s, the sexually inciting aspects of Nazism were forgotten. Admitting to their children or to the rest of the world that they had any particular pleasures during the Third Reich did not fit with one of postwar Germans' most successful strategies for dealing with guilt (whether internally felt or externally imposed) about the Third Reich: the tendency to present themselves as victims of Nazism rather than its supporters and beneficiaries. Stressing that familial and sexual conservatism were timeless German values that transcended political regime changes offered a way of hiding from view and subsequent memory one's own youthful departures from traditional norms, as these were facilitated by Nazism and one's own enthusiasm for Nazism more generally.[42] Moreover, the official re-Christianization of West German culture as it concretely ensued also needs to be seen as a way to manage the metaphysical crisis engendered by mass murder by casting questions of concrete German complicity in cruelty, expropriation, and genocide in deliberately universalizing (and hence no longer specifically German) existential categories of suffering, guilt, and redemption. Christianization, too, although it seemed like a reaction against Nazism, became a way of avoiding responsibility.[43]

Postwar Christians' emphasis on cleaning up sexual mores also provided a convenient means for erasing from popular memory both churches' own complicity with Nazism—especially its antisemitism. Just as disturbingly, the relentless emphasis placed on the moral requirement of premarital heterosexual chastity (which allowed postwar Christians to delineate their difference from Nazism in especially stark terms, since Nazis had been so eager to encourage premarital sex) functioned to distract attention away from the unapologetic perpetuation of Nazi-era laws and attitudes as both homophobia and "eugenic" hostility to the disabled were refurbished and given renewed legitimacy under Christian auspices.[44]

Gradually what evolved under Christian Democratic leadership in the 1950s was a profoundly conservative sexual culture in which female subordination to men was demanded, sexuality before and outside of marriage was treated as intensely shameful (even though it was widely practiced), tens of thousands of homosexuals were registered in police files (and several thousand convicted each year), and one million illegal abortions every year exposed the hypocrisy of denying ready access to contraceptives. And despite a secularizing populace, all of this was justified in the name of Christianity. Conservatives were able to determine the content of sex education curricula until well into the 1960s and rigorous censorship suppressed access to alternative information.

How, ultimately, was this postwar culture of sexual conservatism dismantled? The eventual sexual liberalization of West Germany in the course of the 1960s depended on four key dynamics. One was the medical-technological invention of the birth control pill.[45] A second was the ever-intensifying use of sexual stimuli in advertising and journalism, a dynamic largely intrinsic to economic processes. The third was a process of direct political mobilization against the official culture of sexual conservatism. This mobilization, beginning in the late 1950s and escalating in ardor and strategic effectiveness in the first three or four years of the 1960s, involved both prominent liberal public intellectuals and younger, often left-leaning student activists. While exceedingly critical of the commodification of sex in consumer capitalism, these activists also used the space opened by the contradictions between conservative norms and sexualized marketing to press their own claims.

Yet nothing was more important in helping liberals and leftists redirect the *moral* terms of conversation about sex in West Germany than a fourth factor: the return with full force to public discussion of the Holocaust as its details were made public in the postwar trials of perpetrators. Preeminent among these was the trial of Adolf Eichmann in Jerusalem in 1961 and the trial, held in Frankfurt am Main from 1963 to 1965, of twenty-two SS men and one prisoner *Kapo*—all of whom were perpetrators at Auschwitz. The Auschwitz trial provided a focal point for rewriting the memory and lessons of the Third Reich for liberal-left purposes.

It was precisely in order to emancipate West German society from the claustrophobic and punitive postwar culture of sexual conservatism that liberals and leftists in the early 1960s began to put forward the argument that Nazism had been sexually repressive, and thus that Christians, far from being anti-Nazis, were really not so different from Nazis. In this campaign, which ultimately turned out to be stunningly effective, the Frankfurt Auschwitz trial functioned as Exhibit A. As portrayed in the mass media, the Auschwitz perpetrators seemed like nothing so much as stereotypical petty bourgeois "philistines [*Spiesser*]."[46] As one commentator put it, those who had "celebrated true orgies of sadism" in the camp were seemingly, when outside the camp, law-abiding and conventional in every respect.[47]

As young people growing up in this era would subsequently testify, the similarity between the code of good behavior postwar society demanded and the model evidently exemplified by the executors of genocide sickened them deeply. But it is also clear that identifying this similarity helped them feel as though they could finally understand how "it" had happened, and it gave them something concrete to fight against in their present. Above all, it gave them a way to interpret what was for them one of the most puzzling aspects of older conservative Germans' attitudes: the way these elders acted as though sex was a horribly dirty matter even as they seemed disinclined to support the postwar trials of perpetrators. This misplaced moral emphasis outraged the young. Repeatedly, young leftists began to skewer the hypocrisy of conservatives who found sex and nudity more immoral than antisemitism.[48] They also began to theorize that sexual *re*pression, not expression, was the root of all evil.

From the 1960s on, it became routine to contend that sexual repression was not merely a characteristic of Fascism but rather its very cause—to argue, in short (against all empirical evidence to the contrary)—that "what happened in Auschwitz was typical for a society that suppresses sexuality" or that "in the Fascist rebellion, the energies of inhibited sexuality formed into genocide."[49] Or, as another author put it, under Nazism, "brutality and the lust for destruction became substitutes for bodily pleasure. . . . This is how the seemingly incredible contradiction that the butchers of Auschwitz were—and would become again—respectable, harmless citizens is resolved."[50]

That Nazis had been uptight and anti-sex rapidly became the cultural common sense, and this conviction lent an air of tremendous moral righteousness to the sexual revolution that would sweep Germany in the later

1960s. Over and over, left-leaning and liberal activists asserted that it was obvious there was—as one put it—a "connection between the suppression of sexual drives on the one hand and the antisemitic persecution mania and its raging in manifest cruelty on the other."[51] For West German New Leftists that ubiquitous sixties slogan "Make Love, Not War" was not just a recommendation for a more decent and pleasurable activity than slaughtering other human beings while risking one's own life. It was also a theory of human nature, a deeply held conviction that those who made a lot of love simply would not be interested in hurting or killing others.[52]

Indeed, New Leftists sincerely came to believe, as feminist journalist Ulrike Heider retrospectively summarized it, that "harmless, so-called well-behaved people had . . . been able to become sadistic SA henchmen and concentration camp guards because they had been tormented and sexually repressed by their parents."[53] New Leftists used these ideas as the bases for their own experiments in sexual liberation and anti-authoritarian child-rearing. (In other words, this factually false reading of Nazism as sexually repressive had very concrete effects—from the liberalization of sex-related law to the progressive reform of preschool and elementary education.) For example, as Dietrich Haensch put it in his key text, *Repressive Familienpolitik* (Repressive Family Politics, 1969), capitalist class relations, Fascism, and brutality in wartime were all products of the "genital weakness" induced in those whose natural drives had been coercively distorted and repressed and who had been forced to develop "cramped-up" concepts of honor, duty, and self-control. "The tendency to sadism is maintained," Haensch bluntly informed his readers, "by diverting the libidinal energies away from the sexual drive and toward the drive for destruction and aggression; the necessary fixation on the enemy occurs by diverting the hatred produced by the ambivalent hate-love fixation on the sexual oppressor onto the military opponent."[54]

Similarly, Dieter Duhm, in his much discussed book *Angst im Kapitalismus* (Fear in Capitalism, 1972), also found sexual repression at the source of "the murder orgies of the Third Reich." Like Haensch before him, Duhm tied the potential for aggression to fear and hatred of repressive parents. Referring specifically to the Frankfurt Auschwitz trial, Duhm remarked that "The bestiality of these executioners sits deeply in all human beings who are raised with the instrument of fear and who because of their fear have no possibility of living out in any way their hatred against the oppressors (in the first instance the parents)."[55]

In sum: It was the project of struggling to liberalize sexual mores in West Germany in the 1960s that brought a new and different version of the Third Reich into public discussion. While in the early 1950s Christians had been able to present themselves and their sexually conservative agenda as the *antithesis* of Nazism and its licentious sexual politics, by the mid-1960s Christians and Nazis were increasingly presented as *comparable* in their visceral hostility to sexual freedom.

Already by 1966 the premier liberal news magazine *Der Spiegel* firmly aligned itself with the side of sexual liberation, and for this cause, crucially, it not only attacked the churches (the church fathers' hostility to sex became, according to *Der Spiegel,* "the trauma of a whole culture") but it also invoked Adolf Hitler as a negative counterexample of sexual self-repression and repressiveness. Offering a one-sided reading of *Mein Kampf*—which quoted Hitler's disgust with the "suffocating perfume of our modern eroticism" but did not mention that in the same sentence he had criticized "unmanly" prudery—*Der Spiegel* printed a photograph of Hitler captioned "Sex-Critic Hitler."[56] Along related lines in 1969 the journalist Hannes Schwenger, in an influential book criticizing the "anti-sexual" politics of the Christian churches, could specifically identify the postwar churches' attacks on "free love, premarital intercourse, adultery, and divorce" as speaking "the language of Fascism."[57] What remained in this new configuration of "memory" was a complete inability to understand what had made Nazism so appealing to so many Germans in the first place. That the Nazis themselves had once openly advocated premarital intercourse, adultery, and divorce had become simply unimaginable.

So finally, let me return to my opening puzzle about the juxtaposed pictures in 1975 in *Konkret:* While the New Left clearly felt that a juxtaposition of the beautiful naked Leda with the genocidal *Einsatzgruppen* highlighted a contradiction in Nazism between its surface and its depth, its pretty projected image and its sordid reality, what I want to emphasize instead is the disturbingly smooth fit between the eroticism and the massacres. For it is not I who has dragged together the seemingly incompatible subjects of sex and death, nor is it the hapless and ignorant New Leftists, nor even the postwar Christians eager to clean up Christianity's own image. Bringing together sex with death, pleasure with evil, was at the very heart of Nazism's own project. Its invitations to enjoyment and to cruelty were not at odds but rather operated in tandem.

The conservative sexual culture of the 1950s had itself been an attempt to master Nazism. But the young people growing up in that era had no way of knowing just how recent and novel an invention that conservatism was; they—wrongly but fiercely—believed that the postwar conservatism was a watered-down continuation of Nazism, and they battled that conservatism with a righteous conviction that in so doing they were being excellent anti-Fascists. The 1974 exhibit of Nazi art—which the *Konkret* essay was reviewing—could thus only come as a tremendous and incomprehensible shock.[58] Indeed, so profound has been the resistance to acknowledging the strongly pro-sex elements of Nazism that this resistance has distorted the scholarship on Nazism up to the present day.

Notes

1. Hans Haustein, "Contra Nostalgie," *Konkret* (January 1975), 46–47.
2. See Georg Bussmann, ed., *Kunst im Dritten Reich: Dokumente der Unterwerfung* (Frankfurt am Main: Frankfurter Kunstverein, 1974).

3. For another helpful analysis of both mainstream and left-leaning postwar news magazines' revealing inarticulacy in the face of Nazi nudes, see Silke Wenk, "Hin-weg-sehen oder: Faschismus, Normalität, und Sexismus," in Klaus Behnken and Frank Wagner, eds., *Erbeutete Sinne: Nachträge zur Berliner Ausstellung "Inszenierung der Macht, ästhetische Faszination im Faschismus"* (Berlin: NGBK, 1988).
4. Joachim Hohmann, *Sexualforschung und -aufklärung in der Weimarer Republik* (Berlin: Foerster, 1985), 9; Sabine Weissler, "Sexy Sixties," in Eckhart Siepmann, ed., *CheSchah-Shit* (Berlin: Elefanten Press, 1984), 99; Christian de Nuys-Henkelmann, "Wenn die rote Sonne abends im Meer versinkt," in Anja Bagel-Bohlan and Michael Salewski, eds., *Sexualmoral und Zeitgeist im 19. und 20. Jahrhundert* (Opladen: Leske & Budrich, 1990); Scott Spector, "Was the Third Reich Movie-Made? Interdisciplinarity and the Reframing of 'Ideology,'" *American Historical Review* 106/2 (April 2001), 472. On the emergence in the 1960s of the idea of Nazism as above all sexually repressive, see Dagmar Herzog, "'Pleasure, Sex, and Politics Belong Together': Post-Holocaust Memory and the Sexual Revolution in West Germany," in Lauren Berlant, ed., *Intimacy* (Chicago: University of Chicago Press, 2000).
5. This prevalent argument is summarized in (and given some endorsement by) Erich Goldhagen, "Nazi Sexual Demonology," *Midstream* (May 1981), 11.
6. Jeffrey Herf, "One-Dimensional Man" (review of Herbert Marcuse, *Technology, War and Fascism*), *New Republic* (1 February 1999), 39.
7. Udo Pini, *Leibeskult und Liebeskitsch: Erotik im Dritten Reich* (Munich: Klinkhardt und Biermann, 1992), 9–11. This author further speculates that Germans' willingness to be "distracted away from eroticism and sexuality" was indicative of a deeper and more lasting national sickness, "a political German masochism . . . and . . . willingness to deny one's own feelings," and that the "extremely uptight" state of affairs lasted "until 1968." See also Stefan Maiwald and Gerd Mischler, *Sexualität unterm Hakenkreuz: Manipulation und Vernichtung der Intimsphäre im NS-Staat* (Hamburg and Vienna: Europa Verlag, 1999): "The total state leaves no room in German beds for self-determined sex. The subjects of the NS-state have to forfeit their sexuality unconditionally to the regime" (57).
8. See Angela H. Mayer, "'Schwachsinn höheren Grades': Zur Verfolgung lesbischer Frauen in Österreich während der NS-Zeit," in Burkhard Jellonek and Rüdiger Lautmann, eds., *Nationalsozialistischer Terror gegen Homosexuelle: Verdrängt und ungesühnt* (Paderborn: Schöningh, 2002), 84; Annette Miersch, *Schulmädchen-Report: Der deutsche Sexfilm der 70er Jahre* (Berlin: Bertz, 2003), 69; and John Borneman, "*Gottvater, Landesvater, Familienvater*: Identification and Authority in Germany," in John Borneman, ed., *Death of the Father* (New York: Berghahn Books, 2004).
9. On this last point about pleasure see also Herbert Marcuse, *Technology, War and Fascism: Collected Papers of Herbert Marcuse*, vol. 1, ed. Douglas Kellner (London: Routledge, 1998), 84–86, 90, 162–63; and Arthur Maria Rabenalt, *Film im Zwielicht: Über den unpolitischen Film des Dritten Reiches und die Begrenzung des totalitären Anspruches* (Munich: Copress-Verlag, 1958; reprinted Hildesheim: Ohms, 1978), 26–29.
10. See Ferdinand Hoffmann, *Sittliche Entartung und Geburtenschwund*, 2nd ed. (Munich: J. F. Lehmanns, 1938), 13, 21, 24–25, 34.
11. Paul Danzer, "Die Haltung zum anderen Geschlecht," in *Streiflichter ins Völkische: Ausgewählte Lesestücke für deutsche Menschen aus dem "Völkischen Willen"* (Berlin: Rota-Druck, 1936), 5–6; Dr. Knorr, "Eine noch nicht genügend beachtete weltanschauliche und bevölkerungspolitische Gefahr," *Ziel und Weg: Organ des nationalsozialistischen deutschen Ärtzebundes* 7, no. 22 (November 1937), 570.
12. Hans Endres quoted in George W. Herald, "Sex Is a Nazi Weapon," *American Mercury* 54/222 (June 1942), 661.
13. Carl Csallner, *Das Geschlechtsleben, seine Bedeutung für Individuum und Gemeinschaft* (Munich: Otto Gmelin, 1937), 10.
14. See "Anstössig?" *Das Schwarze Korps* (hereafter *DSK*), 16 April 1936, 13; Dr. Hans Lüdemann, "Neues Stadium der Frauenbewegung?" *DSK*, 19 June 1935, 10; and ". . . Unzucht in der Soldatenzeit," *DSK*, 5 March 1936, 6. See also "Schön und Rein" and

"Geschäft ohne Scham," *DSK*, 20 October 1938, 10, 12. The strategy of displaying images of nude or scantily clad women while chastising "Jews" or the Weimar-era media for their supposed sexual sensationalism was hardly restricted to *Das Schwarze Korps*. Similar double moves can be found, for instance, in "Sie Meinen: Apart und lustig," *Frauenwarte* 8, no. 16 (February 1940); and Karl Eiland, "Deutsche Frauenschönheit," *Neues Volk* 10, no. 9 (September 1942).

15. Michael Kater, "Die deutsche Elternschaft im nationalsozialistischen Erziehungssystem," *Vierteljahresschrift für Wirtschafts- und Sozialgeschichte* 67, no. 4 (1980), 489.
16. Victor Klemperer, *I Will Bear Witness: A Diary of the Nazi Years, 1933–1941*, trans. Martin Chalmers (New York: Random House, 1998), 137.
17. *Deutschland-Berichte der Sozialdemokratischen Partei Deutschlands (Sopade)* (Salzhausen and Frankfurt am Main: Petra Nettelbeck/Zweitausendeins, 1980), report of August 1937, 1070. See also an earlier (1935) report by the Social Democratic Party in exile, to the effect that the so "coarsely" presented "propaganda for racially pure offspring" was leading youth to engage in "uninhibited sexuality." Quoted in Pini, *Leibeskult und Liebeskitsch*, 85.
18. For example, see Walter Brockman, "Illegitimacy in Germany," *Current History* 46, no. 4 (July 1937), 67–70; and S. L. Solon and Albert Brandt, "Sex Under the Swastika," *American Mercury* (August 1939), 428–31.
19. See Walter Menzel, "Ehebruch und ehewidriges Verhalten als Dienststrafvergehen," *Wirtschaft und Recht* 9, no. 6 (15 June 1942), 61–62. (This was a supplement to *Der Deutsche Erzieher*, the official journal for schoolteachers.)
20. See Hartmut Lehmann, "Hitlers protestantische Wähler," in *Protestantische Weltsichten: Transformationen seit dem 17. Jahrhundert* (Göttingen: Vandenhoeck und Ruprecht, 1998), 136–39.
21. Joseph Lortz, *Katholischer Zugang zum Nationalsozialismus, Kirchengeschichtlich Gesehen* (Reich und Kirche, vol. 2) (Münster: Aschendorff, 1933), 9–10.
22. Sellmann quoted in Hans-Georg Stümke, *Homosexuelle in Deutschland: Eine politische Geschichte* (Munich: Beck, 1989), 92.
23. See Julia Roos, "Backlash Against Prostitutes' Rights: Origins and Dynamics of Nazi Prostitution Policies," *Journal of the History of Sexuality* 11, nos. 1-2 (January-April 2002), 81–83; and Matthew Jefferies, "Naturism, Nudity, and the Nazis," *German History* (forthcoming).
24. *Kirche im Volk: Monatsschrift für die katholische Pfarrgemeinde,* January 1934, 31, quoted in Joachim Braun, "Lustprinzip und Sexualität in der Wahrnehmung der Nationalsozialisten" (Diplomarbeit, Freie Universität Berlin, 1991), 107.
25. "Der frische Zug im neuen Staat," *Volkswart* 26 (1933), 170–71, quoted in Roos, "Backlash," 83. Roos argues persuasively that the early Nazi self-presentation as intent on cleaning up the sexual landscape of Germany was directly motivated by the party's effort to reverse the German Catholic leadership's initial skepticism and hostility toward Nazism (81).
26. Weinrich, "Randbemerkungen zum Ehe-Problem," *Monatsschrift für Pastoraltheologie* 30 (1934), 274–79.
27. See John Connelly, "Catholic Opponents of Nazism and the Jewish Question: Vienna in the 1930s," paper delivered at the conference of the American Historical Association, 9 January 2004. The quotes from Muckermann are from his *Volkstum, Staat und Nation eugenisch gesehen* (Essen: Fredebeul und Koenen, 1933).
28. The story is reported in "Anstössig?" 14.
29. The story is reported in "Was ist schamloser?" *DSK*, 20 January 1938, 8.
30. Krupka's remarks in *Weg zum Ziel* no. 18 (1935), quoted and discussed in "Pikanterien im Beichtstuhl," *DSK*, 26 June 1935, 5.
31. See Matthias Laros, *Die Beziehungen der Geschlechter* (Cologne: Staufen-Verlag, 1936), 11–12, 15, 34, 70, 166–77. Laros both described the hedonistic culture in the Germany of his day as an especially dangerous form of "Americanism [*Amerikanismus*]" and tried to use the Nazis' own concepts against Nazi sexual mores, insisting that "ur-Aryan inher-

itance" and the "original source of Germanic essence" were in the process of being ruined (20, 24). Another Catholic author, a Jesuit, in 1939 deplored how "the free intercourse of the two sexes has become so *unbridled* that really no normal human being still sees noble naturalness in it." While the younger generation in Nazi Germany celebrated its own "freedom" and "'unembarrassed naturalness [*unbefangene Natürlichkeit*],'" the author took the view that "this much-vaunted 'unembarrassedness' is nothing but *shamelessness* in the deepest sense of the word." Yet his efforts to put his case in terms the regime would hear reinforced racist and nationalist Nazi values more than challenged them. "There is no question," he argued, "that sexual morality is in bad shape in all strata of our *Volk* and that thereby the physical health and the strength of the *Volk* is threatened. Indeed, moral degeneration has progressed so far that it must necessarily lead to the death of the nation, if a moral renewal of our *Volk* does not take place." B. van Acken, S.J., "Prüderie—Distanzhalten," *Theologisch-praktische Quartalschrift* 92 (1939), 73–79.

32. Wilhelm Stapel, "'Neuheidentum.' Ein Brief und eine Antwort," *Deutsches Volkstum: Monatsschrift für das deutsche Geistesleben* April 1935, 293; and see "Ist das Nacktkultur? Herr Stapel entrüstet sich!" *DSK*, 24 April 1935, 12.

33. Wilhelm Stapel, "Aphoristisches zur Judenfrage," in Gottfried Feder et al., eds., *Das neue Deutschland und die Judenfrage* (Leipzig: Rüdiger, 1933), 172. In 1937 Stapel would once again seek to ingratiate himself with the regime when he published a book that analyzed "the literary dominance of Jews in Germany, 1918–1933." See Wilhelm Stapel, *Die literarische Vorherrschaft der Juden in Deutschland 1918 bis 1933* (Hamburg: Hanseatische Verlagsanstalt, 1937).

34. For a fuller discussion, see Dagmar Herzog, "Sex and the Third Reich," in my *Sex After Fascism: Memory and Morality in Twentieth-Century Germany* (Princeton: Princeton University Press, 2005).

35. See the excellent analyses in Klaus-Dietmar Henke, "Fraternization," in *Die amerikanische Besetzung Deutschlands* (Munich: R. Oldenbourg, 1995), 185–204; John Willoughby, "The Sexual Behavior of American GIs During the Early Years of the Occupation of Germany," *Journal of Military History* 62 (January 1998); Petra Goedde, "From Villains to Victims: Fraternization and the Feminization of Germany, 1945–1947," *Diplomatic History* 23, no. 1 (Winter 1999); and Maria Hoehn, *GIs and Fräuleins: The German-American Encounter in 1950s West Germany* (Chapel Hill: University of North Carolina Press, 2002).

36. See Anton Christian Hofmann, *Die Natürlichkeit der christlichen Ehe* (Munich: J. Pfeiffer, 1951), 5, 9–10, 38–39.

37. For one example among many, contrast the effusively pro-Nazi remarks of Protestant church activist D. Erich Stange in 1933 with his description of Christians as victims of Nazism in 1951. See Stange quoted in Ernst Klee, *"Die SA Jesu Christi": Die Kirchen im Banne Hitlers* (Frankfurt am Main: Fischer, 1989), 26–27; and D. Erich Stange, "Innere Mission und kirchliche Werke," *Evangelische Welt* 5, no. 22 (16 November 1951), 678. But note also that anti-Nazi Christians consistently distorted the relationship between Christianity and Nazism when they emphasized Nazism's anti-Christianity. See, for example, Walter Dirks's remark that "German Catholicism stood on the list of opponents of the German essence that were to be exterminated [*Der deutsche Katholizismus stand auf der Liste der zur Ausrottung bestimmten Widersacher des deutschen Wesens*]"; Dirks in *Frankfurter Hefte* (May 1946), 45. Postwar Protestants, too, regularly remarked that Nazism had planned to "liquidate the church," that Nazism wanted to "destroy the church and exterminate the Christian faith," or that "the persecution of Christians was the direct extension of the battle against the Jews. It would have led to a similar extermination program." See Link, "Königsberg (1945–1948)," *Junge Kirche. Sonderdruck* (January 1950); "Wort des Bruderrates der EKD zur Reinigung der Kirche vom Nationalsozialismus," in Joachim Beckmann, ed., *Kirchliches Jahrbuch für die evangelische Kirche in Deutschland 1945–1948* (Gütersloh: Gütersloher Verlagshaus, 1950), 187; and Otto Fricke, "Wir Christen und die Juden" (1949), in Hans Kallenbach, ed., *Die Juden und wir Christen* (Frankfurt am Main: Lembeck, 1950), 48–49.

38. "Wort der ausserordentlichen Landessynode der Evangelisch-Lutherischen Kirche in Oldenburg an die Gemeinden Oktober 1945," in Beckmann, *Kirchliches Jahrbuch*, 43, 45.
39. "Kundgebung der Landessynode der Evangelisch-Lutherischen Kirche in Bayern in Ansbach, 9.–13. Juli 1946," in ibid., 48.
40. Bishop quoted in Johannes Kleinschmidt, "Amerikaner und Deutsche in der Besatzungszeit—Beziehungen und Probleme." http://www.lpb.bwue.de/publikat/lbesatzer/us-pol6.htm.
41. Johannes Leppich, "'Thema 1,'" in Günther Mees and Günter Graf, eds., *Pater Leppich Spricht: Journalisten hören den "roten" Pater* (Düsseldorf: Bastion, 1952), 43–44.
42. Clearly there were also other reasons for "nesting," not least the strongly felt needs to repair individual partnerships and reconstruct families to the extent that either was possible after the intense disruptions of total war and mass death. A special focus on domesticity was a reasonable response both to years of wartime and postwar deprivation, separation, stress, and loss, and to the Nazi state's aggressive invasion of the private realm alike. Yet as the psychoanalyst Sophinette Becker has pointed out, there was also a more insidious side to this withdrawal into privacy. Dating the onset of the move toward privatization already to the years when World War II was going badly for Germany while the war against the Jews was moving ahead with terrifying speed and effectivity, Becker sees in this privatization a strategy for denial of responsibility for and knowledge of mass murder. See Sophinette Becker, "Zur Funktion der Sexualität im Nationalsozialismus," *Zeitschrift für Sexualforschung* 14, no. 2 (June 2001), 142–43.
43. Y. Michal Bodemann, "Eclipse of Memory: German Representations of Auschwitz in the Early Postwar Period," *New German Critique* 75 (Fall 1998), 61–72, 88–89.
44. For some examples of the postwar persistence of Christian disdain for the disabled, see Meta Holland, *Vor dem Tore der Ehe: Was jede junge Frau wissen muss* (Konstanz: Christliche Verlagsanstalt, 1950), 5, 87–89; Ernst Karl Winter, "Das grosse Geheimnis: Ehe und Familie in der christlichen Zivilisation," *Frankfurter Hefte* (October 1951), 716; Theodor Bovet, *Von Mann zu Mann: Eine Einführung ins Reifealter für junge Männer* (Tübingen: Katzmann, 1955), 47; and Hans March, "Zur Sexual-Ethik," *Stimmen der Zeit* 156 (1955), 297–99. On the influential Catholic Hermann Muckermann's openly advanced post-1945 opinions—including his vociferous concern that the disabled cost society more than the healthy ("the thought is unbearable that hopeless progeny from mentally debilitated hereditary lines would be cared for with greater devotion than the progeny of healthy parents"), see Ernst Klee, *Was sie taten—Was sie wurden: Ärzte, Juristen und andere Beteiligte am Kranken- oder Judenmord* (Frankfurt am Main: Fischer, 1986), 148–49. For examples of the postwar Christian renovation of homophobic ideas promoted under Nazism, see "Not um den Paragraphen 175," *Christ und Welt* 4, no. 20 (1951), 4–5; "Literatur-Umschau," *Kriminalistik* 6, nos. 13-14 (1952), 167–68 (the book under discussion is Gatzweiler, *Das dritte Geschlecht* [Cologne-Klettenberg: Volkswartbund, 1951]); A. Ohm, "Homosexualität als Neurose," *Der Weg zur Seele* 5 (1953), 24–56; and Erich Schröder, *Reif Werden und Rein Bleiben: Briefe eines Arztes an seinen Patensohn* (Konstanz: Christliche Verlagsanstalt, 1956). The churches' resistance to decriminalization of homosexuality was decisive for the failure of the postwar campaign to abolish Paragraph 175. See Mario Kramp and Martin Sölle, "Paragraph 175—Restauration und Reform in der Bundesrepublik," in Kristof Balser et al., eds., *"Himmel und Hölle": Das Leben der Kölner Homosexuellen 1945–1969* (Cologne: Emons, 1995), 126, 132, 139–41.
45. See Dagmar Herzog, "Between Coitus and Commodification: Young West German Women and the Impact of the Pill," in Axel Schildt and Detlef Siegfried, eds., *Between Marx and Coca-Cola: Youth Cultures in Changing European Societies, 1960–1980* (New York: Berghahn Books, forthcoming).
46. As early as 1963, for instance, the mainstream news magazine *Der Spiegel* approvingly cited a comment made by one of the prosecutors in the Frankfurt trial to the effect that Auschwitz had been built by *"Spiesser"*—the term typically used by liberals and leftists to describe not only generally banal and conventional but also sexually uptight conserva-

tives. See "Auf der Rampe," *Der Spiegel,* 18 December 1963, 46–47. For the further impact of this specific assessment of the perpetrators, see the discussion in the section on "legalized criminality" in Arno Plack, *Die Gesellschaft und das Böse: Eine Kritik der herrschenden Moral* (Munich: Paul List, 1967), 304–10.

47. Plack, *Die Gesellschaft und das Böse,* 308.
48. See the discussion of *Konkret* in Ulrike Heider, "Freie Liebe und Liebesreligion: Zum Sexualitätsbegriff der 60er und 80er Jahre," in Ulrike Heider, ed., *Sadomasochisten, Keusche und Romantiker: Vom Mythos neuer Sinnlichkeit* (Reinbek: Rowohlt, 1986), 93.
49. Plack, *Die Gesellschaft und das Böse,* 309; and Michael Rohrwasser, *Saubere Mädel, Starke Genossen: Proletarische Massenkultur?* (Frankfurt am Main: Roter Stern, 1975), 9.
50. Anton-Andreas Guha, *Sexualität und Pornographie: Die organisierte Entmündigung* (Frankfurt am Main: Fischer, 1971), 126–27.
51. Wolfgang Fritz Haug, "Vorbemerkung," *Das Argument* 32 (1965), 30–31.
52. See Dagmar Herzog, "German Ideologies and the Body Politics of 1968," in Jan-Werner Mueller, ed., *German Ideologies Since 1945* (New York: Palgrave Macmillan, 2003).
53. Heider, "Freie Liebe," 94.
54. Dietrich Haensch, *Repressive Familienpolitik: Sexualunterdrückung als Mittel der Politik* (Reinbek: Rowohlt, 1969), 12, 14, 66–67.
55. Dieter Duhm, *Angst im Kapitalismus: Zweiter Versuch der gesellschaftlichen Begründung zwischenmenschlicher Angst in der kapitalistischen Warengesellschaft* (Lampertheim: Kübler, 1972), 100.
56. "Die gefallene Natur," *Der Spiegel,* 2 May 1966, 57–58.
57. Hannes Schwenger, *Antisexuelle Propaganda: Sexualpolitik in der Kirche* (Reinbek: Rowohlt, 1969), 34–36.
58. Tellingly, indeed, New Leftists' first reactions were to be unable to see the Nazi nudes as erotic; instead they insisted on their lack of sensuality. Conversation with Georg Bussmann, 2003; and see Berthold Hinz, *Die Malerei im deutschen Faschismus* (Munich: Hanser, 1974); and Christian Gross and Uwe Grossmann, "Die Darstellung der Frau," in Bussmann, *Kunst im Dritten Reich.*

– *Chapter 12*–

THE GENDER OF GOOD AND EVIL
Women and Holocaust Memory

Sara R. Horowitz

What is the gender of good or of evil? Do moral categories and gender categories intersect in any meaningful way, particularly in the context of the Holocaust? We might be tempted to dismiss the question as ill-posed, pointing to the wide variety of sources that confirm that men and women behaved in a wide range of ways as victims, collaborators, bystanders, rescuers, and perpetrators during the Nazi genocide. But on the level of representations, it is important to note that particular patterns of gendered images of the Holocaust have emerged and proliferated. Shaped by preexisting tropes of male and female good and evil, in addition to cultural norms about who men and women are and what they do, these images play a strong role in shaping cultural memory and meanings of the Holocaust. Beginning with contemporaneous wartime representations and continuing until today, certain gendered images of good and evil—of men or women doing or being good or evil in particularly male or female ways—permeate the vehicles of memory such as historical or literary narratives, documentary and feature films, and the visual and plastic arts. These images play a strong role in memory and memorialization of the Holocaust.

Images of good and evil associated particularly with women under Nazism are shaped by cultural attitudes about women's nature and women's behavior and, in turn, shape our perception of the Holocaust. The tropes of womanly good and evil are linked strongly with women's sexuality, even when framed in contexts not explicitly sexual.

Notes for this section begin on page 176.

The Good

A *New York Times* headline on 8 January 1943 announced, "93 Choose Suicide Before Shame."[1] The article reported an episode involving ninety-three students of the Beth Jacob (or Bais Yakov) school, which was a religious seminary for girls in Krakow (although the *Times* article placed the incident in Warsaw). The students and their teacher, the article recounted, "chose mass suicide to escape being forced into prostitution by German soldiers."

The *Times* story was based on a letter dated 11 August 1942, ostensibly written by a Beth Jacob teacher who died with her pupils and whose name the newspaper withheld "lest relatives [remaining in Europe] . . . be subjected to reprisals." The letter, the *Times* noted, reached a member the Beth Jacob Committee in New York, part of the ultra-Orthodox Agudas Yisroel organization, in early 1943. The *Times* article included the text of the letter translated from the original Yiddish. The letter described how the young women, aged fourteen to twenty-three, were held in a dark room and without food. Eventually, the letter noted, they "were given hot baths and . . . told that German soldiers would come tonight" and then taken to "a big house with bright rooms and nice beds." However, the letter explained, the young women planned to avoid forced prostitution by committing suicide. "All of us have poison. When the soldiers will come we shall drink it," the letter stated. The young women were presented as taking courage from the study of sacred texts. "It is good to live for God, but it is also good to die for Him." The letter ends by enjoining its addressee to recite the memorial prayer on behalf of the Beth Jacob students: "Say Kaddish for us, your 93 children."

The *Times* article offered no explanation for how the teacher managed to smuggle the letter out from the room in which the young women were held captive, nor did it name any of the students. By now most historians agree that the incident described in the *Times* did not occur, although it was initially accepted as a true account of an actual wartime event. However, after its *New York Times* coverage, the story took on a life of its own. Variations of the episode circulated quickly in Orthodox circles in the United States as a particularly trenchant illustration of the horrors confronting the Jews of Europe. In addition to the obvious importance of a firsthand account by a victim amid ongoing atrocity, the story placed the focus on Nazi persecution as aimed against Jews as a religious, rather than a racially defined, people, in addition to affirming the possibility of faith in the darkest hour. In its various retellings the incident was set sometimes in Warsaw, as per the *Times* article, and other times it was placed in Krakow, where the Beth Jacob seminary was located; some versions referred to German soldiers, and others to German officers. The story moved beyond the sphere of Orthodox Judaism and was declaimed from synagogue pulpits and published in various American Jewish publications. Several published versions of the episode refer back to the original letter, whose Yiddish was written in German, rather than Hebrew, characters, and bore the signature "Chaja Feldman."

Two weeks after the publication of the letter in the *Times* a poem by Hillel Bavli appeared in *Ha-Do'ar*, a New York–based Hebrew language newspaper.[2] Bavli, a Hebrew poet and literary scholar from Lithuania who taught at the Jewish Theological Seminary (the New York rabbinical institute of the Conservative movement), drew strongly on the language and imagery of the letter in composing "The Martyrdom of the Ninety-Three Maidens." Ordered to "satisfy the lustful desires" of Nazi soldiers, the young women instead "poured out their hearts in prayer and swallowed poison and returned their breath to God." In March of that year an English translation of Bavli's poem was published in *The Reconstructionist*, the journal of Reconstructionist Judaism, with the suggestion that it be read aloud in synagogues before the recitation of the Kaddish memorial prayer.[3] The request with which the letter closes, posed either as a rhetorical statement or a personal petition to the addressee—"Say Kaddish for us"—is transformed through Bavli's poem into a communal, liturgical imperative.

It is not surprising that Bavli was drawn to the incident. Two months before the *Times* ran the story about the ninety-three Beth Jacob girls, it reported on a special commencement ceremony at the Jewish Theological Seminary to accelerate the ordination of several rabbinical students to meet the need for chaplains in the armed forces.[4] At the ceremony, in which Bavli received an honorary doctorate, the borough president of Manhattan gave a commencement address that emphasized the importance of religious "faith and ideals" both to the morale of the American fighting men and to American society at large as it rebuilt itself after the war.

> The youth of America may return from this war . . . with the spiritual values, the eternal beauty of life dimmed, if not extinguished, unless their faith in God and belief in their religion is maintained. That is the task of all leaders of religion . . . to maintain the faith and belief and trust in god, in religion, and in all spiritual values. It must be done if this war is not to be fought in vain.

The borough president noted that "this is particularly true of those of us of the Jewish faith." The preservation of religious ideals was seen as essential to the continuity of "the ways of American democracy" (to use the language of the *New York Times*) as well as to the continuity of Judaism in America. For Bavli, two months after hearing this exhortation, the image of young women praying at the brink of death must have presented itself as affirming of religious values in just the way that the borough president charged. In defending their sexual chastity against overwhelming odds, the girls turned despair into triumph over evil.

Indeed, this is how the story struck the American Jewish community. By the late 1940s Bavli's poem began to be integrated into Yom Kippur (Day of Atonement) liturgy. It appears, for example, in the 1948 edition of the Reconstructionist High Holiday prayer book and a decade later in Conservative ones, as part of the Yom Kippur Martyrology service.[5] It is utilized today in liberal American synagogues on Yom Kippur and in Holocaust Remembrance Day commemorations. As such, "The Martyrdom of the

Ninety-Three Maidens" has become part of an American Jewish Holocaust canon.⁶

In the poem's liturgical use the ninety-three virgins are employed iconically. The young maidens whose lives are tragically cut short become an emblem of the Holocaust. Holocaust atrocity becomes identified and synonymous with sexual violation. The language of the poem presents the maidens' suicide as an act of *kiddush ha-shem,* literally sanctification of the divine Name, the traditional Jewish term for martyrdom. Martyrdom implies agency and choice; the liturgy emphasizes the element of choice: death over forced prostitution, that is to say, rape. The maidens' prayer before death invokes the near death of the biblical Isaac in the *Akedah,* or binding episode depicted in Genesis 22, the prototype for martyrdom in Jewish medieval poetry. In the Yom Kippur martyrology the poem is placed in the context of historical and legendary Jewish martyrdoms—most notably the ten sages martyred by the Romans in Mishnaic times and the communal suicides in the Crusader era. In strongly linking the deaths of the ninety-three young women during the Holocaust with traditional Jewish archetypes of martyrdom, the poem provides religious comfort and theological meaning. The story it recounts asserts that, despite the horrors of the Shoah, the Holocaust can be absorbed readily into the continuum of Jewish life and religious practices. Theologically speaking, nothing has changed.

Although the poem describes the threat of sexual violation aimed at the body of the Jewess, the real assault is against the spirit of the Jew, which triumphs through martyrdom. In traditional Judaic terminology, the poem implies that forced prostitution be seen as a form of *gilui arayot,* the Talmud's term for forbidden sexual relations. *Gilui arayot* is one of the three categories of transgressive behavior that must be avoided at all costs, even at the price of one's life (the other two being idolatry and murder).⁷ The Talmud's discussion of the conditions under which a person is required to give up his life is the earliest extended articulation of the principles of Jewish martyrdom, one to which I will later return. As the poem describes it, the maidens defend against the degradation of Jewish dignity in a context designed to humiliate Jews. The liturgy thus provides an interpretive framework through which to understand and absorb the implications of the Holocaust. While the poem poignantly mourns the premature death of the ninety-three maidens, it celebrates their ultimate purity of body and soul and deems their death inherently meaningful and necessary to Jewish continuity.

The poem presents a gendered image of good—women triumphing over evil *in extremis.* However, this image of female good invokes a shadow image of female evil. In presenting this possibility for heroic death during the Holocaust, the poem implies that rape or forced prostitution is too high a price to pay for survival. Given today's understanding of the dynamics of rape, the enduring popularity of the poem seems surprising, especially in liberal American congregations whose liturgy features revisions and innovations that reflect contemporary American sensibilities. The general acceptance of the poem's sentiments in commemorative ritual suggests, at the very least, an ambivalence about certain gendered strategies for survival, as well as a reluctance to acknowledge the extent of Nazi atrocity. This ambivalence about sexual atrocity and survival *in extremis* does not simply reflect a clash between contemporary sensibilities and traditional Jewish ideals or an imposition of prurient mores on more authentic concepts of Jewish martyrdom. Rather, the ambivalence is already present in the Talmud's initial development of the concept of martyrdom.

Traditional Jewish sources delineate the boundaries of martyrdom by specifying three categories of transgression that one must not commit even under threat of death.[8] In thinking through this issue, the Talmud explores two distinct but related sets of questions. The first is whether a person may save another person from sinning by killing him before he sins. The second is whether a person is required to accept his own death rather than to transgress (the situation of martyrdom). For example, one should prevent a murder from occurring by killing the person intent on committing murder; correspondingly, a person ordered to murder or be killed himself must accept his own death rather than kill. In other words, the Talmud demands that the life of the potential transgressor (whether oneself or another) be forfeited to prevent that person from actualizing the transgression. However, a certain textual ambiguity arises with regard to the third category, that of *gilui arayot*, which has implications for our reading of "The Martyrdom of the Ninety-Three Maidens" and for the issue of sexual violation during the Shoah more generally.

The Talmud proposes a hypothetical situation in which a man is about to rape a betrothed woman. The text asserts that this potential perpetrator may be killed, not—as the contemporary reader might expect—to save the woman from rape but to save the assailant himself from transgressing. The discussion then merges the question of killing a would-be transgressor with the question of martyrdom, in each instance using the phrase that has come to connote martyrdom in rabbinic texts—*yehareg ve'al ya'avor*, he shall be killed rather than transgress. However, in discussing the rape of the betrothed woman, the text suddenly shifts the gender of the verb, so that *she* rather than *he* is the one who must be killed (*tehareg* rather than *yehareg*).[9] The feminization of the verb seems to suggest not only that one must resist—unto death—becoming a perpetrator, but that one must also resist falling victim. In other words, a person must die rather than *commit* murder, but a woman must die rather than *be raped*.[10]

Reading "The Martyrdom of the Ninety-Three Maidens" against the backdrop of these originary texts on Jewish martyrdom, the liturgical poem seems to depict a self-sacrifice required by Jewish law.[11] Responsa of the war era indicate that rabbis permitted Jews to transgress Jewish law rather than perish. Yet the ninety-three young women must remain sexually inviolate at all costs.

The instance in the Talmud seems to establish an impossible standard, not that women are incapable of chastity even under duress, but that—unlike the situation of a person who may choose whether or not to murder, or to worship false gods, or to rape—it may not be in the power of a rape victim to engineer her own death.[12] The letter from Chaja Feldman indicates that the Beth Jacob girls not only had sufficient poison to select death but also sufficient time during which they were not under surveillance. This easy availability of means and opportunity may hardly be said to be the norm, either for Holocaust victims or rape victims. Moreover, the Talmud is disinclined to codify unattainable law. What could the requirement imposed on the betrothed woman, and by extension on the Beth Jacob girls, mean?

Central to the issue of the trope of the good woman in Holocaust representation is the question of desire. In the Talmud, an absence of desire mitigates the guilt of forbidden sexual relations. In its view male desire is necessary for sexual transgressions to occur, but female desire is not. If a woman is *karka olam,* "like the earth" as a passive receptacle for male lust rather than a proactive agent pursuing her own pleasure, she is not considered a transgressor nor expected to forfeit her life. But the possibility of female desire, even in circumstances of rape, troubles the interlocutors of the Talmud and its later interpreters. In "The Martyrdom of the Ninety-Three Maidens," suicide negates the possibility of (forbidden) pleasure. Returning to "dust of the earth" proves that the maidens are "like the earth"; the dead feel no desire.

Literary representations of the Holocaust frequently link the portrayal of women's sexuality and desire with judgments about moral good. For example, in her 1969 novel *An Estate of Memory,* Ilona Karmel describes a group of four Jewish women in a labor camp who form what Karmel calls a "makeshift family," banding together to keep one another alive and sane under the brutal conditions of camp life. The four women are united by a shared goal. One of them is secretly pregnant, and the others wish to help her keep that pregnancy a secret, deliver the baby, and furtively send it to safety outside the camp. One of the women is repulsed by her companion's condition—not by the possibility that the woman may have been raped, but by the thought that the pregnancy resulted from the woman's own undisciplined desire. However, when she learns that the woman became pregnant on the evening preceding her husband's deportation to mass slaughter—that it was the woman's effort to comfort her husband and quell his fears—her revulsion melts away. Like every other behavior in Karmel's novel, sexual behavior is seen through the prism of ethics. The "good" woman disciplines her desire, especially *in extremis.*

The Evil

French filmmaker Marcel Ophuls has made two powerful films grappling with the dark side of France's history during the Holocaust. *The Sorrow and the Pity,* produced in the 1960s and released in 1971, examines life in German-occupied France, focusing on the memories of people in the small city of Clermont-Ferrand. *Hotel Terminus: The Life and Times of Klaus Barbie,* released in 1988, was made during Barbie's war crimes trial. It focuses on the memories of people who had known the "Butcher of Lyons" before, during, and after the war. Both films explore French collaboration and resistance during the war, probing individual as well as institutional cooperation with the Nazi genocide.

One technique that Ophuls employs to great success is to allow people to speak at length on camera, encouraging or goading them with questions but not commenting directly on or evaluating what they say. The most powerful revelations in his films emerge not from directly confronting a speaker but from juxtaposing conversations with different speakers whose differing memories offer an implicit commentary on or corrective to one another. At times Ophuls assumes a particular speaker's point of view long enough for that person's duplicity or self-deception to become apparent to viewers. Other times, when interviewing someone, Ophuls repeats the speaker's words several times. This draws the viewers' attention to phrases that have profound and disturbing implications, and at the same time draws the speaker into further revelations about the past.

In *Hotel Terminus* Ophuls conducts an extended interview with a woman named Françoise Hemmerle. Hemmerle asserts that during the war she had been a "freedom fighter." Ophuls reminds her (and thereby informs the viewers) that in the period immediately following the war, she had been brought to trial and charged with "national indignity," financially exploiting Jewish families, and conspiring with the enemy. Imprisoned with a sentence that was commuted a number of years later, Hemmerle subsequently wrote and published at her own expense a book defending herself against these charges. The book was titled *De la Boue qui ne touche pas,* or "Mud That Does Not Stain."

In her conversation with Ophuls, Hemmerle refers to Alain Resnais' film, *Night and Fog,* as a "propaganda film." Ophuls does not immediately challenge that description. But in the space of a few short minutes he repeats the phrase "propaganda film" no fewer than three times. Eventually Hemmerle concedes that her use of the phrase "propaganda film" indicates that she believes that reports of Nazi horror have been "exaggerated." She downplays the horrors of Nazi atrocity and sweeps genocide into the general hardships of war. "When a war's declared, all sorts of things go on," she says. This lets the film viewers know how to evaluate Hemmerle's claims to morality and how to understand her claim to having been a "freedom" fighter rather than an enemy of the people (or collaborator). Hemmerle is critical of the ongoing Barbie trial. She is not concerned with a particular legal tactic or maneuver that she finds unfair or distasteful; she thinks that the war crimes trial should not be conducted at all. Hemmerle condemns those who want to prosecute Klaus Barbie four decades after his wartime atrocities. "Why not go all the way back to the burning of Joan of Arc?" she asks facetiously.

In her opinion whatever brutality was inflicted by this vastly "exaggerated" Nazi brutality pales in comparison to the greater brutality inflicted by

Frenchmen upon French collaborators in the period immediately following the collapse of the Vichy government. In fact, the only moment in which Hemmerle displays intense emotion on camera is when she recollects her shock at the degree of animosity turned against French collaborators immediately after the war—most specifically the humiliation of women like herself. She calls it "French on French" violence. She asserts that it is far worse to inflict harm on one's fellow countrymen than on one's enemies. (We might note, of course, that French Jews were rounded up by their compatriots.)

In *Hotel Terminus* Ophuls depicts Hemmerle as reprehensible. Indeed, in her behavior during the war and her distortions after the war she is self-serving, hypocritical, mercenary, and hateful. At the same time, one cannot help but note that the way Ophuls depicts her in his film—that is, the way he conducts the interview and edits the final cut—is very different from the way he treats the other collaborator interviewed in *Hotel Terminus*. The other collaborator, retired police officer Armand Zuchner, served in Lyons when Barbie was in authority. He cooperated with Barbie, rounding up people for interrogation or deportation. Close to the time that the Vichy government collapsed, he managed to rescue a number of people named in Barbie's deportation lists. As the interview progresses, he reveals that all those he rescued were influential people or from influential families. From many of them he received affidavits confirming his role in saving them. These documents helped acquit him of war crime accusations after the war.

Ophuls's cinematic treatment of these two collaborators is very different. Zuchner is presented as a petty, self-serving person of little moral fiber, more silly than dangerous. Hemmerle is presented as an evil woman—that is, evil not in a generic way, but in a specifically female way. In a letter written in late 2002 about the depiction of collaboration in *Hotel Terminus*, Ophuls recollects Zuchner as "an idiot." He remembers Hemmerle as "a witch" who fixed the "evil eye" on him. Indeed, the film shows her warning Ophuls several times that bad things befall people who do her harm.

When Hemmerle thinks back on camera to the war years and their immediate aftermath, she remembers in particular the postwar victimization of French women who were thought to be involved personally with German soldiers. Needless to say, I do not accept her contention that this was far worse than the victimization of Jews and resistors under Nazism. But she is correct in pointing out that there was a particular harshness of judgment reserved for women. This severe negative judgment was attached not only to their political activities but also to their sexuality and undisciplined desire. Ophuls's earlier film, *The Sorrow and the Pity,* for example, shows film footage of French women publicly humiliated, with their heads shaved and clothing torn, for having German lovers.

In many films and books about the war years there is a particular anger reserved for the female collaborator, a special horror at something seen as particularly monstrous, above and beyond the act of collaboration itself. Perhaps this is because our culture wishes to see certain attributes as naturally female—attributes such as being nurturing and compassionate. In the woman collaborator something considered to be "naturally" female has been somehow perverted. When women collaborators are depicted, the fact of collaboration attaches itself to the very womanness of the collaborator, making it seem a horrifying and frightening aspect of female sexuality itself, like the sirens of Greek mythology who lure unsuspecting men to their doom. A salient example of this can be seen in the portrayal of the protagonist in the book *Stella*. American journalist Peter Wyden writes about a Jewish woman he had once known in Berlin during his prewar childhood. During the war Stella collaborated with Germans by identifying other Berlin Jews who were attempting to survive the Nazi genocide by posing as non-Jews. In his remembrance of Stella, whom he had not seen since they were young teenagers in Berlin, Wyden describes "the school's Marilyn Monroe: tall, slim, leggy, cool with light blue eyes, teeth out of a toothpaste ad, and pale satin skin . . . a monument to beauty . . . a fantasy for a pubescent boy."[13] He sees her sexuality and her subsequent conspiratorial activities as part of the same essence. "Where," he wonders, "would [the Gestapo] find another blond, blue-eyed Jewess who could wiggle her way into any male confidence . . . ?"[14] Like Ophuls's recollection of Hemmerle, Stella's perfidy and betrayal strike Wyden as worse than those of male collaborators.

The Gray Zone

A number of recently published memoirs by female Holocaust survivors have begun to explore the intersecting issues of sexual violation, sexual desire, victimization, and collaboration in ways that open up spaces for moral ambiguities rather than simplistic certainties. For example, Fanya Heller's memoir, *Strange and Unexpected Love*, describes a sexual liaison between the author as a teenager and Jan, a Ukrainian militia man who rescued her and her family.[15] While the memoir portrays an affair of the heart, reciprocal and loving, there are sufficient indicators that place it in political context: she, a Jewish adolescent without the right to live; he, a uniformed Ukrainian with the right to grant or to take her life. This imbalance between them precludes any real mutuality. As the repeated urging of her parents to be "nice" to Jan reminds us, love was a viable currency in the genocidal economy.

In addition to recounting her own wartime experience, Heller's memoir suggests that accounts of sexual violation and erotic transactions during the Holocaust are strongly underrepresented in the narratives of women survivors. Heller's aunt, for example, was raped by a German soldier. At the time, the aunt tells only a few family members. Many years later, the aunt decided to keep the episode a secret from her children, to exclude it from the memories of wartime atrocity that she transmitted to them. Under less extreme circumstances it would not be unusual for a woman to decide to keep silent about a rape or other sexual violation—indeed, until very recently, such secrecy has been the norm. However, it is significant that here, in the context of ongoing atrocity, rape should be considered different from other forms of torture and humiliation. The oral history transmitted generationally in the family contains deeply shameful episodes, such as Heller's grandfather betraying his wife's hiding place during a roundup in a desperate but vain attempt to save his own life. The family's transmission of Holocaust narratives encompasses even such events but apparently cannot absorb the memory of a rape.

Unlike the seminary girls depicted in Bavli's poem and in wartime reportage as choosing a martyr's death over forbidden sexual relations, Heller enters into an intense sexual relationship with the Ukrainian militia man who protects her and her entire family at great personal risk and considerable loss of stature in his own family and community. Unlike the transactional sex depicted in Ida Fink's short story "Aryan Papers,"[16] in which a teenaged girl offers up her virginity to a scornful and callous man in return for false documents that may save her and her mother's lives, or Agnieska Holland's film, *Angry Harvest,* where a Jewish wife and mother accepts the unwanted sexual overtures of the Polish farmer who hides her, Heller finds these erotic encounters exhilarating and comforting. "Love-making surprised me: it felt so right, the only right thing in a time of madness."[17] Their relationship, as she recollects it in the memoir, is not an exchange of commodities—sex for protection—but one tenderly nurtured and patiently awaited. "There was something between Jan and me that transcended the physical: we had been allied, entwined, intimately involved with each other for over a year before we made love."[18] In that sense, Heller presents their intimacy as a private and contained world, removed from the horrors occurring outside of it. This feeling of separateness is reinforced by descriptions of the places where their lovemaking occurs: closed spaces, barns, and garrets. At the same time, however, one cannot really remove their intimacy from the political context in which it crystallizes. Were it not for the Nazi genocide, the intellectual Heller would not be interested in illiterate Jan. The barriers of religion, social class, and education would have made the match extremely unlikely. But under the threat of genocide, Jan's ability to protect her—which is also a power to betray her—makes him attractive.

Heller's narrative takes great pains to downplay any sense of threat in Jan's presence by subtly feminizing him. In his initial encounter with Heller he acquires food for her family in the marketplace, an act of nurturance traditionally female. While Jan is Heller's first lover, she describes his lovemaking as so gentle that she cannot locate the precise moment when their love is consummated. "Jan was very gentle, careful not to rush me, passion so well-anointed with affection that during those first three days of our intimacy I could not say precisely when I had stopped being a virgin."[19] While Jan appears frequently in military uniform, his distinguishing physical characteristic is the missing upper joints of two of his fingers, which were lost in a machine accident. In Heller's first glimpse of Jan, he is a "tall man with a rifle and wearing the armband of the Ukrainian militia"; Heller immediately notes "that his ring and pinkie fingers were missing: the two knobs where knuckles and fingertips should have been looked forlorn."[20] If a man under the Reich is defined by his power to kill, which is also a power to coerce sexual compliance, Jan's manhood is compromised by his dismembered fingers, symbolically a displaced castration. Thus the narrative attempts to equalize the relationship between Heller and Jan by equalizing their desire and by introducing a gender ambiguity that diminishes the image of his manhood—which, in this context, is indistinguishable from the ability to murder.

When the war ends, Heller views Jan in an entirely different context. The inequalities between them become newly visible as their cultural and religious differences become more pronounced. Jan's family has always been deeply antisemitic. Heller realizes that to marry him would be to live among people who desired her death, "a lone Jew among Ukrainians, who hated and had murdered my people."[21] Rumors abound that implicate Jan in the murder of Heller's father. Immediately following the war Heller feels powerful pressure to reinvent her past. Her mother exhorts her to recreate her life, to construct a history in which Jan never existed. Before his death, Heller's father had promised, "In Paris no one will know. You'll be clean, I promise you."[22] Her parents' admonitions to forget the portion of the past that involved Jan suggest a sense of sexual shame on behalf of their daughter, and also for themselves as party to an unsavory transaction deemed necessary for the family's survival. In addition, Heller realizes that public knowledge of the affair would diminish her value as a marriage partner after the war.

Heller's personal story, full of ambiguities and shades of gray, depicts a very different reality from that of the chaste heroism depicted in "The Martyrdom of the Ninety-Three Maidens." The maidens are seen as "good," but Heller is not. After the publication of her memoir in the 1990s, Heller came under strong censure from many members of her religious community. The implied negative judgment of her wartime behavior is twofold: if Heller did not love Jan, then she prostituted herself; if she did love him, then she consorted with the enemy. In either event Heller's case is judged without reference to the extreme circumstances of the Holocaust and is condemned for behavior that saved her life, as well as her mother's and brother's. In part this may be due to the wish of the Jewish community to see itself as whole again after the unspeakable trauma of the Holocaust. The irreversible loss of virginity, then, offers the unwanted implication that the body of Israel is no longer intact and that the effect of these losses similarly cannot be reversed. The debasement of the sexually violated woman or the one who trades sexual favors becomes a symbol for the lingering sense of psychological debasement that Holocaust survivors and their progeny wish to leave in the past. While other forms of Holocaust atrocity seem unthinkable in the present world of the survivor, sexual violence continues, and may seem, in retrospect, more ordinary—merely shameful and hence, inexcusable.

These representations of women's experiences during the Holocaust present sets of gendered images in which female sexuality and female desire become a barometer of good and evil. It is useful to pose such images against Jean Améry's assertion, in his famous essay "Torture," that torture is "like a rape." Describing the experience and aftershock of torture at the hands of the Belgian Gestapo, he says the following:

> At the first blow . . . trust in the world breaks down. The other person, *opposite* whom I exist physically in the world and *with* whom I can exist only as long as he does not touch my skin surface as border, forces his own corporeality on me with the first blow. He is on me and thereby destroys me. It is like a rape, a sexual act without the consent of one of the two partners.[23]

In using this metaphor—the only metaphor in the entire essay—Améry signals the powerlessness of the tortured to prevent intrusion into or onto one's body, and the realization that one is no longer sovereign over one's self, over one's very being. In Bavli's liturgical poem rape is presented as a gender-specific trope that ironically (and impossibly) insists on the possibility of choice. The poem has serious and problematic ramifications when used as formal or official Holocaust remembrance. How would a survivor who had made a different choice—a woman who had survived rape or sexual barter—feel at a ceremony that invoked the womanly ideal of "The Martyrdom of the Ninety-Three Maidens"? Perversely, such women are faulted for having "chosen wrongly." Holding a woman accountable for her own sexual victimization is not a new idea. But importing it into the realm of Nazi atrocity is startling. It has made it difficult to bring the experiences of some women into the compass of Holocaust discussion and has caused these women to feel ashamed about circumstances they could not control or prevent. The gendered images of good and evil color the way people regard the women's behavior and women's choices. They simplify complex and ambiguous moral questions, insisting on ultimate judgment rather than on compassion.

Notes

1. "93 Choose Suicide Before Shame," *New York Times* (8 January 1943), 8.
2. *Ha-Do'ar* 22:12 (22 January 1943), 186.
3. *The Reconstructionist* 9:2 (5 March 1943), 23–24.
4. "Faith in God Held Needed for Victory," *New York Times* (10 November 1942), 23.
5. See, for example, Rabbi Jules Harlow, ed., *Mahzor for Rosh Hashanah and Yom Kippur: A Prayerbook for the Days of Awe* (New York: Rabbinical Assembly, 1972), 561–63; *Mahzor Le-Yamim Nora'im: Seder Tefillot le-Yom Kippur/High Holiday Prayerbook*, vol. 2, *Prayers for Yom Kippur* (New York: Jewish Reconstructionist Foundation, 1948), 396–97; Ben Zion Bokser, *The High Holiday Prayer Book* (New York: Hebrew Publishing, 1959), 434–36. According to the notation in these prayer books, the liturgical poem written in Hebrew by Hillel Bavli was based on a letter by Chaya Feldman, part of this Bais Yaakov group, dated *Rosh Hodesh Elul*, 5704 [1943].
6. The story (but not Bavli's poem) also took root among the ultra-Orthodox in Israel. Its meanings for that community differed from the American context. For further discussion, see Menachem Friedman, "The Haredim and the Holocaust," *Jerusalem Quarterly* 53

(Winter 1990), 87–114; and Judith Baumel and Jacob J. Schacter, "The Ninety-three Bais Yaakov Girls of Cracow: History or Typology?" in Jacob J. Shacter, ed., *Reverence, Righteousness, and Rahmanut* (Northvale, NJ: Jason Aronson, 1992), 93–127.

7. While the term *gilui arayot*, or forbidden sexual relations, is generally understood to encompass incest and adultery, not sexual relations with an unmarried (and unbetrothed), unrelated women, the question of the culpability of the biblical Esther, which I discuss below, indicates that carnal relations with a non-Jewish man was also sometimes seen in this category.

8. B. Sanhedrin 74a–75b.

9. Although one might resolve this by explaining that the betrothed woman must give her life rather than commit the sin of adultery, just as someone ordered to kill must give up his or her life rather than commit murder, many commentators have found this text, and the equivalence it appears to posit between the potential murder and the woman about to be raped, to be problematic. Many early commentators resolve this by emending the text to read *yehareg* instead of *tehareg*, a reading affirmed by Nahmonides and others. For a summary of responses to the problem of this text, see Aryeh Cohen, "Towards an Erotics of Martyrdom," *The Journal of Jewish Thought and Philosophy* 7 (1998), 234–35. Cohen's article raises objections similar to mine, but his argument moves in a different direction. On the other hand, the Talmud also insists that sexual transgression is propelled by male desire and male agency and women are *not* to blame. The text points to Queen Esther, who is not condemned for engaging in forbidden sexual relations with King Ahasuerus. In the words of the Talmud, Esther was *karka olam*, "like the earth," a passive object of male lust. Therefore, she is not considered a transgressor and is not expected to forfeit her life rather than enter into a forced, forbidden relation.

10. The hypothetical case discussed in the Talmud involves a betrothed woman, hence the transgression in question is adultery, according to rabbinic law. Bavli's poem, in extending the prohibition to encompass any violation of female chastity, follows a trend in both rabbinic literature and Jewish folk culture.

11. In addition to the three transgressions discussed explicitly in connection with *kiddush hashem*, the passage under discussion also makes a distinction between private and public transgression (the prohibition against public transgression is more stringent) and also notes the more rigorous behavioral strictures during a time of religious persecution, or *shmad*, when a person is required to die rather than commit even a minor transgression—"even to change one's shoe strap" is forbidden. This view is by no means uncontested in Jewish texts. Maimonides, for example, modifies and moderates the definition in *Igeret Ha-shmad*. In the episode recounted in "The Martyrdom of the Ninety-Three Maidens," the girls are not in the public sphere; indeed, part of the poignancy of the story rests in their plight being relegated to obscurity, were it not for the letter smuggled out by one of the girls. Moreover, as Baumel and Schacter observe (see note 6 above), no one else in the Krakow ghetto reported any knowledge of the event. The question of whether the Nazi genocide constitutes what the Talmud saw as a period of *shmad* is a more complex one, and I will address it only briefly here. While some aspects of Nazi atrocity entailed religious persecution—that is, the prohibition of and punishment for specific Jewish practices—the Nazi genocide targeted Jewish life, defined racially and not religiously. In that sense, then, the Nazi genocide would not be defined as a period of *shmad*, requiring Jews to die rather than transgress even minor precepts. The large body of wartime responsa authorizing certain transgressions (for example, eating non-kosher food or desecrating the Sabbath) would seem to corroborate this understanding. While the concept of Jewish martyrology expands and escalates over time, I have confined myself here to its most limited and bounded definition.

12. Cohen makes this point, as well, in, "Towards an Erotics of Martyrdom."

13. Peter Wyden, *Stella* (New York: Simon and Schuster, 1992), 15.

14. Ibid., 152.

15. Fanya Gottesfeld Heller, *Strange and Unexpected Love: A Teenage Girl's Holocaust Memoirs* (Hoboken, NJ: Ktav, 1993).

16. In Ida Fink, *A Scrap of Time*, trans. Madeline Levine and Francine Prose (New York: Pantheon, 1987), 63–68.
17. Heller, *Strange and Unexpected Love*, 139.
18. Ibid., 160.
19. Ibid., 159.
20. Ibid., 64.
21. Ibid., 275.
22. Ibid., 160.
23. Jean Améry, *At the Mind's Limits: Contemplations by a Survivor of Auschwitz and Its Realities,* trans. Sidney Rosenfeld and Stella P. Rosenfeld (Bloomington: Indiana University Press, 1980), 28.

– *Part Three* –

GRAY SPACES:
GEOGRAPHICAL AND
IMAGINATIVE LANDSCAPES

When Primo Levi said that deportation was a decisive impulse behind his writing, it was not only deportation's destination—Auschwitz—that he had in mind. His "journey towards nothingness," as Levi called it, began with "one of those notorious transport trains, those which never return."[1] So Levi opened *Survival in Auschwitz* with a chapter called "The Journey." In that chapter, he drew on memory and imagination to create a detailed word-picture of his transport, which consisted of "twelve goods wagons for six hundred and fifty [persons]; in mine, we were only forty-five, but it was a small wagon."[2]

The journey to Auschwitz took four days. Levi describes how the train started and stopped, how slowly it moved. Through slits in the wagon, he could see "the names of the last Italian cities disappear," then there were "known and unknown names of Austrian cities, Salzburg, Vienna, then Czech, finally Polish names."[3] Levi recalls the train stopping for the last time. He remembers that throughout the entire journey a woman had been crushed against him. Although they had known each other for many years, Levi says that they "knew little of each other," but as the train reached Auschwitz, people "said to each other things that are never said among the living. . . . Everyone said farewell to life through his neighbor."[4] Later, Levi would learn that "of our convoy no more than ninety-six men and twenty-nine women entered the respective camps of Monowitz-Buna and Birkenau, and that of all the others, more than five hundred in number, not one was living two days later."[5] Of the forty-five persons in his particular train car, "only four saw their homes again; and it was by far the most fortunate wagon."[6]

Notes for this section begin on page 183.

Levi thought again about Holocaust trains in *The Drowned and the Saved* and in particular in his powerful chapter about "Useless Violence." Those sealed wagons, "converted from a commercial vehicle into an ambulatory prison or even an instrument of death," were crowded, suffocating, thirst-inflicting, stench-ridden places where German administration of the so-called "Final Solution of the Jewish question" intentionally delivered what Levi called "gratuitous viciousness."[7] The Holocaust involved, in Levi's apt words, many "historical space-times," a variety of geographical and imaginative landscapes, a multiplicity of gray zones. The Holocaust's trains bear witness to that fact, and thus it is not surprising that Levi was by no means the only one to note their importance and their horror. "Almost always, at the beginning of the memory sequence," he wrote, "stands the train, which marked the departure toward the unknown, not only for chronological reasons but also for the gratuitous cruelty with which those (otherwise innocuous) convoys of ordinary freight cars were employed for an extraordinary purpose."[8]

Understandably, the train has become one of the most enduring images associated with the Holocaust. To take two of many other examples, Raul Hilberg showed how central the German railroads—both rolling stock and administration of the rail system—were for the destruction of the European Jews. Images of railroads and discussion of Holocaust-related rail traffic dominate *Shoah*, Claude Lanzmann's film epic about the Holocaust. Trains work as icons of the Holocaust for many reasons; among other things, they underscore the point that victims were often transported from one location to another as part of the killing process. The Holocaust was vast in many ways, and this includes geographical range and variety, including sites of ambiguity and compromise. From the tragic fate of Jews in Rhodes, mentioned earlier in Gerhard Weinberg's essay, to the rare, relatively successful intervention on behalf of the Danish Jews, this is a history that played out across the European continent in a diverse array of environments. To date (and with good reason), the Auschwitz-Birkenau facility has been the most carefully studied space of the Final Solution. Scholars are now venturing out into terrain and to places that until now have escaped scrutiny.

Wendy Lower's essay begins Part 3's discussion of gray zones by examining the Nazis' plans for Ukraine. Noting that the utopia they envisioned was in many ways emblematic of their plans for German colonies throughout Central and Eastern Europe, Lower focuses on the Nazis' efforts with regards to three colonies (with the Germanicized names Hegewald, Halbstadt, and Nikopol). As was often the case in the Third Reich, there was a disjunction between the Nazis' vision and the actualized plans (one thinks of historian David Schoenbaum's distinction between "subjective" and "objective social reality," with the former focusing upon people's perceptions). Wendy Lower argues that the settlements under consideration need to be contextualized within a narrative of Nazi colonialism: the themes of race, frontier, hierarchy, economic exploitation, and progress have a notable history and resonate in powerful ways with regard to the Nazis' plans for Ukraine. The reality of life on the ground in these colonies proved very different than the fantasies: the settlers came from dislocated populations and turned to the spoliation that accompanied the genocide as a means of support. In bringing together, on the one hand, the rich literature on German colonialism and Nazi imperialism, and on the other, new research carried out in Ukrainian archives, Lower sheds light on Nazi Germany's Holocaust-related plans for a region that has long been cast in shadows in the minds of many Western scholars.

Martin Dean analyzes the ghettos of Nazi-occupied Eastern Europe as a gray zone between the relative freedom of the prewar period and the regimented and penal-like quality of the camps. But, as Dean shows, these ghettos are gray zones in other respects: they are mysterious and inaccessible places for contemporary scholars, where much remains unknown. Even the more straightforward questions are difficult to answer: Dean asks, "How many ghettos were there and what was their function?" Like Lower, he utilizes documentation from Eastern European archives. Similarly, he turns to specific case studies as a means of answering the "big" questions. He also examines the complex relationship between Jews and non-Jews in and around these communities (noting how the latter contributed to the eradication of source material for writing this history). In focusing on individual communities, Dean shows how Jews in the ghettos sustained their religious life, relied on a black market to obtain food, and tried to avoid the murderous fate that awaited most inhabitants. This careful examination of some of the "lost ghettos" serves as a kind of journey to a gray zone.

Jean-Marc Dreyfus also takes us to places that are little known to Holocaust scholars. The "almost camps" in Paris constituted one of the most unique, if also bizarre, institutions found in Nazi Germany's networks of persecution. In theory they were satellites of the Drancy transit camp located in the northern section of Paris, but in practice they were facilities that employed forced labor and were associated with the Nazi plundering agency, the Einsatzstab Reichsleiter Rosenberg (ERR)—or more specifically, its *Möbel Aktion,* a program that focused on expropriating household furnishings. Jewish workers were obliged to help process the looted furniture that came from the deportation of French Jews—a fact that echoes Primo Levi's ruminations on the gray zone when he focuses on the collaboration, however inadvertent and unintended, of victims with their German overlords (with its extreme embodied in the *Sonderkommando*). Dreyfus's "almost camps" are sometimes more surreal than demonic, especially in the case of the camp in the elegant *maison* that was once an establishment specializing in *haute couture*. He poses the question, "How does one describe these camps?" They are not transit or concentration camps, but rather more ambiguous. Besides emphasizing points made by Wendy Lower and Martin Dean above—that the Holocaust entailed thousands of places of persecution—and amplifying Primo Levi's theme of forced collaboration, Dreyfus shows how murder and plunder went hand-in-hand for the Nazis.

While some scholars are mapping new terrain in terms of the geographical dimensions of the Holocaust, others are exploring what can be called its diverse imaginative and psychological spaces, whose reality is found not only in the German planning that produced the Holocaust or the victims' coping for survival but also in the Holocaust's aftermath. Cultural historian Gavriel Rosenfeld, for example, analyzes the hold that the Third Reich has over the popular imagination. Rosenfeld looks at cultural products usually ignored by scholars: the books, films, plays, and television programs that offer counterfactual (or "allohistorical") treatments of the Third Reich. One finds in these works questions such as, what if the Nazis had won or Hitler had survived? Rosenfeld argues that these cultural products are not unimportant or meaningless, but central to the construction of master narratives and indicative of the ways in which memory works. He arrives at important insights concerning perceptions about perpetrators, the enduring quest for atonement, and the increasing "normalization" of the National Socialist past.

For decades, Ronald Smelser has been an active figure among scholars of the Third Reich. He has witnessed the transformation of the way in which the Holocaust is treated in popular culture: a relatively marginal topic in the 1950s and 1960s, the genocide has assumed an increasingly important and iconic status, in Smelser's words, "practically absorbing the war" and becoming the "primary leitmotiv" of the twentieth century. The increasing cultural importance of the Holocaust, Smelser contends, comes out of "bundled narratives." Some of them are particularly problematic because they trivialize or relativize the Holocaust, or because they have resulted in Holocaust saturation and stale memorialization. This is the case with certain popular histories that began to emerge in the 1950s, as well as with exculpatory memoirs by German military leaders. Some of these myths have been exploded in recent years: for example, that the *Wehrmacht* was an apolitical professional army untarnished by atrocities in the East. But few scholars understand the origins of and foundations for these myths. Nor are most scholars cognizant of their wildly diverse present-day manifestations: computer games, for example, where players are meant to identify with the Germans against the Soviet "hordes." These myths have helped form what Smelser calls a "counternarrative"—one that challenges the "master narrative" in myriad ways. Smelser shows how these two narratives can coexist, sometimes simultaneously in the thinking of an individual, and that the relationship between them is both complex and darkly fascinating. While focusing on narrative strategies and linguistic tendencies, Smelser does not, in the words of Yehuda Bauer, adopt "a post-modernist stance that would deny factual objectivity and deny the possibility, ultimately, of any historical conclusions."[9] Rather, Ronald Smelser does the opposite and employs an interdisciplinary strategy to demystify and explicate ideas that have taken hold in our contemporary culture.

Just as there has been a gray zone of memoirs and popular military histories (Smelser) and counterfactual narratives (Rosenfeld), there has been one of Holocaust-related humor. This latter topic, in fact, might count among the taboo subjects in the field; the notion of humor has made scholars uncomfortable in a manner similar to that noted by Hilberg with regard to victims' guilt. Sociologist Lynn Rapaport shows how there is much to learn from an analysis of humor as it relates to the Holocaust. Her functional analysis reveals how comedy served as a coping mechanism for individuals, offered a means for political satire, and helped members of society confront devastating collective trauma. Clearly, the subject of popular culture and the Holocaust has emerged as a central concern for scholars. Just as the Holocaust has grown in importance within Western culture, so too has cultural history emerged as a field.

The work of historian and film scholar Lawrence Baron embodies these two trends and is perhaps most evident in his forthcoming book on the Holocaust and cinema. In his essay here, Baron examines director Tim Blake Nelson's 2001 film *The Grey Zone,* which attempted the problematic and controversial feat of taking its viewers into the gas chambers and crematoria as they functioned at Auschwitz-Birkenau in 1944. More specifically, Baron shows how the film occupies its own gray zone between the actual history, Dr. Miklos Nyiszli's memoir, and the creative product of a contemporary filmmaker. Baron analyzes these three threads. In doing so, he offers insights about multiple issues, which range from the challenges of representation to the readiness of an audience to "consume" a cultural product of this nature. This film, as Baron points out, was a box-office flop, which shows that it did not fit neatly into the category for which it was initially intended (a commercial film). It also elicited mixed reviews, with some critics finding it powerful and courageous, while others considered it problematic and sensational. Baron shows how looking at both a cultural product and its reception provides avenues for investigating the myriad kinds of imaginative spaces.

Time and space, geography and imagination, places and memories of them—the Holocaust involved and in large measure compromised and even ruined them all. For Primo Levi, the Holocaust was inseparable from Buna, and on 28 December 1945, he finished a poem with the name of that historical place-time as its title. "Torn feet and cursed earth," he recalls while remembering "the long line in the gray morning" and the smoke from "a thousand chimneys" as "a day like every other day" got under way. Thinking of Buna's prisoners, those who survived and those who did not, he imagines them meeting again, "sweet beneath the sun," and he asks "with what kind of face would we confront each other?"[10] Scholars and students who explore the Holocaust's gray spaces as Lower, Dean, Dreyfus, Rosenfeld, Smelser, Rapaport, and Baron have done in Part 3 are likely to share Levi's wonderment and yearning.

Notes

1. Primo Levi, *Survival in Auschwitz: The Nazi Assault on Humanity,* trans. Stuart Woolf (New York: Simon and Schuster, 1996), 16–17.

2. Ibid., 16.
3. Ibid., 17–18.
4. Ibid., 19.
5. Ibid., 20.
6. Ibid., 18.
7. Primo Levi, *The Drowned and the Saved,* trans. Raymond Rosenthal (New York: Summit Books, 1988), 108, 111.
8. Ibid., 107–8.
9. Yehuda Bauer, "Letter to the Editor," *Holocaust and Genocide Studies* 18/1 (Spring 2004), 183.
10. Primo Levi, "Buna," in his *Collected Poems,* trans. Ruth Feldman and Brian Swann (London: Faber and Faber, 1988), 5.

– Chapter 13 –

HITLER'S "GARDEN OF EDEN" IN UKRAINE
Nazi Colonialism, Volksdeutsche, and the Holocaust, 1941–1944

Wendy Lower

The "New Order," as the Nazis conceived it, entailed a racial classification and "cleansing" of Europe. Although Nazi population policies were aimed at all peoples who fell into German hands, Nazi leaders focused their resettlement and colonization programs on Eastern Europe, which was designated the ideal German "living space." They were not only extremely exclusionary in their taxonomies of people but also narrowly selective in their view of "fertile" geographic spaces where Germans would thrive. As historian Gerhard Weinberg and others have stressed, the joining of race and space was central to the Nazi *Weltanschauung*.[1]

During World War II, the Germans implemented experimental colonial schemes in Poland and Ukraine. In Ukraine they concentrated their efforts in the central region of Zhytomyr at the Hegewald colony and in the southern regions of Dnepropetrovsk and Nikoleav at the Halbstadt and Nikopol colonies. The Hegewald colony was situated strategically in the "backyard" of Himmler and Hitler's secret field headquarters at Vinnytsia and Zhytomyr. The Halbstadt and Nikopol colonies stretched across German civilian-

---

The author wishes to acknowledge staff and former fellows of the United States Holocaust Memorial Museum's Center for Advanced Holocaust Studies, especially Peter Black, Peter Longerich, Martin Dean, Götz Aly, David Furber, and Doris Bergen, who read parts or all of this work, engaged me in discussions of this history, and provided me invaluable research materials. Any opinions or mistakes in this essay are my responsibility alone. The organizers and funders of the Claremont McKenna College conference, "Gray Zones," generously supported my writing of this essay and included me in a very memorable, enlightening conference, for which I am extremely grateful.

Notes for this section begin on page 199.

and military-administered territories in southeastern Ukraine; additional SS-controlled German colonies dotted the Romanian-occupied area of former Soviet Ukraine, which was named Transnistria. In the latter half of 1941 and early 1942 these colonies were "ethnically cleansed" of their Jewish populations. Nearly all of the Jews who resided there for generations were massacred; the Ukrainians who were not retained as forced laborers on the *Volksdeutsche* (ethnic German) and SS-police colonies were deported to labor camps in eastern Ukraine or to the Reich. *Prima facie*, the logic of this destruction seems quite clear and consistent with a European pattern of imperial conquest, mass migration, forced deportations, and a genocidal "displacement" of the "native" population. However, the ideological and causal links between Nazi resettlement programs and the Holocaust were more tenuous even in the colonial context of Ukraine.

This essay focuses on the ambiguous relationship between Hitler's utopian vision of the eastern territories as, in his words, a "Garden of Eden" and the concrete, "on-the-ground" reality of the implementation of the Holocaust and Nazi colonization programs in Ukraine.[2] It explores Nazi *Lebensraum* fantasies and colonialist ambitions in light of German anti-Jewish policies and *Volksdeutsche* resettlement. To what extent can we deepen understanding of the history of the Shoah by contextualizing it within a narrative of Nazi colonialism?

Nazi Colonialist Thinking Toward Ukraine and Eastern Europe

Only a few works, such as Raphael Lemkin's unpublished history of genocide and Hannah Arendt's *Origins of Totalitarianism,* explored the relationship between Nazi imperialism, colonialism, and the Holocaust and its basis in European history. Ostensibly, in the pre-Hitler era the German race for colonies was a short-lived endeavor dating roughly from the Bismarckian era

Wartime film footage of the Volksdeutsche Colony Halbstadt, Nazi occupied Ukraine, date unknown. The author is grateful to David Furber, Regina Longo and Joshua Binder for bringing the German film to my attention and helping to secure these stills from the United States Holocaust Memorial Museum Film Archive. Reproduced with permission of the Buudesarchiv, Filmarchiv/Transit Film GmbH.

to the German defeat in World War I. Yet, as recent sociocultural studies in German history have shown, colonialist thinking in Germany developed from a longer European history of exploration, conquest, migration, and mass destruction of indigenous peoples.[3] Thus one finds in the speeches and writings about *Lebensraum* by Hitler, the leader of the SS Heinrich Himmler, and Reich Minister for the Eastern Territories Alfred Rosenberg references to the North American frontier, the British Empire in India, and the European exploitation of Africa's resources in the late nineteenth century.

The continuity of colonial metaphors of race and frontier combined with hierarchical population schemes and exploitive economic policies (especially forced labor practices) is indeed striking. Heinrich Himmler and his coterie of General Plan East planners described Eastern Europe as Germany's Californian paradise. Alfred Rosenberg encouraged his regional commissars in Ukraine to read colonial travelogues such as Nazi supporter Kurt Freber's *With My Backpack to India* (1927) and Schulz's *In the African Jungle* alongside antisemitic tracts such as Esser's *The Jewish World Plague* (1939).[4] In 1942, children in Hitler's Germany played a board game in which armed farmers competed for the fertile "black earth" of Ukraine.[5] Much more has been written about the colonial roots of Nazi racial science stemming from anthropologists and eugenicists who viewed Africa and Southeast Asia as their laboratories, namely, Eugen Fischer, whose early "fieldwork" included examining the skulls of slain Rehobother Bastards in German Southwest Africa. In the colonies the first debates over intermarriage or "racial mixing" between Germans and "inferior" Africans emerged in 1892, which gave rise to the notion of *Mischlinge*.[6]

The forced labor *Erziehung zur Arbeit* practices in the colonies and exploitive population policies of Wilhelmine colonial lobbyists such as Paul Rohrbach (1869–1956) also reappeared in a modified, more extreme form in Nazi-occupied Europe.[7] In 1942/43 Nazi economic developers established the Togo Ost Society in Zhytomyr, Ukraine, bringing state-controlled agricultural models from Africa to Eastern Europe. In addition to frontier fantasies, economic models, and ideas of race, the Nazis also transferred German Africans to Eastern Europe. In September 1943, as the Red Army advanced toward Poland, Nazi colonial enthusiasts "imported" German settlers from eastern Africa to the Warthegau. According to an account in the *Litzmannstädter Zeitung*, the German Africanists were happy to leave behind the monoculture farming of Africa and enjoy the rich soil and diverse crops of Polish farms. As model pioneers they were supposed to inspire European Germans who were reluctant to relocate to Poland.[8]

Militarily, the German Army and SS-police's application of total and guerrilla-style warfare and their overall veneration of violence had its antecedents in the colonial wars of Kaiser Wilhelm II's General Staff and World War I. During the Great War the Germans occupied Eastern Europe under General Ludendorff's *Ober Ost* administration and pursued empire building through social engineering. According to the recent study of Vejas Liulevicius, Ludendorff's *Verkehrspolitik* furthered the notion that the eastern territories were not a "complicated weaving of lands and peoples, but of spaces and races to be ordered by German mastery and organization."[9] Twenty years later Ludendorff's successors in Hitler's Third Reich returned to Eastern Europe to impose their own racial ordering of society. Nazi leaders may have drawn from European models of imperialism to develop their own revolutionary, criminal approach to colonization, but their fantasies, motivations, and policies were more closely tied to Germany's own history of migration, especially to Eastern Europe.

In the coveted breadbasket of Ukraine the Nazis found territory ripe for German agricultural settlements.[10] Already in the early 1920s, Hitler and his cohorts argued for a new German foreign policy, which they described as a "soil policy of the future" rooted in Germany's medieval history of migration to the east. In *Mein Kampf* Hitler wrote,

> We National Socialists consciously draw a line beneath the foreign policy of our pre-War period. We take up where we broke off six hundred years ago. We stop the endless German movement to the south and west, and turn our gaze to the east. At long last we break off the colonial and commercial policy of the pre-War period and shift to the soil policy of the future.[11]

Combining atavistic "blood and soil" notions of utopia with modern state structures and methods, Hitler, Darré, and other Nazi ideologues played down overseas colonialism and concentrated instead on contiguous German settlements in Eastern Europe and especially Ukraine where the Aryan "soldier-peasant" tilled the soil with a weapon at his side, ready to defend the farm from the "Asian hordes." As for the Ukrainians whom the Nazis pejoratively branded "Negroes," Hitler remarked that the Germans would supply them "with scarves, glass beads and everything that colonial peoples like."[12] After the Germans defeated Poland in autumn of 1939, the newly appointed Reich Commissar for the Strengthening of Germandom, Heinrich Himmler, was instructed "to give shape to the new German areas of colonization" by "eliminating harmful, alien elements from the German Volk and its living space," and "to carry out the settlement of the *Volksdeutsche* on the designated lands."[13] The concept and process of Germanization as Himmler described it was "not in the old sense of bringing the German languages and German laws to the people dwelling in that area, but to ensure that in the east only people of genuinely German, Teutonic blood shall live."[14] As Germany and its allies unleashed the "war of destruction" against the Soviet Union, Hitler asserted in October 1941,

> Ukraine will be a home for twenty million inhabitants besides the natives. In three hundred years, the country will be one of the loveliest gardens in the world. As for the natives, we'll have to screen them carefully. The Jew, that destroyer, we shall drive out . . . our colonizing penetration must be constantly progressive, until it reaches the stage where our own colonists far outnumber the local inhabitants.[15]

The Holocaust and Nazi *Volksdeutsche* Programs in Ukraine, June 1941–42

What was the causal relationship between these two Nazi missions—the colonization of the *Lebensraum* and the destruction of the Jews? Scholars such as Czeslaw Madajczyk and Götz Aly have stressed the importance of Poland in Himmler's General Plan East, which was the Nazi blueprint for "Germanizing" Eastern Europe. When compared with other parts of Nazi-occupied Europe, the causal links between ethnic German resettlement and anti-Jewish practices were strongest in Poland. From the start, the Nazi leadership portrayed the Polish invasion in September 1939 as a rescue mission on behalf of the *Volksdeutsche*.

As Alexander Rossino's *Hitler Strikes Poland* has deftly demonstrated, the Germans often legitimized their anti-Polish and anti-Jewish brutality as acts of revenge for the persecution or murder of *Volksdeutsche*, for example in Bromberg (Bydgoszcz). In Poland where Reinhard Heydrich's *Einwandererzentralstelle* (Immigration Center) and Adolf Eichmann's *Umwandererzentralstelle* (Relocation Center) engineered the deportation machinery of ethnic German resettlement and the Holocaust, the two programs literally intersected. For example, in January 1940 trains of Jewish deportees to Hrubieszow collided with trainloads of Volhynian Germans moving to Lodz. Jews unloaded the baggage of the *Volksdeutsche* arrivees, cleaned out their homes prior to their arrival, and "cared for the resettlers' horses and other livestock."[16]

Ukraine has been largely left out of the postwar studies of SS-police resettlement plans for the East. The omission is odd because it was precisely in Ukraine where Himmler left his individual mark as a colonizer and where Europe's largest Jewish population, after Poland, resided and was destroyed in the Holocaust. According to Himmler's schemes, Ukraine was not to be 100 percent Germanized like the annexed territories of the Reich in the Polish Warthegau. Instead, Himmler's planners conceived of Ukraine as a land of *Siedlungsmarken und Stützpunkte*, or patches of German settlements. They aimed to consolidate the scattered communities of Volhynian Germans located in west-central Ukraine and residing in the Zhytomyr Commissariat, and the so-called Black Sea Germans located in southern Ukraine, including in Crimea (which Hitler dreamed of as a Nazi Riviera). The ethnic German settlements and farms were to be placed along the new autobahns and railway lines running east-west and north-south. On the eve of the Nazi invasion most ethnic Germans who were left in Soviet Ukraine lived in the poorest rural areas and not in the major towns.[17]

The Germans occupied most of Ukraine between the end of June 1941 and early 1942, renaming the area of civilian administration the Reichskommissariat Ukraine (RKU). The Reichskommissariat was home to about two hundred thousand ethnic Germans (out of a total population of 16.9 million civilians). Actually this was about half of the prewar population of

Volksdeutsche in Ukraine because tens of thousands had been deported by Stalin and thousands, particularly the Volhynian Germans, were brought "home to the Reich" after Hitler and Stalin carved up Poland in autumn of 1939. The much larger minority population in Ukraine at this time was the Jewish one, comprising 30 to 50 percent of the population in what was formerly the tsarist empire's Pale of Settlement.[18]

The systematic mass murder of Jews began in Ukraine and the Soviet territories, not in Poland. As of 22 June 1941 the *Wehrmacht* and SS-police arrived in Ukraine with a license to shoot male Jews, which quickly expanded to all Jews, who were vilified as the racial bearers of Bolshevism. The Germans and their accomplices killed between 1.2 and 1.4 million Jews in Ukraine. The survival rate for Jews was less than 4 percent. Most Jews died in or near their hometowns. In a historical Jewish center such as Berdychiv, which was occupied by the *Wehrmacht* on 7 July 1941, the Germans registered approximately thirty thousand Jews (the town's overall population did not exceed sixty thousand). When the Red Army liberated the town in January 1944, only fifteen Jews emerged from the rubble; most had been killed on one day in mid-September 1941.[19] Did the presence of *Volksdeutsche* or plans for Nazi resettlement schemes in these and other parts of Ukraine affect the course of the Holocaust or increase anti-Jewish violence?

In addition to the now well-known *Einsatzgruppen* that invaded the Soviet territories under Reinhard Heydrich's command in the summer of 1941, on 11 July Himmler activated secret task forces, also labeled *Einsatzgruppen,* as part of a special mission code-named "*Sonderkommando Russland.*" The "special commando Russia" was tasked with secret colonization activities that began with the registration of the *Volksdeutsche*. The commando carried out their work with the assistance of personnel from *Einsatzgruppe* C and *Einsatzgruppe* D. According to historian Isabel Heinemann's latest research, there were 277 SS-policemen assigned to *Sonderkommando Russland,* and they represented a conglomeration of SS and police agencies—the Reich Commission for the Strengthening of Germandom (RKF), the Race and Settlement Main Office (RuSHA), the Economic and Administrative Main Office (WVHA), the Ethnic German Liaison Office (VoMi), and the Security Service (SD). Many had worked the previous two years in Poland on resettlement programs. They established headquarters first in Zhytomyr then Odessa, Nikoleav, Crimea, and Kiev.[20] Thus, while the Sipo-SD *Einsatzgruppen* (C and D) focused on security and intelligence operations, above all anti-Jewish measures, these other SS colonization task forces concentrated on three activities: (1) determination of valuable German blood; (2) survey and registration of the land for later SS colonization; and (3) coordination of colonization work with other Himmler agencies in order to secure SS-police strongholds in Ukraine.[21]

Did these two SS-police task forces with distinct missions jointly plan and implement the Holocaust? To what extent did their antisemitic and pro-*Volksdeutsche* activities overlap? Before *Sonderkommando Russland* staff arrived in Zhytomyr in early September 1941, a subunit of *Einsatzgruppe*

C (*Sonderkommando* 4a) began to register the ethnic Germans according to the German People's List.²² Members of Heydrich's secret police units also reported the first news about the dismal state of the *Volksdeutsche* who had survived Stalin's terror.

According to these first reports, the *Volksdeutsche* were scattered around the Zhytomyr region. They were impoverished; few could speak German and grasped what the arrival of the *Wehrmacht* meant.²³ Although 40 percent of the forty thousand ethnic Germans in the region were day laborers and lacked skills, regional German commanders placed them in leading administrative positions, much to the ire of the rest of the population of non-Germans.²⁴ Those who could serve as translators were immediately put to use by the Nazis. In Vasily Grossman's account of the destruction of Berdychiv's Jewish community, he stressed that the new ethnic German mayor of Berdychiv, Reder, and his Ukrainian chief of police, Koroliuk, "took an active part in organizing and conducting the execution."²⁵ One of the more notorious ethnic Germans in *Einsatzgruppe* C was Dr. Arthur Boss; he was a 33-year-old neurologist originally from Odessa who spoke Russian and German. He helped Paul Blobel's *Sonderkommando* 4a with the planning and implementation of the massacre of Zhytomyr's Jews on 19 September, when they shot more than three thousand men, women, and children. According to eyewitness accounts, Boss was Blobel's right-hand man, identifying the Jews, accompanying Blobel to the mass shooting pits, and afterward helping with the distribution of Jewish clothing and linens to Zhytomyr's ethnic German population. Boss also set up a medical practice in Zhytomyr and provided Paul Blobel's shooters with injections to calm their nerves after killing actions.²⁶ Like Arthur Boss, the Becker brothers, Paul and Edmund, who were both in their late teens and came from an ethnic German community near the city called Alter Huette, were also picked up by the SD and put to use in the implementation of the "Final Solution." The Beckers were transferred in the fall of 1941 to the SS training center at Trawniki, where they learned how to be guards at the ghettos and death camps in Poland.²⁷

Unlike in Poland, however, Heydrich's *Einsatzgruppen* in Ukraine rarely exploited their campaign to rescue the *Volksdeutsche* to stir up anti-Jewish or anti-Ukrainian violence. In one rare case in Zhytomyr on 7 August 1941, regional SS-police and military leaders publicly hanged two Jewish men in the marketplace and displayed a poster on the gallows that claimed the two men were former members of the Soviet secret police and as such had killed more than one thousand *Volksdeutsche* and Ukrainians.²⁸ Instead of using pro-*Volksdeutsche* rationales to incite violence against Jews, the Germans used the more popular anti-Bolshevik themes to inflame local antisemitism, themes that appealed to the Ukrainian, Polish, and *Volksdeutsche* population. At the highest levels of the leadership, Reich Minister Rosenberg lobbied to Hitler (in early September 1941) that all Central European Jews should be dumped in the East in retaliation for Stalin's order to deport the Volga Germans.²⁹ While in the killing fields of Ukraine perpetrators seldom argued that the Jews should pay the price for the sorry plight of the ethnic Germans.

The "Black Sea Germans" and the Holocaust in Transnistria (Romanian-Occupied Ukraine)

In southern Ukraine along the Black Sea and in the territory between the Bug and Dniester rivers, *Einsatzgruppe* D under Otto Ohlendorf actively implemented the Holocaust and recruited local ethnic Germans into the Sipo-SD to assist in the mass murder of Jews. One such ethnic German was named Alfons J. Goetzfried. At first he helped with the gassings of Jews in Simferopol; then Goetzfried participated in the ghetto and camp liquidations in Galicia. His career as a Holocaust perpetrator culminated with his dispatch to Lublin (Majdanek) where he participated in the final massacres of Jews in the General Government during early November 1943.[30]

In southern Ukraine, *Sonderkommando Russland* task forces (under Dr. Klaus Siebert's command) registered Ukraine's largest population of so-called Black Sea Germans. More than 130,000 Black Sea Germans greeted the *Wehrmacht,* SS-police, and Romanian troops in July and August 1941.[31] *Sonderkommando Russland* set up its headquarters in Landau, a historic ethnic German settlement that was about fifty kilometers northwest of Nikoleav. From here Siebert's staff established fourteen settlement centers (*Bereichkommandos*) that stretched across German military and civilian and Romanian-occupied territory. According to the Tighina Agreement of 30 August 1941 and a November 1941 pact between Romanian foreign minister Mihai Antonescu and German ambassador to Romania Manfred von Killinger, the *Volksdeutsche* colonies in Romanian territory (formerly in Soviet Ukraine) came under the authority of the Volksdeutsche Mittelstelle (VoMi), which deployed its SS personnel to the historic settlements of Rastatt, Lichtenfeld, Hoffnungsthal, and Bergdorf, among others. Most of these German communities originated with the migrations of Germans to Russia in the late eighteenth and nineteenth centuries.[32] The settlements contained ethnic German mayors, schools, and farms and semi-autonomous German police forces known as *Selbstschutz.*[33]

With minimal prodding from the Reich German and Romanian authorities, the ethnic German auxiliary police forces massacred Jews (and Roma gypsies) who lived in or near the colonies. *Volksdeutsche* farmers exploited Roma laborers, forcing them to live in pigsties and providing them with little to no food in exchange for work. Starving Roma searched for bits of food in the animals' troughs and feces. According to testimony of a former Romanian prefect in Transnistria, in 1942 the inhabitants of the ethnic German colony Schonfeld killed and burned gypsies on their farms.[34]

In the winter of 1941/42, as many as thirty thousand Jews were brought from Odessa to Beresowka, which was not far from a cluster of ethnic German colonies. Romanian and German documents as well as eyewitness accounts reveal that a combination of ethnic German *Selbstschutz,* colonists, Ukrainian militia, and Romanian gendarmes shot eighteen thousand Jews at the death camp of Domanowka south of the Bug River. At the Romanian camp of Bogdanowka, where another forty-eight thousand Jews were forcibly marched, tens of thousands were killed in continuous mass shootings and barn burnings and with hand grenades. Many succumbed in the freezing temperatures to typhus and famine-related illnesses.[35] In summer and autumn of 1942, while Himmler was stationed at his Ukrainian headquarters near Zhytomyr, he and his staff toured the *Volksdeutsche* communities and were so impressed with the work of the *Selbstschutz* in southern Ukraine and Transnistria that they formed similar police training schools and activated *Volksdeutsche* police and *Waffen-SS* units for antipartisan actions in the Reich Commissariat Ukraine.[36]

East of Transnistria, however, Himmler's resettlement staff encountered recurring problems that caused conflicts between the SS-police and *Wehrmacht.* The Nikoleav and Dnepropetrovsk districts contained fluid borders. Steady streams of refugees flowed in from the battle zones. Consequently, local Germanization campaigns were often interrupted, for example, in March 1942 when half of the Halbstadt settlement near Melitopol was suddenly placed under military administration for ten days. At this time twenty-five thousand ethnic Germans found themselves under General von Kleist's rule while fifteen thousand remained in the civilian zone of the Commissariat. The *Wehrmacht* quickly snatched up ethnic Germans to serve as

Reich Führer of the SS and Police Map of the Reich Commissariat Ukraine, May 1942. Original in the Central State Archives, Minsk 393-1-1. Copy courtesy of the United States Holocaust Memorial Museum Film Archives (RG 53.002M, reel 4).

translators or drafted the able-bodied men into cavalry troops, which infuriated Himmler because he wanted these men for his own SS-police forces. By contrast it was westward from the front around the secured elite headquarters at Zhytomyr and Vinnytsia where Himmler made Ukraine's first colonial experiment a priority during the summer and autumn of 1942.

Volksdeutsche in the Reich Commissariat Ukraine, the Holocaust, and Nazi Germanization Experiments in Zhytomyr, Summer 1942–44

By late summer of 1942 most of Ukraine's urban Jews living east of the Zhytomyr district had been killed. Roughly 270,000 remained in ghettos and camps in western centers of the Reich Commissariat Ukraine such as in Rivne, Pinsk, Luts'k, Kowel, and Letychiv. Thousands were scattered in small rural ghettos, and hundreds of individuals and broken families roamed the countryside in search of food and shelter.[37] For the continued implementation of Nazi anti-Jewish measures, the SS-police and civilian rulers known as commissars sought out ethnic Germans to serve as translators and police auxiliaries in the gendarmerie. As unit leaders of the rural units known as *Schutzmannschaften,* ethnic Germans carried out anti-Jewish manhunts in the Commissariat's vast fields and forests. The ethnic German police were relatively few in number but locally quite powerful, usually commanding Ukrainian units and managing the countryside where German *Gebietskommissare* rarely ventured. They communicated Nazi orders to the villagers. Many helped identify individual Jews and Jewish families; some were directly involved in the killing. A female ethnic German translator on the staff of a gendarme post in the Khmil'nyk district shot Jewish children during the ghetto liquidation there. When the ethnic German chief of a *Schutzmannschaft* unit in Ruzhyn, near Zhytomyr, found Jews in hiding in May 1942, he pulled out his own revolver and shot them on the spot.[38]

Historian Martin Dean, whose work appears in this volume, recently traced the career and criminal activities of an ethnic German policeman, Ernst Hering, from the Ustynivka district in the Nikoleav Commissariat. In spring of 1942, after serving a few months in the police, the nineteen-year-old Hering was asked to shoot the Jews from his hometown. Hering's unit rounded up and killed about twenty-five Jewish men, women, and children and twenty half-Jewish children and babies from the smaller villages in the area. The rural police in Ustynivka worked under two ethnic German supervisors: the rayon (county) leader Friedrich Strohmeier and local police chief Alexander Huebner. Hering's cousin Gustav was also in the local police.

Reich German leaders in the Commissariat's field offices tried to integrate the *Volksdeutsche* into the new Nazi racial hierarchy, but most questioned the loyalty of the ethnic Germans. They were skeptical for a number of reasons, not the least of which was that the *Volksdeutsche* were ideologically heterogeneous and on the whole destitute. They were not as expected a unified caste of superior "Aryan" leaders. Under Stalin assimilation was preferable, even a matter of survival. Thus ethnic Germans had intermarried with Ukrainians. Many clung to traditional religious faiths while others embraced new secular ones: they were Catholic, Protestant, Lutheran, Baptist, Mennonite, communist, and socialist. To bring the *Volksdeutsche* into line ideologically and make them more useful in fighting for the Nazi cause, Himmler and his agencies along with representatives of the Nazi Party's Welfare Society (NSV) introduced educational programs that combined ideological indoctrination, racial hygiene, and vocational training.[39]

Ideological indoctrination of the ethnic German police was of great concern to Himmler because he wanted to create an all-German police force in Ukraine and therefore rely less on Ukrainian policemen.[40] In June 1942 Himmler issued a memorandum on the ideological assessment of order police auxiliaries. Accordingly, the chief of police training programs in Kiev provided his regional offices with the educational themes for training local ethnic German and Ukrainian auxiliaries. The themes are striking because they reveal how lower-level police combined Germany's conquest of the East with the so-called war against Judeo-Bolshevism, mimicking the distortions of German history and virulent antisemitism found in the Nazi leadership's writings and speeches. As this Kiev-based police trainer explained it to his men,

> A large part of the blood sacrifice of the German people was given up over the centuries in the incessant battles over the borders of Eastern Europe. What is happening today in the East is already part of the New Order of Europe. German politics in the East are inspired by the memory of Eastern Europe as a land of settlement. When the Germanic-German colonists and merchants penetrated Eastern European countries over the course of centuries, they were called by the rulers of the peoples who lived there. They did not bring robbery and destruction, fire and murder, death and ruin; instead the successes of their works were fertile fields, blooming cities, outstanding buildings, and artistic [and] scholarly works of the highest value.
>
> By contrast, the culture-negating and people-destroying forces of Bolshevism have only failed to promote the cultures that were there and the free development of European peoples in Russia. The Bolshevism that the Lithuanian, Estonian, Latvian, Byelorussian, and Ukrainian people were confronted with was not European, and also not actually Russian in character, but Jewish and Asian in its nature. The Jews brought Bolshevism to power through a tyranny of terror, hunger, crime. . . .[41]

One of the recipients of this memorandum was the *Schutzpolizei* leader in Berdychiv named Albrecht. In his assessment Albrecht wrote that the themes are suitable and effective, but that the ethnic Germans were only slowly becoming convinced of their superiority. The education process was somewhat hindered by the fact that regional SS-police leaders had to rely on Ukrainian teachers and Ukrainian language materials to convey these pro-German messages. Of special interest to our fresh ethnic German and Ukrainian police recruits, he wrote, was the German approach to the Jewish problem. As Albrecht put it, all they had to do is point out that Berdychiv was 72 percent Jewish before the Germans arrived, that most are now gone, and that no one wants to have anything to do with Jews: "Even the prisoners in our labor camps refuse to work side by side with Jews or half Jews." As Albrecht's report suggests, Ukrainian and ethnic German police recruits viewed the Holocaust as an "achievement," one that increased their loyalty if not gratitude toward Hitler's Reich.[42] In other words, Nazi regional leaders discovered that the Holocaust was not to be kept secret. On the contrary, it was a powerful tool for forging closer bonds between Reich Germans and *Volksdeutsche* as well as between Germans and Ukrainians.

Himmler's Experimental Hegewald Colony, September 1942–November 1943

Before Himmler announced his plans to form a *Volksdeutsche* colony at Hegewald in September 1942, the district German leaders in and around Zhytomyr had concentrated the region's forty-five thousand ethnic Germans into small communities. They supplied the ethnic Germans with food, clothing, and housing, as well as German history and language books.[43] While Rosenberg's ethnographers and commissars went from village to village compiling population surveys and local histories, Himmler's men tried to turn the *Volksdeutsche* men into productive, armed farmers who could defend the SS estates and collective farms.[44] The NSV provided missionary-style relief workers, many of them women, who served as kindergarten teachers, nurses, and midwives.[45] These three main "Germanizers" operating in the field worked side by side but not in unison. They vied for the support of the local civilian leaders, the commissars, who controlled the plunder depots, and they competed with one another for recognition from Nazi headquarters in Zhytomyr, Vinnytsia, Rivne, and Berlin. Yet, outside of this core group of activists, the majority of Reich Germans posted to the region doubted the wisdom of and even advised against initiating major resettlement operations until after the war, because the population upheaval increased anti-German sentiment within the Ukrainian majority and interfered with the economy. In short, many local officials viewed the *Volksdeutsche* as more of a welfare burden than a "racial" asset.[46]

By contrast, Heinrich Himmler, who had the upper hand in ethnic German policy-making and exerted his direct influence over the Zhytomyr region, pushed through the resettlement action around his Hegewald headquarters—of course, only after he had gained Hitler's approval. In August 1942 Himmler sought to convince Hitler that his personnel, not Rosenberg's commissars, were best equipped to colonize the Hegewald area. Himmler argued that partisan attackers jeopardized the ethnic German families scattered around the Zhytomyr region and that the *Volksdeutsche* needed to be protected by concentrating them into a settlement around their headquarters. With the fleet of trucks and SS forces at Himmler's disposal he could quickly move the population into the area. Hitler agreed. At his Zhytomyr headquarters Himmler convened his top SS officials (including Dr. Konrad Meyer) to introduce the scheme and initiate implementation plans. Under the direction of the RKF chief Ulrich Greifelt, Ukraine's senior SS-police leader Hans Adolf Pruetzmann, and the SS regional chief of resettlement actions in Zhytomyr, Theo Henschel, local gendarme and VoMi officials rounded up eighteen thousand Ukrainians who lived in the designated space for resettlement. They crammed them onto freight cars and dumped them in labor camps in southern Russia and neighboring regions. Meanwhile, treks of ethnic Germans totaling more than ten thousand persons were moved under police guard by foot and in carriages to the designated colony. At the rest areas along the journey's path, the SS-police forces had cleared the villages of their Ukrainian inhabitants and left many of them in transit camps destined to go to the Reich as forced laborers.[47]

The ethnic Germans who arrived at Hegewald were organized into, as Hitler and Himmler described them, "settlement pearls," which were stretched along the Zhytomyr–Vinnytsia autobahn like a *Kette* or string of pearls. To start, the *Volksdeutsche* who were assigned to the SS-run collective farms were given private plots of land, about one hectare per family. If they proved their diligence they could receive up to twenty-five hectares. The ethnic German farms were subjected to high SS quotas and random confiscations of milk and other produce. Ukrainian and Byelorussian prisoners and forced laborers tilled the reserve farmland not allotted to the German and SS farmers. The entire Hegewald district of two hundred square miles, consisting of twenty-eight villages and collective farms, was administered by ethnic German mayors, SS-policemen, agricultural specialists, and Nazi Party welfare workers and not by Rosenberg's commissars. Thus, on paper Rosenberg's administration provided the administrative framework for governing the eastern territories, yet in reality population policies and the future of colonization experiments lay in the hands of Himmler's SS-police agencies and the Nazi Party.

Photo spreads and articles in the official newspaper of the RKU, the *Deutsche Ukraine Zeitung,* celebrated the Hegewald settlement, proclaiming it a success. However, the reality was quite different. When viewed from the ground, the entire campaign was, as one local official described it, "eine Schweinerei" (an awful mess). The Nazis could not fulfill the propagandized promises to the *Volksdeutsche,* who represented a dislocated population with few skills and resources. Regular and substantial shipments of Jewish belongings arrived in Hegewald from the plunder depots at Lublin, Auschwitz, and even France. Ethnic Germans at Hegewald wore the clothing and slept on the bedding of these Jewish victims of the Holocaust.

But these plundered goods, which the Nazis presented as Christmas gifts to the *Volksdeutsche,* were not enough to make Nazi colonization schemes successful. About six hundred "racially valuable" children, who had been kidnapped according to Himmler's instructions, could not be adequately cared for in the crowded orphanages in and around Zhytomyr. For one community of 3,500 *Volksdeutsche,* SS-police officials established one produce shop. Rations were not available, and when items did arrive they were not distributed with the kind of efficiency that one normally attributes to the Nazi system of destruction. Nazi forced labor raiders swept through the villages and grabbed *Volksdeutsche* who were not supposed to be included among the deportees to the Reich. Soviet partisans targeted the settlements, ransacked the farms, and killed their inhabitants. In the wake of such attacks the ethnic German *Selbstschutz* units at Hegewald took revenge on neighboring Ukrainian villages.[48]

In Ukraine the military setbacks of 1943 compelled Nazi leaders to reduce *Volksdeutsche* programs to regional initiatives and then to abandon them altogether. The evacuation of the Hegewald settlement was hastily carried out a few weeks before the Red Army arrived in November 1943. The Ukrainians and ethnic Germans who were assigned to escort the treks of evacuees heading west were prone to, as the SS-police reported, "plundering and other offensive excesses." Also, Soviet forces overtook and massacred hundreds of ethnic Germans who were trudging westward. By the end of November 1943, *Volksdeutsche* from the settlements in Ukraine were arriving in western Ukraine and Poland where they remained in camps run by the VoMi. When the Red Army uncovered these camps in early 1945, thousands of these *Volksdeutsche* were branded collaborators and deported to Soviet camps in the trans-Ural region.[49]

Conclusion

The formation of Hegewald (as well as other resettlement actions in Dnepropetrovsk and Nikoleav) did not go as smoothly as Nazi leaders had expected. The Nazis were unable to construct colonies based on the pseudo-scientific and mythic notions of race. Many of the contradictions and tensions that lay beneath Hitler and Himmler's fantasies of an Aryan living space in the East revealed themselves at the local level of praxis.[50]

The same regional commissars, SS-policemen who rarely questioned the morality or rationality of eradicating those deemed inferior, remained uncertain, skeptical, and less enthusiastic about their role and the general aim of creating utopian colonies out of ethnic German settlements. Nazi leaders tried to inspire their underlings with pep talks about the unlimited opportunities in the East and praised them as "pioneers of Germandom in the East."[51] They compared them to frontiersmen who settled the American West. However, in reality the German colonizer had no choice about where he settled, which farm he received, or what he could do with it. This was decided by Himmler's proliferating agencies of race and space planning. The German pioneer in the East was racially selected by the state and placed into an artificial society that had been ethnically "cleansed" by Himmler's SS-police killing units.[52]

Besides demonstrating that Nazi racial policy was a devastating failure, the history of Himmler's creation of an experimental colony at Hegewald shows that once under way, resettlement actions in Ukraine were not directly linked to the unfolding of anti-Jewish policy there. The *Volksdeutsche* actions caused the mass deportations of Ukrainian farmers and their families, not of Jews, because by the time these *Volksdeutsche* resettlement actions began, most Jews who resided on the designated colonial spaces were already dead or in camps. Moreover, the earlier anti-Jewish massacres do not seem to have been motivated by widespread empathy for the *Volksdeutsche* or committed as acts of revenge on behalf of the *Volksdeutsche*.

More than an ideological motivator, the *Volksdeutsche* in Ukraine offered Nazi regional leaders with a critical source of labor for carrying out the Holocaust. The *Volksdeutsche* minority had access to a newfound power especially within the lower ranks of the Nazi system where the genocide was actually realized. Some, such as the Becker brothers and Arthur Boss, became perpetrators rather than victims of circumstance, and, as the Nazi leaders desired, were integrated parts of the whole system of destruction.

The Germans were able to carry out the first step in their larger plan of remapping and Germanizing Europe—the destruction of the Jews whom they considered their greatest threat. Of the estimated six million Jews killed in the Holocaust, about five million resided in the eastern regions intended to be the new German "living space." Nazi leaders, ideologues, technocrats, engineers, economic developers, SS-police, military personnel, and academicians accepted or rationalized the Holocaust as a means to a much larger end of securing a German empire in Europe and beyond. On the other hand, many Germans, including the *Volksdeutsche* and certainly most non-German collaborators who participated in the Holocaust and carried out the most horrific atrocities against Jewish women and children, were not motivated by a vague notion of an Aryan *Lebensraum* or guided by a broader vision of a "Germanized" Europe. They supported a genocidal "Final Solution" as an end unto itself.

Notes

1. The Nazi worldview derived from various strands of thought that had become especially popular as of the late nineteenth century. The imperialist threads can be found in the writings of political geographer Friedrich Raetzel, Weimar geopolitical theorist Karl Haushofer, and Nazi ideologue Walter Darré, who was famous for his *Blut und Boden* (blood and soil) theory. In addition to Woodruff Smith's work *The Ideological Origins of Nazi Imperialism* (Oxford: Oxford University Press, 1986), see Holger Herwig's "*Geopolitik:* Haushofer, Hitler and Lebensraum," *The Journal of Strategic Studies* 22 (June/September 1999), 218–241, and Alan Steinweis's "Eastern Europe and the Notion of the 'Frontier' in Germany to 1945," in Keith Bullivant, Geoffrey Giles, and Walter Pape, eds., *Germany and Eastern Europe: Cultural Identities and Cultural Differences* (Amsterdam: Rodopi, 1999). On the Nazis' territorial ambitions and agricultural policies, see Uwe Mai's "*Rasse und Raum*": *Agrarpolitik, Sozial- und Raumplanung im NS-Staat*

(Paderborn: Ferdinand Schoeningh, 2002). In *Mein Kampf* Hitler revealed his aim to acquire more "living space" for Germans by conquering Eastern Europe and Bolshevik Russia. He did not promote acquisition of colonies (territory abroad) but rather land for resettlement that bordered the Reich to "enhance the area of the mother country." See the edition translated by Ralph Manheim (Boston: Houghton Mifflin, 1971), 652.

2. As Hitler put it to his subordinates: "Out of the eastern territories, we must make a Garden of Eden; they [the eastern territories] are vital to us . . . [overseas] colonies play an entirely subordinate role." See Bormann's notes of the 16 July 1941 meeting when Hitler spoke with Rosenberg, Keitel, Lammers, Göring, and Bormann about the political plan of action for the Soviet territories. U.S. National Archives and Record Administration (NARA), Record Group 238, International Military Tribunal at Nuremberg, Document 221-L, reprinted in volume 38, 86–94.

3. Sara Lennox, Sara Friedrichsmeyer, and Susanne Zantop, eds., *The Imperialist Imagination: German Colonialism and Its Legacy* (Ann Arbor: University of Michigan Press, 1998). Also see David Furber, "Going East: Colonialism and German Life in Nazi-Occupied Poland," Ph.D. thesis, State University of New York at Buffalo, June 2003.

4. See Zhytomyr Commissar's memo about books offered by the Nazi Party to the staff. Books listed included P. H. Kuntze, *Das Volksbuch unserer Kolonien* (1938, rev. ed. 1941), Lettow-Vorbeck, *Um Vaterland und Kolonie* (1919), K. Haenel, *Der belgische Kongo*, H. Richter, *Buntes Afrika* (1939), H. Schulz, *Im afrikanischen Dschungel*, K. Freber, *Mit dem Rucksack nach Indien* (1927), and Esser, *Die Jüdische Weltpest* (1939). General Commissar Klemm memo to district commissars dated 27 February 1942, Zhytomyr State Archives, Zhytomyr, Ukraine (hereafter ZSA), P-1151c-1-21. Books for administrators in the Nazi Party library listed in ZSA, P-1151-1-104.

5. According to Götz Aly, the East was a laboratory for establishing the *Volksgemeinschaft*, the space where all Germans regardless of class fulfilled socialist as well as racial dreams of prosperity. This thesis and reference to the children's game "Wehrbauer im Schwarzerdegebiet" in Götz Aly, "Hitlers Volksstaat," in *Rasse und Klasse: Nachforschungen zum deutschen Wesen* (Frankfurt am Main: Fischer, 2003), 230–44.

6. Hitler appointed Fischer the rector of the University of Berlin, and the SS commissioned racial studies from him. On Eugen Fischer's research and influence on Nazi and SS racial policies, see Paul Weindling, *Health, Race and German Politics Between National Unification and Nazism, 1870–1945* (Cambridge: Cambridge University Press, 1993), and Isabel Heinemann, *"Rasse, Siedlung, deutsches Blut": Das Rasse- & Siedlungshauptamt der SS und die rassenpolitische Neuordnung Europas* (Göttingen: Wallstein Verlag, 2003), 20–23.

7. On labor as a "civilizing" form and punitive measure in the Wilhelmine era, see the work of Sebastian Conrad, "Education, Deportation, Extermination: 'Erziehung zur Arbeit' in Colonial Africa and Imperial Germany, 1890–1914," paper presented at the American Historical Association Annual Conference, 9 January 2003, Washington, DC. Paul Rohrbach, a Baltic German and staunch Evangelical Christian, led the Osteuropa movement during World War I, calling for the colonization or Germanization of the Baltics, as well as German settlement in the Middle East and southwest Africa. See Paul Rohrbach's *Deutsche Kolonialwirtschaft* (Berlin, 1907) and *Deutsch Südwest-Afrika ein Ansiedlungs-Gebiet?* (Berlin, 1905, 2nd ed., 1910); also Walter Mogk, *Paul Rohrbach und das "Grössere Deutschland": Ethischer Imperialismus im Wilhelminischen Zeitalter* (Munich: Wilhelm Goldmann Verlag, 1972).

8. *Litzmannstädter Zeitung*, 26 September 1943, United States Holocaust Memorial Museum (USHMM), Collection of Newspapers from Nazi Occupied Poland, reel 13. I am grateful to David Furber for providing me with a copy of this newspaper article.

9. At this time the minorities question focused on autonomous rights (self-determination) and the search for a segregationist coexistence of different autonomous entities within nation-states. The strict racial, more social Darwinistic view that saw homogeneous nation-states in a constant struggle became more widespread in the interwar and WWII eras. See Vejas Gabriel Liulevicius, *War and Land on the Eastern Front: Culture, National Iden-*

tity and German Occupation in World War I (Cambridge: Cambridge University Press, 2000).
10. On the significance of Ukraine in Hitler's foreign policy, see Alexander Dallin, *German Rule in Russia, 1941–1945: A Study of Occupation Policies* (New York: Macmillan, 1957), and Gerhard Weinberg, *The Foreign Policy of Hitler's Germany: 1937–1939* (Chicago: University of Chicago Press, 1980), 475–77, 583.
11. Hitler, *Mein Kampf*, 654.
12. Quote of Adolf Hitler from the Bormann letters, monologue of 17 September 1941. See Adolf Hitler, *Secret Conversations, 1941–1944*, trans. Norman Cameron and R. H. Stevens (New York: Octagon Books, 1972), 29. The lure of the east had its historical antecedents in the medieval-era migrations of Germans to Poland and then the Russian empire under Catherine the Great. But the phrase "Drang nach Osten" became popular in the early twentieth century. Since the late nineteenth century, economic imperialists who espoused the expansionist ideology of *Weltpolitik* also eyed the Ukraine as a new commercial and industrial marketplace. See Wolfgang Wippermann's *Der "Deutsche Drang Nach Osten": Ideologien und Wirklichkeit eine politischen Schlagwortes* (Darmstadt: Wissenschaftliche Buchgesellschaft, 1981).
13. Valdis Lumans, "A Reassessment of *Volksdeutsche* and Jews in the Volhynia-Galicia-Narew Resettlement," in Alan Steinweis and Daniel Rogers, eds., *The Impact of Nazism: New Perspectives on the Third Reich and Its Legacy* (Lincoln: University of Nebraska Press, 2003), 85; and Raphael Lemkin, *Axis Rule in Occupied Europe: Laws of Occupation, Analyses of Government, Proposals for Redress* (Washington, DC: Carnegie Endowment for International Peace, 1944), 21.
14. Lemkin, *Axis Rule,* 21.
15. Monologue of 17 October 1941, *Hitler's Table Talk, 1941–1944, His Private Conversations*, trans. Cameron and Stevens (London: Enigma, 2000), 68. Also see C. Madajczyk, ed., *Generalny Plan Wschodni: Zbior dokumentow* (Warsaw, 1990), 69.
16. Lumans, "A Reassessment," 93. See also Roessler, Schleiermacher, and Tollmien, eds., *Der "Generalplan Ost" Hauptlinien der nationalsozialistischen Planungs- und Vernichtungspolitik* (Berlin: Akademie Verlag, 1993).
17. Meir Buchsweiler, *Volksdeutsche in der Ukraine am Vorabend und Beginn des Zweiten Weltkrieges—ein Fall doppelter Loyalität?* (Tel Aviv: Bleicher Verlag, 1984).
18. For example, one of six administrative districts that comprised the Reichskommissariat Ukraine, the Zhytomyr Generalbezirk (which was in area roughly the size of the combined U.S. states of New Hampshire, Vermont, and Massachusetts contained about 2.5 million inhabitants; Ukrainians made up the vast majority, representing 87.4 percent of the population; the largest minority was Jewish, with more than 9 percent of the population, followed by Poles making up 7.4 percent of the population. The Russian minority decreased during the war, while the ethnic German minority doubled, comprising close to 3 percent of the population in 1942. According to the 1939 Soviet census, there were about 266,000 Jews living in and around the region's centers of Zhytomyr, Vinnytsia, and Berdychiv; an average of 30 percent lived in the cities or larger towns. These figures appear in Mordechai Altshuler's *Soviet Jewry on the Eve of the Holocaust: A Social and Demographic Profile* (Jerusalem: Yad Vashem, 1998). The German figures for Ukrainians, Poles, Russians, and ethnic Germans were printed in *Holos Volyni*, 17 December 1941, ZSA, newspaper collection. On Jews in the Pale, see Zvi Gitelman, *A Century of Ambivalence: The Jews of Russia and the Soviet Union, 1881 to the Present* (New York: YIVO Institute for Jewish Research, 1988), and John Klier and Shlomo Lambroza, eds., *Pogroms: Anti-Jewish Violence in Modern Russian History* (Cambridge: Cambridge University Press, 1992).
19. Ilya Ehrenburg and Vasily Grossman, eds., *The Black Book: The Ruthless Murder of Jews by German Fascist Invaders Throughout the Temporarily Occupied Regions of the Soviet Union and in the Death Camps of Poland During the War of 1941–1945*, trans. John Glad and James Levine (New York: Holocaust Library, 1980), 16. Also see testimonies and segments of the Extraordinary Commission Report in S. Ya. Yelisavetsky,

Berdichevskaya tragediya (Kiev, 1991), 81–85. I am grateful to Asya Vaisman for assisting with the Russian translations. Also see Carol and John Garrard, *The Bones of Berdichev: The Life and Fate of Vasily Grossman* (New York: Free Press, 1996), 23–25.

20. On 21 June (the eve of the outbreak of the Nazi war against the Soviet Union), Himmler instructed his staff of the RKF to incorporate the Soviet territories into the General Plan East. On *Sonderkommando Russland,* see Heinemann, "Rasse, Siedlung, deutsches Blut," 418–20. Also see Götz Aly, *Final Solution: Nazi Population Policy and the Murder of the European Jews* (New York: Arnold, 1999), 189.

21. Priorities as RuSHA chief Otto Hofmann defined them. See Heinemann, "Rasse, Siedlung, deutsches Blut," 422.

22. The German People's List (DVL) consisted of four categories: Group I, represented those deemed racially Aryan and willing to be Germanized; Group II, racially pure Germans who lacked a will to be Germanized but were capable of being Germanized; Group III those with mixed but predominantly Aryan blood and capable of being Germanized, and who could apply for temporary Reich citizenship and then live under racial political surveillance for ten years before receiving citizenship; and Group IV, those with only some German blood, assimilated to other groups and unwilling to become German citizens or considered unfit for Germanization. Persons in this last category were handed over to the Gestapo, sent to camps, or liquidated on the spot. Those who fit into categories I and II were immediately eligible for Reich German citizenship. See Ingeborg Fleischhauer, "The Ethnic Germans Under Nazi Rule," in Ingeborg Fleischauer and Benjamin Pinkus, eds., *The Soviet Germans Past and Present* (New York: St. Martin's Press, 1986), 96–97.

23. See *Einsatzgruppe* C (EGC) Report, 6 September 1941, "Lage der Volksdeutschen in Shitomir," NARA, RG 242 T-175/R 233/2722221-5.

24. See secret field report of Stepan Bandera's activist near Zhytomyr, "RR," 30 July 1941, ZSA, P1151-1-2.

25. Ehrenburg and Grossman, eds., *The Black Book,* 18.

26. See Boss statements of 23 June 1965 and 6 July 1966, Kuno Callsen et al, Ludwigsburg 207 AR-Z 419/62. On the *Volksdeutsche* informant network attached to EGC, see report of 11 September 1941, NARA RG 242 T-175/R 233/2722288. In another case the female ethnic German translator attached to Khmil'nyk gendarme post identified Jews and was also accused of shooting Jewish children during a ghetto clearing action there. See "Abschlussbericht," Litin Commissariat Case, Ludwigsburg 204a ARZ 135/67, 53.

27. Peter Black, "Police Auxiliaries for Operation *Reinhard:* Shedding Light on the Trawniki Training Camp Through Documents from Behind the Iron Curtain," Conference on The Holocaust and Intelligence, City University of New York, 2–4 June 2003. I am grateful to Dr. Black for material on Trawniki guards from Zhytomyr, including the SS personnel and Nazi immigration files on the Becker brothers. On the ethnic German police in the Lublin area, see Peter Black's "Rehearsal for 'Reinhard'?: Odilo Globocnik and the Lublin *Selbstschutz,*" *Central European History* 25 (1992), 204–26.

28. The photo of the poster is reprinted in Ernst Klee, Willi Dressen, and Volker Riess, eds., *The Good Old Days: The Holocaust As Seen by Its Perpetrators and Bystanders* (New York: The Free Press, 1991), 107–17.

29. Rosenberg came up with this plan in response to Stalin's 28 August 1941 order to liquidate the Volga German Republic and ship Volga Germans "as state enemies" to Asia. Rosenberg's deportation plan against German Jews became part of a general discussion among Hitler and his top brass about impending actions against Reich and other European Jews. See Christopher Browning and Juergen Matthaeus, *The Origins of the Final Solution: The Evolution of Nazi Jewish Policy, September 1939–March 1942* (Lincoln: University of Nebraska Press, 2004), 324. On Rosenberg's input, see Andrej Angrick, *Besatzungspolitik und Massenmord: Die Einsatzgruppe D in der suedlichen Sowjetunion, 1941–1943* (Hamburg, 2003), 263–64.

30. The November 1943 massacres occurred at Majdanek, Trawniki, and Poniatowa (Lublin district). See war crimes trial material against Alfons J. Goetzfried, cited in Martin Dean, "The Participation of Soviet Germans in the Holocaust As Members of the German

Police Forces in the Reich Commissariat Ukraine, 1941–1944" in Ray Brandon and Wendy Lower, eds., *The Shoah in Ukraine: History, Testimony and Memorialization* (forthcoming).
31. See the war crimes investigation of Dr. Siebert and his staff, *Zentralstelle Dortmund gegen Dr. Siebert und andere*, 45 Js 26/62, "Verfügung," 15 January 1974, 1–27.
32. The "pacifistic" Mennonites comprised a large number of them. Nazi ethnographers such as Karl Stumpp traced German migration history further back to the medieval conquests of the Goths. Karl Stumpp, *Ostwanderung: Akten über die Auswanderung der Württemberger nach Russland 1816–1822* (Leipzig: S. Hirzel, 1941). This study was the second volume in a series: *Sammlung Georg Leibbrandt, Quellen zur Erforschung des Deutschtums in Osteuropa*. Leibbrandt was Rosenberg's chief of the political department in the Ostministerium, July 1941–1943. See the recent analysis of Stumpp's and Leibbrandt's work in Ukraine and their postwar fate in Eric Schmaltz and Samuel Siner, "The Nazi Ethnographic Research of Georg Leibbrandt and Karl Stumpp in Ukraine and Its North American Legacy," *Holocaust and Genocide Studies* 14 (Spring 2001), 28–64.
33. On Nazi-Romanian diplomacy vis-à-vis the Holocaust in Transnistria, see Jean Ancel's *Transnistria, 1941–1943: The Romanian Mass Murder Campaign* (Tel Aviv: Goldstein-Goren Diaspora Research Center, 2003), volume 1.
34. Radu Ioanid, *The Holocaust in Romania: The Destruction of Jews and Gypsies Under the Antonescu Regime, 1940–1944* (Chicago: Ivan R. Dee, 2000), 232–37. See *Zentralstelle Dortmund gegen Dr. Siebert und andere*, 45 Js 26/62; on the persecution of Roma by ethnic German farmers, see International Office of Migration Restitution Claims, Roma Testimony, Geneva, Switzerland, office.
35. Dalia Ofer, "The Holocaust in Transnistria," in Lucjan Dobroszycki and Jeffrey S. Gurock, eds., *The Holocaust in the Soviet Union: Studies and Sources on the Destruction of the Jews in the Nazi-Occupied Territories of the USSR, 1941–1944* (New York: M. E. Sharpe,1993), 136–38. On German involvement in Transnistria, see Ioanid, *The Holocaust in Romania*, 187–201. Iaonid estimates that 75,000 Jews were killed in the Golta region.
36. Plans for increasing the *Selbstschutz* materialized at Hegewald where Commander von Oelhafen placed about 2,500 ethnic German men into police formations, established four *Selbstschutz* schools, and began training an additional one thousand men. Compare with the sixteen *Selbstschutz* schools in Transnistria, which trained seven thousand men. See undated report, NARA RG 242 T-175/R 72/2589180. Also see Valdis Lumans, *Himmler's Auxiliaries: The Volksdeutsche Mittelstelle and the German National Minorities in Europe, 1933–1945* (Chapel Hill: University of North Carolina Press, 1993), 246–247.
37. For recent research on the German implementation of the Holocaust across Ukraine, see Dieter Pohl's "Schauplatz Ukraine: Der Massenmord an den Juden im Militärverwaltungsgebiet und im Reichskommissariat 1941–1943," in Norbert Frei, ed., *Ausbeutung, Vernichtung, Öffentlichkeit: NS-Lager und Vernichtungspolitik* (Munich: K. G. Sauer, 2000), 135–73.
38. Dean, "The Participation of Soviet Germans," drawn from Zentrale Stelle Ludwigsburg II 204 AR-Z 128/67, vol. 1, 139–40, investigation of Arthur Reglin, police chief in Vchoraishe. Also see Martin Dean's *Collaboration in the Holocaust: Crimes of the Local Police in Belorussia and Ukraine, 1941–1944* (New York: St. Martin's Press, 2000).
39. See the report, "Hauptamt VoMi, Aussenstelle Shitomir: Arbeit und Aufgaben der Volksdeutschen Mittelstelle," September–December 1941, ZSA, P1151-1-120. Also see the Hoffmeyer report of 12 October 1941, NARA RG 242 T-454/R 100/000661-670.
40. This was all done with the Nazi aim, as the gendarme captain in Korosten put it, "of integrating the ethnic Germans into [their] community and strengthening the position of Germans in this country [Ukraine]." From USHMM RG 53.002M, reel 5, 658-1-1. Quoted from Martin Dean's "The Participation of Soviet Germans in the Holocaust as Members of the German Police Forces in the Reich Commissariat Ukraine, 1941–1944," unpublished manuscript, forthcoming in *The Shoah in Ukraine*.
41. BdO (Befehlshaber der Ordnungspolizei; Commander in Chief of the Order Police) Ukraine, Polizeischulungsleiter, 22 August 1942, ZSA, P1151-1-147a. Similar themes appeared in

the training of Sipo-SD elites. See Juergen Matthaeus, Konrad Kwiet, Jürgen Förster, and Richard Breitman, *Ausbildungsziel Judenmord? "Weltanschauliche Erziehung" von SS, Polizei und Waffen-SS im Rahmen der "Endlösung"* (Frankfurt am Main: S. Fischer, 2003).

42. KdO (Kommandeur der Ordnungspolizei; Commander of the Order Police) Shitomir, Schupo Abteilung Berditschew to KdO, Re: Politische Betreuung der Schutzmannschaft, 8 October 1942, ZSA, P1151-1-5, USHMM, reel 5.
43. VoMi Aussenstelle Shitomir, Situation Report, September–December 1941, ZSA, P1151-1-120. *Sonderkommando* R, Hoffmeyer report, 12 October 1941, NARA, T 454, roll 100, frame 000661-670.
44. On Rosenberg's deputies see Schmaltz and Siner, "Nazi Ethnographic Research," 28–64.
45. On the continuity and changes in women's roles as colonizers, see Lore Wildenthal, *German Women for Empire, 1884–1945* (Durham, NC: Duke University Press, 2001), and Elisabeth Harvey, *Women and the Nazi East: Agents and Witnesses of Germanization* (New Haven, CT: Yale University Press, 2003).
46. General Commissar Klemm, Shitomir, Lagebericht, 3 June 1942, Bundesarchiv, R6/310. I am grateful to Dieter Pohl for this document. On the NSV, see Pg. (Party Comrade) Kersten's reports to Berlin, USHMM, RG 31.002m, Kiev Archive October Revolution, roll 6/3206/6/255.
47. General Commissar Leyser, Formation of Hegewald Report, 16 November 1942, ZSA, P1182-1-32.
48. Himmler order to Oswald Pohl regarding Christmas supplies for *Volksdeutsche*, 24 October 1942, NARA, T-175, roll 129, frame 2655141. Also see RKU chief Paul Dargel to Hoffmeyer regarding ethnic Germans in Ukraine, 20 March 1943, NARA, T-175, roll 72, frame 2589146.
49. Wendy Lower, "A New Ordering of Space and Race: Nazi Colonial Dreams in Zhytomyr, Ukraine, 1941–1944," *German Studies Review* (May 2002), 228–54. On the 1943–44 plight of the *Volksdeutsche* and the ambiguous, exploitative nature of the entire classification process, see Doris Bergen's "The Volksdeutsche of Eastern Europe and the Collapse of the Nazi Empire, 1944–1945," in Alan Steinweis and Daniel Rogers, eds. *The Impact of Nazism: New Perspectives on the Third Reich and Its Legacy* (Lincoln: University of Nebraska Press, 2003), 101–28.
50. Valdis Lumans recently came to a similar conclusion that "in practice the two operations unfolded independently and transpired along different paths. Granted these paths occasionally crossed, at times by coincidence, at other times by plan; however, the relationship was not a linear one of cause and effect." See Lumans, "A Reassessment," 82.
51. At Hegewald in September 1942, RuSHA Chief Otto Hoffman told his SS farmers and *Volksdeutsche* that they were "pioneers of Germandom in the East and that when they make decisions in the field as lone colonizers they should ask themselves: What would the Führer or Reichsführer SS do in my place?" See Heinemann, *Rasse, Siedlung, "deutsches Blut,"* 437.
52. Ihor Kamenetsky, *Secret Nazi Plans for Eastern Europe: A Study of Lebensraum Policies* (New York: Bookman Associates, 1961), 72–73.

– Chapter 14 –

LIFE AND DEATH IN THE "GRAY ZONE" OF JEWISH GHETTOS IN NAZI-OCCUPIED EUROPE
The Unknown, the Ambiguous, and the Disappeared

Martin Dean

In more than one thousand cities, towns, and *shtetl* of Nazi-occupied Eastern Europe, Jews were confined to the "gray zone" of the ghetto, a form of holding place and twilight zone, where they suffered humiliation, persecution, and exploitation prior to their destruction. Yet this central theme in the topography of the Holocaust also remains a "gray zone" in its historiography, comparatively underresearched and not fully understood. How many ghettos were there, and what was their function?

Precisely because the ghetto also offered a degree of protection and even self-administration for its Jewish inhabitants, it remains an area of ambiguity and, sometimes, heated controversy. Remnants of Jewish life and culture continued to subsist within the ghetto, with a degree of private space and community not possible in the concentrationcamps and forced labor camps. Even the definition of a ghetto remains disputed and unclear. The rare and inaccessible nature of many of the key sources has added to the difficulties facing historians attempting to penetrate this fog.

What happened during the Holocaust in the many small locations in the occupied Soviet Union and former eastern Poland, where Jews had dominated town life for generations? Is it accurate to describe the brief incarceration of the local Jews before their murder as "ghettoization"?

The opinions stated in this paper are those of the author alone and do not necessarily reflect those of the United States Holocaust Memorial Museum or of the United States Holocaust Memorial Council. Dean is currently the coordinating editor for the ghettos volume of a larger multivolume encyclopedia project on concentration camps, ghettos, and other places of detention in Nazi-dominated Europe, being prepared in the museum's Center for Advanced Holocaust Studies and funded with the support of the Bader Foundation.

Notes for this section begin on page 219.

In terms of Holocaust history, there are many photos, memoirs, and detailed descriptions of events in the larger ghettos such as Lodz, Warsaw, Krakow, or Bialystok. Thus I would be able to present, at least, a black and white image of life in the "gray zone" of the ghetto. But the Nazi destruction of many smaller Jewish communities further to the east still has to be pieced together from the few remaining fragments. Often little more can be found in the current literature than three lines in an encyclopedia or perhaps a short reference from an *Einsatzgruppen* report. Yet one of the most frequently asked questions by visitors to the United States Holocaust Memorial Museum is, what happened to the Jews of this or that small town in Eastern Europe, "where my relatives once lived"?

Therefore, this paper will set out on a painful journey into the unknown, to reconstruct events in some of the more obscure ghettos under Nazi occupation. It starts, for example, with the history of three small and short-lived ghettos in the Pukhovichi county (or rayon), near Minsk, which previously have gained scant notice from even the most diligent of Holocaust historians.[1]

The Pukhovichi, Mar'ina Gorka, and Tal'ka Ghettos

According to *Einsatzgruppen* report 124, dated 25 October 1941, 996 Jews were murdered in Mar'ina Gorka some fifty miles southeast of Minsk and 222 Jews in the nearby town of Tal'ka. These killings were conducted apparently on the orders of the newly appointed civil administrator, *Generalkommissar* Wilhelm Kube in Minsk, under the pretext cited by the *Einsatzgruppen,* the spreading of anti-German propaganda by the Jews in Tal'ka and the reluctance of Jews to work in Mar'ina Gorka.[2] No precise date is given for these massacres, and, as frequently occurs, the available sources disagree, although it was almost certainly in the second half of September 1941.

These bare facts are almost all that has been published about the extinction of the Jewish communities of the Pukhovichi county in the Minsk oblast' of Belarus. In the absence of survivor accounts, it is possible only to reconstruct the final days of these communities on the basis of interviews conducted with non-Jewish local inhabitants and the findings of criminal investigations in Germany and the Soviet Union.

Nevertheless, from these limited sources, viewing events from the outside, a number of revealing details emerge. In each of these three small towns, Mar'ina Gorka, Pukhovichi, and Tal'ka, a makeshift ghetto was established, separating the Jews from their gentile neighbors, just prior to the mass shooting of the Jewish population.

According to the 1939 census there were 786 Jews living in Mar'ina Gorka, probably about six hundred in Pukhovichi, and some two hundred in the town of Tal'ka. The Germans occupied the region in early July 1941, and in August groups of eighty or so Jewish men were arrested and murdered in both Mar'ina Gorka and Pukhovichi. In Mar'ina Gorka local witnesses describe how the Germans humiliated these Jews in the police courtyard for about a week prior to their murder. Subjected to continuous blows, the Jews had their beards cut off, stars cut into their heads, and were forced to crawl on the ground.[3]

It was about this time in late August or early September 1941 that the German authorities established ghettos in all three towns. In Pukhovichi the Jews were assembled and informed that they would soon be sent to Palestine. In preparation for this, they were all moved into a former sanitorium, which formed a makeshift ghetto. Then in the second half of September, the Belarussian mayor of the rayon, Leonid Derban, instructed the local police to surround the "ghetto" in Pukhovichi as a German police unit had arrived. The Jews were told to put on their best clothes and to take their most valuable belongings with them. When the column was ready the Germans and local police escorted the Jews to the nearby collective farm at Blon', where they shot them together with the Jews of Mar'ina Gorka.[4]

In Mar'ina Gorka the Germans had confined about six hundred Jews, mostly women, children, and the elderly, within a ghetto in the area of Gorki Street, May 1 Street, and Soviet Street. The local population was not permitted to enter the ghetto, and Jews were forbidden all contact with their former neighbors.

On the morning of the massacre, a force of about fifty German policemen from Minsk, assisted by local Belarussian police, surrounded the ghetto. The Jews were forcibly assembled and brutally loaded onto trucks to be driven to the Blon' collective farm. One woman, Goda Kogan, called out to a gentile friend as she was driven away, "Live well—we won't see each other again!" Another Jewish woman sprang from the moving truck into the river and was shot by the German guards.[5]

At Blon' the Jews from the two ghettos were made to undress in a pigsty and then taken up the hill of Popova Gorka in groups of ten, where the Germans shot them with machine guns. Children were thrown into the grave and buried alive. According to one account, some women were raped before they were shot. The shootings lasted nearly all day, and the Germans apparently attempted to drown out the noise of gunfire by running tractor engines.

The rayon mayor, Derban, was present at the execution site. Clothing and other goods taken from the victims were loaded onto trucks and taken to Mar'ina Gorka. These items were subsequently sold at the communal shop or stolen by the police. Some sixty-seven Soviet prisoners of war were also taken to the execution site on trucks later in the day and shot in a separate grave nearby.[6]

In early September several hundred Jews from Tal'ka and the surrounding villages were concentrated in a former pioneer camp about one kilometer from town, forming a makeshift ghetto. Those who were too slow in moving into the ghetto were beaten. No food was provided to the Jews and they were made to perform forced labor, such as road construction, that was sometimes beyond their physical capacity. The local police who guarded the ghetto cursed the Jews. When the Jewish elder, Meyer Rabinovich, protested about the treatment of his community, he was shot together with two other Jews.[7]

Then in mid-September 1941 units of the German gendarmerie arrived in Tal'ka and together with the local police surrounded the ghetto. They escorted all the Jews into a forest about five hundred meters away and shot them into a grave in groups of about fifteen. Before the shooting the German officer made a speech condemning the Jewish population and praising the German race.

During the shooting Raisa Surbayeva pleaded for the life of her infant, but a German gendarme shot her together with her child. Another woman attempted to bribe the head of the local police, Kulobizian, with three hundred rubles, but he took the money and shot her anyway. The property of the Jews was taken to Pukhovichi by the gendarmerie, but the local police also stole part of it.[8]

What do these fragmentary accounts tell us about the process of ghettoization and the responses of Jews to the emerging Holocaust? Clearly during this key phase in August/September of 1941, as the German forces crossed the threshold of genocide by beginning to wipe out whole communities, the process of ghettoization facilitated mass murder, especially in communities that were largely unsuspecting. Yet even here, it is not certain that these ghettos were established only with destruction in mind. Both civil and military authorities sought initially to isolate the Jews from the local population and to exploit their labor, applying ghettoization on an ad hoc basis. Yet the failure to supply food, as reported in Tal'ka, clearly created an unsustainable situation that may have accelerated the progress toward genocidal solutions. As my colleague Wendy Lower has commented in an essay on the Ukraine,[9] some ghettos may have accelerated the escalation of mass murder by fostering epidemics or sporadic resistance, if this was only one contributory factor in a complex mix of orders from the center and local initiatives on the ground.

The observations of local gentiles in the Pukhovichi rayon reveal a wide array of responses from the clearly stunned Jewish population. These ranged from official protests by Jewish leaders to refusal to work, resignation, pleading for mercy, attempted bribes, and even desperate escape. Ultimately these all appear to have been unsuccessful. Yet given that the remaining population consisted mainly of women, children, and the elderly, it would be wrong to condemn this merely as passivity. During subsequent ghetto liquidations, when German intentions were more widely suspected, considerable efforts were directed especially toward hiding and escape.

Definition: What Constituted a "Ghetto"?

The above examples raise the question of what constituted a ghetto. Did it have to exist for a certain length of time or be of a certain size to be distinguished from, for example, the "Jewish houses" that were widely established inside the Reich, or other killing sites that were based around specific buildings? In particular, was a fence or wall its defining characteristic, or were there also so-called open ghettos, where Jews were not physically contained but could be shot on sight if they transgressed the boundary of the "Jewish residential district"?

The reason for confronting these difficult questions is that they are central to the comprehensive encyclopedia of ghettos currently in preparation at the Center of Advanced Holocaust Studies (CAHS) at the United States Holocaust Memorial Museum. The first task I have faced as coordinating editor has been to prepare a comprehensive list of all known ghettos.

"Open Ghettos"

From the available evidence there is no doubt that so-called open ghettos were quite common, for example, in the Lublin district of the General Government and also in the Volhynian region of Reichskommissariat Ukraine. These open ghettos, where Jews were forced to live compressed within strictly defined Jewish quarters but remained unfenced, deserve recognition insofar as the Jews were forcibly resettled and collected in a specific area with strict regulations controlling those who entered and left the "ghetto." According to the research of Aleksandr Kruglov, the "Jewish district" was not physically isolated and only lightly guarded (as in the instance of Uman, Ukraine), but Jews were forbidden to leave, and those who did leave were severely punished.[10]

In a number of eastern Belarussian towns, such as Chashniki, the Germans also did not establish enclosed ghettos. In the opinion of Israeli historian Daniel Romanovsky, this was possibly because the entire Jewish population lived in the center of town. Some Jews were resettled and their houses made available to non-Jews. However, all Jewish houses were marked with plywood *Magen Davids,* and all Jews were forbidden to leave the town or communicate with non-Jews. This form of open ghetto was also found elsewhere in Belarus as well as in parts of Ukraine. In Chashniki this situation existed until just prior to the mass shooting of the Jews in mid-February 1942, that is, for about six months.[11] Nevertheless, these open ghettos form a special category that requires some differentiation from the more typical ghettos that were enclosed by barbed wire, wooden fences, or walls.

Critical Defining Elements and Other Indicators

In defining ghettos, three critical elements form necessary prerequisites: the resettlement of Jews into a clearly defined residential area, their physical separation from the surrounding population, and some threatened punishment for leaving this confined space.

To these basic criteria may be added a number of typical indicators for ghettos, for which there may be occasional exceptions. For example, most ghettos were usually in or close to a town or village where Jews had resided previously. Most that existed for more than a few days had some form of Jewish Council or self-administration, although this was true also of some communities where no ghettoization took place. The existence of a fence or barrier, which was usually guarded to prevent escapes or smuggling expeditions, is usually a clear indicator of an enclosed ghetto but is also shared by forced labor and other types of camps. Another important point is the use of ghettos as a concentration point for Jews from the surrounding villages; often this was part of a concerted German policy of clearing the countryside of Jews, usually in preparation for their murder or deportation.

"Destruction Ghettos"

A particular problem with regard to definition is how to handle the many short-lived ghettos, which the Nazi German forces used primarily as staging areas for mass murder. This was especially common in Lithuania, where Jews were forced into communal buildings or held in makeshift camps on the edge of town for just a few days prior to their murder. An additional problem is that there is little information about such ghettos, which had no communal life or a realistic chance for organizing resistance. Nevertheless, the basic research needs to be done to identify such sites and explain briefly what happened in each place, in addition to how these "destruction ghettos" differed from other types of ghettos.[12]

Therefore, a separate category to be discussed is what Roman Mogilanski and others have called "Nazi death traps,"[13] or "destruction ghettos," those short-lived ghettos used primarily to facilitate the mass shootings or deportations. A good indicator for such ghettos, apart from their short duration, is often the complete denial of food to Jews held within them, as seen in Tal'ka. Another example is the ghetto in Khoiniki, in southeastern Belarus, where about two hundred Jews were locked up in a bookshop without food and water for several days before they were shot. When gentile children attempted to give the incarcerated Jews some food and drink in response to their constant pleading, the German forces also threatened them with shooting.[14] Nonetheless, there are cases in which plans for ghettoization initiated by the military, civil, or even the collaborationist administration for local reasons were rapidly overtaken by the intervention of the *Einsatzgruppen* or other police forces, which murdered the inmates abruptly on orders received through a separate chain of command.

As many of these "problematic sites" are referred to specifically as "ghettos" in the available sources, both open ghettos and destruction ghettos will be identified and described as far as possible in the encyclopedia in order to help clarify how they differed from the majority of enclosed ghettos.

Interpreting Ambiguities: The Case of the Tomaszowka Ghetto

Wrestling with these conceptual problems, which have emerged directly from empirical research, only confirms the unavoidable role of ambiguity and uncertainty within the "ghettos universe." In particular, simple data such as the opening and closing dates of specific ghettos or the size of their population are often not available or are riddled with irreconcilable contradictions. It is in fact much easier to come to a firm conclusion on such matters when there is only one source rather than several, all of questionable reliability, which are in stark disagreement with each other.

The case study of the little-known ghetto in Tomaszowka demonstrates well some of the ambiguities and uncertainties that arise when attempting to reconstruct basic data from fragmentary contemporary documentation and sketchy oral accounts.

The small town of Tomaszowka is located today about fifty kilometers to the south of Brest just on the Belarussian side of the border with Poland. Its ghetto is barely mentioned in the available Holocaust literature.[15] My research has only uncovered one detailed survivor statement regarding the ghetto, by a Jew from the neighboring town of Wlodawa who was brought into the Tomaszowka ghetto to conduct construction work on a bridge across the Bug River.

Very little is known about the Jewish population of Tomaszowka prior to the war. No mention can be found in the detailed census of 1921, and the 1931 census has no data on the smaller Jewish settlements. However, a local inhabitant recalled the following details:

> The main industry of Tomaszowka was woodsaw mills, which were owned by Jews. The majority of the working population were Poles, together with some Jews. The few shops in Tomaszowka were owned by Jews. They sold most general goods. The Poles who didn't work at the woodsaw mills and didn't have their own plots of land were employed by the Jews to work in their houses or shops. The relations between the Jews and the local people were good. The Jews were better off, and the rest of the population lived quite poorly. Several Polish, Russian, and Jewish families were deported to Siberia at the end of 1940 or at the beginning of 1941.[16]

The same local inhabitant, Kiril Karvat, has given detailed descriptions of the fate of the ghetto:

> From the very first days of the occupation, the whole Jewish population living in Tomaszowka was herded by the Germans into a camp, which was called a ghetto. The Jewish ghetto was in the western part of the settlement. This area has now been developed and there are no longer any traces of a ghetto. The Germans put up a barbed wire fence around the ghetto. German police and soldiers patrolled the fence the whole time.[17] . . . I can't say exactly how many houses were in the ghetto. The Jews had yellow patches with a star on them, on their clothes, on the chest and the back. Very strict restrictions were introduced, the local people were forbidden to go into the ghetto, if caught they might be shot.[18]

The Jewish survivor Nachum Knopmacher from Wlodawa has described his work in the Tomaszowka ghetto, which was under the control of the Organisation Todt (OT). He was in the ghetto from autumn of 1941 until summer of 1942. His work included bridge and housing construction for the OT. Jews worked outside the ghetto during the day and had to return in the evening. In autumn of 1941 he saw how the local German civil official in charge, Hecht, murdered a Jew named Tuwia in a cruel manner, setting his dog onto the man when he was helpless to resist.

In the early summer of 1942 some four hundred Viennese Jews were brought into the ghetto from the General Government to assist with the forced labor tasks.[19] According to Knopmacher, in April 1942 all the Jews of the ghetto (about 2,500 according to Knopmacher) were assembled, and Hecht selected some eighty women, children, and old men who were then taken out of town and shot nearby. Knopmacher mentions also that some fifty Jewish workers (mostly those from Vienna) were shot at the discretion of the Reich German, Krystop, who was in charge of the bridge construction work.[20]

A shooting at the end of April 1942 is also described by Kiril Karvat, although he believes those Jews shot came from the Domaczewo ghetto:

> We saw three or four German trucks with canvas tops coming from the direction of Tomaszowka towards us. The trucks turned left into a field in which there was a long defensive ditch that had been dug previously by Soviet soldiers. There were three German machine guns mounted on tripods. The people came down from the trucks, guarded by Germans and policemen. I recognized these people as Jews from Domaczewo, men, women and children. We saw that some of them were made to undress and were then forced to get into the ditch in groups of about twenty people. The policemen and the German soldiers stood on the edge of the ditch, they were armed with sub machine guns and they shot the Jews. I heard the screaming of children and women. After each shooting the remaining Jews were made to fill in the ditch. This procedure was repeated about four times until all the Jews were shot. The shooting must have lasted at least two hours.[21]

Ghetto Liquidation

Conflicting dates for the liquidation of the Tomaszowka ghetto are to be found in the available sources. The Soviet Extraordinary Commission Report, based mainly on local eyewitness statements, dates the liquidation as taking place in July 1942 in antitank ditches just off the road from Tomaszowka to Brest.[22] However, there may be some confusion between the ghetto liquidation and the shooting of Jews working on road construction in the area, as the same execution site was used at least twice.

According to a contemporary German report for June 1942, about one thousand Jews (both men and women) were removed from the Tomaszowka ghetto and placed in a separate labor camp nearby, where they were employed by the OT for construction work on the bridge between Wlodawa and Tomaszowka.[23] The Extraordinary Commission Report also mentions some five hundred Jews being taken from the Domaczewo ghetto in May

1942 for work on the Brest-Kowel highway, noting that all those who were exhausted and weakened were shot shortly afterward.[24]

A majority of the eyewitness accounts, however, confirm the dating given in a contemporary German report. The gendarmerie district leader in Brest stated that "on 19 and 20 September 1942 about 2,900 Jews were shot in Domaczewo and Tomaszowka by a special command of the SD in connection with the cavalry squadron stationed in Domaczewo, the gendarmerie, and the *Schutzmannschaft*. The 'Jewish action' took place without any disturbances."[25]

A Jewish survivor from Domaczewo stated that the action in Tomaszowka took place on the day after the liquidation of the Domaczewo ghetto.[26] And a driver for the gendarmerie in Brest dated the ghetto liquidations in Tomaszowka and Domaczewo both in September, adding that in Tomaszowka the Jews were killed in an antitank ditch.[27]

Most significantly, a key local witness from Tomaszewka, the aforementioned Kiril Karvat, who in previous statements had dated the action in the summer of 1942, subsequently confirmed that "in September 1942, together with my friend, we were going to Tomaszowka, and when we arrived there we saw the Jews from the Tomaszowka ghetto being escorted by Gestapo soldiers and policemen. . . . A very big group of Jews from Tomaszowka were shot on that day. The massacre took place in the same field and ditch as the shooting of April 1942. . . ."[28]

Some sketchy information on the ghetto in Tomaszowka is also to be found in statements by Germans who served in the area and were investigated by the federal German authorities after the war. The agricultural leader in the town, Werner Dressler, confirmed the existence of a ghetto and recalls a Jewish interpreter, who worked for him from February 1942, having been assigned to him by the Jewish Council. After about five months Dressler received orders from the district commissar in Brest (Rolle) to terminate his employment.[29]

Other German witnesses served in a cavalry squadron that was based in Tomaszowka and Domaczewo from August 1942. One former member, Vehrenberg, stated, "Jewish artisans and families, about thirty people in all, were accommodated in several houses on the outskirts of Tomaszowka, surrounded by barbed wire. They did all the work that the squadron needed doing."[30] If his recollection is correct, this was either a remnant left after the main action or those left after the bulk had been transferred to a labor camp closer to their work site. Another cavalry squadron member, Erwin Hentschke, recalls that members of the squadron served as perimeter guards during the Tomaszowka ghetto liquidation.[31]

Size of the Ghetto and Numbers Killed

Despite some detailed demographic information available from contemporary sources, it is still not possible to determine precisely how many Jews were confined within the Tomaszowka ghetto, nor how many were killed.

From the scanty prewar description, there were probably only a few hundred Jews living in Tomaszowka before the war.³²

Accounts of the liquidation of the Tomaszewka ghetto, if they are to be believed, estimate that somewhere between 1,500 and 2,000 Jews were killed during this action.³³ This would imply that Jews were brought in from elsewhere, most probably Domaczewo, in addition to the four hundred or so Jews from Vienna who were sent across the Bug in April 1942. According to contemporary German records, in early 1942 there were 3,316 Jews living in the Domaczewo rayon.³⁴ Given that several hundred died or were killed during the course of the summer, the figure of 2,900 killed in Domaczewo and Tomaszowka on 19 to 20 September 1942 seems fairly reliable. The only question is how to divide this figure between the two ghettos. Estimates based on the evidence of German witnesses, who were keen to minimize the scale of the action, mention only some five hundred Jews in Domaczewo at the time of the ghetto liquidation. The Soviet Extraordinary Commission Report, by contrast, gives the figure of 2,700 Jews killed in Domaczewo.³⁵ My own estimate is that there were probably just over one thousand Jews still in Domaczewo and maybe 1,800 in Tomaszowka,³⁶ including any nearby labor camps, at the time of the action. Some Jews were transferred from Domaczewo to Tomaszowka to work on the road and bridge construction there.³⁷

After the ghetto liquidation, according to local inhabitants, "The Germans and policemen brought the clothes and underwear of those who had been shot by lorry into the settlement of Tomaszowka and sold them to the inhabitants for eggs, butter, home-made spirits and bacon."³⁸ Another local inhabitant recalls that after the "action," a local policeman came to her house to check if any Jews were hiding there.³⁹ There is today a monument at the grave site of the Tomaszowka Jews, which was erected in 1954.⁴⁰

Structure

What was the function of ghettos within Nazi plans for the "Final Solution"? Essentially they were never more than a stopgap, a point of concentration and transit, used for exploiting Jewish labor and material resources on the way to mass murder. The German authorities sought the isolation of the Jewish population for a variety of ideological, economic, and practical reasons that resulted in many regional differences in implementation. Forced labor and economic isolation were central to almost all ghettos that existed for more than a few weeks, but at the same time there remained inherent contradictions. Work details left many ghettos on a daily basis, and barter with the non-Jewish population was impossible to prevent.

The Jewish police and the Jewish Councils, which for many survivors have become symbols of Jewish collaboration and betrayal, could also ameliorate conditions and, on occasion, also strengthen the resistance. More than half of all Holocaust victims passed through the ghettos, yet these ephemeral communities have been viewed primarily as a prologue to the destruction that followed.

Internal Life of a Ghetto: The Case of Byten As Seen Through Its Yizkor Book

In some cases where several accounts from survivors are available, especially in the form of a Yizkor book, it is possible to examine the experiences and responses of the Jewish population within the ghetto in some detail. This final narrative of events in the Byten ghetto, just south of Słonim in western Belarus, owes much to the work of Andrew Koss, who assembled most of this detailed account from the Yizkor book and German investigative sources.[41]

On the eve of World War II, there were more than 880 Jews in Byten. With the outbreak of war in 1939, about two hundred Jewish refugees from central Poland settled in the town.[42] After the arrival of the Germans on 25 June 1941, the local military commandant formed a *Judenrat* in mid-July. Rather than trying to find an established authority figure, a German officer simply stopped a Jew on the street one night and ordered him to present within two hours a list of six people who could sit on the *Judenrat*.[43]

In September 1941 a group of German soldiers ordered a few Jews to remove the Torah scrolls and sacred books from the *Beit Midrash* (study house) and place them on a wagon, which the soldiers then set on fire.[44] Forced labor became part of the daily routine for the Jews of Byten. Besides having to work on the roads, many Jews worked taking care of horses or at a variety of other menial tasks. At first, the soldiers supervising the roadwork treated the Jews with relative decency; later on, however, soldiers merely passing through the area would beat Jews they saw at work.[45]

During that winter antisemitic leaflets were distributed and antisemitic posters displayed throughout Byten. There was also a further mass confiscation of Jewish property. Members of the *Judenrat* were summoned to the *Gebietskommissariat* in Słonim, where Dietrich Hick, the section leader for Jewish affairs, demanded they hand over all the valuables they owned, in addition to fixed sums of gold and cash. Three members of the *Judenrat* were held hostage. To meet these demands some Jews in Byten had their gold teeth extracted, while others sold their clothes to raise the necessary cash.[46]

The office of the *Gebietskommissariat* issued the order to form a ghetto in May or June 1942. Hundreds of Jews went to the forests to get wood to build the fence that would imprison them. They constructed it out of wooden beams and barbed wire. They were given less than a week to build the fence and relocate to the ghetto. The ghetto itself consisted of forty-eight houses and the large *Beit Midrash,* which was transformed into a residence. The ghetto had a population of about 1,200 (including refugees from the nearby town of Iwacewicze, where the Jews had all been driven out in March

1942); hence, the overcrowding was extreme. Lack of space and time prevented the Jews from bringing all of their few remaining possessions into the ghetto. The local gentiles quickly looted whatever they had left behind. The gendarmes announced that any Jew caught outside the ghetto without permission would be killed.[47]

Forced labor continued, but now the workers had to come and go in columns under strict German supervision. The rudiments of cultural life continued as well. Because the local synagogues either lay outside the ghetto or were needed for housing, a barn and a stall were turned into ad hoc places of prayer, which held twice-daily services. Rabbi Yafa attended one makeshift synagogue and Rabbi Liberman, along with Rabbi Rakhman, the former rabbi of Iwacewicze, attended the other. Other members of the community continued to provide religious education for the children. Adults gathered in the evenings to chat or discuss the situation. A refugee from Lodz named Dr. Vodnik organized a sanitary commission.[48]

The black market was the only means of obtaining food available to the Jews. Every day, a few peasants would secretly bring food to the ghetto fence and exchange it with Jews—usually for clothing or other goods.[49] On receiving news of the second large "action" that took place in Słonim on 29 June 1942, the Jews in Byten built bunkers and other hiding places in anticipation of the liquidation of the ghetto.[50] On 24 July 1942 rumor spread that peasants from the countryside had been put to work digging pits. The Jews suspected the purpose of these pits and prepared to hide in their bunkers.[51] Before dawn on the next day, one of the Jewish policemen went from door to door telling people to hide, as the ghetto had been surrounded by gendarmes and local police. Not long thereafter, local police and German gendarmes began to round up the Jews. A force of about 80 auxiliaries and a Sipo-SD *Kommando* had been brought in to carry out the action.[52]

The ghetto was searched thoroughly by the local police, who discovered many of the hiding Jews, sometimes shooting them on the spot.[53] The rest of the Jews were either crowded onto trucks and driven in shifts to pits that had been dug between the villages of Zapolie and Rudnia, a few kilometers from Byten, or forced to walk there.[54] The "useful Jews" living outside the ghetto were actually the first to be brought to the pits.[55] There, the SS men shot both groups of Jews and covered the mass graves. It seems that the local gendarmes and the *Hilfspolizei* were primarily involved in transporting the Jews and serving as cordon guards.[56] As in other shooting actions, many were not killed by the gunshots and died of suffocation, buried alive in the graves.[57] The local police also exploited the opportunity to loot. Peasants came and took whatever they left behind.[58] According to one survivor, the Germans announced that 840 Jews had been killed and 360 remained.[59]

After a few days had passed, the Jews who had hidden came out of their bunkers. The gendarmerie gathered them together in the *Beit Midrash* and determined their ability to work. Older Jews shaved their beards or made other efforts to appear younger. They were told they had only one month to live and were put to work clearing out the Jewish houses and bringing whatever they found there to the gendarmes. Surviving artisans were allowed to continue practicing their trades.[60]

On 13 August fifty-six skilled workers were transferred out of the ghetto and told that they no longer had to wear yellow patches. On Saturday, 29 August at 4:00 A.M., an SS unit, accompanied by Lithuanian auxiliaries, arrived and surrounded the ghetto. The Jews realized what was happening right away and hid in their bunkers. A few managed to escape as the action was being carried out. After daybreak, the Lithuanians and SS along with the local police entered the houses of the ghetto, rounded up its residents, and gathered them together. Later that morning, they marched the Jews on foot to the pits near Zapolie, ordered them to undress, and shot them. The gendarmes took first pick of any clothes they wanted and left the rest for the peasants. The plundering of Jewish homes in the ghetto by the local population began immediately.[61] In mid-September the remaining Jewish workers and their families were shot inside the town.[62]

Escape and Resistance During the Ghetto Liquidations

As this description demonstrates, the liquidation of the ghettos during the "second wave" in the summer and autumn of 1942 was sudden and violent. "Resistance" most frequently consisted of silent escape or the attempt to hide behind false walls or in concealed bunkers. The systematic liquidation of the ghettos was carefully organized by the Nazi police and their collaborators, requiring a considerable workforce to conduct house-by-house searches. Inside the ghettos the machinery of destruction still required a personal confrontation between perpetrator and victim. The tense final moments are reflected in the drunken conversations of local policemen looking for loot, recalled by survivors in hiding, fearful of death.[63] Afterward most ghettos were ransacked, dismantled, left to decay, or reoccupied by the gentile population, leaving almost no lasting physical trace.

Conclusions: The Unknown, the Ambiguous, and the Disappeared

What emerges from the detailed study of these small and in some cases "lost ghettos," where the full story will likely never be known? This geographical "gray zone" of the Holocaust is still populated by the unknown, the ambiguous, and the disappeared.

Perhaps the real meaning of the project lies in the little-known facts. Considerable amounts of new research in archives only recently opened to scholars make such a comprehensive project feasible in a way that was not conceivable a few years ago. It is now possible to identify and describe ghettos that existed, however briefly, in little-known locations such as Tal'ka, Tomaszowka, and Byten. Documentation from contemporary German reports, survivor testimonies, and postwar investigations can now be compared directly, though resolving the contradictions still remains a difficult task. So far more than 950 individual ghettos have been identified and more than eighty of these have now been described. In terms of basic research it has been possible to put some "lost ghettos" on the historical map and give a rough estimate of the number of victims and their fate.

Completely resolving the uncertainties and ambiguities of Jewish ghettos in Nazi-occupied Eastern Europe, however, will not be possible. This applies even more so to the moral questions surrounding the role of the Jewish Councils or the Jewish police force. Reconstructing the dilemmas of those caught in the Nazi trap and attempting to understand their perception of events is now more important than engaging in further harsh moral criticism of Jewish responses to this unprecedented threat.[64] For this reason, those rare "Jewish sources" that provide an insight into the internal dynamics within the ghetto, as shown in the case of Byten, are of great significance in describing the complexities of life lived under the threat of extinction.

Much of the pain and ambiguity comes from trying to reconstruct from shards some essence of a now-vanished community in its death throes. The bare facts of the destruction are not sufficient to restore the memory of what has been lost, but they remain a crucial starting point. As the last survivors and bystanders are now passing away, it is important to record the details as fully as possible. In particular, the ghettos have a particularly tenuous grasp within the landscape of memory due to their innately ephemeral existence.

Since most ghetto sites were located in the changing urban landscape and many were ransacked, redeveloped, or simply reinhabited by the non-Jewish population immediately following the massacres, there is rarely an identifiable ghetto site that can be commemorated. Even large ghettos such as Warsaw, Lodz, and Minsk have left little physical evidence that is visible today, and the same applies to the majority of smaller ghettos. Rare exceptions are those such as the "second ghetto" in Mir, which was located in a surviving castle. Here, though, the brief "ghetto history" remains almost entirely subsumed within the broader cultural significance of a historic monument preserved by UNESCO. Those memorials that do exist stand mainly at the grave sites outside the towns, preserving little connection to the bustling urban community that once was.

Thus the "gray zones" of the ghettos have to be carefully reconstructed from sources replete with problems and contradictions. Yet this difficult empirical research can lead to important conceptual breakthroughs as the scope and diversity of experiences in the many small ghettos are pieced together from surviving fragments. In this way historical memory can be salvaged for the generations to come who will have the same questions about the severing of their ancestral roots as well as for historians seeking to map out this shattered landscape.

Notes

1. Christian Gerlach, *Kalkulierte Mord: Die deutsche Wirtschafts- und Vernichtungspolitik in Weissrussland 1941 bis 1944* (Hamburg: HIS, 1999), 587, mentions the shootings of the Jews from these three towns but does not note that the Jews from Pukhovichi and Mar'ina Gorka were killed together in a single action, and as a result his figures are probably inaccurate.
2. Bundesarchiv Berlin-Lichterfelde (BA), R58/217, Ereignismeldung UdSSR No. 124, 25 October 1941.
3. Bundesarchiv, Aussenstelle Ludwigsburg, former Zentrale Stelle der Landesjustizverwaltungen (ZSL), II 202 179/67, Dok. Bd. I, statements of Olga Androsik on 25 March 1968 and Sinaida Bartasevich on 18 December 1945.
4. Ibid., Dok. Bd. II, statements of Mikhail A. Koreny, Anna Biryukova, and Nadezhda I. Syrez in September 1944.
5. Ibid., 87–94, statements of Sinaida Bartasevich and Valentina Cherepko in December 1945.
6. Ibid., Dok. Bd. II, statements of Mikhail A. Koreny and Sinaida K. Bartasevich in September 1944.
7. Ibid., Dok. Bd. I, statements of Semen Panschey and Kondrat Molchan in 1945; Dok. Bd. II, statement of Anna Koreny in September 1944.
8. Ibid.
9. Wendy Lower, "Facilitating Genocide: Nazi Ghettoization Practices in Occupied Ukraine, 1941-1942," forthcoming.
10. Aleksandr Kruglov, draft entry on the ghetto of Uman for the CAHS ghettos encyclopedia volume.
11. Daniel Romanovsky, draft entry on Chashniki, ibid. Other examples of open ghettos in this region include Beshenkovichi and Ostrovno. On Chashniki, see also Romanovsky's essay in *Vestnik Yevreiskogo Universiteta v Moskve* 1 (1992), 157–99.
12. On "destruction ghettos" see especially Lower, "Facilitating Genocide."
13. Roman Mogilanski, ed., *The Ghetto Anthology: A Comprehensive Chronicle of the Extermination of Jewry in Nazi Death Camps and Ghettos in Poland* (Los Angeles: American Congress of Jews from Poland and Survivors of Concentration Camps, 1985).
14. ZSL, 204 AR-Z 121/67 (Orlizek investigation), 225ff., statements of Warwara Latyschkewitsch on 30 January 1968 and Anna Erofeewa on 29 January 1969.
15. It cannot be found, for example, in Shmuel Spector and Geoffrey Wigoder, eds., *The Encyclopedia of Jewish Life Before and During the Holocaust* (Jerusalem: Yad Vashem; New York: New York University Press, 2001), which otherwise is one of the best sources for tracking down little-known ghettos. There is, however, a mention in Marat Botvinnik, *Pamyatniki Genotsida Evreev Belarusi* (Minsk: Belaruskaya Navuka, 2000), 136.
16. Metropolitan Police War Crimes Unit (henceforth WCU), statement of Kiril Petrovich Karvat on 18 February 1997. The records of the WCU are now held by the Public Records Office, Kew, London.
17. ZSL, II 204 AR-Z 472/67, statement of Kiril Petrovich Karvat on 17 June 1968; he was interviewed again in 1997 by officers of the WCU when he elaborated on his previous statements.
18. WCU, statement of Kiril Petrovich Karvat on 18 February 1997.
19. ZSL, II 202 AR-Z 472/67 (Hecht investigation), Bd. I, 31–38, statement of Nachum Knopmacher on 15 June 1965. Knopmacher dates this transfer in March 1942, but it is unlikely to have been before May, as the deportation of 998 Jews to Wlodawa from Vienna (the only deportation from Vienna to Wlodawa) did not leave the city until 27 April 1942. See Florian Freund and Hans Safrian, "Die Verfolgung der österreichischen Juden 1938–1945: Vertreibung und Deportation," in Emmerich Talos et al., eds., *NS-Herrschaft in Österreich: Ein Handbuch* (Vienna: öbv & hpt, 2001), 767–94, here 793.
20. ZSL, statement of Nachum Knopmacher on 15 June 1965.

21. WCU, statement of Kiril Petrovich Karvat on 18 February 1997.
22. Brest Regional (oblast') State Archive (BRSA), 514-1-195, 4–7.
23. BA, R 94/7, Monthly report of Brest District Commissar, section *Arbeitsamt*, for June 1942.
24. BRSA, 514-1-195, 4–7.
25. BA, R 94/7, Gendarmerie District Leader Brest situation report, 6 October 1942.
26. Brest regional KGB Archive (Brest KGB), Criminal File 2905, case no. 69 (against Nikolai K. Lyalko), 40, statement of Boris S. Grunstein on 27 September 1944.
27. Brest KGB, File No. 466 (Criminal Case against Ivan E. Chikun), Vol. 2, 89–93, statement of Ivan S. Khvisyuchik on 16 March 1983. See also the 24 March 1970 statement of Erwin Glass, a former cavalry squadron member, who recalls that his comrades told him that the Jews of Tomaszowka were killed at the same time as those of Domaczewo. ZSL, II 202 AR-Z 472/67, Bd. I, 180–82.
28. WCU, statement of Kiril Petrovich Karvat on 18 February 1997.
29. ZSL, II 204 AR-Z 472/67, Bd. I, 190–91, statement of Werner Dressler on 13 October 1970.
30. See ZSL, 204 AR-Z 369/63 (Hahn investigation), Bd. V, 178–98.
31. See ZSL, Ludwigsburg II 202 AR-Z 472/67, Bd. I, 165–67, statement of Erwin Hentschke on 16 March 1970.
32. ZSL, II 204 AR-Z 472/67, statement of Kiril Petrovich Karvat on 17 June 1968. He estimates some two thousand, but this number is almost certainly too high, given the absence of any census data for the town.
33. See the Soviet Extraordinary Commission Reports for the Domaczewo rayon and accompanying witness statements in BRSA, 514-1-195. There is also mention in one statement of the gassing of Jewish victims in Tomaszowka, but this remains uncorroborated.
34. BA, R 94/7, Situation Report of District Commissar Rolle dated 24 March 1942.
35. See, for example, ZSL, 204 AR-Z 369/63, Bd. I, 194-6; Soviet Extraordinary Commission Report, BRSA, 514-1-195.
36. WCU, officer's information on an interview with Kiril Petrovich Karvat on 10 February 1995. In this interview Karvat gave the figure of 1,800 Jews killed in Tomaszowka.
37. See, for example, the slightly vague comments about his own transfer in WCU, statement of Baruch Greenstein on 9 October 1996. Greenstein's testimony was problematic and was not used during the trial of Andrei Sawoniuk in London in 1999.
38. ZSL, II 204 AR-Z 472/67, statement of Kiril Petrovich Karvat on 17 June 1968.
39. Brest KGB, Criminal File 2905, case no. 69 (against Nikolai K. Lyalko), 60–61, statement of Marya Antonovna Ol'shevskaya on 30 November 1944.
40. Botvinnik, *Pamyatniki Genotsida Evreev Belarusi,* 136; WCU, interview with Anna Karvat in February 1997.
41. Andrew Koss was a research fellow at the U.S. Holocaust Memorial Museum's Center for Advanced Holocaust Studies from May 2002 to May 2004, specializing in Hebrew and Yiddish sources in support of the ghettos encyclopedia volume.
42. Dodl Abramovitsh, "Khurbn un Widershtand" [Destruction and Resistance], in Dodl Abramovitsh and Mordkhay V. Bernshtayn, eds., *Pinkes Biten: Der Oyfkum un Untergang fun a Yidisher Kihile* [The Register of Byten: The Origins and Downfall of a Jewish Community] (Buenos Aires: Bitener Landslayt in Argentine, 1954), 321–412, here 321.
43. Ibid., 322–24. See also Moshe Pitkovski, "Azoy iz Untergegangen di Yidishe Kehile in Biten" [Thus Was the Jewish Community of Byten Destroyed], in *Pinkes Biten,* 207–314, here 209.
44. Pitkovski, "Azoy iz Untergegangen," 209–10, 213.
45. Abramovitsh, "Khurbn," 326; Pitkovski, "Azoy iz Untergegangen," 210–11, 213.
46. Ibid., 219; ZSL, Trial Verdict in the case of Gerhard Erren (II 202 AR-Z 228/59), 4352.
47. Pitkovski, "Azoy iz Untergegangen, 225–27; ZSL, Erren Trial Verdict, 4344, 4352.
48. Pitkovski, "Azoy iz Untergegangen," 227–28.
49. Ibid., 230.
50. Ibid., 214–15, 228.

51. Ibid., 230–32; ZSL, Erren Trial Verdict, 4353.
52. Pitkovski, "Azoy iz Untergegangen," 233–34; ZSL, Erren Trial Verdict, 4343–54.
53. Pitkovski, "Azoy iz Untergegangen," 232–36; ZSL, Erren Trial Verdict, 4345–46.
54. Pitkovski, "Azoy iz Untergegangen," 235–36; ZSL, Erren Trial Verdict, 4345; Report of the Soviet Extraordinary Commission, State Archives of the Russian Federation (GARF), 7021-81-102, 1–31.
55. Pitkovski, "Azoy iz Untergegangen," 229; ZSL, Erren Trial Verdict, 4349.
56. ZSL, Erren Trial Verdict, 4345.
57. Pitkovski, "Azoy iz Untergegangen," 236; Abramovitsh, "Khurbn," 327.
58. Pitkovski, "Azoy iz Untergegangen," 233–34, 239.
59. Ibid., 236–38; one German witness put the number of victims between five and six hundred, while another put it at about 2,800. The trial verdict itself considers the latter figure too high; see ZSL, Erren Trial Verdict, 4346–47. According to the Extraordinary Commission Report, two mass graves were found near Rudnia; one contained nine hundred corpses and the other eighty, coming close to Pitkovski's figure of 840. Perhaps the second grave contains victims of the second *Aktion*. Another account in *Pinkes Biten* gives the figure as "close to 900" (456).
60. ZSL, Erren Trial Verdict, 4354; Pitkovski, "Azoy iz Untergegangen," 236–39.
61. ZSL, Erren Trial Verdict, 4331–43; Pitkovski, "Azoy iz Untergegangen," 240–41, 248–50; *Pinkes Biten*, 3; WCU, interview with Byten survivor Tanya Imber in August 1994; ZSL, II 202 AR-Z 228/59 (Erren investigation) Handakte, Bd. II, 651–57.
62. ZSL, Erren Trial Verdict, 4354; *Pinkes Biten*, 3; WCU, Imber interview.
63. See, for example, Martin Dean, *Collaboration in the Holocaust: Crimes of the Local Police in Belorussia and Ukraine, 1941–1944* (New York: St. Martin's Press, 2000), 90.
64. Shalom Cholawski, *The Jews of Bielorussia During World War II* (Amsterdam: Harwood, 1998), 251–70, gives a balanced account of the role of the Jewish Councils in western Belarus, examining a wide variety of responses within the specific local circumstances.

– Chapter 15 –

"ALMOST-CAMPS" IN PARIS
The Difficult Description of Three Annexes of Drancy—Austerlitz, Lévitan, and Bassano, July 1943 to August 1944

Jean-Marc Dreyfus

On 18 July 1943, 120 Jews, inmates of the transit camp of Drancy in the northern suburb of Paris, were transported by bus to the heart of the French capital, to a building located in the Faubourg Saint-Martin street, standing almost opposite the tenth district city hall. The building had previously been used as a furniture store with the firm name of Lévitan. With the transfer of these Jews the building was turned into a camp, the first of three to be set up in Paris.[1] Austerlitz, the second camp to be created, on 1 November 1943, was located in a warehouse on the *quai de la Gare* behind the famous train station. The first inmates arrived in Bassano in March 1944. It was the third of the camps to be established, located in a beautiful *fin-de-siècle* townhouse in the heart of the bourgeois sixteenth district of Paris.

The three camps in Paris are a part of the history of the Holocaust. Their description, though, has raised many questions, as the camps cannot precisely be defined. They were not concentration camps, since they were never controlled by the SS (though SS men helped to guard them). They were not transit camps, as inmates were not supposed to be sent back to Drancy for deportation, though in reality dozens of prisoners were ultimately removed from the Paris camps and were deported, always through Drancy. The facilities at Austerlitz, Lévitan, and Bassano were not prisons where political prisoners were to be interrogated. They were not special shelters for wealthy or important Jews who could serve as hostages for potential negotiations of exchange. In Western Europe, at least, they remained unique. No such camps were created in the Reich, in Belgium, in the Netherlands,

Notes for this section begin on page 236.

or in Norway.² They remain "in-between," challenging definitions of camp settings and defying all of the current representations of the persecution and destruction of Jews in Europe. Only eight hundred Jews were incarcerated in one (or two) of the three camps. They represent a tiny percentage of European Jewry and even of the Jews in France.³ Moreover, the camps existed only for a limited period of time—thirteen months—compared to Drancy, which was in operation for three years out of Germany's four-year-and-two-month occupation of Paris. They could easily have been set apart from the main historiography of the Vichy regime and the Holocaust in France, and indeed might have been forgotten, as they did not seem to be representative of the levels of violence of the time. But their history tells us a good deal about the Nazi policy in France: the looting of Jewish properties, the classification of Jews in different categories, and the justification of a *"Weltanschauung"* that made the Jews responsible for the suffering of Germans under Allied bombings. As the numerous pictures taken in the camps and found in several archival centers show, Austerlitz, Bassano, and Lévitan appear to be "gray zones." They were not places of unrestricted violence or of killing, but they participated in the general machinery of the Holocaust in France.

Gray also was the certain secrecy to be maintained concerning these camps, according to German orders. The camps were not totally secluded from the rest of the city, but their existence was not publicized (as was the existence of other camps, most significantly Drancy, in the French press due to German propaganda). In July 1943 opposition to the persecution of Jews had risen among the French populace,⁴ and the French collaborationist government of Pierre Laval was no longer eager to help in the organization of deportations and roundups. The period of police collaboration between the German Gestapo and the state secretary of police was about to end.⁵ The Jews who were kept prisoners in Paris were prevented from having contact with the French population (although this restriction was only partially enforced) and were hidden from passersby in the surrounding streets. In all three camps they were rarely permitted to go out of the buildings and were forbidden to approach the windows.⁶ As a punishment they could be immediately sent back to Drancy and from there deported to Auschwitz or Sobibor in the next convoy.⁷ In Lévitan, huge shop windows directly faced the busy street of Faubourg Saint-Martin. Every piece of furniture from the shop that could be seen from the street was left untouched. One might have the impression that the store was closed for temporary reasons and that it would reopen soon. This mock furniture store in the center of Paris is reminiscent of the mock merchant bank in Amsterdam, the Liro (Lippmann, Rosenthal & Co.),⁸ which was in reality a German institution created to confiscate Jewish bank accounts, assets, stocks, and other valuables. Comparison between the two is especially apt because the three camps of Paris were at the center of a major looting operation, the so-called *Möbel Aktion* or "Furniture Operation."

Why These Camps? The *Möbel Aktion*

The *Möbel Aktion* was a gigantic looting operation that affected all Jewish-owned flats and houses in France, Belgium, and the Netherlands.[9] The idea of emptying all Jewish houses of their belongings was launched in Paris by Kurt von Behr, the deputy head of the Einsatzstab Reichsleiter Rosenberg (ERR). The ERR, whose Paris branch was founded as early as July 1940, organized the looting of archives, historical documents, books, and works of art in Western Europe[10] under the supervision of Alfred Rosenberg, the "ideologue" of National Socialism. Kurt von Behr, a shady character who posed as a baron and had a British wife, managed to convince Alfred Rosenberg to support his project. Hitler himself gave the authorization for the effort on 31 December 1940.[11] The official purpose of this vast operation was the furnishing of the newly created German administrations in the eastern part of Europe occupied by the Reich after the June 1941 invasion of the Soviet Union. As the Reich Minister for the Occupied Eastern Territories, Rosenberg was entrusted with this new mission.[12]

To implement the *Möbel Aktion,* a new organization was set up in Paris, the *Dienststelle Westen* (Western Department) of the Ministry of the Eastern Occupied Territories. Hitler gave the order not to loot inhabited Jewish flats and forbade the publication of an official ordinance.[13] The official date of creation for the *Dienststelle Westen* was 17 April 1942.[14] This new office was organized on the same pattern as the ERR with branches in provincial towns and independent departments in Belgium and the Netherlands. Some warehouses were confiscated in order to store the loot. In Paris six of them became permanent. One year later, three were turned into camps. As early as April 1942 trains loaded with confiscated goods left Paris for the East. At least some transports reached the eastern territories, Ukraine for example, and were distributed to German administrations or German colonists.[15] After the massive Allied bombings over Cologne during the night of 30 May 1942, the destination of trains loaded with looted furniture and objects changed: they arrived in the Reich with the official stated reason of lightening the burden of German victims of air raids.[16] It became part of the Nazi propaganda to state that the Jews, being responsible for the war, had to pay for their crimes and compensate the damages caused to the German civilian population with their own property.[17] The same propaganda was used to a somewhat lesser degree by the Vichy regime in France, whose administration was granted the distribution of some loads of furniture. Pictures were displayed in the French press by the official propaganda office of Marshal Pétain.[18] As the main cities of the Reich became the target of repeated air raids, German Gauleiters could turn to Paris and the *Dienststelle Westen* to receive objects and furniture. Boats from the Netherlands arrived in Hamburg.[19] The *Möbel Aktion* was extended to the entire French occupied zone. In the main provincial cities, small branches of the *Dienststelle Westen* were set up, sometimes for a limited period of time, to organize the looting. In some cities these had to compete with the local *Kommandantur,* the *Sicherheitsdienst,* or even French collaborationist movements. The southern zone of France was largely spared, as Kurt von Behr could not get the permission from the *Wehrmacht* to intervene in this region, though he was most interested in the villas of the Côte d'Azur.[20]

The *Möbel Aktion* was continued till the end of the French occupation. Flats were emptied in Paris as late as August 1944. The global appraisal of the operation is difficult to assess with absolute certainty, as documents indicate divergent figures. The last report of the *Dienststelle Westen* gives the figure of 69,619 looted apartments and 26,984 wagons.[21] In Paris and its suburbs 38,000 flats were emptied. This appraisal apparently does not include the looting in the Netherlands. As late as 3 September 1944, seventeen carloads of furniture left Nancy for Offenbach,[22] near Frankfurt am Main, where the ERR had storage facilities.

The *Möbel Aktion* was implemented with very little German personnel, for example, only about 120 people in Paris. It used the local workforce, mostly movers who were drafted but paid. In France the local moving companies worked all through the period to loot Jewish flats.[23] But the cost of the operation, supported by the budget of the Ministry of Occupied Eastern Territories and by the selling of the furniture to the Gauleiters, was apparently too high. Workforce was also lacking in Paris. Jews were subjected to forced labor within the framework of the *Möbel Aktion*. Hence the three camps in Paris were created.

The Inmates: Special Categories

The Jews sent from Drancy to Austerlitz, Lévitan, and Bassano were classified in several "privileged" categories. These "privileged" ones were not to be deported immediately and were thus granted temporary protection from death. The categories were formalized again at the very beginning of July 1943, when the administration of Drancy was entirely taken over by the Germans.[24] Aloïs Brunner, former deputy of Adolf Eichmann and an SS captain *(Hauptsturmführer),* became head of the camp. Jews who were arrested and sent to Drancy were dispatched into the following groups:

A: Non-Jews arrested for having helped Jews, Jews in intermarriage, and half-Jews;
B: the majority of Jews, with no protection;
C: administrators of the camps, who headed the several directions and offices (among these were the Jews who worked at the *Kanzlei* or census office, which kept the main file of the camp and imposed these categories; all of the Jews in this category were French citizens);
C2: foreigners protected by their country: Swiss, Turks, Spaniards, Greeks, Romanians, Hungarians, and Yugoslavians;
C3: Jewish wives of Jewish war prisoners in Germany;

C4: Jews awaiting reunion with their families before being deported, who represented an incentive for the rest of their families to give themselves up to the Gestapo; and

C5: inmates waiting for documents proving that they were not Jewish according to the Nuremberg Laws.[25]

Jews of the categories A and C3 could be sent to other camps in France. On 9 July 1943 three hundred of them were sent to the labor camps of Aurigny Island, a British Channel Island occupied by the Reich.[26]

The majority of the inmates sent to the camps in Paris were Jews in intermarriage. There were also a handful of half-Jews and about one hundred Jewish wives of prisoners of war. Some Jews were also sent to one of the camps just because they had specific professional skills. This was the case for Erna Herzberg, a Jewess from Vienna whose husband was also Jewish, but who was a talented seamstress. She had worked before the war for a prestigious couture house called Paquin. Her knowledge of the latest Parisian fashion was in demand and she worked in two of the three camps to sew uniforms and dresses.[27]

The creation of the camps was permitted by Hitler's temporary decision not to deport Jews in intermarriage, a decision that was implemented only in some parts of the Nazi empire. Numerous discussions arose concerning this statute and the fate of these Jews. In the end they were not deported but rather held in the Reich and subjected to a long list of bans, as were their spouses. They were subjected to forced labor in ammunition factories in Berlin and the lowest categories of jobs in public works, but they survived the Holocaust.[28] Aryan wives of Jews arrested in the *Fabrik Aktion* of February and March 1943 demonstrated in an unorganized way in front of the Rosenstrasse building, where their husbands were kept.[29] In Drancy orders were sent not to deport the Jews in intermarriage. According to a census, there were fifteen thousand in Drancy in March 1943.[30] Half of them were transferred to Austerlitz, Lévitan, and Bassano.

Inmates of the camps in Paris came from all social backgrounds. They were most likely to be French citizens, as the more ancient Jewish presence in France meant a deeper integration into the mainstream population. They were equally divided between men and women. Most of them were isolated from their loved ones because of the Nazi categorization system. They were not interned with their spouses. Only some parents were arrested and transferred to Paris with their children, who were considered to be half-Jewish. Wives of prisoners of war who were arrested with their children remained in Drancy. No children were transferred to the three camps of Paris, but some teenagers were. One condition for the relocation to Austerlitz, Lévitan, and Bassano was a good physical condition, as these camps were labor camps. In Lévitan especially, some inmates were from the higher level of the bourgeoisie and often were Parisian. They constituted a group of persons linked by friendship and social affinities.[31] As part of an affluent milieu, some inmates were sons or daughters of the wealthiest French families. For example, Odette Vernes was the granddaughter of Emile Deutsch de la Meurthe, the founder of the oil refining industry in France.[32] Ironically, the *Dienststelle Westen* had moved into one of the family buildings, 54 avenue d'Iéna in Paris.

The last of the three camps to be opened, Bassano, was set up in a townhouse, a private mansion with luxurious ornamentation that belonged to the heirs of Louis Cahen d'Anvers, a wealthy Parisian banker of the nineteenth century. His granddaughter, Colette de Dampierre, was arrested and transferred to Lévitan.[33] A handful of these high-society Jewish women were married to French aristocrats. Kurt von Behr, the self-styled camp "baron" who was apparently fascinated by the nobility, approached some of them as they worked.

Inmates of the Parisian camps remained administratively connected to those of Drancy, as shown by their personal cards in the Drancy file,[34] and they could be transferred from one camp to another. Bassano was created as an annex of the two other camps, and prisoners could be sent back to Drancy at any moment. In the camps inmates had to work very hard six days a week, but their living conditions were not comparable to the ones in Drancy.

Living Conditions in the Camps

The archives of the Union générale des Israélites de France (UGIF),[35] the notorious Jewish Union in France, give precise insight into the living conditions in the three camps of Austerlitz, Lévitan, and Bassano. The UGIF was created by a French law in November 1941 after months of German pressure on the French government.[36] The Union was deemed to function as a *Judenrat* but did not act as such due to the specific conditions in France and the existence of a more or less autonomous French government in Vichy.[37] The role of the UGIF has been much criticized, though recent research shows that the picture is less severe than as had been previously described. The Gestapo in Paris contacted the Union for help in keeping some of the Drancy Jews in French territory, namely, in the Paris camps. The leaders accepted the proposal.

The Union was in charge of feeding and taking care of the inmates. Every day, the food was cooked in one of the buildings of the UGIF, in the Guy Patin street (it had been a students' hall before the war) and transported by trucks to each of the camps. Though inmates complained about the quality of the food, they did not really suffer from hunger except perhaps in the very last weeks of the camps' existence.[38] They were granted cigarettes, newspapers (mostly collaborationist ones), and small supplies necessary for daily life, such as material for shoe repair. The UGIF also supplied the yellow stars that the inmates had to wear inside the camps. All the testimonies show that the food was better there than at Drancy. Living conditions were harsh in buildings that were not constructed for housing human beings (except for Bassano, although the inmates here lived in an attic ill-suited to their needs). There were rats, little heating, and only one toilet, washbasin, and tap. But living conditions improved over time, and new facilities such as showers were built (and financed) by the UGIF.[39] The UGIF also took care of the laundry.

The main paradox was that the inmates were living among vast quantities of goods. Every day trucks loaded with furniture and boxes full of every kind of object arrived in the camps. Bassano was mostly dedicated to luxury objects as a kind of showroom of the best spoils of the lootings. The Jews held in Bassano could steal some objects, food, medicine, and books for their own use. They were rarely mistreated by the German guards, and their testimonies stand in sharp contrast with the situation in Drancy, where the arrival of Aloïs Brunner worsened the inmates' situation. Drancy inmates lived under the shadows of forced labor, collective punishment, humiliation, and constant threat.[40]

The inmates of the Paris camps could write one letter a week and receive as many as they wanted. They could also receive parcels from outside, and most of them had non-Jewish family members who were living a normal life in the family home. Wives of war prisoners had been the least fortunate inmates, as they were left isolated in the camps, until modest social services were created to grant them a small alimony to complement their food rations. In Austerlitz a kind of grocery store was even created within the camp where the Jews could buy, at the black market price, different kinds of produce. Some inmates gave these objects to the visitors that they were allowed to entertain on Sunday afternoons.

A photograph filed in the Center for Jewish Contemporary Documentation in Paris shows the outside of the Austerlitz camp. In the picture a group of people in winter coats is walking together. A wagon can be seen in the background, as well as a pile of boxes. The people in the picture are not Jews, as they do not wear the yellow star. They are Sunday afternoon visitors leaving the camp. This image does not show the cruelty of camp life and needs to be explained and interpreted within the framework of the Holocaust in France.

Labor in the Three Camps

Jews in the Parisian camps worked very hard. They sorted, cleaned, repaired, and packed the objects and furniture stolen in the *Möbel Aktion*. Jewish flats and houses were totally emptied of everything from school exercise books to sideboards. When the boxes arrived in the camp, their contents were divided into several categories: dishes, fabrics, books, clothes, and so on. Each object was cleaned, examined, and stripped of all markings that would identify its former owner. In Austerlitz a fire burned constantly to destroy the personal papers and family pictures.

The camps were organized like department stores, with counters. The most beautiful objects were displayed on shelves, so that German visitors from Berlin could choose what they liked. These visits by officials, who were often high-ranking officers in the *Wehrmacht,* have been described by the survivors. For example, Sepp Dietrich, commanding general of an SS Panzer division, visited Bassano at least once. A special service was organized in the camps to send the furniture and objects selected directly to furnish apartments and villas in Berlin. The camps were used as special stores (free of charge) for prominent Nazis. They were the authorized means granted to faithful followers and heads of military forces by the regime.[41]

Jews in the camps also fulfilled other duties. Some workshops were created in the camps to repair clothing, shoes, and fine leather goods. They also produced luxury clothes, bags, and shoes. A workshop was even opened to make the boxes that would be filled with looted objects and sent to the Reich. All the luxury and the fashion of Paris was on display and available to German visitors. It was one of the great paradoxes of this camp located in occupied Paris: an annex of the Nazi system of concentration camps was an *haute couture* fashion house.

Before leaving Paris, people in charge of the *Möbel Aktion* burned the archives in one of the storage places in Aubervilliers.[42] The accounting of the looting was lost, as were the statistics on the display of objects and furniture. Only the *Findbücher,* the lists of emptied flats, were sent to Germany, in numerous cars and trucks loaded with boxes that probably contained the remains of the looting. Archival traces of the *Möbel Aktion,* especially on the French side of the operation, can hardly be found. But the *Möbel Aktion* was also administrative, and several different administrations, as described, were involved. The UGIF and the movers kept traces of the existence of the camps, though the German archives are scattered.[43]

Our knowledge of the Paris camps is limited, and the historical writing is sometimes as incomplete as the memory of witnesses. One report of the *Dienststelle Westen* states that the camps were guarded by twenty SS and two hundred "Russian legionaries,"[44] which means soldiers of the Vlassov Army. It is the only written clue we have about the camp's surveillance. We do not know, for example, how the Jews were transferred from one camp to another or if French gendarmes guarded them.[45] Survivors of the camp described their guards as "Chinese" or "Asian," which added to the strangeness of the situation. Asians were not common in occupied France. These Vlassov Army guards probably came from Central Asia or the Caucasus. Not all of them seemed to have worked as camp guards. They were dispatched probably in all six storage sites of the *Möbel Aktion* in Paris to keep watch over the looting of Jewish flats. The three camps were not heavily guarded. The inmates were kept in one single building in each camp, and as they worked in this building, a handful of soldiers was sufficient to watch them. One effective means to deter escape attempts was to impose collective punishment. If a Jew escaped, ten inmates were immediately sent back to Drancy and from there deported to death camps. This happened at least twice, in November 1943 and February 1944.[46] Inmates could be sent back to Drancy even for such minor infractions as looking out a window.

The camps had Jewish leaders that were in charge of contact with the Germans and the UGIF and who assigned the work to be done. Georges Kohn, who had been the Jewish head of Drancy, was appointed to Austerlitz and then to Lévitan until his escape on 6 June 1944.[47] German heads of camps, members of the *Dienststelle Westen,* were also appointed. Their dispositions varied from one individual to another. A simple private like Bruno Kochan, who was suddenly promoted to oversee one of the camps, could become ferocious. Others were happy to be in Paris instead of on the eastern front and seemed to have patiently awaited the end of the war.

Austerlitz and Lévitan were kept secret, but they were not totally closed to the outside world. Trucks arrived at the camps every day with loads of looted properties. Railroad workers for the SNCF, the national French railway company active on the site of Austerlitz, could see what was happening even if they probably did not realize the scope of the operation and the details of its organization. At some points the Jews in Lévitan had contact with the movers. Inmate Colette de Dampierre in fact asked one of these men to bring her sweets to celebrate Christmas of 1943.[48]

Austerlitz, Lévitan, and Bassano were camps, but because inmates were allowed to have occasional visitors, to send and receive mail, and to take leaves to visit a doctor, they are unlike other camps we have studied from this time period. Thus they are more difficult to describe and understand.

The End of the Camps

Beginning on 21 June 1944, all of the inmates in the Parisian camps were sent to Drancy. Their documents were checked, which means that the camp administration once again verified that they could fall into one of the "protected" categories. Aloïs Brunner himself summoned many inmates to his office. He "interviewed" them, asking them to prove in short oral presentations that they were really only half-Jewish or that their spouses were Aryans. Brunner showed once again how the administrative tradition—here an oral interview similar to ones used to hire an employee—meshed with the horror of mass destruction.

The results, however, were not always logical. The majority of the inmates were sent back to the Parisian camps. Thirty-eight of the inmates stayed in Drancy. The purpose of this operation was to find as many Jews as possible suitable for deportation, as a convoy was being prepared. They were deported in Convoy 76 to Auschwitz, which left France on 30 June 1944. Georges Wellers, who had spent months in Austerlitz, was among them. He survived Auschwitz and wrote important and early testimonies on the death camps. The Jewish women whose spouses were prisoners of war were not sent back to Paris. They were all deported to Bergen-Belsen in one of two convoys. The first left Drancy on 21 July and the second on 24 July.

Life and work went on in the three camps in Paris while the *Möbel Aktion* continued late in the month of July 1944. On 31 July eleven inmates of the three camps were deported to Auschwitz. Austerlitz, Lévitan, and Bassano were all evacuated to Drancy on 12 August. The inmates were transported in buses of the RATP, the Parisian transport company. Some Jews escaped the bus.[49] In Drancy, Brunner was trying unsuccessfully to organize a last, huge convoy to the East as the Allied troops were approaching. Brunner left Paris on 17 August with fifty-one Jewish hostages.

Jews of the Parisian camps were liberated in Drancy on 18 August. They walked home, as the Resistance had organized a public transportation system strike. The majority of the inmates of Austerlitz, Lévitan, and Bassano survived the war in France. The majority of the women deported to Bergen-Belsen also returned to France, some even with their children. Only a handful of French Jews deported to Auschwitz returned home. The camps in Paris could be seen as providing limited shelter for the inmates in the heart of Paris due to the circumstances of the liberation.[50] Approximately 21 percent of all the inmates from these camps were deported to Auschwitz or to Bergen-Belsen. Jews were "almost" spared from death. The image created by the camps is again gray. No clear-cut, black and white assessment can be made. The shade of interpretation about the history of the camps in Paris can explain the gray zones of memory surrounding them.

Gray Zones of Memory

In thousands of books that have been published on the Vichy regime and the persecution of the Jews in France, no discussion of the three camps is to be found. Except for Georges Wellers and for the three testimonies published in *Le Monde juif*, it was impossible to find scholarly treatment of Austerlitz, Lévitan, and Bassano, even though French historians of the period knew that they existed. The camps remained neglected by scholars, considered to be only a footnote in history. It was sometimes stated that all of the inmates were saved. The images of high-society Jews being protected from deportation may also have prevented further investigation. The research we conducted and the book that was published from that research are the results of a specific need. It can in no way be understood as a competition between different categories of victims.[51] Only as recently as 1997 did survivors and their families create a small association called *Amicale* from the French for "to be set up." This small group of people struggled to gather testimonies and hired a historian and a sociologist to write the history the camps and of the *Möbel Aktion*, which was in part a commemoration and in part an effort to produce scientific knowledge. After the book was published, the *Amicale* decided to disband.

While beginning to research the camps, we were surprised by the numerous slips in the expression of memory. In interviews, witnesses often said "Auschwitz" when they meant "Austerlitz." Commemoration plaques existed on the sites of Austerlitz and Lévitan, but the first one described a mass deportation from the site that never occurred, and the second disappeared in the 1970s when the heirs of the Lévitan family sold the building. Thus there was no permanent commemoration of what happened in the camps.

What the survivors primarily demonstrated in the interviews was that they have been indirect witnesses of the catastrophe.[52] Their memories were certainly reconstructed once Auschwitz was known of. In the Parisian camps inmates did not know the details of the Nazis' campaign of mass murder, even if they could feel that the fate of deportees was terrible. It is striking to see that the survivors started to testify and to describe what happened in the camps just after their liberation. An article was published as early as September 1944 in a Resistance newspaper.[53] After April 1945, when the European press published numerous articles on the concentration and death camps with descriptions of the gas chambers and photos of corpses,[54] survivors of the three camps stopped talking, as if their testimonies were irrelevant in light of these new descriptions. When we wrote our book, all witnesses insisted that they wanted to testify about the fate of their fellow inmates who had been deported. They saw them leaving Paris for Drancy. They also wanted to express that by having sorted all of the objects and furniture stolen from Jewish flats, they were the last witnesses of the traces of disappeared lives.

This is not totally accurate, as 75 percent of the French Jews survived, while all of the Jews were despoiled of their property: furniture and objects transiting through the camps in Paris were not automatically the ones of dead Jews. Neither were inmates of Austerlitz or Lévitan the last to handle these objects, as they were sent to Germany. The true last witnesses were the Germans who received their share of the lootings. What the survivors now hear, what we also comprehend in the history of these camps, is an echo of what happened in Poland. These camps are connected with the storage places of Auschwitz, the "Kanada" and the "Mexiko" where the luggage of arriving Jews was sorted and repaired by special *Kommandos*. The fire that constantly burns on the site of Austerlitz evokes in our memory the fire of the crematoria.

Curiously enough, there are no traces of testimonies, texts, or diaries written in the camps themselves, except for the diary of Georges Kohn.[55] Some prisoners may have tried to leave written traces of what they saw, but any such records remained out of historians' reach. Some memoirs were written after the war, the majority a long time after liberation, and few were published.[56] Yvonne Redgis-Klug wrote a memoir just after her liberation from Auschwitz (she did not participate in the death march and was freed in the camp). Though there are at least two versions of the text, one in French and a slightly more complete one in English, the French version is supposed to have been written as early as March 1945 in Poland, which was before her repatriation to France.[57] After divorcing her husband and emigrating to California in 1947, Yvonne Redgis-Klug settled in Pasadena where she made a living giving lectures in local clubs. The leaflet advertising her talks explained that Ms. Redgis could speak about such topics as the French view of the United States, the American view of France, the French Resistance, the Auschwitz prison camp, and the latest fashion in Paris.[58]

Whether she mentioned the existence of the Paris camps during her talks is not known.

Though the Jews in the Paris camps did not seem to keep written records of their experiences, they still tried to keep a trace of their internment in Austerlitz, Lévitan, and Bassano. They managed to smuggle out some objects with visitors, such as a copy of a book by Shakespeare. Marc Garguir, a prisoner in Austerlitz, took the time to pack a china cup with a saucer and a silver fork before being sent back to Drancy. Once liberated in Drancy, he walked back to his home in Enghein, a suburb north of Paris, with the china and the silverware in his suitcase. Denise Bernard, his daughter, inherited them and still keeps them in her living room.[59]

These objects are material traces of the vanished existence and memories of the camp. Only a subtext, an explanation, can tell what they are, what they represent. In many cases these objects saved from the camps have been lost or misplaced, but their owners attest to their existence. They are material proof of a slippery remembrance, of a story that did not find a stable framework. The very premise of my book may have only been an attempt to offer this memory a framework. The paradox of this difficult memory is the existence of numerous pictures taken in the camps by the German propaganda office that very precisely show the life and work of the inmates. Piles of objects can also to be seen in this unpublished material. From these documentary traces, the memory of the camps becomes a precise, visual representation, as with other concentration camps such as Terezin.

The Gray Zones of Memory . . . with Photographs

Pictures of the *Möbel Aktion* were taken by German photographers. A minimum of 107 pictures exist, divided between several archives in Germany, France, and the United States. They come from the same sources, the same sets of images. We do not know what the *Dienststelle Westen* intended to do with these pictures. It was not uncommon in the Third Reich for pictures taken for propaganda purposes to go unused for fear of producing an undesired effect on the public. For example, films and pictures taken in the Warsaw ghetto were never used by the German propaganda machine. This is probably also what happened with the photographs taken in the Parisian camps. What do they show us? They document the implementation of the *Möbel Aktion,* following objects from Jewish flats, to French trucks, and finally to their arrival in the camps (all three camps are documented). The process of sorting, cleaning, and packing is shown in detail. The inmates smile at the camera. A visit by high-ranking German officials can be seen with Kurt von Behr leading the walk through the camps. The pictures precisely show what the witnesses described in their oral or written testimonies.

But we also know that the photographs are deceptive. They do not show the inmates' fear or the instability of their lives in the camps. Neither do they show the deportation of the inmates or their fate. We know, thanks

In this photo taken by German authorities at a *M-Aktion* (Möbel-Aktion) depot in Paris, a German officer inspects a crate packed for transport to Germany while Jewish inmates stand by.

to testimonies, that the Jews did not work to make clothes for the German children who were victims of Allied bombing, but that they were exclusively sewing uniforms and party dresses for officers in charge of the *Möbel Aktion*. The pictures are precious as historical documents, but they show only "scraps of reality."[60] For us, they echo the family pictures burned in the camps in Paris, when all traces of individual Jewish lives were to be destroyed, the looted objects turned into anonymous properties.

Because witnesses and writers could not describe the World War II air raids that destroyed much of Germany, it was necessary to add pictures. This is precisely what the German writer W. G. Sebald did in his book on the literature of destruction.[61] Sebald also described one of the Paris camps in his last novel, offering one of the few treatments of the subject. He even gave the name of the camp, Austerlitz, to his book.[62] He inserted photographs, not to prove the reality of his story, but to show that historical reality, and even the imagination of writers, always has gray zones. Sebald knew that a photograph itself can show only a part of what has to be described. At the end of the twentieth century and the beginning of the twenty-first, it is impossible to consider any description of the past, any remembrance, without associating it with a photograph. The photographs of

In this photo taken by authorities at a *M-Aktion* (Möbel-Aktion) depot in Paris, Jewish women inmates at Lévitan mend clothes, seized from Jews in France, before the goods are shipped to the Reich.

World War II and the Holocaust are often in black and white but rarely without literal and metaphorical shades of gray.

Conclusion

Much can be learned from the history of the three small Parisian annexes of Drancy. The main concern of our research was the question of memory. Why did these camps remain in the shadow of memory, even as we are obsessed with memorializing the Holocaust and as Drancy is now identified in France as "a site of memory" of twentieth-century French history? The question is not easy to answer. Documents and testimonies were available. French descriptions of daily life in the camps can be read in the open archives of the UGIF at the Center for Jewish Contemporary Documentation, located not very far from the site of Lévitan.

What makes a topic the subject of historical research? In this case, it was clearly a social demand of a small group of survivors and family members. Confronting the camp testimonies has been both fascinating and challenging. First of all, we often had the impression that we were collecting words spoken for the first time sixty years after the events they described. In many cases these words were being told for the first time to professionals, in order to be recorded, compared to other traces of memory, examined, and eventually criticized. Telling these stories, which were so different from the mainstream camp narratives that have found strong representation in France since the late 1970s, was not easy for the former inmates. For those Jews who have survived Auschwitz, harsh interment in Poland was often easier to describe than the milder of days in Austerlitz, Lévitan, or Bassano, as if the collective memory of the Parisian camps was not solid enough to help support the testimonies. The only testimony about the Parisian camps that we could get from a Jewish woman who also survived Bergen-Belsen was a written one that had been made in front of a tribunal. All the women refused to be interviewed, as if they could not find space in the lives they have rebuilt after the war for the memory of these atypical camps.

Many witnesses and persons involved in the politics of memory explained that the memory of the looted objects was not important: only the victims matter. But is it not much easier for a person living at the beginning of the twenty-first century in a peaceful Europe to identify with an inmate of the Parisian camps than with a survivor of Auschwitz? The banal scenes that the photographs depict could have been taken anywhere. And these piles of objects, whose owners have been killed, bring us in some way closer to annihilation than many of the scenes of Drancy do. The gray pictures showing toys or kitchen tools can prove to be unbearable.

Notes

1. This article is based on the extensive research conducted on the Parisian camp annexes of Drancy, written with Sarah Gensburger. See Jean-Marc Dreyfus and Sarah Gensburger, *Des camps dans Paris: Austerlitz, Lévitan, Bassano, juillet 1943–août 1944* (Paris: Fayard, 2003).
2. In Eastern Europe, some labor camps bore similarities to the camps of Paris, although their organization was never totally identical. In special warehouses and in ghettos after liquidation, Jews worked to clean, sort, and repair objects and furniture. Living conditions in the Paris camps were very different from those in Eastern European labor camps.
3. Jews in France numbered between 300,000 and 330,000 in 1940.
4. On French public opinion in Vichy France, see the seminal work of Pierre Laborie, *L'opinion française sous Vichy* (Paris: Le Seuil, 1992).
5. Pascal Froment, *René Bousquet* (Paris: Stock, 1994), 332.
6. Dreyfus and Gensburger, *Des camps dans Paris*, 190–91. We interviewed twenty survivors or witnesses of the Parisian camps, including family members who had visited their parents in Austerlitz or Lévitan. The testimonies of Jacqueline Jacob-Delmas, Mira Lessovoi, and Michèle Bonnet were published, with a foreword by Lucien Steinberg, in *Le Monde juif*, 146, January-March 1993.
7. Most of the Jewish deportation convoys went to Sobibor and Auschwitz. See the convoy list in Serge Klarsfeld, *Le calendrier de la persécution des Juifs de France 1940–1944* (Paris: The Beate Klarsfeld Foundation, 1993), 1122–24.
8. Gerard Aalders, *Geraubt! Die Enteignung jüdischen Besitzes im Zweiten Weltkrieg* (Cologne: Dittrich Verlag, 2000), 221.
9. For an overview of the *Möbel Aktion*, see Annette Wieviorka and Floriane Azoulay, *Le Pillage des appartements et son indemnisation* (Paris: Mission d'étude pour la spoliation des Juifs de France, La Documentation française, 2000); Anja Heuss, *Kunst- und Kulturgutraub: Eine vergleichende Studie zur Besatzungspolitik der Nationalsozialisten in*

Frankreich und der Sowjetunion (Heidelberg: Universitätsverlag, C. Winter, 2000), 125–30; United Restitution Organization (URO), M. *Aktion, Frankreich, Belgien, Holland and Luxemburg, 1940–1944*. This last reference is a collection of documents on the operation, constituted for the implementation of the law of the German Federal Republic of 1957 *(Bundesrückerstattungsgesetzt)*.

10. The looting of musical instruments by the ERR was thoroughly studied in Willem de Vries, *Sonderstab Musik: Music Confiscations by the Einsatzstab Reichsleiter Rosenberg under the Nazi Occupation of Western Europe* (Amsterdam: Amsterdam University Press, 1996).
11. Dreyfus and Gensburger, *Des camps dans Paris*, 35–36.
12. Andreas Molau, *Alfred Rosenberg: Der Ideologe des Nationalsozialismus. Eine politische Biographie* (Koblenz: Verlag Siegfried Bublies, 1993), 126–35.
13. Dreyfus and Gensburger, *Des camps dans Paris*, 37.
14. Centre de Documentation Juive Contemporaine, Paris, LXIII-17, Vereinbarung des Reichsministerium für die besetzten Ostgebiete, 17 April 1942.
15. See the contribution by Wendy Lower in this volume.
16. On the air raids, see Jörg Friedrich, *Der Brand: Deutschland in Bombenkrieg 1940–1945* (Berlin: Propyläen, 2002), and W. G. Sebald, *Luftkrieg und Literatur* (Munich: Carl Hanser Verlag, 1999).
17. For examples of the way the furniture was distributed, see Ralf Blank, "Ersatzbeschaffung durch 'Beutemachen': Die 'M-Aktionen'—ein Beispiel nationalsozialistischer Ausplünderungspolitik," in Alfons Kenkmann and Bernd-A. Rusinek, eds., *Verfolgung und Verwaltung: Die wirtschaftliche Ausplünderung der Juden und die westfälischen Finanzbehörden* (Münster: Oberfinanzdirektion Münster, 1999), 87–101.
18. Françoise Denoyelle, *La photographie d'actualité et de propagande sous le régime de Vichy* (Paris: CNRS Éditions, 2003), 187.
19. Frank Bajohr, *"Arisierung" in Hamburg: Die Verdrängung jüdischer Unternehmer 1933–1945* (Hamburg: Christians, 1998), 234–35.
20. Centre de Documentation Juive Contemporaine, Paris, CCXXXII-32, Bericht von Schwarze, Gemeinschaftsführer, 16 June 1994.
21. Centre de Documentation Juive Contemporaine, Paris, XIII-47, activity report dated 31 July 1944.
22. Bundesarchiv, NS 30, 12, Abschluss-Bericht, 5.
23. Dreyfus and Gensburger, *Des camps dans Paris*, 50–55.
24. Klarsfeld, *Le calendrier*, 837.
25. Ibid., 835.
26. On Aurigny Island and the other occupied Channel Islands, see Asa Briggs, *The Channel Islands: Occupation and Liberation* (London: Imperial War Museum, 1995), 68.
27. Interview with Erna Herzberg, Paris, 20 June 2002.
28. H. G. Adler, *Der verwaltete Mensch: Studien zur Deportation der Juden aus Deutschland* (Tübingen: Mohr, 1974), 154–65.
29. See Nathan Stoltzfus, *Resistance of the Heart: Intermarriage and the Rosenstrasse Protest in Nazi Germany* (New York: W. W. Norton, 1996); Wolf Gruner, "Die Fabrik-Aktion und die Ereignisse in der Berliner Rosenstrasse: Fakten und Fiktionen um den 27 Februar 1943. 60 Jahre danach," *Jahrbuch für Antisemitismusforschung* 11 (2002), 137–77; Wolf Gruner, *Der geschlossene Arbeitseinsatz deutscher Juden: zur Zwangsarbeit als Element der Verfolgung, 1938–1943* (Berlin: Metropol, 1997), 310–23. Historians do not agree on the real meaning of the demonstration. It apparently went through a reconstruction of memory. Gruner showed that the Gestapo did not intend to deport the intermarried Jews but meant to use them to replace Jews of the administrative body of the community who were deported to Auschwitz.
30. Klarsfeld, *Le calendrier*, 771.
31. Interview with Claude Haymans, daughter of Robert Fabius, an inmate in Lévitan, London, 14 December 2002.
32. The family company, Les pétroles Jupiter, had been sold to Shell at the beginning of the 1930s.

33. Memoirs of Colette de Dampierre, born Cahen d'Anvers, in English, private archives of Christian de Montbrison, Paris.
34. Microfilms of the file are kept at the National Archives in Paris: "Fichier de Drancy et cahier de transfert," F9/5675 to 5749; F9/5781 to 5788.
35. These archives are kept at the Yivo in New York. Microfilms are available at the Centre de Documentation Juive Contemporaine in Paris.
36. *Journal official de l'Etat français* (Official bulletin of the French State), 12 December 1941.
37. On the creation of the UGIF, see Michael R. Marrus and Robert O. Paxton, *Vichy et les Juifs*, trans. Marguerite Delmotte (Paris: Le Livre de Poche, 1981), 157–60; Claudia Steur, *Theodor Dannecker: Ein Fünktionär der "Endlösung"* (Tübingen: Schriften der Bibliotek für Zeitgeschichte, 1997), 64. See also Richard I. Cohen, *The Burden of Conscience* (Bloomington: Indiana University Press, 1987); Maurice Rajfus, *Des Juifs dans la collaboration: l'Union générale des Israélites de France* (Paris: EDI, 1980). A more recent book gives the history of the UGIF from the point of view of its leaders: Michel Laffitte, *Un engrenage fatal: l'UGIF face aux réalités de la Shoah, 1941–1944* (Paris: Liana Levi, 2003).
38. Dreyfus and Gensburger, *Des camps dans Paris*, 206–15.
39. Centre de Documentation Juive Contemporaine, UGIF 18-1194, 1195, and 1198.
40. See, for example, the testimony of Yvonne Redgis-Klug, Centre de Documentation Juive Contemporaine, "Le 8616 revint. Souvenirs d'une rescapée du camp d'extermination d'Auschwitz." Yvonne Klug was born in France, but her father was American. She was arrested on the Côte d'Azur, transferred to Drancy and from there to Lévitan, as her husband was not Jewish. She was later deported to Auschwitz but survived. She moved to California in 1947.
41. Frank Bajohr, *Parvenüs und Profiteure: Korruption in der NS-Zeit* (Frankfurt am Main: S. Fischer, 2001).
42. Bundesarchiv, Berlin, ER, NS 30/28.
43. The archives of the SNCF, the French national railway company, long remained closed to researchers. Although they are officially opened, the documents are not properly catalogued and no inventory is available.
44. Centre de Documentation Juive Contemporaine, Paris, CDXXXVI-10.
45. Archives of the gendarmerie are not sufficiently detailed to provide this information.
46. Dreyfus and Gensburger, *Des camps dans Paris*, 194–95.
47. Kohn left a diary, which has been published in part. See Georges Kohn, *Journal de Compiègne et de Drancy*, ed. Serge Klarsfeld (Paris: Editions de l'Association Les Fils et Filles des Déportés Juifs de France, 1990).
48. Memoirs of Colette de Dampierre.
49. Bonnet testimony.
50. Working on the different files created by the German and the French administrations is not always easy, as they do not match. Few are completed, and errors appear in the cards. Another problem is the repeated surnames—Levy or Blum, for instance—which often lack first names. In addition, the spelling of names is not always consistent from one file to another. See Dreyfus and Gensburger, *Des camps dans Paris*, 265–71.
51. In this matter, we opposed the idea of a competition among victims. See also Jean-Michel Chaumont, *La concurrence des victimes: génocide, identité, reconnaissance* (Paris: La Découverte, 1997).
52. For a comparable case, see the testimony of Madeleine Steinberg on the Vittel camp: Madeleine Steinberg, "Paris, Besançon, Vittel 1941–1944," in *Le Monde juif*, Revue d'histoire de la Shoah, Paris, Centre de Documentation Juive Contemporaine, January–June 2004, No. 180, 315–60. Inmates of Vittel were British and American citizens. In 1944, a convoy of Jewish survivors of the Warsaw ghetto reached Vittel as part of a tentative exchange of prisoners.
53. Georges Geissmann, in *L'Homme libre*, 15 September 1944.
54. Annette Wieviorka, *Déportation et genocide: Entre la mémoire et l'oubli* (Paris: Plon, 1992), 107.

55. But the part of his diary from the time he spent in Austerlitz and Lévitan was not published.
56. Georges Wellers wrote a testimony on Drancy, Austerlitz, and Auschwitz, which was published in 1946. See Georges Wellers, *De Drancy à Auschwitz* (Paris: Editions du Centre, 1946).
57. Redgis-Klug testimony.
58. Private archives of Eddy Francell, nephew of Yvonne Redgis, Atlanta, Georgia.
59. Interview with Denise Bernard, Paris, 29 March 2002.
60. Here we Georges Didi-Hubermann's stimulating reflection in his book on the pictures of the Holocaust. See Georges Didi-Hubermann, *Images malgré tout* (Paris: Les Editions de Minuit, 2003), 54.
61. See Sebald, *Luftkrieg und Literatur.*
62. W. G. Sebald, *Austerlitz* (Arles: Actes Sud, 2002).

– Chapter 16 –

ALTERNATE HOLOCAUSTS AND THE MISTRUST OF MEMORY

Gavriel D. Rosenfeld

We cut off the [Henry Hudson] Drive onto the Goethe Parkway. . . . I still didn't know why we were heading out to Westchester, and to tell the truth I didn't care much. . . .
    "That's Croton-on-Hudson up ahead," Kohler said. "It's not far now."
    You could read the sign from 500 yards, a huge billboard draped with swastika bunting and crested by an Imperial Eagle with the globe clutched in its talons: "Welcome to Croton-on-Hudson. Home of the Final Solution. Visit the Frederick Barbarossa Death Camp, 1 mile ahead, First Right. Admission 35 marks, Children Free. No Dogs Allowed. Picnic areas adjacent. . . ."
    We drove along the road at fifteen or twenty miles an hour, . . . and I looked out at the Barbarossa Camp without any great interest. There wasn't really much to see, just a lot of old barracks and endless coils of rusty barbed wire plus a string of road signs from the local Elks and Rotarians greeting visitors: "Croton-on-Hudson, where Four Million Enemies of the Reich perished." I remember reading that Croton was second only to Auschwitz in its kill ratio, so I guess they had reason for pride, but I didn't care for the commercialization. One big sign was decorated with a blown-up color photograph of an emaciated Jew, . . . [his] drowned eyes luminous with hunger. It was captioned in huge red letters, "If Bread and Water Isn't Enough For You, Visit Schaumberger's Steak House, Rt. 1, 250 yards from the Wesley Overpass."[1]

The image of a Nazi extermination camp turned into a theme park as recounted by New York City detective Bill Halder in Eric Norden's 1973 thriller, *The Ultimate Solution,* provides a particularly chilling answer to a question that has been asked with increasing frequency in recent years: What would have happened had the Nazis won World War II? To ask this counterfactual question is to delve into a new field of historical inquiry that

Notes for this section begin on page 248.

has come to be known as "alternate history."[2] In the last several decades, an increasing number of such counterfactual—or as they are increasingly being called, "allohistorical"—representations of Nazism have appeared in England, the United States, and Germany in the form of highbrow and lowbrow novels, popular films, plays, television broadcasts, and historical essays.[3] In such works as Robert Harris's 1992 novel, *Fatherland,* Armin Mueller-Stahl's 1996 film, *Conversation with the Beast,* and Henry Turner's 1996 article, "Hitler's Impact on History," the practitioners of alternate history have explored a wide range of questions: What if the Nazis had won World War II? What if Hitler had survived his suicide attempt and escaped into the jungles of South America? What if Hitler had been killed as an art student in Vienna in 1913?[4]

Of the more than one hundred narratives that have attempted to answer such questions, very few, significantly enough, have focused on the Holocaust. Only about 5 percent of the allohistorical novels, films, plays, television shows, and comic books on the Third Reich have focused on the Nazis' extermination of the Jews. This near absence is especially striking, as it runs counter to the recent proliferation of historical, literary, and cinematic attention to the Holocaust in academic scholarship and popular culture. Still, over the course of the last two decades, a scattered number of works have addressed a variety of counterfactual questions pertaining to the Holocaust: What if the "Final Solution" of the Jewish question had been completed? What if the Germans had been punished more severely for having perpetrated it? What if the Holocaust could be undone? How would history have been different?

In looking at how allohistorical depictions of the Holocaust have posed these questions, several broad trends emerge. First, nearly all the narratives have focused upon the perpetrators rather than the victims. Second, these accounts have largely revolved around themes of repentance and remembrance. Thus, there have been portrayals of the perpetrators or their descendants attempting to atone for the Holocaust long after its completion. There have also been accounts of the perpetrators being forcibly compelled to atone for the Holocaust. And there have been depictions of rueful perpetrators attempting to undo the Nazi genocide altogether. Despite their diverse themes, however, these narratives have been linked by a pessimistic belief in the impossibility of ever atoning for the crimes of the Holocaust. In the process, these narratives have exhibited a skeptical stance toward the utility of remembrance—one that stands in stark contrast to the hallowed mantra long associated with the study of the Nazi genocide: "Never forget." For this reason postwar allohistorical depictions of the Holocaust seem to suggest the increasing normalization of the Nazi past in Western memory.[5]

The most frequently portrayed allohistorical scenario pertaining to the Holocaust has been the Nazis' successful completion of the Final Solution. The idea of a world without Jews has most often been presented in alternate histories depicting the Nazis winning World War II, such as Eric Norden's *The Ultimate Solution,* Philip K. Dick's *The Man in the High Castle* (1961), Robert Harris's *Fatherland* (1992), and William Overgard's *The Divide* (1980).[6] In all of these works, the Nazis have exterminated all the world's Jews and have moved on to killing blacks, Native Americans, and other unwanted groups. Few of these novels have placed the Holocaust's completion at the center of their narratives, preferring to relegate it to the background. Still, such references to the Final Solution's completion have fulfilled an important moral function by underscoring the barbarism of Nazism and clearly reinforcing the prevailing view that a Nazi-ruled world would have been an utterly horrific place.

Interestingly enough, however, recent works suggest a waning of this sense of horror. This trend was clearly visible in the most prominent recent depiction of a world without Jews, best-selling American writer Daniel Quinn's 2001 novel, *After Dachau*.[7] Set in America two thousand years in the future, *After Dachau* takes place in a world in which the Nazis have exterminated all Jews and other "mongrelized races" in the wake of their decisive victory at the "Battle of Dachau" in the "Great War." This premise was hardly new, but *After Dachau* diverged from earlier narratives by refraining from depicting a Nazi-ruled world as a dystopia and instead projecting an "Aryan paradise." *After Dachau* does this by retelling the past through the eyes of the novel's protagonist, a wealthy American slacker by the name of Jason Tull, who repeatedly hails his nation's virtues to the novel's other protagonist, Mallory, a woman who has been reincarnated into Jason's world from her own twentieth-century past: "We live in a world that is . . . blessedly stable," Jason says, "as it *deserves* to be for the race that is the pinnacle of cosmic development."[8] As the novel unfolds, however, Mallory (who, it turns out, was herself killed by the Nazis) gradually brings Jason to a moral awakening about his nation's criminal past, and he resolves to repent by mounting a campaign to expose the truth about it. Ultimately, however, Jason's crusade for repentance and remembrance meets with total indifference from the society at large. The moral truth about the past thus remains shrouded in historical myth, and the crimes of the past remain ignored and unatoned for.

In arriving at this bleak conclusion, *After Dachau* offers a strikingly normalized portrait of the Holocaust's completion. It is significant that Quinn abandoned the moralistic depiction of a Nazi-ruled world as a horrific place populated by sadistic perpetrators, and instead portrayed it as a contented place populated by the long-dead perpetrators' relatively "normal" (if uninformed) descendants. In effect, Quinn provided literary validation of Saul Friedländer's theoretical contention that, had the Nazis won World War II and completed the Final Solution, they would have emplotted the Holocaust in comic terms as a happy ending.[9] Quinn did this to make a larger point—namely, that history and memory are inherently subjective and thus untrustworthy. As Jason asserts repeatedly in the novel, "History is just an agreed-upon fiction."[10] In submitting this pessimistic, postmodern vision, Quinn most likely hoped to critique the blind spots of contemporary American memory. In a crucial passage of the novel, Jason notes:

Mallory seemed to think that I should live in sackcloth and ashes because my ancestors exterminated the original inhabitants of Asia and Africa to make room for people like me. I made a mental note to ask her if [her friends] . . . lived in sackcloth and ashes because [their] . . . ancestors exterminated the original inhabitants of North America to make room for people like . . . [them].

It isn't just *our* history that is an agreed-upon fiction.[11]

Quinn's comparison of the Nazis' whitewashed view of the past with that of contemporary America is overstated. Yet, it is nonetheless significant. For by instrumentally using the Holocaust to criticize the shortcomings of American memory, and by questioning the integrity of remembrance itself, *After Dachau* exhibits a new level of historical relativism that directly challenged the traditional admonition of "Never forget."

The skepticism toward memory seen in *After Dachau* is also visible in two German-language works dealing with another scenario related to the Holocaust: the Allies' decision to punish the Germans for the Final Solution by imposing the Morgenthau Plan upon the defeated nation. German writer Thomas Ziegler's 1984 novel, *Die Stimmen der Nacht* (Voices of the Night), and Austrian writer Christoph Ransmayr's 1996 novel, *Morbus Kitahara* (translated as *The Dog King*), both focus upon this controversial theme.[12] Both novels depict the allohistorical consequences of the Morgenthau Plan in strongly negative terms. In Ziegler's tale, the Allies' decision to leave Germany in ruins and deport the majority of the German people to Latin America as punishment for their crimes backfires entirely. Instead of inspiring the Germans to repent, the forcible imposition of a punitive peace upon them results in a maniacal German desire for vengeance. Thus as one of the novel's central characters, an American military official named Mr. Splitz, notes, the Morgenthau Plan had only

> . . . strengthened the Germans in their insanity. Hitler now is more popular than before the war. The Germans no longer build tanks and airplanes, but rather . . . tend to their meadows. . . . [T]hey are still Nazis, worse than ever before. Morgenthau achieved the precise opposite of what he wanted. Now the Nazis [in Latin America] are sitting at our front door. . . . And they have not given up their plans.
> They hate us Americans . . . from the depths of their souls, because of Morgenthau and what he did to the Reich, and they are preparing for . . . a holy war against everything Jewish and American and Bolshevist, against the whole world, as once before, except this time they have the bomb . . . and the only thing that's missing is a single spark and the world will explode.[13]

By the end of the novel, the outbreak of nuclear war between the Latin American Nazis (led by Martin Bormann) and the Allies clearly underscores the perils of remembrance and the virtues of amnesia.

Similarly, in Ransmayr's more nuanced novel the Allied imposition of forcible remembrance upon the Germans backfires by making them a self-pitying lot, resentful of their occupiers and utterly incapable of sympathizing with the Nazis' true victims. This reaction is best visible in the character of Bering, a German born at the war's end, who is too young to be guilty of the regime's crimes. Yet after years of being forced to attend ritualized ceremonies of repentance decreed by the American Supreme Court justice Lyndon Porter Stellamour (a thinly veiled Henry Morgenthau), he becomes openly hostile toward remembering the past. This sense of apathy turns into open hostility near the end of the novel, when Bering is displaced from his home in the punitively treated town of Moor and realizes that the surrounding areas of Austria have been spared the Morgenthau Plan and have thrived. When Bering arrives in the lowland town of Brand, for example, he encounters

> cars, tracks, runways! High-tension lines, department stores! Garbage cans full of delicacies. . . . Was that the penitence, the punishment that the great Bringer of Peace had prescribed for the lowlands? . . . Was it? Shit, goddamn bullshit.
>
> Had there been no barracks in the lowlands? No lime pits full of corpses? Brand . . . and Greater Vienna and all those other so-called Reconstruction Zones . . . hadn't they also sent soldiers into war against Stellamour and his allies? . . .
>
> So, then, it was probably only fair that Moor and the lake country were still doing penance now, two and a half decades after the war, . . . while the lowlands got a fireworks show and had a row of limousines standing in every alley. Only fair, right?
>
> Some justice—the lowlands sparkled . . . like a huge amusement park, while . . . under the cliffs of the Blind Shore, . . . banners were unrolled: *Never forget. Thou shalt not kill.* . . . The great penitential spectacle of Stellamour . . . was surely staged only where there wasn't much else to stage. . . .
>
> *Never forget.*
> Forget it all.

Like *Die Stimmen der Nacht,* the novel *Morbus Kitahara* ends on a bleak note. After Bering attempts to flee Germany and its burdensome memories for the new opportunities in Brazil, he ends up murdering his girlfriend and ultimately being killed in an accidental fall off of a mountain cliff.

Ultimately, both *Die Stimmen der Nacht* and *Morbus Kitahara* depict the difficulty of repentance after the Holocaust. Yet they do so in far different fashion from Daniel Quinn's *After Dachau.* Whereas Quinn's novel depicted the inability to repent as the fault of the perpetrators themselves, in *Die Stimmen der Nacht* and *Morbus Kitahara* it is less the fault of the perpetrators than their Allied conquerors. This shift in responsibility reflects a common agenda behind the two novels. By portraying Germany's alternate history under the Morgenthau Plan as turning out worse than real history, Ziegler's and Ransmayr's critiques of the allohistorical Allied policy of compulsory remembrance serve to justify the real historical reconstruction of Germany after 1945. It is well known that the early years of postwar Germany were characterized by a widespread evasion of the Nazi past. Ransmayr's and Ziegler's works, however, endorsed this policy of amnesia by implying that things could have been much worse had the past actually been confronted. Written by novelists who have expressed skepticism about the virtues of remembrance in contemporary German culture, moreover, both novels reflect a conservative exhaustion with memory and a desire to finally arrive at a state of normalcy.[14]

If the tales of Ziegler and Ransmayr portray the stubborn unwillingness of fictional Germans to repent for the Holocaust, three other recent works, Thomas Ziegler's 1991 novella, *Eine Kleinigkeit für uns Reinkarnauten,* British writer Martin Amis's 1991 novel, *Time's Arrow,* and British actor and writer Stephen Fry's 1996 novel, *Making History,* depict an obsessive German yearning to repent by undoing the Holocaust altogether.[15] Set in the middle of the twenty-first century, Ziegler's novella focuses on the visit of a wealthy but dying German industrialist, Karl von Hutten, to the Los Angeles–based Institute for Reincarnation Science in order to be sent back in time to the village of Braunau-am-Inn on 20 April 1889 in order to be reincarnated as a newborn infant by the name of Adolf Hitler. Hutten hopes that, through a "post-hypnotic decree," he can transform Hitler into a more "rational" antisemite who will decide at the Wannsee Conference to use the Jews "merely" for forced labor instead of killing them.[16] Driving Hutten, the most powerful man in "reunified Germany," is the desire to undo the event that "has sullied Germany's name in the whole world for centuries" and "branded [it with] the mark of Cain."[17] In short, the plan is driven by the desire to normalize German history and German identity. In the end, however, this Faustian plan comes to naught as a conspiratorial cell of Palestinian Islamic fundamentalists, fearing that the unmaking of the Holocaust will pave the way for a second Holocaust of the Palestinian nation, kills Hutten before he can be reincarnated as Hitler.

With this conclusion, *Eine Kleinigkeit für uns Reinkarnauten* illustrates the ongoing tension between the Germans' desire both to confront the Holocaust and to be done with it finally. While the story's basic premise expresses the fantasy of many Germans for normalcy, its ending seems to offer a cautionary message that the attempt to flee from the responsibilities of memory can only lead to disaster. On the face of it, then, Ziegler's novel seems to offer an eloquent plea to resist normalization. But the novel's ultimate message was more ambiguous. Since the text clearly shows that it is the Germans' constant brooding over the past that leads to the yearning for absolution and normalcy in the first place, Ziegler ultimately blames memory itself for the novella's disastrous conclusion and thus seems to recommend a healthy dose of amnesia to cure the problem at its source.

While *Eine Kleinigkeit für uns Reinkarnauten* stops short of undoing the Holocaust, Martin Amis's *Time's Arrow* pursues this scenario to its logical conclusion. Hardly a traditional work of alternate history, *Time's Arrow* does not so much alter the historical record as completely reverse it. Amis's novel is distinguished by its backwards narrative, beginning with the end and ending with the beginning of the life of its protagonist, Tod T. Friendly, a man who (the reader learns midway through the novel) had served as a German medical doctor under Josef Mengele at Auschwitz during World War II. As the narrative careens backward in time, *Time's Arrow* embarks upon the bizarre, if logically consistent, description of the Holocaust's unmaking.

Thus, by the end of the novel, Tod witnesses how all the Holocaust's victims have come "back from Auschwitz-Birkenau-Monowitz, from Ravensbruck . . . from Buchenwald and Belsen and Majdanek," to their places of origin.[18] In short, from the narrative perspective of Tod's soul—the novel's narrator who experiences the backward flow of time in a forward-looking sense—the passage of time from the 1940s to the 1930s logically *improves* the course of history.

On the face of it, *Time's Arrow* partook of the fantasy of undoing the Holocaust and thus dovetailed with the recent trend of narrating the event through the prism of redemptive endings à la Steven Spielberg's film *Schindler's List* or Roberto Benigni's *Life Is Beautiful*. Yet the novel's conclusion is ultimately much more ambiguous—especially with respect to what was perhaps its central theme: the impossibility of atonement after the Holocaust. Amis never explains *why* Tod's soul separates from his body at his death and travels backward in time. But in all likelihood, Tod (who is increasingly plagued by guilt near the end of his life) most likely wills his life into reverse to make amends for the past. In the end, though, Amis casts doubt upon the possibility of atonement. For in the novel's last line, as Tod is unborn (and reenters his mother's womb), his soul witnesses with horror an arrow flying forward, point first. Here, Amis seems to suggest that history is now resuming its regular—and tragic—course all over again. The Holocaust, in short, will occur as once before. Tod's efforts to atone fail, thus exposing memory as a curse rather than a blessing.

Finally, this same pessimistic conclusion was endorsed by Stephen Fry's novel *Making History*. In this work, two academics at Cambridge—a nebbish history graduate student, Michael Young, and a German scientist, Leo Zuckermann—send a birth control pill back in time to render Alois Hitler impotent and prevent the birth of her son, Adolf. While the goal of the two men is to improve the course of history, Leo's specific motive resembles that of Karl von Hutten and Tod T. Friendly, insofar as he embodies the role of the German perpetrator desperate to atone for his nation's historical crimes (in the novel, Leo is the guilt-ridden son of an SS doctor at Auschwitz). In the end, moreover, Leo fails just as miserably as Hutten and Friendly. As the novel shows, even without Hitler the German people end up embracing a different dictator who uses his superior rationality to succeed where the irrational Führer failed, developing the atomic bomb and using it to conquer all of Europe and to complete the Final Solution. In short, by portraying remembrance leading to catastrophe, Fry echoed the conclusions of Ziegler and Amis.

Overall, recent allohistorical works about the Holocaust reveal surprising conclusions about its evolving place in Western memory. The conventional wisdom today among most scholars, of course, is that the Holocaust has progressively gained a larger place within the broader Western memory of the Third Reich.[19] If the Holocaust was largely ignored as a historical event in the early decades of the postwar world, the years since the late 1970s have witnessed such a proliferation of Holocaust-related films, memorials, museums, and commemorative holidays that the genocide of the Jews has become regarded as the signature event of the entire Nazi experience.[20] At the same time, however, signs of a backlash against the increasingly central place of the Holocaust in Western consciousness have become apparent in recent years, as various scholars—Peter Novick, Norman Finkelstein, David Stannard, Martin Walser, Stefan Courtois, and Amos Elon being the most prominent—have accused it of being, among other things, an *ersatz* source of Jewish identity, a geopolitical tool for suppressing Palestinian rights, a crude method of financial blackmail, a politically correct moral cudgel, and a bad-faith excuse for ignoring other horrific cases of genocide.[21] Having diagnosed a surfeit of memory, these scholars and other observers have preached the virtues of forgetting.[22]

Alternate histories of the Holocaust seem to dovetail with this burgeoning backlash against Holocaust memory. Most notably, they have challenged the reigning notion that memory represents the path to salvation. Indeed, by depicting memory as a burden that leads to frustration if not outright disaster, these accounts have challenged the long-held belief in the necessity of remembrance. The significance of this trend is difficult to interpret. On the one hand, these alternate histories may be seen as *descriptive* accounts of the difficulty in coping with the Nazi past. On the other hand, the impatience with memory that suffuses them may well reflect a *prescriptive* desire to be done with the Holocaust once and for all.

This supposition is supported by recalling that the authors in question have largely chosen to present their narratives from the perspective of the perpetrators (or their guilt-ridden descendants) instead of the victims. Moreover, the perpetrators in these accounts—whether Jason Tull, Karl von Hutten, the soul of Tod Friendly, or Leo Zuckermann—have been depicted in strikingly sympathetic fashion as engaged in the admirable struggle to atone for the crimes of the past. At the same time, the victims have seldom found mention in these accounts. And where they have appeared, they have been depicted negatively as bitter slaves to memory. On balance, by rehabilitating the perpetrators and criticizing the victims, recent alternate histories have challenged the maxim that remembrance is the closest approximation to justice for the crimes of the Holocaust.

By failing to consider this ethical function of memory, these works have revealed a reluctance to explore the Holocaust's most profound moral implications and instead have displayed a tendency to exploit it as a vehicle for separate agendas. In the cases of Quinn, Ransmayr, and Ziegler the agenda has involved a critique of their respective societies' cultures of remembrance. In the case of Amis (who, according to critics, apparently came to write about the Holocaust by accident), the agenda may have had more to do with careerism.[23] Regardless of the underlying agenda, all of the novels in question have been characterized by an emotionally distanced relationship to the Holocaust, which is treated with considerable superficiality. In the end, it is the instrumental use of, and the emotionally disengaged relationship to, the Holocaust that seems to suggest the presence of an increasingly normalized perspective to the event.

Whether or not these works signal a new trend is difficult to determine. But it is notable that many of them have been critical as well as commercial successes. Ransmayr's and Ziegler's novels won important literary prizes.[24] And the works of Amis, Fry, and Quinn have garnered significant praise as well.[25] This positive reception suggests a general receptivity to their broader mnemonic conclusions. At the same time, however, the endorsement of these novels was hardly unanimous. *Making History* and *Time's Arrow* were vehemently attacked by many critics, some of whom likened the latter to a form of Holocaust denial.[26] Meanwhile, doubts were also expressed about the extent to which Ransmayr and Ziegler were committed to the cause of remembrance.[27]

This criticism notwithstanding, the works in question have drawn enough positive reviews to suggest that we are at a transitional point in the broader evolution of Holocaust memory. Many observers have pointed out that we are currently witnessing the displacement of "authentic" Holocaust memories with those of a more "vicarious" sort, the latter produced by individuals belonging to the second and third postwar generations who never experienced the event themselves.[28] Alternate histories of the Holocaust represent an extreme form of vicarious memory, for they depict events that not only were not personally experienced but never happened at all. While all acts of fictionalization play with the factuality of history, the extreme playfulness of alternate history in representing an event long seen, for both moral and aesthetic reasons, to be at the limits of representation reveals an increasingly normalized relationship to the Nazi experience.

Notes

1. Eric Norden, *The Ultimate Solution* (New York: Warner Books, 1973), 71–73.
2. The scholarly literature on alternate history is small but growing. Historians as well as literary scholars have contributed important works. Among the pioneering studies by historians are Alexander Demandt, *History That Never Happened: A Treatise on the Question, What Would Have Happened If . . . ?* (Jefferson, NC: McFarland, 1993, German original, 1984) and Niall Ferguson, ed., *Virtual History: Alternatives and Counter-Factuals* (London: Picador, 1997). Studies by literary scholars include Jörg Helbig, *Der parahistorische Roman: Ein literarhistorischer und gattungstypologischer Beitrag zur Allotopieforschung* (Frankfurt: P. Lang, 1987); Christoph Rodiek, *Erfundene Vergangenheit: Kontrafaktische Geschichtsdarstellung (Uchronie) in der Literatur* (Frankfurt: Klostermann, 1997); Karen Hellekson, *The Alternate History: Refiguring Historical Time* (Kent, OH: Kent State University Press, 2001); William Joseph Collins, *Paths Not Taken: The Development, Structure, and Aesthetics of Alternative History* (Ph.D. dissertation, University of California, Davis, 1990); Edgar V. McKnight, Jr., *Alternative History: The Development of a Literary Genre* (Ph.D. dissertation, University of North Carolina, Chapel Hill, 1994); see also Johannes Bulhof, "What If? Modality and History," *History and Theory* 2 (1999), 145–68; and finally, Gavriel D. Rosenfeld, "Why Do We Ask 'What If?' Reflections on the Function of Alternate History," *History and Theory* (December 2002), 90–103.
3. See Gavriel Rosenfeld, *The World Hitler Never Made: Alternate History and the Memory of Nazism* (Cambridge: Cambridge University Press, 2005).

4. Robert Harris, *Fatherland* (New York: Random House, 1992). Henry Turner, "Hitler's Impact on History," in David Wetzel, ed., *From the Berlin Museum to the Berlin Wall: Essays on the Cultural and Political History of Modern Germany* (Westport, CT: Praeger, 1996), 109–26.
5. The concept of "normalization" is a central one in current scholarship on memory, but it has rarely been systematically defined. The term has most frequently appeared in studies of German memory and has also been invoked to refer to national identity. Among the few that have made efforts to discuss the term conceptually are Aleida Assmann and Ute Frevert, *Geschichtsvergessenheit, Geschichtsversessenheit. Vom Umgang mit deutschen Vergangenheiten nach 1945* (Stuttgart: Deutsche Verlags-Anstalt, 1999), 59–63; Jeffrey K. Olick, "What Does It Mean to Normalize the Past?" *Social Science History* (Winter 1998), 547–71; Stefan Berger, *The Search for Normality: National Identity and Historical Consciousness in Germany Since 1800* (Providence: Berghahn Books, 1997); Siobhan Kattago, *Ambiguous Memory: The Nazi Past and German National Identity* (Westport, CT: Praeger, 2001).
6. Philip K. Dick, *The Man in the High Castle* (New York: Vintage Books, 1961); and William Overgard, *The Divide* (New York: Jove, 1980).
7. Daniel Quinn, *After Dachau* (New York: Context Books, 2001).
8. Ibid., 137–38.
9. Friedländer made this point in response to the historian Hayden White, who, when discussing the "limits" of representing the Holocaust in the early 1990s, conceded that "in the case of an emplotment of the events of the Third Reich in a 'comic' or 'pastoral' mode, we would be eminently justified in appealing to 'the facts' in order to dismiss it from the lists of 'competing narratives' of the Third Reich." To this statement, Friedländer replied: "White's theses . . . appear untenable . . . , [for] what would have happened if the Nazis had won the war? No doubt there would have been a plethora of pastoral emplotments of life in the Third Reich and of comic emplotments of the disappearance of its victims, mainly the Jews." Quoted in Saul Friedländer, ed., *Probing the Limits of Representation* (Cambridge: Harvard University Press, 1992), 40, 10.
10. Quinn, *After Dachau,* 126.
11. Ibid., 137–38.
12. Thomas Ziegler, *Die Stimmen der Nacht* (Frankfurt: Heyne Verlag, 1984). Ransmayr's *Morbus Kitahara* appeared in English as *The Dog King,* trans. John Woods (New York: Alfred A. Knopf, 1997). All quotes in this essay come from the English edition.
13. Ziegler, *Die Stimmen der Nacht,* 23.
14. Ransmayr has openly opposed what might be called "organized memory"—that is, any state-imposed program of remembrance—declaring that "every attempt to facilitate comprehension . . . for the suffering . . . of people in the form of an organized . . . program . . . is destined to remain hopeless." See Christoph Ransmayr, "'. . . das Thema hat mich bedroht,'" in Uwe Wittstock, ed., *Die Erfindung der Welt: zum Werk von Christoph Ransmayr* (Frankfurt: Fischer, 1997), 218. Ziegler has noted: "Sticking to the past can make you blind for the future; it distorts . . . perception and lets you see [only] shadows instead of . . . light." Thomas Ziegler, e-mail message to author, 10 December 2001.
15. Thomas Ziegler, "Eine Kleinigkeit für uns Reinkarnauten," in *Eine Kleinigkeit für uns Reinkarnauten* (Windeck: Blitz Verlag, 1997), 83–173. Originally written in the winter of 1987, this story was first published in 1988 and thereafter in English in the 1991 anthology, edited by Uwe Anton, entitled *Welcome to Reality: The Nightmares of Philip K. Dick* (Cambridge, MA: Broken Mirror Press, 1991), 125–75. All quotations are my own translations from the 1997 German edition. Martin Amis, *Time's Arrow* (New York: Harmony Books, 1991). Stephen Fry, *Making History* (New York: Random House, 1996).
16. Ziegler, "Eine Kleinigkeit für uns Reinkarnauten," 159.
17. Ibid., 161.
18. Amis, *Time's Arrow,* 153.
19. This trend has held true across national lines. Peter Novick has pointed to the paradox of the Holocaust gaining in attention the more that the event has faded into the past. Peter

Novick, *The Holocaust in American Life* (Boston: Houghton Mifflin, 1999). Y. Michael Bodemann, *In den Wogen der Erinnerung: Jüdische Existenz in Deutschland* (Berlin: Deutsche Taschenbuch Verlag, 2002). Norbert Frei, "Vom Alter der juengsten Vergangenheit. Die deutsche Reaktion: leider 'aus dem Ruder gelaufen,'" *Die Süddeutsche Zeitung*, 30 January 2003, 17.

20. See, for example, Annette Insdorf, *Indelible Shadows: Film and the Holocaust*, 3rd ed. (Cambridge: Cambridge University Press, 2003); Jeffrey Shandler, *While America Watches: Televising the Holocaust* (New York: Oxford University Press, 1999); James Young, *The Texture of Memory: Holocaust Memorials and Meaning* (New Haven, CT: Yale University Press, 1993); Dora Apel, *Memory Effects: The Holocaust and the Art of Secondary Witnessing* (New Brunswick, NJ: Rutgers University Press, 2002).

21. See Novick, *The Holocaust in American Life*; Norman Finkelstein, *The Holocaust Industry: Reflections on the Exploitation of Jewish Suffering* (London: Verso, 2000). See also David Stannard, "Uniqueness as Denial: The Politics of Genocide Scholarship," in Alan Rosenbaum, ed., *Is the Holocaust Unique? Perspectives in Comparative Genocide* (Boulder, CO: Westview Press, 1996), 163–208. Many of these critical voices have focused their attacks on the concept of the Holocaust's uniqueness. See Gavriel Rosenfeld, "The Politics of Uniqueness: Reflections on the Recent Polemical Turn in Holocaust and Genocide Scholarship," *Holocaust and Genocide Studies* 1 (Spring 1999), 28–61. See also the introduction of Stefan Courtois's edited work, *The Black Book of Communism: Crimes, Terror, Repression* (Cambridge: Harvard University Press, 1999), 23; Amos Elon, "The Politics of *Repression* Memory," *The New York Review of Books* (7 October 1993), 3–5.

22. Charles Maier's essay "A Surfeit of Memory? Reflections on History, Melancholy and Denial," *History and Memory* (Winter 1993), 136–51, takes issue with the general memory boom of the 1990s but pays special attention to the subject of the Holocaust. A convincing retort can be found in John Torpey, "'Making Whole What Has Been Smashed': Reflections on Reparations," *Journal of Modern History* (June 2001), 333–58, who argues that it is precisely the increasing attention to the Holocaust in the last decade that explains the world's greater sensitivity to contemporary atrocities. For a general discussion of memory and forgetting see Avishai Margalit, *The Ethics of Memory* (Cambridge: Harvard University Press, 2002).

23. There is considerable evidence that Amis stumbled upon the theme of the Holocaust more or less by accident. As one journalist who interviewed the author reported, "Amis is candid to say that he had already decided to write a backward-in-time story and was, so to speak, shopping for a suitable theme to go with it." Charles Trueheart, "Through a Mirror, Darkly," *Washington Post* (26 November 1991), B1. Amis is quoted as having said, "I'd always been very interested in the Holocaust . . . but it never occurred to me I would write about it."

24. Christoph Ransmayr's *Morbus Kitahara* shared Europe's coveted Aristeion Prize with Salman Rushdie's novel *The Moor's Last Sigh* in 1996. *Morbus Kitahara* appeared on a variety of "must-read" and best-seller lists as well. "Die Schimmel- und Grass-Messe," *Bunte* (28 September 1995), 96. "Die SWF-Bestenliste im Oktober," *Süddeutsche Zeitung (SZ)* (30 September 1995). Among the many positive reviews were Ursula K. Le Guin, "The Beasts in the Jungle," *Washington Post* (10 August 1997), X5; Gilbert Taylor in *Booklist* (1 April 1997); *Kirkus Reviews* (1 March 1997). Not much farther down the list, however, were Thomas Ziegler's *Die Stimmen der Nacht* and *Eine Kleinigkeit für uns Reinkarnauten*, both of which won the top prizes in the German science fiction world. *Die Stimmen der Nacht* snagged the prestigious Kurd Lasswitz Prize in 1984 (for its original version) as well as in 1994, for a slightly updated version. *Die Stimmen der Nacht* enjoyed respectable commercial success, selling more than six thousand copies in its 1994 version published by the Heyne Verlag. Letter from Martina Geissler of the Heyne Verlag to author, 14 November 2001. Ziegler won the prize in 1990 for best short story for *Eine Kleinigkeit für uns Reinkarnauten*. http://www.epilog.de/Dokumente/Preise/SF/Lasswitz/Index.html.

25. Martin Amis's *Time's Arrow* was nominated for (though did not receive) Britain's prestigious Booker Prize. Positive reviews have included Leslie Epstein, "Ceaselessly Into the

Past," *Washington Post* (27 October 1991); X1; David Chute, "When the Clock Runs Backwards," *Los Angeles Times Book Review* (10 November 1991), 3; Frank Kermode, "In Reverse," *London Review of Books* (12 September 1991), 11. Stephen Fry's *Making History* was a best-seller in England. Daniel Quinn's *After Dachau* was called "fascinating," "intelligent," and "provocative" and was favorably compared to the work of Ray Bradbury and Robert Heinlein. See Dolores Derrickson, "Quinn Draws Eerie, Fascinating World," *Rocky Mountain News* (18 March 2001), 2E. Review of *After Dachau* in *Publishers Weekly* (15 January 2001), 54. Heather Lee Schroeder, "Hitler as Victor Will Make You Think," *Capital Times* (Madison, WI, 23 March 2001). Elizabeth Hand, review of *After Dachau*, in *Voice Literary Supplement* (April 2001). Scott Brown, review of *After Dachau*, in *Entertainment Weekly* (2 April 2002).

26. "Scream First, Pain Later," *The Economist* (5 October 1991), 101. Michiko Kakutani, "Time Runs Backward to Point Up a Moral," *New York Times* (22 October 1991), C17. Frances Gertler, "Black Comedy Genre," *Jerusalem Post* (27 December 1991). The charge of denial is cited in Claire Tham, "This Arrow Is Amis," *Straits Times* (27 June 1992), 17. Tham concluded: "even as one marvels at Amis' bag of tricks, there is a lingering reservation about any literary response which manages to suggest, even ironically, that the Nazis were 'helping' the Jews."

27. Thomas E. Schmidt, "Dunkelgrüner Granit, brüchig, beinahe schon zu Schotter zerbröselt," *Die Frankfurter Rundschau* (11 October 1995), B3; Ulrike Gottwald, "Review of *Die Stimmen der Nacht*," in *Grundwerk* (February 1989), 1–2. Review of *Die Stimmen der Nacht* in www.sf-rezension.de/htmlversion/stimmen.html.

28. On the concept of vicarious memory, see James Young, *At Memory's Edge: After-Images of the Holocaust in Contemporary Art and Architecture* (New Haven, CT: Yale University Press, 2000). See also Efraim Sicher, "The Future of the Past: Countermemory and Postmemory in Contemporary American Post-Holocaust Narratives," *History and Memory* (Fall/Winter 2000), 56–83.

– Chapter 17 –

LAUGHTER AND HEARTACHE
The Functions of Humor in Holocaust Tragedy

Lynn Rapaport

> Two Jews are being marched to the gas chamber. As they approach the door of the building, one of the Jews begins to scream in terror, "No! No! I don't want to die!" The other Jew turns to him and says, "Quiet, Moishe! We don't want to make trouble!"

Obviously, there is nothing funny about people being led to gas chambers. While comedy is the flipside of tragedy, is there a role for humor in Holocaust studies? What are the aesthetic and ethical questions regarding laughter amidst mass death? Humor plays an important role in the human condition, though it is often taken for granted as a communications medium. Humor can serve as social commentary, thus providing a venue for change by lending comedians a forum to discuss social, political, religious, and sexual issues safely. Humor can also help society work through unspeakable difficulties by giving a name and face to evil.[1]

Anthropologist Mary Douglas describes the role of the joker as a privileged person who can say certain things in certain ways with immunity. Safe within the permitted range of attack, the joker lightens the oppressiveness of social reality, demonstrates its arbitrariness, and expresses creative possibilities of the situation.[2] According to a tale in the Talmud, the prophet Elijah said that there will be a reward in the next world for those who bring laughter to others in this one.[3] Humor can function as a vehicle for critical

---

I am grateful to Lawrence Baron, Stephen Feinstein, and Stephen Lebowitz for their helpful comments on an earlier draft of this paper. I also thank Jonathan Petropoulos and John Roth for inviting me to participate in the Gray Zones conference and this edited volume.

Notes for this section begin on page 266.

thought, promoting group solidarity and helping people survive in a hostile world. This essay focuses on the various functions of humor—as political satire, as coping mechanism, and as a subtle form of opposition to Nazi oppression.

Humor As Political Opposition Against the Nazi Regime

Even before the Nazis came to power in Germany in 1933, artists, comedians, and entertainers were among the first to critique Hitler and his party. Political cartoons began attacking Hitler in the mid-1920s. They appeared in both daily newspapers with mass circulation (including international publications after the mid-1930s) and in the more specialized or low-circulation daily newspapers (primarily in German publications until 1933).[4] Cabaret performers were also doing satirical sketches about Hitler and his storm troopers. The last four years of the Weimar Republic were rife with cabarets. Some were purely amusement dives or strip clubs; others, including student cabarets, were more politically oriented, battling the increasing power of the National Socialists and their ideology of racial purity as well as exposing the nature and existence of concentration camps and other aspects of Nazi terror.[5]

In Munich, for instance, cabaret performer Weiss Ferdl would bring out *large* photographs of Hitler, Göring, and other Nazi leaders and muse, "Now, should I hang them or line them up against the wall?" He also joked about the new concentration camp, Dachau. "I took a walk around the Dachau camp," he told his audience. "Most impressive and well-protected, I must say. The walls are ten meters high with barbed wire along the top, electrically charged, and machine-gun towers at every corner—still, I only have to say a word or two, and I'll be inside in a jiffy!" That story was told all over Germany.[6] Other cabaret comedians walked onto the stage with a gag over their mouths, sat silently on a chair for several minutes, then stood up and walked off the stage. The master of ceremonies would then say, "Ladies and gentlemen, now that the political part of our program is over, we come to the entertainment."[7]

One of the most popular comedians was Werner Finck. His cabaret, *Die Katakombe* (The Catacombs), moved to a small hall on the premises of the Scala variety theater in Berlin in 1932. His cabaret was opened, closed, reopened, and reclosed several times by the Nazis. It was in a small cellar-like space with wooden tables and chairs, a meager stage, and improvised costumes. The troupe's gift for literary parody and social satire, as well as Finck's unique personality, won over a wide audience. On opening night Finck explained to his public why *Katakombe* had been chosen as the cabaret's name: "Two thousand years ago, the catacombs provided a place of refuge for the first Christians; today it is a place of refuge for the last."[8]

Finck recounts in his memoirs that quite by chance the *Katakombe*'s performers were completely Aryan.[9] When someone did not like his political material and shouted from the audience, "Dirty Jew," Finck would respond, "I only look this intelligent." When he spotted Gestapo observers in the audience, he would ask them, "Am I speaking too fast for you?"[10] By 10 May 1935 his cabaret was closed. The *Völkischer Beobachter*, the Nazi paper, described the closure as follows:

> They mocked military and party uniforms, ridiculed the organization of the Party, and dragged the national service through the mud. A racially pure Jew, who enjoys only a guest status in Germany, dares to make critical remarks on political events in Germany. Consequently the audience mainly consists of Jews and other elements destructive to the state.[11]

Eventually the Nazis closed all the cabarets. Some of the performers who had fled the Third Reich attempted to perform in exile, and cabarets sprang up in Vienna, Prague, Zurich, Paris, and London.[12] Other performers, including Finck, were sent to prison and concentration camps, where cabaret humor reappeared.

On 24 April 1934 the Nazis established the *Volksgerichtshof*, or People's Court, based in Berlin, to sentence offenders charged with treason and other political violations. Treason included espionage *(Spionage)*, acts undermining Germany's military power *(Wehrkraftzersetzung)*, assisting enemy forces *(Feindbegünstigung)*, and crimes affecting Germany's external and internal security. Acts of treason ranged from murdering or attempting to murder government officials to harboring an enemy prisoner or maintaining social contact with one. It also included spreading propaganda among the German population and armed forces and publicly insulting or slandering "the Führer and Reich Chancellor."[13] Telling a political joke was considered an act of treason, and both teller and listener were subject to sentences ranging from imprisonment to capital punishment. For instance, between 1934 and 1945 the People's Court handed down 5,286 death sentences, many of which went to political joke tellers.[14] On 26 June 1943 a young war widow was prosecuted and sentenced to death for telling political jokes. One of her jokes featured Göring and Hitler sitting on top of the Berlin broadcasting tower, whereby Göring asks Hitler to do the German people a favor and jump off. In another incident, a priest told an artisan a joke about a dying soldier, who asked to see those for whom he had to die. A picture of Hitler was placed on one side of the soldier and one of Göring on his other side. The soldier said that now he was dying like Christ. The judgment against the priest read as follows:

> with his authority as a priest he has directed the most vulgar and dangerous attacks against our confidence in the Führer, an attack which can reduce the readiness of our people to risk its life for the life of the Volk. And he did not do this only once, because what he has said before us points in the same direction! And he did it while we are engaged in the gravest of battles. Such behavior is not only an irresponsible misuse of the authority of a priest, it is more than that: it is treason to Volk, Führer and Reich. Such treason causes external loss of honor. To

deter others anxious to do the same, such an attack on the morale of our war effort can be punished with nothing other than death.[15]

Throughout Hitler's reign of terror overt opposition resulted in swift reprisals. Nonetheless, covert opposition found a voice underground in the form of *Flüsterwitze,* or whispered jokes. These jokes provided some therapeutic value, a welcome emotional release from the pressures and restrictions of living in a totalitarian state. For example, when the Nazi government introduced its race laws—the Laws for the Protection of German Blood—in 1935, they stipulated that only people of the "Aryan" race could be German citizens, thus outlawing all Jews, gypsies, and other people of alien origin. A great search for "Aryan grannies" began. One whispered joke retold the Little Red Riding Hood fairy tale: She meets the big bad wolf in the forest. "Where are you going?" asks the wolf. "I'm looking for my grandmother," replies the girl. "Aren't we all?" sighs the wolf.[16] Another joke was as follows: A woman in a Jewish cemetery is busy pouring water from a watering can onto several graves. An attendant comes along and asks her what she is doing. "I am baptizing my ancestors," she replies.[17]

There were also jokes about the old regime—President Paul von Hindenburg,[18] Secretary of State Otto Meissner, former chancellor Franz von Papen, and Economic Minister Hjalmar Schacht. There were jokes about Hitler—his background, his appearance, his path to power, his personal life, his personal traits like being superstitious and vindictive, his success, and ultimately, his decline. Jokes about other personalities—Hermann Göring, Joseph Goebbels, Rudolf Hess, Ernst Röhm, Joachim von Ribbentrop, Robert Ley—were also popular. Indeed, jokes about Göring were the first to circulate throughout the Third Reich, and Göring, in contrast to Hitler, had a good sense of humor. There were rumors that he collected jokes about himself, paying ten marks for any new joke.[19] There were many jokes about the Nazi Party, the storm troopers, the SS, the Gestapo, concentration camps, the Judiciary, the *Staatsbeamte* (Civil Service), the Hitler Youth, and the military. Jews were the subject of many of these jokes. Some jokes revealed the absurdity of Hitler's antisemitism, with the enactment of the Nuremberg Laws, and the meaning of the word "Aryan." Others were produced by Jews themselves, enabling them to laugh at the Nazis as well as to cope with the tragedy of their situation. One theme of the jokes was to laugh at the intolerance, bureaucracy, and ignorance of the Nazis, while showing how Jews could outwit them. For instance,

Two Jews meet on the street.
"I have good news for you," says the one, "partly good and partly bad."
"Please tell me the good news first."
"Hitler is dead!"
"Excellent! Now the bad news?"
"It's not true."[20]

Another one was as follows:

A Jew is arrested during the war, having been denounced for killing a Nazi at 10 P.M. and even eating the brain of his victim. This is his defense: In the first place a Nazi hasn't got any brain. Secondly, a Jew doesn't eat anything that comes from a pig. And thirdly, he could not have killed the Nazi at 10 P.M. because at that time everybody listens to the BBC broadcast.[21]

Since conversations criticizing the regime and telling jokes about leading Nazis were risky, rendering one liable to end up in a concentration camp or be sentenced to death, whispered jokes were examples of contemporary political satire—a form of opposition whose value became even more significant once war broke out.

Humor As a Coping Mechanism During the Holocaust

In *Children and Play in the Holocaust,* George Eisen, writing about the Vilna ghetto, notes that "a graveyard is no place for [children's] merriment."[22] Yet children still found "Games Among the Shadows" a necessity. Lucjan Dobroszycki chronicles how in the Lodz ghetto chairman Mordecai C. Rumkowski personally inspected a series of building sites in the summer of 1941 searching for a location suitable for a children's playground.[23]

How could children play amidst suffering, hunger, and annihilation? Eisen explains that children's play behavior was not divorced from the reality they were experiencing. On the contrary, it was reflective of it, and articulated skills for survival. Fantasy and play helped remove one, even momentarily, from the bleakness and horror of the moment. Playing was a life-affirming act, offering mental and physical health, a psychological buffer, social stability, and order in the face of crises.

Adults living through the Holocaust experienced a need similar to children.[24] Any activity that would—if only for a short time—transport one to another world, allowing mental detachment from their immediate circumstances, helped inmates survive. Humor existed in the ghettos and concentration and death camps. For example, in the beginning of the German Nazi occupation of Poland, the Nazi authorities allowed a wide range of cultural activities in the ghettos. These included vocational courses, Hebrew schools, choral groups, and cabarets. In the Warsaw ghetto, five cabarets opened, two in Yiddish and three in Polish, all concentrating on comedies and reviews.[25] "However poor the talent and trashy the content," writes Lucy Davidowicz, this "impoverished entertainment heightened ghetto morale simply by releasing the audiences for a brief span from their day-to-day anxieties."[26]

Cabarets also existed in concentration and holding camps. For instance, Westerbork was inaugurated by the Dutch government in 1939 as a holding camp for Jewish refugees from Germany. Several hundred German Jews lived there until July 1942, when the camp was taken over by the SS. Thereafter its population burgeoned to several thousand at any one time, as it became a way station for Dutch Jews being transported to Auschwitz, Sobibor,

Bergen-Belsen, and Theresienstadt. Between July 1943 and June 1944 six cabarets were staged there. Writing about the first revue, Philip Mechanicus, a Dutch journalist whose diary chronicled life in Westerbork, noted, "The revue was a mixture of antiquated sketches and mild ridicule of the conditions and circumstances prevailing at the camp. Not a single sharp word, not a single harsh word, but a little gentle irony in passing, avoiding the main issues. A compromise."[27] The second revue, *Humor und Melodie* (Humor and Melody) opened on 4 September 1943. It was a mixture of mild satire about camp conditions and pure diversion. It had skits imitating the outdoor roll calls of camp inmates, and other numbers dealing with crowded barracks. The shows were well rehearsed and props and costumes were often elaborate, leading Mechanicus to write that "Westerbork has the best cabaret in Holland."[28]

Konrad Gemmeker, Westerbork's camp commandant, encouraged the cabaret by allotting large sums of money for props and costumes. "On one occasion he came three times in succession to see the same performance and roared with laughter at the same old jokes each time," according to Etty Hillesum, who chronicled life in the camp.[29] Although the performances were popular with inmates and invariably sold out, they were still controversial. Many inmates saw them as part of a larger strategy of manipulation that ensured the proper functioning of Westerbork—and Westerbork's main function was to fulfill a weekly quota of transporting Jews and others to concentration camps in Poland. If one were in the cast, he or she would be exempt from deportation. The fact that most revue performers were German Jews created resentment on the part of Dutch Jews. Thus, there were many debates about the propriety of attending the shows. Some Jews saw the reviews as tasteless at best and sacrilegious at worst. Some believed that the shows were offensive to a sense of Jewish self-respect. The shows were performed in the registration hall where one had to go to apply for exemption from deportation, and wooden boards from the old synagogue of Assen were used for constructing the stage. Other Jewish attendees believed the shows provided both a temporary diversion and the mental strength to carry on.

In Dachau a play satirizing the Nazis was performed for six weeks in the summer of 1943. The lead character, Count Adolar, was a thinly disguised Hitler. The SS were seated at the front as "honored guests." Rudolf Kalmar, the writer of the play, survived the camp and became a popular actor in East Germany after the war. Another survivor described the impact of this satire on the camp inmates: "Many of them, who sat behind rows of the SS each night and laughed with full heart, didn't experience a day of freedom. But most among them took this demonstration of strength to endure their situation. . . . They had the certainty, as they lay that night on their wooden bunks: We have done something that gives strength to our comrades. We have made the Nazis look ridiculous."[30]

Even in Auschwitz cabarets were improvised from time to time. Viktor Frankl describes:

> A hut was cleared temporarily, a few wooden benches were pushed or nailed together and a program was drawn up. In the evening those who had fairly good positions in the camp—the Capos and the workers who did not have to leave the camp on distant marches—assembled there. They came to have a few laughs or perhaps to cry a little; anyway, to forget. There were songs, poems, jokes, some with underlying satire regarding the camp. All were meant to help us forget, and they did help. The gatherings were so effective that a few ordinary prisoners went to see the cabaret in spite of their fatigue even though they missed their daily portion of food by going.[31]

The most developed cabaret and theater in the camps was at Theresienstadt in Czechoslovakia. Poets, actors, and musicians entertained the camp with songs, skits, and music, doing special performances for the sick. As Rabbi Erich Weiner, spiritual leader of the prisoners, observed, the cabaret "strengthened their will to survive as well as infused their power to resist."[32] Frankl writes of his experiences in Auschwitz, "Humor was another of the soul's weapons in the fight for self-preservation. It is well known that humor, more than anything else in the human make-up, can afford an aloofness and an ability to rise above any situation, even if only for a few seconds."[33]

David Bergman, who as a twelve-year-old boy from Czechoslovakia spent fourteen months in Auschwitz and other concentration camps, describes how humor helped him cope with the situation:

> When I was held captive early in the death camps, a few of us victims who somehow managed to maintain a positive outlook on life would get together secretly after work just to exchange humorous stories. These exchanges helped us to temporarily numb the horrors we faced, thus making it possible for us to make it through another difficult and trying day.[34]

Many Holocaust memoirs written in the aftermath approach the trauma with a note of wry, black humor to embody the absurdity of their world. For instance, the opening stories of Primo Levi's *Survival in Auschwitz* (1959) and Tadeusz Borowski's *This Way for the Gas, Ladies and Gentlemen* (1967), among other works, describe macabre episodes that brought them to laughter as well as anger, when depicting their journey and life in hell. "We kept our morale through humor," said philosopher Emil Fackenheim of his experiences in Auschwitz.[35]

Indeed, based on a study of in-depth interviews with fifty-five Jewish Holocaust survivors in Israel, Chaya Ostrower argues that humor served various functions for survivors during the Holocaust. Most importantly, it functioned as a defense mechanism through self-humor and gallows humor. "Without humor we would all have committed suicide," explained one respondent. "We made fun of everything. What I'm actually saying is that that helped us remain human, even under hard conditions."[36] Another had this to say:

> When I was interviewed for Spielberg and they asked me what I thought was the reason I survived, they probably expected me to answer good fortune or other

things. I said that I thought it was laughter and humor. Not to take things the way we were living, but to dress them up as something different. That was what helped me. I wasn't thinking about miracles . . . I only thought how not to take things seriously. . . . And I guess it [this attitude] helped me. Because it was absurd all that time, it was inconceivable, that they could do those things to people.[37]

While humor did not reduce survivors' sense of the atrocity or horror, it facilitated coping with it. One laughed at the impossible predicament, wondering if it could become any worse. As documented in survivor studies, strong social bonds, whether familial or through friendship, helped create a support network within the camp. This meant releasing the tension in dangerous situations through humor, story-telling, utterances, songs, cabarets, caricature paintings and drawings, reminiscences, and fantasies. Humor functioned as a survival mechanism—buoying up those inmates who had lost their reserves of mental endurance. Humor helped victims maintain morale—key elements central to strengthening the will to live, thus increasing chances of survival.[38] Sociologist and Auschwitz survivor Anna Pawelczyńska argues that every moment of laughter and every joke was part of the arsenal of collective defense, and thus an element of resistance.[39]

Humorous Media Portrayals of Hitler and the Holocaust During Hitler's Lifetime

During his lifetime there were many portrayals of Hitler in film and drama that glorified and deified the Führer.[40] *Thingspiele* or Third Reich passion plays, like Richard Euringer's *Deutsche Passion* (1933), that presented Hitler as a Christ figure were common. Yet there were also satires in which the dictator was portrayed as a comic figure, a buffoon whose actions had tragic consequences. Some plays like Stanislaw Ignacy Witkeiewicz's *The Cuttlefish* (1922) and *Gyubal Wahazar* (1921) forecasted the rise of Hitler and his reign of terror. Others, like Bertolt Brecht's *Roundheads and Peakheads* (1934) and *The Resistible Rise of Arturo Ui* (1941), lampooned the class struggle that allowed Hitler to rise to power and dictatorial rule. Brecht focused on Hitler's antisemitism, explaining Germany's acceptance of racial policy in economic terms.[41] Nonetheless, Hitler resisted seeing himself portrayed on screen. Under Nazi control the German film industry forbade characterizations of Hitler or episodes of his life to be used as subject matter for film. Hitler was only to appear in newsreels and documentaries, and neither did he want artificial Hitlers as rivals.

Moreover, the United States, in the throes of the Great Depression, followed an isolationist foreign policy to keep out of the war. Most Americans were unwilling to be drawn into European power struggles or to take sides between Hitler and his intended victims. When World War II erupted in 1939, a Gallup poll showed that 96 percent of Americans opposed entering the war.[42] Despite the widespread presence and significant influence of Jews in the American film industry during the 1930s, Hollywood discreetly avoided making overtly anti-Nazi films. During this period Hollywood faced a dilemma regarding how to depict the Nazis and their Allies. The Jewish studio heads worried that any mention of Nazi antisemitism might be construed as covert propaganda designed to edge the United States into the war to save their fellow Jews. These moguls also feared that humorous treatments of Nazis, more than drama, would reveal an anti-Nazi tilt. They were reticent to fan the flames of domestic antisemitism or exacerbate problems for Jews in Germany.[43] This attitude remained unchanged until the Japanese attack on Pearl Harbor in December 1941.[44]

In 1938 Charlie Chaplin decided to openly defy the Nazis when he envisioned the plot for a film about a mustached Jewish barber mistaken for the Führer. Hollywood's self-policing Motion Picture Producers and Distributors of America, the Hays Office, told United Artists, the distribution company, that Chaplin "would run into censorship trouble."[45] After a long gestation period, Chaplin did not begin shooting the film until September 1939, when war broke out in Europe. Before the script was even written, the German consulate in Los Angeles complained.[46] German sympathizers threatened to vandalize theaters showing Chaplin's film and set off stink bombs in them. In *My Autobiography,* Chaplin confesses, "Had I known of the actual horrors of the German concentration camps, I could not have made *The Great Dictator;* I could not have made fun of the homicidal insanity of the Nazis."[47]

While feature films were being heavily scrutinized for their anti-Nazi and anti-foreigner content, the "shorts" shown before the full-length feature movie were not regulated in the same way. In mid-1939 Jules White, head of Columbia Pictures Short Department and longtime producer and director of the Three Stooges comedies, walked into his brother Sam's office at Columbia Studios and said that he was planning a comedy about Hitler. Moe would be Hitler, Curly would be Göring, and Larry would be Goebbels. Sam told his brother that it was a grim situation in Europe and asked if he could make it funny. "I'll make it funny," Jules replied.

The Three Stooges short, *You Nazty Spy,* was finished on 31 October 1939, two months after war was declared in Europe. The film cost about $18,500 to make and preceded the release of Charlie Chaplin's *The Great Dictator* by nine months. The Three Stooges went unnoticed or ignored by the censors.[48] Moe Howard of the Three Stooges was the first American actor to lampoon Hitler on film.[49] It was also his favorite Three Stooges short. *I'll Never Heil Again,* a sequel, was released before the Japanese attack on Pearl Harbor.

Ernst Lubitsch's *To Be or Not to Be* (1942), staring Jack Benny and Carole Lombard, was a comedy about the Nazi occupation of Poland, whereby a band of Polish actors never stop "performing" amidst the thunder of applause or bombs.[50] *To Be or Not to Be* initially received unfavorable reviews. For example, the *Philadelphia Inquirer* called it a "callous, tasteless effort to find fun in the bombing of Warsaw." The National Board of Review warned that "sensitive people won't like it," and one critic even labeled the work a propaganda piece for Goebbels. Because of the viciousness of the attacks, Lubitsch felt it necessary to defend himself:[51]

> When in *To Be or Not to Be* I have referred to the destruction of Warsaw, I have shown it in all seriousness; the commentation under the shots of the devastated Warsaw speaks for itself and cannot leave any doubt in the spectator's mind what my point of view and attitude are toward those acts of horror. What I have satirized in this picture are the Nazis and their ridiculous ideology. I have also satirized the attitude of actors who always remain actors regardless of how dangerous the situation might be, which I believe is a true observation.[52]

Using comic form, an important goal for all of these films was to shatter the image of Hitler and the Nazis. By turning its leaders into buffoons, these films confront the Nazis by making people laugh at the absurdity of the "master race." Humor was used as a weapon to make the enemy small and thus to expose conventional norms and empower society's outcasts. For instance, in the Three Stooges' shorts confrontations between the Axis partners who are struggling over control of the world are portrayed as games—checkers and basketball. Hitler and the Nazis pose a threat to the social order, and this physical and ideological conflict is resolved by their eradication, as the films reach narrative resolution with the demise of Hitler, the Nazis, and the Axis powers.

Moreover, Jewish impersonations of Hitler, like Chaplin's and Moe Howard's of the Stooges, represent boundary crossings that serve several purposes. Within the precincts of Jewish humor, the masquerade is derived from the spirit of Purim, in which for one day each year saints and villains become interchangeable through an exchange of clothing and other theatrical gestures. This demonstrates an awareness of Jewish powerlessness in the fight against Hitler and a strategy for empowerment for society's outcasts and helpless victims.

Once America entered the war, comic depictions of Hitler and the Nazis were rampant. For instance, Theodor Seuss Geisel, better known as Dr. Seuss, responded to early reports of Nazi atrocities in Europe and produced hundreds of political cartoons reflecting the wartime zeitgeist.[53] Hollywood also joined the war effort by making movies with Nazis in sinister roles. These films were entertaining and profitable and served as propaganda for the Allied cause. For instance, the Disney studio made a series of propaganda cartoons including *Education for Death: The Making of a Nazi* (1943). Based on a book of the same title by Gregor Ziemer, this cartoon follows Hans, a little boy growing up in Nazi Germany, and shows his degrading attitude about the value of human life as he becomes indoctrinated with Nazi ideology. Disney also produced a series of Donald Duck propaganda shorts including *Donald Gets Drafted* (1942), *The Vanishing Private* (1942), *Sky Trooper* (1942), *Der Fuehrer's Face* (1942), *Fall Out—Fall In* (1943), *The Old Army Game* (1943), and lastly, *Commando Duck* (1944). Their goal was to make Americans less afraid of the enemy.

Donald was most effective in ridiculing the enemy in *Der Fuehrer's Face* (1942). "In this war, humor and fantasy have enlisted on the side of the united nations. They're fighting, fighting hard—and their smash-Hitler weapon is the animated cartoon. No other weapon of propaganda can ridicule the Axis, expose its absurdities, as deftly," stated Joe Grant and Dick Huemer, scriptwriters for *Der Fuehrer's Face*.[54] Originally titled *Donald Duck in Nutziland,* the eight-minute cartoon features a German "oom-pah" band parading through a German town singing the "virtues" of the Führer. They awaken Donald Duck, who regrettably has to work in a Nazi munitions factory. After a frantic workday of making bombs and saluting Hitler, Donald awakens from this nightmare to find that he is still living in the good old United States of America. Spike Jones's title song, "Der Fuehrer's Face," was an instant hit, and the cartoon won an Academy Award for best short subject.

Postwar Humorous Depictions of Nazis and the Holocaust

Following World War II the revelation of the enormity of Nazi atrocities put the Holocaust beyond the reach of the comic imagination. Indeed, Terrence Des Pres noted that Holocaust etiquette "dictates that anything pertaining to the Holocaust must be serious, must be reverential in a manner that acknowledges (and supports) the sacredness of its occasion."[55] Some critics and scholars see comic depictions of the Holocaust as an affront to historical, ethical, and aesthetic sensibilities, thus trivializing the horror. Lawrence Baron calculates that after the end of World War II, no comedies were produced until 1958, when *Me and the Colonel* and Kurt Hoffman's *Aren't We Wonderful* appeared.[56] Nonetheless, Des Pres defends the use of laughter as "life-reclaiming" and argues that a comic response in art "is more resilient, more effectively in revolt against terror and sources of terror than a response that is solemn or tragic."[57]

Nazi-bashing persisted in American media during the 1960s, exemplified by Mel Brooks's 1968 film *The Producers* and the television series *Hogan's Heroes*, which aired on CBS from 1965 to 1971. While *Hogan's Heroes* was set in a German Nazi-run POW camp (not a concentration camp) and might not constitute "Holocaust comedy," many viewers thought it was a comedy about a concentration camp and it generated considerable controversy.[58] In 1967 *MAD* magazine lampooned the series by setting it in Buchenwald, thus exacerbating the confusion.[59] Ironically, actor Robert Clary, who played Corporal Louis LeBeau on the series, was a Holocaust survivor who, as a Jewish Parisian teenager, spent thirty-one months in German concentration camps.[60]

Mel Brooks's *The Producers* (1967), which reappeared on stage in 2001 to win twelve Tony Awards, is a film (and play) in which the Jewish characters, however unappealing they may be, are far more sympathetic than the characters they exploit. In the film and play, the characters Max Bialystock and Leo Bloom seduce rich old ladies to obtain funds beyond the cost of production to put on the worst possible play—*Springtime for Hitler*—so that they can close the play early and reap the profits. The audacity to present a musical called *Springtime for Hitler*, with outrageous song lyrics, satirizes an American public willing to find humor, however grotesque, in the Third Reich. *The Producers* was a late manifestation of "sick comedy" associated since the late 1950s with many Jewish stand-up comedians—Mort Sahl, Shelly Berman, Mike Nichols and Elaine May, Tom Lehrer, and Lenny Bruce. Indeed, Lenny Bruce had a routine, "Hitler and the M.C.A.," in which two talent agents in 1930, desperate to find a dictator, discover and recruit a handy house painter.[61] When *The Producers* opened in Los Angeles and New York, there were no recorded complaints in the Anti-Defamation League's Los Angeles or New York offices.[62]

In 1972 Jerry Lewis cowrote and directed *The Day the Clown Cried*, about a clown in a concentration camp forced to lead children into the gas chambers. Shot in Paris and Sweden, "The Clown in the movie is a sort of Pied Piper who doesn't really get along with the other internees," says Lewis, and is "assigned to try to keep the kids in the camp happy—and ignorant of the crimes being committed by Hitler. And it is he who, in the end, is expected to lead the children—and himself—to the ovens."[63] The film ran into financial trouble, was never released, and to this day sits in the vaults of Stockholm's AB Europa Film.

Lawrence Baron calculates six Holocaust comedies released in the 1970s, constituting 5 percent of all Holocaust feature films.[64] For example, *Harold and Maude* (1971), a cult classic because of its controversial love affair between a teenage boy and an eighty-year-old female Holocaust survivor, signals the Holocaust through a shot of the numbers tattooed on Maude's arm and her memories of prewar Vienna. Maude, who has witnessed death, teaches Harold, who is obsessed with funerals and suicide, to enjoy life.[65] Furthermore, Lena Wertmuller's *Seven Beauties* (1975) was the first film to extract laughter from the plight of an inmate in Auschwitz, when, to get an extra ration of food, Pasqualino seduces his repulsive female commandant.[66] Other films like *Genghis Cohn* (1958), *The Nasty Girl* (1991), *Europa, Europa* (1991), and *My Mother's Courage* (1996) made humorous subplots set in the context of the Holocaust more commonplace. The combination of laughter and lies told to keep people ignorant of the gas chambers was central to three Holocaust comedies produced in the late 1990s. *Life Is Beautiful* (1998), *Jakob the Liar* (1999), and *Train of Life* (1998) center around lies that enable Jews to survive their ordeal.

For instance, *Life Is Beautiful* is about a father who tries to shield his son from Nazi atrocities by lying to him about their internment in a concentration camp. Guido (Roberto Benigni), an Italian Jew, is sent to a concentration camp with his wife and young son. Wanting to protect his son from the reality of the Nazis' concentration camp atrocities, including separation from the little boy's mother, Guido tells him that they and the Nazis are playing an elaborate game. In the midst of the struggle merely to survive, the father makes his son (and the audience) laugh with his eccentric antics.[67] While *New Yorker* critic David Denby described *Life Is Beautiful* as "a benign form of Holocaust denial,"[68] it received worldwide acclaim and won numerous awards, including a 1998 Oscar for best foreign-language film.[69]

Jakob the Liar, a remake of the 1974 East German film *Jakob der Lügner*, is set in a Jewish ghetto in Nazi-occupied Poland. While detained at Gestapo headquarters, Jakob (Robin Williams) overhears a news broadcast signaling Soviet military successes against the Nazis. He reports this back to the ghetto, and rumors spread that he has a radio—an offense punishable by death. Despite the danger, Jakob continues to fabricate news bulletins about Allied advances. These lies keep hope alive—the suicide rate drops, spirits are lifted, and optimism is reborn. The Nazis learn of the mythical radio and search for the resistance hero operating it.

Radu Mihaileanu's *Train of Life* tells the story of a Jewish village faking its own deportation to escape the Nazis. When Schlomo, the village idiot, learns that Nazi troops are descending on his *shtetl,* he convinces the rabbi that the villagers should buy their own train, disguise themselves as Nazis and prisoners, and fake their own deportation. Embarking on a wild train ride toward the Russian border with Palestine as the goal, the Nazis resemble those of *Hogan's Heroes* and the Jews those of *Fiddler on the Roof*.

Those of the "second generation," or children of Holocaust survivors, have made their own contributions to Holocaust humor.[70] Beginning in 1990 children of Holocaust survivors began performing comedic material about their experiences. For example, the Canadian film *Punch Me in the Stomach* (1994) is based on Deb Filler's autobiographical one-woman stage show, where in comedic form she plays thirty-six different characters from her extended family. In the story Deb's father, a concentration camp survivor, asks her to accompany him on a tour of the camps in which he was incarcerated during the Holocaust. She relates this experience, but only after telling a wide range of other stories about her own family and growing up.

Adam Melnick and Josh Tarjan, both children of Holocaust survivors, were inspired by Helen Epstein's book *Children of the Holocaust* to write their own play, *Camp Holocaust*. In October 2000 the Present Company Theatorium, an off-Broadway theater, debuted this play about Dave and Ed, children of Holocaust survivors who decide to build a concentration camp in Poland as an "adventure" destination for American Jews. Described as a "darkly comic and deadly serious play," the characters represent different groups of people—Americans, Germans, and Poles, with different points of view within each group. Characters include a survivor parent and a rabbi, both of whom are against the boys' going to Poland; some people who want to forget the Holocaust; and others who are militant in their remembering— insisting the camp be run by Germans behaving cruelly.

While there are numerous other examples of humorous portrayals of the Holocaust in popular culture, one thing is certain: it is becoming a mainstream phenomenon. Nazi iconography and imagery—like Seinfeld's soup

Nazi, Holocaust jokes in Woody Allen films,[71] and Holocaust stories that incorporate wit and humor—have been appropriated into mainstream popular culture.[72]

Conclusion

Is laughter the best medicine for the mind and body? Preliminary scientific research is demonstrating that laughter and humor boost immunity, diminish pain, and help people deal with life's stresses. For instance, medical studies are beginning to explore the means by which laughter can cut the risk of heart disease as it prevents damage to the protective barrier lining blood vessels. When this is impaired, as it is with too much mental stress, it is thought to trigger an inflammatory reaction that causes fat and cholesterol to build up in the arteries.[73] Preliminary studies on children with cancer and AIDS show that when they laugh there was significant improvement in pain management and the body's natural defense mechanisms. There was also a direct response to the autonomic nervous system responsible for involuntary action, which can be damaged by illness. While laughter is not a cure for illness, it can have positive effects in reducing stress hormone levels.[74]

Mary Douglas argues that joking allows for purification through the catharsis of laughter. Moreover, joking challenges the relevance of the dominant structure, as the joker performs with immunity the act that wipes out the venial offense.[75] Psychiatrist Sigmund Freud argues that jokes can serve a hostile purpose, representing a rebellion against the authority, a liberation from its pressure.[76] "By making our enemy small, inferior, despicable, or comic, we achieve in a roundabout way, the enjoyment of overcoming him."[77]

Political jokes reflect a certain level of collective anxiety about public matters. They externalize anxieties about the public domain and the links between what C. Wright Mills called public issues and private troubles.[78] "In a tyranny, political jokes are acts of defiance and of great courage," writes Steven Lukes in *No Laughing Matter: A Collection of Political Jokes*.[79] Egon Larson argues that the political joke is a safety valve, a way in which an oppressed people preserves its sanity. Humor also serves a postwar purpose—it provides a mechanism through which society can confront cultural traumas.

In conclusion, humor was present before, during, and after the Holocaust, serving many important functions to its tellers and listeners. Through gallows humor, Jewish humor, and political satire, humor enabled Holocaust victims to cope with the absurdity and horror of their situation. Laughter itself could be thought of as an act of resistance by boosting morale and strengthening the will to live. Moreover, while political jokes may not be able to topple a dictatorial regime, there is one important point that adds to their effectiveness—the oppressors have no defense against it. If they try to fight back, they only appear more ridiculous.[80]

Notes

1. Gary Goshgarian, *Understanding Language* (New York: Addison Wesley Longman, 2001), 167.
2. Mary Douglas, "Jokes," in Chandra Mukerji and Michael Schudson, eds., *Rethinking Popular Culture* (Berkeley: University of California Press, 1991), 305.
3. As cited in John Morreall, "Humor in the Holocaust: Its Critical, Cohesive, and Coping Functions," in Marcia Sachs Littell, ed., *Annual Scholars' Conference on the Holocaust and the Churches, 1990–2000*, CD-ROM (Stamford, CT: Vista-Intermedia, 2001).
4. For a good overview, see Zbyněk Zeman, *Heckling Hitler: Caricatures of the Third Reich* (Hanover, NH, and London: University Press of New England, 1987).
5. Lisa Appignanesi, *The Cabaret* (New York: Universe Books, 1976), 158.
6. Egon Larson, *Wit As a Weapon: The Political Joke in History* (London: Frederick Muller Limited, 1980), 46.
7. Steve Lipman, *Laughter in Hell: The Use of Humor During the Holocaust* (New Jersey: Jason Aronson, 1993), 36.
8. Appignanesi, *The Cabaret*, 159.
9. Ibid.
10. See Morreall, "Humor in the Holocaust."
11. Appignanesi, *The Cabaret*, 159.
12. They had somewhat limited success in cities such as Zurich, Paris, Prague, Vienna, and London. See Peter Jelavich, "Cabaret in Concentration Camps," in Michael Balfour, ed. *Theatre and War, 1933–1945* (New York: Berghahn Books, 2001), 137.
13. H. W. Koch, *In the Name of the Volk: Political Justice in Hitler's Germany* (London: I. B. Tauris Publishers, 1989), 93. See also *The Statutory Criminal Law of Germany*, War Department Pamphlet No. 31-122, U.S. Government War Office, August 1946.
14. Lipman, *Laughter in Hell*, 34.
15. Ibid., 141.
16. Larson, *Wit As a Weapon*, 48–49.
17. Ibid., 74.
18. Hindenburg was president of the Weimar Republic beginning in 1925. By 1932, the last year of the Weimar Republic, political jokes centering on Hindenburg circulated at an ever-increasing rate. See F. K. M. Hillenbrand, *Underground Humour in Nazi Germany, 1933–1945* (London: Routledge, 1995), 1.
19. Ibid., 22.
20. Ibid., 78.
21. Ibid., 77.
22. George Eisen, *Children and Play in the Holocaust* (Amherst: The University of Massachusetts Press, 1988), 5.
23. Lucjan Dobroszycki, ed., *The Chronicle of the Łódź Ghetto, 1941–1944*, trans. Richard Lourie et al. (New Haven, CT: Yale University Press, 1984), 49.
24. Sheng-mei Ma, "The Great Dictator and Maus: 'The Comical' Before and After the Holocaust," *Proteus: A Journal of Ideas* 12 (1995), 47.
25. Lipman, *Laughter in Hell*, 151.
26. As cited in ibid., 151.
27. As cited in Peter Jelavich, *Berlin Cabaret* (Cambridge: Harvard University Press, 1993), 263–64.
28. Ibid., 264–65.
29. Ibid., 265.
30. As cited in Lipman, *Laughter in Hell*, 73.
31. Viktor Frankl, *Man's Search for Meaning* (New York: Washington Square Press, 1984), 65.
32. See Morreall, "Humor in the Holocaust."
33. Ibid.

34. Jim Davidson, "Holocaust Survivor Found Solace in Humor," *Newton Kansan*, 24 February 2003.
35. As cited in Morreall, "Humor in the Holocaust."
36. Chaya Ostrower, "Humor as a Defense Mechanism in the Holocaust," Ph.D. dissertation abstract (Tel Aviv University, 2000), 5.
37. Ibid.
38. Shamai Davidson, "Human Reciprocity Among the Jewish Prisoners in the Nazi Concentration Camps," in Yisrael Gutman and Avital Saf, eds., *The Nazi Concentration Camps: Structure and Aims, The Image of the Prisoner, The Jews in the Camps*, Proceedings of the Fourth Yad Vashem International Historical Conference (Jerusalem: Daf-Chen Press, 1984), 568–69.
39. Anna Pawelczyńska, *Values and Violence in Auschwitz* (Berkeley: University of California Press, 1979), 120.
40. For instance, in Nazi Germany, *Thingspiele*, or Third Reich passion plays, usually glorified Hitler. See, for example, Johannes Reichl, *Das Thingspiel: über den Versuch einer nationalsozialistischen Lehrstück-Theater* (Frankfurt am Main: Misslbeck, 1988), and Boguslaw Drewniak, *Das Theater im NS-Staat: Szenarium deutscher Zeitgeschichte, 1933–1945* (Düsseldorf: Droste, 1983).
41. Alvin Goldfarb, "Adolf Hitler as Portrayed in Drama and Film During His Lifetime," *Journal of Popular Culture* 13 (1979), 55–66.
42. David Robinson, *Chaplin: His Life and Art* (New York: Da Capo Press, 1994), 506.
43. Lipman, *Laughter in Hell*, 236–37.
44. There were some exceptions. For example, in 1937 when Larry Blake, a Brooklyn-born actor, was cast as Hitler in *The Road Back*, an adaptation of Erich Maria Remarque's sequel to his novel *All Quiet on the Western Front*, the Nazis launched an all-out campaign against Universal Studios to abandon the production. The screenplay was strongly anti-Nazi and told the story of the conditions faced by defeated German soldiers of World War I upon returning home. Although the Nazis had a strong but clandestine influence in Hollywood, Carl Laemmle, Jr., Universal's studio head, resisted the pressure. After Laemmle lost managerial control over Universal, the new regime under Charles R. Rogers yielded to many of the Nazis' demands. *The Road Back* was gutted, all Hitler scenes were removed or destroyed, and extensive cuts were made to the anti-Nazi tone of the picture. Larry Blake's performance of Hitler was never seen by more than a limited number of personnel at Universal Studios.
45. Lipman, *Laughter in Hell*, 236.
46. On 31 October 1938, Dr. Georg Gyssling, Consul of Germany, wrote to Mr. Joseph Breen, the director of the Production Code Administration of the Motion Picture Producers and Distributors of America, about a newspaper article announcing Chaplin's plans for a new film, *The Great Dictator*. Quoting from the article whose caption reads: "Charlie Chaplin will burlesque Hitler," Gyssling writes that according to the article Chaplin will play a "defenseless little Jew, who is mistaken for a powerful dictator, while in the other role you will see him as the dictator himself." The article further states that "while naturally Hitler is not mentioned, it doesn't take any Salomon or Sherlock Holmes to see it is the Führer, whom Chaplin is burlesquing," writes Gyssling. Gyssling asks the Association of Motion Pictures to look into this matter, for Chaplin's film "will naturally lead to serious troubles and complications." Gyssling had also complained about the possible production of the Warner Brothers film *Confessions of a Nazi Spy*, based on the sworn testimony given at a trial in the Federal District Court in New York City, resulting in the conviction of espionage of several foreign agents.
47. As cited in Sheng-mei Ma, "The Great Dictator and Maus," 48.
48. See Don Morlan, "The Three Stooges Contribution to World War II Propaganda: Moe Hailstone & Adenoid Hynkel's Race to the Screen," *The Three Stooges Journal* 63 (Fall 1992) and 64 (Winter 1992).
49. Robert Kurson, *The Official Three Stooges Encyclopedia* (Chicago: Contemporary Books, 1998), 364.

50. Mel Brooks did a remake of the film in 1983.
51. Lester D. Friedman, *The Jewish Image in American Film* (Secaucus, NJ: Citadel Press, 1987), 133.
52. As quoted in Annette Insdorf, *Indelible Shadows: Film and the Holocaust* (Cambridge: Cambridge University Press, 1983), 70.
53. See Richard Minear, *Dr. Seuss Goes to War: The World War II Editorial Cartoons of Theodor Seuss Geisel* (New York: The New Press, 1999).
54. Joe Grant and Dick Huemer, "Laughter Knows How to Fight," *Dispatch from Disney's*, Vol. 1, Number 1, Walt Disney Productions, 1943.
55. Terrence Des Pres, *Writing Into the World. Essays: 1973–1987* (New York: Viking, 1991), 278.
56. Lawrence Baron, *Projecting the Holocaust into the Present: Trends in Holocaust Feature Films Since 1990* (Lanham, MD: Rowman and Littlefield, in press).
57. Des Pres, *Writing Into the World*, 281.
58. It is often difficult to distinguish clearly between representations that could be viewed solely as anti-Nazi and those that solely depict the Holocaust, as the boundaries blur in representing the historical moment. For instance, some could argue that *Hogan's Heroes* or *The Producers* deals with the "mindset" of the perpetrators in a humorous manner, and are thus appropriate to include in a paper on Holocaust humor. I take a more inclusive approach and have chosen humorous depictions that are either popular or interesting to illustrate my points.
59. Jeffrey Shandler, *While America Watches: Televising the Holocaust* (New York: Oxford University Press, 1999), 144-5.
60. See Robert Clary, *From the Holocaust to* Hogan's Heroes: *The Autobiography of Robert Clary* (Lanham, MD: Madison Books, 2002).
61. J. Hoberman, "When the Nazis Became Nudniks," *New York Times*, 15 April 2001.
62. Ibid.
63. See A. H. Wiler's article in the *New York Times*, 7 November 1971.
64. Other films include the British comedy *Hard Battles, Soft Beds* (1974), the German film *Jakob der Lügner* (1975), and *Son of Hitler* (1978).
65. See Baron, *Projecting the Holocaust into the Present*.
66. Ibid.
67. For a strong condemnation of *Life Is Beautiful* see, for example, Sander Gilman, "Is Life Beautiful? Can the Shoah Be Funny? Some Thoughts on Recent and Older Films," *Critical Inquiry* 26 (Winter 2000).
68. David Denby, "In the Eye of the Beholder: Another Look at Roberto Benigni's Holocaust Fantasy," *The New Yorker* 75 (15 March 1999), 99.
69. Benigni also won an Academy Award for Best Actor, and the film also won for Best Dramatic Score.
70. For a good overview on the novels and films of the second generation, see Alan Berger, *Children of Job* (Albany: State University of New York Press, 1997).
71. See, for example, "My Worst Fears Realized: Woody Allen and the Holocaust," in Renee R. Curry, ed., *Perspectives on Woody Allen* (New York: G. K. Hall & Company, 1996), 218–36.
72. Alan Dundes and Thomas Hauschild document Holocaust jokes that were current in West Germany in the 1980s. Rather than gallows humor (jokes about Jews told by Jews), they document "executioners' humor," jokes enabling perpetrators to laugh at Jewish victims. Such jokes have appeared throughout Europe, North and South America, and elsewhere. For instance, jokes such as "How many Jews can you fit into a Volkswagen? Fourteen. Two in the front, two in the back, ten in the ashtray," were circulating in Europe and the United States in the 1980s. These jokes reflect group attitudes, and they are important barometers of antisemitism. At the time of this writing, a Web search on "Holocaust jokes" brought up numerous examples of this kind.
73. A study at the University of Maryland questioned 150 healthy people and 150 people who had suffered a heart attack, and found that even in positive situations those who suf-

fered heart disease were less likely to laugh. Moreover, the initial results of a five-year study at UCLA of the effects of laughter for children with cancer and AIDS showed that watching comedy videos and listening to jokes substantially lowered their stress hormone levels (*The Sunday Times Style Magazine*, 3 March 2002).
74. Ibid.
75. Douglas, "Jokes," 306.
76. Sigmund Freud, *Jokes and Their Relation to the Unconscious*, trans. James Strachey (New York: W. W. Norton, 1960), 105.
77. Ibid., 103.
78. Itzhak Galnoor and Steven Lukes, *No Laughing Matter: A Collection of Political Jokes* (London: Routledge & Kegan Paul, 1985), xi.
79. Ibid., vii.
80. Larson, *Wit As a Weapon*, 3.

– Chapter 18 –

THE HOLOCAUST IN POPULAR CULTURE
Master-Narrative and Counter-Narratives in the Gray Zone

Ronald Smelser

Napoleon is alleged to have said, "History is lies agreed upon." Historians would generally not subscribe to this cynical observation, but it does remind us that history is always contested: that there are different and competing narratives; that they are always in flux depending on surrounding circumstances; that there tend to be master-narratives, peripheral narratives, sub-rosa narratives, and bundled narratives; and that these narratives play off each other and change with regard to their influence and tenacity.

The history of the Holocaust in popular culture illustrates this set of concepts. In the early postwar period through the 1950s and into the 1960s, there was practically no Holocaust narrative. Early textbooks on World War II did not use the word, said little about the extermination camps as central to Nazi motives, and never mentioned Jews.[1] The diary of Anne Frank in the 1950s certainly had an impact, but she was viewed in the popular mind as a sole and universal figure.[2] That began to change dramatically in the 1960s, particularly in the wake of the Eichmann trial. Far from scarcely being mentioned in World War II narratives, the Holocaust has practically absorbed the war itself to become its central theme of the war in popular culture.[3]

The prevalence of this master-narrative in film, novels, memoirs, documentaries, plays, TV programs, museums, and even comic books has caused some to raise the question: Is the Holocaust being overdone?[4] The master-narrative is really an example of "bundled" narratives, that is, narratives in different media that are bundled together in the popular mind and often tend to reinforce one another. Certainly there are a number of problems

Notes for this section begin on page 283.

connected with the master-narrative that bear on its breadth, depth, ubiquity, complexities, contradictions, and misuses to make it potentially vulnerable to counter-narratives. Some of these include:

1. Trivialization: some critics felt that movies like *Life Is Beautiful* do not evince the necessary gravitas to deal with such an immense tragedy as the Holocaust;[5]
2. Relativization: the often unseemly spectacle of competing victim narratives that challenge the exclusivity of the larger Jewish one. A master-narrative that includes some people, but not all people;[6]
3. Saturation: the mind and senses becoming dulled by the ubiquity of the master-narrative;[7]
4. Memorialization: with respect to memorials and museums, Tim Cole has pointed out that "There is a sense perhaps, in which the immortalization of memory in stone leads towards a process of distancing and forgetting. Rather than a memory being alive and fluid, it becomes dead, fixed, and forgotten. . . . We will perhaps stand at the end of the twenty-first century and look upon the 'myth' of the Holocaust as largely irrelevant to the present, and live lives surrounded by Holocaust memorials which have become meaningless";[8]
5. The appearance of children/grandchildren literature, which involves the personal problems of the descendants of victims. These can be valuable in showing the ripple effect of the Holocaust over several generations, but can also represent Holocaust story-telling as therapy;
6. Fraud: cases such as Jerzy Kosinski's *The Painted Bird* and Binjamin Wilkomirski's *Fragments,* which cast doubt on the accuracy of parts of the master-narrative;[9] and
7. What some view as the misuse of the Holocaust story for doubtful personal gain, as Norman Finkelstein has pointed out in connection with slave labor and bank account lawsuits.[10]

These aspects present problems. Do they mean that the master-narrative is surfeited? No, but they do reveal a kind of vulnerability that one would expect to find in any master-narrative that shoulders the kind of responsibility as does that of the Holocaust: context for World War II and leitmotiv of the twentieth century.

Part of that potential vulnerability arises from other narratives. There are two other narratives of this period in what one might call the gray zone of popular culture—one in the United States, the other primarily in Germany but moving to the United States. These narratives are peripheral, yet each has the potential—under certain circumstances—to challenge the master-narrative. The former might be called "the Romance of the *Wehrmacht*" and the latter "The Germans as Victims."

The master-narrative, one is reminded, took thirty to forty years after the war's end to attain a predominant position, due in part to the international climate.[11] Important changes in the international context were necessary before the master-narrative could emerge. Similarly, changes in the larger context permitted the emergence of one of our counter-narratives—the myth of the "clean" *Wehrmacht*—in the 1950s. The Cold War changed attitudes dramatically in the West. Our former Allies, the Russians, were swiftly transformed into enemies, while the Germans, our former enemies and main perpetrators of the Holocaust, became friends and allies. With the vast majority of the senior officers of the newly created *Bundeswehr* having served in Hitler's *Wehrmacht,* it was inconvenient to recall that they had served in an institution that had been implicated in Hitler's murderous policies. The Adenauer regime, meanwhile, also largely abandoned the pursuit of justice vis-à-vis the former German military in exchange for the relatively easy assimilation of millions of German soldiers into the newly created West German democracy.[12] In this climate, it was not propitious to emphasize the Nazi mass murder of the Jews nor to remember the *Wehrmacht* as a criminal institution.

Just at the point in history when a comprehensive narrative on the Holocaust could not yet effectively emerge, a counter-narrative that cast the "Germans as Heroes" was developing in the American context. It represents the second use of the "Lost Cause Myth" in American history for political purposes. The first was the romanticization of the Confederacy in the wake of the Civil War as a method of reuniting a people riven by civil conflict. Men like Lee and Jackson, who had been traitors in the war, leading a rebellion to destroy the Union, became in later decades tragic heroes fighting a noble struggle against an overwhelming military and industrial machine. This theme became an integral and dominant part of American popular culture from the late nineteenth century to the civil rights era of the mid-twentieth century and is still with us as a strong peripheral narrative. One notes, however, that the rapprochement that this "Lost Cause mythology" permitted and furthered took place on the backs of the African-American population in both the American South and North. That the South stood for slavery was either forgotten entirely or that sordid institution was itself romanticized in films such as *Gone with the Wind.*[13]

Similarly, within the context of the Cold War, a romanticization of the German military, primarily in its war against the Soviet Union, took place, which ultimately portrayed the *Wehrmacht* as well as the *Waffen*-SS as valiant soldiers fighting for their Fatherland against a malevolent foe, who prevailed only because of an overwhelming superiority in masses of men and material. Like an earlier myth, this Cold War one permitted a rapprochement: this time between Germans and Americans, but on the backs of the victims of the Holocaust, who were either not mentioned or relegated to a shadow world peopled only by SS and police villains.

This romanticization was fed from a number of streams, again bundled narratives, all of which flowed into American mainstream popular culture. The most important of these was the military's. Hundreds of studies were completed for the Americans by German officers in the late 1940s and into the 1950s under the direction of Franz Halder, former chief of the German

General Staff, which portrayed the war in the East from the point of view of the German military. This view cast the Russians in the role of barbarian, Asiatic hordes from whom the *Wehrmacht* tried to save Western civilization. Absent from these narratives was any reference to the *Wehrmacht*'s complicity in Nazi war crimes, which, when they were mentioned at all, were laid entirely at the feet of the party and the SS (but not the *Waffen*-SS, who remained "soldiers like any other"). The view communicated here was one of a group of professionals whose efforts were frustrated by the irrational interference of a rank amateur, Hitler.[14] That we were receptive to this point of view is attested to not only by a host of popular books and memoirs that emerged under the impact of these studies but also by the fact that Halder was the only German general ever to be decorated both by Adolf Hitler and by a president of the United States. In 1960 John F. Kennedy presented Halder, who had received a military medal from Hitler, with the Civilian Service Award, the highest civilian award this country had to offer for his services.[15]

Another stream that continues to feed this narrative was that of exculpatory memoirs of German generals like Heinz Guderian, Erich von Manstein, Hans von Luck, and F. W. von Mellenthin. Far from being obscure sources in the libraries of West Point and the Pentagon, these were and remain best-sellers, always included as primary or secondary selections of national book clubs. A well-publicized edition of Guderian's *Panzer Leader* was re-released in 2002 as a main book club selection on the fiftieth anniversary of its original appearance.[16] The book, written by one of Hitler's favorite generals, who accepted Hitler's gift of an estate worth RM 1,240,000, continues the heroic and exculpatory narrative propounded by most of the former German generals from "the other side of the hill," in the words of British historian Basil Liddell-Hart, himself complicit in the mythologizing.[17]

Among the usual disclaimers, Guderian claims not to have heard of the infamous Commissar order. Part of the sales success of Guderian's book over the last fifty years has been the legitimization given it by prominent American and British scholars. The cover of the new edition has the names of three scholars who "legitimize" Guderian: B. H. Liddell-Hart, who wrote the original foreword; Kenneth Macksey, who wrote the introduction; and Stephen Ambrose's cover blurb: "This brilliant memoir is a mesmerizing read. . . . A great book by a great soldier." On the back cover John Eisenhower, son of the former president, proclaims that Guderian's book "belongs on the shelf of every serious student of this violent twentieth century." Dwight Eisenhower, as NATO commander, in a sense set in motion this mythologizing of the German military by famously giving it a clean bill of health in 1951. His son continues this tradition.[18]

Another classic in which the myths are retold is the memoir from the pen of former major general F. W. von Mellenthin, *Panzer Battles,* which went through six printings in the United States between 1956 and 1976 and continues to be a very popular read.[19] As late as 1943, he contends, German soldiers were still being welcomed as friends by Ukrainians and White Russians, "who even after the numerous and disastrous setbacks the German armies received during the Winter of 1942–3, took up arms to free Russia from the yoke of Communism." Unfortunately, only the cruel policies of Gauleiter Koch, Hitler's paladin in the Ukraine, ruined this promising alliance. In any case, the Germans were "faced by a ruthless enemy, possessed of immense and seemingly inexhaustible resources." Mellenthin is no admirer of the Russian soldier who comprised these masses and whom he views through racial glasses. "The stoicism of the majority of Russian soldiers and their mental sluggishness make them quite insensible to losses. The Russian soldier values his own life no more than those of his comrades. . . . Life is not precious to him. He is immune to the most incredible hardships, and does not even appear to notice them; he seems equally indifferent to bombs and shells."[20]

No wonder, since many of the Russian soldiers were "Asiatics dragged from the deepest recesses of the Soviet empire." The author waxes eloquently on the racial defectiveness of the Russian soldier. "He is essentially a primitive being, innately courageous, and dominated by emotions and instincts. . . . He lacks any true religious or moral balance, and his moods alter between bestial cruelty and genuine kindness." His other qualities include "dullness, mental rigidity, and a natural tendency toward indolence." That the Germans were nevertheless kind to the Slavic subhumans, according to Mellenthin, was partly reflected in their humane policy with regard to the evacuation of Russian civilians. "The most important point was traffic control, for these wandering masses had to be very carefully handled." The policy was a great success. "No serious losses were suffered and military operations were not greatly hindered." This humane German policy toward refugees Mellenthin contrasts with that of the Russians who would drive tanks through the columns. That the Germans lost in the end to the *Untermenschen* had to be explained. Mellenthin's answer in brief: "The achievements of the German soldier in Russia clearly prove that the Russians are not invincible. . . . Even in the critical years of 1944–5 our soldiers never had the feeling of being inferior to the Russians—but the weak German forces were like rocks in the ocean, surrounded by endless waves of men and tanks which surged around and finally submerged them."[21]

Another Mellenthin book on his comrades in World War II is a long paean of praise to the German generals. One of his favorites is Erich von Manstein, father of the 1940 victory over France and a man of honor and principle, who, when he heard Hitler announce in March 1941 that the upcoming Russian campaign would be a war without mercy, "found himself facing a conflict between obedience and his conscience, and he told the commander of Army group North that he could not carry out such instructions, which were against his sense of honor as a soldier." This sense of honor was further evidenced, according to Mellenthin, in Manstein's concern about the "accommodation and feeding of the enormous numbers of prisoners of war" and "the needy civilian population of the Crimea." This is the same Manstein who, in November 1941, issued an order to his troops—a variation of Reichenau's infamous 10 October order—that exactly corresponded to Hitler's announcement of the previous March. The order noted that "the food supply situation in the homeland makes it necessary that the troops live off the land as much as possible and that, over and above that, the greatest possible stocks be made available to the homeland. Especially in the enemy cities, a large part of the population will have to starve. . . ." The German soldiers are exhorted to "summon up understanding for the necessity of harsh punishment of Jewry, the spiritual carrier of Bolshevik terror."[22]

Alexander von Stahlberg, Manstein's adjutant, revealed in his memoirs, *Bounden Duty,* how shocked his boss was when he discovered that Jews were being shot in large numbers in the army's rear area in the Crimea. Jörg Friedrich and other historians have revealed, to the contrary, that Manstein knew exactly what was going on all along and in fact had quarreled with the SS (*Einsatzgruppe* D) over who should get custody of the pocket watches of the 23,000 Jews who had been murdered in the Crimea while Manstein was commander of the 11th Amy there. Manstein also issued an order on 20 November 1941 demanding that "The soldier must understand the need to take harsh reprisals on Jewry, the intellectual support of Bolshevik terror."[23]

The production of memoirs has continued as German officers of ever-lower rank produce their own memoirs in print for American audiences, always reinforced by the reprints of those of their deceased seniors. Colonel Hans von Luck's *Panzer Commander* appeared in 1989 complete with an adulatory introduction by—again—the ubiquitous Stephen Ambrose.[24] Von Luck admits in his preface that without the encouragement from his friend, Ambrose, the memoirs "would never have been written." He "forced me to relate my experiences, and constantly gave me the heart to continue." Ambrose in his introduction writes, "Except for General Eisenhower I have never met a veteran I liked or admired more." As for those von Luck fought alongside, he writes, "But the real hero of this book is the German soldier. . . . They were remarkable for their endurance, tenacity, boldness, comradeship and loyalty. So was Colonel von Luck. One of the outstanding soldiers of World War II, he has written a memoir that is simply superb, an instant classic that will be read for decades to come." In his memoirs von Luck once again repeats the enduring myths: friendly Russians who welcomed the Germans, who reopened the churches; unfortunate Russian prisoners, who were too numerous for the Germans to provision properly, despite their best efforts; and, of course, the derogatory descriptions of the Russians, who "were like children who could tear the wings off a fly one minute, and in the next, cry over a dead bird. They might share their last crust of bread one moment and then hit the same person over the head."[25]

A reinforcing stream is that of popular histories, particularly illustrated ones. One especially egregious case of this is the books by Paul Carell. Carell's books on World War II, which appeared in America in the 1960s and continue to be commercial successes, have sold in the millions, both in Germany and in the United States. They overshadow scholarly books by a wide margin in terms of numbers of books sold. The two best known on the Eastern front are *Hitler Moves East 1941–1943* (1965) and *Scorched Earth* (1966). *Hitler Moves East* went through no fewer than five printings between February 1965 and January 1967 alone.

In his books Carell presents the *Wehrmacht* as heroes fighting for a lost cause, as tragic yet valiant after Stalingrad. The pictures follow suit: clean, handsome, forward-looking, heroically posed, physically vigorous, smiling, and determined young German soldiers making sanitized war. The only ugliness is in the Russian POWs. There is nothing here of *Einsatzgruppen*, massive theft of food and clothing, laying waste to cities and villages, shooting of hostages, or depredations against the civilian population. Civilians are in fact portrayed as welcoming the Germans and, in turn, being helped by them, the equivalent of GIs handing out candy bars and cigarettes. [26]

When the SS appears in Carell's books, they are depicted only as fighting troops, soldiers like all the others. Later in the war, the Germans are depicted as disheveled but unbowed, fighting desperately with all the means at their disposal against overwhelming material and labor resources, determined to prevent or to delay as long as possible the arrival of the Asiatic hordes in the Fatherland. The war in the East is portrayed as a preventive strike, the Russian victory largely owing to American aid. Turning points in the war, such as Stalingrad or Kursk, are portrayed with a subtext that suggests regret that they did not turn the other way. The text reflects the shibboleths developed right after the war. A competent, professional army leadership was thwarted by an erratic, amateur dictator who was responsible for all the mistakes the generals would have avoided if war had nevertheless broken out. The narrative is an engaging, dramatic one that lends itself to a mass readership.

Who was this Paul Carell? His real name was Paul Karl Schmidt, and his past reveals something of his motivation in "educating" several generations of Germans and Americans about the war.[27] Schmidt was Ribbentrop's press spokesman in the Foreign Ministry (Chief of the Press Section), a convinced Nazi who joined the party at the age of twenty during his student years and advanced to *Gauführer* of the NS *Studentenbund*. In 1934 he joined the SS and rose to the rank of SS-*Obersturmbannführer*. As press spokesman in the Foreign Ministry, Schmidt rivaled the other two media competitors, Otto Dietrich and Hans Fritsche over at the Propaganda Ministry. He was in charge of presenting the Third Reich to the foreign media. His leitmotivs under the rubric "Europe for the Europeans" were the elimination of Bolshevism, the elimination of the Jews, and the removal of England and Roosevelt from Europe as the "pimps of Bolshevism." In formulating propaganda, Schmidt maintained close relations with the *Wehrmacht* leadership. He also created a publishing empire, which he ran through a holding company, anticipating his postwar career.

With respect to the Holocaust Schmidt made his own modest propaganda contribution. He was quoted in July 1943 as saying, "Jewry must be combated, wherever it appears, because it is a political pathogen, ferment for the decay and death of any national organism." Ten months later, informed by his friend SS-*Brigadeführer* Edmund Veesenmayer that the Jews of Budapest were about to be deported to Auschwitz for extermination, Carell, mindful of public opinion in the European countries he was courting, made the following suggestion on 27 May 1944:

> I gather from a very good overview of the Jewish actions in Hungary, planned and underway, that a major action is planned for the Budapest Jews in June. This action will be sufficiently extensive so as to excite much attention and be the occasion of a powerful reaction. Our opponents will scream and refer to the hunting down of human beings, etc., and use horror stories to get the neutrals all worked up. Thus, I would like to suggest that we might prevent these things by creating pretexts and explanations for the action, for example, finding explosives in Jewish clubs and synagogues, plans for organized sabotage, coups d'états, assaults on policemen, big-time shady deals with currency to undermine the Hungarian economy. The keystone of such an action would have to be a particularly flagrant case which would justify the big roundup.[28]

After the war he wrote articles on the war for the popular journal *Kristall,* part of Axel Springer's right-wing publishing empire. In the 1950s, then, he began to publish highly popular illustrated histories of World War II, many of which appeared in English translations in the United States and, as we have seen, sold in huge numbers. Carell was still spreading his mythology as recently as 1992 (he died in 1997) with books like *Stalingrad Sieg* and *Untergang der 6. Armee.*

Recently reinforcing these popular histories are the memoirs of ordinary German soldiers. These men, who were boys during the war and who are now retired from jobs and professions, do not have the necessary perspective to formulate sophisticated arguments about causation and responsibility, strategy and operations. None of them ever sat at a conference table next to Hitler. Moreover, they are writing half a century after the events they describe. Interestingly, nearly all of these memoirs depict events on the Eastern front. No other theater of war comes into the picture, except occasionally peripherally.

What these memoirs convey is the filth and fear and death of war on the ground against an implacable, often invisible foe. The style is simple; the prose is colorful and turgid. The stories resemble closely those related for decades in Germany in the popular Landser series but never translated into English. Some sample titles include Günter Koschorrek, *Blood Red Snow: The Memoirs of a German Soldier on the Eastern Front* (2002); Henry Metelmann, *Through Hell for Hitler* (2000); Werner Adamczyk, *Feuer! An Artilleryman's Life on the Eastern Front* (1992); Gottlob Bidermann, *In Deadly Combat: A German Soldier's Memoir of the Eastern Front* (2000); Alfred Novotny, *The Good Soldier* (2003); Armin Scheiderbauer, *Adventures in My Youth: A German Soldier on the Eastern Front, 1941–45* (2003); Gerhardt B. Thamm, *Boy Soldier: A German Teenager at the Nazi Twilight* (2000), to mention only a few. Most are translations; some are from the pens of men who emigrated to America after the war.

These memoirs reinforce the war in the East from the German perspective. The Russians are a distant, anonymous foe. Since conditions were so barbaric in the East, the memoirs also arouse the sympathy of the reader. Absent entirely are the depredations of the *Wehrmacht* against the civilian population, which is invariably depicted as friendly to the Germans. Some of these men became prisoners, and this experience gives them the opportunity in retrospect to excoriate the Soviet system. All in all, this flood of recent enlisted men's memoirs not only paints a sympathetic picture of the Germans in the East and reinforces the mythology of the generals' memoirs from the grassroots perspective but also joins the emerging narrative of "Germans as victims."

Most of the soldiers' memoirs are from *Wehrmacht* veterans. But one is by an unreconstructed, unrepentant *Waffen*-SS veteran named Hans Schmidt: *SS Panzergrenadier: A True Story of World War Two* (2001). Ironically, Schmidt fought first on the western front in the Battle of the Bulge, then in the final battle for Hungary, then was taken prisoner by the Americans. Schmidt, unlike the others, spices his narrative with ideological observations that demonstrate his unrepentant nature. He served temporarily with Jochen Peiper, perpetrator of the infamous Malmedy Massacre on captured American soldiers, an incident that Schmidt denies ever happened.[29]

Schmidt contends that "concepts like honor, loyalty and chivalry have been eliminated from Western civilization by Bolshevism and Western 'Liberalism.'" When shown pictures of Dachau and Buchenwald by one of his American captors, he responds, "My reaction was not unlike that of today when viewing the same: I shrugged my shoulders." To him this was, and remains, obviously propaganda. In conversation with this same American, Schmidt was at pains to defend Germany. "Fortunately, I was able to tell this American soldier as much as I knew about Germany and the Third Reich, and why, in my opinion, we had been the true defenders in the war we had just lost." In a tribute to his *Wehrmacht* comrades he says, "It was mainly the common soldiers of the Army who from 1941 to 1945 held the 1000-mile front from the Baltic to the Black Sea and thereby prevented the Bolshevists from overrunning Europe. Without the sacrifice of these brave men, Europe, the cradle of Western Civilization, would by now have descended into total darkness. It is doubtful whether the United States could have withstood the succeeding assault." Finally, he excoriates the Americans for their treatment of German POWs right after the war in "Eisenhower's death camps," buying into the myth developed by James Bacque in his book *Other Losses*.[30]

What is particularly disturbing here is the fact that this book glorifies Nazi Germany, demonizes the Soviets, denies the Holocaust, and excoriates the Americans. It features as blurbs on the dust jacket rave reviews from Byron de la Beckwith, the murderer of Medgar Evers, and John Schmitz, retired USMC colonel, former right-wing congressman from Orange County and Libertarian Party candidate for president in 1972, who hopes that this book "will be mandatory reading at all American military academies." Clearly this book is more on the margins of the gray zone than those mentioned above and yet has been assimilated into the mainstream by the "bundling" phenomenon, whereby Internet booksellers include it with more mainstream books in their advertising: "Customers who bought this book also bought: [followed by titles]." In addition, enthusiastic comments from an often clueless readership included in the ad for the book lend it even more respectability. This is something I have observed for years, as these counter-narratives appeared side by side with respectable mainstream scholarship in catalogues such as Hamilton, but reaching a much larger audience here.

I will include here a word about the Internet, which has emerged as incredibly important in disseminating books with the counter-narrative. I have identified hundreds of Web sites devoted to romanticizing the German Eastern front experience during World War II and—most disturbingly—disproportionately the *Waffen*-SS. Virtually every former *Waffen*-SS division has its own devotees and Web sites. Web pages have quizzes: Which commanders served where and when? There are several "panzer of the month" pages and a "choose your favorite German commander" page. On one Web site enthusiasts can send in their personal information and receive authentic *Wehrmacht* pay books and dog tags made to order; they literally "morph" into a German soldier. Chat rooms mourn the loss of strategic battles like Kursk and Stalingrad. Endless discussions range from minutiae over German uniforms and artillery specs to "what if" speculations about crucial turning points in the war in the East, which might have gone the other way. Medals, uniform parts, and other "icons" are available in proliferation for purchase. Only by examining the number of "hits" on these Web sites have the true dimensions of this subculture begun to emerge.

It is also proving to be a morally troubled world, as the "romanticizers" become increasingly aware of the Holocaust and its horrors. Many Web sites include disclaimers; they are not "Nazis," they claim, nor are they disseminating the "Nazi line," whatever they understand that term to mean. Many reluctantly admit that the Germans committed crimes, but quickly add that so did the Russians and the Americans. Generally, though, they try to exculpate their real heroes—the *Waffen*-SS. The recent "Crimes of the *Wehrmacht*" exhibit in Germany they find offensive in the extreme. The conversations also champion unsung heroes, often highly decorated junior *Waffen*-SS officers. One of their universal heroes, inexplicably, is Jochen Peiper, whose SS unit was responsible for the massacre of U.S. soldiers at Malmedy. They are fascinated with the ultimate icons of their culture—living German veterans who join them in their chat rooms. Many of these veterans have joined in the conversation in cyberspace with their own Web sites.

This "glorification" (not too strong a word) of the German military continues in the popular literature, in war gaming, on the Internet, resonating with hundreds of thousands if not millions of Americans who read these books, play these games, and surf the Web. It represents something more than just the "pop fascism" to which Alvin Rosenfeld has alluded, although he is certainly correct in maintaining that "the eye and the ear remain hungry for visual representations of the Hitler period and apparently are far from being sated."[31] Particularly seductive, I would maintain, are the visual images. Wolf Kansteiner insightfully analyzed the Guido Knopp documentaries on the Nazis shown on German television, but his point remains valid for much of what I am talking about here in America, including television (and Knopp's work is appearing in the United States as well).[32] He points out that Knopp makes Nazi kitsch, and that he gives the audience the opportunity to "play Nazi" in the visuals while keeping the text safely in the conventional realm. The historical facts and contextualization of the Nazi period tend to get lost in a world of images. Images once accompanied the text; now they virtually shove it aside. Knopp also brings the voice of the wartime German into the public arena, which previously had been limited to venues like *Landser* magazine. Thus, even documentaries, which should be designed to continue and refine the master-narrative, instead can serve the counter-narrative. This offering of images without contextualization unfortunately plays an important role in our public schools, when teachers without sufficient knowledge of historical facts and interpretations routinely bring to class objects—war souvenirs, flags, helmets, captured firearms and uniforms, and so on—that only contribute to the romanticization of Fascism in the minds of adolescents. *Triumph of the Will,* which for decades in America was the most widely shown film on the Nazis, illustrates this phenomenon quite dramatically.

No one suggests that this narrative is anywhere close to challenging the master-narrative at this point in time. It remains on the margins but is by no means negligible. Nor are the people who are captured by this mythology Holocaust deniers. They share in the same mass culture that watches *Schindler's List* and reads *The Diary of Anne Frank.* But there still run two narratives, I think, in separate compartments. The counter-narrative I have just described is not fading. On the contrary, the Internet has given it new vibrancy and extended numbers of adherents. The many similar titles that reflect it are "bundled," especially in online bookseller ads. It may never challenge the master-narrative. But we must remember that which narrative predominates does not depend on its moral power alone, but also on circumstances, national and international. Nor does this narrative deny the Holocaust; it just does not mention it or, if it does, confines the villains to Hitler and the SS-police.

It is ironic that while in a part of the American popular culture over a number of decades the German military could be elevated to the level of beleaguered heroes, in Germany the victim narrative—the second gray-zone narrative I will describe here—was cast into the shadows, again by surrounding circumstances. At the end of World War II most West Germans were in a state of shock and denial so that an adequate narrative of their suffering could only slowly gain traction in the national popular culture, although it remained in the folk discourse and in many local publications.[33] (In talking to older Germans during my first visits to Germany in the 1960s, had I known nothing about World War II, I could have been forgiven for thinking that the conflict had begun in 1944 with an Anglo-American-Soviet invasion of Central Europe).

When the victimization theme did appear in novels, films, and other venues, the focus was on the fate of expellees and missing *Wehrmacht* prisoners in Russia. Bombing of German cities got short shrift, not surprisingly, since the first two were largely the result of Soviet actions in the East, while the bombing was an Anglo-American undertaking, and the West Germans were hesitant to accuse their protectors. In any case, what is telling is that postwar West German accounts did establish a moral equivalency between the suffering of Germans and that of the Jews. After a flowering in the 1950s, the "Germans as Victims" narrative tended to fade with the gradual integration of expellees, repatriation of the last POWs, and the rebuilding of cities, although it never disappeared entirely. The revelations that came in the wake of the Eichmann and Auschwitz trials brought a new awareness to West Germans as to the crimes of the Nazi regime and brought the master-narrative of the Holocaust into a predominant position in the minds of West Germans to the point where the narrative of their own victimization did not again take center stage, partly out of a widespread sense of guilt and shame over the German perpetrator role.

In recent years, however, with a new generation in power that had scarcely been born during the war, in addition to a reunited nation, many of whose members feel that expiation has been sufficient, a twin victim narrative has come out of the shadows and achieved a great deal of circulation in Germany. Here two narratives have emerged most dramatically and have been "bundled" into a powerful combination: the firebombing of German cities and the expulsion of millions of Germans from Eastern Europe. It was a discussion opened in the late 1990s by W. G. Sebald's critique of West German literature for ignoring the firebombing of World War II, in which 620,000 Germans, mostly women, children, and the elderly, perished.[34]

The publication of Jörg Friedrich's *Der Brand* in 2002 intensified the discussion, as had the appearance in 1999 of Gert Ledig's *Vergeltung*, the very graphic description of the bombing of a German town written in 1956. Friedrich's book, which deals with the raid on Hamburg in July 1943—Operation Gomorrah—is especially controversial for his use of specific Holocaust terminology with respect to the bombing. Allied Bomber Group V becomes *Massenvernichtungsgruppe #5;* an air raid basement becomes a *Krematorium;* cities to be bombed are *Hinrichtungsstaetten;* the bombing of libraries is *Bücherverbrennung;* cores of bombed cities are called *Vernichtungszentren*. The Allies plan a *Kolossalmassaker* from the air, which, in turn, is a tempered version of the "gas and bacteria attack" on sixty German cities planned by Winston Churchill. Prior to his account of the demolition of each city, Friedrich gives a tender description of a soon to be obliterated historical landscape evocative of laments over the disappearance of Jewish culture in Eastern Europe.[35] This is ironic in that Friedrich is a leftist liberal whose other work exposed the criminal nature of the *Wehrmacht* in the East. This narrative has come to our shores of late. Sebald has been translated into *On the Natural History of Destruction,* after having been featured in the *New Yorker.* Günter Grass's *Crabwalk* is also available in English. Ledig's *Vergeltung,* first published and largely ignored in Germany in 1956, then republished with greater fanfare and resonance in 1999, has recently appeared in English as *Payback*.³⁶

The discussion of Germans as victims was given tremendous impetus by the 2002 publication of Grass's *Crabwalk,* which treats the sinking of the *Wilhelm Gustloff* by a Russian submarine in January 1945. The ship was full of refugees, mostly young women, more than nine thousand of whom went down with the ship. The publication of this account—ironically by someone on the political left—allowed a discourse that had been marginalized and largely limited to rightist nationalists to enter the mainstream. It did so mainly in the context of the mainstreaming of another victim narrative that had remained in the German gray zone: the expulsion of 14 million Germans from East-Central and Eastern Europe at the end of the war, most dramatically that of 3.5 million Sudeten Germans from Czechoslovakia. Unlike their counterparts from other parts of Europe, the Sudetens became and have remained a potent political force in Germany, particularly in Bavaria, where conservative politicians ignore them at their peril.

The expulsion discussion has a particularly sharp cutting edge—the plans that have been advanced by Erika Steinbach and Peter Glotz to build a large *Zentrum gegen Vertreibungen* (Center against Expulsions) in Berlin, which would, in a moral sense, rival the recently constructed Holocaust memorial there. The advocates put their plans into a larger European context and use the language of the European community, but the center clearly represents a renationalization of the expellee question.³⁷ What emerges from this literature and these activities is a kind of moral equivalency in the twin narratives, which threatens to rival the moral message that has long been part of the Holocaust master-narrative.

While still overwhelmingly a German popular culture theme, the "Germans as Victims" narrative has the potential to link up with the "Germans as Heroes" theme in American popular culture to form a compelling story—if circumstances permit. Certainly, much of the refugee memoir material has been translated and published in the United States, although it has not yet achieved a critical mass. Some titles include Wolfgang W. E. Samuel's *German Boy: A Child at War* (2001)—this book has also received an American imprimatur with a long and sympathetic introduction by the omnipresent Stephen Ambrose; Lali Horstmann's *Nothing for Tears* (2000); Erich Anton Helfort's *Valley of the Shadow* (1997); Eva Krutein's *Eva's War: A True Story of Survival* (1990); Luisa Lang Owen's *Casualty of War* (2003); and Elizabeth Walter's *Barefoot in the Rubble* (2000). Active in Chicago, Walter was the American Legion Auxiliary Woman of the Year in 1998 and had sufficient clout to have an exhibit based on her book displayed in the Russell Senate Office Building Rotunda in Washington, DC, during that same year. Alfred de Zayas, an author, attorney, and activist on behalf of the victimized Germans who has been trying for years to bring Americans the story of German expellees in a number of sympathetic books, must be experiencing a feeling of vindication.[38] There has not yet, however, been a major film that could make this set of narratives "gel."[39]

Again, no one expects either the "Germans as Victims" theme or the continued romanticization of the *Wehrmacht* to displace the massively present and continuing master-narrative of the Holocaust. But, as we have seen, historical memory is quite malleable and subject to historical circumstance. What once emerged from the gray zone to mastery could, under certain circumstances, return. It is but a short journey from silence to salience and back.[40]

Notes

1. See Donald Schilling, "Representing the Holocaust in the General Histories of World War II," in Ronald Smelser, ed., *Lessons and Legacies V: The Holocaust and Justice* (Evanston, IL: Northwestern University Press, 2000), 279–95.
2. See Alan Mintz, *Popular Culture and the Shaping of Holocaust Memory in America* (Seattle: University of Washington Press, 2001), 16–18; also Peter Novick, *The Holocaust in American Life* (Boston: Houghton Mifflin, 1999), 117–18.
3. In the words of Yehuda Bauer, "Whether presented authentically or inauthentically, in accordance with the historical facts or in contradiction to them, with empathy and understanding or as monumental kitsch, the Holocaust has become a ruling symbol in our culture. I am not sure whether this is good or bad, but it seems to be a fact." "The Significance of the Final Solution," in David Cesarani, ed., *The Final Solution: Origins and Implementation* (London: Routledge, 1994), 306.
4. This question is raised rhetorically by movie reviewer Michael Medved in his review of *Max* and *The Pianist* with the words, "Two more Holocaust movies: Earnest, artful . . . but unnecessary?" WorldNetDaily.com, 10 January 2003.
5. See comments by Susan Magminas on the occasion of the debate between Judith Doneson and Stuart Liebman, "Life Is Beautiful . . . But Is It Accurate?" www.peacemagazine.org/0001/jagminas.htm, 24 June 2003.
6. For the debate on this issue leading up to the opening of the United States Memorial Holocaust Museum, see Novick, *The Holocaust in American Life*, 216–20.
7. See Frank Rich, "Journal: The Holocaust Boom. Memory As an Art Form," *New York Times*, 7 April 1994, who talks about the "limited shelf life" of Holocaust representations.
8. See Tim Cole, *Selling the Holocaust: From Auschwitz to Schindler: How History Is Bought, Packaged, and Sold* (New York, Routledge, 1999), 5–6. His point can also apply to many all-too-familiar and iconic photographs of the Holocaust.
9. See Norman Finkelstein, *The Holocaust Industry: Reflections on the Exploitation of Jewish Suffering* (London: Verso, 2000), 55–62.
10. Ibid., chapter 3.
11. Novick, *The Holocaust in American Life*, chapter 5, discusses the Holocaust narrative under the impact of the Cold War.
12. See Norbert Frei, *Adenauer's Germany and the Nazi Past: The Politics of Amnesty and Integration* (New York: Columbia University Press, 2002).
13. There is an abundance of literature on this topic. See Gary W. Gallagher and Alan T. Nolan, eds., *The Myth of the Lost Cause and Civil War History* (Bloomington: Indiana University Press, 2000); also Tony Horwitz, *Confederates in the Attic: Dispatches from the Unfinished Civil War* (New York: Pantheon, 1998).
14. On the Halder project see Christian Greiner, "'Operational History (German) Section' und 'Naval Historical Team.' Deutsches militärstrategisches Denken im Dienst der ameri-

kanischen Streitkräfte von 1946 bis 1950" in *Militärgeschichte: Probleme, Thesen, Wege* (Stuttgart: 1982), 409–35; also Charles Burdick, "Vom Schwert zur feder. Deutsche Kriegsgefangene im Dienst der Vorbereitung der amerikanischen Geschichtsschreibung über den Zweiten Weltkrieg," in Donald S. Detweiler, ed., *Militärgeschichtliche Mitteilungen* 2/1971, 69–80. Detweiler edited 213 of these studies in twenty-four volumes in World War II German Military Studies (New York: Garland, 1979). On the Russians as conveyed by the German generals, see in particular volume 19.

15. See Gerd R. Überschär, *Generaloberst Franz Halder. Generalstabschef, Gegner und Gefangener Hitlers* (Zürich: Muster-Schmidt Verlag, 1991), 101.
16. Heinz Guderian, *Panzer Leader* (Cambridge, MA: Da Capo, 2002).
17. On Guderian's corruption see Gerd Überschär and Winfried Vogel, *Dienen und Verdienen: Hitlers Geschenke an seine Eliten* (Frankfurt: S. Fischer, 1999), 168–74; Alexander von Stahlberg describes a conversation between Guderian and Manstein in which Manstein was supposedly "speechless" at Guderian's description of his gift from the Führer. See Alexander von Stahlberg, *Bounden Duty: The Memoirs of a German Officer, 1932–45* (New York: Brassey's, 1990), 372. Guderian allowed the following after the war in a conversation with fellow captured officers, monitored by the Americans, with regard to National Socialism: "The fundamental principles were fine." Seventh Army Interrogation Center, 26 July 1945. In U.S. National Archives and Records Administration (NARA), RG 319, Box 71A, Vol. 5, Folder 3.
18. See Klaus von Schubert, *Wiederbewaffnung und Westintegration: Die innere Auseinandersetzung um die militärische und aussenpolitische Orientierung der Bundesrepublik 1950–1952* (Stuttgart: Dt. Verl.-Anst., 1970), 82f.
19. F. W. von Mellenthin, *Panzer Battles: A Study of the Employment of Armor in the Second World War* (New York: Ballantine, 1976).
20. F. W. von Mellenthin, *Panzer Battles: A Study of the Employment of Armor in the Second World War* (Norman: University of Oklahoma Press, 1956), 255–56, 259, 281.
21. Ibid., 319, 350, 352, 292–93, 365.
22. F. W. von Mellenthin, *German Generals of World War II: As I Saw Them* (Norman: University of Oklahoma Press, 1977), 28, 32.
23. Stahlberg, *Bounden Duty,* 312–14. On the watch story, see Jörg Friedrich, *Das Gesetz des Krieges: Das deutsche Heer in Russland 1941 bis 1945. Der Prozess gegen das Oberkommando der Wehrmacht* (Munich: Piper, 1993), 669–71. The Manstein quote is from Manfred Messerschmidt, "Forward Defense," in Hannes Heer and Klaus Naumann, eds., *War of Extermination: The German Military in World War II, 1941–1944* (New York: Berghahn Books, 2000), 392.
24. Hans von Luck, *Panzer Commander* (New York: Dell Publishing, 1989).
25. Ibid., viii, 2–3, 70–72.
26. For a much more accurate portrayal of the *Wehrmacht* behavior on the ground in Russia see Christoph Rass, *"Menschenmaterial": Deutsche Soldaten an der Ostfront. Innenansicht einer Infanteriedivision, 1939–1945* (Paderborn: Schoeningh Verlag, 2003), esp. 333–85.
27. On Schmidt/Carell see Peter Longerich, *Propagandisten im Krieg: Die Presseabteilung des Auswärtigen Amtes unter Ribbentrop* (Munich: R. Oldenbourg, 1987), 88, 144–45, 152–55, 167–70, 284–91.
28. "*Notiz für Herrn Staatssekretär,*" Staatsarchiv Nürnberg NG-2424, quoted in Otto Köhler, *Wir Schreibmaschinentäter. Journalisten unter Hitler und danach* (Cologne: Pahl-Rubenstein, 1989), 105–6 (author's translation).
29. Hans Schmidt, *SS Panzergrenadier: A True Story of World War Two* (Pensacola, FL: self-published, 2001), 259.
30. Ibid., 296, 305–6, 309. See James Bacque, *Other Losses: An Investigation into the Mass Deaths of German Prisoners at the Hands of the French and Americans After World War II* (Toronto: Stoddart, 1989), 325ff.
31. Alvin Rosenfeld, "The Holocaust in American Popular Culture," *Midstream* (June/July 1983), 53–59, esp. 53.

32. Wolf Kansteiner, "The Radicalization of German Memory in the Age of Its Commercial Reproduction: Hitler and the Third Reich in the TV Documentaries of Guido Knopp," presented at the annual German Studies Association meeting, 18–23 September 2003, New Orleans, Louisiana, Panel 137.
33. On this theme see Robert G. Moeller, *War Stories: The Search for a Usable Past in the Federal Republic of Germany* (Berkeley: University of California Press, 2001).
34. W. G. Sebald, *Luftkrieg und Literatur* (Munich: Carl Hanser Verlag, 1999).
35. Jörg Friedrich, *Der Brand: Deutschland im Bombenkrieg, 1940–1945* (Munich: Propyläen, 2002). See the review of Friedrich's book by Jörg Arnold in H-German, 3 November 2003, 354, 388, 358.
36. W. G. Sebald, *On the Natural History of Destruction*, trans. Anthea Bell (New York: Random House, 2003); Günter Grass, *Crabwalk* (London: Harcourt, 2002); Gert Ledig, *Payback*, trans. Shaun Whiteside (London: Granta Books, 2003).
37. See the *New York Times* online article by Richard Bernstein, "Honor the Uprooted Germans? Poles Are Uneasy," 15 October 2003. A Bundestag majority voted to erect such a center. See www.german-foreign-policy.com, 17 May 2002.
38. De Zayas has written a number of books on this theme, including *A Terrible Revenge: The Ethnic Cleansing of the East European Germans, 1944–1950* (New York: St. Martin's Press, 1994); *The German Expellees: Victims in War and Peace* (New York: St. Martin's Press, 1993); and *Nemesis at Potsdam: The Expulsion of the Germans from the East* (Lincoln: University of Nebraska Press, 1989), among others.
39. On the importance of film and memory, see Judith Doneson, *The Holocaust in American Film*, 2nd ed. (Syracuse, NY: Syracuse University Press, 2002). "Yet interest in this Jewish past," Doneson writes, "might have remained dormant, as we have seen, without American cinematic representations of the Holocaust casting their Hollywood shadow over European history" (220).
40. See Mintz, *Popular Culture and the Shaping of Holocaust Memory in America*.

– Chapter 19 –

THE GREY ZONE
The Cinema of Choiceless Choices

Lawrence Baron

The Grey Zone
Directed by Tim Blake Nelson
(United States: The Goatsingers, Killer Films,
Martien Holdings, Millennium Films, 2001)

> We do not believe in the most obvious and facile deduction: that man is fundamentally brutal, egoistic and stupid in his conduct once every civilized institution is taken away, and that the Häftling is consequently nothing but a man without inhibitions. We believe, rather, that the only conclusion to be drawn is that in the face of driving necessity and physical disabilities many social habits and instincts are reduced to silence.
>
> —Primo Levi, *Survival in Auschwitz*

Based on Dr. Miklòs Nyiszli's Auschwitz memoir and Primo Levi's trenchant essay "The Gray Zone," Tim Blake Nelson's *The Grey Zone* constitutes the most graphic cinematic portrayal to date of the death camp at Birkenau.[1] Nyiszli occupied a privileged position among the camp's inmates in return for performing autopsies on twins who died as a result of Josef Mengele's experiments. As a reward for his services, Nyiszli obtained permission to save his wife and daughter from liquidation by securing them a transfer to a "safer" work camp. The beneficiaries of ample food and living quarters, the Hungarian Jews of the Twelfth *Sonderkommando* delayed their deaths by four months by supervising the stripping of Jews before their executions, removing the cadavers from the gas chambers, and incinerating them in open pits or crematoria. Although coerced to do these repugnant

Notes for this section begin on page 291.

tasks, the "special squadron" and the doctor enabled Auschwitz-Birkenau to function respectively as an efficient extermination factory and a medical research clinic.

Nelson's image of the camp as a factory pervades the film. A grayish cloud of ashen emissions from the crematoria chimneys darkens the already drab colors of the heaps of bodies, the uniforms of the guards and inmates, and the interiors of the undressing rooms and gas chambers. The main characters employ industrial euphemisms about their heinous duties to shield themselves from the reality that they are killing and burning human beings.[2] Nelson deleted panoramic shots of the camp to evoke a feeling of claustrophobia that the *Sonderkommando* experienced as it abetted the Germans in herding multitudes of Jews into the gas chambers, confiscating their belongings, and carrying their corpses to the crematoria for disposal.[3]

The ambient noise consists of the roar and crackling of fires, occasional gunshots in the background, the hum of electrical generators, and the air rushing into exhaust fans removing the lethal fumes of the gas in the chambers. Nelson intended to make it impossible for the characters to ever forget that they are "inside the very organs of the most massively lethal killing apparatus ever assembled."[4]

The Grey Zone plunges its audience into the netherworld of amoral choices facing the members of the *Sonderkommando*. A handheld camera glides through dimly lit corridors, tracing the steps of Nyiszli rushing to save a comatose man who had overdosed on sedatives to kill himself. Later in the film, a flashback recalls the events that had culminated in his suicide. The man belonged to the *Sonderkommando* and carted bodies to the furnaces. Dumping the deceased in front of a grate, he recognized his wife and daughter among the corpses. Devastated by the loss of his entire family, he had lost the will to live. An inmate named Hoffman summoned Nyiszli to revive the expiring man. Other *Sonderkommandos* resent that the doctor would deny someone the right to die under such circumstances. While one prisoner physically restrains Nyiszli, another smothers the man with a pillow. A third comments, "It's what he wanted, that's all." Should the doctor have tried to prolong the life of the suicidal man? Were the inmates murderers because they had honored his wish? Nelson refrains from judging either.[5]

After showing the disintegration of moral standards at Auschwitz, Nelson introduces the sights and sounds of a typical workday in the camp. Tossed over the shoulder of a former comrade, the suffocated man is carried down into a tunnel to the furnaces. The sound of the fires gets louder as the ovens come into view. An outdoor shot of the chimneys brightens the night sky with leaping flames. Juxtaposed to this iconographic image is a daytime picture of an innocuous-looking red-brick building, which houses the machinery of death. The lawn in front of the structure is green, trimmed, and well watered by sprinklers. Most of the people walking around its perimeter are wearing civilian clothing and not striped uniforms. Pieces of furniture await storage in the camp's warehouses. Inside a gas chamber, inmates hose away the blood, excrement, and urine left behind by the last group of Jews poisoned there. Other prisoners scrub and repaint the walls in preparation for the next trainload of Jews. In a nearby office, Mengele compliments Nyiszli on his professionalism and informs him that the "volume" of their research will be increasing soon.

A transport carrying the next shipment of Jews rumbles toward the camp. The camera focuses first on the frightened eyes of a Jewish girl inside a cattle car. As she looks around at the faces of the other Jews penned in there with her, the camera replicates her gaze. They look more dazed than frightened. In the Union Munitions Plant at Auschwitz the women workers are smuggling gunpowder out of the factory. They hide it on the bodies of dead Jews so it can be collected by the *Sonderkommando*. The conspirators realize that their clandestine activity jeopardizes the lives of all the women in their work detail. Their leader, Rosa Robota, has become so inured to suffering by her ordeal that she callously remarks, "What's the fucking difference when you're dead anyway?"

As Rosa's remark indicates, Nelson injects brusqueness and contemporary swearwords into the conversations the prisoners conduct among themselves. He resorts to profanities and staccato exchanges to illustrate the breakdown of civility and temporality rather than to replicate the way inmates actually spoke to one another: "Characters interrupt one another in the film; they don't have time to listen. Their interactions are never sentimental or quaint. They curse, cut one another off."[6]

This crude discourse contrasts sharply with the sanitized terminology the inmates use when they talk about the nature of their duties. They parrot the innocuous euphemisms the Nazis invented to camouflage the ghastly purpose of the extermination facility. According to Nelson, "institutional language reflects and can even forge institutional behavior, and the people forced to work inside the crematoria learned quickly . . . that to survive they had to treat their tasks just as the Nazis taught them to describe them: as 'work' and nothing more."[7]

Meanwhile, the cycle of death and disposal continues. Two SS men empty a canister of Zyklon B into a slot in the gas chamber's roof. Muffled screams follow. Jews in long lines calmly file down the steps to their demise to the strains of a Strauss waltz played by an orchestra consisting of inmates. This adds a surreal quality to the scene but diminishes its credibility. At Auschwitz orchestras did entertain the SS, greet Jewish transports, and perform marches for inmates marching to their work assignments. They never, however, serenaded Jews descending into the inner sanctum of the gas chambers.[8] An aerial shot reveals the flames and smoke pouring out of the chimneys, which are the final destination of the Jews standing in the lines. The crematorium room looks like a foundry with the *Sonderkommando* stoking its fires with human carcasses. A truck dumps the ashes of incinerated Jews, which in turn are shoveled into the Vistula River. Nyiszli suggests to Commandant Muhsfeld that his severe headaches and heavy drinking are caused by the recent increase in the level of "cargo."

The casual reference to "cargo" segues into a scene of the *Sonderkommando* feasting upon food and liquor confiscated from the new arrivals. Several prisoners debate whether they should use the weapons and gunpowder they have procured to blow up the crematoria or escape to testify about the atrocities they have seen. Hoffman pointedly asks, "Do you want to look anyone in the face, if any of your family is even alive, and tell them what you have done for a little more life, for vodka and bed linens?" This actually never was a matter of contention among the *Sonderkommando*.[9] Similarly, Nelson artificially heightens the suspense by having the SS torture Dina to force her to disclose what she knows about the impending attempt to sabotage the crematoria. The interrogations and the delayed hanging of the women implicated in the plot, however, occurred after the revolt.[10]

The transport finally pulls into Auschwitz. The camera work again acts as a proxy for the eyes of the girl on the cattle car. Her group is ordered to undress and put their clothes and shoes on numbered hooks to help them locate their belongings after taking a delousing shower. An agitated man demands that Hoffman admit that the new arrivals will soon be exterminated. Hoffman fails to allay his suspicions, and the man calls him a "Nazi liar." When Hoffman notices that the man still possesses a wristwatch, he commands him to surrender it. Enraged and ashamed by the man's truthful accusations, Hoffman seizes upon the watch as a pretext to pummel him into a bloody pulp in front of his hysterical wife. An SS guard shoots her in the head and smiles as he hands the watch to Hoffman. The girl watches in astonishment. Appalled by his own brutality, Hoffman crouches on the floor, realizing he has overstepped the limits of what is acceptable behavior even for a *Sonderkommando*.

The camera returns to the girl's gaze as she enters the gas chamber. Panic sets in among those condemned to die. The door is closed shut by the *Sonderkommando*. The bloodcurdling screams of the victims resound in the ears of the distraught Hoffman. As his crew hauls away bodies, Hoffman detects that the girl is still breathing. Somehow she survived in an air pocket on the wet floor. A subsequent flashback replicates what she saw as she lay choking at the bottom of a pile of corpses. Saving her becomes Hoffman's opportunity to redeem himself.

As her face becomes visible for the first time, the audience cannot help but perceive that this teenager bears a striking resemblance to Anne Frank. In his director's notes, Nelson indicates that reading Primo Levi convinced him that people are not basically "good at heart" as Anne Frank hoped.[11] Casting an actress who looks like Anne Frank may have been motivated by Nelson's intent to challenge the optimism of Anne before she endured incarceration at Auschwitz and Bergen-Belsen.

The leaders of the *Sonderkommando* argue over whether keeping the girl alive is a "distraction" from the uprising or proof that they are not murderers. The story of the girl who survived a gassing is true, but the insertion of it as a factor in the *Sonderkommando* rebellion is something Nelson does to heighten "dramatic tension."[12] At a time prior to the insurrection, Muhsfeld rejected Nyiszli's pleas to spare her and summarily shot her in the back of the neck about a half hour after learning of her existence.[13] In the movie Muhsfeld forces the nameless girl to witness the reprisal executions of the Twelfth *Sonderkommando*. Hoffman and Max console themselves by the thought that at least "we did something." Driven to madness, the girl runs toward the electrified fence but is gunned down before she reaches it.

Paradoxically, the most moving scene in *The Grey Zone* jettisons the film's graphic realism in favor of a more stylized look and imaginary monologue. The new *Sonderkommandos* carry the girl's body to the crematorium. Filmed at a slightly slower speed with a soft focus, the figures incinerating her appear more like automatons than human beings. The girl's voice-over stoically describes her own immolation:

> I catch fire quickly. The first part of me rises in dense smoke that mingles with the smoke of others. Then there are the bones, which settle in ash, and these are swept up to be carried to the river, and the last bits of our dust, that simply float there in air around the working of the new group.
>
> These bits of dust are grey. We settle on their shoes and on their faces, and in their lungs, and they begin to get so used to us that soon they don't cough and they don't brush us away. At this point, they're just moving. Breathing, and moving, like anyone else still alive in that place. And this is how the work continues.[14]

The Grey Zone received mixed reviews.[15] Even its harshest critics conceded that it was a well-intentioned attempt to dramatize the moral morass in which the Jewish *Sonderkommandos* of Auschwitz were mired. What distinguished the positive from the negative reviews was whether the critic believed that the depths of human depravity manifested in the operation of the extermination camp could ever be authentically represented. Roger Ebert gave the movie four stars for its devastating realism: "I have seen a lot of films about the Holocaust, but I have never seen one so immediate, unblinking, and painful in its materials." Elsewhere he opines, "there cannot be a happy ending except that the war eventually ended."[16]

Manohla Dargis of the *Los Angeles Times* doubted that any movie could convey what transpired at Auschwitz. She contended, "It isn't just that there's something unsettling about a film that aestheticizes a crematorium; it's that there's something trivializing about the very effort." She reveals her biases against the feasibility of ever capturing the horror of a Nazi death camp on film by confiding that "the crimes committed at Auschwitz . . . were beyond what cinema entertainment, which demands realism but not necessarily truth, can show us." Dargis questions casting David Arquette as Hoffman because he starred in Wes Craven's *Scream* trilogy, not distinguishing between the type of audiences who go to films like *The Grey Zone* and those who attend teenage slasher movies.[17]

Dargis finds flaws in the casting, filming, and scripting of *The Grey Zone* because she shares Claude Lanzmann's belief that the Holocaust defies representation in fictional forms. Nelson anticipated this sort of specious criticism. In the preface to his screenplay, he states, "Of course, those in the

Lanzmann camp will claim there are no events like the Holocaust, that it stands alone. It most certainly does. Yet to extend sanctimoniously the place it occupies to an area so far beyond that of other tragedies that it becomes untouchable for certain forms of artistic expression is not only self-righteous, but also self-defeating."[18] Nelson acknowledges that his "jagged and hard realism" is not the only way to depict the Holocaust and refers to the differing but affecting approaches taken by Roberto Benigni in *Life Is Beautiful* and Steven Spielberg in *Schindler's List*.[19]

Whether the movie compels the viewer to think "this is how it must have been"[20] or to dismiss it for being "nowhere horrible enough,"[21] *The Grey Zone*'s grueling assault on the emotional, moral, and visual sensibilities of its audience destined the film for box-office failure.[22] It was not booked at many theaters and quickly disappeared from release.[23] Advertisements for the movie did not conceal its grim subject matter. The poster tagline, "The story you haven't seen," was positioned beneath a close-up of the haunting face of the girl. The preview began with this frank voice-over: "We can't know what we're capable of, any of us. How can you know what you'd really do to stay alive, until you're asked? I know now that the answer for most of us is anything." Even the uprising is placed in this defiled perspective: "In order to survive, they did the unthinkable, but it gave them the chance to attempt the impossible."

When *The Grey Zone* appeared on videotape and DVD, it was marketed as a movie about resistance despite Nelson's explicit wish that it not be misconstrued as a heroic film.[24] On its jacket, the recognizable faces of actors Harvey Keitel, Mira Sorvino, David Arquette, and Steve Buscemi hover above the tagline: "While the world was fighting . . . a secret battle was about to erupt." The narrator on the trailer declares, "Their freedom was lost; their hope was shattered, until the sight of one girl inspired a people to rebel."[25] By fabricating a causal relationship between these two events, the film's distributors obliterated the gray zone between historical authenticity and truth in advertising.

Notes

1. See the chapter on "The Gray Zone" in Primo Levi, *The Drowned and the Saved*, trans. Raymond Rosenthal (New York: Summit Books, 1988), 36–69; Miklòs Nyiszli, *Auschwitz: A Doctor's Eyewitness Account*, trans. Tibère Kremer and Richard Seaver (New York: Arcade Publishing, 1993).
2. Tim Blake Nelson, *The Grey Zone: Director's Notes and Screenplay* (New York: Newmarket Press, 2003), 145.
3. "Deleted Scenes," *The Grey Zone*, DVD (United States: Lions Gate Home Entertainment, 2003).
4. Nelson, *Director's Notes*, 165.
5. Ibid., 141.
6. Ibid., 158.
7. Ibid., 145.

8. Danuta Czech, "The Auschwitz Prisoner Administration," in Yisrael Gutman and Michael Berenbaum, eds., *Anatomy of the Auschwitz Death Camp* (Bloomington: Indiana University Press, 1994), 367–68.
9. Nyiszli, *Auschwitz*, 114–25.
10. Nelson, *Director's Notes*, 157–58; Hermann Langbein, "The Auschwitz Underground," in Gutman and Berenbaum, eds., *Anatomy of the Auschwitz Death Camp*, 502.
11. Nelson, *Director's Notes*, ix.
12. Ibid., 155–56.
13. Nyiszli, *Auschwitz*, 88–92.
14. Nelson, *Director's Notes*, 120–21.
15. "*The Grey Zone*," www.metacritic.com. This site assigns numerical averages to reviews by leading movie critics in the United States and then weights them according to the influence of the reviewer. On a scale of 0 to 100, *The Grey Zone* received an average score of 61.
16. Roger Ebert, "*The Grey Zone*," www.suntimes.com (25 October 2002).
17. Manohla Dargis, "Meticulous Details Add Up to Holocaust Trivia in *Zone*," www.calendarlive.com (18 October 2002), 1–2.
18. Nelson, *Director's Notes*, xii. Nelson never capitalizes *holocaust*, apparently as a way to dispute its absolute uniqueness and unrepresentability.
19. Ibid., 163.
20. Joe Leydon, "Shades of Grey," *San Francisco Examiner* (25 October 2002).
21. Dargis, "Meticulous Details," 1.
22. Martin A. Grove, "Nelson's Passion Key to 'Grey' Reaching Screen," www.hollywoodreporter.com (18 October 2002). In this article, Nelson remembers one of the movie's financial backers telling him, "We don't plan on making all our money back. We simply must be involved in the making of this film."
23. *The Grey Zone*, "Box Office and Business Data," www.IMDb.com. *The Grey Zone* grossed slightly more than US$500,000. It cost US$5,000,000 to produce. It played at movie theaters for only nine weeks. The most screens on which it was ever shown nationally in any one week was 36.
24. Nelson, *Director's Notes*, 158–59.
25. *The Grey Zone* (United States: Lions Gate Home Entertainment, 2003). See "Posters" and "Trailers" for *The Grey Zone*, www.IMDb.com.

– *Part Four* –

JUSTICE, RELIGION, AND ETHICS DURING AND AFTER THE HOLOCAUST

Throughout *The Drowned and the Saved* and particularly in its chapter on "The Gray Zone," a crucial tension emerges between Primo Levi's caution about making moral judgments and his persistent use of ethical evaluations. Levi understood that human cravings for simple understanding include the need "to separate evil from good, to be able to take sides, to emulate Christ's gesture on Judgment Day: here the righteous, over there the reprobates."[1] The gray zone, however, defied such neat separations. Indeed, Levi argued, it ought to "confuse our need to judge."[2]

Nevertheless, moral judgments resound in Levi's writing. He never hesitated, for example, to call the creation of the *Sonderkommando* a "demonic crime," the worst committed by National Socialists.[3] Recalling and quoting from his introduction to the German edition of *Survival in Auschwitz*, Levi said that he had written that book "to bear witness, to make my voice heard by the German people, to . . . remind them of what they have done, and say to them: 'I am alive, and I would like to understand you in order to judge you.'"[4] Levi added that he did not hate the German people, but then he delivered a comment whose moral critique was as devastating as it was understated: "I cannot say I understand the Germans."[5]

That statement contained an ethical judgment that went much deeper than conventional moral evaluations, which assume that people are more or less in agreement about shared rights and responsibilities, even though they may violate those norms. For Levi, the Germans were not understandable because, as he put it, they had willingly abandoned civilization. Levi clarified these points in comments that he made about collective guilt in 1961:

Notes for this section begin on page 297.

> The very expression "collective guilt" is a contradiction in terms, and it is a Nazi invention. Every person is singly responsible for their actions. Every German (and non-German) who took part in the murdering is fully guilty; their accomplices are partially guilty . . . ; less guilty but still contemptible are the many who did nothing in the full knowledge of what was happening, and the mass who found ways of not knowing because of their hypocrisy or poverty of spirit.
>
> In this way, we can build up a picture which belies the heroic inventions of Nazi propaganda: not collective guilt, but collective cowardice, a collective failure of intellectual courage, a collective foolishness and abandonment of civilization.[6]

Responsibility had to be assessed case by case, individual by individual, but when Levi took those steps, the accumulated judgments led him to see that moral reasoning could not comprehend Nazi Germany, at least not completely.

Levi's ethical analysis did not stop there. Acknowledging that he lacked trust in "the moral instinct of humanity, in mankind as 'naturally' good,"[7] Levi warned that the existence of Nazi Germany and the Holocaust meant that realities akin to them could appear again—were even likely to do so—because no community had guaranteed immunity against them.[8] What could humankind do, he wondered, to keep such threats at bay? One of Levi's responses was to study the gray zone and to grasp why there must be caution as well as boldness in making moral judgments. The existence of the *Sonderkommando,* for example, raised questions for those who wanted simple understanding: "Why did they accept that task? Why didn't they rebel? Why didn't they prefer death?"[9] Historical inquiry, Levi emphasized, had done much to put such questions to rest. "Not all did accept," he rightly stated, "some did rebel, knowing they would die."[10] As for those who went on to do the miserable work, Levi asserted that "no one is authorized to judge them, not those who lived through the experience of the Lager and even less those who did not."[11]

Levi did not find that imperative applicable to all prisoners in the *Lager.* Especially when the gray zone was under consideration, moral evaluations had to be made. Otherwise, important differences of power and privilege would be ignored, significant distinctions between individuals and their responsibilities overlooked. On the whole, however, Levi urged careful deliberation about any moral assessment of prisoner behavior, and he held that view for multiple reasons. First, quite apart from the Holocaust, it was illogical to think that ordinary men and women would behave like "saints and stoic philosophers."[12] If the *Lager*'s realities were taken into account, Levi thought that the prisoners' behavior could be called "rigidly preordained. In the space of a few weeks or months the deprivations to which they were subjected led them to a condition of pure survival, a daily struggle against hunger, cold, fatigue, and blows in which the room for choices (especially moral choices) was reduced to zero."[13] Levi strengthened his argument for caution about making moral judgments by adding two more reminders: "one is never in another's place," he emphasized, and "nobody can know for how long and under what trials his soul can resist before yielding or breaking."[14]

Levi's position harbored danger, if not some inconsistency. While defending the *Lager*'s victims against inappropriate moral judgments, would his appeal to human frailty and even to a kind of behavioral determinism open the door too widely for rationalizations that undermined the moral accountability he so much wanted to support? However unintentionally, was Levi handing the Holocaust's perpetrators and bystanders lines of reasoning that they could use to excuse themselves? To disarm the danger, Levi brought attention back to the pressurized structure of the gray zone. "Certainly," he argued, "the greatest responsibility lies with the system,"[15] but the system was neither abstract nor anonymous, and it was definitely not something that its victims had chosen or created, even though their entrapment meant that they would contribute to weaving its ensnaring web. Levi minced no words about German murderers and their accomplices, the experts at planning and implementing the "useless violence" that was rife in the Holocaust.[16] They were the ones who initiated, built, and maintained the system. Apart from them—from Hitler and Himmler to Muhsfeld and Pannwitz—it had no reality, but with them the degradation and killing went on and on.

Levi's ethics is instructive. By learning to restrain moral judgment appropriately, by not misdirecting it in ways that blame the victims, one can better focus where the ethical critique and its accompanying senses of moral obligation belong. Moral judgment should focus on the persons and decisions, the institutions and policies that created the Holocaust and every other form of genocide. Accompanying that judgment should be an intensification of responsibility to resist such people and to intervene against those circumstances, to honor those who do so, to embrace the survivors with compassion, to mourn and remember those who were murdered, and to restore—as far as possible—what was lost.

Levi's moral agenda is demanding. One reason, as he knew, is that restoring what the Holocaust took away is not only difficult but in many ways impossible. So when Levi asks what we can do to prevent further abandonment of civilization, he is aware that this work must be done in ruins where words such as *justice, religion, ethics,* and even *civilization* itself are deeply wounded, and not least because National Socialism co-opted them all. Nazism appealed to justice, used religion for its own ends, advanced its aims as ethical, and envisioned a new civilization even as it drew on science, technology, art, music, literature, and philosophy to attract its following. Levi's gray zone of Auschwitz, then, creates additional gray zones of the Holocaust and its aftermath when we think about the meaning of such elemental concepts and developments.

The essays in Part 4 respond to those challenges. Three of them deal with people who were more or less Levi's contemporaries. Noting that Levi's chapter on "The Gray Zone" discusses only one "gray-zoner" at length, Richard Rubenstein refocuses attention on Chaim Rumkowski, head of the Jewish Council in the Lodz ghetto. Rubenstein is interested in Rumkowski as a bureaucrat who served masters intent on the massive destruction of human life, including even the life of Rumkowski's Jewish people. Rubenstein argues instructively, and his view is largely supported by Levi, that Rumkowski, try as he might to save Jewish lives, was not only put in positions of choiceless choice but also took decisions of his own that were corrupting and lethal. Showing that gray can turn into black, Rubenstein's case study of Rumkowski as "a bureaucrat serving a genocidal conqueror" brings moral judgment to bear in ways that are not identical to Levi's but that complement and amplify his moral outlook because they clarify how destructive decision-making can be.

Related concerns govern the essays by Jeffrey Lewis and Jonathan Petropoulos, which concentrate on questions about justice concerning Nazi personnel and assets. Lewis traces the careers of two German scientists—Adolf Butenandt and Georg Melchers—to illustrate how "shades of gray best describe the relationship between researchers such as Butenandt and Melchers and the Nazi government." Implicated to greater or lesser degrees in scientific study that advanced the Third Reich's interests, these men also provide instructive case studies about the development, politics, and ethics of Germany's post-Holocaust scientific community. Petropoulos, who argues convincingly that the Nazi regime was "a kleptocracy of the first order," uncovers additional moral dilemmas by exploring the postwar compromises the Allies made in dealing with the material assets of significant Nazi figures. The limitations on justice revealed by this chapter in the history of denazification reverberate in contemporary life.

Primo Levi did not live to see it, but as the twentieth century drew to a close, an extensive international campaign of reparation and restitution was launched to compensate Holocaust victims and their families for the massive losses, including property of diverse kinds, that Nazi Germany and its collaborators had inflicted. Desires to restore at least a modicum of justice motivated these initiatives, but in the process Levi's insight would again loom large: "The greater part of historical and natural phenomena are not simple, or not simple in the way that we would like."[17] Michael Bazyler explores gray-zoned features of these compensation procedures, noting how their successes were accompanied by consequences that proved to be "detrimental, or at least morally ambiguous." If the post-Holocaust reparation and restitution campaign is to be a model for responses to other demographic catastrophes, including possible effects as a deterrent to genocide, then not only its successes but also its pitfalls will continue to deserve attention.

Rubenstein, Lewis, Petropoulos, and Bazyler detail why the Holocaust made *justice* a gray-zoned word. It might be hoped that religion and ethics could rescue that situation, but again such matters are far from simple. As Victoria Barnett points out, the Holocaust not only compromised religion, but in many ways its fury depended upon its Christian forms in particular. Understanding how and why that happened, a complex process to which Barnett contributes significantly, is crucial if integrity is to be restored to the Christian tradition after Auschwitz. "One of the lasting lessons of the Holocaust," she concludes, is that "the quest for ethical clarity and historical truth go together." Picking up on that motif, John Roth finds the historical truth to be that ethics is in a double bind after the Holocaust. Drawing on the work of the Holocaust survivor-philosopher Sarah Kofman, his essay explores how the Holocaust produces an obligation to make ethics stronger and yet also creates the choking feeling that "too much harm has been done for a good recovery to be made." Study of the Holocaust's gray zones suggests that no question is more important than how—or even whether—ethics can be restored after Auschwitz.

Primo Levi was not sure that ethics could be restored after Auschwitz, but he knew that the failure to try would exact a price higher than humankind could pay. That theme is illustrated in "News from the Sky," which appeared in *L'altrui mestiere* (1985), a volume of Levi's essays that was translated into English as *Other People's Trades* (1986 UK, 1989 US). There Levi notes that Immanuel Kant, the famous German philosopher, emphasized two wonders in creation: the starry sky above and the moral law within. "I don't know about the moral law," Levi muses. "Does it dwell in everyone? . . . Every passing year augments our doubts."[18] The starry sky seemed to be another matter, but even those considerations gave Levi pause. The stars remain, but the sky—the territory of bombers, missiles, hijacked planes that can unleash terror and death—has become an ominous place because of World War II, the Holocaust, and that which followed.

"The universe is strange to us, we are strange in the universe," wrote Levi, and "the future of humanity is uncertain."[19] Nevertheless, Levi had his hopes. "There are no problems that cannot be solved around a table," he said, "provided there is good will and reciprocal trust."[20] Much hinges on that qualification, for good will and reciprocal trust remain in short supply. That scarcity is one result of the Holocaust's gray zones. As the essays in Part 4 spell out, humanity's future depends on our responses to them.

Notes

1. Primo Levi, *The Drowned and the Saved*, trans. Raymond Rosenthal (New York: Summit Books, 1988), 37.
2. Ibid., 42.
3. Ibid., 53.
4. Ibid., 173–75.
5. Ibid., 174.
6. Primo Levi, *The Voice of Memory: Interviews, 1961–1987*, ed. Marco Belpoliti and Robert Gordon; trans. Robert Gordon (New York: The New Press, 2001), 180–81.
7. Ibid., 180.
8. See Levi, *The Drowned and the Saved*, 199.
9. Ibid., 58.
10. Ibid.
11. Ibid., 59.
12. Ibid., 49.
13. Ibid., 49–50.
14. Ibid., 60.

15. Ibid., 44.
16. See Levi's chapter on "Useless Violence" in *The Drowned and the Saved*, 105–26.
17. Levi, *The Drowned and the Saved*, 37.
18. Primo Levi, *Other People's Trades*, trans. Raymond Rosenthal (New York: Summit Books, 1989), 20.
19. Ibid., 22–23.
20. Levi, *The Drowned and the Saved*, 200.

– Chapter 20 –

GRAY INTO BLACK
The Case of Mordecai Chaim Rumkowski

Richard L. Rubenstein

In *Moments of Reprieve* and elsewhere Primo Levi observes that totalitarian regimes typically "create a vast zone of gray consciences that stand between the great men of evil and the pure victims."[1] However, Levi discusses only one gray zone character at any length, Mordecai Chaim Rumkowski (1877–1944), who served as the Nazi-appointed *Älteste der Juden* (Elder of the Jews) in Litzmannstadt from October 1939 to August 1944.[2] Nor was Levi alone among writers, novelists, and historians in taking a special interest in Rumkowski.[3] The latter's career during the Nazi occupation exemplifies some of the most corrupting issues confronting a bureaucrat serving a genocidal conqueror.

Our attempt to understand Rumkowski through Levi's eyes may be helped by a consideration of some aspects of Levi's life. According to Massimo Giuliani, an Italian authority on Levi and an important Jewish thinker, Levi spoke of his own true identity as being that of a centaur, a hybrid mixture of the rational and moral and amoral animalism. Moreover, Levi insisted that every human being is a centaur.[4] Nevertheless, Levi believed that men and women could overcome their animal side by making order where chaos had reigned, or *tikkun 'olam*, the restoration of the world so that Auschwitz might never be repeated. Writing about Auschwitz was Levi's way of doing precisely that.

According to Giuliani, Levi regarded the fostering of *tikkun 'olam* as his path to *salvazione*, a term that had for him absolutely no religious overtones. For Levi, there were two types of *salvazione: la salvazione del capire* (salvation of understanding) and *la salvazione del riso* (salvation of laugh-

Notes for this section begin on page 308.

ter). Giuliani therefore proposes to translate the term by a neologism, "salvaction," a strictly human endeavor, with no reference to divinity, which is realizable through actions that belong only to human beings, namely, understanding and laughter.[5] In Levi's case it is through words and reflection that he finds his "salvaction."

Levi's *salvazione* leaves no room for any attempt either to mythologize or to appeal to Transcendence concerning Auschwitz. This is brutally apparent in his description in *The Drowned and the Saved* of the shock of his initial arrival in the camp where atomized inmates felt no hint of solidarity with him as a newcomer. Levi discerned a continuum of good and evil that extended from the victims to the perpetrators.[6] With the same objectivity that he brought to his scientific endeavors, Levi sought to depict and to understand the behavior of human beings in extreme situations.

Of all of Levi's efforts at such understanding, none has been arguably as painful as his analysis of the area of collaboration between the victims and the perpetrators. This was not appreciated by Elie Wiesel, who characterized as "unfair" Levi's analysis of the gray zone and who argued that, by speaking of the "relativity" of the victims' innocence, Levi was attenuating the guilt of the killers.[7] Giuliani insists that this is a clear distortion of Levi's thought, that Levi did not discharge guilt, but rather that he sought to explore the truth of human beings in desperate situations. Giuliani concludes his rejoinder by reminding us that Levi's approach was "rational [and] demythologizing" and that the difference in approach makes Levi "a kind of anti-Wiesel."[8] Not surprisingly, Levi disliked and rarely used the term "Holocaust," and, to the best of my knowledge, Wiesel discusses Rumkowski only once and briefly.[9]

I first became familiar with the person of Rumkowski in 1961 through reading Raul Hilberg's discussion of Rumkowski and the *Judenräte* in *The Destruction of the European Jews*.[10] Rumkowski appeared to exemplify the degree to which a conqueror's bureaucracy could co-opt the bureaucracy of a conquered people and make it complicit in the destruction of the conquered. Much of the debate concerning the *Judenräte* deals implicitly with that issue which is interwoven with the issue of hope in extreme situations. Every conquered people suffers much at the hands of its conquerors in the hope that the day of liberation may eventually arrive. Until then, suffering is to be expected, and the conquered community's leaders are faced with a terrible calculus: they may be compelled to sacrifice a part of the community so that a remnant may ultimately survive.

Moreover, for almost two thousand years Jewish culture and religion had been that of a defeated and conquered community that had developed relatively successful survival strategies under conditions of powerlessness.[11] The fundamental premise upon which that culture rested was that its overlords could more or less be trusted not to abuse their power in exchange for Jewish obedience and subordination. If Jewish sovereignty could not survive the catastrophic military defeat of the Judeo-Roman wars of C.E. 66–70, at least Jewish religion and culture could.

As Raul Hilberg has pointed out, the willingness of the Jews of Europe to follow the *Judenräte* was not something new. It was rooted in centuries-old experience and culture. I believe it rested ultimately on the culture of rabbinic Judaism.[12] Unfortunately, during the years of the Third Reich, most European Jews did not understand until too late that a radically different kind of overlord had arisen who was determined to use his power not to dominate but to exterminate. In the ghettos and the camps, Jews came to understand that the survival of at least a remnant rested on their enemy's defeat. Until then degrading strategies of submission were, of necessity, the order of the day. This was the condition under which the entrance of so many into the gray zone can be understood.

Nevertheless, Rumkowski took the historic Jewish strategies of submission to a new level, something that Adam Czerniakow, chairman of the Warsaw *Judenräte*, was ultimately unable or unwilling to do.[13] As is well known, Rumkowski's basic strategy was to make the Lodz ghetto so productive for the Germans that they would understand that their wartime economic interests were best served by allowing the ghetto's inhabitants to survive. The strategy held greater promise in Lodz than elsewhere in Poland because it was that country's most important manufacturing center. By 1914, 175 factories (33.3 percent of the total) were owned by Jews; 150 of those were textile mills. Jews also owned 18,954 small workshops (27.7 percent), 18,476 being textile enterprises. In the years immediately before World War II, of Lodz's 27,385 Jewish workers (32.9 percent of the labor force), 26,845 were employed in textile industries. In 1939 Lodz had twelve hundred enterprises and two million spindles.[14]

When the Germans first established the Lodz ghetto early in 1940, its inhabitants had few, if any, economic resources with which to stave off starvation other than the sale of their rapidly diminishing possessions at grossly disadvantageous prices. The Lodz ghetto was wholly cut off from the surrounding population, which rendered smuggling, forbidden commerce, and other forms of contact with them impossible. The ghetto was wholly dependent for its food supply on the Germans, who could open or close the spigot at will. Understanding the gravity of the situation, in April 1940 Rumkowski proposed to Dr. Karl Marder, the *Oberbürgermeister* of Litzmannstadt (the German name of occupied Lodz), that he be empowered to organize ghetto production in order to purchase food for the ghetto poor. Initially, the Germans showed little interest in Jewish labor or productivity, believing that it would hinder the development of Lodz's wartime textile industry.[15] Although Marder gave Rumkowski permission to impose forced labor on the ghetto's inhabitants, the Germans expected very little from Rumkowski's efforts.[16] They also expected that the ghetto would be evacuated in August and the Jews deported, in all likelihood to Madagascar.[17]

Contrary to German expectations, Rumkowski's plan began to work. Some Jews had been productively employed in the ghetto from the start and Rumkowski was seeking quickly to increase their number. However, in July 1940 Rumkowski reported to Hans Biebow, head of the German *Gettover-*

waltung ("Ghetto Administration"), that the ghetto's funds for purchasing food were almost exhausted and that poverty was rapidly increasing. Biebow took a skeptical, wait-and-see attitude initially. By August 1940, 70 percent of the population lacked the means to purchase food and were entirely dependent on the community. The community's funds were also depleted at the end of August, and the Germans halted deliveries for some days in September in the belief that the Jews were secretly hoarding valuables that starvation would force them to release.[18]

By early October 1940 Biebow's views had changed. He became convinced of the need to supply the ghetto with funds for food in order to facilitate Rumkowski's self-maintenance plans. At about the same time the German authorities realized that deportation was neither feasible not imminent. On 18 October 1940 they concluded "that the ghetto in Lodz must continue to exist and everything must be done to make the ghetto self-sustaining."[19]

The decision constituted a new development in the occupying power's relations with the ghetto. Lodz was officially incorporated into the Reich on 8 November 1939. Germany's initial population policy in both the old and newly annexed Reich was deadly in its simplicity: *Germans in—Jews out.* However, within a month the German authorities recognized that immediate evacuation of the Jews from the Wartheland, the newly annexed territory, was impossible. Consequently, Friedrich Übelhoer, the Nazi leader in the area, gave secret orders for the construction of a ghetto on 10 December 1939. Nevertheless, the ghetto was regarded as a temporary expedient until its inhabitants could be transferred either "further east" or to Madagascar, which, for a short time after the fall of France in 1940, was regarded by the Nazi leadership as the likeliest location for the resettlement of Europe's Jews. As noted, by mid-October the Germans recognized that transfer neither to the East nor to Madagascar was feasible and that the ghetto had to become economically self-sustaining.[20]

Thus, in the early months of the war, official German policy was resettlement, not genocide. In attempting to come to judgment concerning Rumkowski, it is important that we regard his initial decision to work with the Germans as they appeared to be in autumn of 1939, not what they revealed themselves to be in 1942 and later. When Rumkowski first sought ghetto leadership, he may have been a collaborationist making a questionable bargain with a brutally abusive occupying power, but he was not making a devil's bargain with a regime he knew to be unremittingly genocidal. Scholars are divided as to when the decision was taken to exterminate Europe's Jews, but, apart from the Soviet Union, two of the most eminent scholars in the field, Christopher Browning and Christian Gerlach, hold that the decision was taken either in October or December 1941.[21] In spite of the regime's brutality, in autumn of 1939 some measure of reluctant cooperation with the occupying authorities made sense. Rumkowski undoubtedly understood that many Jews would perish, but the threshold separating even the most vicious occupying power from a conqueror with genocidal intent had yet to be crossed. Rumkowski's original proposal was thus made to an occupying power that, with a measure of delusive wishful thinking, could be regarded as within the range of normal occupying powers, albeit one of the most vicious.

The first response by the occupying power to Rumkowski's proposal came on 30 April 1940 when the *Oberbürgermeister* of Litzmannstadt, Dr. Karl Marder, delegated to him "the task of taking all steps that are necessary for the maintenance of order in the Jewish residential life. In particular, you are responsible for an orderly economic life, the supply of food, the division of labor, health care and welfare."[22] Marder stipulated that "all dealings with German authorities" would take place *solely* through Rumkowski or his representative. To secure internal control, Rumkowski established, with German approval, a Jewish police force of twelve hundred, the *Ordnungsdienst*. Its responsibilities included the normal duties of maintaining what passed for law and order in a lawless situation, in addition to such extra-legal tasks as the confiscation of foreign currency, merchandise, gold, silver, and diamonds either on orders from Rumkowski or the German criminal police (*Kripo*).[23] The force included the *Sonderabteilung* ("Special Squad") that was established toward the end of June 1940 and cooperated with the Germans in the deportation of the Jews from the ghetto to the camps.[24] Because of its constant contact with all kinds of German police, the *Sonderabteilung* gained both influence and a measure of independence even of Rumkowski. In 1944, the year of the final deportations, the *Sonderabteilung* had the power to decide on exemptions from deportation, which were in any event only temporary.[25] Nevertheless, Rumkowski effectively claimed the power of arrest, right of seizure by oral command, and the right to grant amnesty.

As long as Rumkowski did the bidding of his German masters, there could be no successful challenge to his power from within the ghetto in spite of widespread protests, strikes, and other forms of resistance.[26] Rumkowski was in effect a one-man *Judenrat* with total control over the ghetto population. Hilberg has succinctly described the situation:

> [V]iewed internally, the ghettos were not cities but city-states and totalitarian ones at that. Each *Judenrat* operated large economic enterprises (in the case of Lodz, all economic enterprises). Each *Judenrat* had the power to impress labor. During the deportations, it became clear that each *Judenrat* also held powers of life and death.[27]

In reflecting on the testimony given at the trial of Adolf Eichmann in Jerusalem in 1961, Hannah Arendt argued:

> The whole truth was that if the Jewish people had really been unorganized and leaderless, there would have been chaos and misery but the total number of victims would hardly have been between four and a half and six million people.... About half of them could have saved themselves if they had not followed the instructions of the Jewish councils.[28]

Whatever might have been true elsewhere in Eastern Europe, Arendt's judgment does not hold for Lodz. There was absolutely no possibility that a greater number of the Jews in Lodz would have survived had they been leaderless and without organization. Locked up as they were in total isolation, their survival was always dependent on the success of Rumkowski's fundamental strategy—namely, by submission to the Germans, a portion of the community might survive Germany's ultimate defeat. As Dr. Israel Milejkowski, an inmate of the Warsaw ghetto, observed in 1942, "Endurance and survival must be our current slogan."[29] The strategy was at best a wager against extreme odds that did not pay off. Still, the ghetto inmates had no other viable choice. Disordered and disorganized, the ghetto would have descended in utter desperation into a "war of all against all," a state of nature far worse than any Thomas Hobbes could have imagined. Moreover, it is fair to ask whether, given the situation of the ghetto inmate, a less totalitarian regime could have made the ghetto economically viable, even if only temporarily.

Rumkowski started from scratch under the most miserable conditions imaginable, but within six months he could, with some justice, claim that the ghetto had become self-sufficient. Between November 1940 and August 1942 the German *Gettoverwaltung* under Hans Biebow reported a net profit from productivity and confiscations of RM 20,000,000 after deducting RM 33,000,000 for "maintenance of the ghetto." From September 1942 to September 1944, the *Gettoverwaltung* reported a net profit of RM 26,211,485 after deducting RM 43,232,813 for maintaining the ghetto's inhabitants. The ghetto provided Germany with tons of munitions, telecommunications equipment, military uniforms, boots, lingerie, temporary housing, carpets, and many other goods.[30] And, because of its productivity, it was the longest-lasting ghetto in the Nazi empire. Had a less capable and a less dictatorial administrator governed, it is highly unlikely that the ghetto could have turned out the volume of goods that it did.

Unlike the Warsaw ghetto, the enclosed Lodz ghetto was almost completely isolated from the outside world. Even those who accidentally strayed close to the ghetto fence were likely to be shot and killed on the spot. Going to the fence actually became a convenient way to commit suicide. All currency was converted into ghetto currency bearing Rumkowski's signature, currency worthless outside of the area of his control. He was also empowered to confiscate and distribute all food supplies and to seize and secure "all Jewish property" save for food, clothing, and apartment furnishings.[31] Moreover, Jews were required to work without pay, a measure that effectively made them slaves, dependent as they were upon the food, housing, and health allotment available solely at Rumkowski's discretion.

Rumkowski thus had the power to feed his favorites well and to condemn to near starvation those who measured poorly in terms of utilitarian calculation or were out of favor altogether. He controlled the ghetto police and security services, whose willingness to carry out the most draconian Nazi decrees was guaranteed by the privileges granted to them and their families. There was also little, if any, distinction between the police and the system of justice. Nor was there any possibility of appeal above Rumkowski since he was the sole intermediary between the ghetto and the Germans.[32]

Rumkowski's mindset was basically bourgeois. He assumed that economic utility would trump all other values for the Nazis. As we have seen, his assumption was initially not without a measure of plausibility. Indeed, some German leaders were prepared to let the ghetto's productive workers survive because of the needs of the military. Albert Speer may have been one of them. He later claimed that he had a "long discussion" with Hitler on 7 June 1944 in which he made Hitler aware of the "production losses that could be expected" from the total liquidation of the ghetto.[33] The respite did not last long. Two months later Himmler ordered the final liquidation of the Lodz ghetto, save for the workers required for post-liquidation clean up.

Like many others, Rumkowski failed to understand that for the Nazi leadership, at least until the racial war was won, ideological aims would trump rational economic policy, even if it entailed losing the war in the field. As Götz Aly has pointed out, in Hitler's Reichstag speech of 6 October 1939, he asserted that the "most important task" facing wartime Germany was the creation of a "new order of ethnic constellations, meaning a resettlement of nationalities so that at the conclusion of this development better lines of division arise than exist today."[34] This is not the occasion to discuss fully Nazi population policy, but one thing was certain.[35] Whatever might be the ultimate fate of Europe's Jews, the Nazis always intended that the Reich proper, which to them included the Warthegau, would be *Judenfrei*.

On 4 September 1942 Rumkowski delivered one of the most extraordinary speeches ever uttered by a Jewish leader in all of history. The day before, he told his audience, he had been given the order "to send away more than 20,000 Jews from the ghetto." He warned that the Germans would do it themselves if he refused to comply. Using the majestic plural "we," Rumkowski declared that "we" were "guided not by the thought: 'How many will be lost?' but 'How many can be saved?'" He concluded, "I must cut off limbs in order to save the body."

Rumkowski was brutally frank about the effects of his compliance. Since Rumkowski regarded productivity as the key to survival, children and the elderly were "useless eaters" (*unnütze Esser*) and he was prepared to sacrifice them. He bragged about one small victory. He had been ordered to register nine-year-old children, but succeeded in limiting the registration to children ten and over. He did suggest that there was a possible way out, which he characterized as perhaps "a satanic plan" and "perhaps not." Noting that many ghetto inhabitants were suffering from tuberculosis and their "days or perhaps weeks are numbered," he pleaded, "Give me these sick people, and perhaps it will be possible to save the healthy in their place. ... Common sense dictates that the saved must be those who have a chance of being saved and *not those whom there is no chance of being saved in any case*. ..." Apparently Rumkowski could not resist adding a note of self-pity. He told his audience, "I share your pain. I suffer because of your anguish, and I don't know how I'll survive this—where I'll find the strength to do so."[36]

The speech exemplifies Rumkowski's mindset and *modus operandi*. Save for his favorites, he had concern only for that remnant of the group likely to survive the ordeal of the war. He had no concern for the individual. To an extent apparently unsurpassed by any other Nazi-appointed Jewish leader, he was the Führer of his tiny kingdom for much of his reign, a role he appears at times to have savored. For example, Leon Hurwitz, an engineer whose diary survived the war (even though he did not), reported that Rumkowski told an associate, "'What do you know about power? Power is sweet, power is everything in life.' And with a fanatical gleam in his half-crazed eyes, he finished, 'But woe to him who makes the slightest attempt to wrest power from me.'"[37] Moreover, there is at least one report indicating that for a time Rumkowski expected a Nazi victory and hoped to lead the surviving Jewish remnant in that empire.[38]

Hurwitz describes the transformation in Rumkowski once he became assured of his power over his mini-kingdom:

> New strength poured into his old man's body, along with power. Looking fit and well-fed, he radiates energy in every direction. He wears new, military-style boots, perfectly tailored trousers and a classy, rather sporty fur coat. He strides proudly from his winter residence to the Balut Market. There he listens to reports from the police, from secret agents, from regular informers, from all sorts of schemers itching for a position. He revels in the organization he has created in such a short time. And everyone lives in fear of him.[39]

Indeed, Rumkowski appears to have exemplified to an extraordinary degree the psychological mechanism identified by Anna Freud in *The Ego and the Mechanisms of Defense* as identification with the aggressor. According to Freud, by identifying with the aggressor, the victim "transforms himself from the person threatened into the person who makes the threats."[40] Rumkowski's identification became so complete that he was reported to have adopted the oratorical techniques of Hitler and Mussolini in his speeches as well as in the unrestrained narcissistic omnipotence with which he conducted both his office and the compulsory adoration he demanded of courtiers and schoolchildren.[41]

Moreover, in many respects, Rumkowski's thinking was close to, if not identical to, that of the Nazis. If he himself was not philosophically a social Darwinist, his policies were. As the head of the ghetto he was committed unconditionally to the *Führerprinzip* and used the levers of power permitted to him by the Nazi leadership to assure his dominance over the ghetto. His was a totalitarian police ministate.

As noted, with his direct experience of the *Lager* and its overlords, Primo Levi withheld judgment on Rumkowski. He concedes that no tribunal would have exonerated Rumkowski, but that there were extenuating circumstances and cites especially National Socialism's "frightful power of corruption" that degrades its victims, making them similar to itself. Levi concludes that "We are all mirrored in Rumkowski; his ambiguity is ours, our second nature . . . his fever is ours, the fever of our Western civilization."[42]

Levi's judgment is consistent with his fundamental view of man as a centaur, but must we accept Levi's *impotentia judicandi*? I think not. It is one thing to govern harshly with a sense of the tragic necessity of the measures one must take under hitherto unimaginable conditions for the survival of one's community; it is a very different matter to separate oneself from one's community and maintain a regal, Messianic persona as the leader of that community. One can understand the impossible compromises that Rumkowski was compelled to make as long as he was ignorant of the Nazis' true intentions, either through their capacity to deceive or his own blindness, but there came a time when blindness, if that it was, became criminal in one who had accepted the responsibility of communal leadership. As Adam Czerniakow came to realize, there are circumstances under which a leader has no choice but death rather than to be complicit in the destruction of his own community.

Perhaps the most inexcusable aspect of Rumkowski's career as *Älteste der Juden* is that, whatever his frequently stated conflicts, he came to enjoy his job and the power that it entailed. Photographs always depict him as well fed and impeccably dressed, hardly surprising given Jewish supremacy in Poland's needle trades. He lived well even as the ghetto was progressively starving.

There was a religious response to Rumkowski's policies. When Rumkowski asked the *Vaad HaRabbanim* to participate in the selection process, they refused.[43] From the point of view of the rabbis, Rumkowski was guilty of murder for his participation and that of his police in the deportations if he knew the fate of those being deported.[44] Moses Maimonides (1135–1204), one of the greatest rabbinic authorities of all time, wrote, "If they should say, 'Give us one of you and we will kill him and if not we will kill all of you,' the Jews should allow themselves to be killed and not hand over a single life."[45] Rumkowski's "Give me your children" speech of 4 September 1942 indicates that he was under no illusions concerning the fate of the deportees. The speech also gives expression to his rationalization of the grisly task, "We sacrifice a part so that the whole might survive." Unfortunately, he maintained that logic even in the final deportation, implemented by his Jewish police, when there was no longer any chance of survival.

Conventional wisdom sometimes says more than elaborately worked out legal or ethical systems. During World War II, Orthodox Jewish military personnel in the American military forces inquired of the rabbinate whether it was permissible to eat pork products if no other food was available. The rabbinic response was that it was permissible as a matter of survival during wartime, but they counseled, "*Lecht nicht die bayner*—Don't lick the bones." The logic of the Orthodox rabbis was that when confronted with a genuinely life-threatening situation, it was permissible to do what was necessary to survive, but under no circumstances ought one to delight in the transgression.

Rumkowski's behavior is in stark contrast to that of the *Sonderkommandos,* a group composed almost entirely of Jews who were assigned the grisly task of running the crematoria. Levi characterizes the *Sonderkommandos* as "National Socialism's most demonic crime," its attempt to shift the burden of guilt to others.[46] He rightly asked that we view the *Sonderkommandos* "with pity and rigor" and suspend judgment.[47] Can anyone imagine that the *Sonderkommandos* in any way enjoyed their terrible work? Nor would anyone regard them as traitorous outcasts. The same cannot be said of Rumkowski, who, as noted, seemed to have savored his position. If for no other reason, and there are other reasons, he warrants our condemnation. Like Primo Levi, Elie Wiesel condemns Rumkowski, but he also sees him, as does Levi, as a victim. Wiesel asks rhetorically:

> But what about Chaim Rumkowski, "king" of the Lodz ghetto? Is he, too, defensible? No, he lived too comfortably, too "luxuriously," for me to speak on his behalf. Yet I consider him a victim too, a victim of oppression, of the murderous, dehumanizing order the hangmen imposed on the entire Jewish people.[48]

While I agree that Rumkowski was a victim like every other Jew, he nevertheless voluntarily accepted the responsibilities entailed in being the leader of the ghetto. That act imposed upon him greater obligations than those of ordinary Jews. Even, nay especially, under the harshest of circumstances, leadership has unique obligations. For that reason, I do not share with either Levi or Wiesel the mitigation of his being a victim. In Rumkowski the gray zone had turned black.

Notes

1. Primo Levi, *Moments of Reprieve,* trans. Ruth Feldman (New York: Viking Penguin, 1987), 171.
2. During the occupation, Germans called the conquered Polish city of Lodz Litzmannstadt.
3. The novelist Leslie Epstein has written a novel about Rumkowski, whom he calls I. C. Trumpelman: *King of the Jews: A Novel of the Holocaust* (New York: Coward, McCann & Geoghan, 1979). A documentary film, *Lodz Ghetto* (118 min.), edited by Alan Adelson and Kathryn Taverna, was presented on PBS in 1989.
4. Massimo Giuliani, *A Centaur in Auschwitz: Reflections on Primo Levi's Thinking* (Lanham, MD: Lexington Books, 2003), 7, 28.
5. Ibid., 33.
6. Primo Levi, *The Drowned and the Saved,* trans. Raymond Rosenthal (London: Sphere Books, 1989), 24–25.
7. Elie Wiesel, *And the Sea Is Never Full: Memoirs, 1969–,* trans. Marion Wiesel (New York: Alfred A. Knopf, 1999), 346; Giuliani, *A Centaur in Auschwitz,* 3.
8. Giuliani, *A Centaur in Auschwitz,* 4.
9. Elie Wiesel, *All Rivers Run to the Sea: Memoirs,* trans. Marion Wiesel (New York: Alfred A. Knopf, 1995), 65. For this reference, I am indebted to Professor Carole Lambert of Azusa Pacific University.
10. Raul Hilberg, *The Destruction of the European Jews* (Chicago: Quadrangle Books, 1961). An excellent earlier study in English by Professor Solomon F. Bloom had appeared in *Commentary,* but it had escaped my notice.

11. See "Rabbi Yochanan's Bargain" in Richard L. Rubenstein, *Power Struggle: An Autobiographical Confession* (New York: Charles Scribner's Sons, 1974), 171–93.
12. Ibid.
13. See Raul Hilberg, Stanislaw Staron, and Josef Kermisz, eds., *The Warsaw Diary of Adam Czerniakow* (New York: Stein and Day, 1979), 70; Abraham I. Katsch, ed., *Scroll of Agony: The Warsaw Diary of Chaim A. Kaplan* (New York: Macmillan, 1965), 384–85.
14. "Lodz," *Encyclopedia Judaica* (Shaker Heights, OH: Judaica Multimedia International, 1997), CD-ROM edition.
15. See Christopher R. Browning, *The Origins of the Final Solution: The Evolution of Nazi Jewish Policy, September 1939–March 1942* (Lincoln: University of Nebraska Press, 2004), 116.
16. Ibid., 116, 117.
17. On the Madagascar Plan, see Christopher R. Browning, "Madagascar Plan," in Walter Laqueur, ed., *The Holocaust Encyclopedia* (New Haven, CT: Yale University Press, 2001), 407–9.
18. Browning, *The Origins of the Final Solution*, 117, 118.
19. Ibid., 119.
20. For a brief overview of German population policy toward the Jews in the early stages of the war, see Richard L. Rubenstein and John K. Roth, *Approaches to Auschwitz: The Holocaust and Its Legacy*, rev. ed. (Louisville: Westminster John Knox Press, 2003), 149–52, 158–66.
21. Browning suggests the October date, Gerlach December. See Browning, *The Origins of the Final Solution*, 318; Gerlach, "The Wannsee Conference, and Hitler's Decision in Principle to Exterminate All European Jews," *Journal of Modern History* 70 (December 1998), 759–812. For a discussion of conflicting views, see Rubenstein and Roth, *Approaches to Auschwitz*, 186–94.
22. Office of the *Oberbürgermeister* (signed Schiffer) to Rumkowski, 30 April 1940. See Raul Hilberg, *Destruction*, 167; Alan Adelson and Robert Lapides, eds., *Lodz Ghetto: Inside a Community Under Siege* (New York: Penguin Books, 1989), 47.
23. Isaiah Trunk, *Judenrat: The Jewish Councils in Eastern Europe Under Nazi Occupation* (New York: Stein and Day, 1977), 480.
24. Michael Checinski, "How Rumkowski Died," *Commentary* 67, no. 5 (May 1979), 63.
25. Trunk, *Judenrat*, 482.
26. On resistance to German-appointed Jewish councils, see, for example, ibid., 451–547.
27. Hilberg, *Destruction*, 154.
28. Hannah Arendt, *Eichmann in Jerusalem: A Report on the Banality of Evil* (New York: Viking Press, 1964), 125.
29. Adelson and Lapides, eds., *Lodz Ghetto*, 149.
30. Ibid., 45.
31. Ibid., 47.
32. Ibid., 51.
33. Albert Speer, *Infiltration: How Heinrich Himmler Schemed to Build an SS Industrial Empire*, trans. Joachim Neugroschel (New York: Macmillan, 1981), 288.
34. See Götz Aly, *"Final Solution": Nazi Population Policy and the Murder of the European Jews*, trans. Belinda Cooper and Allison Brown (New York: Arnold, 1999), 34; Aly, "'Jewish Resettlement,'" in Ulrich Herbert, ed., *National Socialist Extermination Policies: Contemporary German Perspectives and Controversies* (New York: Berghahn Books, 2000), 59.
35. See Rubenstein and Roth, *Approaches to Auschwitz*, 143–66.
36. Mordecai Chaim Rumkowski, "Address at the Time of the Deportation of the Children from the Lodz Ghetto, September 4, 1942," http://www.yad-vashem.org.il/about_holocaust/documents/part2/doc109.html.
37. Adelson and Lapides, eds., *Lodz Ghetto*, 94.
38. Ibid., xvi.
39. Ibid., 94.

40. Anna Freud, *The Ego and the Mechanisms of Defense,* trans. Cecil Baines (New York: International Universities Press, 1946).
41. See Solomon F. Bloom, "Dictator of the Lodz Ghetto: The Strange History of Mordecai Chaim Rumkowski," *Commentary* (February 1949), 115, 116.
42. Levi, *The Drowned and the Saved,* 50.
43. Adelson and Lapides, eds., *Lodz Ghetto,* 490.
44. Ibid.
45. Maimonides, *Sefer Hamada,* chapter 5, *Hilchoth Yesoday HaTorah Halacha* #5 (Jerusalem: Pardes Publishing Company, 1955).
46. Levi, *The Drowned and the Saved,* 37.
47. Ibid., 41.
48. Wiesel, *All Rivers Run to the Sea,* 65. Here again, I am indebted to Professor Carole Lambert.

– Chapter 21 –

CATALYZING FASCISM
Academic Science in National Socialist Germany and Afterward

Jeffrey Lewis

For many years, the history of science in Nazi Germany would probably have been viewed as an inappropriate topic for a project dedicated to studying ambiguity and compromise in the Holocaust. The reason for this is simple. Scientists themselves, and many of the scholars who study and interpret their work, have tended to stress the clarity of scientific research as a vocation. Somewhat simplified, the reasoning goes as follows: Scientists examine the natural world in an effort to produce knowledge about that world. If all goes according to plan, the knowledge produced by scientific communities, and by individual scientists, provides insights into the world that transcend languages, cultures, and politics. From these basic assumptions it is a short step to equate the transcendent character of scientific knowledge with the scientists themselves, conflating the *product* of scientific inquiry with the human *process* of scientific research. However tempting it might be to lump the two together, this contributes to neither our understanding of scientific knowledge nor of the cultural context in which it is produced.[1] From the perspective of a historian of science in modern Germany, the most dangerous consequence of such an uncritical examination of the scientific enterprise is that it provides scientific researchers with a rhetorical tool for portraying themselves as removed from human society and the quotidian business of politics, which therefore can be used to absolve them of social responsibility.

Used in this manner, this rhetorical tool proved to be exceedingly useful for German scientists in the aftermath of World War II and the Holocaust. As the German people sought to remember the past selectively, in an

Notes for this section begin on page 321.

exculpatory fashion, scientists had a built-in advantage—they could draw on the prestige of their occupation and its perceived objectivity to "prove" that they had not been complicit in the crimes of Nazi Germany. They fashioned an interpretation of their profession that argued that good science is fundamentally independent of political ideology. Good scientists, they argued, cannot simultaneously have been devoted Nazis. In fact, some went so far as to argue that open scientific inquiry was by its very nature a kind of resistance to the irrational, anti-intellectual Nazis.[2] In specific cases when scientists had clearly collaborated with the Nazi government, the individuals in question were depicted as frauds or outcasts—the exceptions that proved the rule.[3] The Western allies themselves were sympathetic to the notion of science as an apolitical activity, so more often than not they accepted the claims of the German scientific community at face value, and for the most part, German scientists re-established themselves with little difficulty in the Western zones of occupation.[4]

Only recently has German society begun to confront the reality that many of its most successful postwar researchers and organizations did in fact contribute in some manner to the Nazi regime. It was not until 2001 that a leading figure in the German scientific community, former Max Planck Society president Hubert Markl, publicly apologized to surviving victims of Nazi medical experiments. Interestingly, Markl apologized not only for the conduct of German scientists during the Nazi era but also for their conduct in the postwar era, when they continually denied any responsibility for the abuses of science and medicine that took place under their watch.[5] Markl's apology came in the aftermath of a significant public controversy surrounding Adolf Butenandt, one of Germany's most prominent postwar researchers and president of the Max Planck Society from 1960 until 1972. After his death in 1995, Butenandt's Nazi Party membership, denied by him during his lifetime, became widely known and generated fierce public controversy between his supporters and those more critical of science and scientists in twentieth-century Germany.[6]

Butenandt's career is thus a very natural departure point for a brief inquiry into the role of scientists in the Third Reich and afterward. In order to provide some perspective on Butenandt's behavior during this time, I shall examine it in comparison with the behavior of his colleague Georg Melchers. Melchers was another of Germany's leading researchers whose active career, like Butenandt's, spanned the decades from the 1930s to the 1990s. Unlike Butenandt, however, Melchers never joined the Nazi Party and has deservedly been remembered as an opponent of Nazism. By comparing the choices of these two outstanding scientists, I hope to demonstrate that the behavior of scientific researchers during the Nazi era and afterward should not be viewed as a stark, black and white contrast between true scientists and fraudulent supporters of the regime. Instead, shades of gray best describe the relationship between researchers such as Butenandt and Melchers and the Nazi government.

Adolf Butenandt was born in 1903. He began his education at Marburg University in 1921, and in 1924 he continued his studies at the University of Göttingen. His primary field of study was organic chemistry, but he also took a strong interest in biology, and throughout his career his research reflected this combined interest. After passing his doctoral exams in 1927, Butenandt remained in Göttingen, where he began a successful research program focusing on the isolation of sex hormones. He also began taking on his own doctoral students and running his own lab. In 1933 he accepted an offer to move to the Technische Hochschule of Danzig, at that time a free city administered by Poland as part of the territorial settlement after World War I. He had no interest in the Nazi Party in its early years; instead, his political attitude can best be summed up as conservative and *bürgerlich*. He opposed the Versailles treaty and disliked the Weimar Republic, although as a citizen he felt obligated to support it.[7]

Butenandt kept his distance from the Nazi Party until late 1935; at that point he and a number of other faculty members at the Technische Hochschule decided collectively to apply for party membership. They seem to have hoped that this would lead to increased financial support from the Reich, for in the early 1930s the school was constantly short of funding, and there was even talk of closing it down and moving the faculty to Königsberg. This soon proved to be an advantageous time for Butenandt to reconcile himself with the Nazi Party, for in early 1936 he became one of the candidates to head the Kaiser Wilhelm Institute for Biochemistry in Berlin. His scientific credentials were above reproach, but at that point he was seen as politically unreliable since he had made no effort to affiliate himself formally with the party.[8] His decision to join apparently placated his political opponents, and on 1 May 1936 he officially became the director of the Kaiser Wilhelm Institute for Biochemistry as well as Nazi Party member number 3716562.

The following autumn Butenandt moved his research group to Berlin and enjoyed lavish support. His entire institute was rebuilt according to his own specifications, and he received a generous salary along with a large house complete with stables for his horses.[9] Intellectually he had the opportunity to work in close contact with the best minds in Germany and in this environment he flourished. Although he was no antisemite and disliked the way his Jewish colleagues had been persecuted by the Nazi government, he found himself on the whole able to tolerate the politics of the Nazi Party throughout the late 1930s. His own prosperity, coupled with his approval of Hitler's aggressive foreign policy, made it easy for him to shut his eyes to the regime's other qualities.

By 1939, however, Butenandt began to pay a price for his association with the Nazi government. He regretted the outbreak of war; he supported Hitler's aggressive nationalism, but not to the extent of open warfare. Furthermore, the outbreak of hostilities severed Butenandt's contact with important foreign colleagues. After the German declaration of war on the United States, Butenandt's scientific work suffered from the lack of foreign contact;

in particular Butenandt and his colleagues were cut off from the lab of the American chemist Wendell Stanley, whose own work had been essential in motivating Butenandt to move into the subject of virus research.[10] More importantly, the Nazi government temporarily cost Butenandt the greatest achievement of his scientific career—the Nobel Prize. Butenandt was awarded the Nobel Prize in chemistry in 1939 for his hormone research. Hitler, however, had forbidden German citizens from accepting Nobel Prizes, and Butenandt was given a letter to sign and return to the Nobel committee, formally rejecting the prize. He did so, certainly with no small regret. He eventually received the prize in 1949 but without the cash award that ordinarily accompanies it.[11]

Despite his personal misgivings Butenandt continued to support the Nazi government until the end of the war. According to one contemporary, he sometimes appeared publicly wearing Nazi insignia and on at least one occasion publicly praised the importance of chemistry for Germany's war effort.[12] From Butenandt's personal perspective, this was the sensible course of action. His salary and institutional budget came from the Reich Ministry of Education. Hundreds of thousands of Reichsmarks in additional funding for other research projects came from other various government ministries.[13] Since he had not been forced to participate in any work that he found to be morally repugnant—there is no evidence that he participated directly in medical experiments involving concentration camp inmates, for example, although he must have been aware that such activities were taking place—he could focus on his own research and convince himself that he ultimately bore no responsibility for what was happening around him.

After the war Butenandt sought to leave the Nazi past behind him as much as possible, both for his own sake as well as for the professional rehabilitation of German science as a whole. He was treated very well in the immediate postwar months. Beginning in 1943 he and his colleagues were evacuated to the city of Tübingen in southwest Germany, so when the war ended they came under the jurisdiction of the French occupation. The French were surprisingly benevolent, and Butenandt lost no research time at all on account of the French military government. He and his colleagues also enjoyed the unstinting support of local German officials and received significant material and financial support throughout the occupation.[14]

Nevertheless, Butenandt understood that the success of the scientific profession in postwar Germany would depend to a large extent on the ability of scientists to absolve themselves of complicity with Nazism. On some occasions Butenandt simply lied about his own past. He repeatedly denied his party membership, and instead said that he had never been more than a candidate (*Anwärter*) for membership in the party.[15] He also served as a character witness for scientists who were considerably more compromised than he was. The most glaring example of this behavior took place in September 1949, when Butenandt and three other researchers produced an affidavit (*Persilschein*) clearing Otmar Freiherr von Verschuer of wrongdoing during the Nazi era. Verschuer had certainly been involved in experiments with concentration camp inmates. He had become a public burden for the newly founded Max Planck Society, so Butenandt and the others cleared his professional reputation in order to allow the Max Planck Society to shuffle Verschuer off to a university position where his notoriety would no longer be a nuisance.[16]

Georg Melchers was only three years younger than Butenandt, but during the Nazi era he was very much Butenandt's junior in professional matters. Born in 1906, Melchers studied botany in Freiburg before moving to Kiel and finally to Göttingen, where he completed his doctoral work under the direction of Fritz von Wettstein. When Wettstein moved to Berlin to accept a position in the Kaiser Wilhelm Institute for Biology in 1934, Melchers accompanied him as a scientific assistant. During the war Melchers distinguished himself through his research, and by the postwar era he was one of the leading experts on plant viruses in Germany. After Wettstein's death in 1945, Melchers succeeded his mentor as one of the directors of the Kaiser Wilhelm Institute for Biology. In this capacity Melchers helped lead one of the most innovative biology institutes in West Germany; both he and his students achieved excellent international reputations in the fields of virology and microbiology. He was also an active member of the Social Democratic Party and corresponded with leading SPD politicians such as Carlo Schmidt and Willy Brandt. At one point he was even considered for the position of cultural minister of the Land of Baden-Württemberg.[17]

Melchers earned his reputation as a leader in plant virology as one of the leaders of an extraordinary research group, the Arbeitsstätte für Virusforschung, which was established by Butenandt, Wettstein, and Alfred Kühn in 1937.[18] The group was innovative because it emphasized interdisciplinary research combining the expertise of botanists, biologists, biochemists, and geneticists, which was a dramatic contrast with the rigid disciplinary boundaries of the German university system. The research group was very generously funded and therefore had access to the most expensive and sophisticated laboratory equipment in the world. Melchers and his colleagues published a number of important papers during the war years, but more significantly, the research community of which they were a part became the foundation of West Germany's most successful biological research community. However, as was the case with Butenandt, Melchers's career was hindered as well as helped as a result of the actions of Nazi Germany. Beginning in 1943, when the research group was evacuated to Tübingen, Melchers's ability to carry out his own research was seriously constrained by the lack of research facilities, until a new institute was built for him in 1950.

Melchers never joined the Nazi Party.[19] He had been a member of the SPD during his youth and kept a liberal political attitude throughout the Third Reich era. When the war ended he was one of the few German scientists who still had an excellent reputation abroad as an opponent of National Socialism. Years later, Gunther Stent, a Jewish émigré from Nazi Germany who became one of America's leading molecular biologists, wrote of Melchers, "Melchers was the only senior German biologist of whom Max [Delbrück] was dead certain that he had never been a Nazi—a judgment for which, having known and admired Melchers for forty-five years, I would thrust my own hand into the fire."[20] Melchers was also one of the few German scientists who advocated that the German scientific community critically examine its own past and make efforts to exclude those whose behavior in the Nazi era was unacceptable rather than cover up for them. Since Melchers had excellent contact with foreign scientists, he understood that Germany's postwar reputation would hinge upon the behavior of the Germans themselves; he became convinced of this while participating in the Eighth International Congress of Genetics, held in Stockholm in 1948. Upon returning to Germany, Melchers wrote to Otto Hahn, then president of the Max Planck Society, urging him to take an aggressive stance against what Melchers called the "re-nazification" of German science. In Melchers's opinion, the resumption of normal relations with foreign colleagues depended upon the Germans taking this responsibility on themselves.[21] Melchers was also one of the few German scientists who insisted that the Max Planck Society compensate scientists who had been driven from their positions by the racial politics of the Nazis.

Overall his opinions were highly valued, and both German and foreign officials sought his advice regarding the conduct of his colleagues during the Nazi era. Interestingly, when Butenandt was a candidate for a biochemistry position at the University of Basel, a representative of the state education department wrote to Melchers to ask him his opinion of Butenandt's political behavior during the Third Reich. Melchers replied that because of his position, it had been impossible for Butenandt to steer completely clear of formal entanglements with the Nazi government. In his opinion Butenandt was not a supporter of the Nazi government, but neither had he been an opponent. In Melchers's estimation, Butenandt would fare well in the democratic political culture of Switzerland.[22]

Up to this point the image of these two men that I have portrayed probably seems to be a study in contrasts between the upright, moral Melchers and the opportunistic Butenandt. While true to an extent, the difference between the two men was perhaps not as great as might seem on the surface, and I suggest that the two men's behavior is best viewed as different shades of gray with Butenandt certainly the darker of the two. As a scientific assistant with little real authority, Melchers was not subjected to the same kind of pressures and choices as was Butenandt, the leader of a high-profile institute responsible for dozens of workers and commanding a budget of hundreds of thousands of Reichsmarks. After the war Melchers admitted that his adviser, Wettstein, sheltered him during the Nazi era, protecting him from the more difficult choices that Butenandt faced. In addition, all of Melchers's excellent pre-1943 research would have been impossible without the generous support of government ministries, and Melchers himself played a significant role in the ongoing task of securing patronage from the Nazi government. For example, when the Kaiser Wilhelm Institutes for Biology and Biochemistry were evacuated to Tübingen in 1943, they were described as carrying out important war-related research for the German armed forces by none other than Albert Speer himself. Melchers deliberately made use of Speer's name and support in an effort to pressure the rector of Tübingen University to construct experimental greenhouses for him, similar to those he had left behind in Berlin.[23] In truth, none of the research carried out by Melchers or his close colleagues was directly relevant to the military. Instead, the term "war-related" was a rhetorical tool that they used to convince a government at war to support them. The point here is that Melchers was willing to declare his support for the war effort and associate himself with important figures in the Nazi government in order to secure material support for his own research.

These were the kinds of concessions that many in Nazi Germany made in order to accommodate themselves with an arbitrary, dictatorial government. However understandable, though, concessions such as these seriously undercut Melchers's moral authority among his colleagues in the postwar era. For many of them, he was at best a nuisance and at worst a hypocrite because of the support he and his colleagues had received for their work. For example, after the war Melchers opposed the reinstatement of a Dr. Schlösser, who had been an advocate of racial hygiene during the Nazi era. Schlösser was outraged that Melchers was trying to bring up the past—he wrote, "I ask you openly, from where do you get the moral right to disturb my work and my life in such a fashion?" Schlösser believed that since Melchers had received lavish support at the public's expense during the Nazi period, he had no such moral right.[24] Since the two men had known each other fairly well since the mid-1930s, Schlösser closed with a personal taunt by suggesting that even Melchers's wife would be ashamed of his behavior if she only knew about it.

In his indignation Schlösser failed to note that there was in fact a qualitative difference between keeping one's mouth shut and taking what the Nazis had to offer, and enthusiastically providing scientific legitimacy for the ideology of racial hygiene that contributed to the extermination of millions of people. Schlösser, however, was not unique in trying to equate his own support for the Nazis with the lack of opposition shown by many others. In a postwar world where many German scientists were searching for any excuse to feel sorry for themselves, the seeming contradiction between Melchers's deeds and words provided the excuse his opponents needed to rationalize their own complicity with the Nazi government. Melchers's lack of open resistance thus seriously undercut his campaign to impose a sense of historical responsibility on his colleagues after the war.

By the time of this exchange of letters, the obstacles facing any effort to persuade the German scientific community to police itself regarding its past had already become very clear. In autumn 1949 both Butenandt and Melchers found themselves in a situation that required them to make an explicit choice between their own material and professional well-being or taking a moral stance against the legacy of National Socialism.[25] In 1946 the Kaiser Wilhelm Society had been refounded as the Max Planck Society for the

Advancement of the Sciences in the British zone of occupation. In February 1948 the society spread to include former Kaiser Wilhelm Institutes in the American zone. Significant hurdles prevented the inclusion of institutes from the French zone of occupation until the end of 1949, however. The directors of the French zone institutes, led by Melchers and Alfred Kühn, focused their opposition to the Max Planck Society on the society's general secretary, Ernst Telschow. They opposed Telschow first of all because he was a centralizing bureaucrat who tended to subordinate the authority of individual institutes and their directors to the society's general administration in Göttingen. This tendency had been on ready display during Telschow's previous tenure as general secretary of the society before and during the war. Second, they opposed Telschow because he had been an enthusiastic member of the Nazi Party, having joined in 1933.

After the war, Telschow managed to convince the British that he had joined the Party in order to protect the Kaiser Wilhelm Society, and they allowed him to become perhaps the most significant figure in transforming this organization into the Max Planck Society. However, the French zone Kaiser Wilhelm Institute directors, including Butenandt and Melchers, were not as forgiving. They implicitly threatened to make Telschow's Nazi association public and in doing so hoped to pressure the Max Planck Society into removing him as a precondition for the inclusion of their institutes in the society. Melchers had no reservations about publicly discrediting Telschow and the entire Max Planck Society if need be. In autumn of 1949 he wrote to his friend Anton Lang, "All the trump cards were in our hands. It would have been fully unthinkable to have to explain in public that the institutes for biochemistry . . . , biology . . . , private law . . . , and physics . . . would not join the Max Planck Society because it chose to stand fast by the old Nazi Telschow."[26]

However, in October 1949 Max Planck Society president Otto Hahn offered Butenandt a position as senator in the society; placated, Butenandt switched sides and the Tübingen opposition collapsed. Melchers was outraged at Butenandt, calling his actions treason. Thus began a long feud between two of West Germany's most prominent biological researchers, one that was not settled until the early 1990s. Melchers, however, did not follow through with his threat to discredit Telschow publicly. It seems as though he had too much to lose, personally and professionally, to make a lone stand against his colleagues in Tübingen as well as his adversaries in Göttingen. He truly did believe that it was a disgrace that a man such as Telschow led the administration of West Germany's most prestigious research organization, but his moral outrage was counterbalanced by his practical side. He stood to gain very little by prolonging the conflict. He had already lost nearly seven years' worth of productive research time. Despite his protestations, high-ranking Nazi Party and even SS officials flowed steadily back into the German universities and the Max Planck Society. Renazification would take place whether or not he embarrassed Telschow publicly, so he kept his silence but vowed to carry on a cold war against Telschow and other former Nazis behind the scenes, a promise he kept in the following years.

In the postwar world the easiest choice for most scientists was to use the rhetoric of science as an apolitical activity to distance themselves from the Nazi government. Isolating and excluding specific individuals aided this process; so did covering up for individuals like Verschuer. However, when Butenandt, Melchers, and their Tübingen colleagues threatened to embarrass the Max Planck Society publicly, they threatened the very illusion that had allowed German scientists as a whole to make the transition into the postwar era relatively easily. They therefore had to make a choice between their professional lives and their sense of what was right. For some this choice was more difficult than for others.

The German scientific institution as a whole had been faced with a similar choice sixteen years earlier. Confronted with a government that many of them detested, they offered their services in order to safeguard and advance their professional careers. Since the initiative often came from scientists themselves, there was no need for the state to control them; their dependence ensured that they would collaborate. This has been described as the "self-mobilization" of scientists under Nazism.[27] I suggest that the behavior of Butenandt and Melchers illustrates a similar phenomenon in postwar German science—another example of the self-mobilization of scientists, only in this case they voluntarily, if not always happily, supported a society and culture that was devoted to ignoring its complicity with National Socialism.[28]

To conclude we need to return to the question of exactly what role researchers such as these played in Nazi Germany in order to understand how they contributed to the power and legitimacy of a criminal government. In his recent two-volume biography of Adolf Hitler, Ian Kershaw concerned himself with precisely this phenomenon—the origins and nature of Hitler's power. Examining German society as a whole, Kershaw argues that direct control from the top down did not characterize the Nazi dictatorship. Instead, Hitler's power flowed from the bottom up; Kershaw suggests that "Hitler's personalized form of rule invited radical initiatives from below and offered such initiatives backing, so long as they were in line with his broadly defined goals." He continues:

> In the Darwinist jungle of the Third Reich, the way to power and advancement was through anticipating the "Führer will," and, without waiting for directives, taking initiatives to promote what were presumed to be Hitler's aims and wishes. . . . But, metaphorically, ordinary citizens denouncing neighbors to the Gestapo, often turning personal animosity or resentment to their advantage through political slur, businessmen happy to exploit anti-Jewish legislation to rid themselves of competitors, and the many others whose daily forms of minor cooperation with the regime took place at the cost of others, were—whatever their motives—indirectly "working towards the Führer."[29]

Konrad Jarausch noted a similar phenomenon in his study of the legal, teaching, and engineering professions in Nazi Germany. In this case, though, it was not so much individuals working toward the Führer, but rather professionals trying to resolve an ethical dilemma. Jarausch writes that "maintaining professional standards did create an apolitical refuge and serve persecuted clients, curious pupils, and trusting customers. But such competent performance also helped to support dictatorship at home and aggression abroad."[30] I believe that the role of the academic sciences in Nazi Germany was similar to that of the other educated professions as noted by Jarausch. They were not necessarily taking initiatives to bring themselves in line with Hitler's ideological goals, but through the competent execution of their professional duties they did contribute to the power of the Nazi government in the undirected, bottom-up mechanism discerned by Kershaw.

Understanding how this pursuit of individual interests, even those seemingly unrelated to the goals of National Socialism, contributed to the radicalization of German society is one of the most important lessons to be learned from the example of scientific research in the Third Reich. I believe that the best way to understand the role of people such as Butenandt and Melchers in Nazi Germany is to see them collectively as catalysts for National Socialism. In chemistry, a catalyst does not actually become involved as a participant in the reaction, but instead makes the reaction take place more quickly and easily than in its absence. If one views the increasing radicalization of Nazi Germany as a political reaction spiraling out of control, then researchers like Butenandt and Melchers can be seen as playing such a role.

Just as a catalyst is not an integral part of a chemical reaction, these researchers were not an integral part of the National Socialist movement prior to 1933. Neither had joined party groups before 1936, and one of the most surprising aspects of their research is the extent to which it did *not* reflect the racial biology of the Nazi leadership. They were willing to work with Nazism, however, so long as they received financial support and scientific freedom. Butenandt, Melchers, and German scientists in general needed the National Socialist government in order to continue their professional lives. The converse, however, was not true: scientists were not essential to the success of Nazism. In his review of John Heilbron's biography of Max Planck, Mark Walker noted that scientists such as Planck were "very useful if not necessary . . . to the National Socialist leadership."[31] They tended not to support the party in its early years, and toward the war's end, they did not produce the technologically advanced wonder weapons of Hitler's fantasies. However, whatever their true intentions or beliefs, scientists made National Socialism more successful than it would have been in their absence. At the very least they showed by their own example that decent, intelligent human beings, even those with no formal party affiliation, could work with it under conditions of relative normalcy. Furthermore, by standing by as Nazi Germany descended into genocide, they helped ensure that nothing would hold the reaction in check. If Germany's best thinkers were not expected to condemn genocide, who could be?

I find the catalyst metaphor to be illuminating for a number of reasons. First of all, it provides the mechanism linking competent performance of professional duties to the crimes of the Nazi government. Applied specifically to the case of the physical and biological sciences, it allows us to understand how researchers could produce useful, accurate, "objective" knowledge while at the same time occupying a moral gray zone. Furthermore, it automatically implies the "useful but not necessary" relationship between academic scientists and the Nazi government noted above. The idea of a catalyst also implies continuity. Catalysts are neither consumed nor altered in a chemical reaction; they emerge from it essentially unchanged. Such continuity is descriptive of the biological research community surrounding Butenandt and Melchers. I have already noted one continuity, that of the phenomenon of self-mobilization in both the Nazi and postwar eras. Another fundamental continuity is worth mentioning as well: the research program pioneered by Butenandt, Melchers, and their colleagues beginning in 1937 continued entirely intact and in fact achieved its greatest successes in the Federal Republic of Germany.

Finally, and most importantly, the catalyst metaphor ascribes the element of agency to those Germans whose feelings toward the Nazi Party were noncommittal without demonizing them. These researchers were not the passive onlookers they claimed to be, but neither were they true believers in the Nazi cause. They may not have been working toward the Führer, but they certainly were not opposing him, either. The problem with scientists in the Third Reich, then, was not that they were corrupted by Nazism, but instead that they proceeded as normally as they could and worked *with* the National Socialist government. Thus the metaphor illustrates the ease with which normal human behavior can unintentionally contribute to inhuman actions, and in doing so demonstrates that in Nazi Germany selfishness and apathy were in some ways as dangerous as hatred and racism.

Notes

1. Space constraints prohibit me from providing a more extensive philosophical discussion of scientists, the knowledge they create, and the ways in which they interact with both the human and natural worlds. For a more thorough account of my own ideas on the subject, see Jeffrey Lewis, "Continuity in German Science, 1937–1972: Genealogy and Strategies of the TMV/Molecular Biology Community" (Ph.D. diss., The Ohio State University, 2002), esp. 11–20. The works that have been most influential in shaping my thinking on this topic are Ronald N. Giere, *Science Without Laws* (Chicago: University of Chicago Press, 1999); Alfred Gierer, *Im Spiegel der Natur erkennen wir uns Selbst* (Reinbeck bei Hamburg: Rowohlt Verlag, 1998); and David L. Hull, *Science As a Process: An Evolutionary Account of the Social and Conceptual Development of Science* (Chicago: University of Chicago Press, 1988).
2. Herbert Mehrtens has argued that the idea of pure research offered scientists a symbol with which they could identify that was independent of the social context in which they were operating, allowing them to declare that they were apolitical even when working for the interests of the state. Herbert Mehrtens, "Irresponsible Purity: The Political and Moral Structure of Mathematical Sciences in the National Socialist State," in Monika Renneberg and Mark Walker, eds., *Science, Technology, and National Socialism* (Cambridge: Cambridge University Press, 1994), 332.

3. Michael Schüring, "Ein 'unerfreulicher Vorgang.' Das Max-Planck-Institut für Züchtungsforschung in Voldagsen und die gescheiterte Rückkehr von Max Ufer," in Susanne Heim, ed., *Autarkie und Ostexpansion. Pflanzenzucht und Agrarforschung im Nationalsozialismus* (Göttingen: Wallstein Verlag, 2002), 288–89.
4. Otto Gerhard Oexle, *The British Roots of the Max-Planck-Gesellschaft* (London: German Historical Institute, 1995); Mark Walker, *German National Socialism and the Quest for Nuclear Power, 1939–1949* (Cambridge: Cambridge University Press, 1989), 189. Also see the following two articles by David Cassidy: "Controlling German Science I: US and Allied Forces in Germany, 1945–1947," *Historical Studies in the Physical and Biological Sciences* 24 (1994) and "Controlling German Science II: Bizonal Occupation and the Struggle Over West German Science Policy, 1946–1949," *Historical Studies in the Physical and Biological Sciences* 26 (1996).
5. The Max Planck Society has published a brief report on the symposium called "Symposium in Berlin: *Biowissenschaften und Menschenversuche an Kaiser-Wilhelm-Instituten—Die Verbindung nach Auschwitz*" (Munich, August 2001).
6. Butenandt's ties to individuals who had taken part in medical crimes were documented by Ernst Klee in his *Auschwitz, die NS-Medizin, und ihre Opfer* (Frankfurt am Main: S. Fischer Verlag, 1997). The controversy that emerged regarding Butenandt was not confined to the role of scientists during the Nazi period. In fact, the American Nobel Prize winner James Watson argued that it was Butenandt's unwillingness in the postwar era to admit the extent of his cooperation with the National Socialist government that was causing ongoing public distrust of the German scientific community. James D. Watson, "Leichte Schatten über Berlin. Die Deutschen und ihre Genetiker: Anmerkungen eines amerikanischen Nobelpreisträgers," *Frankfurter Allgemeine Zeitung*, 19 July 1997. The publicity generated about Butenandt became so negative that teachers in a school named after him began to question whether he should be honored in such a manner. *Weser-Kurier* (Bremen), 31 August 1998.
7. The most thorough biography of Butenandt was written by one of his former students, Peter Karlson, and has been criticized for omitting or softening details concerning Butenandt's relationship with the Nazi Party. The American historian Robert Proctor has recently provided a much more critical account. As part of the Presidential Commission on the history of the Kaiser-Wilhelm-Gesellschaft under National Socialism, Proctor was the first scholar to have access to Butenandt's files in the archives of the Max Planck Society. Based as it was on a relatively fast examination of an immense collection of papers, Proctor's article was not the final word and has been the subject of some criticism. The most thorough critical examination of Butenandt's life and science is the collection of essays in Wolfgang Schieder and Achim Trunk, eds., *Adolf Butenandt und die Kaiser-Wilhelm-Gesellschaft: Wissenschaft, Industrie, und Politik im "Dritten Reich"* (Berlin: Wallstein Verlag, 2004). I have relied on a preliminary draft of Wolfgang Schieder's chapter in this volume, as well as my own doctoral research, for the biographical information on Butenandt presented in this essay. Also see Peter Karlson, *Adolf Butenandt: Biochemiker, Hormonforscher, Wissenschaftspolitiker* (Stuttgart: Wissenschaftliche Verlagsgesellschaft, 1990); Robert Proctor, "Adolf Butenandt (1903–1995): Nobelpreisträger, Nationalsozialist, und MPG-Präsident. Ein erster Blick in den Nachlass," *Forschungsprogramm "Geschichte der Kaiser-Wilhelm-Gesellschaft im Nationalsozialismus,"* Ergebnisse 2 (2000).
8. Also see Kristie Macrakis, *Surviving the Swastika: Scientific Research in Nazi Germany* (New York: Oxford University Press, 1993), esp. 115–18. Macrakis wrote her book when Butenandt was still alive; out of respect for his privacy she chose not to name him, but it is very clear in this chapter to whom she is referring.
9. Butenandt's salary and perks are described in several documents in his personal papers in the Archives of the Max Planck Society (henceforth MPG Archive); in particular, see compensation package signed by Society General Secretary Ernst Telschow, dated 14 August 1936, and Butenandt's contract with the Ministry of Education, dated 28 October 1936. MPG Archive, Abt. II, Rep. 1A, Nr. 2-3.

10. The negative impact that the isolation of the war years had on the German scientific community is a major theme of Ute Deichmann's *Biologists Under Hitler*, trans. Thomas Dunlap (Cambridge: Harvard University Press, 1996); for the specific example of the virus research community centered on Butenandt and Melchers, see Lewis, "Continuity in German Science," 179–82.
11. This incident is discussed in Elizabeth Crawford, "German Scientists and Hitler's Vendetta Against the Nobel Prizes," *Historical Studies in the Physical and Biological Sciences* 21 (1999), 42–47.
12. Author interview with Carsten Bresch, Freiburg, 9 June 2000; Adolf Butenandt, "Die biologische Chemie im Dienste der Volksgesundheit," *Preussische Akademie der Wissenschaften Vorträge und Schriften, Heft 8* (Berlin: Verlag Walter de Gruyter, 1941).
13. In particular, the research group that Butenandt helped to create for the study of viruses was very generously supported throughout the war years. Called the Arbeitsstätte für Virusforschung, financial support came from ministries in the federal government and the state government of Prussia; the greatest single contributor was the Reichsministerium für Ernährung und Landwirtschaft (RMEL), which provided RM 60,000 in 1941, RM 55,000 in 1942, and RM 141,100 for the 1944 fiscal year, of which half was probably never dispersed. The researchers also received funds from I. G. Farben and the Deutsche Forschungsgemeinschaft. The total budget for the group grew steadily during the war years and exceeded RM 200,000 in 1943. Arbeitsstätte für Virusforschung, Berlin Dahlem, *Bericht über die Prüfung des Rechnungsabschlusses*, 1941, 1942, 1943 fiscal years. MPG Archive, I. Abt., Rep. 1A, Nr. 2907(3), Nr. 2908(2), Nr. 2908(3).
14. Jeffrey Lewis, "Kalter Krieg in der Max-Planck-Gesellschaft: Göttingen und Tübingen—eine Vereinigung mit Hindernissen, 1948–1949," trans. Birgit Kolboske, in Schieder and Trunk, eds., *Adolf Butenandt*, 404–9.
15. Butenandt lied, very deliberately, on this topic in a letter to his friend Emil Aberhalden, dated 9 January 1947. MPG Archive, Abt. III, Rep. 84/2, Nr. 2.
16. Carola Sachse, "*'Persilscheinkultur': Zum Umgang mit der NS-Vergangenheit in der Kaiser Wilhelm/Max-Planck-Gesellschaft,*" in Bernd Weisbrod, ed., *Akademische Vergangenheitspolitik: Beiträge zur Wissenschaftskultur der Nachkriegszeit* (Göttingen: Wallstein Verlag, 2002). Also see Hans-Peter Kröner, *Von der Rassenhygiene zur Humangenetik: Das Kaiser-Wilhelm-Institute für Anthropologie, menschliche Erblehre und Eugenik nach dem Kriege* (Stuttgart: Gustav Fischer Verlag, 1998).
17. Peter Overath, "Nachruf: Georg Melchers," *MPG Berichte und Mitteilungen* (1998), 191–93, and Georg Melchers, "Ein Botaniker auf dem Weg in die Allgemeine Biologie auch in Zeiten moralischer und materieller Zerstörung," *Berichte der Deutschen Botanischen Gesellschaft* 100 (1987). Also see Lewis, "Continuity in German Science," esp. 75, 364–67. Melchers discussed the possibility of taking the position of cultural minister in a letter to his friend Anton Lang, dated 12 November 1951. MPG Archive, Georg Melchers Papers, Abt. III, Rep. 75, Ordner 2.
18. Hans-Jörg Rheinberger, "Virusforschung an den Kaiser-Wilhelm-Instituten für Biochemie und für Biologie," in Doris Kaufmann, ed., *Geschichte der Kaiser-Wilhelm-Gesellschaft im Nationalsozialismus: Bestandsaufnahme und Perspektiven der Forschung* (Göttingen: Wallstein Verlag, 2000); Christina Brandt, "Metaphor und Experiment: Zur Forschung am Tabakmosaikvirus in Deutschland, 1940–1965" (Ph.D. diss., Technischen Universität Braunschweig, 2002); and Jeffrey Lewis, "From Virus Research to Molecular Biology: Tobacco Mosaic Virus in Germany, 1936–1956," *Journal of the History of Biology*, forthcoming.
19. Melchers's denazification certificate is included in his papers in the Max Planck Society. On 12 September 1949 he was officially judged "Nicht Betroffen," having never been a member or candidate for party membership. MPG Archive, Georg Melchers Papers, Abt. III, Rep. 75, Ordner 2.
20. Gunther Stent, *Nazis, Women, and Molecular Biology: Memoirs of a Lucky Self-Hater* (Kensington, CA: Briones Books, 1998), 352.

21. Melchers to Otto Hahn, 26 July 1948. MPG Archive, Georg Melchers Papers, Abt. III, Rep. 75, Ordner 1. Also see Schüring, "Ein 'unerfreulicher Vorgang,'" 287–91, 293–94.
22. Melchers to Dr. Miville, Basel, 3 June 1948. MPG Archive, Georg Melchers Papers, Abt. III, Rep. 75, Ordner 1.
23. *Georg Melchers an Seine Magnifizenz den Herrn Recktor der Universität Tübingen*, 10 September 1943. Tübingen Universitätsarchiv, Sig. 117/13634.
24. Schlösser to Melchers, 17 February 1950; Melchers to Schlösser, 27 May 1950. MPG Archive, Georg Melchers Papers, Abt. III, Rep. 75, Ordner 2.
25. For a more thorough account of this incident, see Lewis, "Kalter Krieg in der Max-Planck-Gesellschaft."
26. Melchers to Anton Lang, 1–5 November 1949. MPG Archive, Melchers Papers, Abt. III, Rep. 75, Ordner 1.
27. Helmuth Trischler, "Self-Mobilization or Resistance? Aeronautical Research and National Socialism," in Monika Renneberg and Mark Walker, eds., *Science, Technology, and National Socialism* (Cambridge: Cambridge University Press, 1994). Also see Dieter Hoffmann, "Carl Ramsauer, die deutsche Physikalische Gesellschaft und die Selbstmobilisierung der Physikerschaft im 'Dritten Reich,'" in Helmut Maier, ed., *Rüstungsforschung im Nationalsozialismus. Organisation, Mobilisierung, und Entgrenzung der Technikwissenschaften* (Göttingen: Wallstein Verlag, 2002).
28. Lewis, "Kalter Krieg in der Max-Planck-Gesellschaft," 440–42.
29. Ian Kershaw, *Hitler 1889–1936: Hubris* (New York: W. W. Norton, 1998), 530.
30. Konrad H. Jarausch, *The Unfree Professions: German Lawyers, Teachers, and Engineers, 1900–1950* (New York: Oxford University Press, 1990), 169.
31. Mark Walker, "Science, National Socialism, and the *Longue Durée*," *Historical Studies in the Physical and Biological Sciences* 24 (1994), 395–402, here 397.

– Chapter 22 –

POSTWAR JUSTICE AND THE TREATMENT OF NAZI ASSETS

Jonathan Petropoulos

In August 2002 the *New York Times* ran a front-page story under the heading, "Hitler, It Seems, Loved Money and Died Rich."[1] Despite the breathless, "stop-the-presses" tone of this article, this was an instance of journalists following the lead of scholars: over the past two decades, historians have documented Hitler's vast wealth and effectively countered the parts of the "Führer Myth" that portrayed him as ascetic and unconcerned about material possessions.[2] Indeed, it is now clear that all of the Nazi leaders were exceedingly wealthy and that the regime was a kleptocracy of the first order. Despite this realization, there is little understanding of what happened to the assets of the Nazi leaders and their high-ranking accomplices. To what extent were these individuals denuded of their wealth after the war? In other words, were they able to preserve it, and is this another instance in which one finds continuity between the Third Reich and the postwar period?

This essay examines the manner in which the Allies approached the assets belonging to Nazis—both high-ranking leaders and the rank and file. I will argue that the initial intentions of depriving Nazis of their wealth gave way to compromise, and that what started off as a legal regimen with stiff financial penalties ended up as one with mild sanctions—especially for those who were not at the pinnacle of the Nazi state. Most Nazis were able to preserve their wealth, even when it had been generated through the persecution of victims and the invasion of neighboring lands. For a variety of reasons the Western Allies and the authorities in the Federal Republic were

---

The author would like to thank Rebecca Boehling for her assistance with this essay.
Notes for this section begin on page 336.

unwilling to effect a redistribution of wealth in western Germany. I will also argue that the limited financial penalties had implications for the issue of victims' compensation—certainly symbolically and, one can argue, in terms of actual sums.

In order to understand this failure—the diluted sanctions that made denazification the very embodiment of the gray zone—it is necessary to examine the Allies' initial intentions with regard to the Nazi leaders' assets. The origins of the United States' policies with regard to Nazi property lie in the wartime measures that aimed at strangling Germany economically. While there were a number of agencies that contributed to this effort, one can point to the Office of Foreign Funds Control within the Treasury Department, the Office of Alien Property Custodian established by President Roosevelt in March 1942, and the Foreign Exchange and Blocking Control Branch within the State Department, which was also charged with securing enemy assets and then administering them.[3] Operation Safehaven, an interagency program formulated in 1944, aimed, among other things, "to block Germany from transferring assets to neutral countries, to ensure that German wealth would be accessible for war reparations and for the rehabilitation of Europe, to make possible the return to legal owners of properties looted from countries once occupied by the Germans, and to prevent the escape of strategic German personnel to neutral havens."[4] Subsequently, the important directive of April 1945, known as JCS-1067, in which the U.S. Joint Chiefs of Staff provided the commander in chief of the U.S. occupation forces with guidelines for a military government in Germany, also included specific provisions aimed at seizing "property, real and personal, owned or controlled by the Nazi Party, its formations . . . and by all persons subject to arrest under the provisions of paragraph 8 . . . [Adolf Hitler, his chief associates, other war criminals, and all persons who have participated in planning or carrying out Nazi enterprises. . . .]."[5] U.S. policy also permitted troops to requisition property belonging to Nazis so far as they were justified by military necessity. This practice of utilizing Nazi Party members' assets continued into the post-surrender period, and it was not uncommon to see army officers furnish their quarters with furniture, rugs, table services, and the like.[6]

After the defeat of Germany in May 1945, a series of laws and decrees were passed that elaborated on the means by which Nazis would be divested of their assets. For example, Military Government Law No. 52 (the Blocking Control Law) of mid-May 1945 "blocked all property owned or controlled directly or indirectly in whole or in part by the Reich or any political subdivision or agency thereof, the Nazi Party and affiliated organizations, all persons who were high in the political and economic life of Germany, and persons residing outside of Germany." It also blocked property that had been acquired under duress. Under MG Law No. 52, the Military Government had the right to seize any such property.[7] The subsequent MG Law No. 53 (the Foreign Exchange Control Law) of 31 May 1945 prohibited financial transactions involving persons inside Germany with those outside and provided for the surrender of all foreign assets to local branches of the Reichsbank. Because similar policies had been in place throughout the Supreme Headquarters Allied Expeditionary Force (SHAEF) occupation period (ending in July 1945), there were comparable measures in place in the British and French zones (the Russians had similar provisions that permitted the seizure of assets).

It is important to recognize that the forfeiture of property lay at the heart of the judicial strategy of the Allies. Indeed, this was a principle that all four victorious powers could agree upon. Control Council Law No. 10, which was ratified by military representatives of all four Allied Powers on 20 December 1945, listed the sanctions for those found guilty of the various charges that emerged at Nuremberg and in the subsequent trials: (a) death; (b) imprisonment for life or a term of years with or without hard labor; (c) fines; (d) forfeiture of property; (e) restitution of property wrongfully acquired; and (f) deprivation of some or all civil rights.[8] Well into 1946 U.S. officials discussed schemes to extract compensation from wealthy Nazis—an idea that continued to attract supporters until at least 1947. For example, after some of the jewels stolen from the Princes von Hessen were recovered and the thieves prosecuted, these valuables belonging to high-ranking Nazis were transported to the United States with an eye to seizing them as a contribution toward German reparations.[9]

The principle of levying fines was also embedded in the crucial 5 March 1946 Law for Liberation from National Socialism and Militarism. This law, which was at the centerpiece of what Hans Woller called General Lucius Clay's "not uncontroversial policy of 'turn-it-over-to-the-Germans,'" provided that every resident in the U.S. zone would be required to fill out a *Meldebogen* (questionnaire), which would then be assessed by German authorities.[10] Of the 13.5 million who filled them out, more than 6 million would appear before a *Spruchkammer*, where they were placed in one of five categories, with category I (major offender) being the most culpable and category V (exonerated) standing at the other end of the spectrum. While 98 percent of those who went through denazification were placed in category IV (fellow traveler or *Mitläufer*) or category V, more than one million Germans were in the former.[11] All individuals placed in categories I through IV paid some kind of fine. As Earl Ziemke noted in his study written for the Center of Military History in the United States, "Those who were exonerated or paid fines were considered denazified and recovered their full civil rights."[12] In other words, the forfeiture of property was part of the denazification process from a very early stage.

The five categories of complicity that lay at the core of the March 1946 Law for Liberation from National Socialism and Militarism provide a useful organizing schema with which to approach the property sanctions levied against Nazi Party members. Most observers recognize that the categorization was highly imperfect—and more specifically, too lenient, as seriously compromised individuals were let off as mere "fellow travelers." Historian Lutz Niethammer aptly titled his path-breaking study "the fellow traveler factory" (*Die Mitläufer-fabrik*).[13] Nonetheless, by February 1950 denazification had yielded the following verdicts: nearly 1,700 were found to be major offenders (category I); 23,000 were offenders (category II); 150,400 were classified as lesser offenders (category III); 1,006,000 were declared fellow travelers (category IV); and 3,939,000 had their cases dismissed (category V).[14]

Not surprisingly, Allied and West German authorities were most effective in securing the property of the major offenders in category I—although, even here, it is far from clear that all 1,700 lost their assets. The Major War Criminals who went on trial at the International Military Tribunal lost most but not all of their assets. Family members were permitted to keep most of the property that they possessed prior to 1933. This principle meant that individuals like Emmy Göring pursued property that had belonged to her husband, and that the appeals process often continued throughout the 1960s and 1970s.

With regard to the property of category I offenders, it is striking to see how the sanctions figured into the legal process and to note that rather elaborate mechanisms were developed to handle this property. With regard to the first, even Hitler's estate was liquidated: on 15 October 1948 a denazification board heard the dictator's case (his profession was listed as "painter and decorator"), and his estate, which was valued at the astonishingly low sum of DM 200,000 (the equivalent of US$625,000 today) was ordered confiscated (this applied to his wife Eva Braun's property as well). Two empty chairs were placed in the courtroom to symbolize the presence of the two.[15]

With regard to individuals placed in categories II through IV, we have a different picture: individuals in these categories by and large retained their wealth. Just as denazification became increasingly less effective in bringing perpetrators to justice, the associated financial penalties were watered down so as to become essentially meaningless.[16] The roots of the failure predated the transfer of authority to the West Germans. U.S. officials increasingly sought to disengage from the tasks of restitution and justice, and the French and British were even less inclined to deprive former Nazis of resources. Historian Ian Turner noted that "the British opposed the radical and comprehensive measures proposed by the Americans" as they "tried instead to strike a balance between the needs of security and the demands of a shattered economy."[17]

The large number of Germans who were subject to denazification—in the American zone, 28 percent of adults required vetting—and the shortage of personnel to carry out the process also undermined efforts at justice.[18] This created a backlog of cases at a time when there was a labor shortage. Indeed, it became a conscious policy to try those who appeared less incriminated first so that they could return to work. Historian Rebecca Boehling has shown that "the trials of the least incriminated came at a time when punishment was most stringent."[19] This enabled many of the "bigger fish" to get off the hook. The amnesties that the Western Allies initiated beginning in late 1947—for example, the American amnesty for the young and socially disadvantaged and the French one for "all merely nominal National Socialists"—set a tone and established a significant precedent.[20] In the Soviet zone, denazification ended altogether with the decree of 26 February 1948.[21]

While the origins of the policy of diminished penalties lie in the period of the Allies' occupation, the key developments occurred once the Germans took over. Historian Norbert Frei writes about an "unmistakable collapse of punitive morale so soon after the emergence of the Federal Republic" in 1949.[22] There are a number of factors that contributed to the diminished penalties: fatigue with the trials; the wish to forget crimes and transgressions; the focus on rebuilding the country and the need for a capitalist elite; the abilities of skilled attorneys who represented wealthy defendants; and a judicial system that did not feature financial compensation as an instrument of justice. It was the judges and the prosecutors who bore ultimate responsibility for the "extraordinarily mild judgments," but "undoubtedly they could feel their reluctance [to levy stiff penalties] to be in harmony with the prevailing public and political mood."[23]

In West Germany there was initially a system of fining those found guilty, although there were some disagreements between the Germans and the American occupation authorities. The fine was supposed to go to a restitution fund *(Wiedergutmachungsfond)*. For *Mitläufer* in category IV, this fine was set at RM 2,000 (note that there was no set amount for those in categories I–III). Those found responsible (hence, all those not placed in category V) were also supposed to pay court costs, which were set according to a table that took into account the income and wealth of the defendant.[24] Disagreements arose between Germans and Americans over the fines: somewhat surprisingly, many German officials thought the RM 2,000 fine was inadequate (it was roughly the same as a carton of cigarettes on the black market, but could also be the equivalent of a month's salary of a low-ranking employee). General Clay remained committed to the RM 2,000 fine and argued that in the case of the wealthier defendants, the court costs would be raised so as to penalize them in a significant way. But court costs exceeded the mandatory *Mitläufer* fine in only 4 percent of the cases—and the court cost revenues were not directed to the victims.[25] Granted, there were instances, such as that experienced by a wealthy salesman *(Grosskaufmann)*, where the fine of RM 2,000 was combined with court costs of RM 21,000, but his case was a rarity.[26] Lutz Niethammer concluded, "After the implementation of the March 1946 Law of Liberation the original sense of the American denazification directives was reversed: the hardest hit were neither the German elite nor the holders of high office during the Third Reich, but individual workers, low-ranking civil servants, housewives, and the socially indefinable."[27]

Also deserving special mention in the dilution of sentences and fines are the Courts of Appeal *(Berufungskammern)*. All individuals who went through denazification had recourse to an appellate body—one that had a trained jurist as its chair—and it was customary to avail oneself of this right.[28] In most cases, the *Berufungskammer* would knock the individual down a category: art dealer Karl Haberstock, for example, used his appeal to move from a lesser offender (category III) to a "fellow traveler" (category IV). This not only enabled him to resume his profession but also entailed a reduction in his fine from DM 200,000 to DM 127,000.[29] Prince Philipp von Hessen, a key figure in my study of German princes during the Third Reich, was initially placed in category II and sanctioned with the loss of 30 percent of his property and the forfeiture of any public funds, pensions, or rents.[30] This penalty was consistent with many other prominent but second-rank figures in the Third Reich.[31] Because his assets were valued at more than DM 600,000, this was a considerable sum. To pay it he would have had to sell off a number of family properties and/or possessions. In February 1949 an appeals court showed him leniency by lowering his classification to category III and reducing his fine to DM 36,568 (including court costs).[32] In order to pay this bill, Prince Philipp transferred ownership of Schloss Belvedere in Kassel—his official residence when he was *Oberpräsident* of Hessen-Nassau—to the state. In that it was badly damaged by Allied bombs and was associated with painful memories (especially with those of his wife, Princess Mafalda, who had perished during the war), relinquishing Schloss Belvedere was a modest sanction.

Several other factors also obstructed the seizure of Nazis' assets. Zonal boundaries enabled some who had been found guilty to avoid payment: if they moved from one zone to another there were often inadequate mechanisms in place to pursue shirkers.[33] At other times individuals simply pleaded poverty and the fines were listed as unrecoverable. The currency reforms of June 1948 also presented certain opportunities: many perpetrators had delayed payment and then found that with the conversion to the Deutschmark, the amount of the fine had been reduced.[34] What started as a tendency in the courts became policy in 1954: the 17 July 1954 Law Concerning Release from Punishments and Fines and the Cancellation of Punitive and Fining Proceedings released virtually all former Nazis from the threat of paying monetary penalties for their deeds.[35]

While the denazification courts showed a lack of will with regard to imposing fines, there were other areas concerning denazification where authorities—both Allied and German—were quite tough. In Hesse, denazification cashiered 52 percent of the elementary school teachers, and student-teacher ratios of one to 120 were common (with instructors responsible for three shifts a day).[36] An even higher percentage of teachers were sacked in Bavaria—largely due to the May 1945 MG Law No. 8, which prohibited employing Nazis "either in the private or in the public sector in any capacity other than common laborer."[37] Millions of books were also pulped. In short, there were some areas, such as re-education, where authorities exhibited greater firmness.

The decision not to deprive many Nazis of their property reflected fundamental political beliefs held by the Western Allies and most Germans (while noting that there were genuine differences of opinion). Former OSS analyst and later renowned historian Carl Schorske noted in 1948 that the Americans and British had developed an occupation policy that was based on a conception of the nature of Nazism as a thing of the mind, an evil idea that would have to be rooted out through the elimination of the bearers of the idea and the re-education of the German people as a whole. This conception of Nazism involves the introduction of no change in the fundamental structure of society. Property relations are unchanged. Administration has been largely entrusted to putatively non-political, middle-class technicians. Thus the continuity of the social structure of Imperial, Weimar, and National Socialist Germany is maintained the Western Zones.[38]

Schorske recognized that the Western Allies were not about to embark upon a restructuring of society—certainly not in the threatening Cold War context. They would rather have former Nazi elite retain their wealth, and similarly, permit former Nazi functionaries to return to their old jobs. In short, the Western Allies backed away from what some called "an artificial revolution"—the redistribution of assets away from elites who had supported the Nazi regime.[39]

Despite the increasingly inadequate measures to penalize former Nazis and deprive them of their property, the West German authorities still recovered assets with considerable value. The question arises, where did these assets go? The simple answer is that they were divided between the federal and provincial governments, with the latter receiving the majority of the property. The principle that evolved was that if a Nazi leader used official funds to acquire something, then it became the property of the Federal Republic. If the property was determined to have been acquired with personal resources, then it was transferred to the provincial government. Because so many high-ranking Nazis had residences in Bavaria, and because so much of their property was stored there at war's end (especially art), the state of Bavaria became the chief beneficiary when it came to the seizure of property. For example, Hitler's residences in Munich on the Prinzregentenstrasse and on the Obersalzberg were both given to the state of Bavaria (as were the rights for *Mein Kampf*).[40] This property was sometimes referred to by Bavarians as "KRD50-*Vermögen*" (short for *Kontrollratsdirektive* Nr. 50 *Vermögen*, or Control Council Directive No. 50 Property), and the state often engaged trustees to administer the property. The Bavarian state also received many works of art in this way, including eight hundred to nine hundred that are currently housed in the Bavarian State Painting Collections based in Munich. The museum recently published a study of the 128 paintings from this group that came from Hermann Göring's collection.[41]

As noted above, the artwork acquired by Nazi leaders as part of official projects passed to the federal government. This included the objects intended for the Führermuseum in Linz as well as the Göring estate, Carinhall, just outside of Berlin (which he claimed he intended to turn into a museum). In 1952 these objects became the responsibility of the Treuhandverwaltung für Kulturgut (Trustee Administration for Cultural Objects), an agency that came under the aegis of the Foreign Ministry in Bonn. The Treuhandverwaltung existed until 1962 and referred to the works in its care as the "Linz List" (even though, as noted above, some works came from the collection of Göring and others). Until its dissolution, the Treuhandverwaltung continued to restitute works from the "Linz List" when owners came forward.[42] In other cases it loaned important works to West German museums, and many works once in Nazi leaders' collections continue to grace the walls of notable museums; this includes Lucas Cranach the Elder's *Golden Age,* Watteau's *La Danse* (both in Berlin in the new Gemäldegalerie), and Rembrandt's *Portrait of Saskia* (in the Frankfurt Städel Museum).[43] The works belonging to Nazi leaders that were deemed private property and therefore passed to the *Länder* are also often in the same museums. Very few visitors understand the codes and phrases that differentiate the two: for example, works that belong to the state of Bavaria have the notation "transferred from the state" *("aus Staatsbesitz überwiesen"),* while those from the "Linz List" feature the phrase "loan of the Federal Republic of Germany" *("Leihgabe der BRD").* Most museum guidebooks and publications were produced before the issue of Holocaust victims' assets became a public concern and do not provide specific information about provenance.[44] The distinction between these two categories has been even more difficult to preserve in cases when the works have been sent on loan to offices of government officials, including that of the chancellor. Then again, this may be intentional: it is unlikely that Gerhard Schröder or any other chancellor would want it known that a painting gracing their august office was purchased by Hitler or Göring.

With regard to the property of the top Nazis, three points deserve emphasis. First, there was a lot of it and it was extremely valuable. Even after the restitution process had run its course—and this included returning all objects acquired abroad between 1939 and 1945 to the country of origin—costly assets remained. With regard to art, the Americans transferred approximately twenty thousand objects to the Germans, including 3,800 works acquired by Hitler and his agents and intended for the Linz museum and between three and four hundred from Hermann Göring's collection.[45] There were also thousands of coins and books belonging to Nazi leaders.[46] Second, the top Nazi leaders and their families did not keep much of their property. In short, financial penalties worked fairly well for category I offenders. Third, the seized property was handled in a manner that was less than transparent and was inadequate as a symbolic gesture. There were opportunities to create a program that would have benefited victims of National Socialism in a more direct and meaningful way. Indeed, it is instructive to examine some of the alternative proposals.

One of the most intriguing and serious suggestions for this artwork came from Dr. Philipp Auerbach, the leading German government authority on the compensation of Holocaust victims in the immediate postwar period. Auerbach had a number of titles within the constantly evolving German state bureaucracy that developed after 1945; perhaps most notably, he was *Staatskommissar* for the Racially, Politically, and Religiously Persecuted. Auerbach himself was a survivor of Auschwitz and Buchenwald and was also a leading figure in the remaining Jewish community in West Germany. He fought relentlessly for the compensation of Holocaust victims—

an effort that yielded the most tangible results in 1952 when the Federal Republic signed the Luxembourg Pact and committed to pay reparations to Israel and the Jewish Material Claims Conference.

Prior to this agreement, which was both hard-fought and controversial from the German perspective, Auerbach had advanced a plan to raise funds to compensate victims. The Auerbach plan, as some called it, emerged in 1949 and entailed taking the remaining works belonging to Nazi leaders then in the Central Collecting Point (CCP) in Munich and shipping them to the United States to be auctioned off.[47] Auerbach, who was no art historian or dealer, estimated that the sale would yield US$100–200 million (a wide range but still a considerable sum at that time—one multiplies by a factor of ten to arrive at approximate present-day equivalents).[48] Philipp Auerbach reasoned that the United States was the only country with the financial resources to pay good prices for the artwork. In a sense he tried to actualize an argument of some contemporary observers who believed that the Germans should not benefit from the art-collecting efforts of the Nazi leaders. For example, Francis Henry Taylor, the director of the Metropolitan Museum of Art in New York, argued in 1947 that the art acquired by Nazi leaders should not remain in Germany and benefit the aggressor country but rather should come to the United States against dollar payment for the reconstruction of German cities and relief of the German population.[49] In Auerbach's plan, the Allies would pay for the objects and also help struggling Holocaust victims: 80 percent would go to victims in Bavaria and 20 percent to victims living abroad.[50]

Auerbach's plan elicited criticism from the beginning. Art experts—both German and American—discounted his estimate that the auction would bring US$200 million. Ernst Hanfstaengl, the general director of the Bavarian State Painting Collections, estimated that 75 percent of the works were nineteenth- and early-twentieth-century German art, for which there was limited interest and demand in the United States. He admitted that the 15 percent that were Dutch masters would fare well but thought that Auerbach's estimate was pure fantasy.[51] U.S. Monuments, Fine Arts, and Archives officer Stephan Munsing concurred and thought that the sale might bring US$200,000. Despite this sniping, there was still interest in the proposal by the art experts and government officials who were overseeing the restitution process. Rose Valland, the famed French museum curator who had continued to work in the Nazis' plundering headquarters in the Jeu de Paume and had resisted them to the best of her ability, argued for an international commission to study the plans to help victims. She appeared intrigued by the Auerbach proposal and was keen to do something with the art other than give it to the German state. She also suggested that the works might be used to "satisfy the not-yet-fulfilled claims of damaged nations."[52]

Auerbach lobbied everyone with influence whom he could reach, but his plan was quashed with one decisive blow by the highest-ranking U.S. official in West Germany, High Commissioner John McCloy. McCloy wrote the Bavarian Minister President Hans Ehard in August 1950,

In view of the large number of those items which are still unidentified and the fact that several unsatisfied external restitution claims have not yet been acted upon, we are not prepared at this time to entertain any new proposals affecting the disposition of objects at the Collecting Point in a manner inconsistent with present policies and procedures. I would therefore appreciate it if you will bring these facts to the attention of Dr. Auerbach and request that, for the time being, at least, he discontinue any further efforts along those lines.[53]

McCloy and the other top brass had a vision of restitution in which the United States would not appear self-interested. They did not want to give rise to charges that they had exploited the postwar situation, and they rejected all proposals that aimed at enriching U.S. collections in a manner that was too direct. As far as compensation of Holocaust victims was concerned, the American officials supported the return of all Jewish property—including heirless objects to Jewish successor organizations—and pushed for the West German government to provide compensation, but that was as far as they were prepared to go.

Auerbach's program was thus sunk. A tragic conclusion to the story came in 1952, when Philipp Auerbach was charged with mismanagement of his office.[54] Bavarian authorities removed him from his position and tried him for fabricating claims (using forged documents) and for receiving reimbursement from the state of Baden-Württemberg.[55] Subjected to a humiliating high-profile trial, he was found guilty in 1952 by a panel of judges, of whom at least three out of five were "rehabilitated" Nazis who, like so many, continued their careers after the Third Reich. Shortly after hearing the verdict, Auerbach committed suicide by overdosing on sleeping pills. So ended the life of one of the first and most important officials working for victims' compensation.

The "Auerbach case" also dealt a blow to restitution efforts in general. As William Daniels of the office of the U.S. High Commissioner for Germany noted in 1951, "The whole affair is having a most unfortunate effect on the General Claims program and on Restitution, as well, which are inseparable in the public mind."[56] The imbroglio coincided with a renewal of U.S. officials' efforts to extricate themselves from the restitution process—a shift captured in the title of Constantin Goschler's essay, "The United States and *Wiedergutmachung* for Victims of Nazi Persecution: From Leadership to Disengagement."[57]

Much of the artwork that had entered the collections of Nazi leaders belonged to a gray zone that fell between restitution to the victims and their heirs, on the one hand, and the accession into the regular collections of museums on the other. With their curious status revealed only through a kind of code, they sit in limbo on the walls of German museums. Furthermore, in the 1960s Bavarian authorities embarked on a program of selling some of the works in their possession that had once belonged to Nazi leaders. Museum officials determined that certain paintings were not of museum quality. With the approval of state officials, they put them up for auction in what amounted to clandestine sales. To de-accession these works, the government turned to auction houses that had existed during the Third Reich and had profited handsomely as the Nazi leaders amassed their collections. These compromised vendors therefore profited again as they sold works from Nazi leaders' collections: in another act that falls somewhere in the gray zone, they did not reveal the provenance of the artworks to buyers. This resulted in customers purchasing works that once adorned the homes of Hitler, Göring, Goebbels, Bormann, and others, and not knowing about the works' prior history.[58] More importantly, the revenue from these sales of works belonging to Nazi leaders went to the museums themselves. They used the revenue to fill holes in their collections—especially modern works that had been sold off during the Third Reich.

It bears mentioning that there is now a precedent for taking works that were acquired by Nazi leaders, as well as those that were found at war's end and whose owners were not identifiable, and selling them for the benefit of victims. In 1996 Austrian authorities took artwork of this kind that had been housed in the Mauerbach repository outside Vienna and had Christie's auction it off. The sale brought US$14.6 million that was given to Jewish groups. This art had also once passed through the CCP and had been handled by the Austrian government in a problematic manner (few survivors and heirs were permitted to inspect the artwork or relevant documents, some who recovered paintings in the 1970s were charged storage fees, and there was a general tendency to underestimate the artwork's value).[59] The Germans' share of the CCP remaining stock was significantly greater than that of the Austrians. One should also emphasize that many valuable works belonging to Nazi leaders are still in German museums and that it would not be difficult to sell them for the benefit of the victims.

While one must recognize that the West Germans (and then the unified Germans) have paid a considerable sum in compensation to victims of National Socialism—more than US$60 billion to date has been distributed to more than five hundred thousand victims around the world—one can also identify areas where reparations have been inadequate.[60] The history of denazification, where an early firmness and idealism gave way to a kind of passivity and cynicism, shows the limitations of justice in the wake of the Third Reich. Just as surviving victims and heirs ended up in a gray zone with partial restitution and modest compensation, so too did perpetrators emerge with much of their wealth intact. Historians have long known that nearly all of those who went through denazification were categorized as "exonerated" or "fellow travelers," but even those in categories II and III were put in a position that facilitated the rehabilitation of careers and the return to prosperity. It was only the major war criminals and a very few others who endured a significant loss of property. And, as discussed above, even in the cases where forfeiture occurred, the final disposition raises such serious questions as to leave much of the property in a kind of limbo. The treatment of Nazis' assets does constitute a kind of gray zone between the white of just penalization and the black of irresoluteness and expediency, but it is a dark shade of gray.

Notes

1. Steven Erlanger, "Hitler, It Seems, Loved Money and Died Rich," *New York Times* (8 August 2002).
2. See, for example, the popular works of Wulf Schwarzwäller, e.g., *Hitler's Geld: vom armen Kunstmaler zum millionenschweren Führer* (Vienna: Überreuter, 1998); and James Pool, *Hitler and His Secret Partners: Contributions, Loot, and Rewards, 1933–1945* (New York: Pocket Books, 1997).
3. Presidential Commission on Holocaust Assets in the United States, *Plunder and Restitution: The U.S. and Holocaust Victims' Assets* (Washington, DC: U.S. Government Printing Office, 2000), SR-31-45.
4. William Slany, *U.S. and Allied Efforts to Recover and Restore Gold and Other Assets Stolen or Hidden by Germany During World War II* (Washington, DC: Department of State, 1997), 15. See also Robert Lester, ed., *The Safehaven Program* (Bethesda, MD: University Publications of America, 2002).
5. "Directive of the United States Joint Chiefs of Staff to the Commander-in-Chief of the United States Forces of Occupation Regarding the Military Government of Germany (JCS 1067)," in Beate Ruhm von Oppen, ed., *Documents on Germany Under Occupation, 1945–1954* (London: Oxford University Press, 1955), 13–27.
6. See, for example, the utilization of property from castles belonging to the Princes von Hessen; more specifically, a General Saunders is cited as removing objects for his quarters in a villa at Königstein. Heinrich von Hessen, *Der kristallene Lüster. Meine deutsch-italienische Jugend, 1927–1947* (Munich: Piper Verlag, 1994), 203.
7. See www.ushmm.org/uia-cgi/uia_doc/art/x9-46?hr=null. The records of the Foreign Exchange and Blocking Control Branch are located in NARA, RG 260 (Theater of Operations Records). See also *Plunder and Restitution*, SR-102.
8. Control Council Law No. 10 ("Punishment of Persons Guilty of War Crimes, Crimes Against Peace, and Against Humanity"), at http://www.ess.uwe.ac.uk/documents/cntrl10.htm. Prior to that, there was Directive CCS 551, issued by the Combined Chiefs of Staff on 28 April 1944 (according to Ian Turner, "the first recorded expression of Anglo-American denazification policy"), which aimed at "destruction of Nazism-Fascism and the Nazi hierarchy." See F. S. V. Donnison, *Civil Affairs and Military Government: North West Europe, 1944–1946* (London: HMSO, 1961), 359; and Lutz Niethammer, *Entnazifizierung in Bayern* (Frankfurt: S. Fischer, 1972), 57. Also Ian Turner, "Denazification in the British Zone," in Ian Turner, ed., *Reconstruction in Post-War Germany: British Occupation Policy and the Western Zones, 1945–1955* (Oxford: Berg, 1989), 245.
9. Wolfgang von Hessen, *Aufzeichnungen* (Kronberg/Taunus: Privatdruck, 1986), 226–28.
10. Hans Woller, *Gesellschaft und Politik in der amerikanischen Besatzungszone: Die Regionen Ansbach und Fürth, 1945–1949* (Munich: R. Oldenbourg, 1986), 118. The original quote reads, "nicht unumstrittenen Politik des 'Turn-it-over-to-the-Germans.'"
11. Christian Zentner and Friedemann Bedürftig, eds., *The Encyclopedia of the Third Reich* (New York: Macmillan, 1991), 190.
12. Earl Ziemke, *The U.S. Army in the Occupation of Germany, 1944–1946* (Washington, DC: Center of Military History, United States Army, 1975), 430.
13. Lutz Niethammer, *Die Mitläufer-fabrik: Die Entnazifizierung am Beispiel Bayerns* (Berlin: J. H. W. Dietz, 1982).
14. Zentner and Bedürftig, eds., *Encyclopedia of the Third Reich*, 190.
15. Julia Pascal, "Unbanning Hitler," *The New Statesman* (25 June 2001).
16. See J. H. Herz, "The Fiasco of Denazification in Germany," *Political Science Quarterly* 63/4 (December 1948), 560–94; W. E. Griffith, "Denazification in the United States Zone of Germany," *Annals of the American Academy of Political and Social Science* 267/1 (January 1950), 68–76.
17. Turner, "Denazification in the British Zone," 239.
18. Rebecca Boehling, "Denazification in Theory and Practice in the United States Occupation Zone in Post–World War II Germany," unpublished paper.
19. Ibid.

20. For the U.S. amnesty of 17 November 1947 and the French military governor's amnesty of 13 July 1948, see Zentner and Bedürftig, eds., *Encyclopedia of the Third Reich*, 190.
21. Timothy Vogt, *Denazification in Soviet-Occupied Germany: Brandenburg, 1945–1948* (Cambridge, MA: Harvard University Press, 2000).
22. Norbert Frei, *Adenauer's Germany and the Nazi Past: The Politics of Amnesty and Integration* (New York: Columbia University Press, 2002), 67.
23. Ibid.
24. Niethammer, *Die Mitläufer-fabrik*, 651.
25. Ibid., 651–52.
26. Ibid., 651.
27. Ibid., 547. The German reads, *"Der ursprüngliche Sinn der amerikanischen Entnazifizierungsdirektiven war nach der Duchführung des BefrG [Befreiungsgesetz] ins Gegenteil verkehrt: Am stärksten betroffen waren weder die deutsche Elite noch die höheren Amtsträger des NS, sondern einzelne Arbeiter, kleine Beamter und Angestellte, Hausfrauen und sozial undefinierbare."*
28. Ibid., 645.
29. See Jonathan Petropoulos, *The Faustian Bargain: The Art World in Nazi Germany* (New York/London: Oxford University Press, 2000), 96.
30. Hessisches Hauptstaatsarchiv Wiesbaden (HHSAW), Denazification file of Prince Philipp, #519563, Spruch for Prince Philipp, 17 December 1947, 1. See also IfZG, Munich, clipping file of Prince Philipp von Hessen, article of unspecified newspaper, 19 December 1947.
31. Hans Woller, *Gesellschaft und Politik*, 146. Woller gives the example of the Kreiswart bei KdF named Mühler who received the same penalty in July 1947.
32. HHSAW, Denazification file of Prince Philipp, #519563, Dr. Ortweiler, Berufungskammer Begründung, 10 February 1949.
33. Niethammer, *Die Mitläufer-fabrik*, 651.
34. Ibid.
35. Frei, *Adenauer's Germany*, 68.
36. James Tent, *Mission on the Rhine: Reeducation and Denazification in American-Occupied Germany* (Chicago: University of Chicago Press, 1982), 168.
37. Ibid., 51.
38. Carl Schorske, "The Dilemma in Germany," *Virginia Quarterly Review* 24/1 (Winter 1948), 30. Schorske is cited in Rebecca Boehling, "Denazification in Theory and Practice."
39. J. D. Montgomery, *Forced to Be Free: The Artificial Revolution in Germany and Japan* (Chicago: University of Chicago Press, 1957).
40. Erlanger, "Hitler." Indeed, the state of Bavaria received all of Hitler's assets after the war, including the rights for *Mein Kampf*—except for the English language edition, which was bought by Hutchinson in the United Kingdom (which was subsequently purchased by Random House, which was acquired by Bertelsmann). Pascal, "Unbanning Hitler."
41. Elizabeth Hoefl-Hielscher, "Auf Spurensuche nach der Beutekunst," *Süddeutsche Zeitung* 19 (24 January 2001), L3.
42. Letter from Harold König of the *Oberfinanzdirektion* Berlin to the author, 23 February 2001.
43. In Munich's Neue Pinakothek, Hans Makart's *Die Falknerin* (which was Göring's private property—a birthday gift from Hitler in 1938) and Ferdinand Waldmüller's *Junge Bäuerin mit drei Kinder* (part of photographer Heinrich Hoffmann's collection) are displayed next to Ferdinand Waldmüller's *Vorbereitung zum Weinlesefest* and his *Der Wildbach Strubb bei Ischl*, which Hitler acquired for Linz. These latter two are among the fourteen works on loan from the federal government to the Bavarian State Paintings Collection.
44. The most popular catalogues for the Alte and Neue Pinakotheken from Munich, which were produced in 1983 and 1989, respectively, say very little about previous ownership. See, for example, the *Bayerischen Staatsgemäldesammlungen, Neue Pinakothek München* (Munich: BSGS, 1989), 206, 360, for the entries concerning the Makart and Waldmüller works noted above.
45. Anja Heuss, *Kunst- und Kulturgüterraub: Eine vergleichende Studie zur Besatzungspolitik der Nationalsozialisten in Frankreich unter der Sowjetunion* (Universitätsverlag C. Winter, 2000), 16–23.

46. Bayerisches Hauptstaatsarchiv (BHSA), MK 51498, Dieter Sattler, "Vermerkung," 26 February 1949. As noted above, these objects were then divided between the Federal Republic, which according to a 1969 report had 2,708 paintings and frescos among other works. The other paintings noted above would presumably have gone to the states, most notably Bavaria, as the property of Nazi leaders and the Party. This is presented in the background information at www.lostart.de.
47. BHSA, MK 50871, Philipp Auerbach, "Considerations for the Use of Confiscated National Socialist Assets and of Frozen Funds Belonging to the Beneficiaries of Compensation or Restitution for the Benefit of the Victims of National Socialism and of the State of Bavaria," April 1949.
48. In the above-cited document (note 47), he reduced the estimate to US$100–150 million, but in other discussions (see Sattler's "Vermerkung" in note 46), he used the sum of US$200 million.
49. For a discussion of U.S. museum directors seeking an opportunity to acquire works from German state museums, see Kenneth Lindsay, "Official Art Seizure Under the Military Cloak," *Art Antiquity and Law* 3/2 (June 1998), 128. See also National Archives Record Administration (NARA), RG 59, Lot 62D-4, box 28, Ardelia Hall, "Proposed Sale of Public German Art Collections," 30 March 1948. The chief curator of the National Gallery in Washington, DC, John Walker, another important adviser who helped shape U.S. policy concerning looted art, was also suspected as having designs for works recovered in Europe. Many believed that he hoped that some or all of the 202 pictures removed from Germany in 1946 and shipped to the United States would end up in his institution. General Lucius Clay, for example, wrote General Noce on 4 April 1948, "From the very beginning I have had serious doubts as to the real desires and intent of the directors of the National Gallery of Art. Their representatives on an early visit talked about the possibility of obtaining these pictures either in reparations or in payment of occupation costs." J. E. Smith, ed., *The Papers of General Lucius D. Clay* (Bloomington: Indiana University Press, 1974), vol. 2, 615–16, cited by Lindsay, "Official Art Seizure," 128.
50. Auerbach, "Considerations."
51. Sattler, "Vermerkung."
52. Ibid. The German reads, "die überreste aus diesen Sammlung zur Befriedigung der noch nicht verantworteten Ansprüche der geschädigten Nationen zu verwenden."
53. BHSA, Staatskanzlei 14249, John McCloy to Hans Ehard, 3 August 1950.
54. Constantin Goschler, "Der Fall Philipp Auerbach. Wiedergutmachung in Bayern," in Ludolf Herbst and Constantin Goschler, eds., *Wiedergutmachung in der Bundesrepublik Deutschland* (Munich: R. Oldenbourg, 1989), 77–98.
55. NARA, RG 466 (Records for the High Commissioner for Germany), box 2, William Daniels to Alex Kiefer, 24 March 1951.
56. Ibid.
57. Constantin Goschler, "The United States and *Wiedergutmachung* for Victims of Nazi Persecution: From Leadership to Disengagement," in Axel Frohn, ed., *Holocaust and Shilumin: The Policy of Wiedergutmachung in the Early 1950s* (Washington, DC: German Historical Institute, Occasional Paper No. 2, 1991).
58. See Jonathan Petropoulos, "For Sale: A Troubled Legacy," *ARTnews* 100/6 (June 2001), 114–20.
59. Andrew Decker, "A Legacy of Shame," *ARTnews* 83/10 (December 1984), 54–76. See also Oliver Rathkolb, "From 'Legacy of Shame' to the Auction of 'Heirless' Art in Vienna: Coming to Terms 'Austrian Style' with Nazi Artistic Booty," at http://www.museum-security.org/ww2/Legacy-of-Shame.html.
60. Stuart Eizenstat, *Imperfect Justice: Looted Assets, Slave Labor, and the Unfinished Business of World War II* (New York: Public Affairs, 2003), 15. See also Hans Günter Hockerts, "*Wiedergutmachung* in Deutschland 1945–2000," *Vierteljahrshefte für Zeitgeschichte* 49/2 (2001), 167–214; and Susanna Schrafstetter, "The Diplomacy of *Wiedergutmachung:* Memory, the Cold War, and the Western European Victims of Nazism, 1956–1964," *Holocaust and Genocide Studies* 17/3 (2003), 459–79.

– Chapter 23 –

THE GRAY ZONES OF HOLOCAUST RESTITUTION
American Justice and Holocaust Morality

Michael J. Bazyler

The end of the twentieth century brought a completely unexpected chapter to the postwar consequences of the Holocaust. Beginning in 1995, a half-century after the end of World War II, a campaign took place to try to obtain monetary compensation for the material losses suffered by Jews and other persecuted groups during the war. To everyone's surprise, even to the participants themselves, this campaign would become a major political issue not only in Europe but also in the United States. One illustration of the prominence of the Holocaust restitution movement was that more news articles were published about the Holocaust between 1995 and 2000 than during the fifty preceding years, and most of these articles focused on Holocaust restitution.

Another major surprise was that the locus of the campaign did not take place in Europe, where the Holocaust occurred, but rather in the United States. As a result, the American justice system has been the prime mover behind the numerous agreements concluded between 1998 and 2001 that resulted in compensation being paid to (1) individuals whose families' bank accounts had been looted either during or after the war; (2) former slaves of German companies seeking payment for their wartime labor; and (3) survivors whose claims to benefits of insurance policies issued to their family members who perished during the war had been earlier denied. A fourth subject of Holocaust restitution, also taking place in the United States and often in American courts, involved competing claims to Nazi looted art. Art and cultural objects looted from Jews by the Germans and others are only now being returned by museums, galleries, and private owners to the

Notes for this section begin on page 356.

prewar owners or their families from whom the art was stolen during the Nazi era.[1]

The agreements brought about by the United States government and before U.S. judges since August 1998, when the first settlement took place, reached by 2001 a figure of somewhere between US$8 and 11 billion, depending on the method of calculation. While these settlements came nowhere close to fully compensating still-living Holocaust victims or heirs for their, or their families', wartime material losses, the sheer size of the settlements and their unexpected occurrence so long after the end of the war qualifies them as a major victory for surviving victims and others seeking to right as best as possible the horrible financial wrongs committed during the war.

Not all, however, is positive. The campaign for Holocaust restitution also produced some morally ambiguous results that, within the terminology of this book, can rightly be called the gray zones of Holocaust restitution. This essay will focus on the gray zones arising from the Holocaust restitution campaign. The purpose of the discussion of these gray zones is not to provide answers to the difficult questions raised during the movement. These hard issues, as will be shown, are not amenable to easy solutions. However, it is critical that they be discussed, and done so openly, so that this latest legacy of the Holocaust may be fully understood.

The Gray Zones Implicated by Holocaust Restitution

This section will identify and analyze the gray zones of the Holocaust restitution movement. Five such controversial issues will be discussed.

1. Does seeking restitution funds diminish the memory and distort the history of the Holocaust?

Almost from the beginning, the efforts to collect monetary compensation from the European corporate wrongdoers produced strong controversy; this is not at all surprising considering, as one writer observed, the "minefield of passions that lies beneath this issue."[2]

The question of whether victims of genocide should seek monetary compensation from the perpetrators and other wrongdoers raises important questions, among them: Does the taking of monies by the survivors demean the memory of the deceased victims? Does it allow the perpetrators or their heirs to now claim that their debt has been paid and any moral guilt extinguished?

The Jewish activists pondering these questions in the late 1990s—as they were considering whether to seek compensation from the Swiss banks, German industry, and other European corporate wrongdoers—failed to realize, however, that they were reinventing the wheel. These were, in fact, the very same issues hotly debated by an earlier generation of Jews.

At the end of the war, the surviving victims had to decide whether they should accept restitution from a willing West Germany, or if the acceptance of such funds would bring dishonor to the six million Jews killed by the

Nazis. The postwar debate was raucous, with opponents labeling such payments as "blood money." It most clearly manifested itself in Israel, where many of the destitute survivors came to start new lives. Street demonstrations, led by both opponents and proponents, showed the terrible rift in the Israeli populace over the issue. The controversy was mirrored outside Israel, as American Jewry and surviving European Jews also held angry exchanges as to how to respond to the West German offer.[3]

Pragmatism eventually won out. Israel was in dire financial straits, needing an estimated US$1.5 billion to resettle the refugees from Europe. It was agreed that West Germany would pay US$1 billion of that amount. This led to the next stage of payments, where certain limited classes of Holocaust survivors residing in the West began receiving lifetime monthly payments from West Germany. These payments still continue today. To date, Germany has paid approximately US$60 billion to Jews worldwide through its various reparations programs.

While this amount came nowhere close to compensating the material losses suffered by European Jewry during World War II—never mind the loss of life—the debate over whether to accept financial restitution appeared to have been settled by the late 1950s. This, however, did not prove to be true. It emerged again with the same full force during the course of the Holocaust restitution litigation.

The first publicly raised misgivings over the litigation and claims for monetary damages appeared in December 1998. Abraham Foxman, head of the U.S.-based Anti-Defamation League and himself a child Holocaust survivor who was hidden by a Polish Catholic family, wrote an opinion piece for the *Wall Street Journal*,[4] labeling the litigation against the Swiss banks as undignified. In an oft-repeated statement, he decried that this struggle for restitution from the private corporate defendants made money the "last sound bite" of the Holocaust. According to Foxman, this is a "desecration of the victims, a perversion of why the Nazis had a Final Solution, and too high a price to pay for justice we can never achieve."[5] In a later interview, he explained that the litigation "trivialized the Holocaust, skewed it and made it to be that Jews didn't die because they were Jews but because they had Monets, Swiss bank accounts, Stradivarius violins. The fact is that a tiny, tiny, tiny, tiny, tiny percentage had Swiss bank accounts. [For the perpetrators, t]his was a perk of the genocide, not the cause of it. I am worried that the last sound bite of the century not be that the Jews were killed for their gold teeth."[6]

Foxman was not alone. Soon, other prominent critics joined their ranks. Journalist and author Leon Wieseltier published an angry piece in *The New Republic,* disparaging lawyers and other activists who sought restitution from wartime financial losses. Wieseltier related telling his mother, a Holocaust survivor, to "spit at it," when she showed him the application she received for benefits from the Swiss.[7]

Despite these concerns, it is argued here that the move to collect restitution funds was worthwhile. Not seeking financial restitution in the face of documented proof that financial giants worldwide are sitting on billions of dollars of profits made on the backs of World War II victims, which they then invested and reinvested many times over during the last half-century, amounts to an injustice that cannot be ignored. Allowing these corporate concerns to escape financial liability amounts to unjust enrichment. Equally significant, forcing a wrongdoer to pay up is a form of retributive justice. As Stuart Eizenstat, President Clinton's chief envoy on Holocaust restitution, has observed, "I think there is a certain symbolic quality that only money can convey to repair the injustices."[8] Moreover, outside of criminal punishment, the only other remedy that can be imposed upon a wrongdoer, even one committing or enabling genocide, is to make the wrongdoer pay. As Eizenstat, who is a diplomat and lawyer, points out,

> In every developed nation on earth, the accepted method of compensating the victim when a civil wrong has been committed, a contract breached, or labor extracted under duress is the award of money. Victims of negligent and reckless acts of all types, including radiation exposure, oil spills, medical malpractice, and smoking-related illness routinely bring lawsuits asking for money damages for themselves and for others who have suffered the same injuries. . . . Why should the victims [of the Holocaust] not have the same right to sue for justice as victims of other and lesser catastrophes?[9]

Richard Cohen, in a *Washington Post* opinion column appropriately titled "The Money Matters," also accurately answers criticism that seeking compensation and making the wrongdoers pay demeans the memory of the Holocaust:

> An immense calamity was committed in Europe, a moral calamity that left a black hole in the middle of the twentieth century. Money is the least of it. But money is part of it. Holocaust victims paid once for being Jewish. Now, in a way, they or their heirs are being asked to pay again—a virtual Jewish tax, which obliges them not to act as others would in the same situation. But in avoiding one stereotype, they adopt a worse one—perpetual victim.[10]

Elie Wiesel goes even further, indicating that failure to deal with the monetary losses from the Holocaust amounts to a suppression of history. Quoted in a 1997 *Time* magazine article, he makes clear that "if all the money in all the Swiss banks were turned over, it would not bring back the life of one Jewish child. But the money is a symbol. It is part of the story. If you suppress any part of the story, it comes back later with force and vengeance."[11]

As to the danger posed that the restitution campaign fueled antisemitism in Europe, antisemites will seize every opportunity to promote their hate message. As *Jerusalem Post* columnist Hirsh Goodman puts it, "The anti-Semites looking for reasons to hate the Jews call us Shylocks. Who cares? . . . If those living in countries now under scrutiny feel uncomfortable, that is the price of living with thieves. As one [survivor has] said: 'I will not allow the anti-Semites to dictate our agenda.' How right he was."[12]

Eizenstat aptly illustrates the anomalous and simply unjust result of using the fear of antisemitism as a reason not to seek restitution.

> Polish Catholics who worked in a Nazi munitions factory under terrible conditions . . . should be repaid for their forced labor, but the Jews who worked beside them should not. Why not? Because it is crass, unseemly—in short, "bad for the Jews," as the saying goes—to seek compensation for Holocaust injuries; because doing so exacerbates anti-Semitism by reinforcing the age-old stereotypes that equate Jews with greed.[13]

Despite some early concerns, it is clear that the Holocaust restitution movement has not diminished the memory of the Holocaust or distorted its history.

2. Who is a "Holocaust survivor" and thereby entitled to distribution proceeds?

Another "hot button" issue surrounding the Holocaust restitution movement has been how to allocate the funds received. The simple answer, of course, is that the monies should go to the still-living Holocaust survivors. This reply, however, begs another important and even more sensitive question: Which individuals can rightfully be called "Holocaust survivors"?

Those who survived concentration camps, ghettos, and death camps claim that only they can be called Holocaust survivors.[14] Individuals who lost their entire families, never mind all their assets, but who managed to personally escape the Nazi onslaught by emigration or flight vehemently challenge this view. Then there are the so-called "child survivors"—infants and up who either were hidden by righteous gentiles or survived under false identities. They passionately and correctly claim the status of "Holocaust survivor." For example, who would deny Anne Frank the status of survivor if she and her family had survived the war without being betrayed? As for the assertion by those captured by the Nazis that the hidden ones "had it better" during the war, the child survivors point, not the least, to the daily fear of being exposed and then shipped off to death.

The definitional dispute is reflected in demographic studies. One survey, conducted by Hebrew University demographer Sergio DellaPergola, found 1,092,000 Holocaust survivors alive today. A contrasting study by American demographer Jacob Ukeles estimated the world's survivor population to be only 687,900.[15]

While the definitional debate may have remained in the theoretical sphere before the Holocaust restitution settlements, it acquired practical importance after the resolution of the litigation. Since billions of dollars now needed to be distributed to Holocaust survivors, it became necessary to decide who is qualified to receive the funds.

The definitional dilemma became most prominent during the controversy about how to distribute the Swiss bank settlement funds. In 2000 Brooklyn federal judge Edward Korman, acting on the recommendation of the settlement's Special Master Judah Gribetz, allocated US$800 million out of the

US$1.25 billion settlement for the deposited assets claims. The amount is proving to be a gross overestimate. By 2005 the Swiss Claims Resolution Tribunal in Zurich, in charge of processing the claims of depositors or their heirs to dormant wartime accounts in Swiss banks, distributed approximately US$220 million. As it became clear that more than US$500 million was going to be left over, a mad scramble ensued for the remaining funds.

The first to make a claim for these funds was an organization titled the Holocaust Survivors' Foundation–USA (HSF-USA), claiming to represent the interests of the "true survivors" of the Holocaust. Created in the late 1990s specifically to provide a voice for survivors with regard to the distribution of the various Holocaust restitution settlements, HSF-USA sought to distinguish itself from the Claims Conference for the Material Claims Against Germany (Claims Conference), the organization created in 1951 to negotiate with West Germany (later, unified Germany) regarding reparation payments to Jewish survivors and to distribute such payments to the survivors worldwide. According to the HSF-USA organizers and others, the Claims Conference for many years had not been representing the interests of the survivors, but was instead involved in self-dealing, handing out proceeds to its favorite charities and various Jewish communal organizations that made up the Claims Conference.[16]

Most upsetting to the HSF-USA founders was that the Claims Conference was distributing vast amounts to Jews in the former Soviet Union (FSU). Many of these still-living elderly Jews managed to flee or were evacuated from Soviet territory before it became occupied by the Nazis. Some even served in the Red Army during the war. According to HSF-USA, however, these FSU Jews are not actual survivors of the Holocaust because the Nazis never directly persecuted them. Not being "true Holocaust survivors," they should not be receiving, claimed HSF-USA, any of the Holocaust restitution funds.[17] Moreover, according to HSF-USA, there was a measure of self-dealing in the distribution of funds to the FSU Jews, since those funds were being distributed by the Joint Distribution Committee (JDC), itself a major participant in the Claims Conference.

Gribetz, in his initial recommendation in 2000 to Korman on how to allocate the US$1.25 billion Swiss settlement, did not agree. Following the terms of the settlement agreement reached with the Swiss banks, he classified FSU Jews as eligible for distribution of the Swiss bank settlement funds. Moreover, he found these survivors to be most in need of assistance. After the fall of the Soviet Union, the social safety net collapsed in the FSU and mega-inflation robbed these aged pensioners of their savings.

For this reason, out of the initial US$100 million allocated in 2000 for humanitarian purposes, Gribetz recommended that 75 percent go to the survivors in the FSU. Survivors in Israel were allocated 13 percent of the humanitarian funds, with the remainder divided among survivors in the rest of the world. Survivors in the United States were allocated 4 percent of the funds, a travesty, according to HSF-USA and others. Two later humanitarian distributions were made. Eventually US$205 million in humanitarian funds from the Swiss bank settlement were distributed along the same lines. HSF-USA, with a major base of support in South Florida (sometimes called the sixth borough of New York City because of the high concentration of Jewish retirees from New York), retained Sam Dubbin, a Miami attorney who had worked in the Justice Department during the Clinton administration, to convince Judge Korman that Gribetz's distribution formula was unfair. Instead of adopting Gribetz's needs-based formula, whereby the humanitarian funds would be divided among segments of survivors' groups worldwide based on need, Dubbin urged that the judge adopt a population-based formula. Under this formula, any humanitarian distributions were to be divided according to the percentage of survivors found in each country. Since approximately 25 percent of the worldwide population of Holocaust survivors live in the United States, this percentage of US$ 205 million, claimed Dubbin, should be allocated to U.S. survivors.

Judge Korman stuck with Gribetz's plan, and he also agreed with Gribetz that Jews in the FSU who fled from the Nazis, fought in the war, or survived the various sieges of Soviet cities during the war should also be considered Holocaust survivors. HSF-USA initially appealed the decision, but then dropped the appeal. The US$205 million was allocated based on needs, not upon survivor population count, and a definitional formula used by Gribetz counted Jews in the FSU who survived the war as "Holocaust survivors."

In 2004, when it became clear that the greater bulk of the US$800 million allocated for the dormant account claimants would remain unclaimed and would now also be used for humanitarian purposes, Dubbin urged Judge Korman to allocate a greater proportion of these leftover funds to survivors in the United States, in effect to make up for the alleged shortfall to the U.S. survivors when the original US$205 million humanitarian distribution was made.

As a first step, in September 2003 Dubbin filed a petition with Korman seeking an immediate distribution of US$50 million to survivors in the United States. According to Dubbin's papers, "There is over $670 million under the court's control right now, sitting in the bank, helping no one other than the bankers. This money is legally and morally the survivors' money."[18] The proposed funds were to be used for a seemingly worthy goal: providing home health care to aging U.S.-based survivors during the last years of their lives.

In March 2004 Judge Korman issued a ruling refusing the request to make this interim distribution. (Korman also questioned whether HSF-USA had the capacity to represent the survivors in the United States).[19] A month later, Gribetz in his report to Judge Korman agreed that a secondary distribution of humanitarian funds was premature, since it was still possible that the Swiss banks could be forced to release additional wartime accounts information, and this could lead to a whole new set of claimants coming forward with a demand for a portion of the US$800 million.[20]

In recommending how to distribute eventually any remainder of the US$800 million, Gribetz stuck to the same distribution formula he recommended to Judge Korman for the disbursement of the initial US$205 million in humanitarian funds. As with the previous humanitarian funds distributions, Gribetz recommended that the first priority should be to allocate any leftover portion of the US$800 million to the neediest of the needy survivors, the vast majority of whom are the elderly Jews in the FSU.

According to Gribetz, 85 percent of the survivors who are in need of food aid and other basic necessities for survival are in the FSU.[21] In contrast, for survivors in places like the United States and Israel, their food needs were taken care of through their government's social welfare programs, with their unmet needs limited to such matters as home health care or better access to medicines. For this reason, reasoned Gribetz, the limited funds should be channeled primarily to survivors in the FSU who could starve or freeze to death without outside financial assistance. Explained Gribetz: "In sum, assistance that helps survivors live—food, winter relief and in many cases emergency grants—should take priority over all other aid programs, even those that add to survivors' comfort and relieve some of the burdens for those who have difficulty with personal care."[22] Before making a final decision whether to apply Gribetz's formula to the leftover funds, Korman gave outside parties an opportunity to give their input. As with the original preallocation period in 2000, when outside parties had a chance to submit proposals to Korman for the distribution of the US$1.25 billion settlement, more than one hundred proposals came in on how to distribute the leftover funds.[23]

During the original allocation decision, Israel stayed on the sidelines. This time, Israeli officials weighed in, urging that Israel, containing the largest population of Holocaust survivors, should receive 48 percent of the leftover funds both to aid Israeli survivors and for Holocaust education and remembrance projects in Israel. As support, Israeli officials claimed that 48 percent of worldwide survivors live in Israel.[24]

Israel's petition brought an angry editorial from *Forward*, a respected New York–based Jewish weekly newspaper. Its lead editorial, "Israel and the Swiss Banks," accused Israeli officials of misrepresenting the number of Holocaust survivors by counting "as Nazi victims persons who lived during World War II in countries like Egypt and Iraq where the local populace sympathized with Hitler." Returning again to the definitional question of "Who is a Holocaust survivor?" the editorial commented: "With all due respect, that's not what is meant by Holocaust victims."[25]

The editorial characterized Israel's petition for the largest share of the Swiss leftover funds as "carry[ing] an unfortunate odor of opportunism." It explained,

> It is true, as Israel argues, that a significant number of the destitute survivors in the Soviet Union have relocated to Israel in recent years, increasing Israel's burden. That's why Gribetz increased Israel's share of future humanitarian funds from 14 percent to 20 percent in his latest round of recommendations.
>
> But many other Israeli arguments are specious. The crisis in social welfare is largely a result of government cuts driven by neoliberal, Thatcherite economics. . . . It's not clear that this is the sort of hardship for which the Swiss humanitarian funds were intended. . . .

It looks as though Israel sees these looted Holocaust-era bank accounts as an available pool of money to close its budget gap, and it wants that money. That's the last thing the world needs to hear right now.[26]

Anger and accusations continued to dominate the question of the leftover distribution. Judge Korman scheduled a hearing for 29 April 2004 to have interested parties appear before him and present their views.[27] HSF-USA took this as a signal for action. Prior to the hearing, ads began appearing in New York–area Jewish newspapers, including *Forward*,[28] urging Holocaust survivors to attend a rally in front of the Brooklyn courthouse where the hearing to urge Korman to allocate a greater amount to the survivor population in the United States would be held. The ad explained,

> On 29 April Judge Korman of the Swiss Banks' settlement will hold an open hearing on how to allocate unclaimed funds likely to exceed $600 million. So far, Special Master Gribetz has recommended, and the Judge agreed, that *70 to 75 percent* be given to the "HESED" program administrators, for residents in the Former Soviet Union—FSU.
>
> The United States Holocaust Survivors have received, as of the latest reports, about *4 percent of the funds* from the interest on the funds sitting in the bank, even thought reliable population studies have reported that *up to 25 percent* of the Holocaust Survivors have incomes below the federal poverty level.
>
> Many have to make painful choices between buying food or medication, between getting a few hours of home-care or paying rent & utilities. Judge Korman has stated that the needs of Holocaust Survivors living in the United States do not measure up to those living in the FSU, and therefore survivors here are entitled *only to a minimal share*.[29]

Pitting seemingly actual Holocaust survivors in the United States against alleged impostors in the FSU, the ad then stated, "We say that all true Holocaust Survivors in need, wherever they live, ought to get assistance they need, and that survivors ought not be penalized because they live in the United States." It concluded: "If you believe, as we do, that Survivors in need in the U.S.A. have as much right to help from the Swiss settlement funds *as Survivors anywhere else,* please JOIN US IN OUR RALLY."[30]

The debate did not just stay within the community of survivors or even within the Jewish community. The "dirty laundry" began to be aired in the mainstream media when the *New York Times* and other major media outlets published prominent stories on the issue and also covered the 29 April hearing and the protests outside.[31]

At the day-long hearing more than fifty speakers, including Holocaust survivors, members of Jewish organizations, and other advocates, each gave Korman their suggestion on how the leftover funds should be distributed. According to one account, "There were passionate requests to release unclaimed funds only after more bank account holders and their heirs are found, and equally passionate requests to release more money now. Some people wanted funds for remembrance, some wanted help for other survivors and some, it seemed, just wanted to share their stories."[32] At the hearing, "questions bled easily into raw emotional appeals and painful discussions, including one about the definition of a survivor."[33]

The State of Israel appeared through Natan Sharansky, the former Soviet dissident and now Israel's Minister of Diaspora Affairs, who in a video call during the hearing asked for a substantial increase in the percentage of the funds going to survivors residing in Israel.[34]

The *Financial Times,* in its coverage of the hearing, praised Judge Korman. Describing Korman as "the long suffering Brooklyn judge with the Solomonic task of overseeing the Swiss banks' $1.25 billion settlement with Holocaust survivors," its editorial noted that "[d]ozens of claimants [at the hearing] made their case; a few opted to hurl abuse at him. Korman seemed to maintain his sense of humour. . . . And then there was that patience. He started his hearing at 10:00 A.M. and did not call a recess for a bathroom break until just before 5:30 P.M. That's when the court loved everything about him."[35]

The HSF-USA leaders took a different view. In an angry letter sent to the *New York Law Journal* shortly before the hearing, they accused Korman of "continu[ing] to rule against the American survivors, ignoring the desperate needs of thousands who are dying alone without adequate care or basic necessities."[36] For its part, Israeli officials likewise criticized Gribetz's allocation formula, publicly announcing, as the Jewish Telegraphic Agency reported, that "the Gribetz report reflects a total ignorance of the needs of survivors in Israel and throughout the world except those in the FSU."[37]

Forward sadly commented in a lead editorial that "[s]omething that began as a struggle for justice—forcing Switzerland and other European nations to give up billions of dollars looted from the victims of Nazism—has turned into an unseemly scramble by competing Jewish interests to grab a piece of the pie."[38] In another story, it noted that the "emotions on display in the courtroom suggested that the Swiss bank case has, for many survivor activists, become a stand-in for the frustrations and failures of the entire 50-year reparations process."[39]

It was a no-win situation. Korman either had to stick with the original needs-based formula and allocate most of the leftover funds to the poverty-stricken Jews in the FSU, or shift more funds in this second distribution to the survivor populations in the United States and Israel, where genuinely needy survivors are also present. As of this writing, Korman appears to have chosen the former. In his March 2004 ruling, he noted that while many survivors in the United States and Israel indeed do not have adequate home health care and medicines, the level of needs of the survivors in the FSU is much more acute, since many of these survivors lack such basic necessities as food and shelter.[40] Moreover, he noted that survivors in the West have been receiving reparations payments from Germany for the past half-century, amounting to over US$50 billion, while survivors in the FSU, living until recently behind the Iron Curtain, were left out of the German reparations distribution scheme. As Korman explained during the hearing, "Survivors in the United States have actually gotten the long end of the stick, while survivors in the old Soviet Union have 'gotten next to nothing.'"[41]

In the midst of this sad drama an important point should be kept in mind. As Gribetz explained in his allocation report, "members of the Looted Assets Class [meaning, as explained above, all Jewish and other survivors of Nazi persecution], who already have received funds [from the US$205 million humanitarian distribution] and many now be the beneficiaries of residual funds [from the US$800 million] properly belonging to the Deposited Assets Class, probably would have received nothing at all had the case continued to trial."[42] In other words, Gribetz seemed to be saying to the unhappy survivors, "Be happy with what you got." As he correctly noted, whatever assistance needy survivors are receiving from the Swiss banks settlement is, in fact, all "found money."

3. Should restitution funds be used for Holocaust remembrance and education?

Another emotionally charged issue brought out by the Holocaust restitution settlements was whether any of the settlement funds should be used for matters other than direct assistance to survivors.

Soon after the Swiss banks settlement, various proposals began to be made suggesting that a portion of the funds received should be spent on Holocaust remembrance and education. For example, Miles Lerman, former chair of the United States Holocaust Memorial Council and himself a survivor, stated at the time, "Survivors are entitled to get what was stolen from them or their parents. . . . But we believe Holocaust education is more important; we believe the last chapter of the Holocaust cannot be gold and it cannot be bank accounts."[43]

In the German slave labor settlement, the German payers insisted that DM 700 million (approximately US$325 million) of the DM 10 billion fund go to Holocaust education and remembrance, especially since they titled their foundation the Remembrance, Responsibility and the Future Foundation. According to Count Otto Lambsdorff, the lead German negotiator, "When the survivors have passed away, their memory and their legacy can be kept alive with projects financed by the interest that has accrued on the Future Fund's capital."[44]

Likewise, in the French banks settlement a portion was allocated, at the banks' insistence and with the support of the French government, to perpetuate the memory of the Shoah and other historic examples of man's inhumanity to man. In contrast, in the Swiss banks settlement, Judge Korman, following the recommendation of his Special Master Judah Gribetz, refused to allocate any funds from that settlement to educational and remembrance programs. According to Gribetz, the needs of survivors are so overwhelming that all funds should be used to directly benefit the survivors.[45]

The allocations for educational and remembrance programs have been controversial. Many Holocaust survivors and their supporters argue that, as long as there is one needy survivor still alive anywhere in the world, all monies must be used strictly for the benefit of survivors. Many survivors also feel that the funds belong only to them, since they were sought on their behalf and in the name of the suffering and degradation they experienced, and, therefore, only they should decide how the unanticipated billions now flowing in should be distributed.

The position that none of the funds should be used for Holocaust education and remembrance is strongly challenged by leaders of many Jewish organizations, especially the World Jewish Congress (WJC). These leaders argue that the heirs of the six million murdered are the entire body of worldwide Jewry, or at least descendants of those killed. The most forceful proponent of this view is Israel Singer, rewarded with the job of running the Claims Conference on the heels of his victories as the WJC leader most responsible for the Holocaust restitution settlements. In the June 2002 issue of *Sh'ma,* a respected Jewish monthly, Singer explained,

> Holocaust survivors are not the only persons charged with making decisions for the Jewish people about how to use monies that will not be needed after they die. While our first obligation is to take care of Holocaust survivors, the remainder of any monies should be spent to ensure the existence of the Jewish people—not necessarily the existence of Jewish organizations. These decisions, which are about the future rather than the past, affect the entire Jewish people.[46]

Invoking his authority "as a child of survivors and having worked for them my entire life," Singer then asserts:

> The entire Jewish people are the heirs of survivors. . . . Survivors have tremendous institutional memory—without which the Jewish people couldn't understand their existence in this time. However, survivors should not decide all questions about funds restored to the Jewish people from the Holocaust.[47]

Many Holocaust survivors are livid when they hear Singer and others make the claim that the "entire Jewish people are the heirs of survivors" and, as such, the Holocaust restitution funds belong to worldwide Jewry. HSF-USA president David Schaecter, a Holocaust survivor and long-time Jewish activist from Florida, responded to Singer in the same issue of *Sh'ma:*

> The organizations that negotiated in the name of survivors are pushing to be the organizations that decide how to distribute the "leftover" money. . . . While voicing empty rhetoric about "taking care of survivors first," they have given paltry support for the real social service needs of survivors today. . . . How dare these institutions presume to spend "restituted" funds for their favored "philanthropic" projects into the next century, using money claimed from the most terrorized victims of the past century.[48]

Singer would create "a new body that would include the [Claims Conference], the World Jewish Restitution Organization, and the government of Israel, along with Holocaust survivors, Jewish educators, and innovative thinkers"[49] to make all distribution decisions. The mandate of the new organization, which Singer has called "Fund for the Jewish People" or a "Jewish People's Fund," should be to address the future needs of the Jewish people; for example, education—creating an innovative voucher system for every Jewish child to attend Jewish schools—would be a welcome initiative. The purpose of this effort would be to create a new future for the Jewish people. This restitution should be used to rebuild the Jewish soul and spirit. This has never been done effectively in the Diaspora.[50]

Given the panoply of groups claiming to represent the "Jewish people" and the diversity of their interests, it is doubtful that Singer's proposal would ever reach fruition—even if there was complete backing of his proposal by Holocaust survivors.

Another distribution proposal, greatly appealing to genocide scholars and those working to help all genocide victims, is to have the monies collected used to assist victims of more recent genocides. As columnist Jeff Jacoby suggested in the *Boston Globe:*

> All Jews, including Holocaust survivors, should reject the funds; instead, the monies should be distributed to survivors of other, more recent human rights tragedies (such as to the victims of the Rwandan massacres and the Bosnian conflict of the 1990s, and the Khmer Rouge Cambodian auto-genocide of the 1970s).[51]

Jacoby further explained:

> I propose an entirely different idea, one that emerged in a conversation with Dennis Prager, a Los Angeles broadcaster renowned for his writings on ethics and Judaism: Once the cheated depositors have been paid, let the Jewish people relinquish any claims to the balance of the money. Let it be used instead to help human beings whose lives have been shattered by genocide and ethnic slaughter. Rather than earmarking the money for Jewish causes, spend it to heal the still-suffering survivors of the Rwandan massacre. Or the deeply scarred victims of the Cambodian holocaust. Or the Bosnian women brutalized in Serbia's rape camps. "We Jews wanted to awaken the world to what the Swiss did," Prager says. "We don't want to profit by it."[52]

While this proposal did not get a great deal of publicity, there seems to be strong opposition to it, both inside and outside the survivor community. According to Leo Rechter, a child survivor and a leader of HSF-USA,

> ASTOUNDING! Jacoby has empathy for the formerly wealthy survivors; he has empathy for the victims of other genocides, but to try and ameliorate the final days of needy Shoah survivors does not cross his mind.... It is of course easy to be magnanimous with someone else's money, even though it is plainly evident that it is often desperately needed by the latter.[53]

William Elperin, son of survivors and president of the 1939 Club, a California-based organization of survivors and their children, comments,

> I believe that position is a mere extension of the *shtetl* philosophy. "Let's not rock the boat too much. Let's show everyone that we're good people because we're giving them money and maybe they won't criticize us (or kill us)." Can you imag-

ine any other group entitled to restitution saying "We don't want all of it. Let's give it to the Jews." We should live so long![54]

The personal predilection of this author is to take up the Jacoby and Prager scheme and devote at least some portion of the received funds to help survivors of the post-Holocaust genocides. At the least, it is preferable to spend monies on these living victims of other genocides than to build another Holocaust museum or memorial, since it comports with the governing motto of "monies for persons, not projects." Moreover, it also sends a universalist message that Jews, and foremost survivors of the Holocaust, are ready to help others who suffered like them. "Never again" is not just a cry calling to prevent another genocide to Jews, but "never again" to humankind.

4. Should attorneys prosecuting the Holocaust restitution cases be entitled to attorneys' fees?

There is an additional controversy in the Holocaust payouts scene. Rubbing salt into the wound of the current recipients is the millions reaped by plaintiffs' lawyers who filed the suits. True, it could not have been done without them since, until the lawsuits were filed, the various European corporate concerns were glad to ignore the half-century-old financial claims.

The lawyers all took on the cases on a contingency basis, that wonderful invention of American law that opens the American courthouse to those who cannot afford to hire a lawyer to prosecute their case. Under the contingency fee system, the lawyer gets paid only if the case is resolved successfully, with the lawyer taking a percentage of the award recovered. In class action litigation, such fees must also be approved by the court.

While the Swiss banks class action cases were settled first, Judge Korman declined to approve any attorneys' fees until a significant portion of the claimants received payment from the Swiss settlement. Three of the principal lawyers in the Swiss banks litigation took on the case *pro bono* and did not seek any fees. The remainder collected fees of US$22.5 million, which amounted to less than 2 percent of the US$1.25 billion of the Swiss banks settlement. As a comparison, in typical class action settlements, fee awards generally range between 15 and 22 percent of the total settlement amount, which in this case would have been at least US$180 million.[55]

Many of the same attorneys who prosecuted the Swiss banks cases also represented the claimants in the German litigation. Here, all the lawyers made applications to be paid for their work. Why did the lawyers not take on these cases *pro bono*? The most common answer given by the lawyers was that they could not afford to continue prosecuting further Holocaust restitution suits without compensation. The litigation was becoming quite expensive; the German companies, like the Swiss banks, hired top-notch counsel to defend them. As in the Swiss banks litigation, the defense attorneys filed voluminous motions to have the cases dismissed. The prosecuting lawyers insisted that in order to be able to devote their time and the time of their associates, paralegals, historians, and other experts to these suits, they needed to be paid.

In June 2001 the fee awards were issued to the lawyers involved in the German litigation. Fifty-one lawyers were awarded fees totaling US$59.9 million. While the amount may appear large, it is about 1.2 percent of the total US$5 billion settlement. In a typical class action settlement, the lawyers would be awarded at least US$750 million.

Soon after, Paul Spiegel, a leader of Germany's Jewish community, issued a public appeal to the lawyers urging them to donate their fees to the German Fund, to help increase the payments to the survivors. According to Spiegel, "I am convinced that the lawyers have a legal right to their money, but not a moral right. I am not saying that the lawyers are greedy. It is just immoral when the highest payments to survivors are about $7,000 and the lawyers are getting millions."[56]

The lawyers were not interested. Michael Witti, a German lawyer working on some of the cases and awarded about US$4 million for his work, chose to publicly respond to Spiegel's proposal. Witti explained that the fees will enable him to continue representing survivors for other wartime claims, such as helping to recover confiscated property in Eastern Europe. The fees are needed, Witti elaborated, "so I can hire experts, so I can travel and have office staff. And this money gives me the support for this." He concluded: "If you are not [fiscally] responsible, you run away and take commercial cases. But I have an obligation to do human rights cases."[57]

Diane Leigh Davison, a Baltimore class action lawyer also working on the German cases, had a more straightforward explanation why she was charging her Holocaust survivor clients. "You don't say to a surgeon, 'Don't take your fee.'"[58] The lawyers also pointed out that without their intervention, the Germans would not have settled. One example: After the settlement, some survivors in Britain made noises about filing their own separate lawsuits in European courts.[59] It was all a bluff. No English lawyer was willing to take such a case. Only the lawyers in America were bold enough to take on the Germans.

5. Should Jewish lawyers have defended the Holocaust restitution suits?

The ethical issue of whether a lawyer should decline to represent a certain client because of the behavior of which the client is being accused also presented itself in the Holocaust restitution litigation. Many companies being sued by Holocaust survivors hired Jewish lawyers from some of the most prominent law firms in the United States to defend them, often retaining counsel with important connections to the organized Jewish community.

For instance, the Italian insurance carrier Assicurazioni Generali, when sued for failing to honor Holocaust-era insurance policies issued to Holocaust victims, hired Kenneth Bialkin, a partner at the powerhouse New York firm of Skadden, Arps, Slate, Meagher & Flom. During his lengthy career, Bialkin has also led several prominent Jewish institutions, among them the Anti-Defamation League. Defending his decision to take the case, Bialkin stated, "I'm in it to see if we can bring it to closure, and everybody gets out of it in a dignified way."[60]

Countered William Shernoff, a lead plaintiffs' counsel in the insurance litigation, "I just think there's something wrong here, that these pillars of the Jewish community-type of people—well-connected, well-respected—are taking money [in legal fees] from this insurance company to try to beat down and destroy the claims of these survivors. What the hell am I missing here?"[61]

The *Jerusalem Post* quoted an unnamed representative of the Holocaust claimants, as follows:

> I feel [Bialkin] is using years of service to the Jewish community to now perform a great disservice to Holocaust survivors. A Jewish lawyer can be a Jewish lawyer for anyone, but someone who calls himself a Jewish leader . . . has no business trying to defend the position of those who did not pay Holocaust victims. Period.[62]

Countered Bialkin:

> I'm doing what I think is right, I'm going to try to perform it honorably, I think in the end it will be viewed as a service to the Jewish people, but I recognize that it can blow up in my face. . . . I'm a big boy, I did what I thought was appropriate. . . . and I'm prepared to be judged by my peers.[63]

Generali was not the only defendant in the Holocaust restitution suits to find it worthwhile to retain Jewish lawyers as defense counsel. Other corporate defendants also hired top-notch American law firms to defend them, with the Jewish lawyers in those firms likewise faced with the moral dilemma of whether they, or even their firms, should be involved in these cases.

The private misgivings first became public in a 1997 story published by the *Washington Post* titled "N.Y. Law Firm to Advise Swiss Bank Accused of Laundering Nazi Loot." The story described how, "[o]ver the heated objections of many of its lawyers, the high-priced New York law firm of Cravath, Swaine & Moore is representing a Swiss bank that wartime U.S. officials described as 'the most frequent violator' of rules against laundering looted Nazi gold." Cravath's representation of the bank, Credit Suisse, led to "an angry internal dispute that then-presiding-partner Samuel C. Butler said has no precedent in the law firm's history."[64] According to Butler,

> There were a fair number of partners, some of them Jewish, who said, 'Do we really want to do this? There was a lot of soul searching.' . . . After an hour and a half of discussion, the very strong consensus was we should take it on because, very frankly, they [Credit Suisse] are trying to do the right thing.[65]

The decision to go ahead with the representation was not accepted quietly. As further described by the *Washington Post,*

> One Cravath employee, speaking on condition of anonymity, said yesterday that a number of associate lawyers at Cravath remain angry, but are afraid to speak out for fear of being denied promotions to partner. "If we are so generous-minded on this subject, why not represent Holocaust survivors?" said the employee, self-described as "angry and I also happen to be Jewish."[66]

Cravath's involvement in the Holocaust restitution litigation can be considered minor, however, compared to the work done on these cases by another blue-chip law firm, Wilmer, Cutler & Pickering (which, through a megamerger with another large firm in 2004 became Wilmer, Cutler, Pickering, Hale & Dorr). The firm's founder, Lloyd Cutler, is one of the most prominent Jewish lawyers in the United States. Roger Witten and Marc Cohen, the two Wilmer lawyers leading the defense team, are both Jewish.

As with Cravath, Wilmer's representation of the Swiss banks in suits filed by Holocaust survivors accusing the banks of profiting from the Holocaust led to a great deal of soul searching on the part of some of the other Jewish lawyers in the firm. The Wilmer partners quickly called a meeting "to suppress any dissent before it manifested itself."[67] As explained by Jane Schapiro in her account of the Swiss banks litigation, the partners drew a distinction between defending cigarette companies and the Swiss banks. "Everyone should understand, the banks were not like the cigarette makers who were killing people with their cigarettes and had no intention of stopping. The Swiss bankers wanted to correct the situation, and they had a specific proposal to prove it."[68] Their argument that the Swiss banks wanted to make it right apparently convinced the dissenting lawyers.[69] Wilmer went on to represent the Swiss banks not only in this litigation but also throughout the much longer stage of effectuating the settlement.

Wilmer's successful representation of the Swiss banks also led to the firm being asked to represent other European defendants sued for Holocaust-era wrongs. This time, however, the clients would not be Swiss banks, whose country was neutral during the war, but rather German companies who worked hand in hand with the Nazis. The companies were being sued by Holocaust survivors who were slaves of these companies during the war. For these suits, the Wilmer partners could not keep the internal controversy private. It spilled out into the open through another story in the *Washington Post*. As that article explained,

> For the firms' many Jewish lawyers, the real problem was the inescapable sense that they were on the wrong side. Wilmer, Cutler's work for Krupp, for instance, put them at odds with people such as Rachel Grunebaum, a Romanian-born 75-year-old who is a plaintiff in one of the [slave labor] class action lawsuits. . . . Jewish groups contend that companies that used forced laborers weren't reluctantly playing by the rules foisted on them by an immoral regime. Krupp and others, they say, badgered the Nazis for more bodies, eager to boost profits.[70]

The firm's partners, nevertheless, decided to take on the defense of the German firms. For the next four years Wilmer, Cutler & Pickering became the leading law firm in the United States defending corporate Europe for its nefarious dealings during the war.

> In the end, Wilmer, Cutler & Pickering decided to represent Siemens AG, Krupp AG and other German companies accused of exploiting forced laborers during the Nazi era. But there is lingering anger among some of the firm's rank and file,

and sympathy for an associate who disclosed during the arguments that his Jewish grandfather had been a forced laborer at Siemens. "It came down to issues of conscience warring against issues of business," said one Wilmer lawyer, who requested anonymity. "And business won."[71]

In contrast, Stuart Eizenstat, now in private practice, indicated that if he had been asked by the European defendants to be their lawyer, he would have declined the representation.[72]

Conclusion

The Holocaust restitution campaign can be viewed on many levels as an important triumph. Elderly Holocaust survivors and other wartime victims received compensation for losses that appeared to be forgotten for more than a half-century. For many victims, this was the first time that they received any damages for their wartime suffering. With compensation also came recognition of the survivors' claims, as the payments became potent symbols to the victims that the wrongdoers finally acknowledged their wartime misdeeds.

The campaign also unearthed valuable new information about the wartime behavior of many nations and private corporate entities during World War II. The newly discovered documentation has yet to be fully analyzed by Holocaust historians. This new treasure trove of knowledge may be found either to support or refute our long-held beliefs about the financial crimes and other events committed during the war.

Last, the Holocaust restitution campaign has become a model for other campaigns to right other historically acknowledged wrongs. Again, how transferable the Holocaust restitution model is to other historical claims is yet to be seen. The campaign, however, even strictly within the confines of Holocaust history and memory, also produced a number of detrimental, or at least morally ambiguous, consequences. Often this came about because, in the words of Elie Wiesel, a decision needed to be made that presented "the impossible task of judging between right and right."[73] How well these decisions have been handled can only be fully evaluated once all the settlements are concluded. Nevertheless, even if history does judge these settlements as not fully satisfactory, they add another important chapter to the story of the gray zones of the Holocaust and its aftermath.

Notes

1. Three major studies have been published on the Holocaust restitution movement. In 2002, two journalists who covered the Holocaust restitution story for the *Financial Times* wrote a journalistic account of the movement. See John Authers and Richard Wolffe, *The Victims' Fortune: Inside the Epic Battle Over the Debts of the Holocaust* (New York: HarperCollins, 2002). In early 2003, Stuart Eizenstat, President Clinton's chief envoy on

Holocaust restitution issues, wrote a memoir setting out his own account of the movement. See Stuart E. Eizenstat, *Imperfect Justice: Looted Assets, Slave Labor, and the Unfinished Business of World War II* (New York: Public Affairs, 2003). This author published in mid-2003 a study of the movement. See Michael J. Bazyler, *Holocaust Justice: The Battle for Restitution in America's Courts* (New York: New York University Press, 2003). Last, that same year journalist Jane Schapiro published an account of the Swiss banks litigation from the perspective of attorney Michael Hausfeld, one of the lead plaintiffs' counsel in the Swiss banks and subsequent Holocaust restitution litigation. See Jane Schapiro, *Inside a Class Action: The Holocaust and the Swiss Banks* (Madison: University of Wisconsin Press, 2003). All of these contain detailed discussions of the Holocaust restitution movement.
2. Roland Stephen, "Controversy: Holocaust Reparations," *Commentary* (17 January 2001), 17.
3. Elazar Barkan, *The Guilt of Nations: Restitution and Negotiating Historical Injustices* (New York: W. W. Norton, 2000), 9, 23–27.
4. Abraham H. Foxman, "The Dangers of Holocaust Restitution," *Wall Street Journal* (4 December 1998), A18.
5. Ibid.
6. Naftali Bendavid, "Is the Meaning Lost in Court?" *Chicago Tribune* (12 August 2001), 1.
7. Leon Wieseltier, "Assets," *The New Republic* (8 November 1999), 98.
8. Richard Wolffe, "Putting a Price on the Holocaust," *Irish Times* (16 March 1999), 15.
9. Stuart Eizenstat, "Controversy: Holocaust Reparations," *Commentary* (17 January 2001), 10.
10. Richard Cohen, "The Money Matters," *Washington Post* (8 December 1998), A21.
11. Quoted in Lance Morrow, "The Justice of the Calculator," *Time* (24 February 1997), 45.
12. Hirsh Goodman, "Atrocities Beyond Compensation," *Jerusalem Post* (22 October 1999), 8B.
13. Eizenstat, "Holocaust Reparations," 10.
14. For support of the view that only those imprisoned under Nazi occupation are Holocaust survivors, see Thane Rosenbaum, "Whose Money Is It?" *New York Jewish Week* (7 May 2004). The author, a novelist, law professor, and son of Holocaust survivors, approves of "a narrower definition of Holocaust survivors—the way such a designation is more conventionally understood, not as mere targets of Nazism, but rather those who were either in concentration camps, ghettoes or subject to slave labor. . . ."
15. Joe Berkofsky, "Israeli Officials Jump into Fray Over Use of Swiss Bank Settlement," *JTA [Jewish Telegraphic Agency] News* (26 April 2004).
16. For articles discussing criticisms of the Claims Conference see, for example, Isabel Vincent, "Who Is a Holocaust Survivor? Jewish Groups Argue Over Hundreds of Millions in Restitution Payments," *National Post* (Canada) (24 January 2004), 1; Jay Bushinsky, "Holocaust Panel Vilified," *Washington Times* (22 October 2003), A18; "More Light, More Justice—Holocaust Restitution and the Claims Conference," *The Economist* (23 August 2003), 47.
17. Joe Berkofsky, "UJC Seeks to Mediate Between Claims Conference and Survivors," *JTA News* (2 July 2003). See also Dwight Owen Schweitzer, "I Accuse," *Jewish Star Times* (19 June 2002), 4. Schweitzer, the publisher of a local South Florida Jewish weekly, accuses the Claims Conference, among others, "of complicity in the continued suffering of the victims of the Holocaust who remain alive, and not keeping faith with the millions who have died and will continue to die."
18. Motion for Immediate Interim Distribution of Swiss Settlement Proceeds, filed 11 September 2003.
19. In re Holocaust Victim Assets Litigation, 302 F.Supp.2d 89 (E.D.N.Y. 2004).
20. Judah Gribetz and Shari C. Reig, "Special Master's Recommendations for Allocation of Possible Unclaimed Residual Funds," 16 April 2004, available at www.swissbankclaims.com (hereafter Gribetz Allocation Report).
21. Gribetz identified three categories of basic survival needs faced by Holocaust survivors: (1) assistance with the purchase of food; (2) winter relief, such as winter clothing and util-

ity payments for delivery of heat; and (3) emergency financial assistance "for sudden and unexpected crises (such as the need for a medical procedure or a device for which no other source of payment exists)." Gribetz Allocation Report, 11.
22. Ibid.
23. The proposals can be located at www.swissbankclaims.com. They are summarized in Appendix D of the Gribetz Allocation Report, also available at this Web site.
24. Because tens of thousands of FSU Jews emigrated to Israel over the last twenty years, many of whom are elderly Jews who lived through World War II, it was in the interest of the Israeli officials in their papers sent before Judge Korman to label these individuals as "Holocaust survivors."
25. Editorial, "Israel and the Swiss Banks," *Forward* (30 April 2004), 6.
26. Ibid.
27. Earlier, Korman issued an opinion denying Dubbin's request for attorney fees to be paid out of the Swiss banks settlement funds. In the opinion, Korman ruled that Dubbin is not entitled to any fees because he made no worthwhile contribution to the settlement of the litigation against the Swiss banks. In re Holocaust Victim Assets Litigation, 2004 WL 717243, *3, available at www.westlaw.com.
28. Ad (quarter-page), "All Holocaust Survivors Rally," *Forward* (16 April 2004), 3.
29. Ibid. (emphasis in original).
30. Ibid. (emphasis and all capital letters in original).
31. See, for example, William Glaberson, "Judge Is Assailed Over Holocaust Fund," *New York Times* (30 April 2004), B1; John Authers, "Holocaust Survivors Ask Why Justice Has Taken So Long," *Financial Times* (29 April, 2004), 3; David Mermelstein, "Holocaust Survivors Speak Out Against Injustice," *The Miami Herald* (12 April 2004), 24; "Holocaust Survivors Plead for Swiss Accounts," *Newsday* (10 April 2004), A22; Amy Dockser Marcus, "Group Says Survivors Come First," *Wall Street Journal Europe* (15 January 2003), 1.
32. David Hafetz, "Holocaust Survivor Stories Aired in Brooklyn Court," *New York Sun* (30 April 2004), 1.
33. Nathaniel Popper, "Passions Flare at Swiss Banks Hearing," *Forward* (7 May 2004), 3.
34. Itamar Levin, "Israel Intervenes in U.S. Swiss Bank Deposit Payout Hearing," *Israel Business Arena* (2 May 2004), 1.
35. "Sitting Judge Observer," *Financial Times* (3 May 2004), 12. Others have also compared Judge Korman's task to that of the dilemma faced by the biblical King Solomon. See, for example, Netty C. Gross, "Playing Solomon," *The Jerusalem Report* (12 January 2004), 31.
36. "Holocaust Survivors Upset with Restitution," *New York Law Journal* (27 April 2004), 2.
37. Berkovsky, "Israeli Officials Jump into Fray," quoting Sallai Meridor, co-chairman of the World Jewish Restitution Organization and chairman of the Jewish Agency for Israel.
38. Editorial, "Justice, At Last," *Forward* (16 January 2004), 10.
39. See Popper, "Passions Flare."
40. Meridor disagreed with this assessment. "You could not say that giving food is more important than giving mental health assistance or assistance to the disabled survivor who cannot get out of bed, or giving a home to a survivor who made *aliyah* [emigrated to Israel] but has no place to live." See Berkovsky, "Israeli Officials Jump into Fray."
41. Quoted in Hafetz, "Holocaust Survivor Stories Aired," 1.
42. Gribetz Allocation Report, 13.
43. Quoted in James D. Besser, "Seeking Moral Restitution," *Jewish Journal* (4 December 1998), 22.
44. Hearing of the Committee on Banking and Financial Services of the U.S. House of Representatives, 106th Cong. (9 February 2000), 6. The relevant testimony is by Dr. Otto Graf Lambsdorff.
45. Gribetz Allocation Report, 11–13, 34–75.
46. Israel Singer, "Transparency, Truth, and Restitution," *Sh'ma* (June 2002).

47. Ibid.
48. David Schaecter, "Use Restituted Funds for Urgent Survivors' Needs," *Sh'ma* (June 2002).
49. Singer, "Transparency, Truth, and Restitution."
50. Ibid.
51. Jeff Jacoby, "Jews Can Set a Moral Example with Holocaust Funds," *Boston Globe* (7 December 1998), A15.
52. Ibid.
53. Email from Leo Rechter to author, 10 July 2002.
54. Email from William Elperin to author, 4 July 2002.
55. For an excellent article discussing the excessive fees received by plaintiffs' lawyers in some cases, especially the recent tobacco litigation settlements, see Alex Beam, "Greed on Trial," *The Atlantic Monthly* (June 2004), 96 (discussing a tobacco litigation settlement where plaintiffs' attorneys, in addition to receiving fees amounting to US$7,700 an hour, went to court seeking for the state of Massachusetts to honor an agreement under which the lawyers would be entitled to an additional US$1.3 billion in fees).
56. Toby Axelrod, "Lawyers for Nazi-era Slave Laborers Urged to Use Fees to Help Survivors," *JTA Newswire* (26 June 2001).
57. Ibid.
58. Jonathan Weisman, "Redress Sought in Nazi-era Labor," *Baltimore Sun* (23 August 1999), 1A.
59. Marilyn Henry, "Slave Labor Pact Reached with Germany," *Jerusalem Post* (24 March 2000), 7A ("British survivors said yesterday that they would pursue their claims in Europe an courts.").
60. Alan Abrahamson, "Searching for Justice," *Los Angeles Times Magazine* (20 June 1999), 35.
61. Ibid.
62. Elli Wohlgelernter, "Lawyers and the Holocaust," *Jerusalem Post* (2 July 2002), 4B.
63. Ibid.
64. Blaine Harden and Saundra Torry, "N.Y. Law Firm to Advise Swiss Bank Accused of Laundering Nazi Loot," *Washington Post* (28 February 1997), A3.
65. Ibid.
66. Ibid.
67. Schapiro, *Inside a Class Action*, 19.
68. Ibid.
69. Whether the Swiss banks really wanted to, and actually did, "make it right" remains doubtful. In February 2004, Judge Korman issued an opinion castigating both the Swiss banks and the Wilmer lawyers for deliberately issuing misinformation in the case during the settlement process. In re Holocaust Victim Asset Litigation, 302 F.Supp.2d 59 (E.D.N.Y. 2004). In an angry tone, Korman explained: "What compelled me to write is that over the past year-and-a-half, the bank defendants have filed a series of frivolous and offensive objections to the distribution [of the settlement] process. . . . These objections bring to mind the theory that 'if you tell a lie big enough and keep repeating it, people will eventually come to believe it.' The 'Big Lie' for the Swiss banks is that during the Nazi era and its wake, the banks never engaged in substantial wrongdoing. . . . [Their] statements continually distort and obscure the truth, and . . . I am forced to address them."
70. David Segal, "Past v. Future: Nazi-Related Suits Put Law Firms on Defensive," *Washington Post* (9 March 1999), E1.
71. Ibid.
72. Author's conversation with Stuart Eizenstat, Washington, DC, 7 February 2003.
73. Letter from Elie Wiesel to Judge Korman, quoted in David Hafetz, "Miami Lawyer Draws Fire from Judge in Holocaust Case," *New York Sun* (29 April 2004), 1.

– Chapter 24 –

THE CREATION OF ETHICAL "GRAY ZONES" IN THE GERMAN PROTESTANT CHURCH
Reflections on the Historical Quest for Ethical Clarity

Victoria J. Barnett

One of the most haunting pictures to emerge from the Nazi concentration camps is Primo Levi's description of the "gray zone," rendered even more poignant by the depression and self-doubt that finally drove Levi himself to suicide in 1987. The Nazis' humiliation, brutalization, and destruction of their victims were not confined to the external violence experienced by Levi and others in the concentration camps. For many victims, that devastation continued until the end of their lives in the form of internalized violence and shame. Many survivors of the camps felt guilty for surviving when so many in their families had died. They felt shame about their helplessness at the time, about compromises they made, about the humiliation of being driven by hunger to steal bread or driven by fear to save themselves, even as those around them were dying. Surely one of the Nazis' cruelest crimes was this corruption of their victims through extreme dehumanization—a kind of double victimization by which the victims eventually internalized the contempt with which they had been treated. Years later, Levi would describe the difficulty of surviving this process, "the demolition of a man": "Nothing belongs to us any more; they have taken away our clothes, our shoes, even our hair; if we speak, they will not listen to us, and if they listen, they will not understand. They will even take away our name: and if we want to keep it, we will have to find ourselves the strength to do so, to manage somehow so that behind the name something of us, of us as we were, remains."[1]

Clearly, we would say, these human beings were victims; just as clearly, we would see them, in ethical terms, as innocent. Yet in Levi's writings about the "gray zone" he went on to describe an even more insidious process by

Notes for this section begin on page 370.

which the innocence of the victims was compromised. Some victims actually became participants in the process of genocide, forced by the Nazi leaders of the camps and the ghettos to become complicit in the suffering of their fellow inmates. Certain Jews were selected to be in the "special units" that ran the crematoria; in the Lodz ghetto a Jew named Chaim Rumkowski was made leader of the ghetto—a role that compelled him to collaborate with the enemies of his people, even as it gave him privileges and power that ultimately, of course, proved to be illusory.

Most of us who study the Holocaust are moved both by compassion and horror at the plight of these victims who were driven into the "gray zones"—a realm in which, as Lawrence Langer wrote, "One is plunged into a world of moral turmoil that may silence judgment. . . . As one wavers between the 'dreadful' and the 'impossible,' one begins to glimpse a deeper level of reality in the death camps, where moral choice as we know it was superfluous and inmates were left with the futile task of defining decency in an atmosphere that could not support it."[2]

The topic of this essay is a different kind of "gray zone," the ethical gray zones created by ordinary Germans at the time and later: first, as they came to terms with Nazism and became active participants in the Nazi universe, and second, after 1945 as they sought to understand their past in a way they could live with. This gray zone is far removed from that into which the victims were forced, and yet the two are related, for both these realms—the coerced gray zone of victims and the constructed gray zone of the complicit—were part of the Nazi universe, albeit on different points of the spectrum. More importantly, both gray zones corrupted and destroyed those within them and made a mockery of ideals, of ethical principles, of moral decisions. Wherever they stood in the Nazi universe, victims and collaborators alike were changed, and ethical choices inevitably begin to look different through the lens of such a change. Human moral behavior is complex, particularly in times of political terror and turbulence. The fact that evil comes in shades of gray does not make it any less reprehensible, but it does make it more disconcerting and difficult to address, ethically speaking. Particularly because the evil that was the Holocaust was so cataclysmic, overwhelming, and unambiguous, it is difficult to acknowledge that evil, examined more closely, often proves to be the product of human complicity, duplicity, and rationalization, as well as even more mundane motives like fear and ambition.

Yet evil corrupts; as Levi observed, it could even corrupt its victims. Among the nonvictims, the Nazi capacity to create a new ethical system in which the murder of human beings was viewed as a social "good" testifies to the pervasiveness of this corruption among the German population and their social and political institutions. "The Holocaust," writes philosopher Peter Haas, "became ethically possible because the basic character of ethical argumentation remained unchanged. . . . It is not that they [the Germans] had lost the ability to behave ethically; they simply evaluated certain activities in a different, yet still ethically coherent, way."[3] Thus, although the experience of Levi and others in the camps was fundamentally different from that of ordinary Germans and the institutions of which they were a part, the dynamics of the "gray zone" in both instances were actually quite similar. This may be one reason why, after 1945, the process of dealing with the past followed a parallel trajectory for victims and bystanders alike, moving from the silence and denial of the 1950s to the gradual emergence and confrontation with the history that has continued until today.

This is not, I would suggest, simply because the past was painful (although that is one reason) but because ethical reflection, in the case of events such as the Holocaust, can never be done independently of honest historiography. It is only with the accumulation of historical documentation and detail that we are confronted with our alibis, our lies, and our rationalizations. Because it is so crucial to establish agreement about the truth of what happened, the facts are important. Recognition of this has become widespread in the past few decades, as different forms of "truth commissions" have become a primary means for the reestablishment of civil society in the wake of serious human rights abuses and genocide in places such as Rwanda, South Africa, Paraguay, and Brazil. The necessary tasks of justice, accountability, apology, grieving, reparations, and restitution cannot be fulfilled without the creation of some consensus about what happened, both historically and morally, to everyone involved in that history.

For that reason, the history of Nazism and its aftermath in Germany is instructive, particularly the history of the German Protestant Church, which is a striking case study in the dynamics of the "gray zone" and the way in which the ethical discourse created in the course of compromise with evil shapes all subsequent ways to address it. In 1945 the German Protestant Church emerged as one of the few sectors in German society that *appeared* to have maintained its integrity between 1933 and 1945. This was largely due to the prominence of the Confessing Church, an opposition movement within the German Protestant Church that had actively fought the Nazification of that church, but this positive postwar picture was soon extended to the German Protestant Church as a whole. The Confessing Church initially emerged in opposition to the pro-Nazi German Christian movement, and Confessing Christians in many parts of the country were harassed by Nazi authorities; in a few cases, they went farther than that and actually became part of underground resistance or rescue networks.[4] Some of the more prominent members of the Confessing movement (the most famous being Dietrich Bonhoeffer, a pastor and theologian who was executed in 1945 for his role in the resistance group that tried to kill Hitler) were imprisoned or executed by the Nazis.

Yet, because the Confessing Church had always remained a part of the German Protestant Church, and because many Protestant bishops had at some point been part of the movement, the mantle of resistance was quickly donned by many church members whose actual behavior was characterized much more by complicity and compromise than by resistance. Most Protestant leaders, in fact, had followed a course of deliberate caution during the

Nazi era. They sought to keep their churches free of state or party control but, at the same time, wanted to avoid antagonizing the Nazi state. Most of them shared Nazism's nationalist aspirations and tolerated, if not embraced, its anti-Jewish rhetoric. Church leaders actually defended many of the early Nazi laws against the Jews, and the church's treatment of its own "non-Aryan" members (Christians affected by the Nazi racial laws) was a shameful exercise in cowardice by which the church eventually abandoned them as state pressures intensified.

The theological and political biases of most Protestant leaders made their responses to Nazism ambivalent at best and complicit at worst. Yet, at the same time, the churches endured enough harassment under Nazism—particularly in the battle to retain control of the institutional church against theological extremists within the church—that many did view themselves as a kind of opposition group within Nazi Germany. The church's postwar self-characterization as a resistance group against Nazism, then, was quite a turnabout; but it was also in many ways simply an extension of the rationalizations and self-justifications that had begun in 1933. Even where such resistance actually existed, it had been primarily for the sake of church independence within a situation of dictatorship. After the defeat of Nazi Germany, with the evidence of the concentration camps before the world and an international clamor for justice and accountability, the story of the Protestant battle to save the institutional church was amplified into a much greater story that portrayed the churches as far more decisively anti-Nazi than they had ever been.

Thus, church leaders in 1945 created an ethical gray zone as they sought not to understand their behavior or repudiate it, but instead to justify and explain it. In all too many cases, this meant creating an ethical interpretation of their history—in effect, a falsified version of history—that they could live with in the new post-Nazi situation. The dominant portrait that emerged for both the Catholic and Protestant churches was one that portrayed the churches as victims of Nazism, and church leaders—from the pope to the bishops to the clergy—as people who had offered spiritual (and in some cases political) resistance to the Nazi regime and its measures. Leaders such as Berlin's bishop Otto Dibelius, who had served as church superintendent of Berlin's Protestant churches and had also been a member of the Confessing Church, emphasized the pressures and restrictions they had endured under the Nazi state—not mentioning (in the case of Dibelius) their initial enthusiasm for the Third Reich and their early outspoken defense of Nazi anti-Jewish legislation.

The larger historical context of this "gray" version of history was the immediate postwar period in Germany. Germans did indeed suffer during those initial years; like people throughout Europe, their cities had been bombed, family members were missing, and there was sometimes not enough to eat. In the summer and fall of 1945, there was widespread chaos in the East as millions of Germans fled the regions occupied by the Soviet army; tensions were already growing between the Soviet Union and the other Allies.

Moreover, for the second time in thirty years, Germany was vanquished by foreign armies and despised by its neighbors.

Under these circumstances, Germans soon began to view themselves as victims, and this became the dominant ethical framework from which the churches, too, interpreted the German experience. On Good Friday in 1947 the German theologian Helmut Thielicke preached a widely reprinted sermon titled "The German Passion," in which he compared the postwar suffering of Germans with that of Christ on the cross: despised by all nations, isolated, and utterly dependent upon the mercy of God. Thielicke was challenged by Hermann Diem, a former member of the Confessing Church and one of the few who called upon the Germans in that early postwar period to acknowledge their guilt,[5] yet the sentiments Thielicke expressed were shared by a large sector of the German population. As observers like Hannah Arendt (who paid her first postwar visit to Germany in 1949) and Alexander and Margarete Mitscherlich noted, the Germans in the late 1940s were in no mood to confront issues of guilt or responsibility. Most Germans put the Nazi past behind them by denying it or—where they confronted it at all—by focusing on their own personal experience, separated from its larger political context.[6] The suffering of the Jews and other victims of Nazism, where addressed at all, was conflated into the general rubric of "wartime suffering," a framework that ignored the historical reality of what had happened and erased any sense of personal or collective responsibility for that history.

This interpretation prevailed throughout the 1950s, the same era in which Theodor Adorno began to study the authoritarian personality and Hannah Arendt wrote her seminal work on totalitarianism. The focus of both studies was the process by which human individuals and their institutions could succumb to a totalitarian dictatorship and become isolated, morally paralyzed, and otherwise complicit in evil. The philosopher Karl Jaspers, in his famous essay on German guilt, concluded, "Once a dictatorship has been established, no liberation from within is possible."[7] These insights emerged in the immediate wake of Nazism, and all these authors had experienced Nazism firsthand—Adorno as a concentration camp inmate and Arendt and Jaspers as refugees. They were also, of course, writing in an era of growing awareness and anxiety about the totalitarian realities of Stalinism in the Soviet Union.

Such interpretations of the recent past, however, converged in Germany with the daily realities of suffering, hardship, and uncertainty to create an ethical gray zone with respect to the Nazi past. The focus on the power of mass movements and dictatorships, tied to the relative powerlessness of individuals, was a relatively comfortable perspective for viewing recent history, but it led to a weak ethic—a gray ethic, as it were, that ignored the victims, protected the perpetrators, and comforted the bystanders. This was exacerbated not only by the churches' sense of German victimization (as exemplified in Thielicke's sermon) but also by their emphasis on Christian teachings about reconciliation and forgiveness, which became another dominant theme in early postwar church statements. This was most striking during the period immediately following the fall of Nazism, when Confessing Church leaders, with very few exceptions, condemned Allied denazification policies and were quite critical of the Nuremberg trials and subsequent war crimes trials. Martin Niemöller, an outspoken Confessing Church pastor who had spent six years in concentration camps, led the charge, calling denazification a "witch hunt" and even comparing the Allied authorities in their ideological zeal to the Nazis.[8] The churches took a similar approach with regard to actual former perpetrators, emphasizing the importance of forgiveness and lack of retribution.[9] In many of their statements, church leaders spoke about the "gray areas" of life in a dictatorship—the difficulty of making moral decisions, the challenge of moral courage, and the churches' obligation to minister to everyone, saint and sinner alike.

In those instances where the churches did address the issue of guilt, the issue of responsibility and the identification of the victims and perpetrators remained comfortably vague. The August 1945 Stuttgart Declaration of Guilt issued by the German Protestant Church, while acknowledging the guilt of the German nation before its European neighbors, also stressed that the churches had fought against "the spirit that found horrible expression in the violent National Socialist regime," and emphasized the need for a "new beginning."[10] The document made no reference at all to the persecution and genocide of the Jews. The 1947 Darmstadt statement of guilt was more politically concrete (written in the very early days of the Cold War, it sought primarily to ease tensions between the eastern and western sectors of Germany) but it, too, omitted any mention of the Jews.

The absence of reference to the victims—essentially an evasion of any responsibility for their suffering—was coupled with an avoidance of confronting the perpetrators and collaborators with the specificity of their guilt. Despite his opposition to denazification, Pastor Martin Niemöller was virtually the only church leader to speak regularly and openly about Christian complicity with the Nazi regime. The first official acknowledgment of the German churches' political and theological guilt in the Holocaust came in 1950 at the Weissensee synod of the Protestant Church of Germany. It came at the urging of Adolf Freudenberg, who as a refugee from Nazi Germany had directed the Protestant office for refugees in Geneva, Switzerland, and in that capacity had worked closely there with Gerhard Riegner, the head of the World Jewish Congress. It was at Weissensee in 1950 that the two central factors in the churches' behavior under Nazism were first addressed in an official capacity: (1) their dismal record with regard to the persecution and genocide of the Jews, and (2) the theological underpinnings of that record. Yet Weissensee remained an anomaly in the general postwar picture. Not until the 1981 Rhineland synod did a regional Protestant synod in Germany confront the issue of guilt and officially repudiate the anti-Jewish teachings of the church.

In Germany and internationally the discussion begun at Weissensee has continued to this day, and it is a discussion in which history, ethics, and theology intersect. The trajectory of Christian ethical reflection on the Holocaust has moved from the early phase of ignorance and denial to a much more thorough historical documentation and analysis of the churches' political, ideological, and theological biases that affected its behavior under Nazism. This in turn has led to a rethinking, revising, and in some cases repudiation of Christian theological teachings that, by denying the validity of the Judaic faith, legitimated prejudice and hatred and thus helped pave the way to actual genocide.

In much of this work and in most writing in general about the complicity of the Christian churches in the Holocaust, the emphasis has been on the role of Christian theology and in particular Christian teachings about Judaism. This emphasis is not misplaced—indeed, it is crucial for understanding the churches' role at the time, and it is the starting point of any post-Holocaust Christian theology. Nonetheless, the "gray zone" in which the churches found themselves under Nazism was not simply the product of theological teachings about the Jews. Like Levi's gray zone, it emerged from the very process by which Protestants had become participants in the history of their times; the gray zone in which they lived before 1945 shaped their actions at the time as well as their capacity to think critically about those actions in retrospect.

The one German theologian who wrote about this at length was Dietrich Bonhoeffer. Because of his role in the German resistance and his execution by the Nazis, Bonhoeffer is generally viewed as a hero and martyr of the period, and his theological writings carry enormous power even today because he articulates and rethinks certain Christian teachings in a way that is enormously helpful and provocative for contemporary Christians. Most of his writings, of course, were based upon his own experience under Nazism. Nonetheless, the historical examination of Bonhoeffer, like that of his church, has become more critical in recent years.[11] Consistent with the general focus on theological anti-Judaism, much of this critique has been focused on the existence of such prejudice in Bonhoeffer's own early theological writings, particularly in his 1933 essay, "The Church and the Jewish Question," which, despite the fact that it was one of the first statements to discuss the necessity of church resistance to Nazism, nonetheless defended the legitimacy of traditional Christian supercessionist teachings.

While this aspect of Bonhoeffer's thought cannot be ignored, one problem in discussing the historical Bonhoeffer is that his theological writings, his role in the resistance, and the history of the Holocaust as it unfolded around him have been conflated into a narrative in which these three aspects form an ethically coherent whole. Yet this both distorts and simplifies the complexity of his life and thought, particularly the ways in which his thinking changed between 1933 and 1945. A far more relevant aspect for any discussion of "gray zones" is his own struggle, particularly during his period in the resistance, with the interrelatedness of ethics and history. Bonhoeffer was one of very few Protestants in Germany (or anywhere) at the time to recognize the challenge Nazism posed for religious belief, and this led him to struggle both with his own tradition and with the historical challenges to that tradition. Thus, his resistance-era writings (particularly his book *Ethics,* written in 1941) portray a "gray zone" in which Bonhoeffer directly confronts the complexity of acting responsibly in a historical situation of complicity and compromise.

Even before his entry into the resistance in 1939, Bonhoeffer vacillated between decisive public opposition to Nazism and privately made compromises. In 1933 he was perhaps the most outspoken voice in the Confessing Church against the "Aryan Paragraph," which incorporated the guidelines of the early Nazi racial laws into church law. As late as 1939, however, his seminarians were filling out "Aryan Certificates" for parishioners, and Bonhoeffer had no critical comment to make on the matter, although during the same period he was quite outspoken and uncompromising on a number of other issues confronting the church.[12] Bonhoeffer himself produced an "Aryan Certificate" in order to retain his teaching position at Berlin University; according to his friend and biographer Eberhard Bethge, "He viewed this not as a timid compromise but as a necessity" that would allow him to continue to teach his students.[13]

Bonhoeffer, then, made some of the same compromises made by many others in his church; perhaps the greatest difference was that he began to write about what this meant in ethical terms. By the time he joined the resistance, Bonhoeffer seems to have understood that his life, his theological work, his ministry, and his resistance were being lived out in the "gray zone," and in the early 1940s he began to write about this. The tone of these wartime writings was so different that after his death some former students claimed that he had written under psychological duress—that this wasn't the "real Bonhoeffer." His book *Ethics* was actually a collection of manuscript fragments that were written, as he put it, "in the domain of relativity, the twilight which the historical situation spreads over good and evil," a period in which people were being forced to choose not just "between right and wrong and between good and evil, but between right and right and between wrong and wrong."[14] In his seminal chapter on "History and the Good" in that volume, Bonhoeffer concluded that the ethical choices made during such historical periods necessarily reflected "ultimate ignorance" of whether they would be judged good or evil by later generations. Human ethics and moral decisions, he wrote, could not be understood apart from the historical context in which they were made.[15]

Bonhoeffer's conclusions here were very grounded in his Christian faith, calling for an ultimate reliance upon grace; yet the bottom line of his reflections was that human beings ultimately had to assume and claim full historical responsibility for their actions. They could not depend upon God's sanction for what they did, nor could they seek comfort by denying the ugly realities of which they had become a part. It was in *Ethics* that Bonhoeffer wrote his own confession of guilt for the churches, noting that Christians in Germany had become complicit in the deaths of the Jews,[16] and where he pondered what it meant "to tell the truth" in an age dominated by lies and duplicity. In another document from 1943, a letter he wrote to his fellow conspirators, Bonhoeffer asked:

> We have been silent witnesses of evil deeds: we have been drenched by many storms; we have learnt the arts of equivocation and pretence; experience has made us suspicious of others and kept us from being truthful and open; intolerable conflicts have worn us down and even made us cynical. Are we still of any use?[17]

This brutal honesty with himself and his religious tradition emerged, I believe, from the honesty with which Bonhoeffer confronted his own gray zones. What is striking throughout these writings was his emphasis on the importance of history—for, in general, it was the work of historians that began to bring the true record of the churches to light, by correcting the false early historical pictures rendered within these "created" gray zones. Bonhoeffer had discovered that ethical reflection and action must be done both from within the context of history and as a response to history.

This point is underscored by the fact that, in the decades since the Holocaust, ethical reflection and historiography have gone hand in hand. Good historiography has given scholars a more critical understanding of the behavior of the churches and other institutions in Nazi Germany. The gradual shift from a "gray" historical understanding of peoples' ethical options and choices began during the 1960s, with events such as the 1961 trial of Adolf Eichmann and other war crimes trials, the provocative portrayal of the Catholic Church in Rolf Hochhuth's play *The Deputy*, and the coming of age of a younger generation of Germans who began to challenge their parents' version of history. In 1967 a doctoral student named Wolfgang Gerlach wrote a critical dissertation about the widespread anti-Judaism in the Confessing Church and the complicity of many of its leaders and pastors.[18] Gerlach's work was so controversial (and many of those about whom he wrote were still alive) that it did not find a publisher until 1987. Yet while the more critical examination of the churches' record was only beginning, Germans in general were beginning a more extensive and honest examination of their history. This trend continued throughout the 1970s, supplemented by the growing body of scholarship about the Holocaust in general and by increasing research into the churches' record.[19]

In the ensuing decades the Holocaust has become the most examined phenomenon in history; there are few aspects of this event that have not been documented and studied in at least a preliminary fashion. Yet, while this historical work has dismantled the early comfortable myths that portrayed the Holocaust as the work of only a few Nazi leaders or rendered a heroic picture of the churches, historiography can never completely eradicate the ethical "gray zones." To a great extent, this is because—as Jaspers, Arendt, Adorno, and Bonhoeffer realized—difficult ethical dilemmas arise in dictatorships. The "gray zones" existed not only in the camps but also throughout the Nazi universe. The stories of people such as Oskar Schindler and Kurt Gerstein, the studies of "ordinary men," and the dynamics observed among "bystanders" raise more questions than they answer. They suggest that all human beings are capable of both great good and terrible evil, and the haunting next question, of course, is: under what circumstances? The historical reality of the Holocaust was defined at numerous levels by "gray zones" that tend to subvert any universal ethical conclusions one might draw. The essential ethical dilemma that we face, however, is that we hope to respond to what is clearly a case of documented, unambiguous evil with equally unambiguous ethical interpretations of what happened, and this is not always possible when confronted with the complexities of real history. All too often this tension between historical complexity and the need for a clear ethical interpretation leads either to a superficial picture that ignores the "gray zones" or to a picture that, in acknowledging the historical complexity, succumbs to ethical rationalization.

To use the social scientists' distinction between "explaining" and "understanding," history helps to explain, while ethics is connected to understanding. Any ethical discourse thus brings us into a gray area, for when we begin to understand human behavior we begin to have compassion, if not empathy, for the perpetrators and bystanders, which is morally problematic. This was at the heart of the ethical questions that Jaspers, Arendt, and Adorno addressed, and it was precisely the factor that led many German church leaders in the early postwar period to absolve their parishioners of any culpability in what had happened. How much of the ethical burden falls upon the individual, and how much derives from the situation in which people find themselves? What is the ethical significance of "collective guilt" for how we think about individuals and how we understand the role and complexity of the historical situation? These questions, in turn, are related to the larger ethical questions that are the legacy of the Holocaust as we confront similar situations today: How do we prevent genocide from happening? How, when it is under way, do we stop it? And in its wake how do we do the work of reconciliation and justice? How do we offer justice in proper measure to all those emerging from its shadows: to the survivors, to the families of the victims, and to the perpetrators and the bystanders? To a greater extent than we like to think, those are very pragmatic and political questions that bring us into the "gray zones."

In the early decades following Nazism the churches and their leaders permitted their knowledge of the gray zones—of the actual moral complexity that people did indeed face in the Nazi years—to "gray over" their ethical judgment and, as a result, their own version of history. In the process ethics itself became an act of complicity that promoted and actually legitimized a falsified picture of history. In turn the work of historians began the process of dismantling the ethical cover-up. History, done well, helps to keep us ethically honest by keeping the truth of the record out there. It confronts us with the facts, the documents, with human behavior as it was, not as we wish it had been—even when it often raises more questions than it answers.

Likewise, ethics, to be done well (which, as Bonhoeffer wrote, means to be done responsibly) must always be done in conjunction with history; it is not an ahistorical (or an "über-historical") set of principles to be applied.

But ethics is not just about what we do, but about how we understand what we do. The practice of history, like the practice of ethics, can naturally be manipulated for ideological purposes; and there are histories of the Holocaust that, in their quest for ethical certainty, divide the people of that age into clear villains and heroes—a historical picture that is false because it denies the complexity of human behavior. To be done well, history must acknowledge and confront us with the gray zones, and ethics needs to retain that same capacity: to face the tough questions and, where necessary, rethink fundamental questions about religious belief as it is lived out in history. One of the lasting lessons of the Holocaust is that the quest for ethical clarity and historical truth go together.

Notes

1. Primo Levi, *Survival in Auschwitz,* trans. Stuart Woolf (New York: Collier Books, 1993), 26.
2. Lawrence Langer, *Versions of Survival: The Holocaust and the Human Spirit* (Ithaca: State University of New York Press, 1982), 75.
3. Peter J. Haas, *Morality After Auschwitz: The Radical Challenge of the Nazi Ethic* (Philadelphia: Fortress Press, 1988), 7.
4. The story of the Confessing Church and the ideological battles within German Protestantism cannot be told in the scope of this essay. See my own work *For the Soul of the People: Protestant Protest Against Hitler* (New York: Oxford University Press, 1992); Doris Bergen, *Twisted Cross: The German Christian Movement in the Third Reich* (Chapel Hill: University of North Carolina Press, 1996); and Robert Ericksen and Susannah Heschel, eds., *Betrayal: German Churches and the Holocaust* (Minneapolis: Fortress Press, 1999). A good overview of the role of the churches in general during the Nazi era can be found in Carol Rittner, Stephen Smith, and Irena Steinfeldt, eds., *The Holocaust and the Christian World* (London: Kuperard, 2000).
5. Thielicke's sermon and Diem's response were both reprinted in a booklet, *Die Schuld der Anderen: Ein Briefwechsel zwischen Helmut Thielicke und Hermann Diem* (Göttingen: Vandenhoeck & Ruprecht, 1948).
6. See the Mitscherlichs' book, *Inability to Mourn: Principles of Collective Behavior* (New York: Grove Press, 1975). Arendt shared many of their impressions in her report on postwar Germany, "Aftermath of Nazi Rule," published in *Commentary* in October 1950. A more recent reflection that addresses many of the same issues commented on by the Mitscherlichs and Arendt is W. G. Sebald, *On the Natural History of Destruction,* trans. Anthea Bell (New York: Random House, 2003).
7. Karl Jaspers, *The Question of German Guilt,* reprint ed. (Westport, CT: Greenwood Press, 1978), 99.
8. See my discussion of this in *For the Soul of the People,* 209–39.
9. Two recent studies of this question are Katharina von Kellenbach, "The Gospel of Cheap Grace: Rituals of Forgiveness in German Prisons After the Holocaust," paper presented at the American Academy of Religion, 21 November 2003; and Suzanne Brown-Fleming, "Cardinal Aloisius Muench and the Guilt Question in Germany, 1946–1959," paper presented at the German Studies Association, October 2001.
10. Reprinted in *For the Soul of the People,* 209.
11. See especially Kenneth Barnes, "Dietrich Bonhoeffer and Hitler's Persecution of the Jews," in Ericksen and Heschel, eds., *Betrayal,* 110–29; and Stephen Haynes, *The Bonhoeffer Phenomenon: Portraits of a Protestant Saint* (Minneapolis: Fortress Press, 2004).
12. See *Illegale Theologenausbildung: Sammelvikariate 1937–1940,* Dietrich Bonhoeffer Werke, vol. 15 (Gütersloh: Chr. Kaiser, 1998), 119, n. 3. Another reference to this by one

of Bonhoeffer's students, Gerhard Vibrans, is in Eberhard Bethge, ed., *So ist es gewesen: Briefe im Kirchenkampf* (Gütersloh: Chr. Kaiser, 1995), 240, 291f.
13. Eberhard Bethge, *Dietrich Bonhoeffer: A Biography*, 2nd and rev. ed. (Minneapolis: Fortress Press, 2000), 515.
14. Dietrich Bonhoeffer, *Ethics* (New York: Collier Books, 1986), 13, 249.
15. Ibid., 214–15, 234.
16. Ibid., 110f.
17. Dietrich Bonhoeffer, "After Ten Years," in his *Letters and Papers from Prison*, ed. Eberhard Bethge (New York: Macmillan, 1971), 16–17.
18. Published in English as *And the Witnesses Were Silent: The Confessing Church and the Jews* (Lincoln: University of Nebraska Press, 2000).
19. One sign of this was the Annual Scholars' Conference on the Holocaust and the Churches, which began in 1975 and soon drew an international body of scholars.

– Chapter 25 –

Gray-Zoned Ethics
Morality's Double Binds During and After the Holocaust

John K. Roth

> *How is it possible to speak, when you feel . . . a strange* double bind: *an infinite claim to speak,* a duty to speak infinitely, *imposing itself with irrepressible force, and at the same time, an almost physical impossibility to speak, a* choking *feeling.*
>
> —Sarah Kofman, *Smothered Words*

The German philosopher Immanuel Kant, one of the most important thinkers in Western civilization, suggested that three questions define philosophy: What can I know? What should I do? What may I hope? Much hinges on whether people can rightly claim to possess knowledge. Scarcely an hour passes without our wondering whether we ought to do some things and not others. Those issues keep people thinking and hoping about the future. Questions about the meaning and destiny of our lives—individual and collective—are never far behind.

Ethics or moral philosophy revolves around Kant's second question: What should I do? In one way or another, everyday experience puts that question before us. We deal constantly with factual matters, but we also make value judgments, issue prescriptive statements, and formulate normative appraisals. In short, we try to figure out what we ought to do, what is good and right. We distinguish these factors from what we consider wrong and simply the way events turn out. How *should* they come out, we ask.

Many factors enter into such evaluations: our cultural backgrounds, historical situations, religious training or the lack of it, the influences of parents, teachers, and friends, to mention but a few. Ethics or moral philosophy takes those factors into account. But when philosophers explore variations on the question "What should I do?" they want to learn, for example, whether

Notes for this section begin on page 385.

our attitudes about right and wrong are simply the traditional assumptions of our culture or whether they rest on critically examined and rationally defensible judgments. They wonder, too, whether all men and women have rights and duties in common. Philosophers try to discover what a good life involves and to see if the qualities of justice that make life good are valid regardless of time and place. They may also ask whether human history makes any moral progress. Philosophy, in turn, asks us to decide how we can educate people so that they are more likely to achieve worthwhile goals.

This description of ethics or moral philosophy emphasizes clarity and understanding as the aims of inquiry. Life's complexities and confusions make it difficult to obtain those outcomes, but the philosophical quest typically assumes that clarity and understanding are obtainable. If reason works long and hard enough, it is possible, at least in principle, to "get things right." Primo Levi, the Auschwitz survivor who explored what he called "the gray zone," makes one reconsider that assumption. Although Levi has not obtained Kant's canonical status, and in spite of the fact that he said of philosophy, "no, it's not for me," I regard him as a very important philosopher.[1] He, too, sought clarity and understanding but in ways that diverged significantly from philosophy's conventional paths and assumptions.

If clarity and understanding were to be obtained, Levi contended that they would have to reckon with "the gray zone." As he experienced and explored that Auschwitz region, Levi stressed that it contained surprises and shocks that revealed a "world" that was not only "terrible . . . but also indecipherable: it did not conform to any model."[2] His brilliant chapter on "The Gray Zone" in *The Drowned and the Saved* helped to make that region decipherable, at least in part, but his honesty made it impossible—at least for him—to remove completely the ambiguity and compromise that blocked the hope that full clarity and understanding could be obtained, even in principle. Rejecting the speculative claim that Holocaust studies sometimes evoke—"in my depths there lurks a murderer"—Levi did not hesitate to say that "I was a guiltless victim and I was not a murderer."[3] Nor did Levi mince words about the fact that the Holocaust epitomized wrongdoing, and never more so, in his judgment, than when the Germans created the *Sonderkommando*, those units of predominantly Jewish prisoners whose task it was to man the Auschwitz crematoria. "Conceiving and organizing [those] squads," he said, "was National Socialism's most demonic crime."[4] Those clear and distinct moral judgments, however, mixed and mingled with two other dimensions of awareness that make Levi a much more complicated and profound ethical thinker.

First, Levi saw that gray-zone behavior could not be neatly analyzed in terms of right and wrong, at least not as most traditions of philosophical ethics might try to do. Arguably, those traditions could still be used to judge the National Socialist perpetrators of the Holocaust, but no Kantian categorical imperative, Aristotelian theory of virtue, or utilitarian calculations about consequences were of much relevance for judging those who were conscripted into the *Sonderkommando,* let alone for determining what those hapless men should do, condemned as they were to a fate of choiceless choices, before they too were murdered.

Next, Levi saw how the gray zone revealed a tragic dysfunctionality for ethics. That dysfunctionality had at least two parts. First, traces of idealism about treating one's neighbor as oneself or of refusing to steal might remain in the gray zone, but within that region of experience such teachings lost their appeal. As Levi put the point: "The physiological reserves of the organism were consumed in two or three months, and death by hunger, or by diseases induced by hunger, was the prisoner's normal destiny, avoidable only with additional food. Obtaining that extra nourishment required a privilege—large or small, granted or conquered, astute or violent, licit or illicit—whatever it took to lift oneself above the norm."[5] Second, if the most basic ethical teachings lost their appeal in the gray zone, then that fact scarcely inspired confidence—then or now—that the world had a fundamental moral structure that could be trusted. True, Levi thought that "at least sometimes, at least in part, historical crimes are punished," and that the Nazi project had been suicidal.[6] But Levi's book *The Drowned and the Saved* was written, overall, in a minor key, and its chapter on the gray zone ends as follows: "Willingly or not we come to terms with power, forgetting that we are all in the ghetto, that the ghetto is walled in, that outside the ghetto reign the lords of death, and that close by the train is waiting."[7]

Levi knew that a kind of "logic" governed Nazi thinking. He did not unpack, however, something implied by his insight, something that others have underscored in ways that not only are consistent with Levi's outlook but also create additional worries about and for ethics, especially after the Holocaust. In 1988 Peter J. Haas identified what he called "the Nazi ethic."[8] Fifteen years later, the historian Claudia Koonz has written about "the Nazi Conscience." That concept, she joins Haas to show, "is not an oxymoron." On the contrary, Koonz argues persuasively, "The popularizers of antisemitism and the planners of genocide followed a coherent set of severe ethical maxims derived from broad philosophical concepts."[9] Both Haas and Koonz help to show that ethical reasoning can take forms that are not only multiple but at lethal odds with one another. Koonz makes the point by referring to the German political theorist Carl Schmitt, who rejected universal human rights and argued in May 1933 that, in Koonz's translation, "Not every being with a human face is human."[10] One can and must argue that such reasoning is false and wrong, but arguments do not guarantee the triumph of rationality, especially when what counts as rational is not only arguable but also a factor in struggles for power and political control. Neither philosophy nor ethics can take much comfort from saying, after its devastation was wreaked, that the Holocaust was wrong.

In more ways than one, the Holocaust leaves ethics gray-zoned. This essay considers how ethics might respond to the ambiguous and compromised condition that the Holocaust expanded and intensified for moral philosophy, even if that condition was not created originally by that genocide. As the existence of Primo Levi's gray zone helps to show, the Holocaust signifies an immense human failure. It did enormous harm to ethics by showing how ethical teachings could be overridden, rendered dysfunctional, or even subverted to serve the interests of genocide. To the extent that philosophers—moral philosophers in particular—have paid close attention to the Holocaust (not many, unfortunately, have done so), a significant version of the double bind that Sarah Kofman (1934–1995) identified in *Smothered Words* is definitely in effect. One feels a duty to speak, an obligation to make ethics stronger and less subject to overriding, dysfunctionality, or subversion, an insistence not only to drive home the difference between right and wrong but also to influence action accordingly. Yet such work can produce a choking feeling, a sense that too much harm has been done for a good recovery to be made, a suspicion that ethics may be overwhelmed by the challenges it faces. The bind is double, for the sense of ethical responsibility, real though it is, remains hopelessly optimistic and naive unless it grapples with the despair that encounters with the Holocaust and other genocides are bound to produce. To be touched by that despair, however, scarcely encourages one to believe that ethical responsibilities will be accepted and met. Caught between the post-Holocaust need to speak for ethics and above all to speak ethically and boldly, on the one hand, and the feeling that the key elements of ethics—words, arguments, appeals to reason, persuasion through the example of moral action—may be inadequate, on the other, the question persists: Given what happened to ethics during the Holocaust, what can and should be made of ethics after Auschwitz?

It is doubtful that such a question can be answered, at least if one expects answers to bring finality and closure. But there can be responses, and that is what this essay attempts to provide, albeit only in part and even in fragmented form. The attempt consists of two parts: (1) consideration of some of Sarah Kofman's contributions to post-Holocaust ethics, and (2) reflections stimulated by her contributions, which point toward what she called "the possibility of a new ethics."[11] Kofman did not use the term, but her hints about a new ethics suggest that such an outlook would need to be a gray-zoned ethics in the sense that moral philosophy would have to take the gray zone seriously in ways akin to those that Irving Greenberg had in mind about theology when he set forth his now well-known working principle that "no statement, theological or otherwise, should be made that would not be credible in the presence of the burning children."[12] No philosophy, one could argue, could be either new or ethical if it failed to take account of the gray zone. The two parts of my exploration in this essay contend especially that gray-zoned ethics must take seriously the fragility of ethics and foster awareness that nothing good ought to be taken for granted.

Knotted Words

What can words say? What can they do? Words can be put to many uses. They can make statements and ask questions. They can mystify and deconstruct; they can be used against themselves. Speeches, propaganda, orders, laws—these are only a few of the ways in which language can advance mass murder. Testimonies, memoirs, poems, stories—these are only a few of the ways in which language can bear witness to atrocity. Words can kill. They are also memory's voice. Without words, there could have been no Holocaust. Words, however, cannot do everything. One reason is that words can be smothered or, as Sarah Kofman sometimes said, words can be knotted. The Holocaust produced knotted words, especially for the survivors, because such words, Kofman suggests, are "demanded and yet forbidden, because for too long they have been internalized and withheld." Knotted words, she went on to say, "stick in your throat and cause you to suffocate, to lose your breath"; they "asphyxiate you, taking away the possibility of even beginning."[13]

Kofman understood all too well what she was saying, for this French philosopher was a Holocaust survivor. Like four other important writers who also endured that catastrophe—Jean Améry (1912–1978), Tadeusz Borowski (1922–1951), Paul Celan (1920–1970), and Primo Levi (1919–1987)—she took her own life. Kofman left behind a rich collection of philosophical works, among them significant writings on Sigmund Freud and Friedrich Nietzsche—especially the latter's outlook affects in varied ways Kofman's moral philosophy—as well as major contributions to feminist theory. Her voice, which was often heard on French radio and in political debate, earned its prominence in an influential generation of French philosophers that has included Jacques Derrida, Emmanuel Levinas, and Jean-Luc Nancy, who said of Kofman that "Fidelity was for her the very course of life. Not 'truth' but fidelity, the truth of fidelity, which has no final sense but the sense of its very course. Truth that returns to life and not the converse."[14]

Kofman is better known in many philosophical and literary circles than the other survivor-suicides mentioned above, but in the field of Holocaust studies it has thus far been her fate to be overlooked and too little appreciated. True, she wrote less—or at least less directly—about the Holocaust than some survivors, including Charlotte Delbo (1913–1985), arguably the woman who has written the most impressively in French about the Holocaust.[15] Kofman's explicit works about the Holocaust consist primarily of two small books, *Paroles suffoquées* (1987), a reflection focused on her father, Berek Kofman, a Parisian rabbi who was deported to Auschwitz in 1942, and *Rue Ordener, Rue Labat* (1994), her memoir about antisemitism, family separation, and hiding during the German occupation of her native France.[16]

Ann Smock, one of her translators, notes that Kofman began writing *Rue Ordener, Rue Labat* during the winter of 1992–93. She was almost sixty at the time. The memoir takes its title from two Parisian streets, which, Kofman observes, were separated by one Métro stop.[17] The family home had been on Rue Ordener, but everything changed when Kofman's father was caught in the roundup of some thirteen thousand Parisian Jews that took place on 16–17 July 1942.[18] Subsequently Sarah's mother, who survived the

Holocaust, had to find hiding places for the children. Kofman's turned out to be on Rue Labat with a Christian widow named Mémé.[19]

Meanwhile Kofman never saw her father again. In *Smothered Words,* Kofman sums up the bare facts of her father's fate as follows:

> My father: Berek Kofman, born on October 10, 1900, in Sobin (Poland), taken to Drancy on July 16, 1942. Was in convoy no. 12, dated July 29, 1942, a convoy comprising 1,000 deportees, 270 men and 730 women (aged 36–54); 270 men registered 54,153 to 54,422; 514 women selected for work, registered 13,320 to 13,833; 216 other women gassed immediately.[20]

The ending of the five-page chapter that contains those words mentions the memorial register created by Serge Klarsfeld, a French historian of the Holocaust and a hunter of Nazi war criminals. Kofman reproduces a portion of its double-columned, alphabetized list of the French deportees. There, in the left-hand column between the names of Simone Klempen and Grange Kohn, one finds Berek Kofman. Klarsfeld's memorial list, with "its endless columns of names ... takes your breath away," says Kofman. "Its 'neutral' voice summons you obliquely; in its extreme restraint, it is the very voice of affliction, of this event in which all possibility vanished, and which inflicted on the whole of humanity 'the decisive blow which left nothing intact.' This voice leaves you without a voice, makes you doubt your common sense and all sense, makes you suffocate in silence: 'silence like a cry without words; mute, although crying endlessly.'"[21]

Her father's death suffocated Kofman, stifled her words. It did so, however, not simply because it was her father's death, grievous enough though a father's death can be for anyone. "Because he was a Jew," as her stifled voice expresses it, "my father died in Auschwitz."[22] Kofman's emphasis on smothered words, moreover, shows that it was inseparable from the memory of how her father died in Auschwitz. "My father, a rabbi," she writes, "was killed because he tried to observe the Sabbath in the death camps; buried alive with a shovel for having—or so the witnesses reported—refused to work on that day, in order to celebrate the Sabbath, to pray to God for them all, victims and executioners, reestablishing, in this situation of extreme powerlessness and violence, a relation beyond all power. And they could not bear that a Jew, that vermin, even in the camps, did not lose faith in God."[23]

"Because he was a Jew, my father died in Auschwitz." Her father's suffocation and her own produce the double-binding questions that follow: "How can it not be said? And how can it be said?"[24] Not just a father's death but a particular Jewish father's death in its Auschwitz specificity—that event, which Kofman calls "my absolute," made the suffocating difference. She elaborates what she means by suggesting that integral to that difference is the awareness that "death in Auschwitz was worse than death."[25]

Kofman's point is not restricted to the brutality of that place or even to the systematic, assembly-line character of the mass murder that took place in Birkenau's gas chambers and crematoria. When she says that an Auschwitz death was worse than death, she is not mystifying death, let alone denying that death is death. She points instead to the smothering, even the death, of words such as *human* and *humanity*. After Auschwitz, Kofman claims, people "do not really die" because death itself—in the sense that the death of every man, woman, and child is the death of a human being—was degraded and mocked by Nazi Germany's "Final Solution." Auschwitz meant that people died *differently* in the sense that the Nazi extermination camps, whose mass killing went on for months and years, were a devastating assault on the very idea of a shared humanity that puts us all on a common ground of rights and responsibilities, of dignity and respect.

This tragic insight is not solely a lament about the loss of humanity conceived generically, universally, or in terms of some fixed philosophical essence, for, in the words of the philosopher Richard Rorty, "most people—especially people relatively untouched by the European Enlightenment—simply do not think of themselves as, first and foremost, a human being."[26] The loss of humanity involves a destruction of particularity, difference, and the potential for personal development—ingredients without which humanity is an abstraction. Not simply wanton but calculated and intended again and again by Nazi Germany and its collaborators, the destruction of Berek Kofman—a particular Jewish rabbi with a distinctive social identity, a specific name and a singular face whose difference is definitive of his humanity—constitutes the assault on humanity that is also the death of human death. There was, could be, only one Berek Kofman. The Nazi assault on humanity was systematic, extensive, and devastating. It could only be what it was by destruction that murdered particularity and difference—social and personal—as it destroyed children, women, and men *en masse* but also one by one by one. Post-Holocaust people, Kofman indicates ironically and tragically, have survived death only to discover, if they will, that reviving suffocated *humanity* is a task that indeed puts us, and perhaps philosophers and ethicists in particular, in "a strange *double bind:* an infinite claim to speak, *a duty to speak infinitely,* imposing itself with irrepressible force, and at the same time, an almost physical impossibility to speak, a *choking* feeling."[27]

All she has left of her father, Kofman observes at the beginning of *Rue Ordener, Rue Labat,* is his fountain pen. "Patched up with Scotch tape," it can produce words no more, but "right in front of me on my desk," she says, that mute pen "makes me write, write."[28] As she penned those words, Kofman was trying to do what she had not done overtly very much before. "Maybe all my books," she observed, "have been the detours required to bring me to write about 'that.'"[29] *That* included her father's death, the Holocaust, the loss of humanity, the death of death. Kofman had written about some of these matters already and in ways many and diverse, but a direct encounter with the Holocaust, unavoidably including the particularity of her father's death and her own identity in relation to that disaster, created in her something akin to the predicament felt by Robert Antelme, a member of the French Resistance, who was arrested by the Germans in June 1944, sent to Buchenwald, and eventually liberated at Dachau. In his philosophical memoir, *The Human Species,* which was originally published in

French as *L'Espèce humaine* (1957), he wrote that his "liberation" from Dachau left him to see that "it was impossible to bridge the gap we discovered opening up between the words at our disposal and that experience which, in the case of most of us, was still going forward within our bodies. How were we to resign ourselves to not trying to explain how we had got to the state we were in? For we were yet in that state. And even so, it was impossible. No sooner would we begin to tell our story than we would be choking over it."[30]

Confronting this double bind, but not paralyzed—at least not completely—by it, Antelme told his story, and Kofman examined the message that she took from it. Antelme saw that the more Adolf Hitler and his followers tried to destroy an inclusive sense of *humanity* through their genocidal antisemitism and racism, the more undeniable the "indestructible unity" of humanity became, or, as Antelme himself put it, "there is only one human race." The SS, continued Antelme, "can kill a man, but he can't change him into something else."[31] Kofman seems to share what she calls Antelme's "pleasure in tearing the Nazis' power to shreds and overturning their mastery," but as much as she admires his resistance, his determination not to permit the Nazis or even his own devastating experience to choke his words completely, Kofman appears to find Antelme's affirmative understanding of the persistence of a single humanity less than sufficient and therefore not entirely convincing.[32] It is not that she denies the unity but that Antelme may not have emphasized enough how Nazism wreaked havoc on *community*.

Her father's death never far from her consciousness, Kofman starts to draw out what remained only implicit in Antelme's *The Human Race*. The value of a shared sense of humanity, of our belonging to a human species, depends on whether that belonging binds us together in mutual respect and caring, whether it draws people together in community. As Kofman sizes up the situation, however, the connections between the unity implied by the word *humanity* and the senses of community that may or may not follow are tenuous and even problematic. First, she points out, "No community is possible with the SS."[33] With a vengeance, Nazi ideology rejected the idea of an inclusively shared humanity. Regarding difference—especially alleged racial difference—as profoundly threatening, its genocidal impulses took the world to Treblinka and Auschwitz. Nazi Germany, of course, took pride in its own sense of community, which underscores that community is not necessarily humanity's ally, especially if *humanity* is understood to be pluralistic and diverse. So Kofman makes a second point: It is crucial to support "the community (of those) without community."[34]

Those without community are outsiders, but Kofman's thinking does not stop with a call to defend and protect those who are threatened and harmed because they are left out. More radically and fundamentally, she rejects all senses of community that are based on "any specific difference or on a shared essence" such as reason.[35] The right forms of community, she seems to be saying, are those that consciously accept a double bind. This bind acknowledges that every community is particular, different, finite, even exclusive in one way or another, but no community should rest on assumptions about immutable superiority or inferiority. On the contrary, the particularity of one community ought to affirm, protect, and encourage the particularity of others. At its best, she contends, community depends on "a shared power to choose, to make incompatible though correlative choices, the power to kill *and* the power to respect and safeguard the incommensurable distance, the relation without relation."[36]

Here Kofman's words are not smothered or knotted, but they remain less than fully expressed. They remain hints, allusions, or signposts pointing to an ethical outlook that would not be the same as old humanisms that appealed to human nature, to the essence of humanity, or to reason as humankind's most decisive characteristic. Instead, she suggests that everyday realities and actions—things such as choices and keeping or betraying one's word—reveal our humanity and make all the difference. The Holocaust reaffirmed that all of those caught in it—perpetrators, victims, bystanders, and more—were human. In some sense, humanity survived the Holocaust, if only to testify, as the French philosopher Maurice Blanchot put it, how human indestructibility reveals "that there is no limit to the destruction of man."[37] But if humanity is to mean more than that, if humanity is to be what Kofman thinks it ought to become, then the destruction of old humanisms must make possible the willful reconstitution of a "new kind of 'we,'" even "a new 'humanism' one might say, if it were still acceptable to use this trite and idyllic word."[38]

Unknotted Words?

What about Kofman's guarded hope, her hint of "community (of those) without community," which could be based on "a shared power to choose"? Kofman glimpsed the possibility of a new humanism and a new ethics, but the Holocaust scholar Raul Hilberg seemed to emphasize a different theme, even one that disagreed with hers, when he spoke at a conference on ethics after the Holocaust at the University of Oregon in 1996.[39] Explaining that he did not consider himself a philosopher or theologian, Hilberg asserted that ethics is the same today as it was yesterday and even the day before yesterday; it is the same after Auschwitz as it was before and during the lethal operations at that place. Especially with regard to needless and wanton killing, he emphasized, ethics is the same for everyone, everywhere. Hilberg left no unclarity. Such killing is wrong. We know that "in our bones," he said, for such knowledge is the heritage of many years.

Kofman, I think, would accept Hilberg's claims only up to a point, and she would be right before conceding that Hilberg's bold pronouncement unknots the words that ethics after Auschwitz needs to express. True, senses of right and wrong are real. The Holocaust helps to focus them. Even the SS leader Heinrich Himmler knew as much. He and the other perpetrators of the Holocaust were aware of the psychological turmoil created by their orders to kill. They did their best to make those tasks easier, more "humane," by distancing the killers from their victims. Thus, they substituted mass gassings for the shootings of the *Einsatzgruppen*. But did Himmler and the other perpetrators know "in their bones" that what they were doing was wrong? In some cases, there is evidence that says so. The perpetrators covered their tracks as best they could. Many of the killers numbed themselves with alcohol. Some Germans refused orders to kill Jews, especially when children were the targets.

On the other hand, such evidence is mostly circumstantial. It was not very often enhanced by admissions of guilt or expressions of remorse. Far more common were excuses that referred to orders that must be obeyed or to fears of punishment if obedience was not forthcoming. For the most part, Nazi leaders and Holocaust perpetrators remained unrepentant. At the end of the day, their behavior does not show that they knew that their killing of the Jews was wanton, needless, and wrong. On the contrary, their behavior suggests that they believed their killing to be right and good, albeit extremely difficult, even loathsome to do. It would be comforting if Hilberg's convictions were true, but the Holocaust does not inspire confidence that all human beings know—in their bones or in any other way—that mass killing and genocide are wrong. Kofman was right: no community was possible with the SS because it did not know better than it thought it did. That knowledge, as Kofman also understood, depended on an entirely different approach to choosing and fidelity than Nazism required.

To the extent that knowledge of wrongdoing complicated the killing that the perpetrators carried out month after month, year after year, moral sensitivity did have to be overridden. Himmler and his henchmen could rely on an ally of vast authority: human consciousness itself.[40] Humanity's capacity to think is amazingly pliable, especially so in its ability to justify whatever the powers that be want done. The explanations offered by German industrialists to warrant their use of slave labor—for example, Germany was fighting for its life, what else could one do?—were only one strand in a web of rationalization and repression that did much to ensure that dissenting moral scruples would be subordinated to "higher" necessities or even that the dictates of morality and mass murder would coincide.[41] The Nazis were not totally successful in this regard. But when one remembers that the persons responsible for the Holocaust were a cross-section from virtually every profession, skill, and social class, then the persistence with which the Final Solution went forward without effective moral dissent is the more striking. Absent the force of will, what Kofman called the "shared power to choose" that makes "incompatible though correlative choices, the power to kill *and* the power to respect and safeguard the incommensurable distance, the relation without relation," nothing guarantees that ethics will not be smothered after the Holocaust as it was with such devastating results during that disaster.

"The owl of Minerva," wrote the philosopher Hegel, "spreads it wings only with the falling of the dusk." He meant that human reason and philosophy in particular achieve understanding only in retrospect; they are hard pressed to give "instruction as to what the world ought to be."[42] If Hegel is correct, the tools of moral philosophy and religious ethics are meager. Still, they have a role to play that nothing else can duplicate. Moral reflection, for example, can clarify and intensify feelings of wrong prompted by the Holocaust. Such thinking can show the importance of those feelings by revealing what happens when they fail to work their way into practice. Yet that understanding alone does little to change the world as long as societies concretely reward activities that kill and take punitive action toward those who refuse to cooperate. If one wants to affirm the United Nations' declaration that "everyone has the right to life, liberty, and security of person," one must realize that such claims are as frail as they are abstract.

The same is true of the United Nations Convention on the Prevention and Punishment of the Crime of Genocide, which was submitted to the UN's membership in December 1948. The United States became the ninety-seventh nation to approve the treaty when the Senate ratified the pact on 19 February 1986. The long delay was occasioned by fears that if the United States agreed to the treaty that makes genocide a crime, the nation might be indicted by its adversaries. Meanwhile, history continues to testify that it is power, not pacts, that facilitates or mitigates mass killing. Rights, liberty, and security of person are real only in specific times and places, only in actual political circumstances. Apart from such concrete settings those ideals are only that. Granted, they are ideals that attract. They can bring out the best in people. They can rally powerful forces behind them. They may even have a transcendent status ordained by God. To assume, however, that they are more than ideals until men and women take responsibility to make them a concrete reality may well be an illusion.

In our pluralistic world, in which cultural, religious, and philosophical perspectives vary considerably, a widely held belief is that values are so relative to one's time and place that the "truth" of moral claims is much more a result of subjective preference and political power than a function of objective reality and universal reason. That relativistic outlook meets resistance in the Holocaust, for there is a widely shared conviction that the Holocaust was *wrong*. It was something that should not have happened, and nothing akin to it should ever happen again. Michael Berenbaum puts the point effectively when he emphasizes that the Holocaust has become a "negative absolute." Even if people remain skeptical that rational agreement can be obtained about what is right, just, and good, the Holocaust seems to reestablish conviction that what happened at Auschwitz and Treblinka was wrong, unjust, and evil—period. More than that, the scale of the wrongdoing, the magnitude of the injustice, and the devastation of the Holocaust's evil are so radical that we can ill afford not to have our ethical sensibilities informed by them. As another Holocaust scholar, Franklin Littell, has stressed, "Study of the Holocaust is like pathology in medicine."[43] Pathology seeks to understand the origins and characteristics of disease and the conditions in which it thrives. If such understanding can be obtained, the prospects for resistance against disease, and perhaps even a cure, may be increased.

Unfortunately, to identify the Holocaust as a negative absolute that reinstates confidence in moral absolutes is a step, as the gray zone reminds us, that cannot be taken easily. No one is advised to rush to judgment that study of the Holocaust can obtain the hopeful results of medical pathology at its best. To reiterate the point with which this essay began, the Holocaust signifies an immense human failure. It did harm to ethics by showing how ethical teachings could be overridden, rendered dysfunctional, or even subverted to serve the interests of genocide.[44] When Berenbaum calls the Holocaust a "negative absolute," the absoluteness involved means that not even ethics itself was immune from failure and, at times, complicity in the pathological conditions and characteristics that nearly destroyed Jewish life and left the world morally scarred forever.

The gray-zoned status of ethics after the Holocaust is far from settled. One might argue that Nazi Germany's defeat shows that right defeated wrong and that goodness subdued evil, thus showing that reality has a fundamentally moral underpinning. The Holocaust, however, is far too awesome for such facile triumphalism. The Nazis did not win, but they came too close for comfort. Even though the Third Reich was destroyed, it is not so easy to say that its defeat was a clear and decisive triumph for goodness, truth, and justice over evil, falsehood, and corruption. Add to those realizations the fact that the Nazis themselves were idealists. They had positive beliefs about right and wrong, good and evil, duty and irresponsibility. The Final Solution was a key part of the Nazi ethic, perhaps the essence of its practice, which took place with a zealous, even apocalyptic, vengeance.[45] It would be too convenient to assume that the Nazi ethic's characteristic blending of loyalty, faith, heroism, and even love for country and cause was simply a passive, mindless obedience. Defensible though the judgment would be, it remains too soothing to say only that the Nazi ethic was really no ethic at all but a deadly perversion of what is truly moral, or that the Nazi conscience had nothing to do with ordinary language references to that reality. Most people are unlikely to serve a cause unto death unless that cause makes convincing moral appeals about what is good and worthy of loyalty. Those appeals, of course, can be blind, false, or even sinful, and the Nazis' were. Nevertheless, the perceived and persuasive "goodness" of the beliefs that constituted the Nazi ethic—the dedicated SS man embodied them most thoroughly—is essential to acknowledge if we are to understand why so many Germans willfully followed Hitler into genocidal warfare.

Paradoxically, the Final Solution threatens the status, practical and theoretical, of moral norms that are contrary to those that characterized the Nazi ethic, whose deadly way failed but still prevailed long enough to call into question many of Western civilization's moral assumptions and religious hopes.[46] Adolf Hitler and his Nazi regime intended the annihilation of Jewish life to signify the destruction of the very idea of a common humanity that all people share. Another philosopher-survivor, Jean Améry, was thinking in a vein akin to Kofman's when he wrote that the Nazis "hated the word 'humanity.'"[47] He amplified his point when he said, "Torture was no invention of National Socialism. But it was its apotheosis."⁴⁸ Améry meant that the Third Reich aimed to produce men, women, and children whose hardness would transcend humanity in favor of a so-called racially pure and culturally superior form of life that could still appropriately be called Aryan or German but not merely "human."

Insofar as *humanity* referred to universal equality, suggested a shared and even divine source of life, or implied any of the other trappings of weakness and sentimentality that Hitler and his most dedicated followers attributed to such concepts, National Socialism intentionally tried to go beyond humanity. Such steps entailed more than killing allegedly inferior forms of life that were thought to threaten German superiority. Moving beyond humanity made it essential to inflict torture—not only to show that "humanity" or "subhumanity" deserved no respect in and of itself, but also to ensure that those who had moved beyond humanity, and thus were recognizing the respect deserved only by Germans or Aryans, had really done so. Hitler and his Nazi followers did not succeed completely in implementing their antisemitism, but they went far enough in establishing what Améry aptly called "the rule of the anti-man" that none of our fondest hopes about humanity can be taken for granted.⁴⁹

As Sarah Kofman helped to show, our senses of moral and religious authority have been weakened by the accumulated ruins of history and the depersonalized advances of "civilization" that have taken us from a bloody twentieth century into an even more problematic twenty-first. A moral spirit and religious commitment that have the courage to persist *in spite of* humankind's self-inflicted destructiveness are essential, but the question remains of how effective those dispositions can be in a world where power, and especially the power of governments, stands at the heart of that matter. To find ways to affect "the powers that be" so that their tendencies to lay waste to human life are checked, ethics after Auschwitz will need to become gray-zoned in the sense that it will have to draw on every resource it can find: appeals to human rights, calls for renewed religious sensitivity, respect and honor for people who save lives and resist tyranny, and attention to the Holocaust's warnings, to name only a few. Those efforts will need to be accompanied by efforts that build these concerns into our educational, religious, business, and political institutions.

If one considers human rights after the Holocaust, it is unlikely that humankind will ever reach full agreement on a single worldview that will ground belief in such rights. But it does not follow that appeals to human rights are dashed as well. If people feel the need to ground appeals to human rights, a variety of options—philosophical and religious—may remain credible even if they will not be universally accepted. More importantly, there may be considerable agreement—especially after the Holocaust—about what the functional interpretation of human rights ought to be. Here, too, there will not be universal agreement, but the Holocaust itself has had an important impact in helping to clarify what ought not to happen to human beings. If we think about what ought not to happen to human beings, moreover, we may find considerable agreement about what should happen.

Sarah Kofman never forgot what the Nazi assault meant, namely, that after 16 July 1942, she never saw her father Berek again. In the afterword to *Nightfather,* a remarkable novel about a young daughter's poignant attempt to understand her father, a Holocaust survivor, the Dutch writer Carl Friedman—whose father was a survivor—quotes the poet Remco Campert, another author from the Netherlands. "Resistance does not start with big words," Campert says, "it starts with small deeds. Asking yourself a question / that is how resistance starts / then putting that question to somebody else."[50] Nazism and its Holocaust were an assault on the values that human beings hold most dear when we are at our best. Resistance to protect them came too late then; hence resistance continues to be urgent now, and it begins perpetually with small deeds, the raising of critical questions among them. Sarah Kofman, her smothered words, the Holocaust's double binds, Kofman's sense that "after Auschwitz there is no word tinged from on high . . . that has any right unless it has undergone a transformation"—each and all, her hard-earned perspectives underscore that nothing human, natural, or divine guarantees respect for those values.[51] Nothing, though, is more important than our commitment to defend them, for they remain as fundamental as they are fragile, as precious as they are endangered. These insights are among those made clearer by Primo Levi's gray zone and by Sarah Kofman's smothered words, her guarded hope, her hint of "community (of those) without community," and her glimpses of the possibility of a new humanism and a new ethics that might emerge from the Holocaust's gray-zoned double binds.

Notes

1. See "The Essential and the Superfluous," Levi's 1987 interview with Robert Di Caro, in Primo Levi, *The Voice of Memory: Interviews, 1961–1987,* ed. Marco Belpoliti and Robert Gordon; trans. Robert Gordon (New York: The New Press, 2001), 175.
2. Primo Levi, *The Drowned and the Saved,* trans. Raymond Rosenthal (New York: Summit Books, 1988), 38.
3. Ibid., 48.
4. Ibid., 53.
5. Ibid., 41. In *Jewish Resistance During the Holocaust: Moral Uses of Violence and Will* (New York: Palgrave Macmillan, 2004), James M. Glass shows how the Holocaust produced a disintegration of ethics akin to the outcomes that Levi witnessed in Auschwitz. He describes two types of Jewish resistance to that disintegration. One form, spiritual resistance, did not eliminate useless suffering and death, but it allowed the dying a modicum of dignity and perhaps helped to keep ethical hopes alive. The other form, violent resistance, developed an ethic of its own, one that gave priority to survival and legitimated what was necessary to improve the odds for it. Glass's lucid and realistic account helps to show how the status and content of understandings of right and wrong are influenced by power configurations.
6. Levi, *The Drowned and the Saved,* 202.
7. Ibid., 69.

8. See Peter J. Haas, *Morality After Auschwitz: The Radical Challenge of the Nazi Ethic* (Philadelphia: Fortress Press, 1988). For further discussion on this important theme, see also John K. Roth, ed., *Ethics After the Holocaust: Perspectives, Critiques, and Responses* (St. Paul, MN: Paragon House, 1999).
9. Claudia Koonz, *The Nazi Conscience* (Cambridge: Harvard University Press, 2003), 1.
10. Ibid., 2.
11. Sarah Kofman, *Smothered Words*, trans. Madeleine Dobie (Evanston, IL: Northwestern University Press, 1998), 73.
12. Irving Greenberg, "Cloud of Smoke, Pillar of Fire: Judaism, Christianity, and Modernity after the Holocaust," in Eva Fleischner, ed., *Auschwitz: Beginning of a New Era?* (New York: Ktav Publishing House, 1977), 23.
13. Kofman, *Smothered Words*, 39.
14. Jean-Luc Nancy, "Foreword: Run, Sarah!" in Penelope Deutscher and Kelly Oliver, eds., *Enigmas: Essays on Sarah Kofman* (Ithaca, NY: Cornell University Press, 1999), ix. Deutscher and Oliver provide helpful background—biographical and philosophical—about Kofman in "Sarah Kofman's Skirts," their introduction to *Enigmas*, which also contains a detailed bibliography of Kofman's publications. See 1–22 and 264–75.
15. See especially Charlotte Delbo, *Auschwitz and After*, trans. Rosette C. Lamont (New Haven, CT: Yale University Press, 1995). Delbo was not Jewish, but her activity in the French Resistance led to her arrest and deportation to Auschwitz, which took place on 24 January 1943. She survived Auschwitz and Ravensbrück, a Nazi camp established especially for women.
16. For the English translations of these books, see Kofman, *Smothered Words*, and Sarah Kofman, *Rue Ordener, Rue Labat*, trans. Ann Smock (Lincoln: University of Nebraska Press, 1996). Kofman's memory of her father plays an important part in both. *Smothered Words* is dedicated to him and also to the philosophers Maurice Blanchot (1907–2003) and Robert Antelme (1917–1990). Blanchot's controversial career included the prewar articles that he wrote for right-wing, antisemitic publications, but also assistance to French Jews during the German occupation and postwar reflections on the Holocaust, particularly *L'Ecriture du désastre* (1980), which influenced Kofman considerably. Antelme was arrested by the Germans because of his work in the French Resistance. His survival of Buchenwald and Dachau led to *L'Espèce humaine* (1957), a philosophical memoir that made an especially strong impression upon Kofman. "To have to speak without being able to speak or be understood, to have to choke," wrote Kofman in *Smothered Words* (39), "such is the ethical exigency that Robert Antelme obeys in *The Human Race*." For the English translations of the books by Blanchot and Antelme, see Maurice Blanchot, *The Writing of the Disaster*, trans. Ann Smock (Lincoln: University of Nebraska Press, 1986), and Robert Antelme, *The Human Race*, trans. Jeffrey Haight and Annie Mahler (Evanston, IL: The Marlboro Press/Northwestern University Press, 1998). All citations from Antelme and Blanchot as well as from *Rue Ordener, Rue Labat* and *Smothered Words* are from the English editions I have noted.
17. Kofman, *Rue Ordener, Rue Labat*, 31.
18. Kofman adds the following information about her father: "On 16 July 1942, my father knew he was going to be picked up. It had been rumored that a big roundup was planned for that day. He was rabbi of a small synagogue on the Rue Duc in the 18th arrondissement. He had left home very early that day to warn as many Jews as he could to go into hiding immediately.

"Then he came home and waited: he was afraid that if he too were to hide his wife and six young children would be taken in his place. He had three girls and three boys between two and twelve years old.

"He waited and prayed to God that they would come for him, as long as his wife and children could be saved" (*Rue Ordener, Rue Labat*, 5).

About eighty thousand Jews from France were killed in Nazi Germany's extermination camps, mostly at Auschwitz. Approximately one-third of them were French citizens;

the majority were immigrants and refugees. Foreign Jews were first deported from France to Auschwitz on 27 March 1942. Facilitated by French police, the roundups and deportations intensified during the summer of 1942. For more background and detail, see David Weinberg, "France," in Walter Laqueur, ed., *The Holocaust Encyclopedia* (New Haven, CT: Yale University Press, 2001), 213–22.

19. Among the multiple double binds that the Holocaust created were the complex dilemmas of identity encountered by hidden children. Kofman illustrates an aspect of that bind when she briefly describes the journey that took her from Rue Ordener, her home street, to a place of hiding and relative safety on Rue Labat. Her reaction seems to run as deep as it was physical. Short in distance and time though it was, that journey "seemed endless to me, and I vomited the whole way." Kofman indicates that Mémé, her rescuer, was "not without anti-Semitic prejudices." She also detached Kofman from her mother and Judaism. Yet Kofman says that she came to love Mémé "more than my own mother." Ending *Rue Ordener, Rue Labat* with Mémé on her mind, Kofman writes, "I was unable to attend her funeral. But I know that at her grave the priest recalled how she had saved a little Jewish girl during the war" (*Rue Ordener, Rue Labat,* 31, 47, 58, 85).
20. Kofman, *Smothered Words,* 10.
21. Ibid., 10–11. In this passage Kofman includes two quotations from Blanchot, whose words, along with Antelme's, are frequently quoted in *Smothered Words.* The first quotation is from "After the Fact," Blanchot's afterword to his *Vicious Circles,* trans. Paul Auster (Barrytown, NY: Station Hill Press, 1985), 68. The second passage is from *The Step Not Beyond,* trans. Lycette Nelson (Albany: State University of New York Press, 1992), 61. Elsewhere Blanchot amplifies and complicates the point made in the first passage quoted by Kofman. "The disaster ruins everything," he writes, "all the while leaving everything intact." That relationship epitomizes another of the Holocaust's double binds, which are so vividly illustrated in Kofman's life and authorship. See Blanchot, *The Writing of the Disaster,* 1.

   In "A Note on Translation," which helps to introduce *Smothered Words,* Madeleine Dobie observes that Kofman's frequent use of quotations, a style often found in her later writings, "may be seen to attenuate the mastery of the narrative voice through the interposition of the voices of others, and thereby of the Other, the style that Kofman, following Blanchot, calls 'writing without power.' . . . *Paroles suffoquées*," continues Dobie, "is at once a scholarly piece that develops arguments supported by quotations and footnotes, and a meditation in the style of Blanchot, in which the conventional privileging of the signified—arguments or ideas—over the signifier—form or the very process of writing itself—is called into question" (xxiv). My essay's discussion of Kofman, replete with quotation of her words, modestly tries to emulate her style in that regard.
22. Kofman, *Smothered Words,* 9.
23. Ibid., 34.
24. Ibid., 9.
25. Ibid. Kofman cites Theodor Adorno's *Negative Dialectics* as an influence on her thinking about this point.
26. See Richard Rorty, "Human Rights, Rationality, and Sentimentality," in Patrick Hayden, ed., *The Philosophy of Human Rights* (St. Paul, MN: Paragon House, 2001), 251.
27. Kofman, *Smothered Words,* 39.
28. Kofman, *Rue Ordener, Rue Labat,* 3.
29. Ibid.
30. Antelme, *The Human Race,* 3.
31. See Kofman, *Smothered Words,* 58, and Antelme, *The Human Race,* 220.
32. Kofman, *Smothered Words,* 66.
33. Ibid., 70.
34. Ibid.
35. Ibid.
36. Ibid.

37. Kofman ends *Smothered Words* with this quotation from Blanchot (see 73). The quoted passage comes from *The Infinite Conversation,* trans. Susan Hanson (Minneapolis: University of Minnesota Press, 1993), 135.
38. Kofman, *Smothered Words,* 73. Kofman adds an intriguing note to her allusion about a new "humanism." She writes as follows: "In spite of everything that makes this word unacceptable for us today—after 'the death of God' and the end of man that is its correlate—I nonetheless want to conserve it, while giving it a completely different meaning, displacing and transforming it. I keep it because what other, new 'word' could have as much hold on the old humanism?" (89–90). Here one thinks of the Nietzschean theme of the revaluation of values.
39. The discussion in this part of my essay is adapted from the epilogue to Richard L. Rubenstein and John K. Roth, *Approaches to Auschwitz: The Holocaust and Its Legacy,* rev. ed. (Louisville: Westminster John Knox Press, 2003), 365–77.
40. For instructive sociopsychological discussions about rationalizations and interpersonal dynamics that expedited the Holocaust and facilitate the potential for future genocides, see Christopher R. Browning, *Ordinary Men: Reserve Police Battalion 101 and the Final Solution in Poland* (New York: HarperCollins, 1992); Daniel Jonah Goldhagen, *Hitler's Willing Executioners: Ordinary Germans and the Holocaust* (New York: Alfred A. Knopf, 1996); Ervin Staub, *The Roots of Evil: The Origins of Genocide and Other Group Violence* (Cambridge: Cambridge University Press, 1989); and James Waller, *Becoming Evil: How Ordinary People Commit Genocide and Mass Killing* (New York: Oxford University Press, 2002).
41. For a useful discussion of the various defense mechanisms employed by Nazis to justify their actions in the Holocaust, see Raul Hilberg, "The Nature of the Process," in Joel E. Dimsdale, ed., *Survivors, Victims, and Perpetrators: Essays on the Nazi Holocaust* (Washington, DC: Hemisphere, 1980), 5–54. See also Robert Wolfe, "Putative Threat to National Security As Nuremberg Defense for Genocide," in Irene G. Shur, Franklin H. Littell, and Marvin E. Wolfgang, eds., *Reflections on the Holocaust* (Philadelphia: The American Academy of Political and Social Science, 1980), 46–67. As he sized up the excuses that German industrialists offered, Benjamin Ferencz, an American prosecutor at the Nuremberg trials, added that as far as German businessmen were concerned, "it was only those who had nothing to be ashamed of who expressed a sense of guilt and culpability." See Benjamin B. Ferencz, *Less Than Slaves: Jewish Forced Labor and the Quest for Compensation* (Cambridge: Harvard University Press, 1979), 192.
42. G. W. F. Hegel, *Philosophy of Right,* trans. T. M. Knox (New York: Oxford University Press, 1967), 12–13.
43. The quotation is from Littell's concluding plenary speech at Remembering for the Future 2000, a major international conference on the Holocaust held in Oxford, England, 16–23 July 2000. See John K. Roth and Elisabeth Maxwell, eds., *Remembering for the Future: The Holocaust in an Age of Genocide,* 3 vols. (New York: Palgrave, 2001), 3:8–9.
44. On these points see Zygmunt Bauman, *Modernity and the Holocaust* (Ithaca, NY: Cornell University Press, 1991), and Jonathan Glover, *Humanity: A Moral History of the Twentieth Century* (New Haven, CT: Yale University Press, 2000).
45. For an important discussion of these themes, see Haas, *Morality After Auschwitz* and Roth, ed., *Ethics After the Holocaust.*
46. Even with respect to Berenbaum's appealing idea that the Holocaust is a negative absolute, this judgment remains valid. There is no guarantee that universal moral reason or intuition exists or that, if they do, they will automatically conclude without disagreement that the Holocaust is a negative absolute. In ethics, the human will is decisive in determining how good and evil, right and wrong are understood. Reason and intuition inform our willing and choosing, but without the latter, our senses of good and evil, right and wrong, lack the force that gives them full reality and makes them effective. Willing and choosing alone do not determine what is ethical, but in the fullest sense no determination of right and wrong takes place without them. For a careful and important ethical study that emphasizes rationality in a more universalistic way, see David H. Jones, *Moral Respon-*

sibility in the Holocaust: A Study in the Ethics of Character (Lanham, MD: Rowman & Littlefield, 1999).

47. Jean Améry, *At the Mind's Limits: Contemplations by a Survivor on Auschwitz and Its Realities*, trans. Sidney Rosenfeld and Stella P. Rosenfeld (Bloomington: Indiana University Press, 1980), 31. After Nazi Germany annexed his native Austria in March 1938, Améry fled to Western Europe. During the German occupation of Belgium, he joined the resistance movement in that country and was arrested and tortured by the Germans in 1943. He survived Auschwitz and Bergen-Belsen, where he was liberated in April 1945. *Jenseits von Schuld und Sühne* (Beyond Guilt and Atonement) appeared in 1966. The English translation noted above was first published in 1980. Améry stressed that his experience of torture and the Holocaust caused him to lose what he called "trust in the world" (28).
48. Ibid., 30.
49. Ibid., 31.
50. Carl Friedman, *Nightfather*, trans. Arnold and Erica Pomerans (New York: Persea Books, 1994), 134.
51. Kofman, *Smothered Words*, 73. Kofman mistakenly attributes the quoted phrase to Antelme, but as her translator points out, Theodor Adorno's *Negative Dialectics* is the correct source. "After Auschwitz," he said, "there is no word tinged from on high, not even a theological one, that has any right unless it underwent a transformation." See Theodor Adorno, *Negative Dialectics*, trans. E. B. Ashton (New York: Seabury Press, 1973), 367.

EPILOGUE
An Intense Wish to Understand

Jonathan Petropoulos and John K. Roth

I leave a lot of uncompleted work . . .

—Primo Levi, "Unfinished Business"

In September 1986, less than a year before Primo Levi's untimely death, the novelist Philip Roth arrived in Turin, Italy, to renew the conversation that was later reported as an afterword to the 1996 American edition of *Survival in Auschwitz*, the classic Holocaust memoir that has provided some of the linking threads for *Gray Zones*. Philip Roth offered his opinion that much more than luck had determined Levi's survival. He felt that Levi's "professional character," his scientific curiosity and precision, his desire to discern order, and his refusal to accept what Roth called the "evil inversion" of everything that Levi valued had all done their parts to save Levi's life. "The scientist and the survivor," said Roth, "are one."[1]

Levi accepted Philip Roth's equation only in part. No general rule governed survival in Auschwitz, he insisted, "except entering the camp in good health and knowing German. Barring this, luck dominated." Levi did not take himself to be an exception, but he acknowledged that "for me thinking and observing were survival factors." Although they were not enough to explain his survival, let alone to ensure it, Levi said to Roth that he remembered "having lived my Auschwitz year in a condition of exceptional spiritedness. I don't know if this depended on my professional background, or an unsuspected stamina, or on a sound instinct." What did remain clear to Levi was that he "never stopped recording the world and people around me, so much so that I still have an unbelievably detailed image of them."

Notes for this section begin on page 394.

Levi insisted that he was "constantly pervaded by a curiosity ... the curiosity of the naturalist who finds himself transplanted into an environment that is monstrous but new, monstrously new." He underscores that he had "an intense wish to understand."[2]

Levi's intense wish to understand was less than fulfilled. "I have a lot of uncompleted work," he had written in a poem called "Unfinished Business," which he completed on 19 April 1981.[3] The Holocaust was too vast to encompass, its gray zones too full of ambiguity and compromise to fathom completely, and then there were the experiences that had been forgotten or repressed—"human memory," said Levi, "is a marvelous but fallacious instrument"[4]—as well as the unforgotten horrors that eluded description and muted language.

In various ways, all of the contributors to this volume have encountered versions of those realities. This book reflects that fact. It has done so by showing why few reflections about the Holocaust are more important than Primo Levi's about the gray zone, a region in which moral ambiguity and compromise were pronounced. Levi located the gray zone primarily, though not exclusively, in Auschwitz. Not only did Levi rightly caution against premature closure in historical and ethical analysis of the Holocaust, but also his account of the gray zone suggested that there were many zones and degrees of "gray" during and after that disaster. In multiple ways, as this volume's essays attest, his insights about the complexity of human behavior and relationships in Auschwitz have influenced scholarship and even popular understanding about the Holocaust.

In this book twenty-five Holocaust scholars have explored a variety of gray zones. Accomplished scholars in their fields, they have brought a necessary interdisciplinary focus to bear on timely and often controversial topics in cutting-edge Holocaust studies. While each essay has utilized a particular methodology and has argued for its own thesis, the volume as a whole advances the claim that the more we learn about the Holocaust, the more complex that event turns out to be. This complexity often has much to do with the ambiguities and compromises that characterized the persons, places, perspectives, and policies that created the Holocaust and its aftermath. Only if these ambiguities and compromises are identified, explored, and at times allowed to remain—lest resolution deceive us—will our awareness of the Holocaust and its implications be as full as possible.

As mentioned in the prologue, *Gray Zones* emerged from a conference that was held in Claremont, California, in February 2004. Although the contributors have had the opportunity to revise their texts and take advantage of the criticism and discussion offered during the conference, no volume can capture all facets of the exchanges that took place. More specifically, there are two individuals who contributed greatly to the conference but who thus far have not been represented in this book. A word about them makes a fitting conclusion for a book whose governing epigraph is Levi's gray-zoned insight that "the greater part of historical and natural phenomena are not simple, or not simple in the way that we would like."[5]

The first, Dario Gabbai, provided one of the most memorable and moving moments of the conference when he spoke about his experiences in Auschwitz-Birkenau. Gabbai's talk took place on the opening evening of the conference and caught most of the participants by surprise. This is not an easy thing to do: while few would label the assembled scholars a jaded group, they had abundant experience in listening to survivors and testimony about the Holocaust. Indeed, most of the scholars turn to survivors when they teach their courses on the Holocaust, in much the same way that Dario Gabbai has become a mainstay of the Holocaust courses taught at Claremont McKenna College. But Dario Gabbai is special, as we all learned that evening.

Gabbai was a member of the last *Sonderkommando* to work in Auschwitz-Birkenau. More precisely, he had arrived in Auschwitz in April 1944 on a transport of Greek Jews and had immediately been sent to Crematorium II, where he and the others in the *Sonderkommando* worked to "process" the influx of Hungarian Jews. Gabbai was and is many things: cultured (he speaks perfect Greek, Italian, and English), sensitive, generous, and physically diminutive. But there are other dimensions to him: he is a tough man who is nevertheless deeply saddened and wracked by feelings of guilt.

On that February night when the "Gray Zones" conference began, Gabbai, his voice quivering with emotion, told the audience that "there are two men inside of me." There is the person that people ordinarily see—sympathetic and modest, among the adjectives noted above—and there is the "other" part of him. This part resulted from his seeing what virtually no one else has seen, from doing what virtually nobody else has done. Day after day, who else has hooked a belt around an Auschwitz corpse and dragged it to a raging oven? Week after week, who else has searched body cavities for valuables? During a lifetime, who else has faced the choiceless choices and done the devastating things that were required of him in Auschwitz if his life was to be prolonged?

Dario Gabbai is a survivor who combines incredible strength with a vulnerability and fragility that become apparent when he bears witness. The former found expression in Auschwitz, where he not only endured the horrifying work detail but also a highly dangerous situation that resulted from the uprising of *Sonderkommandos* in October 1944. Gabbai's unit in Crematorium II was prepared to participate in the revolt, but other *Sonderkommandos,* acted prematurely—before word had been sent to Gabbai and his fellow prisoners so that they could act in concert. The rebels who had acted were overpowered, killed, and then "processed" by the surviving *Sonderkommando*—Gabbai had to participate in their disposal, too. The SS guards then planned to liquidate his unit, but before that could happen, Gabbai and some of his comrades managed to escape from their special compound and meld in with the other inmates. The SS searched for them. They tried to find these witnesses so that these bearers of secrets could never tell what they knew. Nevertheless, Gabbai survived, enduring even the brutal winter death march that took him to the Austrian Salzkammergut. When liberated at Ebensee, he weighed sixty-seven pounds. He has also survived the terrible memories and the nightmares that he frequently experiences.

Dario Gabbai is special for many reasons—for surviving what he did, for rebuilding a life in California, for enduring the pain of repeatedly telling his story. He is also special because he was a *Sonderkommando,* and he saw aspects of the Holocaust witnessed by few others. Other survivors know that he is special, although they struggle with that fact and what it means. After Gabbai's presentation on the opening night of the conference, one of the scholars present tried to acknowledge Gabbai's uniqueness. The formulation was somewhat clumsy and suggested, however inadvertently, that Gabbai was a better or more valuable witness of the genocide than other survivors who had been at Auschwitz but not in the *Sonderkommando.* This remark elicited a critical response from another Auschwitz survivor in the audience. He strongly rejected any rankings among survivors, but even more may have been going on as that commentary unfolded. The encounter suggests that there are many more gray-zoned dimensions to the Holocaust than even Primo Levi and the contributors to this book have documented.

The Auschwitz survivor who rejected rankings among survivors was Theodore ("Zev") Weiss, a remarkable man who has devoted himself to encouraging Holocaust education and research by establishing and leading the Holocaust Educational Foundation, whose headquarters is in Skokie, Illinois. Through its Lessons and Legacies program and other international initiatives, Weiss's foundation supports scholars, academic travel, and conferences, including the one that led to this book. A man of vision, Weiss is also gentle, humane, and characterized by an often surprising sense of humor. His comments on that February night in Claremont, however, were marked more by intense and perhaps even hidden feelings. While his words rejecting rankings among survivors may have been directed to the scholar who had paid tribute to Dario Gabbai, some in the audience felt that Weiss was addressing Gabbai himself, although Gabbai had made no claims about his uniqueness, let alone his superiority.

Around the bar at the conference hotel later in the evening, some of the scholars at the conference tried to make sense of the exchange they had witnessed. What *had* been said? What had *not* been said? One scholar ventured an opinion: Zev Weiss had lost family members at Auschwitz, including a brother in late 1944. Was it possible that Dario Gabbai had "processed" Zev Weiss's brother? Probably neither Gabbai nor Weiss could ever know for sure.

* * * * * * *

"There now, it's finished: there's no more to be done," wrote Primo Levi in a poem called "The Work," which concludes with the question "What to do now?"[6] As *Gray Zones* draws to a close, it also testifies that much remains to be done in Holocaust studies. That work of study and scholarship, which always entails dealing with the Holocaust's complexity, requires finding out, clarifying, and getting right as much as we can. It also involves pondering the unanswerable questions created by the Holocaust and the ambiguities and compromises left in its wake.

Notes

1. See Philip Roth's "A Conversation with Primo Levi," in Primo Levi, *Survival in Auschwitz: The Nazi Assault on Humanity,* trans. Stuart Woolf (New York: Simon and Schuster, 1996), 180.
2. Ibid.
3. Primo Levi, "Unfinished Business," in his *Collected Poems,* trans. Ruth Feldman and Brian Swann (London: Faber and Faber, 1988), 47.
4. Primo Levi, *The Drowned and the Saved,* trans. Raymond Rosenthal (New York: Summit Books, 1988), 23.
5. Ibid., 37.
6. Primo Levi, "The Work," in *Collected Poems,* 56.

Select Bibliography

As the chapter notes indicate, many sources have informed the contributors' work. Listed below are some of the books that have most influenced their interpretations of the Holocaust's gray zones.

Adler, Stanislaw. *In the Warsaw Ghetto, 1940–1943*. Jerusalem: Yad Vashem, 1982.
Aly, Götz. *"Final Solution": Nazi Population Policy and the Murder of the European Jews*. Translated by Belinda Cooper and Allison Brown. London: Arnold, 1999.
Améry, Jean. *At the Mind's Limits: Contemplations by a Survivor of Auschwitz and Its Realities*. Translated by Sidney Rosenfeld and Stella P. Rosenfeld. Bloomington: Indiana University Press, 1980.
Angier, Carole. *The Double Bond: Primo Levi, a Biography*. New York: Farrar, Straus and Giroux, 2002.
Anissimov, Myriam. *Primo Levi: Tragedy of an Optimist*. Translated by Steve Cox. Woodstock, NY: Overlook Press, 1998.
Auschwitz-Birkenau State Museum. *KL Auschwitz Seen by the SS: Rudolf Höss, Pery Broad, Johann Paul Kremer*. Translated by Constantine FitzGibbon and Krystyna Michalik. Oświęcim: Cieszyńska Drukarnia Wydawnicza, 1996.
Authers, John, and Richard Wolffe. *The Victim's Fortune: Inside the Epic Battle Over the Debts of the Holocaust*. New York: HarperCollins, 2002.
Barkai, Avraham. *"Wehr Dich!": Der Centralverein deutscher Staatsbürger jüdischen Glaubens 1893–1938*. Munich: Beck, 2002.
Barkan, Elazar. *The Guilt of Nations: Restitution and Negotiating Historical Injustices*. New York: W. W. Norton, 2000.
Bazyler, Michael. *Holocaust Justice: The Battle for Restitution in America's Courts*. New York: New York University Press, 2003.
Benz, Wolfgang, ed. *Dimension des Völkermords: Die Zahl der jüdischen Opfer des Nationalsozialismus*. Munich: Oldenbourg, 1991.
Bonhoeffer, Dietrich. *Ethics*. New York: Collier Books, 1986.
Bourke, Joanna. *Dismembering the Male: Men's Bodies, Britain and the Great War*. Chicago: University of Chicago Press, 1996.
Breitman, Richard. *Official Secrets: What the Nazis Planned, What the British and Americans Knew*. New York: Hill and Wang, 1998.
Browning, Christopher. *Collected Memories: Holocaust History and Postwar Testimony*. Madison: University of Wisconsin Press, 2003.
———. *Nazi Policy, Jewish Workers, German Killers*. New York: Cambridge University Press, 2000.
———. *Ordinary Men: Reserve Police Battalion 101 and the Final Solution in Poland*. New York: HarperCollins, 1992.
———. *The Origins of the Final Solution: The Evolution of Nazi Jewish Policy, September 1939–March 1942*. Lincoln: University of Nebraska Press, 2004.

Chaumont, Jean-Michel. *Concurrence des Victimes: Génocide, Identité, Reconnaissance.* Paris: Editions de la Découverte, 1997.
Cholawski, Shalom. *The Jews of Bielorussia During World War II.* Amsterdam: Harwood, 1998.
Dean, Martin. *Collaboration in the Holocaust: Crimes of the Local Police in Belorussia and Ukraine, 1941–1944.* New York: St. Martin's Press, 2000.
Demandt, Alexander. *History That Never Happened: A Treatise on the Question, What Would Have Happened If . . . ?* Jefferson, NC: McFarland, 1993.
Dobroszycki, Lucjan, ed. *The Chronicle of the Łódź Ghetto, 1941–1944.* Translated by Richard Lourie et al. New Haven, CT: Yale University Press, 1984.
Dreyfus, Jean-Marc, and Sarah Gensburger. *Des Camps dans Paris: Austerlitz, Lévitan, Bassano, juillet 1943–août 1944.* Paris: Fayard, 2003.
Eizenstat, Stuart. *Imperfect Justice: Looted Assets, Slave Labor, and the Unfinished Business of World War II.* New York: Public Affairs, 2003.
Ferguson, Niall, ed. *Virtual History: Alternatives and Counter-Factuals.* New York: Basic Books, 1999.
Finkelstein, Norman. *The Holocaust Industry: Reflections on the Exploitation of Jewish Suffering.* London: Verso, 2000.
Frei, Norbert. *Adenauer's Germany and the Nazi Past: The Politics of Amnesty and Integration.* New York: Columbia University Press, 2002.
Fremont, Helen. *After Long Silence.* New York: Delta, 1999.
Friedlander, Henry. *The Origins of Nazi Genocide: From Euthanasia to the Final Solution.* Chapel Hill: University of North Carolina Press, 1995.
Friedländer, Saul. *Kurt Gerstein: The Ambiguity of Good.* Translated by Charles Fullman. New York: Knopf, 1969.
———. *Quand vient le Souvenir . . .* Paris: Editions du Seuil, 1978.
Gerlach, Wolfgang. *And the Witnesses Were Silent: The Confessing Church and the Jews.* Lincoln: University of Nebraska Press, 2000.
Giuliani, Massimo. *A Centaur in Auschwitz: Reflections on Primo Levi's Thinking.* Lanham, MD: Lexington Books, 2003.
Grau, Günter, ed. *Homosexualität in der NS-Zeit: Dokumente einer Diskriminierung und Verfolgung.* Frankfurt am Main: Fischer Taschenbuch Verlag, 1993.
Greif, Gideon. *Wir weinten tränenlos . . . : Augenzeugenberichte des jüdischen "Sonderkommandos" in Auschwitz.* Frankfurt am Main: Fischer Taschenbuch Verlag, 1999.
Guderian, Heinz. *Panzer Leader.* Cambridge, MA: Da Capo, 2002.
Haas, Peter. *Morality After Auschwitz: The Radical Challenge of the Nazi Ethic.* Philadelphia: Fortress Press, 1988.
Haensch, Dietrich. *Repressive Familienpolitik: Sexualunterdrückung als Mittel der Politik.* Reinbek: Rowohlt, 1969.
Hayes, Peter. *From Cooperation to Complicity: Degussa in the Third Reich.* New York: Cambridge University Press, 2004.
Haynes, Stephen. *The Bonhoeffer Phenomenon: Portraits of a Protestant Saint.* Minneapolis: Fortress Press, 2004.
Heinemann, Isabel. *"Rasse, Siedlung, deutsches Blut": Das Rasse- und Siedlungshauptamt der SS und die rassenpolitische Neuordnung Europas.* Göttingen: Wallstein Verlag, 2003.
Heller, Fanya Gottesfeld. *Strange and Unexpected Love: A Teenage Girl's Holocaust Memoirs.* Hoboken, NJ: Ktav, 1993.
Heuss, Anja. *Kunst- und Kulturgutraub: Eine vergleichende Studie zur Besatzungspolitik der Nationalsozialisten in Frankreich unter der Sowjetunion.* Heidelberg: Universitätsverlag C. Winter, 2000.
Hilberg, Raul. *The Destruction of the European Jews.* 3rd ed. New Haven, CT: Yale University Press, 2003.
———. *Sources of Holocaust Research: An Analysis.* Chicago: Ivan R. Dee, 2001.
Hillenbrand, F. K. M. *Underground Humour in Nazi Germany, 1933–1945.* London: Routledge, 1995.

Höhn, Maria. *GIs and Fräuleins: The German-American Encounter in 1950s West Germany.* Chapel Hill: University of North Carolina Press, 2002.
Ioanid, Radu. *The Holocaust in Romania: The Destruction of Jews and Gypsies Under the Antonescu Regime, 1940–1944.* Chicago: Ivan R. Dee, 2000.
Jellonnek, Burkhard. *Homosexuelle unter dem Hakenkreuz: Die Verfolgung von Homosexuellen im Dritten Reich.* Paderborn: F. Schöhningh, 1990.
Kalib, Goldie Szachter. *The Last Selection: A Child's Journey Through the Holocaust.* Amherst: University of Massachusetts Press, 1991.
Kattago, Siobhan. *Ambiguous Memory: The Nazi Past and German National Identity.* Westport, CT: Praeger, 2001.
Kershaw, Ian. *Hitler 1889–1936: Hubris.* New York: W. W. Norton, 1999.
———. *Hitler 1936–1945: Nemesis.* New York: W. W. Norton, 2000.
Klee, Ernst. *Auschwitz, die NS-Medezin, und ihre Opfer.* Frankfurt am Main: S. Fischer, 1997.
———. *Was sie taten—was sie wurden: Ärtzte, Juristen und Andere Beteiligte am Kranken- oder Judenmord.* Frankfurt am Main: Fischer Taschenbuch Verlag, 1986.
Kofman, Sarah. *Rue Ordener, Rue Labat.* Translated by Ann Smock. Lincoln: University of Nebraska Press, 1996.
———. *Smothered Words.* Translated by Madeleine Dobie. Evanston, IL: Northwestern University Press, 1998.
Koonz, Claudia. *The Nazi Conscience.* Cambridge: Harvard University Press, 2003.
Laffitte, Michel. *Un Engrenage Fatal: l'UGIF Face aux Réalités de la Shoah, 1941–1944.* Paris: Liana Levi, 2003.
Lambert, Raymond-Raoul. *Carnet d'un témoin.* Paris: Fayard, 1985.
Langbein, Hermann. *People in Auschwitz.* Translated by Harry Zohn. Chapel Hill: University of North Carolina Press, 2004.
Langer, Lawrence L. *Admitting the Holocaust.* Oxford: Oxford University Press, 1995.
———. *Versions of Survival: The Holocaust and the Human Spirit.* Albany: State University of New York Press, 1982.
Larson, Egon. *Wit As a Weapon: The Political Joke in History.* London: Frederick Muller Limited, 1980.
Levi, Primo. *The Drowned and the Saved.* Translated by Raymond Rosenthal. New York: Summit Books, 1988.
———. *Moments of Reprieve: A Memoir of Auschwitz.* Translated by Ruth Feldman. New York: Penguin Books, 1987.
———. *The Periodic Table.* Translated by Raymond Rosenthal. New York: Schocken Books, 1984.
———. *Survival in Auschwitz: The Nazi Assault on Humanity.* Translated by Stuart Woolf. New York: Simon and Schuster, 1996.
———. *The Voice of Memory: Interviews, 1961–1987.* Edited by Marco Belpoliti and Robert Gordon and translated by Robert Gordon. New York: New Press, 2001.
Lipman, Steve. *Laughter in Hell: The Use of Humor During the Holocaust.* Northvale, NJ: J. Aronson Inc., 1991.
Macrakis, Kristie. *Surviving the Swastika: Scientific Research in Nazi Germany.* New York: Oxford University Press, 1993.
Marks, Jane. *The Hidden Children: The Secret Survivors of the Holocaust.* New York: Fawcett Columbine, 1993.
Matthäus, Jürgen, Konrad Kwiet, Jürgen Förster, and Richard Breitman. *Ausbildungsziel Judenmord?: "weltanschauliche Erziehung" von SS, Polizei und Waffen-SS im Rahmen der "Endlösung".* Frankfurt am Main: Fischer Taschenbuch Verlag, 2003.
Melson, Robert. *False Papers: Deception and Survival in the Holocaust.* Urbana: University of Illinois Press, 2000.
Mildenberger, Florian. *In der Richtung der Homosexualität Verdorben: Psychiater, Kriminalpsychologen und Gerichtsmediziner über Männliche Homosexualität 1850–1970.* Hamburg: MännerschwarmSkript-Verlag, 2002.

Mintz, Alan. *Popular Culture and the Shaping of Holocaust Memory in America.* Seattle: University of Washington Press, 2001.
Mogilanski, Roman, ed. *The Ghetto Anthology: A Comprehensive Chronicle of the Extermination of Jewry in Nazi Death Camps and Ghettos in Poland.* Los Angeles: American Congress of Jews from Poland and Survivors of Concentration Camps, 1985.
Müller, Filip. *Eyewitness Auschwitz: Three Years in the Gas Chambers.* Edited and translated by Susanne Flatauer. Chicago: Ivan R. Dee, 1999.
Neumann, Oscar. *Im Schatten des Todes: Vom Schicksalskampf des slowakischen Judentums.* Tel Aviv: Edition 'Olamenu,' 1956.
Novick, Peter. *The Holocaust in American Life.* Boston: Houghton Mifflin, 1999.
Nyiszli, Miklós. *Auschwitz: A Doctor's Eyewitness Account.* Translated by Tibère Kremer and Richard Seaver. New York: Arcade Publishing, 1993.
Petropoulos, Jonathan. *The Faustian Bargain: The Art World in Nazi Germany.* New York: Oxford University Press, 2000.
Plack, Arno. *Die Gesellschaft und das Böse: eine Kritik der Herrschenden Moral.* Munich: Paul List, 1967.
Presidential Commission on Holocaust Assets in the United States. *Plunder and Restitution: The U.S. and Holocaust Victims' Assets.* Washington, DC: U.S. Government Printing Office, 2000.
Renneberg, Monika, and Mark Walter, eds. *Science, Technology, and National Socialism.* Cambridge: Cambridge University Press, 1994.
Rigg, Bryan Mark. *Hitler's Jewish Soldiers: The Untold Story of Nazi Racial Laws and Men of Jewish Descent in the German Military.* Lawrence: University Press of Kansas, 2002.
Rood, Coen. *"Wenn ich es nicht erzählen kann, muss ich weinen": Als Zwangsarbeiter in der Rüstungsindustrie.* Frankfurt am Main: Fischer Taschenbuch Verlag, 2002.
Roth, John K., and Elisabeth Maxwell, eds. *Remembering for the Future: The Holocaust in an Age of Genocide,* 3 vols. New York: Palgrave, 2001.
Rubenstein, Richard L., and John K. Roth. *Approaches to Auschwitz: The Holocaust and Its Legacy,* rev. ed. Louisville: Westminster John Knox Press, 2003.
Schapiro, Jane. *Inside a Class Action: The Holocaust and the Swiss Banks.* Madison: University of Wisconsin Press, 2003.
Sebald, W. G. *On the Natural History of Destruction.* Translated by Anthea Bell. New York: Random House, 2003.
Spiliotis, Susanne-Sophia. *Verantwortung und Rechtsfrieden: Die Stiftungsinitiative der deutschen Wirtschaft.* Frankfurt am Main: Fischer Taschenbuch Verlag, 2003.
Spoerer, Mark. *Zwangsarbeit unter dem Hakenkreuz.* Stuttgart: Deutsche Verlags-Anstalt, 2001.
Steinweis, Alan, and Daniel Rogers, eds. *The Impact of Nazism: New Perspectives on the Third Reich and Its Legacy.* Lincoln: University of Nebraska Press, 2003.
Tálos, Emmerich, et al., eds. *NS-Herrschaft in Österreich: Ein Handbuch.* Vienna: öbv & hpt, 2001.
Thomson, Ian. *Primo Levi: A Life.* New York: Henry Holt, 2002.
Trunk, Isaiah. *Judenrat: The Jewish Councils in Eastern Europe Under Nazi Occupation.* New York: Macmillan, 1972.
Waller, James. *Becoming Evil: How Ordinary People Commit Genocide and Mass Killing.* New York: Oxford University Press, 2002.
Weinberg, Gerhard. *A World at Arms: A Global History of World War II.* Cambridge: Cambridge University Press, 1994.
Wellers, Georges. *De Drancy à Auschwitz.* Paris: Editions du Centre, 1946.
Wiesel, Elie. *All Rivers Run to the Sea: Memoirs.* Translated by Marion Wiesel. New York: Alfred A. Knopf, 1995.
Wyden, Peter. *Stella.* New York: Simon & Schuster, 1992. Young, James. *At Memory's Edge: After-Images of the Holocaust in Contemporary Art and Architecture.* New Haven, CT: Yale University Press, 2000.

ABOUT THE EDITORS AND CONTRIBUTORS

Editors

Jonathan Petropoulos is the John V. Croul Professor of European History at Claremont McKenna College, where he also serves as director of the Gould Center for Humanistic Studies and the associate director of the Center for the Study of the Holocaust, Genocide, and Human Rights. He is the author of *Art As Politics in the Third Reich* and *The Faustian Bargain: The Art World in Nazi Germany,* and he is the coeditor of *A User's Guide to German Cultural Studies.* Petropoulos has also served as research director for art and cultural property on the Presidential Commission on Holocaust Assets in the United States, where in 2001 he helped draft the report, *Restitution and Plunder: The U.S. and Holocaust Victims' Assets.* He has helped organize art exhibitions, including *Degenerate Art: The Fate of the Avant-Garde in Nazi Germany,* which opened at the Los Angeles County Museum of Art in 1991, and he has served as a consultant for a number of Holocaust victims who are trying to recover lost artwork. Petropoulos is currently completing a book about German princely families during the Third Reich.

John K. Roth is the Edward J. Sexton Professor of Philosophy and the director of the Center for the Study of the Holocaust, Genocide, and Human Rights at Claremont McKenna College, where he has taught since 1966. In addition to service on the United States Holocaust Memorial Council and on the editorial board for *Holocaust and Genocide Studies,* he has published hundreds of articles and reviews and more than thirty-five books, including *Holocaust Politics, Pope Pius XII and the Holocaust,* and *Will Genocide Ever End?* as well as *After-Words* and a revised edition of *Approaches to Auschwitz: The Holocaust and Its Legacy,* which Roth coauthored with Richard L. Rubenstein. Roth has been visiting professor of Holocaust studies at the University of Haifa, Israel, and his Holocaust-related research appointments have included a 2001 Koerner Visiting Fellowship at the Oxford Centre for Hebrew and Jewish Studies in England as well as a 2004–5 appointment as the Ina Levine Invitational Scholar in the Center for Advanced Holocaust Studies at the United States Holocaust Memorial Museum, Washington, DC. In 1988 Roth was named U.S. National Professor of the Year by the Council for Advancement and Support of Education and the Carnegie Foundation for the Advancement of Teaching.

Contributors

Lawrence Baron is the Abraham Nasatir Professor of Modern Jewish History and director of the Lipinsky Institute for Judaic Studies at San Diego State University. He is the author of a study of German-Jewish archivist Erich Mühsam and more than sixty articles on modern Jewish history. His edited volumes include *Embracing the Other: Psychological, Philosophical, and Historical Perspectives on Altruism* and *Martin Buber and the Human Sciences*. Baron's book *Projecting the Holocaust into the Present: The Changing Focus of Contemporary Holocaust Cinema* will appear in 2005.

Victoria J. Barnett is associate general editor of the complete English edition of Dietrich Bonhoeffer's works, which is being published by Fortress Press. She has also lectured and taught extensively on the history of the churches during the Holocaust. Since 1994 she has been a consultant to the Church Relations Department of the United States Holocaust Memorial Museum in Washington, DC. In 2004 she became that department's head. Barnett is the author of *For the Soul of the People: Protestant Protest Against Hitler* and *Bystanders: Conscience and Complicity During the Holocaust*. She is also editor and translator of Wolfgang Gerlach's *And the Witnesses Were Silent: The Confessing Church and the Jews* and the revised English edition of Eberhard Bethge's *Dietrich Bonhoeffer: A Biography*. She is author of an essay on Bonhoeffer that was commissioned by the United States Holocaust Memorial Museum and published on the Museum's Web site in 1997, and she has published more than seventy articles, book chapters, and book reviews.

Michael J. Bazyler, professor of law at Whittier Law School, has also been a research fellow at the Holocaust Education Trust in London and at the Center for Advanced Holocaust Studies, United States Holocaust Memorial Museum, Washington, DC. He is the author of more than fifty articles dealing with the international law of human rights, and his book, *Holocaust Justice: The Battle for Restitution in America's Courts,* was published in 2003.

Michael Berenbaum has served as president of Steven Spielberg's Survivors of the Shoah Visual History Foundation, as deputy director of the President's Commission on the Holocaust, and as project director of the United States Holocaust Memorial Museum. He is currently the president of the Berenbaum Group, a consulting firm specializing in the development of museums and historical films. Also serving as adjunct professor of theology at the University of Judaism in Los Angeles, he directs the university's Sigi Ziering Institute. Among the most recent of his many Holocaust-related books is *A Promise to Remember: The Holocaust in the Words and Voices of Its Survivors.*

Christopher R. Browning is the Frank Porter Graham Professor of History at the University of North Carolina at Chapel Hill. Before taking up this position in the fall of 1999, he taught for twenty-five years at Pacific Lutheran University. Browning is the author of seven books: *The Final Solution and the German Foreign Office; Fateful Months: Essays on the Emergence of the Final Solution; Ordinary Men: Police Battalion 101 and the Final Solution in Poland; The Path to Genocide; Nazi Policy, Jewish Workers, German Killers; Collected Memories: Holocaust History and Postwar Testimony;* and *The Origins of the Final Solution: The Evolution of Nazi Jewish Policy, September 1939–March 1942.* Browning has been the J. B. and Maurice Shapiro Senior Scholar and Ina Levine Senior Scholar at the United States Holocaust Memorial Museum. In addition to delivering the George Macaulay Trevelyan Lectures at Cambridge University and the George L. Mosse Lectures at the University of Wisconsin—Madison, he has served as an expert witness in war crimes trials in Australia, Canada, and Great Britain and in two "Holocaust denial" cases: the second Zundel trial in Toronto (1988) and David Irving's libel suit against Deborah Lipstadt in London (2000).

Martin Dean is currently an applied research scholar at the Center for Advanced Holocaust Studies, United States Holocaust Memorial Museum, Washington, DC, where he also was the Pearl Resnick Fellow in 1997–98. Dean has also held senior research positions at the Metropolitan Police War Crimes Unit in New Scotland Yard, London, at the Australian Special Investigations Unit. His book, *Collaboration in the Holocaust: Crimes of the Local Police in Belorussia and Ukraine, 1941–1944,* appeared in 2000. In addition, Dean is the author or editor of numerous publications, including Holocaust-related articles in *Holocaust and Genocide Studies, German History,* and *Economic History Review.*

Jean-Marc Dreyfus is a historian who has specialized on the economic "Aryanization" of Jewish property during the Holocaust. In addition to teaching at the Institute for Political Sciences in Paris, he has held research fellowships from the Minda de Gunzburg Center for European Studies at Harvard University and the Centre Marc Bloch in Berlin. He is the author of two books: *Pillages sur ordonnances,* which describes the Nazi looting of banks in France, and *Des camps dans Paris,* which is the first study of the Drancy subcamps at Austerlitz, Lévitan, and Bassano.

Eva Fleischner, professor emerita at Montclair State University, has been involved in teaching and research on the Holocaust since the late 1960s. At the age of twelve she left Austria in 1938 after the *Anschluss,* completing her high school education at a Catholic boarding school in England before joining her family in the United States at the age of eighteen. Throughout her career she has received numerous awards, including the Second *Nostra Aetate* Award in 1997 from Seton Hall University for distinguished work on Catholic-Jewish relations and the Distinguished Alumna of the Year award in 2002 from Marquette University, where she earned her Ph.D. Fleischner is a board member of the National Catholic Institute for Holocaust Education, Seton Hall University, and served from 1999 to 2001 on the International Historical Commission established by the Vatican, where she was the only woman among six commission members appointed. She is the author or editor of numerous books and articles on the Holocaust, including *Auschwitz: Beginning of a New Era?* and *Cries in the Night: Women Who Challenged the Holocaust.*

Geoffrey J. Giles teaches German history at the University of Florida, where he has been a professor since 1978. His numerous publications include *Students and National Socialism in Germany.* In addition to holding positions on editorial boards and scholarly associations such as the German Studies Association, he has led traveling seminars for faculty to Eastern Europe on behalf of the Holocaust Educational Foundation. In 2000–1 he was the J. B. and Maurice C. Shapiro Senior Scholar in Residence at the Center for Advanced Holocaust Studies at the United States Holocaust Memorial Museum in Washington, DC. He spent the 2003–4 academic year as an Alexander von Humboldt Fellow at the Ludwig-Maximilians-Universität in Munich, where he completed a forthcoming book on homosexuality and the Nazis.

Gideon Greif, an Israeli historian, has worked at the Yad Vashem Holocaust Memorial, Israel, for more than twenty-five years. A central topic in his research on the Shoah is the history of the extermination camp Auschwitz-Birkenau, and in particular the history of the *Sonderkommando,* a special Jewish prisoner detail in Auschwitz. His book on that topic, *"We Wept Without Tears": Testimonies of the Jewish* Sonderkommandos *in Auschwitz,* has been published in Hebrew, German, and Polish and appeared in English in 2005. In addition to his numerous other publications, Greif has produced radio documentaries and several documentary films about the Holocaust.

Peter Hayes is professor of history and German and the Theodore Z. Weiss–Holocaust Educational Foundation Professor of Holocaust Studies at Northwestern University, where he has taught since 1980. He is the author or editor of eight books, including the prize-winning titles *Industry and Ideology: IG Farben in the Nazi Era* and *Lessons and Legacies: The Meaning of the Holocaust in a Changing World.* His most recent books are *From Cooperation to Complicity: Degussa in the Third Reich,* which appeared in 2004, and his forthcoming work *Profits and Persecution: German Big Business and* *the Holocaust.* Hayes serves on the academic advisory board of the German Society for Business History and on the Academic Committee of the United States Holocaust Memorial Council. In addition to holding fellowships from the German Academic Exchange Service, the Social Science Research Council, and the Harry Frank Guggenheim Foundation, he was the 1997–98 J. B. and Maurice C. Shapiro Senior Scholar in Residence at the United States Holocaust Memorial Museum.

Dagmar Herzog is professor of history at the Graduate Center, City University of New York. She is the author of *Intimacy and Exclusion: Religious Politics in Pre-Revolutionary Baden* and *Sex After Fascism: Memory and Morality in Twentieth-Century Germany.* Her edited works include *Sexuality and German Fascism* and *The Holocaust in the International Perspective.* Her current projects include a transnationally comparative investigation of the Christian churches' responses to the sexual revolution across the postwar West and a study of postwar theologians' engagement with the challenges of popular secularization. Her research has been supported by grants and fellowships from the Ford Foundation, the Frederick Burkhardt Fellowship Program of the American Council of Learned Societies, the Social Science Research Council, the National Endowment for the Humanities, and the Andrew W. Mellon Fellowship Program at Harvard University.

Raul Hilberg retired as the John G. McCullough Professor of Political Science at the University of Vermont in 1991. From his graduate student days he has searched for documents about the Holocaust in archives and on microfilm. His principal work, *The Destruction of the European Jews,* was first published in 1961. The third edition appeared in 2003. His other books include *Perpetrators Victims Bystanders; The Politics of Memory;* and *Sources of Holocaust Research.* From 1978 to 1979 he served on the President's Commission on the Holocaust, and from 1980 to 1986 he was a charter member of the United States Holocaust Memorial Council. Over the years he also testified as an expert witness in Holocaust-related cases in the courts of the United States and foreign countries.

Sara R. Horowitz is associate director of the Centre for Jewish Studies at York University (Canada), and she teaches comparative literature and Jewish studies in the Division of Humanities. She is the author of *Voicing the Void: Muteness and Memory in Holocaust Fiction,* which received the *Choice* Award for Outstanding Academic Book, as well as coeditor of *Encounter with Appelfeld,* a collection of essays on Aharon Appelfeld. She has published extensively on Holocaust literature, women survivors, Jewish American fiction, and pedagogy. Currently, she is completing a book called *Gender, Genocide, and Jewish Memory.*

Jeffrey Lewis teaches in the international studies program at Ohio State University. His research focuses on Germany's scientific community in the twentieth century and, in particular, on the role of science and scientists during the Third Reich. He has been the recipient of research fellowships from the Fulbright Program, the German Academic Exchange Service (DAAD), the Max Planck Society for the Advancement of the Sciences, and Phi Alpha Theta history honors society. He has published on the history and philosophy of biology more generally as well as on the history of biological research in Germany.

Wendy Lower teaches history at Towson University. Her Holocaust-related research includes analysis of the German implementation of the Holocaust and the creation of *Volksdeutsche* colonies in Zhytomyr. In addition to her articles in *German Studies Review* and *Holocaust and Genocide Studies*, she has also written on the history of Nazi ghettoization practices in Ukraine, the bureaucratic language of Nazi perpetrators in Ukraine, and a comparison of German colonizers in Wilhelmine Southwest Africa (1904–8) and in Nazi-occupied Ukraine (1941–44). Before taking her position at Towson University, Lower directed the Visiting Scholars Program at the United States Holocaust Memorial Museum's Center for Advanced Holocaust Studies.

Robert Melson, professor of political science at Purdue University, has done extensive research on the Holocaust, genocide, and ethnic conflict. His published works include *Revolution and Genocide: On the Origins of the Armenian Genocide and the Holocaust,* which received the 1993 PIOOM-Amnesty International Award from Leiden University (Netherlands) for its contribution to the field of human rights, and *False Papers: Deception and Survival in the Holocaust,* which was a finalist in the 2001 competition for the National Jewish Book Awards. Melson's contributions have also included a term as president of the International Association of Genocide Scholars.

Lynn Rapaport is professor of sociology at Pomona College, where she chairs the sociology department. She is the author of *Jews in Germany After the Holocaust: Memory, Identity, and Jewish-German Relations,* which won the 1998 Most Distinguished Publication Award in the Sociology of Religion from the American Sociological Association. She is currently working on a project on how the Holocaust is portrayed in popular culture.

Bryan Mark Rigg, whose scholarly training took place at Yale University and Cambridge University, teaches history at the American Military University. He has also served in the Israeli military and in the United States Marine Corps. *Hitler's Jewish Soldiers,* his book about half- and quarter-Jews who served in the Third Reich's *Wehrmacht,* appeared in 2002. That work brought Rigg the 2003 William E. Colby Award for the best military history book of the year by a first-time author. In 2004 he published *Rescued from the Reich: How One of Hitler's Soldiers Saved the Lubavitcher Rebbe.*

Gavriel D. Rosenfeld is associate professor of history at Fairfield University, where he has taught modern German and European history since 2000. A specialist in the history and memory of the Third Reich and the Holocaust, Rosenfeld is the author of *Munich and Memory: Architecture, Monuments, and the Legacy of the Third Reich*, which appeared in 2000 and then was translated into German in 2004. His current book project, *The World Hitler Never Made: Alternate History and the Memory of Nazism*, examines counterfactual literary, cinematic, and historical representations of the Nazi era and their role in normalizing the memory of the Nazi past in the West since 1945.

Richard L. Rubenstein is president emeritus, Distinguished Professor of Religion, and a life member of the Board of Trustees at the University of Bridgeport. He is also Distinguished Professor Emeritus at Florida State University, where, in 2001, that university established the Richard L. Rubenstein Professorship in Religion in his honor. His first book, *After Auschwitz*, which was published in 1966, focused the contemporary debate on the meaning of the Holocaust in religious thought, both Jewish and Christian. A revised, expanded edition of *After Auschwitz* appeared in 1992. Rubenstein's other Holocaust-related books include *The Cunning of History*, *The Age of Triage*, and *Approaches to Auschwitz*, coauthored with John K. Roth.

Ronald Smelser is professor of history at the University of Utah, where he has taught since 1974. He is the author of more than thirty-five scholarly articles, and he has authored or edited numerous books, including *Robert Ley: Hitler's Labor Front Leader*; *The Sudeten Problem, 1933–1938: Volkstumpolitik and the Formulation of Nazi Foreign Policy*; and *The Holocaust and Justice*. His current book project is entitled *The Myth of the Eastern Front: An American Perspective*. Active in numerous scholarly societies, Smelser has served as president of the German Studies Association.

Gerhard L. Weinberg retired as the William Rand Kenan, Jr., Professor of History at the University of North Carolina at Chapel Hill in 1999. He is the author or editor of ten books, including *Germany, Hitler, and World War II*; *A World at Arms: A Global History of World War II*; *World in the Balance: Behind the Scenes of World War II*; *The Foreign Policy of Hitler's Germany: Starting World War II, 1937–1939*; and *The Foreign Policy of Hitler's Germany: Diplomatic Revolution in Europe, 1933–1936*. In addition to his many other writings—articles, book chapters, introductions, and reviews—he has held fellowships from the Rockefeller Foundation, the Guggenheim Foundation, and the National Endowment for the Humanities. He was the J. B. and Maurice C. Shapiro Senior Scholar in Residence at the United States Holocaust Memorial Museum from 2001 to 2002. He has been awarded many prizes for his writing, including the Herbert Hoover Book Award for 1994 from the Herbert Hoover Presidential Library Association.

INDEX

A

Adamczyk, Werner, 277
Adorno, Theodor, 364, 368, 369
Adventures in My Youth: A German Soldier on the Eastern Front (Scheiderbauer), 277
After Dachau (Quinn), 242–43, 244
After the Long Silence (Fremont), 116
Agudas Yisroel, 166
Albania, Jewish population in, 74
Allen, Woody, 265
alternate Holocaust histories, 240–48
Althoff, Willi, 30, 31
Aly, Götz, 189, 305
Ambrose, Stephen, 273, 282
American Historical Review, 70
Améry, Jean, 176, 376, 383
Amicale, 231
Amis, Martin, 245–46, 248
Angry Harvest, 174
Angst im Kapitalismus (Duhm), 158
Antelme, Robert, 378
Anti-Defamation League, 263
Antonescu, Mihai, 192
Anvers, Louis Cahen d', 227
Arendt, Hannah, 186, 303, 364, 368, 369
Aren't We Wonderful, 262
Aronson, Shlomo, 76
Arquette, David, 290, 291
art collections, Nazi confiscation of, 224–36, 330–35, 339–40
"Aryan Papers" (Fink), 174
Assicurazioni Generali, 353
Auerbach, Philipp, 332–34
Auerbach Program, 332–34
Auschwitz, 17, 28, 37, 41, 44, 46–47, 157, 223, 232, 256–58, 286–91, 379, 382
Austerlitz camp, 222–36

B

Bacon, Yehuda, 52, 55
Bacque, James, 278
Baerwind, Ernst, 9, 10
Baeyer, Dr. von, 139
Barbie, Klaus, 171
Barefoot in the Rubble (Walter), 282
Barkai, Avraham, 78
Baron, Lawrence, 262, 263
Bassano camp, 222–36
Battle of the Bulge, 278
Baumgarten, Kurt Otto, 31–32
Bavli, Hillel, 167, 174, 176
BDM (Bund Deutscher Mädel), 151
Becker, Bernhard, 18
Becker, Edmund, 191, 199
Becker, Paul, 191, 199
Becker, Walter, 29
Beckwith, Byron de la, 278
Behr, Kurt von, 224, 225, 227, 233
Belarus, Jewish ghettos in, 205–18
Belgium, Nazi looting operations in, 223–25
Belzec, 63, 66, 67, 68, 99
Benigni, Roberto, 246, 291
Benny, Jack, 260
Benz, Wolfgang, 79
Berenbaum, Michael, 382–83
Bergen-Belsen, 230, 236, 256
Bergman, David, 258
Berman, Shelly, 263
Bernard, Denise, 233
Bethge, Eberhard, 367
Beth Jacob Committee, 166
Bialkin, Kenneth, 353–54
Bialystok ghetto, 206
Bidermann, Gottlob, 277
Biebow, Hans, 301–02, 304
Birkenau, 33, 34, 45, 48, 61, 286

Black Sea Germans, 192–94
Blanchot, Maurice, 380
Blass, Guta, 32
Blobel, Paul, 191
Blood Red Snow: The Memoirs of a German Soldier on the Eastern Front (Koschorrek), 277
Boehling, Rebecca, 328
Bogdanowka camp, 193
Bonhoeffer, Dietrich, 362, 366–68
Bormann, Martin, 132
Borowski, Tadeusz, 258, 376
Borsig Coking Works, 10, 17
Boss, Arthur, 191, 199
Boston Globe, 351
Bourke, Joanna, 128
Boy Soldier: A German Teenager at the Nazi Twilight (Thamm), 277
Brandt, Willy, 315
Brauchitsch, Walther von, 120, 129
Brecht, Berolt, 259
Brooks, Mel, 262–63
Browning, Christopher, 302
Bruce, Lenny, 263
Brunner, Alöis, 225, 228, 230, 231
Buchenwald, 262, 378
Buscemi, Steve, 291
Butcher of Lyons, 171
Butenandt, Adolf, 312–21
Butler, Samuel C., 354
Byten ghetto, 215–17, 218

C

cabarets, 253–54, 256–57
CAHS (Center for Advanced Holocaust Studies), 209
Campert, Remco, 385
Camp Holocaust, 264
carbon black, wartime production of, 7–21
Carell, Paul, 275–77
Casualty of War (Owen), 282
Catholicism
  Jewish children hidden in households of, 107–16
  relationship with Nazi past, 151–53, 363–64
CCP (Central Collecting Point), 333, 335
Celan, Paul, 376
Center for Jewish Contemporary Documentation, 228, 235
Chaplin, Charlie, 260
Chashniki ghetto, 209
Chazan, Shaul, 38, 41, 43, 54
Children and Play in the Holocaust (Eisen), 256

Children of the Holocaust (Epstein), 264
"choiceless choices," 27
Christian religion
  Jewish children hidden in households of, 107–16
  reshaping history during Nazi regime, 147–59, 360–70
Churchill, Winston, 281
Ciechanower, Mordechai, 56
Civil War, 272
Claims Conference for the Material Claims Against Germany, 344
Clary, Robert, 262
Clay, Lucius, 327, 329
Clendinnen, Inga, 46
Clinton, William J., 342
Cohen, Leon, 41, 43, 54
Cohen, Marc, 355
Cohen, Richard, 342
Cold War, 272
Cole, Tim, 271
Columbia Studios, 260
Commando Duck (1944), 261
Confessing Church, 362–363, 365–68
Conversation with the Beast (1996), 241
Courtois, Stefan, 247
Crabwalk (Grass), 282
Csallner, Carl, 150
Cutler, Lloyd, 355
The Cuttlefish (Witkeiewicz), 259
Czerniakow, Adam, 301

D

Dachau, 253, 257, 378, 379
DAF (German Labor Front), 12, 16, 18
Dampierre, Colette de, 227, 230
Daniels, William, 334
Dargis, Manohla, 290
Das Schwarze Korps, 150
Davidowicz, Lucy, 256
Davison, Diane Leigh, 353
The Day the Clown Cried, 263
Dean, Martin, 194
de Crinis, Max, 141–43
Degussa, use of slave/forced labor, 9–21
De la Boue qui ne touche pas (Hemmerle), 171
Delbo, Charlotte, 376
DellaPergola, Sergio, 343
denazification, 325–35
Denby, David, 264
The Deputy (Hochhuth), 368
Derban, Leonid, 207
Der Brand (Friedrich), 281
Der Fuehrer's Face (1942), 261–62

Derrida, Jacques, 376
Der Spiegel, 158–59
Des Pres, Terrence, 262
destruction ghettos, 210–11
The Destruction of the European Jews (Hilberg), 26, 70, 75, 300
Deutsche Passion (Euringer), 259
DGW (Deutsche Gasrusswerke), use of slave/forced labor, 9–21
The Diary of Anne Frank, 280
Dibelius, Otto, 363
Dick, Philip K., 242
Die Katakombe, 253
Diem, Hermann, 364
Dienststelle Westen, 224–25, 229–30, 233
Die Stimmen der Nacht (Ziegler), 243
Dietrich, Otto, 276
Dietrich, Sepp, 229
Dirlewanger Brigade, 134
Disney studio, 261
The Divide (Overgard), 242
Dobroszycki, Lucjan, 256
Domaczewo ghetto, 212–14
Domanowka camp, 193
Donald Duck, 261–62
Donald Gets Drafted (1942), 261
Douglas, Mary, 252, 265
Dragon, Abraham, 38, 55
Dragon, Shlomo, 38, 42, 43, 67
The Drowned and the Saved (Levi), 37, 57, 300, 373, 374
Dubbin, Sam, 345
Duhm, Dieter, 158

E
Early, Hilary, 77
Eastern Europe, Nazi ghettoization and destruction in, 205–218
Ebert, Roger, 290
Eckell, Johannes, 9, 10, 11, 19
Education for Death: The Making of a Nazi (1943), 261
The Ego and the Mechanisms of Defense (Freud), 306
Ehard, Hans, 333–34
Eichmann, Adolf, 157, 189, 225, 270, 281, 303, 368
Eine Kleinigkeit für uns Reinkarnauten (Ziegler), 245
Einsatzgruppe, 77, 99, 159, 191–92, 206, 276, 381
Eisen, George, 256
Eisenhower, Dwight D., 273, 275
Eisenhower, John, 273
Eisenschmidt, Eliezer, 42, 44, 51, 55, 63

Eizenstat, Stuart, 342, 343, 356
Elon, Amos, 247
Elperin, William, 351
Endres, Hans, 150
Enesmann, Shlomo, 28, 31
England, Jewish population in, 74
Epstein, Helen, 264
Erntefest massacre, 28, 33
ERR (Einsatzstab Reichsleiter Rosenberg), 224
Esser, Hermann, 187
An Estate of Memory (Karmel), 170
ethical clarity and historical truth, 360–70
Ethics (Bonhoeffer), 367
Euringer, Richard, 259
Europa, Europa (1991), 263
Eva's War: A True Story of Survival (Krutein), 282
Evers, Medgar, 278
Evidence, 64

F
Fackenheim, Emil, 258
factory slave labor camps, 7–21, 26–34
Fall Out-Fall In (1943), 261
Fatherland (Harris), 239, 242
Feldman, Chaja, 166, 170
Feldman, Gerald, 8–9
Ferdl, Weiss, 253
Feuer! An Artilleryman's Life on the Eastern Front (Adamczyk), 277
Fiddler on the Roof, 264
Filler, Deb, 264
Finck, Werner, 253–54
Fink, Ida, 174
Finkelstein, Norman, 247, 271
Fischer, Eugen, 187
Flüsterwitze, 255
Foreign Government Information, 76
Forward, 346, 347
Foxman, Abraham, 108, 341
Fragments (Wilkomirski), 271
France
  atypical camps in, 222–36
  Austerlitz, Lévitan, and Bassano camps in, 222–36
  Drancy transit camp in, 222–36
  during the Holocaust, 170–73
  Jewish population in, 72–73, 78
  Nazi looting operation in, 223–36
Frank, Anne, 270, 289, 343
Frankl, Viktor, 257–58
Freber, Kurt, 187
Frei, Norbert, 329
French Resistance, 378

Freud, Anna, 306
Freud, Sigmund, 265, 376
Freudenberg, Adolf, 365
Frick, Wilhelm, 127
Friedlander, Henry, 79
Friedländer, Saul, 67, 111, 242
Friedman, Carol, 385
Friedrich, Jörg, 275, 281
Friedrichsen, Konrad, 18
Fritsch Affair, 128
Fritsche, Hans, 276
Fry, Stephen, 245, 246, 248
(FSU) former Soviet Union, 344–47, 348
Fuchs, Erwin, 119

G

Gabai, Yaakov, 37, 42, 49–52, 54, 57
Gabbai, Dario, 392–93
Garguir, Marc, 233
Geisel, Theodor Seuss, 261
Gemmeker, Konrad, 257
Genghis Cohn (1958), 263
Gerlach, Christian, 75, 302
Gerlach, Wolfgang, 369
German Boy: A Child at War (Samuel), 282
German businesses
  practices during the Third Reich, 7–21
  use of slave/forced labor by, 7–21
German Democratic Republic, 78
German Fund, 353
German Labor Service, 11
German People's List, 191
German Protestant Church, during the Nazi regime, 362–70
German Remembrance Initiative, 20
Germany
  denazification in, 325–35
  mythologizing of military, 271–72
  postwar restitution process in, 325–35
  reparation programs of, 341–56
Gerstein, Kurt, 66–67, 368
Gestapo, 131, 255
ghettoization, in Eastern Europe, 205–218
The Gifts of the Jews (Cahill), 116
Giuliani, Massimo, 299–300
Glogover, Stanley, 56
Glotz, Peter, 282
Godlewska, Irena, 104
Godlewska, Pani Maria, 104
Godlewska, Wanda, 104
Goebbels, Joseph, 255, 261
Goetzfried, Alfons J., 192
Gone With the Wind, 272
Goodman, Hirsh, 342

The Good Soldier (Novotny), 277
Gorges, Johann, 47
Göring, Emmy, 328
Göring, Hermann, 139, 253–54, 255, 331–32
Göring, Matthias, 137, 139
Goschler, Constantin, 334
Gradowski, Zalman, 44, 45, 55
Grant, Joe, 262
Grass, Günter, 282
The Gray Zone (2001), 286–91
"The Gray Zone" (Levi), 286, 390
Great Depression, 259
The Great Dictator, 260
Great War, 187
Greif, Gideon, 64
Greifelt, Ulrich, 197
Gribetz, Judah, 343, 344–48, 349
Grossman, Vasily, 191
Gruner, Wolf, 75
Guderian, Heinz, 273
Gwardia Ludowa, 27
gypsy population, 192
Gyubal Wahazar (Witkeiewicz), 259

H

Haas, Peter, 361, 374
Haberstock, Karl, 330
Ha-Do'ar, 167
Haensch, Dietrich, 158
Hahn, Otto, 316, 318
Halder, Franz, 272–73
Hamberger, Heinrich, 125
Hanfstaengl, Ernst, 333
Harold and Maude (1971), 263
Harris, Robert, 241, 242
Hawryluch, Anastazja, 63
Hays Office, 260
Hazan, Shaul, 62
Hegel, Georg Wilhelm Friedrich, 381–82
Heider, Ulrike, 158
Heilbron, John, 320
Heinemann, Isabel, 190
Helfort, Erich Anton, 282
Heller, Fanya, 173–75
Hemmerle, Françoise, 171–72, 173
Henschel, Theo, 197
Hentschke, Erwin, 213
Herf, Jeffrey, 149
Hering, Ernst, 194
Hering, Gustav, 194
Hermann Göring Werke, 28, 29
Herzberg, Erna, 226
Hess, Rudolf, 255
Hessen, Philipp von, 330

Index 411

Heydrich, Reinhard, 77, 131, 189, 190, 191
Hick, Dietrich, 215
Hilberg, Raul, 26, 70–79, 300–01, 303, 380, 381
Hillesum, Etty, 257
Himmler, Heinrich, 28, 71, 128, 131, 132, 134, 187–90, 193–98, 305, 380
Hindenburg, Paul von, 255
Hirzchmann, Chaim, 63
history
    alternate portrayals of the Holocaust, 240–48
    historical truth and ethical clarity, 360–70
Hitler, Adolf
    authorization of *Möbel Aktion*, 224
    colonialist policy of, 186–87, 188
    Führer Myth of, 325
    on homosexuals in the *Wehrmacht*, 127–44
    jokes and political humor about, 253–54, 255
    media portrayal of, 259–62
    on *Mischlinge* in the *Wehrmacht*, 119–26
    policy of global Final Solution, 70–73, 240–42
    sexual politics of, 159
Hitler, the Allies, and the Jews (Aronson), 76
"Hitler and the M. C. A.", 263
Hitler Moves East 1941–1943 (Carell), 276
"Hitler's Impact on History" (Turner), 241
Hitler Strikes Poland (Rossino), 189
Hitler Youth, 151, 255
Hochhuth, Rolf, 368
Hoffman, Kurt, 262
Hofmann, Anton, 154
Hogan's Heroes, 262, 264
Holland, Agnieska, 174
Holocaust
    allohistorical scenarios of, 240–48
    compensation to victims of, 325–35, 339–56
    double bind and moral ethics of, 375–85
    etiquette in depictions of, 262
    function of humor during, 252–65
    master-narrative and counter-narratives of, 270–83
    media portrayal of, 259–62
    in popular culture, 270–83
    restitution movement related to, 339–56
Holocaust Educational Foundation, 393
Holocaust Remembrance Day, 167
Horstmann, Lali, 282
Höss, Rudolf, 17, 38, 41

Hotel Terminus: The Life and Times of Klaus Barbie (1988), 171, 172
Howard, Moe, 260, 261
HSF-USA (Holocaust Survivors' Foundation-USA), 344–45, 347, 348, 350, 351
Huebner, Alexander, 194
Huemer, Dick, 262
Hueter, Colonel, 16
The Human Species (Antelme), 378–79
humor
    coping function of, 252–65
    media portrayal of Hitler and the Holocaust, 259–65
    of *Sonderkommando*, 51
    as treason, 254–55
Humor und Melodie, 257
Hungary, Jewish population in, 76, 278
Hurwitz, Leon, 306
Hustek, Josef, 47

I

I'll Never Heil Again, 260
In Deadly Combat: A German Soldier's Memoir of the Eastern Front (Bidermann), 277
International Military Tribunal, 328
Internet, 279
In the African Jungle (Schulz), 187
Ioanid, Radu, 75
Israel, Holocaust survivors in, 341, 344, 345, 346–48
Italy, Jewish population in, 74, 78
Itzkowitz, Sam, 61–63, 66, 68

J

Jacob, Erich, 131
Jacoby, Jeff, 351, 352
Jakob the Liar, 263, 264
Janiszow camp, 27
Jarausch, Konrad, 319–20
Jaspers, Karl, 364, 368, 369
JCS-1067, 326
JDC (Joint Distribution Committee), 344
Jerusalem Post, 342, 354
Jewish Council, 210, 214
Jewish ghettos
    characteristics and functions of, 208–15
    documenting "lost ghettos," 205–218
    in Nazi-occupied Eastern Europe, 205–18
Jewish identity
    defined by Jewish law, 118–19
    of hidden children, 107–16
    of Jews serving in the *Wehrmacht*, 118–26

Jewish Telegraphic Agency, 348
Judenrat, 28–29, 75, 215, 227, 300–01

K
Kaiser Wilhelm Institute for Biochemistry, 313, 315, 316
Kalmar, Rudolf, 257
Kansteiner, Wolf, 280
Kant, Immanuel, 372, 373
Kapos, 39, 44, 46
Karmel, Ilona, 170
Karvat, Kiril, 211, 212, 213
Keitel, Wilhelm, 129, 130, 132, 133, 137
Kemnitz, Georg, 10, 11
Kennedy, John F., 273
Kershaw, Ian, 123, 124, 319
Kesselman, Morris, 50, 51, 54
Khoiniki ghetto, 210
Killinger, Manfred von, 192
Klarsfeld, Serge, 377
Kleist, Paul von, 193
Klempen, Simone, 377
Klemperer, Victor, 151
Knopmacher, Nachum, 212
Knopp, Guido, 280
Koch, Gauleiter, 274
Kochan, Bruno, 230
Kofman, Berek, 376, 377, 378, 385
Kofman, Sarah, 375, 376–80, 381, 383, 384–85
Kogan, Goda, 207
Kohn, Georges, 230, 232
Kohn, Grange, 377
Kolditz, Walter, 32
Konkret, 147–48, 149, 159
Koonz, Claudia, 374
Korman, Edward, 343, 345–48, 349, 352
Koschorrek, Günter, 277
Kosinski, Jerzy, 271
Koss, Andrew, 215
Kraepelin, Emil, 132
Krakow ghetto, 206
Kristall, 277
Kruglov, Aleksandr, 209
Krutein, Eva, 282
Kube, Wilhelm, 206
Kühn, Alfred, 315, 318
Kurt Gerstein: The Ambiguity of the Good (Friedlander), 67

L
Lager, 98
Lagerpolizei, 30, 31, 32, 33
Lagerrat, 30, 32
Laks, Izak, 29

Lambsdorff, Otto, 349
Landser, 280
Langer, Lawrence, 27, 361
Langfuss, Leib, 44
Langsleben, Szaja, 32
Lanzmann, Claude, 290–91
Laros, Matthias, 153
Larson, Egon, 265
Laval, Pierre, 223
Law for Liberation from National Socialism and Militarism, 327
Laws for the Protection of German Blood, 255
Ledig, Gert, 281, 282
Lehmann, Dr., 132
Lehrer, Tom, 263
Lemkin, Raphael, 186
Le Monde juif, 231
Leppich, Johannes, 155
Lerman, Miles, 349
L'Espèce humaine (Antelme), 379
Levi, Primo, 37, 39, 52, 57, 64, 97, 106, 258, 286, 299–300, 306–308, 360–61, 373–74, 376, 390–91, 393
Levinas, Emmanuel, 376
Lévitan camp, 222–36
Lewental, Zalman, 44
Lewis, Jerry, 263
Ley, Robert, 255
Liberman, Rabbi, 216
Liddell-Hart, Basil, 273
Life is Beautiful (1998), 246, 263–64, 271, 291
Lifton, Robert Jay, 65
Linz List, 331–32
Littell, Franklin, 382
Litzmannstadt, 299–308
Liulevicius, Vejas, 187
Lodz ghetto, 206, 216, 218, 256, 301–308, 361
Lombard, Carole, 260
Los Angeles Times, 290
Lost Cause mythology, 272–83
Lubitsch, Ernst, 260–61
Luck, Hans von, 275
Ludendorff, Erich, 187
Lukes, Steven, 265

M
Macksey, Kenneth, 273
MAD, 262
Madajczyk, Czeslaw, 189
Mafalda, Princess, 330
Maimonides, Moses, 307
Majdanek, 33, 47, 192

Majowka slave/forced labor camp, 30
Making History (Fry), 245, 246, 248
Malmedy Massacre, 278, 279
The Man in the High Castle (Dick), 242
Manstein, Erich von, 273, 274–75
Marder, Karl, 301, 303
Mar'ina Gorka ghetto, 206–208
Markl, Hubert, 312
Marranos, 109–16
"The Martyrdom of the Ninety-Three Maidens" (Bavli), 167–68, 169, 175, 176
Marxism, 150
Max Planck Society, 312, 315, 316, 318
May, Elaine, 263
McCloy, John, 333–34
Me and the Colonel, 262
Mechanicus, Philip, 257
Meissner, Otto, 255
Melchers, Georg, 312, 315–21
Mellenthin, F. W. von, 273–74
Melnick, Adam, 264
memory
    displacement of authentic Holocaust memories, 240–48
    in Holocaust narratives, 233–35, 236, 270–83
Mendel, Gregor, 124
Mendelsohn, Julius, 101
Mendelsohn, Natalia, 99–102
Mendelsohn, Sylvio, 99
Mendelsohn, Wolf, 99
Mengele, Josef, 56, 286
Metelmann, Henry, 277
Mettenheim, Clara von, 120
Mettenheim, Dieter von, 120
Meurthe, Emile Deutsch de la, 227
MG Law No. 52, 326
MG Law No. 53, 326
Middle East, Jewish population in, 71, 72, 78
Mihaileanu, Radu, 264
Milejkowski, Israel, 304
Mills, C. Wright, 265
Mincburg, Simcha, 28
Minsk ghetto, 218
Mischlinge, 118–26
Mitscherlich, Margarete, 364
Möbel Aktion, 223–25, 228–31, 233–35
Mogilanski, Roman, 210
Moll, Otto, 42, 47, 48–49
Moments of Reprieve (Levi), 299
Moral Purity Association, 152
Morbus Kitahara (Ransmayr), 243, 244
Mordowicz, Czeslaw, 45

Morgenthau Plan, 243
Motion Picture Producers and Distributors of America, 260
Muckermann, Hermann, 152
Mueller-Stahl, Armin, 239
Muhsfeld, Erich, 51, 56–57, 288, 289–90
Müller, Filip, 48–49, 53
Munsing, Stephan, 333
museum collections, Nazi confiscation of, 330–35, 339–40
My Autobiography (Chaplain), 260
My Mother's Courage (1996), 263

N
Nancy, Jean-Luc, 376
The Nasty Girl (1991), 263
National Board of Review, 260
National Labor Service, 12
National Socialism, victims of, 39, 40, 325–35, 373
The Nazi Doctors (Lifton), 65
Nazi ethic, 374
Nazi Party
    humor about, 255
    members of, 12, 311–21
    postwar interpretation of, 147–59, 311–21
Nazi regime
    Allied seizure of wartime assets of, 325–35
    alternate histories of, 240–48
    behaviors of scientific researchers during, 311–21
    colonization plans of, 185–99
    ethical gray zones during, 360–70
    National Office for Economic Expansion of, 9
    "New Order" of, 185–99
    racial laws of, 118–26, 149–50
Nazi War Crimes Disclosure Act, 75–76
Nelson, Tim Blake, 286–91
Nencel, David, 62
Netherlands, Nazi looting operation in, 223–25
Neuborne, Burt, 8
The New Republic, 341
New Yorker, 264, 282
New York Law Journal, 348
New York Times, 166, 167, 325, 347
Nichols, Mike, 263
Niemöller, Martin, 365
Niethammer, Lutz, 327, 329
Nietzsche, Friedrich, 376
Night and Fog, 171
Nightfather (Friedman), 385

1939 Club, 351
Nobel Prize, 314
No Laughing Matter: A Collection of Political Jokes (Lukes), 265
Norden, Eric, 240, 242
Nothing for Tears (Horstmann), 282
Novick, Peter, 247
Novotny, Alfred, 277
NSV (Nazi Party's Welfare Society), 195
Nuremberg Laws, 119, 255
Nyiszli, Miklos, 51, 52, 56–57, 286, 287, 290

O

Oberkapos, 39
Office of Alien Property Custodian, 326
Office of Foreign Funds Control, 326
Ohlendorf, Otto, 77
The Old Army Game (1943), 261
On the Natural History of Destruction (Sebald), 282
open ghettos, 209
Operation Barbarossa, 136
Operation Gomorrah, 281
Operation Safehaven, 326
Ophuls, Marcel, 170, 171, 172, 173
Order Police, 77, 99
Origins of Totalitarianism (Arendt), 186
Ostrower, Chaya, 258
Other Losses (Bacque), 278
OT (Organisation Todt), 12, 122, 123, 212
Overgard, William, 242
Owen, Luisa Lang, 282

P

The Painted Bird (Kosinski), 271
Palestine, 71, 72
Panzer Battles (Mellenthin), 273
Panzer Commander (von Luck), 275
Panzer Leader (Guderian), 273
Papen, Franz von, 255
Paquin, 226
Paraguay, 362
Paris
  atypical camps in, 222–36
  Nazi looting operation in, 223–36
Paroles suffoquées (Kofman), 376
Pawelczyńska, Anna, 259
Payback (Ledig), 282
Peakheads (Brecht), 259
Peiper, Jochen, 278, 279
Pétain, Marshal, 224
Philadelphia Inquirer, 260
Planck, Max, 320
Platka, Bess, 68

Pliszko, Lemke, 42–43, 50, 51, 52, 54–55
Pohl, Dieter, 75
Poland
  Jewish ghettos in, 97–106, 205–218
  Nazi colonization programs in, 9, 185–86, 256
  slave/forced labor camps in, 27
  SS activities in, 190–91
Ponczek, Leon, 99, 104
Ponczek, Natalia, 99
Ponczek, Stefania, 99, 104
Prager, Dennis, 351, 352
The Producers, 262–63
Pross, Robert, 11, 12–18, 20–21
Pruetzmann, Hans Adolf, 197
Pukhovichi ghetto, 206–208
Punch Me in the Stomach (Filler), 264

Q

Quackernack, Walter, 47
Quinn, Daniel, 242–43, 244, 247, 248

R

Rabinovich, Meyer, 207–8
race theory, 40
Rakhman, Rabbi, 216
Ransmayr, Christoph, 243, 244–45, 247, 248
Reading the Holocaust (Clendinnen), 46
Rechter, Leo, 351
The Reconstructionist, 167
Reder, Rudolph, 63, 65, 68
Redgis-Klug, Yvonne, 232
Reich Labor Service, 151
Reichskommisariat, 147
Remembrance, Responsibility and the Future Foundation, 349
Repressive Familienpolitik (Heider), 158
The Resistible Rise of Arturo Ui (Brecht), 258
Resnais, Alain, 171
restitution movement
  activism in the US, 339–56
  controversial issues related to, 340–56
Retze, Ewald von, 12
Ribbentrop, Joachim von, 255, 276
Riegner, Gerhard, 365
RKF (Reich Commission for the Strengthening of Germandom), 190, 197
RKU (Reichskommissariat Ukraine), 189, 197
Robota, Rosa, 288
Röhm, Ernst, 128, 133, 255
Rohrbach, Paul, 187

Roloff, Otto, 147–48
Romanovsky, Daniel, 209
Rood, Coen, 12–13
Rorty, Richard, 378
Rosenberg, Alfred, 187, 191, 197, 224
Rosenfeld, Alvin, 279
Rosin, Arnost, 45
Rossino, Alexander, 189
Roth, Philip, 390
Roundheads (Brecht), 259
rubber industry, wartime, 7–21
Rue Ordener, Rue Labat (Kofman), 376, 378
Rumkowski, Mordecai Chaim, 256, 299–308, 361
RuSHA (Race and Settlement Main Office), 190
Russia, 11
Rwanda, 362
Ryk, Georg van, 47

S
Sabey, Pete, 114–16
Sackar, Joseph, 41, 45, 55, 67
Sahl, Mort, 263
Samuel, Wolfgang W. E., 282
Sandkühler, Thomas, 75
Saving Private Ryan, 118
Schacht, Hjalmar, 255
Schaecter, David, 350
Schapiro, Jane, 355
Scheiderbauer, Armin, 277
Schillinger, Josef, 47, 68
Schindler, Oskar, 368
Schindler's List, 118, 246, 280, 291
Schloss Belvedere, 330
Schlösser, Dr., 317
Schlosser, Hermann, 9
Schmidt, Carlo, 315
Schmidt, Hans, 278
Schmidt, Paul Karl, 276–77
Schmitt, Carl, 374
Schmitz, John, 278
Schneider, Kurt, 138
Schorske, Carl, 330–31
Schröder, Chef des Sanitätswesens der Luftwaffe, 139–41
Schröder, Gerhard, 332
Schrott, Willi, 32
Schulz, H., 187
Schwenger, Hannes, 159
Schwertner, Leopold Rudolf, 29
scientific research by Nazi Germany, 311–21
Scorched Earth (Carell), 276

SD (Security Service), 190
Sebald, W. G., 234, 281–82
The Secret, 109
Segal, Tobias, 68
Seinfeld, Jerry, 265
Sellmann, Adolf, 152
Seven Beauties (1975), 263
Seven Departments of Hell (Stabholz), 47
SHAEF (Supreme Headquarters Allied Expeditionary Force), 327
Sharansky, Natan, 348
Shernoff, William, 354
Sh'ma, 350
Siebert, Klaus, 192
Silberberg, Yaakov, 44–45
Silberklang, David, 27
Singer, Israel, 350–51
Sky Trooper (1942), 261
slave/forced labor
  liquidation of, 28
  pecking order within, 31, 34
  restitution for unpaid wages, 19, 325–35
Smock, Ann, 376
Smothered Words (Kofman), 375, 377
Sobibor, 67, 68, 223, 256
Social Democratic Party, 151
Sonderabteilung, 303
Sonderkommando
  duties at Auschwitz, 37–60, 61 68, 286, 287, 288, 289, 290, 308, 373, 392–93
  Nazi invention of, 39, 40
  surviving or suicide, 43–44, 62
The Sorrow and the Pity (1971), 170–73
South Africa, 362
Soviet Extraordinary Commission Report, 212, 214
Soviet Ukraine (Transnistria), 186, 189, 192–94
Soviet Union
  Holocaust survivors in, 344–47, 348
  Jewish ghettos in, 205–18
SPD (Social Democratic Party), 29, 315
Speer, Albert, 317
Spiegel, Paul, 353
Spielberg, Steven, 118, 246, 291
Springer, Axel, 277
Springtime for Hitler, 263
SS Panzergrenadier: A True Story of World War Two (Schmidt), 278
SS troops
  jokes about, 255
  Lithuanian, 49–50
  notorious members of, 47
  supervision of the death houses, 46–47
  takeover of factory camps by, 16–18

SS troops, *continued*
  Technical Disinfections Department of, 67
Stabholz, Tadeusz, 47
Stahlberg, Alexander von, 275
Stalin, Joseph, 75, 191, 195
Stalingrad Sieg (Carell), 277
Stanley, Wendell, 314
Stannard, David, 247
Stapel, Wilhelm, 153
Starachowice Factory Slave Labor Camp, survivors of, 26–34
Steinbach, Erika, 282
Stella (Wyden), 173
Stent, Gunther, 315
Stiewitz, Friedrich, 47
Stockholm Syndrome, 53
Strange and Unexpected Love (Heller), 173–75
Strelnica slave/forced labor camp, 30
Strohmeier, Friedrich, 194
Surbayeva, Raisa, 208
survival, ambiguities and shame with, 97–106, 360
Survival in Auschwitz (Levi), 258, 390
Swiss Claims Resolution Tribunal, 344

T
Tal'ka ghetto, 206–208, 210, 218
Talmud, 168–69, 252
Tarjan, Josh, 264
Taylor, Francis Henry, 333
Telschow, Ernst, 318
Terezin, 233
Thamm, Gerhardt B., 277
Theresienstadt, 256, 258
Theweleit, Klaus, 128
Thielicke, Helmut, 364
Thingspiele, 259
Third Reich
  German corporate world during, 7–21
  sexual politics of, 147–59
This Way for the Gas, Ladies and Gentlemen (Borowski), 258
Three Stooges, 260, 261
Through Hell for Hitler (Metelmann), 277
Tighina Agreement, 192
Tikkun 'olam, 299
Time, 342
Time's Arrow (Amis), 245–46, 248
To Be or Not to Be (1942), 260–61
Togo Ost Society, 187
Tomaszowka ghetto, 211–14, 218
"Torture" (Améry), 176
Train of Life (1998), 263, 264

Treblinka, 28, 30, 47, 67, 68, 105, 379, 382
Treuhandverwaltung, 331–32
Triumph of the Will, 280
truth commissions, 362
Turner, Henry, 124, 241
Turner, Ian, 328

U
Übelhoer, Friedrich, 302
UGIF (Union générale des Israélites de France), 227–28, 235
Ukeles, Jacob, 343
Ukraine
  German destruction of Jewish populations in, 189–92, 194–96
  Hegewald Colony in, 185, 196–98, 199
  Nazi colonization programs in, 185–86
  SS activities in, 190–91
Ukrainian guards, 30, 32
The Ultimate Solution (Norden), 240, 242
UN Convention on the Prevention and Punishment of the Crime of Genocide, 382
UNESCO, 218
"Unfinished Business" (Levi), 391
Union Munitions Plant, 288
United Artists, 260
United States
  in Allied occupation of Germany, 325–35
  Holocaust restitution movement in, 325–35
United States Holocaust Memorial Council, 349
United States Holocaust Memorial Museum, 206, 209
Untergang der 6. Armee (Carell), 277

V
Valland, Rose, 333
Valley of the Shadow (Helfort), 282
The Vanishing Private (1942), 261
Vashem, Yad, 76
Veesenmayer, Edmund, 277
Velde, Theodore van de, 152
Vergeltung (Ledig), 281, 282
Vernes, Odette, 227
Verschuer, Otmar Freiherr von, 314–15, 319
victims' compensation/restitution, 325–35, 339–56
Vilna ghetto, 256
Vodnik, Dr., 216
Völkischer Beobachter, 152–53, 254

Volksgerichtshof, 254
VoMi (Ethnic German Liaison Office), 190, 192, 197, 198
von Luck, Hans, 273
Vorarbeiter, 39, 44, 47, 55
Vrba, Rudolf, 45

W

Waffen-SS, mythologizing of, 272–73, 278–79
Walker, Mark, 320
Wall Street Journal, 341
Walser, Martin, 247
Walter, Elizabeth, 282
Wannsee Conference, 73, 74, 131, 245
Warsaw ghetto, 206, 218, 256, 304
Washington Post, 342, 354, 355
Wehrmacht
    homosexual soldiers serving in, 127–44
    Mischlinge serving in, 119–26
    mythologizing of, 272–83
Weinberg, Gerhard, 185
Weiner, Erich, 258
Weiss, Theodore, 393
Wellers, Georges, 230
Wenck, Alexandra, 78
Wertmuller, Lena, 263
Westerbork camp, 256, 257
Wettstein, Fritz von, 315
Wetzler, Alfred, 45
White, Jules, 260
White, Sam, 260
Wierzbnik Ghetto, 26–34
Wiesel, Elie, 300, 308, 342, 356
Wieseltier, Leon, 341
Wilczek, Avraham, 32
Wilczek, Jeremiah, 30, 31–32, 34
Wilhelm Gustloff, 282
Wilhelm II, 187
Wilkomirski, Binjamin, 271

Wilmer, Cutler & Pickering, 355
With My Backpack to India (Freber), 187
Witkeiewicz, Stanislaw Ignacy, 259
Witten, Roger, 355
Witti, Michael, 353
WJC (World Jewish Congress), 350, 365
Wolfowicz, Rachmiel, 28, 29, 31
Woller, Hans, 327
women
    as collaborators, 172–73
    in context of the Holocaust, 165–76
    execution of Jewish women, 147–48
    forced prostitution of, 166
    as martyrs, 165–76
    memoirs of Holocaust survivors, 173–76
    in slave/forced labor, 14–16, 18
"The Work" (Levi), 393
World Jewish Restitution Organization, 350
Wuth, Otto, 128–29, 132–39, 141
WVHA (Economic and Administrative Main Office), 190
Wyden, Peter, 173

Y

Yad Vashem Quarterly, 27
Yafa, Rabbi, 216
Yizkor book, 215–17
You Natzy Spy, 260

Z

Zamojski, Boguslaw, 99
Zamojski, Jan, 99–102
Zamojski, Janina, 99–102
Zayas, Alfred de, 282
Ziegler, Thomas, 243, 244–45, 247, 248
Ziemer, Gregor, 261
Ziemke, Earl, 327
Zilberberg, Ya'akov, 62
Zuccotti, Susan, 75
Zyklon B, 40, 44, 67, 288

www.ingramcontent.com/pod-product-compliance
Lightning Source LLC
Chambersburg PA
CBHW071213080526
44587CB00013BA/1355